How to access the supplemental web resource

We are pleased to provide access to a web resource that supplements your book, *Lesson Planning for High School Physical Education.* This resource offers printable versions of all the lesson plans found in the book plus four lesson plan modules not in the book. It also includes a lesson plan template.

Accessing the web resource is easy!
Follow these steps if you purchased a new book:

1. Visit **www.HumanKinetics.com/LessonPlanningforHighSchoolPhysicalEducation**.

2. Click the <u>first edition</u> link next to the book cover.

3. Click the Sign In link on the left or top of the page. If you do not have an account with Human Kinetics, you will be prompted to create one.

4. If the online product you purchased does not appear in the Ancillary Items box on the left of the page, click the Enter Key Code option in that box. Enter the key code that is printed at the right, including all hyphens. Click the Submit button to unlock your online product.

5. After you have entered your key code the first time, you will never have to enter it again to access this product. Once unlocked, a link to your product will permanently appear in the menu on the left. For future visits, all you need to do is sign in to the book's website and follow the link that appears in the left menu!

→ Click the Need Help? button on the book's website if you need assistance along the way.

For technical support, send an e-mail to:
support@hkusa.com . . . . U.S. and international customers
info@hkcanada.com . . . . Canadian customers
academic@hkeurope.com . . . . European customers

D1299870

HUMAN KINETICS

9-2017

Product: Lesson Planning for High School Physical Education web resource

Key code: MACDONALD-R8Y6U7-OSG

This unique code allows you access to the web resource.

Access is provided if you have purchased a new book. Once submitted, the code may not be entered for any other user.

HUMAN KINETICS WEB RESOURCE

Lesson Planning for High School Physical Education

Meeting the National Standards & Grade-Level Outcomes

Lynn Couturier MacDonald, DPE
State University of New York College at Cortland

Robert J. Doan, PhD
University of Southern Mississippi

Stevie Chepko, EdD
University of Nebraska at Omaha

Editors

SHAPE America SOCIETY OF HEALTH AND PHYSICAL EDUCATORS®

health. moves. minds.

HUMAN KINETICS

Library of Congress Cataloging-in-Publication Data

Names: MacDonald, Lynn Couturier, 1959- editor. | Doan, Robert John, editor. | Chepko, Stevie, editor.

Title: Lesson planning for high school physical education : meeting the national standards & grade-level outcomes / Lynn Couturier MacDonald, DPE, State University of New York College at Cortland, Robert J. Doan, PhD, University of Southern Mississippi, Stevie Chepko, EdD, University of Nebraska at Omaha, editors.

Description: Champaign, IL : Human Kinetics, [2017] | Includes bibliographical references.

Identifiers: LCCN 2017018112 (print) | LCCN 2017040605 (ebook) | ISBN 9781492552291 (e-book) | ISBN 9781492547846 (print)

Subjects: LCSH: Physical education and training--Study and teaching (Secondary)--United States. | Physical education and training--Curricula--United States. | Lesson planning.

Classification: LCC GV365 (ebook) | LCC GV365 .L46 2017 (print) | DDC 613.70712--dc23

LC record available at https://lccn.loc.gov/2017018112

ISBN: 978-1-4925-4784-6 (print)

Acquisitions Editor: Scott Wikgren; **SHAPE America Editor:** Joe McGavin; **Senior Managing Editor:** Amy Stahl; **Managing Editor:** Kirsten E. Keller; **Copyeditor:** Patricia L. MacDonald; **Permissions Manager:** Dalene Reeder; **Graphic Designer:** Whitney Milburn; **Cover Designer:** Keith Blomberg; **Photograph (cover):** © Human Kinetics; **Photographs (interior):** © Human Kinetics, unless otherwise noted; p. 74 (adult mayfly) © ECTORWORKS_ENTERPRISE/Shutterstock.com; p. 74 (adult caddis fly) © Kirsanov Valeriy Vladimirovich/Shutterstock.com; p. 74 (adult stone fly) © troutnut/Shutterstock.com; **Photo Asset Manager:** Laura Fitch; **Photo Production Manager:** Jason Allen; **Senior Art Manager:** Kelly Hendren; **Illustrations:** © Human Kinetics; **Printer:** Sheridan Books

SHAPE America – Society of Health and Physical Educators
1900 Association Drive
Reston, VA 20191
800-213-7193
www.shapeamerica.org

Printed in the United States of America   10 9 8 7 6 5 4 3 2 1

The paper in this book is certified under a sustainable forestry program.

Human Kinetics
P.O. Box 5076
Champaign, IL 61825-5076
Website: www.HumanKinetics.com

In the United States, e-mail info@hkusa.com or call 800-747-4457.

In Canada, e-mail info@hkcanada.com.

In Europe, e-mail hk@hkeurope.com.

For information about Human Kinetics' coverage in other areas of the world, please visit our website: www.HumanKinetics.com

E7036

Contents

Preface   v

Preface

This book is designed to complement *National Standards & Grade-Level Outcomes for K-12 Physical Education* (SHAPE America – Society for Health and Physical Educators, 2014) and to help you develop and implement lesson plans that will help your students attain those outcomes. SHAPE America's National Standards and Grade-Level Outcomes are intended to produce **physically literate individuals**; that is, young adults who have "the knowledge, skills and confidence to enjoy a lifetime of healthful physical activity" (p. 11). As a physical education teacher, you are positioned ideally to help students become physically literate. You can educate the *whole* person by providing learning experiences in the **psychomotor, cognitive**, and **affective learning domains**. This holistic education requires a high-quality physical education program, in which students demonstrate content mastery in all three learning domains through formal assessment. The National Standards and Grade-Level Outcomes delineate the grade-specific content that students should learn and master. At the same time, the outcomes provide a structure for you to use in developing meaningful learning experiences for your students.

The lesson plans in this book have been contributed primarily by current or former practitioners who are experienced in teaching high school–level physical education content that is driven by the National Standards and Grade-Level Outcomes. Each lesson plan addresses specific Grade-Level Outcomes; provides deliberate, progressive practice tasks; integrates appropriate assessments to evaluate and monitor student progress; and includes resources, references, equipment lists, and student assignments, as appropriate. You can implement the lesson plans in this book as they are, but they will be more effective if you modify them to meet the needs of your students. In fact, these lesson plans are intended to be used as models for creating your own lessons and learning activities, as well as providing a framework for the curriculum development process.

HOW TO USE THIS BOOK

The content in this book is divided into two parts: Part I, Planning for Student Success in High School (Chapters 1 through 4) and Part II, Lesson Plans for High School Physical Education (Chapters 5 through 11). Part II of the book corresponds with and expands upon Chapter 5 in *National Standards & Grade-Level Outcomes for K-12 Physical Education* (SHAPE America, 2014), which explores the Grade-Level Outcomes for high school.

As stated, chapters 5 through 11 contain lesson plans, arranged in modules (instruction units) of 15 or 16 lessons each, with each chapter covering one of these types of activity: dance and rhythms, individual-performance activities, outdoor pursuits, net/wall games, target games, fitness activities, and designing fitness and physical activity plans. The chapters are organized by category of activity rather than by national standard. While it is possible to teach a lesson or module on a particular standard, it's more realistic to integrate the appropriate outcomes under various standards within the activity being taught. For example, you can teach Standard 4 outcomes, which center on personal and social responsibility, during lessons on net/wall games or fitness or dance, etc. For more information on embedding outcomes within lessons, see Chapter 2.

While this book contains a wide variety of modules and lesson plans, it does not include all possible activities that you might want to teach in your physical education program. You can think of these lesson plans as models for developing your own lesson plans when teaching new or different activities. An accompanying web resource includes an editable lesson plan template as well as all lesson plans in PDF format for easy printing and easy accessibility from a computer or tablet. The Rock Climbing, Tennis Doubles, Line Dance, and Pilates Modules appear on the web resource only. To view these modules, visit www.HumanKinetics.com/LessonPlanningForHighSchoolPhysicalEducation.

Many resources are available to help you increase your content knowledge in new activities, including conferences, books, activity-specific websites, and movement-oriented applications. We hope that you will exercise your passion for lifelong learning to extend the materials offered in this book into new areas for your students and your own professional development.

eBook
available at
HumanKinetics.com

OUR COMMITMENT: 50 MILLION STRONG BY 2029

Approximately 50 million students are enrolled in America's elementary and secondary schools (grades pre-K to 12). SHAPE America is leading the effort to ensure that, by the time today's preschoolers graduate from high school in 2029, all of America's students will have developed the skills, knowledge, and confidence to enjoy healthy, meaningful physical activity. 50 Million Strong is a call to action for all of America's health and physical educators to unite and focus on a common purpose: helping and inspiring all of the nation's children to be physically active, enthusiastic and committed to making healthy lifestyle choices.

PART I

Planning for Student Success in High School

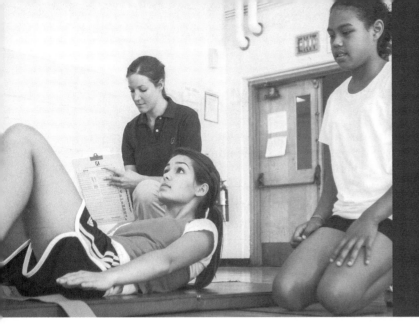

CHAPTER 1

The Importance of Teaching for Student Learning in High School

National Standards & Grade-Level Outcomes for K-12 Physical Education (SHAPE America – Society of Health and Physical Educators, 2014) provides important guidance for high school teachers to enable student learning. In fact, the book's underlying premise is that student learning is the essence of physical *education*. Students at any grade level cannot attain the National Standards and Grade-Level Outcomes without learning taking place, and student learning cannot take place without effective lessons, learning experiences, and assessments.

As physical educators, we believe that physical education is a critical component of student development and the overall school curriculum. We can support that belief, however, only if we take an educational approach, as opposed to a recreational or a public health approach, in our physical education programs (Ennis, 2011, pp. 11-12). In the educational approach, student learning is the primary instructional goal. Simply keeping students "busy, happy and good" (Placek, 1983) will not lead to their becoming physically literate individuals, as prescribed in *National Standards & Grade-Level Outcomes for K-12 Physical Education*. Also, without instruction and learning, physical education diverges from schools' core mission (Ennis, 2011, p. 16) and can be marginalized too easily. With accountability measures on the rise in public education, physical educators must be prepared to both articulate and demonstrate what students have *learned* in physical education. If we are not able to provide evidence of student learning, the credibility of our subject area and our position in schools could be jeopardized.

FACTORS THAT INFLUENCE STUDENT LEARNING

Many factors influence student learning and the subsequent development of physical literacy, including elements such as student engagement, motor skills competency, gender differences, and instructional environment (SHAPE America, 2014). Student engagement refers to the level of personal involvement in the learning activity; in other words, the degree to which a student is engrossed physically, cognitively, and/or socially in the learning experience. A passive bystander in a soccer game is not necessarily "engaged," even though that student might technically be "participating" in the activity. The list that follows summarizes what researchers have determined will affect student engagement in any subject area. For more detail about each point, please review the studies under each topic area in the topic-area resources listed in the back of the book.

Students are more likely to engage in an activity if

■ they believe that they have the skills to succeed in the activity,

■ the learning activity is interesting, and

■ the learning experience provides a socially supportive and inclusive climate.

Having the Skills to Succeed in an Activity

Skill competency and perceived competency are *both* critical for student engagement and learning. When students believe that they have the skills to participate successfully in an activity, they approach it with more interest and confidence, and they are more willing to put effort into the task. When students do *not* believe they have the skills to participate successfully in an activity, they are less willing to put themselves at risk of possible negative social comparisons with their peers and, accordingly, are less likely to engage in the activity (Garn, Cothran, & Jenkins, 2011; Ommundsen, 2006). Those social comparisons often occur in activities in which students perform individually while other students observe (e.g., batting in softball) or in competitive games.

Skill competency and perceived competency are just as important for students to *continue* participating in a physical activity and in fitness as they are for students to engage initially. Researchers have found that kindergarten children who are proficient in motor skills are more physically active than those children who are not as proficient (Kambas et al., 2012), that skillful children are more likely to be fit and physically active as adolescents than are less-skilled children (Barnett et al., 2008a; Barnett et al., 2008b), and that a positive relationship exists between motor skill competence and health-related fitness in young adults (Stodden, Langendorfer, & Robertson, 2009). In other studies, skillful middle school students were found to be more active and more effective during game play than less-skilled students (Bernstein, Phillips, & Silverman, 2011). The less-skilled students often were excluded from game play, resulting in their developing negative attitudes toward it. In general, game play led to fewer skill practice opportunities, lower levels of perceived competence, and a lack of engagement for less-skilled students. Similarly, high school students who lack skill are more likely than those with skill to disengage from physical activity and, thereby, avoid possible embarrassment or social comparisons (Garn, Ware, & Solmon, 2011; Portman, 2003). Stodden et al. (2008) hypothesized that as children mature, the relationship between motor competence and physical activity strengthens. In that model, those who are not skillful are less likely than skillful peers to participate and, therefore, they become less fit, leading to a "negative spiral of disengagement" (p. 296).

The development of competence, then, is a key strategy for promoting long-term physical activity and fitness. Indeed, "SHAPE America considers the development of motor skill competence to be the highest priority in the Grade-Level Outcomes" (SHAPE America, 2014, p. 9). The fundamental movement patterns form the foundation for physical activity, and those skills require instruction and practice from qualified teachers and coaches (Strong et al., 2005, p. 736). As a physical education teacher, you play a critical role in ensuring that all your students develop motor skill competence through the progressive and sequential development of learning experiences and high-quality lesson plans.

Offering Learning Activities That Are Interesting

Students' interest in any particular activity is influenced by their individual interests, situational interest, choice, and challenge. **Individual interest** is a relatively stable construct and depends on each student's personal characteristics and experiences. **Situational interest** is more variable and is influenced by the learning environment. As a teacher, you can increase students' situational interest by manipulating the level of cognitive demand or challenge (Chen & Darst, 2001; Smith & St. Pierre, 2009) and by providing choices to students. It's essential, then, to design learning experiences that require exploration, problem solving, and/or higher levels of thinking (e.g., applying skills to a new situation, synthesizing knowledge from different areas) in order to increase the likelihood that the activities you present to your students will interest them and engage them in learning. If your lesson activities are too basic or are mindlessly repetitive, students will be bored and will check out mentally. An activity has to contain enough challenge to hold your students' attention and motivate them to apply effort to the practice tasks.

Providing choice in the instructional experiences is essential to attracting and maintaining student interest, as well as appealing to students' sense of autonomy (Bryan et al., 2013; Ntoumanis et al., 2004). Allowing students to make some choices leads them to invest a bit of themselves in the task at hand. This can be as simple as allowing students to pick their own partners or pieces of equipment. You also can offer students more complex choices, such as choosing between modified game play and additional practice tasks, or selecting a practice task from several of varying difficulty (**differentiated instruction**). A well-planned elective program could offer high school students choices of different activities. In each case, careful planning is necessary in order to offer meaningful instructional choices to students.

Providing a Socially Supportive and Inclusive Instructional Climate

Most students prefer to engage in physical education when the instructional environment is inclusive and feels supportive (**relatedness**) (Zhang et al., 2011). To be inclusive, the learning environment should offer learning experiences that are welcoming to students of all ability levels (differentiated instruction) and that accommodate a variety of student interests. Often—especially for less-skilled students—a curriculum that is oriented toward competitive team sports does not feel inclusive or supportive. A competitive instructional environment allows highly skilled students to dominate, reducing practice opportunities for other students and increasing their chances of being embarrassed (Bernstein, Phillips, & Silverman, 2011; Hill & Hannon, 2008). Less-skilled students prefer cooperative and noncompetitive activities that allow them to participate on more even footing.

Beginning with adolescence, gender preferences become an important consideration for inclusiveness. Substantial evidence suggests that adolescent girls are dissatisfied with the traditional physical education curriculum. With the exception of those who are highly skilled, most adolescent girls prefer activities such as dance, fitness, and cooperative activities to traditional team sports (Grieser et al., 2006; Hannon & Ratcliffe, 2005). In addition, girls are more likely than boys to perceive the physical education environment as a barrier to participation, indicating that sweating as well as showering and changing clothes in a locker room discourage their involvement in class (Couturier, Chepko, & Coughlin, 2007; Xu & Liu, 2013). Given that girls' physical activity levels are lower than boys' in general, and that those activity levels drop off further in adolescence, teachers must attend to gender differences and preferences in planning learning experiences for their students. The curriculum that you design must have the potential to engage *all* students, regardless of skill level, gender, or personal interest.

THE INSTRUCTIONAL ENVIRONMENT

Ultimately, your challenge is to create an environment that maximizes student engagement and skill development. To accomplish that, you will need to create a mastery climate for instruction, one that emphasizes

- skill acquisition,
- effort,
- individual improvement, and
- assessment of student performance.

Skill Acquisition

Mastery climates reflect effective learning experiences, with progressive, sequential practice tasks as the core of the lesson plan and instructional unit. You must plan the learning tasks in a way that affords students the maximum number of practice opportunities possible, because acquiring skill requires repetition. You can employ many strategies for maximizing practice opportunities, such as providing enough equipment for everyone to participate at once, modifying the task environment or conditions, and using small-sided games to increase the number of touches for each student. The practice tasks should resemble the performance context, but simplified at first, followed by gradual increases in complexity. For example, if the skill is hitting a forehand in tennis, practicing from a dropped ball in a stationary position will not transfer to the performance condition (match), in which students must be able to hit the ball at varying speeds from varying locations. Instead, you could plan practice tasks in which the hitter strikes a forehand from a ball tossed by a partner. After the hitter experiences some success, the tosser could vary the speed of the toss and the distance the hitter must move to hit the ball. Then, the tosser could feed the ball with a controlled hit instead of a toss, again varying angles, speed, and distance. As hitters become more skillful, they can rally with a partner and/or focus on the intended target. In such a series of practice tasks, the learning experiences always reflect the conditions of performance but become increasingly complex. For more examples and information about planning deliberate practice tasks, see Chapter 7 of *National Standards & Grade-Level Outcomes for K-12 Physical Education* (SHAPE America, 2014).

Effort

We physical educators often focus on making activities fun, but fun doesn't necessarily lead to learning and competency. Your students simply cannot improve their skills without effort and practice; they have to *work* at it. Grit, or persistence, is essential for acquiring skill and for attaining long-term goals such as physical literacy (Duckworth et al., 2007). It's all about repetition, repetition, repetition. In fact, becoming an expert performer at anything requires more than 10,000 hours of deliberate practice, although some people can establish basic competence with as few as 50 hours of training (Ericsson, 2006). Obviously, you don't have enough class time for students to reach expert levels of performance, but basic competence is within reach and should be the goal. You also can foster a mastery climate by emphasizing and rewarding effort and persistence among your students.

Individual Improvement

Focusing on improvement rather than competition is another element of a mastery climate (Garn, Ware, & Solmon, 2011; Stuart et al., 2005). A competitive environment inevitably yields losers as well as winners, but when the lesson focuses on improvement, all students can succeed. For a focus on individual improvement to be effective in a mastery climate, you will need to plan differentiated instruction for students of all ability levels. Each practice task will need modifications to simplify it, or make it more complex, depending on your students' skill levels. Practice tasks should be challenging but achievable. It helps if students realize that they probably won't have a lot of success at the beginning and that they should expect some failure. Your assessments will help you identify individual students' areas of weakness, which you must communicate to each of them, along with how they can improve. With a focus on improvement, students are less concerned about how their performance compares to that of other students, and physical education becomes a more positive, supportive climate for learning.

Assessment of Student Performance

Implementing a mastery-oriented instructional climate isn't possible without assessment. You will need to conduct frequent formal and informal assessments to measure student improvement and mastery of the content. You should assess students before instruction to establish what they already know and can do. This pre-assessment establishes your baseline for planning and implementing instruction. You also should integrate assessment throughout the instructional unit to measure progress between lessons (**formative assessment**) as well as cumulative learning at the end of the unit (**summative assessment**). As the teacher, you are engaged in a cycle of assessing, analyzing the results, and applying your analysis through corrective feedback or modification of learning experiences. For more information about assessments, see Chapter 8 of *National Standards & Grade-Level Outcomes for K-12 Physical Education* (SHAPE America, 2014).

Physical literacy–driven physical education is all about student learning, and you are the key to delivering the experiences that lead to that student learning. Fortunately, many of the variables that influence student learning are within your control because *you* shape the learning environment (Subramanian, 2009). By keeping your focus on what students are learning, and by using the National Standards and Grade-Level Outcomes as guideposts, you can help students become physically literate and physically active for a lifetime.

HOW THE GRADE-LEVEL OUTCOMES ARE CODED

As you dig deeper into the Grade-Level Outcomes for high school students, you will see that each outcome has a number code. The code signifies the National Standard, level, and grade with which each outcome is associated. As an example, S2.H1.L1 refers to Standard 2, High School Outcome 1, Level 1 (SHAPE America, 2014, p. 12). You will find this coding helpful in identifying the relationship between standards and outcomes, as well as locating particular outcomes within each grade level.

UNDERSTANDING THE SCOPE & SEQUENCE FOR K-12 PHYSICAL EDUCATION

To help you develop your own lessons, this book replicates SHAPE America's Scope & Sequence of Instruction for K-12 Physical Education from *National Standards & Grade-Level Outcomes for K-12 Physical Education,* applies to all grade levels, not just high school (see table 1.1). The table is designed to give you a quick visual representation of when to teach the skills and content specified in the Grade-Level Outcomes. Each skill is coded with "E" for "emerging," "M" for "maturing" and "A" for "applying" (SHAPE America, 2014, p. 65). **Emerging** indicates when skills and knowledge should be introduced and practiced. **Maturing** indicates when students should be able to demonstrate the critical elements of the skills or knowledge while continuing to refine them. **Applying** indicates when students should be able to demonstrate the critical elements of the skill or knowledge in a variety of physical activity settings. Table 1.1 also provides a framework for a continuum of instruction and learning from the earliest grades through high school graduation, so that you and your colleagues at other grade levels can ensure that everyone is on the same page for curriculum development.

TABLE 1.1 Scope & Sequence for K-12 Physical Education

Standard 1. Motor skills & movement patterns

	Kindergarten	Grade 1	Grade 2	Grade 3	Grade 4	Grade 5	Grade 6	Grade 7	Grade 8	High School
Hopping	E	M	A							→
Galloping	E	M	A							→
Running	E	→	M	A						→
Sliding	E	M	A							→
Skipping	E	→	M	A						→
Leaping		E	→	M	A					→
Jumping & landing	E	→		M	A					→
• Spring & step					E	M	A			
• Jump stop							E	M	A	→
• Jump rope	E	→		M	A	→	i	i	i	i
Balance	E	→		M	→	A				→
Weight transfer			E	M	→		A			→
Rolling	E	→				M	A			→
Curling & stretching	E	→	M	→		A				→
Twisting & bending		E	M	→		A				→
Throwing										
• Underhand	E	→	M	→			A			→
• Overhand	E	→				M	A			→
Catching	E	→			M	A				→
Dribbling/ball control										
• Hands	E	→			M	A				→
• Feet		E	→			M	A			→
• With implement				E	→	M	A			→
Kicking	E	→			M	→	A			→
Volleying										
• Underhand	E	→			M	A				→
• Overhead					E	→	ii	ii	ii	ii
• Set								E	→	M
Striking—with short implement	E	→			M	A				
• Fore/backhand							E	→	M	A
Striking—with long implement			E	→		M	A			→
• Fore/backhand								E	→	M
Combining locomotors & manipulatives					E	→	M	→	A	→
Combining jumping, landing, locomotors & manipulatives							E	M	A	→
Combining balance & weight transfers			E	→			M	→	A	→

[i]Jump rope becomes a fitness activity after grade 5 and is absorbed into Standard 3. Engages in fitness activities.

[ii]Overhead volley becomes a specialized skill for volleyball—setting—that begins being taught in middle school.

(continued)

(continued)

	Kindergarten	Grade 1	Grade 2	Grade 3	Grade 4	Grade 5	Grade 6	Grade 7	Grade 8	High School
Serving										
• Underhand							E	M	A	→
• Overhand							E	⟶	⟶	M
Shooting on goal						E	⟶	⟶	M	*
Passing & receiving										
• Hands						E	→	M	→	*
• Feet					E		⟶	⟶	M	*
• With implement							E	→	M	*
• Forearm pass							E	→	M	A
• Lead pass						E	→	M	→	*
• Give & go							E	M	→	*
Offensive skills										
• Pivots							E	M	A	*
• Fakes							E	→	M	*
• Jab step							E	→	M	*
• Screen									E	*
Defensive skills										
• Drop step							E	→	M	*
• Defensive or athletic stance							E	→	M	*

*Teaching team sports skills is not recommended at the high school level.

Standard 2. Concepts & strategies

	Kindergarten	Grade 1	Grade 2	Grade 3	Grade 4	Grade 5	Grade 6	Grade 7	Grade 8	High School
Movement concepts, principles & knowledge	E	→			M	→	A	→		
Strategies & tactics				E	→		M	→	A	→
Communication (games)							E	→	M	A
Creating space (invasion)										
• Varying pathways, speed, direction							E	M	A	*
• Varying type of pass							E	M	A	*
• Selecting appropriate offensive tactics with object							E	→	M	*
• Selecting appropriate offensive tactics without object							E	→	M	*
• Using width & length of the field/court							E	→	M	*
• Playing with one player up (e.g., 2v1)							E	→	M	*
Reducing space (invasion)										
• Changing size & shape of the defender's body							E	M	A	*
• Changing angle to gain competitive advantage							E	→	M	*
• Denying the pass/player progress							E	→		*
• Playing with one player down (e.g., 1v2)							E	→		*
Transition (invasion)							E	M	A	*
Creating space (net/wall)										
• Varying force, angle and/or direction to gain competitive advantage							E	→	M	A
• Using offensive tactic/shot to move opponent out of position							E	→		M
Reducing space (net/wall)										
• Returning to home position							E	→	M	A
• Shifting to reduce angle for return							E	→		M
Target										
• Selecting appropriate shot/club							E	→	M	A
• Applying blocking strategy							E	→		M
• Varying speed & trajectory							E	→	M	A
Fielding/striking										
• Applying offensive strategies								E	→	*
• Reducing open spaces							E	→	M	*

*Teaching team sports skills is not recommended at the high school level.

(continued)

Standard 3. Health-enhancing level of fitness & physical activity

	Kindergarten	Grade 1	Grade 2	Grade 3	Grade 4	Grade 5	Grade 6	Grade 7	Grade 8	High School
Physical activity knowledge	E	→			→	M	→		A	→
Engages in physical activity	E	→			→	M	→			A
Fitness knowledge	E	→			→	M	→			A
Assessment & program planning				E	→	M	→		A	→
Nutrition	E	→					→	M	→	A
Stress management							E	→		M

Standard 4. Responsible personal & social behavior

	Kindergarten	Grade 1	Grade 2	Grade 3	Grade 4	Grade 5	Grade 6	Grade 7	Grade 8	High School
Demonstrating personal responsibility	E	→		M	→		A	→		→
Accepting feedback	E	→		M	→		A	→		→
Working with others	E	→		M	→		A	→		→
Following rules & etiquette			E	→		M	→	A	→	→
Safety	E	→	M	→		A	→			→

Standard 5. Recognizes the value of physical activity

	Kindergarten	Grade 1	Grade 2	Grade 3	Grade 4	Grade 5	Grade 6	Grade 7	Grade 8	High School
For health			E	→			M	→		A
For challenge			E	→			M	→		A
For self-expression/enjoyment	E	→				M	→			A
For social interaction				E	→		M	→		A

Reprinted, by permission, from SHAPE America – Society of Health and Physical Educators, 2014, *National standards & grade-level outcomes for K-12 physical education* (Champaign, IL: Human Kinetics), 66-69.

CHAPTER 2

Teaching to Standards: Planning Lessons Using the Grade-Level Outcomes

Planning effective lessons is a challenge that integrates an understanding of your students, your mastery of the content, and your application of sound pedagogical skills and instructional strategies. *National Standards & Grade-Level Outcomes for K-12 Physical Education* (SHAPE America – Society of Health and Physical Educators, 2014) is a tool that makes this process somewhat easier by providing a structure—a scope and sequence—to use when developing your lesson content and your curriculum. This chapter focuses on the process of planning lessons for modules, often called units, for high school physical education that align with SHAPE America's National Standards and Grade-Level Outcomes. This process will include three components:

1. Planning for the module
2. Planning for individual lessons
3. Planning for embedded outcomes

PLANNING FOR THE MODULE

Before planning your lessons, consider what your intended outcomes are for the module and how that module fits within the context of your high school curriculum. In general, your students can attain the Grade-Level Outcomes through a variety of learning activities, so it's important to consider how the outcomes you select will address their needs and interests. How do the outcomes build on the skills your students learned and the knowledge they acquired in middle school? How do the learning activities fit with the geographical opportunities available to your students, to their cultural backgrounds, and to the gender preferences of students within each class? Don't forget to factor in any constraints that you might have, such as limitations on the number of lessons that you can teach and the amount of time that you have to teach each lesson, as well as the facilities and equipment that you have at your disposal.

In this book, most of the modules contain 15 or 16 lessons, as recommended for the high school level in *National Standards & Grade-Level Outcomes for K-12 Physical Education* (SHAPE America, 2014). Each lesson is designed to fit a 70- to 90-minute time block, because block periods represent a common type of schedule in high schools. They also have certain advantages, such as allowing time for you to enhance instruction related to concepts and knowledge while maintaining at least half of the instructional time for moderate to vigorous physical activity for students (MVPA), as well as allowing your students enough time to change clothes and shower.

Once you have determined which outcomes to include in your module, and what constraints that you and your class will face, you can create a block plan, which lists the outcomes and objectives for each individual lesson in your module (see table 2.1). One of the many techniques that you can use to create your block plan is "backward mapping," which is simply a process by which you start at the end point (in this case, the outcomes for the module) and work your way back to the first lesson to determine what students should know and be able to do at each step along the way. Figure 2.1 illustrates what using backward mapping to create a block plan would look like.

After selecting the outcomes that you want your students to attain by the end of the module, determine what summative assessment(s) you will use to measure students' progress toward those outcomes. It's essential that you know how you will evaluate student learning before designing the learning activities. By first determining how you will evaluate student learning, you can align the instructional activities closely with the assessment. For example, if you choose Outcome S3.H12.L1 (Designs a fitness program, including all components of health-related fitness, for a college student and an employee in the learner's chosen field of work), you most likely will ask students to develop and implement a health-related fitness program that you will evaluate. You will need to define all of the components that students must include in the plan, as well as create a scoring guide for how you will evaluate it. As you determine all the components of the assessment, you will need to think about all the skills and knowledge that students will need to complete it successfully, such as applying the FITT principle correctly, differentiating among different types of exercise, and implementing safe techniques. You also might take note of other outcomes that you can address readily in this module, such as S1.H3.L1 (Demonstrates competency in 1 or more specialized skills in health-related fitness activities), S2.H1.L1 (Applies the terminology associated with exercise and participation in selected individual-performance activities, dance, net/wall games, target games,

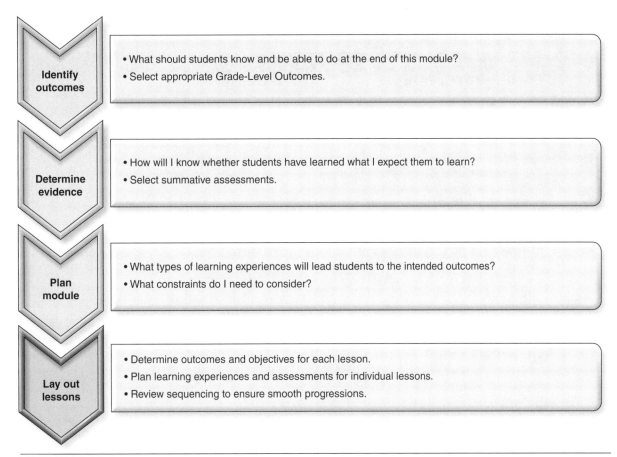

FIGURE 2.1 Backward mapping for module block plans.

Reprinted, by permission, from SHAPE America, 2017, *Lesson planning for middle school physical education* (Champaign, IL: Human Kinetics), 14.

aquatics and/or outdoor pursuits appropriately), and S4.H1.L1 (Employs effective self-management skills to analyze barriers and modify physical activity patterns appropriately as needed), just to name a few possibilities.

Once you've selected or created the assessment, you can move on to thinking about the types of learning experiences that fit into the context of your learning environment. Perhaps you will have students write drafts of their plans and share them with peers to critique. You might consider showing them a completed plan and having them practice aspects of it. Finally, you will want to lay out the number of lessons in the module and specify the outcomes and objectives for each lesson plan. You also might want to include formative assessments in your block plan.

A simple chart with boxes for each lesson can help you create an outline for the entire module that will allow you to check off all the important concepts and skills that the lessons in the module will cover. Knowing that students usually don't get enough practice time in one class period to master the skills or knowledge addressed in most lessons, you should expect to address the same outcomes for multiple lessons and, most likely, multiple modules throughout the year. In table 2.1, you will see that the outcomes from the first part of the Fitness Assessment and Program Planning Module are repeated, even though the lesson objectives change. The practice tasks will change, as well. Once you have completed an outline of the outcomes and objectives, you can design the learning activities and formative assessments that you want to include in each lesson.

TABLE 2.1 Sample High School Block Plan for Fitness Assessment and Program Planning

Lesson	Grade-Level Outcomes	Lesson Objectives
1	**Assessment & Program Planning** Designs a fitness program, including all components of health-related fitness, for a college student and an employee in the learner's chosen field of work. (S3.H12.L1) **Safety** Applies best practices for participating safely in physical activity, exercise and dance (e.g., injury prevention, proper alignment, hydration, use of equipment, implementation of rules, sun protection). (S4.H5.L1)	**The learner will:** • review vocabulary and provide good examples of activities/exercises for each definition. • identify and differentiate the components of health-related and skill-related fitness concepts. • correlate heart rate to exercise intensity.
2	**Fitness Knowledge** Designs a fitness program, including all components of health-related fitness, for a college student and an employee in the learner's chosen field of work. (S3.H12.L1) **Safety** Applies best practices for participating safely in physical activity, exercise and dance (e.g. injury prevention, proper alignment, hydration, use of equipment, implementation of rules, sun protection). (S4.H5.L1)	**The learner will:** • log his or her physical activity over three days, using Activitygram. • perform proper curl-ups and push-ups during the assessment. • identify breaks in form (the cues) of curl-ups and push-ups when assessing partners.
3	**Fitness Knowledge** Designs a fitness program, including all components of health-related fitness, for a college student and an employee in the learner's chosen field of work. (S3.H12.L1) **Safety** Applies best practices for participating safely in physical activity, exercise and dance (e.g., injury prevention, proper alignment, hydration, use of equipment, implementation of rules, sun protection). (S4.H5.L1)	**The learner will:** • perform a dynamic warm-up with proper form. • define and provide examples of the elements of the FITT principle. • examine how he or she runs the mile, using lap time splits.
4	**Fitness Knowledge** Designs a fitness program, including all components of health-related fitness, for a college student and an employee in the learner's chosen field of work. (S3.H12.L1) **Safety** Applies best practices for participating safely in physical activity, exercise and dance (e.g., injury prevention, proper alignment, hydration, use of equipment, implementation of rules, sun protection). (S4.H5.L1) **Rules & Etiquette** Exhibits proper etiquette, respect for others and teamwork while engaging in physical activity and/or social dance. (S4.H2.L1) **Fitness Knowledge** Demonstrates appropriate technique on resistance-training machines and free weights. (S3.H7.L1) **Fitness Activities** Demonstrates competency in 1 or more specialized skills in health-related fitness activities. (S1.H3.L1)	**The learner will:** • discuss the importance of the weight room rules and abide by them. • demonstrate the stations properly and discuss the muscle groups being exercised. • demonstrate proper form and alignment.

Lesson	Grade-Level Outcomes	Lesson Objectives
5	**Assessment & Program Planning** Designs a fitness program, including all components of health-related fitness, for a college student and an employee in the learner's chosen field of work. (S3.H12.L1) **Safety** Applies best practices for participating safely in physical activity, exercise and dance (e.g., injury prevention, proper alignment, hydration, use of equipment, implementation of rules, sun protection). (S4.H5.L1) **Fitness Knowledge** Demonstrates appropriate technique on resistance-training machines and free weights. (S3.H7.L1) **Fitness Activities** Demonstrates competency in 1 or more specialized skills in health-related fitness activities. (S1.H3.L1)	**The learner will:** • determine his or her modified 1 repetition maximum (RM) for selected exercises on task sheet using table. • perform weight training activities properly, using good form and proper alignment. • spot his or her peers properly to ensure safety.

The process of planning modules is important for assuring effective learning experiences for students, but once you've planned your modules, you will need to remain flexible. Your students will progress at different rates, and even the best plans will need to be adjusted to meet student needs.

PLANNING FOR INDIVIDUAL LESSONS

A comprehensive yet flexible lesson plan template is an important tool for developing your lessons. All of the lessons included in this book were developed from a common template, although some lessons might contain slight variations, depending on the lesson content. That template appears for your use in figure 2.2.

We also offer some guidance on what is meant by each heading in the template so that you will understand the various sections in the same way that those who contributed the lesson plans to this book understood them. We realize that we could have included many other sections in this template, but we tried to limit the template to just those elements that are critical for addressing students' attainment of the Grade-Level Outcomes. Therefore, it will be up to you to include other elements such as warm-ups, cool-downs, instant activities, and routines. Finally, we hope that you will find this template to be user-friendly and adaptable to your needs. Of course, you might already have a lesson plan format that you prefer, so feel free to continue to use it when developing your own lessons and modules.

SETTING UP THE LESSON

The top portion of the lesson plan template establishes the framework for the instructional tasks that will follow. Within the five text boxes at the top, list the outcomes that you've targeted, the lesson's objectives, the materials and equipment that you will need, and how you will introduce the lesson. Select the outcomes from table 3.1. Consider them to be longer-term objectives for the module or curriculum, as they are designed to be met by the end of the grade level. It's likely that you will address the same outcomes in several modules throughout the year so as to provide students with enough learning and practice opportunities to

FIGURE 2.2 LESSON PLAN TEMPLATE

Grade-Level Outcomes	Lesson Objectives
	The learner will: • • •
Embedded Outcomes	**Equipment and Materials**

Introduction

Instructional Task	Practice Task *Add as many as appropriate*	Student Choices/ Differentiation	What to Look For
	Extension(s) Refinement(s) *Guiding questions for students* *Embedded outcome(s)*		
Instructional Task	**Practice Task** *Add as many as appropriate*	**Student Choices/ Differentiation**	**What to Look For**
	Extension(s) Refinement(s) *Guiding questions for students* *Embedded outcome(s)*		
Instructional Task	**Practice Task** *Add as many as appropriate*	**Student Choices/ Differentiation**	**What to Look For**
	Extension(s) Refinement(s) *Guiding questions for students* *Embedded outcome(s)*		

| Formal and Informal Assessments |
| Resources |
| Closure |
| Reflection |
| Homework |

From L.C. MacDonald, R.J. Doan, and S. Chepko, eds., 2018, *Lesson planning for high school physical education* (Reston, VA: SHAPE America; Champaign, IL: Human Kinetics).

attain them. Each individual lesson and learning activity should move students closer to the selected outcomes. The Lesson Objectives section is where you will write the objectives that align with the outcomes that you've selected and will lead students to attain the outcomes. While it's usually a good idea to include the task, situation, and criteria when writing lesson objectives, most of the objectives in the lessons in this book have been simplified and might not include all of those components. The criteria should be set locally, based on student ability, experience, and pre-assessment data. Table 2.2 contains an example from a lesson plan in the Fly Fishing Module found in chapter 5.

The Equipment & Materials and Introduction sections in the lesson plan template are there to help you list all of the instructional materials that you will need for each lesson and to help you prepare to introduce the lesson. Your introduction of the lesson should capture students' attention and outline what students will learn in the lesson. You also can include an instant activity in your introduction to start the lesson. Try to think of ways to link the content in each lesson to what students have learned previously or to connect it somehow with their interests. Here is an example of these sections from the same fly fishing lesson:

Equipment & Materials

- 15 fly rods, reels, lines
- 15 rod tubes
- 15 targets (plastic hoops work well)
- Journals
- Writing implements
- *Testament of a Fisherman*, by Robert Traver

Introduction

What did you learn about the culture of fly fishing from your reading? Today, we will become part of that culture by learning about the fly rod and how to make a basic cast.

Introduce the fly rod, basic cast, and equipment expectations. Then, have students practice basic casts with the fly rods. At the end of the lesson, introduce the fly fishing journal assignment and expectations by reviewing the rubric with students.

Note: Once you have completed this portion of the lesson plan, you will have a clear direction for planning your instructional tasks.

TABLE 2.2 Sample Lesson Plan Objectives

Grade-Level Outcomes	Lesson Objectives
Lifetime Activities	**The learner will:**
Demonstrates competency and/or refines activity-specific movement skills in 2 or more lifetime activities (outdoor pursuits, individual-performance activities, aquatics, net/wall games or target games). (S1.H1.L1)	• identify six components of a fly rod.
	• identify the components of a successful basic cast.
Rules & Etiquette	• explain the rules of using fly fishing equipment.
Exhibits proper etiquette, respect for others and teamwork while engaging in physical activity and/or social dance. (S4.H2.L1)	• complete a basic fly cast successfully.
Movement Concepts, Principles & Knowledge	• create a fly fishing journal to be used to support student learning and connect students to the fly fishing culture.
Applies the terminology associated with exercise and participation in selected individual-performance activities, dance, net/wall games, target games, aquatics and/or outdoor pursuits appropriately. (S2.H1.L1)	

Instructional Plan

This part of the template is where you will specify each learning task for the lesson as well as the progressions associated with it. Use the Instructional Task section in the template to list the lesson's "big ideas," also thought of as the main skills, concepts, and/or behaviors that students are expected to learn. Use the Practice Task section to indicate *how* students will learn the skills in each instructional task. You will notice that the Practice Task section carries a note that reads, "Add as many as appropriate." That is to encourage you to think about multiple practice tasks related to the original one. Remember, you want students to master the task, and that doesn't happen if you offer one practice task and then move on to the next lesson or skill. To master any skill, students will need a carefully planned sequence of deliberate practice tasks.

The Extensions and Refinements sections within the Practice Task area reinforce the need for this type of planning. The progression should move from a simplified version of the task to a more complex version. You can think of this as moving students from a controlled practice environment to a less-controlled environment or modifying the initial practice task to be easier or more difficult. In the end, you might place only a few practice tasks in the lesson, but each might have several extensions or refinements. Table 2.3 is an example from a lesson plan in the Tennis Doubles Module that appears on the web resource.

Within the Practice Task section, you also will see a note about *Guiding Questions for Students*. Sometimes, practice tasks lend themselves to guided exploration, and if you want to use that approach, the template encourages you to plan for it. Here are some examples of guiding questions on punch serves, from the tennis lesson.

■ Does the swing path resemble another type of skill? (Answer: overhand throw)

■ How can you hit the ball with more power?

Asking questions like those helps students engage cognitively in the activity and helps them draw connections to concepts that they have learned in other activities. Placing *guiding questions* within your practice tasks will help enhance the learning experience for students.

TABLE 2.3 Sample Instructional Task and Practice Tasks

Instructional Task	Practice Tasks
Forehand strike with partner	Students pair up and stand across from each other on the service line on one side of the T (four students per court). One partner drop-hits three forehands across the net while the partner uses footwork from last class to catch the balls. Partners trade roles.
	Extensions:
	Students perform the same task, except that they move back to the baseline.
	Students perform the same task, except that they try to keep a rally going while striking with rackets (no catching).
	Students perform the same task, except that they set a goal for consecutive forehands in a row.
	Refinements:
	A big concern with this task is that, when students are at the service line, they will abbreviate the movement pattern in order to reduce force on the ball. If this is the case, encourage them to use a lower-density ball.
	Another concern is ball control while two rallies are going on at the same time. Encourage students to follow through pointing the racket at the target (partner).

The instructional plan area of the template also includes a section for Student Choices/Differentiation. The content in this section should look different from the Extension/Refinement(s) in the Practice Task section. This is where you indicate how students will be able to participate in the practice tasks at their own levels. The following examples from the Tennis Doubles Module in Chapter 7 help illustrate student choices.

- Students choose goals for consecutive groundstrokes and modify the goals as needed.
- Students may choose to change partners.
- Students may choose to start with a lower-density ball.
- Students may choose racket size.

Other possibilities include modifying the size of practice areas, practicing with or without a net, altering the speed of the movements, grouping students by ability, and encouraging students to stay with an earlier progression rather than moving to a more difficult one. Although you won't always make use of this section, planning for differentiation is an important tool for creating a mastery environment that is inclusive of all ability levels.

The final section in the instructional planning area is What to Look For, which should force you to think about the critical elements of the task or skill during the lesson's planning phase. These elements form the basis of the corrective feedback that you will provide during the lesson to help students improve their performance. This section also should cause you to consider how you evaluate student performance during the practice task, including the critical elements associated with the skills or concepts. The practitioners who contributed the lesson plans in this book did not include these critical elements because most teachers have developed their own ways of providing those elements through teaching cues and key phrases. In addition, these cues are readily available from other resources, such as video clips of correct technique found online. In many cases, the lesson plan contributors listed resources through which to find this type of information.

The rest of the instructional plan is structured in rows, with the first being the Assessments section. Because assessment is the key to evaluating student progress and learning, it is essential that you plan for it in each lesson, even if it is to be informal assessment, formative assessment, or both. You should assess students formally against the outcomes for each module (summative assessment) at least once, and ideally, you would pre-assess students' knowledge and abilities before planning the lessons. Many types of assessments are available to teachers, including exit slips, checks for understanding, peer assessments, analytic rubrics, written tests, fitness tests, and portfolios. If you are using a published assessment (e.g., *PE Metrics*, Fitnessgram), familiarize yourself with the testing protocols before trying to use the assessment in class. Also, students should have the opportunity to practice assessments and protocols before being scored or graded. For more information on creating and using assessments, see Chapter 8 of *National Standards & Grade-Level Outcomes for K-12 Physical Education* (SHAPE America, 2014).

The Resources section in the lesson plan template is there for you to list any materials that might enhance student learning and could include any websites, books, handouts, visual aids, DVDs, etc., that you used to help prepare the lesson plan or that you want to bring to the attention of interested students. The Closure section is there to help you think about how to pull the various tasks within the lesson together and focus students on what they learned. It also gives you an opportunity to preview the next lesson in the module. Pre-planning some initial questions is a good way to focus students on the important aspects of the day's lesson, as this example from the Fly Fishing Module illustrates.

Closure

- After equipment is put away, the class meets to review the rod components and expectations, and the key concepts.
- Why is it important to load the rod?
- What happens to the line if you don't load it properly?
- Challenge question: In what ways can the fly caster manipulate the casting loop?
- We will continue to work on our casting in our next class.

While the Closure section pulls it together for students, the Reflection section of the template is there to pull it together for *you*. It provides an opportunity for you to evaluate student progress at the end of the lesson and to consider what you might want to do differently (or the same) the next time you teach the lesson. This example from the Fly Fishing Module provides some guiding questions to consider after teaching.

Reflection

- Were students able to make a basic cast?
- Were they able to use the cues from the rubric effectively?
- Are they able to transfer their knowledge as evaluators to their own casting?

The questions are aligned closely with the outcomes and objectives targeted in the lesson, and your assessment of how well students attained those outcomes and objectives might cause you to consider adjusting your next lesson. If students are not "getting it," you might need to take a step back in your progressions before moving on to new content.

The final component of the instructional plan is the Homework section. As with other subject areas, homework can play a vital role in reinforcing skills and knowledge acquired in physical education classes. It also can encourage students to adopt desirable behaviors outside of the school day, such as being physically active in formal or informal activity settings, keeping a physical activity log, and investigating community-based opportunities for active recreation, to name a few. By setting up homework as an expectation, you can extend the reach of physical education beyond your classroom and into family and community settings.

Homework: Fly Fishing Journal Entry

- How does the length of the backcast affect the casting loop?
- Applying what you know about the basic cast, how could we lengthen the casting distance effectively?

PLANNING FOR EMBEDDED OUTCOMES

During your planning, it is important to think about what other Grade-Level Outcomes students might work toward attaining while concentrating on the primary outcomes targeted in the lesson. We call these "other" outcomes **embedded outcomes**, and they differ from "teachable moments" because they don't just happen. You have to plan for—and teach—these secondary outcomes as part of each lesson. For example, you can embed an outcome on responsibility and respect (Standard 4) during skill instruction for a self-defense lesson (Standard 1). The choice of which outcomes to embed into your lessons depends on the content and types of practice tasks that you plan for teaching the primary outcomes. The Embedded Outcomes section appears in the template to remind you to plan for these outcomes as you develop instructional tasks (see figure 2.3).

Embedding outcomes can play an important role in attaining the National Standards. *National Standards & Grade-Level Outcomes for K-12 Physical Education* (SHAPE America, 2014) presents 60 outcomes for the high school level. Even if your students had physical education every day of the school year, you would be hard-pressed to plan individual lessons for all 60 outcomes. In fact, doing so is probably not a good idea. Teaching to every outcome separately would obscure the connections between and among different skills and knowledge, leading to compartmentalization of physical education content. While the outcomes are organized by standard, the content cannot be taught without considering the context in which it takes place. For example, students can pursue and appreciate

FIGURE 2.3   EMBEDDED OUTCOMES

Grade-Level Outcomes	Lesson Objectives
	The learner will:
Embedded Outcomes	**Equipment and Materials**
Introduction	

From L.C. MacDonald, R.J. Doan, and S. Chepko, eds., 2018, *Lesson planning for high school physical education* (Reston, VA: SHAPE America; Champaign, IL: Human Kinetics).

the challenge (Standard 5) of rock climbing, but they also must have specialized skills such as belaying (Standard 1) and must exhibit responsible personal and social behaviors (Standard 4) to participate in a climb indoors or out. The process of integrating or "embedding" outcomes from different standards in lesson plans is the focus of the remainder of this chapter.

OPTIMIZING LEARNING THROUGH EMBEDDED OUTCOMES

According to Holt/Hale and Hall (2016), embedded outcomes "are best described as secondary objectives that you place within the learning experience to maximize teaching effectiveness and student learning" (p. 18). Embedded outcomes are rooted in the learning or practice task by the very nature or challenge of the learning experience. You should not think of these outcomes as by-products of or incidental to the primary objective or task, but rather as opportunities to meet more than one outcome during the learning or practice task. These opportunities are part of everyday school practice, and you should exploit them to optimize learning.

While teaching for skill development or refinement, you have opportunities to embed outcomes from both the cognitive and affective domains into motor competency learning experiences. For example, during practice tasks designed to increase both skill and tactical competency for net/wall game play, you can embed affective outcomes specific to communication and etiquette without sacrificing time devoted to practicing skill and tactics. Without communication and etiquette, for example, teammates will not succeed in doubles play. You shouldn't assume, though, that students will learn communication and etiquette just because you have planned a doubles practice task. You have to *teach* those outcomes and provide feedback on them in the context of the doubles practice task.

Mastery Environment and Embedded Outcomes

The key to embedding outcomes is creating a mastery environment, in which students seek to improve their skills based on the required skill or competency. For example, when working on chipping in golf, students can practice hitting to a chipping target with rings placed around it (1 foot, 3 feet, and 6 feet). Students chip a set number of balls, trying to land them as close to the target as possible. They track their own scores, receiving 5 points for each ball placed within the 1-foot ring, 3 points for each ball placed within the 3-foot ring, and 1 point for each ball placed within the 6-foot ring. They can challenge themselves by setting a higher goal for points on the next set of practice chips. In a mastery environment, students try to improve upon their best performances. The focus is on personal improvement and not on comparing scores with other classmates. This emphasis on a mastery environment allows physical educators to provide feedback on the skills required for the practice task (chipping) while incorporating other important aspects of the game, such as etiquette or safety.

Golf provides many opportunities to teach students about movement concepts such as force, speed, and rotation. After each group of students has completed two cycles of the practice task, you could ask students to identify why their scores did or did not improve. Students could brainstorm ways to improve their scores, which might include changing the amplitude of the swing rather than the speed to alter the distance or keeping their wrists firm at contact to improve consistency. As students are brainstorming in the discussion, you also could check their understanding of the relationship between club loft and ball flight, or trajectory, and roll after impact. You should consider how to capitalize on opportunities to teach embedded outcomes during practice tasks for any activity. For each practice task you plan for a lesson, ask yourself, "What else can I teach in conjunction with this task?"

While teaching a module on dance (Outcome S1.H2.L1), you could embed fitness and physical activity outcomes, such as applying rates of perceived exertion (RPE) (Outcome S3.H3.L2). Students could explore this by recording their RPE values at different points in the lesson to learn about the cardiorespiratory. You also could embed outcomes from Standard 5, as different forms of dance provide opportunities for students to learn about self-expression (Outcome S5.H3.L1) and social support (S5.H4.L1). The latter is particularly true in partner or social dance. If you teach to these embedded outcomes through dance, students will begin to apply important fitness concepts outside of typical "fitness" activities. They also can enhance their interpersonal skills and begin to appreciate movement as a tool for expression and creativity, leading to more competent and physically literate students. Here is an example from the Line Dance Module in Chapter 9.

Instructional Task

Sequence 2: Knee raises, medium and high, with quarter turn to left.

■ PRACTICE TASK

Step 3: Two medium-height knee raises, alternating knee, starting with right knee (right, left).
Two high knee raises, one with the right knee and one with the left knee, while completing a quarter turn to the left. Practice sequence without music.
Step 4: Put whole dance sequence together.

EMBEDDED OUTCOME: S5.H3.L1. Encourage students to use arms in their own way once they have the steps down. For example, clap above head to allow for individual expression.

The examples that we've offered so far have involved embedding cognitive or affective outcomes into motor competency tasks, but embedding can work in the other direction, as well. When teaching a sequence of learning experiences with the primary focus on problem solving or critical thinking (Outcome S4.H4.L1), you will have many opportunities for sharing skill cues with participants, which addresses components of motor competency (Outcome S1.H1.L1). If the primary focus is on developing and implementing a fitness plan (Outcome S3.H12.L1), it's easy to find openings for providing feedback to students about their skill competency (Outcome S1.H3.L1). How students execute the exercise or activity will have a direct impact on the effectiveness of their fitness plans.

Implementing Embedded Outcomes

Using embedded outcomes also can increase practice and activity time during a lesson. Because you don't have to plan separate learning activities for every outcome, you can use instruction and management time more efficiently. One practice task, or a sequence of practice tasks, can address more than one outcome, leaving more time for practice attempts and moderate to vigorous activity. As noted earlier, though, these opportunities require careful planning before the lesson, as well as attention to delivery during the lesson, to be effective. It's also critical that you assess embedded outcomes at some point during the module to track student progress, just as you would for other outcomes. These assessments don't have to be complex. You can use checks for understanding and exit slips for many types of embedded outcomes. Peer assessments also can be very effective, as can other, more formal forms of assessment, such as rubrics and checklists.

All of the modules in this book use the approach of including embedded outcomes from multiple standards to take advantage of opportunities presented by the content. For example, in the Yoga & Stress Management Module in Chapter 10, most of the primary outcomes come from Standard 1, but the embedded outcomes come from Standards 3, 4 and 5. But you could take another approach to embedding outcomes by selecting one national standard as a theme for the entire module. For example, the Yoga & Stress Management Module could just as easily incorporate outcomes from Standard 3 only, because the intent is to illustrate how yoga contributes to fitness and physical activity knowledge and skills. Each approach has its advantages and disadvantages. Pulling embedded outcomes from multiple standards allows you a great deal of flexibility because you can choose from many outcomes. However, it may be difficult to track how well students attain those embedded outcomes across the grade level if you haven't created a pattern for including them. Conversely, identifying a theme for the module simplifies your assessment and monitoring of outcomes across the year, although using outcomes from only one standard might be more difficult to align with some of your lesson content. Either approach can work, but you should decide what makes the most sense for the content that you are teaching.

Embedding outcomes is not about changing what we do, but about leveraging our teaching effectiveness through careful planning and maximizing the opportunities available to us in every lesson. Thinking about embedding outcomes will help you integrate the skills, knowledge, and behaviors from the five National Standards for K-12 Physical Education in a meaningful way for your students. In the end, a physically literate individual experiences physical literacy in a multi-dimensional way, not one standard at a time. So, as you plan or reflect on your lessons, remember to ask yourself, "What more can I teach through this learning experience?"

SUMMARY

Everything we've covered in this chapter comes down to planning. Careful and thorough planning for the module before instruction begins will help you ensure a comprehensive and effective learning experience for your students. Without a doubt, the first time that you teach a module, the planning phase will be labor-intensive. Backward-mapping the module and developing your block plan will take time, as will developing individual lessons and embedding outcomes. However, a good structure will allow you to see gaps in your instructional plan before you even begin implementing it. With a strong framework in place, you will be able to refine and improve your lessons more easily as you move through the module, as well as when you re-teach it in the future.

CHAPTER 3

Meeting the National Standards and Grade-Level Outcomes in High School

As a high school teacher, you play a critical role in students' progress toward the goal of becoming physically literate individuals. You help them refine their middle school competencies into the knowledge, skills, and behaviors that they will need to be physically active in adulthood. This means increasing the complexity of, and the expectations for, student learning. To help students negotiate this transition successfully, you will need to design and implement effective lessons that are based on the Grade-Level Outcomes for high school students. These outcomes form the foundation for planning modules and developing curricula, so it's important that you have a thorough understanding of their content and structure. To facilitate that understanding, the first section of this chapter presents information that differentiates the outcomes for high school students from the outcomes for middle school students. You can find out more about the high school–level outcomes in Chapter 5 of *National Standards & Grade-Level Outcomes for K-12 Physical Education* (SHAPE America – Society of Health and Physical Educators, 2014). At the end of this chapter, you will find a table containing the high school–level outcomes for your reference.

HIGH SCHOOL IS DIFFERENT

The lifelong utilization stage of motor development is at the core of the Grade-Level Outcomes for high school (Gallahue, Ozmun, & Goodway, 2012). In this particular stage, students have a greater awareness of their skills and abilities than they did in the application stage (middle school) and seek to participate in activities of their choice. Skills and knowledge become more specialized, as students learn or refine motor competencies that they will use in adulthood (Gallahue, Ozmun, & Goodway, 2012). By high school, students have made decisions about the types of physical activity that they enjoy, and they have a good understanding of the role that a physically active lifestyle can play in their lives.

The lifelong utilization stage intersects with many of the variables that influence students' learning and engagement, as discussed in Chapter 1. Factors such as competence and perceived competence, gender differences, autonomy (choice), relatedness (social support), cognitive challenge, and instructional climate were important considerations in SHAPE America's development of the Grade-Level Outcomes because those factors affect how students interact with the curriculum (SHAPE America, 2014). The high school–level outcomes reflect an assimilation of students' developmental characteristics, as well as the research on student learning and engagement. The outcomes provide a progression from the competencies expected in middle school to the goal of physical literacy, with consideration given to the environment in which most high school physical education is taught.

THE PROGRESSION FROM MIDDLE SCHOOL

The outcomes for high school students expand on many of the competencies developed in middle school, while shifting the focus to equipping students for a lifetime of physical activity. That approach is aligned with the lifetime utilization stage and the goal of physical literacy. For example, the outcomes for high school students under Standard 1 (*The physically literate individual demonstrates competency in a variety of motor skills and movement patterns*) include lifelong activities only, such as dance, fitness activities, outdoor pursuits, individual-performance activities, aquatics, net/wall games, and target games (SHAPE America, 2014, p. 56). These activity areas, indeed, are present in the middle school–level outcomes, but they take on added emphasis in the high school–level outcomes, which prescribe how students can augment and refine the skills and knowledge they will need to pursue activities in those areas beyond graduation. The prominence of dance and fitness activities in the high school–level outcomes under Standard 1 addresses the activity preferences of many high school girls, which often are overlooked in traditional team sport curricula (Couturier, Chepko, & Coughlin, 2007; O'Neill, Pate, & Liese, 2011). These activities, along with outdoor pursuits, individual-performance activities, and aquatics, lend themselves to cooperative or noncompetitive approaches, which girls and less-skilled students often prefer (Garn, Ware, & Solmon, 2011; Portman, 2003). These activities also have the advantage of offering opportunities for students to support or interact positively with one another, which addresses relatedness, another factor that affects engagement (Ruiz et al., 2010).

Unlike the outcomes for middle school students, the high school–level outcomes don't emphasize games and sports. In particular, invasion games and fielding and striking games are excluded in the high school–level outcomes because those sports typically are not considered lifetime activities and because the literature on student engagement provides evidence that such activities appeal mainly to highly skilled students (SHAPE America, 2014, p. 54). Although highly-skilled students might enjoy the opportunity to demonstrate their proficiency in sport-based activities during physical education classes, the traditional team sport curriculum holds little interest for many high school students, particularly girls (Gao, Lee, & Harrison, 2012; Hannon & Ratcliffe, 2005). And, although many people play some fielding/striking games, such as softball, long after high school, such games are not included in the outcomes under Standard 1 for high school students because they don't provide many opportunities for moderate to vigorous physical activity, and they place less-skilled students in a performance environment that leads to peer comparisons. As noted in Chapter 1, those comparisons can alienate less-skilled students: the very students who most need to be engaged (Garn, Ware, & Solmon, 2011). For more information on gender and skillfulness, see the topic-area references at the end of this book.

The other outcomes for high school students also build on the foundation laid in middle school by increasing the complexity of knowledge and skills that students are to acquire. Outcomes under Standard 2 (*The physically literate individual applies knowledge of concepts, principles, strategies and tactics related to movement and performance*) achieve that by exposing high school students to basic concepts in motor learning, biomechanics, and socio-cultural elements of movement (SHAPE America, 2014, p. 57). High school students learn complex concepts in other subject areas and we have no reason to expect anything different in physical education. These subdisciplines of our field provide valuable conceptual knowledge for lifelong participation in physical activity and help provide the cognitive demand and stimulation that students need to stay engaged.

Outcomes under Standard 3 (*The physically literate individual demonstrates the knowledge and skills to achieve a health-enhancing level of physical activity and fitness*) provide similar challenges in the cognitive area by addressing more difficult fitness and physical activity content than do the outcomes for middle school students. In addition, Standard 3 is a special area of emphasis within the high school–level outcomes, particularly those associated with planning, assessing, and implementing physical activity and fitness plans (SHAPE America, 2014, p. 54). Developing these types of plans requires students to synthesize skills and knowledge from many different areas related to wellness. It demonstrates student mastery of fitness skills and knowledge while preparing students for independent participation in physical activity after high school.

The focus of the outcomes under Standard 4 (*The physically literate individual exhibits responsible personal and social behavior that respects self and others*) is refining self-management and problem-solving skills that students developed at the middle school level. Both of those competencies are tied closely to students' attainment of the outcomes under Standard 3 and should be emphasized at the high school level (Corbin, 2002). The high school-level outcomes under Standard 5 (*The physically literate individual recognizes the value of physical activity for health, enjoyment, challenge, self-expression and/or social interaction*) focus on enhancing students' appreciation of physical activity for health, challenge, self-expression, enjoyment and social interaction (SHAPE America, 2014, p. 58-60), as do the outcomes for middle school students.

HIGH SCHOOL INSTRUCTIONAL ENVIRONMENT

The requirements for high school physical education in terms of minutes per week vary widely across the United States (NASPE & AHA, 2012). Some states require only one or two semesters of physical education for high school students, while others require four years of physical education. With that in mind, the Grade-Level Outcomes for high school students are structured differently from those for middle school students in grades 6, 7, and 8. Instead, the outcomes for high school students have only two levels of competency: Level 1 and Level 2. While it would be possible to develop outcomes for grades 9, 10, 11, and 12 individually, teaching toward that many outcomes wouldn't be very practical or even achievable for programs that require only minimal physical education participation in high school. As a result:

> Level 1 outcomes reflect the minimum knowledge and skills that students must acquire to be ready to pursue an active lifestyle in college or after they enter a career. Level 2 outcomes allow students to build on Level 1 competencies by augmenting knowledge and skills considered desirable for pursuing an active lifestyle through college and/or into a career (SHAPE America, 2014, p. 55)

Using this two-level structure, teachers with limited instructional time can focus on the Level 1 outcomes, and those with more time can integrate the Level 2 outcomes into their lessons. Also, the two-level structure is well suited to planning for differentiated instruction for a range of skill levels in your classes. It's important to pre-assess students to determine their levels of competency before beginning any module. If students haven't mastered some of the middle school–level outcomes, you will need to work on those before moving on to the high school Level 1 and Level 2 outcomes. You know your students best, and you should always consider how the modules might be adjusted to meet the needs of your students.

High schools often use block scheduling, which can offer real benefits for physical education when implemented well. Obviously, you can't expect students to be *vigorously* physically active for the entire period, but block scheduling does allow you time for formal instruction as well as sufficient time for deliberate practice and moderate to vigorous physical activity (SHAPE America, 2014, p. 55). By devoting more time to instruction and deliberate practice, you increase the likelihood that students will become competent and will continue to participate in activities outside of and beyond high school. Longer block periods also can help you address environmental barriers to participation, which are particularly relevant for high school girls and revolve around issues of appearance and hygiene (Cockburn, 2001; Derry, 2002). Block periods permit you to carve out enough time for students to change clothes, shower, and get ready for the next class, which can alleviate some of their concerns.

Keep in mind that the advancement of motor skill competence is the most important goal of the Grade-Level Outcomes for high school students, and that you are trying to help students attain the outcomes by the end of the high school program, not in any one module or lesson. Students' perceptions of their competence play a role in how willing they are to engage in physical education and physical activity (SHAPE America, 2014, p. 9; Stuart et al., 2005). Competence and/or perceived competence can be crucial in combatting the well-documented decline in physical activity during the high school years (Patnode et al., 2011; Yli-Piipari et al., 2012). For more information on competence and perceived competence and on engagement, see the topic-area references at the end of this book.

The modules in this book are organized around several activity categories: outdoor pursuits, fitness activities, and aquatics; dance and rhythmic activities; and net/wall games and target games. Many activities could fit into more than one category, depending on the focus of the outcomes applied. Swimming, for example, could be considered an aquatics activity, a fitness activity, or both. Given the developmental level of high school students and the length of time needed to attain skill and knowledge competency, SHAPE America recommends that modules at the high school level consist of 15 or 16 lessons (SHAPE America, 2014, p. 55). That's twice the minimum number recommended for middle school–level modules. This longer time frame for high school modules allows students more practice opportunities to acquire the skills and knowledge that they need to attain physical literacy and is aligned with the intent of the Common Core State Standards to teach for greater depth. It also simulates physical activity classes in college or health club settings, preparing students to succeed in adult physical activity environments.

The modules and lesson plans for high school that appear in the chapters that follow are designed to be implemented in a block period format of 70 to 90 minutes, including time for changing and showering. If your school doesn't offer block periods, you can adjust the quantity of content in the lesson plans to fit the length of your class periods. You might not be accustomed to teaching modules of this length, and it might be challenging at first. You will need to apply your knowledge of student-engagement factors to retain student interest over the course of the module. Fostering a mastery-oriented instructional environment, incorporating appropriate levels of challenge, and allowing for student choice through differentiation and a well-designed elective program will help you succeed.

GRADE-LEVEL OUTCOMES FOR HIGH SCHOOL STUDENTS (GRADES 9-12)

By the end of high school, the learner will be college- or career-ready, as demonstrated by the ability to plan and implement different types of personal fitness programs; demonstrate competency in two or more lifetime activities; describe key concepts associated with successful participation in physical activity; model responsible behavior while engaged in physical activity; and engage in physical activities that meet the need for self-expression, challenge, social interaction, and enjoyment (SHAPE America, 2014, p. 56).

TABLE 3.1 High School Outcomes (Grades 9-12)

Standard 1. The physically literate individual demonstrates competency in a variety of motor skills and movement patterns.

Standard 1	Level 1	Level 2
Lifetime activities		
S1.H1	Demonstrates competency and/or refines activity-specific movement skills in 2 or more lifetime activities (outdoor pursuits, individual-performance activities, aquatics, net/wall games or target games).[i] (S1.H1.L1)	Refines activity-specific movement skills in 1 or more lifetime activities (outdoor pursuits, individual-performance activities, aquatics, net/wall games or target games).[ii] (S1.H1.L2)
Dance & rhythms		
S1.H2	Demonstrates competency in dance forms used in cultural and social occasions (e.g., weddings, parties), *or* demonstrates competency in 1 form of dance (e.g., ballet, modern, hip hop, tap). (S1.H2.L1)	Demonstrates competency in a form of dance by choreographing a dance or by giving a performance. (S1.H2.L2)
Fitness activities		
S1.H3	Demonstrates competency in 1 or more specialized skills in health-related fitness activities. (S1.H3.L1)	Demonstrates competency in 2 or more specialized skills in health-related fitness activities. (S1.H3.L2)

Standard 2. The physically literate individual applies knowledge of concepts, principles, strategies and tactics related to movement and performance.

Standard 2	Level 1	Level 2
Movement concepts, principles & knowledge		
S2.H1	Applies the terminology associated with exercise and participation in selected individual-performance activities, dance, net/wall games, target games, aquatics and/or outdoor pursuits appropriately. (S2.H1.L1)	Identifies and discusses the historical and cultural roles of games, sports and dance in a society.[iii] (S2.H1.L2)
S2.H2	Uses movement concepts and principles (e.g., force, motion, rotation) to analyze and improve performance of self and/or others in a selected skill.[iv] (S2.H2.L1)	Describes the speed/accuracy trade-off in throwing and striking skills.[v] (S2.H2.L2)
S2.H3	Creates a practice plan to improve performance for a self-selected skill. (S2.H3.L1)	Identifies the stages of learning a motor skill. (S2.H3.L2)
S2.H4	Identifies examples of social and technical dance forms. (S2.H4.L1)	Compares similarities and differences in various dance forms. (S2.H4.L2)

Standard 3. The physically literate individual demonstrates the knowledge and skills to achieve a health-enhancing level of physical activity and fitness.

Standard 3	Level 1	Level 2
Physical activity knowledge		
S3.H1	Discusses the benefits of a physically active lifestyle as it relates to college or career productivity. (S3.H1.L1)	Investigates the relationships among physical activity, nutrition and body composition. (S3.H1.L2)
S3.H2	Evaluates the validity of claims made by commercial products and programs pertaining to fitness and a healthy, active lifestyle.[vi] (S3.H2.L1)	Analyzes and applies technology and social media as tools for supporting a healthy, active lifestyle.[vii] (S3.H2.L2)
S3.H3	Identifies issues associated with exercising in heat, humidity and cold.[viii] (S3.H3.L1)	Applies rates of perceived exertion and pacing.[ix] (S3.H3.L2)
S3.H4	Evaluates—according to their benefits, social support network and participation requirements—activities that can be pursued in the local environment.[x] (S3.H4.L1)	*If the learner did not attain the Outcome in Level 1, it should be a focus in Level 2.*
S3.H5	Evaluates risks and safety factors that might affect physical activity preferences throughout the life cycle.[xi] (S3.H5.L1)	Analyzes the impact of life choices, economics, motivation and accessibility on exercise adherence and participation in physical activity in college or career settings. (S3.H5.L2)
Engages in physical activity		
S3.H6	Participates several times a week in a self-selected lifetime activity, dance or fitness activity outside of the school day. (S3.H6.L1)	Creates a plan, trains for and participates in a community event with a focus on physical activity (e.g., 5K, triathlon, tournament, dance performance, cycling event).[xii] (S3.H6.L2)
Fitness knowledge		
S3.H7	Demonstrates appropriate technique on resistance-training machines and with free weights.[xiii] (S3.H7.L1)	Designs and implements a strength and conditioning program that develops balance in opposing muscle groups (agonist–antagonist) and supports a healthy, active lifestyle.[xiv] (S3.H7.L2)
S3.H8	Relates physiological responses to individual levels of fitness and nutritional balance.[xv] (S3.H8.L1)	Identifies the different energy systems used in a selected physical activity (e.g., adenosine triphosphate and phosphocreatine, anaerobic glycolysis, aerobic).[xvi] (S3.H8.L2)
S3.H9	Identifies types of strength exercises (isometric, concentric, eccentric) and stretching exercises (static, proprioceptive neuromuscular facilitation (PNF), dynamic) for personal fitness development (e.g., strength, endurance, range of motion).[xvii] (S3.H9.L1)	Identifies the structure of skeletal muscle and fiber types as they relate to muscle development.[xviii] (S2.H9.L2)
S3.H10	Calculates target heart rate and applies that information to personal fitness plan. (S3.H10.L1)	Adjusts pacing to keep heart rate in the target zone, using available technology (e.g., pedometer, heart rate monitor), to self-monitor aerobic intensity. (S3.H10.L2)[xix]
Assessment & program planning		
S3.H11	Creates and implements a behavior-modification plan that enhances a healthy, active lifestyle in college or career settings. (S3.H11.L1)	Develops and maintains a fitness portfolio (e.g., assessment scores, goals for improvement, plan of activities for improvement, log of activities being done to reach goals, timeline for improvement).[xx] (S3.H11.L2)
S3.H12	Designs a fitness program, including all components of health-related fitness, for a college student and an employee in the learner's chosen field of work. (S3.H12.L1)	Analyzes the components of skill-related fitness in relation to life and career goals, and designs an appropriate fitness program for those goals.[xxi] (S3.H12.L2)
Nutrition		
S3.H13	Designs and implements a nutrition plan to maintain an appropriate energy balance for a healthy, active lifestyle. (S3.H13.L1)	Creates a snack plan for before, during and after exercise that addresses nutrition needs for each phase. (S3.H13.L2)
Stress management		
S3.H14	Identifies stress-management strategies (e.g., mental imagery, relaxation techniques, deep breathing, aerobic exercise, meditation) to reduce stress.[xxii] (S3.H14.L1)	Applies stress-management strategies (e.g., mental imagery, relaxation techniques, deep breathing, aerobic exercise, meditation) to reduce stress.[xxiii] (S3.H14.L2)

Standard 4. The physically literate individual exhibits responsible personal and social behavior that respects self and others.

Standard 4	Level 1	Level 2
Personal responsibility		
S4.H1	Employs effective self-management skills to analyze barriers and modify physical activity patterns appropriately, as needed.[xxiv] (S4.H1.L1)	Accepts differences between personal characteristics and the idealized body images and elite performance levels portrayed in various media.[xxv] (S4.H1.L2)
Rules & etiquette		
S4.H2	Exhibits proper etiquette, respect for others and teamwork while engaging in physical activity and/or social dance. (S4.H2.L1)	Examines moral and ethical conduct in specific competitive situations (e.g., intentional fouls, performance-enhancing substances, gambling, current events in sport).[xxvi] (S4.H2.L2)
Working with others		
S4.H3	Uses communication skills and strategies that promote team or group dynamics.[xxvii] (S4.H3.L1)	Assumes a leadership role (e.g., task or group leader, referee, coach) in a physical activity setting. (S4.H3.L2)
S4.H4	Solves problems and thinks critically in physical activity and/or dance settings, both as an individual and in groups. (S4.H4.L1)	Accepts others' ideas, cultural diversity and body types by engaging in cooperative and collaborative movement projects. (S4.H4.L2)
Safety		
S4.H5	Applies best practices for participating safely in physical activity, exercise and dance (e.g., injury prevention, proper alignment, hydration, use of equipment, implementation of rules, sun protection). (S4.H5.L1)	*If the learner did not attain the Outcome in Level 1, it should be a focus in Level 2.*

Standard 5. The physically literate individual recognizes the value of physical activity for health, enjoyment, challenge, self-expression and/or social interaction.

Standard 5	Level 1	Level 2
Health		
S5.H1	Analyzes the health benefits of a self-selected physical activity. (S5.H1.L1)	*If the outcome was not achieved in Level 1, it should be a focus in Level 2.*
Challenge		
S5.H2	*Challenge is a focus in Level 2.*	Chooses an appropriate level of challenge to experience success and desire to participate in a self-selected physical activity.[xxviii] (S5.H2.L2)
Self-expression & enjoyment		
S5.H3	Selects and participates in physical activities or dance that meet the need for self-expression and enjoyment. (S5.H3.L1)	Identifies the uniqueness of creative dance as a means of self-expression. (S5.H3.L2)
Social interaction		
S5.H4	Identifies the opportunity for social support in a self-selected physical activity or dance. (S5.H4.L1)	Evaluates the opportunity for social interaction and social support in a self-selected physical activity or dance.[xxix] (S5.H4.L2)

[i]Manitoba Education and Training, School Programs Division, 2000, www.edu.gov.mb.ca/k12/cur/physhlth/grade_10.html?print.

[ii]Ibid.

[iii]NASPE, 1992, p. 15.

[iv]Ibid.

[v]Mohnsen, 2010).

[vi]NASPE, 1992, p. 16.

[vii]NASPE, 2012, p. 20.

[viii]Ibid., p. 9.

[ix]Ibid., p. 5.

[x]NASPE, 1992, p. 15.

[xi]Ibid.

[xii]NASPE, 2012, p. 27.

[xiii]Ibid., p. 6.

[xiv]Manitoba Education and Training, School Programs Division, 2000, www.edu.gov.mb.ca/k12/cur/physhlth/grade_9.html?print.

[xv]NASPE, 2012, p. 15.

[xvi]Ibid., p. 16.

[xvii]Manitoba Education and Training, School Programs Division, 2000, www.edu.gov.mb.ca/k12/cur/physhlth/grade_9.html?print.

[xviii]Ibid.

[xix]NASPE, 2012, p. 23.

[xx]*(Ohio) Physical Education Standards.* (p. 113).

[xxi]Superintendent of Public Instruction, Washington, 2008, p. 101.

[xxii]Manitoba Education and Training, School Programs Division, 2000, www.edu.gov.mb.ca/k12/cur/physhlth/grade_10.html?print.

[xxiii]Ibid.

[xxiv]NASPE, 2012, p. 25.

[xxv]NASPE, 1992, p. 16.

[xxvi]Manitoba Education and Training, School Programs Division, 2000, www.edu.gov.mb.ca/k12/cur/physhlth/grade_10.html?print.

[xxvii]Ibid.

[xxviii]*(Ohio) Physical Education Standards.* (p. 115).

[xxix]Ibid.

Reprinted, by permission, from SHAPE America, 2014, *National standards & grand-level outcomes for K-12 physical education* (Champaign, IL: Human Kinetics), 56-60.

OPERATIONAL DEFINITIONS OF ACTIVITY CATEGORIES (SHAPE AMERICA, 2014, P. 61)

Following are operational definitions of the activity categories used in this book.

Outdoor pursuits: The outdoor environment is an important factor in student engagement in the activity. Activities might include recreational boating (e.g., kayaking, canoeing, sailing, rowing); hiking; backpacking; fishing; orienteering or geocaching; ice skating; skateboarding; snow or water skiing; snowboarding; snowshoeing; surfing; bouldering, traversing, or climbing; mountain biking; adventure activities; and ropes courses. The selection of activities depends on the environment-related opportunities within the geographical region.

Fitness activities: Activities with a focus on improving or maintaining fitness. Fitness activities might include yoga, Pilates, resistance training, spinning, running, fitness walking, fitness swimming, kickboxing, cardio kick, Zumba, and exergaming.

Dance and rhythmic activities: Activities that focus on dance or rhythms. Dance and rhythmic activities might include dance forms such as creative movement or dance, ballet, modern, ethnic or folk, hip hop, Latin, line, ballroom, social, and square.

Aquatics: Might include swimming, diving, synchronized swimming, and water polo.

Individual-performance activities: Might include gymnastics, figure skating, track and field, multi-sport events, in-line skating, wrestling, self-defense, and skateboarding.

Games and sports: Includes the games categories of invasion, net/wall, target, and fielding and striking.

CHAPTER 4

Developing an Electives-Based Program for High School Students

Addressing students' interests and providing students with choices is an important aspect of meeting the National Standards and Grade-Level Outcomes for high school (SHAPE America – Society of Health and Physical Educators, 2014, p. 54). During the high school years, which coincide with the lifelong utilization stage of development (Gallahue, Ozmun, & Goodway, 2012), students are more cognizant of their abilities than ever before and have developed preferences for certain physical activities. The literature on student engagement and learning makes it clear that students are more motivated, interested, and involved when they are allowed to choose activities and/or learning experiences than when they are not involved in those choices (Bryan et al., 2013; Hannon & Ratcliffe, 2005; Ntoumanis et al., 2004). Providing students with choices also enhances perceptions of autonomy, which can lead to higher levels of satisfaction (Ntoumanis et al., 2004).

As students progress through the scope and sequence of an effective physical education program and become increasingly physically literate, they should be given the opportunity to choose the physical education and wellness topics that make up their high school physical education experience. In fact, Outcome S5.H3.L1

Aaron Hart is a lecturer at the State University of New York College at Cortland and is director of educational programs for US Games.

states that high school students should develop the competency to select and participate in "physical activities or dance that meet the need for self-expression and enjoyment" (SHAPE America, 2014, p. 60). One common method for providing high school students with such choices is to offer an electives program so that students can select the activities that interest them the most. Well-planned electives-based physical education programs allow teachers and their students to measure and progress toward this critical outcome. With that in mind, this chapter offers two focused suggestions for programs that are exploring ways to begin, or expand, an electives-based physical education program:

1. Thematic strands
2. Personalized curriculum design

WHY CONSIDER ELECTIVES-BASED PHYSICAL EDUCATION?

As physical educators, we strive to instill within our students a sense of intrinsic motivation that will drive them to participate in physical education and activity because they find it interesting and enjoyable, and to embrace the curriculum because it offers opportunity for learning (Vallerand et al., 1992). It's also important that they possess a degree of self-regulation based on their internalized value of physical education participation (Ryan & Deci, 2000). That is, they participate because they understand the importance of physical literacy for their overall health and lifetime wellness (Ntoumanis, 2005).

What does this all mean for the practitioner? Stated simply, it means that we have to plan lessons and modules that students will enjoy, find challenging, and see as relevant to their overall health, wellness, and lifestyle. In 2014, high school physical educator Tracy Krause—who contributed the three outdoor pursuits modules in chapter 5—described his school's student survey as a critical tool for developing a departmental vision and overall curriculum plan that aligned with the values and interests of both the students and the community (Krause, 2014). Further, Krause explains that these data exposed the importance of intentional and focused decision making. Honest teacher reflection, strategic re-thinking, intentional planning, and mindful assessment are all requirements for physical educators striving toward highly effective curriculum development and implementation. Fortunately, tools such as Google Forms make it easier than ever to use student surveys as a method for gathering critical information to help teachers make informed curriculum decisions.

Start With a Survey

To move forward with an intentional focus on student participation and motivation, programs can start with a student survey based on Standard 5 (SHAPE America, 2014, p. 60). Even when there are potential barriers to immediate change (e.g., funding, facilities, equipment, administrative support), starting the process with a short survey is an act that will begin to build an important bridge between you and your students.

Planning survey questions based on the Grade-Level Outcomes under Standard 5 helps ensure that you're using backward-design principles and are indeed starting with your learning goals in mind. Table 4.1 provides a series of sample survey questions that you can use as a starting point for your own customized student survey.

TABLE 4.1 Sample Survey Questions Based on Grade-Level Outcomes

Standard 5 Grade-Level Outcome	Related survey questions
Health *Analyzes the health benefits of a self-selected physical activity. (S5.H1.L1)*	What activities would you like to participate in during physical education to help you improve or maintain your health and wellness? What activities and programs do you participate in outside of school that can help you improve or maintain your health and wellness?
Challenge *Chooses an appropriate level of challenge to experience success and desire to participate in a self-selected physical activity. (S5.H2.L2)*	What physical activities and programs do you enjoy that also challenge your skill or fitness levels?
Self-expression and enjoyment *Selects and participates in physical activities or dance that meet the need for self-expression and enjoyment. (S5.H3.1)*	What physical activities do you enjoy because they help express who you are as a person? What types of dances do you enjoy?
Self-expression and enjoyment *Identifies the uniqueness of creative dance as a means of self-expression. (S5.H3.L2)*	What characteristics of creative dance do you enjoy? Briefly explain why.
Social interaction *Identifies the opportunity for social support in a self-selected physical activity or dance. (S5.H4.L1)*	What physical activities do you enjoy participating in with family and/or friends? What physical activities have helped you meet new friends?
Social interaction *Evaluates the opportunity for social interaction and social support in a self-selected physical activity or dance. (S5.H4.L2)*	How important to you is being with friends during physical activity? In what ways could having options for physical activities during physical education class help you feel included and/or socially accepted?

Examine Your Resources

Once you have a baseline understanding of what students want and need during their physical education experience, take an honest and creative look at the resources that are available to you.

Teachers are a program's greatest resource. Often, the physical activity options that physical education teachers value match the resources available within the community, but if that's not the case, teacher interest and passion can overcome many obstacles to new offerings. Although curriculum design and implementation should be a collaborative effort among teachers, each member of a department can take ownership of an activity category that interests him or her most. It's also likely that there will be an essential category (or categories) that no one is particularly passionate about. However, the fire and energy created in the process of planning a favorite module or category can carry over into the planning of important topics that may not be particularly favored.

Once your teaching team is excited about content possibilities, take a look at the equipment and facilities available. If fitness swimming rises to the top of the survey results and is a passion for one of the teachers, then take time to examine how the department can gain access to a pool. Community partnerships and grant programs may help make this option a real possibility. However, it's also important to spend time and effort on activity options that are realistic and sustainable. As you begin working toward an electives-based design, it's okay to provide relevant options that fit within program limitations while working to secure the resources for future activity options. You certainly will want to work closely with your school's administrators to secure their buy-in for community partnerships, grant applications, or changes in program direction.

The final resource to be considered is time, and this resource is affected both by school scheduling policy and by the number of teachers available in each period. Lay out a blank block plan before determining the type of design you will implement. It's possible that, because of scheduling parameters, you might choose one design for grades 9 and 10 and another design for grades 11 and 12. Scheduling can be frustrating. It's important to stay positive and be creative during this phase of the planning process.

SELECT A DESIGN, CREATE A PLAN, AND THEN IMPLEMENT THE PROGRAM

The thematic strand design provides two or more pathways from which students can choose, with each pathway containing a series of physical activity and wellness topics that work collectively to meet students' interests and motivational needs, as well as the curricular outcomes. For example, strands could follow the *activity categories* provided by SHAPE America, offering students a choice between pathways in outdoor pursuits, fitness activities, lifetime sports, dance, and individual-performance activities (SHAPE America, 2014, p. 61). Each strand will be subject to the resources available to the school community as well as the experience and expertise of the physical education staff. However, even schools with limited resources and small physical education departments have been creative and resourceful in finding ways to provide content that meets students' interests and needs. You can offer pathways as full-year or split-year pathway options.

Full-Year Multiple-Pathway Option

Students select a pathway to follow at the start of the year and then follow that course of study for the entire year. Table 4.2 lists five possible pathways from which to choose: outdoor pursuits, fitness activities, individual-performance activities, lifetime sports, and dance. If the students in your school receive more than one year of physical education, you can encourage or require them to choose a different pathway during each year of their physical education experience.

Split-Year Dual-Pathway Option

Students select a pathway to follow for the first half of the year. At the end of the first half, students then choose again. Table 4.3 provides an example of how to organize a split-year dual pathway. Although dance and individual-performance activities do not appear in this example, they could be used just as easily as the types of activities that do appear. To ensure that students receive adequate fitness instruction, programs may opt to require fitness activities in either the first or second half of the year. You should encourage students to explore a different pathway in the second half of the year.

Use the flow chart in Table 4.4 and yearly block plans as examples or templates of thematic elective strands (full-year multiple pathway or split-year dual pathway) as a structure.

TABLE 4.2 Example of a Full-Year Multiple-Pathway Option Using SHAPE America Activity Categories

Module	Outdoor pursuits	Fitness activities	Individual performance activities	Lifetime sports	Dance
1	Fitness assessment and program planning	Fitness assessment and program planning	Fitness assessment and program planning	Fitness assessment and program planning	Fitness assessment and program planning
2	Climbing	Fitness walking or fitness swimming	In-line or ice skating	Pickleball or badminton	Social or ballroom dance
3	Snowshoeing or cross-country skiing	Strength/resistance training	Tai chi	Archery or recreational target games	Folk or square dance
4	Hiking and geocaching	Yoga or Pilates	Dance or creative dance	Volleyball	Hip-hop or Latin dance
5	Fly fishing or canoeing or kayaking	Cardio kick or kickboxing	Self-defense	Golf or disc golf	Ballet or modern dance
6	Mountain biking and summer fitness planning	Spinning or cycling and summer fitness planning	Multi-sport (triathlon) and summer fitness planning	Tennis and summer fitness planning	Performance dance or choreography and summer fitness planning

TABLE 4.3 Example of a Split-Year Dual-Pathway Option Using SHAPE America Activity Categories

First half	Outdoor pursuits	Fitness activities
Module 1	Hiking and geocaching	Fitness assessment and program planning
Module 2	Mountain biking	Yoga
Module 3	Climbing	Strength training
Second half	**Fitness activities**	**Lifetime sports**
Module 4	Fitness assessment and program planning	Tennis
Module 5	Pilates and core	Volleyball
Module 6	Fitness swimming	Golf

TABLE 4.4 Examples of Two-Year Student Flow Chart for Full-Year Multiple-Pathway Option and One-Year Student Flow Chart for Dual-Pathway Option

Full-year multiple-pathway option (two-year student flow chart)		
Year 1: Student selects an activity category pathway.	Throughout year 1, student completes all of the activity modules listed in the selected pathway.	
Year 2: Student selects a different activity category pathway.	Throughout year 2, student completes all of the activity modules listed in the selected pathway.	X
Advantage: Students are immersed in an activity category, gaining maximum experience within areas that interest them the most. Teachers can focus on crafting learning experiences and assessment tools in a single activity category.		
Split-year dual-pathway option (one-year student flow chart)		
First half of the year: All students choose between one of two pathways.	Throughout the first half of the year, students complete all of the activity modules listed in the selected pathway.	
Second half of the year: All students choose between one of two pathways. (Students who do not complete a fitness activity pathway in the first 20 weeks must select a fitness activity pathway for the second 20 weeks.)	Throughout the second half of the year, students complete all of the activity modules listed in the selected pathway.	X
Advantage: This design works well in schools with only two physical education teachers. Students still experience immersion in self-selected activity categories while gaining critical fitness knowledge.		

PERSONALIZED CURRICULUM DESIGN

A personalized curriculum design offers a more modular approach to program development, with a framework that allows students to build their own course of study by choosing from a variety of physical activity and wellness options that guide students toward curriculum outcomes.

At the start of the year, give students a blank physical education plan. Each student's plan has an empty physical education course map containing activity category headers as guides. Students are also given a yearly block schedule of module options to use as they select and map out their year.

To help ensure that students acquire and hone the specialized physical skills and knowledge that they will use in adulthood (SHAPE America, 2014, p. 53), provide guidelines that will result in a well-balanced physical education plan that offers a variety of choices across multiple activity categories. Use the sample yearly block schedule and physical education plan in tables 4.5 and figure 4.1 as templates for creating similar documents that work with your district resources and scheduling requirements.

TAKE THE FIRST STEP

Planning and implementing any electives-based design will take a lot of collaborative effort and must involve all members of a physical education department. For those beginning this journey, here's a summary of this chapter's suggested workflow.

1. Survey students. Starting here will help ensure relevancy to your students and your community.

2. Examine your resources. What are the strengths of each teacher? What equipment and facilities are available? What options can be programmed into your school's scheduling format?

3. Select a design and create a plan. Whether you choose thematic strands or personalized curriculum design, invest the time during the initial planning stages to create a detailed road map that students will enjoy and understand easily while working toward prioritized outcomes.

4. Implement the program. Electives-based physical education can present an opportunity to continually energize and fully engage both students and teachers while offering that critical component of choice to students.

SUMMARY

Designing an effective high school physical education curriculum that is both relevant and challenging for all students is an endeavor worth starting and maintaining (Doolittle, 2014). For programs considering an electives-based design, the suggestions in this chapter can serve as a starting point for departmental discussion and exploration. It's important to remember that no two designs will be exactly alike. Each and every program should be unique. Allow your program to encompass and exemplify the personalities, character, and values of teachers, students, and the entire school community.

TABLE 4.5 Sample Yearly Block Schedule

Module	Elective 1	Elective 2	Elective 3
1	Fitness assessment and program planning (required)	Fitness assessment and program planning (required)	Fitness assessment and program planning (required)
2	Hiking (outdoor pursuits)	Tennis (lifetime sports, net/wall)	Yoga (fitness activities)
3	Party dances (dance)	Creative dance (dance)	Skateboarding (individual performance)
4	Badminton (lifetime sports)	Strength training (fitness activities)	Self-defense (individual performance)
5	Snowshoeing (outdoor pursuits)	Fitness walking (fitness activities)	In-line skating (individual performance)
6	Hip-hop (dance) Summer fitness planning (required)	Rock climbing (outdoor pursuits) Summer fitness planning (required)	Golf (lifetime sports/target) Summer fitness planning (required)

FIGURE 4.1 SAMPLE PHYSICAL EDUCATION PLAN TEMPLATE

Student name: _____ Class: _____

Instructions: Write in the name of your elective choice, along with its activity category. Record each of your selections appropriately in the Activity Category Tracker at the bottom of this page.

You must schedule at least one elective in each activity category.

Module 1	Module 2	Module 3
Fitness assessment and program planning (required)	Choice: _____ Activity category: _____	Choice: _____ Activity category: _____
Module 4	**Module 5**	**Module 6**
Choice: _____ Activity category: _____	Choice: _____ Activity category: _____	Choice: _____ Activity category: _____

Category	List all elective choices scheduled above
Outdoor pursuits	
Fitness activities	
Individual performance	
Lifetime sports	
Dance	

From L.C. MacDonald, R.J. Doan, and S. Chepko, eds., 2018, *Lesson planning for high school physical education* (Reston, VA: SHAPE America; Champaign, IL: Human Kinetics).

PART II

Lesson Plans for High School Physical Education

CHAPTER 5

Extending Students' Skills and Knowledge to Outdoor Pursuits

If you have the good fortune to teach near a park or other beautiful recreation area, you will want to take advantage of those natural resources to help your students engage in outdoor pursuits. With young people spending less and less time engaged with nature and ever-increasing amounts of time in front of screens, teaching them the fundamental skills for enjoying the natural world can be a powerful tool (Louv, 2008). Outdoor pursuits provide opportunities for lifelong physical activity, challenge, team building, adventure, reflection, and appreciation of the natural world. They include a wide range of activities, from snow sports (skiing—Nordic or alpine, snowshoeing, skating, snowboarding) to hiking, mountain biking, kayaking, canoeing, fishing, surfing, and many more. As a teacher, you will want to identify activities that you and your classes can pursue in your geographical area and that, ideally, are culturally relevant to your community so that students will find them meaningful and interesting.

This chapter includes three modules for outdoor pursuits: integrated fly fishing, hiking, and rock climbing, each contributed by Tracy Krause, a physical education teacher at Tahoma High School in Maple Valley, Washington. The Rock Climbing Module is available in the e-book and web resource only. The three modules have a strong emphasis on developing skill competency (Outcome S1.H1. L1), applying new terminology and concepts (Outcomes S2.H1.L1 and S2.H2. L2), and recognizing the value of the activities (Standard 5). The Integrated Fly Fishing Module is somewhat unique in that it is taught in an interdisciplinary format and includes an emphasis on appreciating fly fishing culture (Outcome S2.H1.L2). The contributor worked closely with the school's science and English language arts teachers to integrate the readings, assignments, and content for all three areas. For example, students learn about fly casting at the same time that they read a novella in which fly fishing plays a prominent role. Concurrently, in science class, they also learn about the insects the fish eat and the biology of the environment in which they fish. To make this approach work, teachers must work together closely and must have the support of their principal. Even if you don't teach fly fishing, the module offers a great model for creating an interdisciplinary unit for your students and will excite them about the possibilities of making connections to other subject areas.

The Hiking Module allows for great flexibility, as students can hike in any natural setting. The module includes two popular variations on hiking that use technology: orienteering and geocaching. Students also learn about outdoor ethics and etiquette (Outcome S4.H2.L1) through the Leave No Trace philosophy that underpins the module. By necessity, the Rock Climbing Module, available in the e-book and web resource only, carries a strong focus on safety (Outcome S4.H5. L1), and the instructor must be highly trained in safety procedures for belaying and climbing. Both modules include important team-building skills, such as communication and problem solving (Outcomes S4.H3.L1 and S4.H4.L1). For easy reference, each module begins with a block plan chart of the Grade-Level Outcomes that are addressed in the lessons.

All three modules include a short field trip so that students can practice their skills and knowledge in an authentic environment. If you have the training and scheduling flexibility to take more extensive field trips, you can lengthen the modules by including those trips, which will further enhance students' learning experiences.

When teaching outdoor pursuits, the cost of equipment and access to facilities sometimes can be an obstacle. One way to address that is to develop community partnerships, through which students benefit but also contribute through volunteer work. One of the hiking lessons, for example, has a local parks official giving time to the class and students reciprocating by engaging in a trail-maintenance project. In one of the rock climbing lessons, students benefit by gaining access to a local indoor climbing facility, while facility owners can showcase what their facility has to offer for new climbers. For some outdoor pursuits, such as fishing, grant programs can help you buy equipment and some also provide training. Finally, don't overlook local businesses and booster clubs. They often are eager to support local activity programs.

INTEGRATED FLY FISHING MODULE

Lessons in this module were contributed by **Tracy Krause**, a physical education teacher at Tahoma High School in Maple Valley, WA.

Grade-Level Outcomes Addressed, by Lesson	1	2	3	4	5	6	7	8	9	10	11	12	13	14	15
Standard 1. The physically literate individual demonstrates competency in a variety of motor skills and movement patterns.															
Demonstrates competency and/or refines activity-specific movement skills in 2 or more lifetime activities (outdoor pursuits, individual-performance activities, aquatics, net/wall games or target games). (S1.H1.L1)	P	P	P	P	P	P	P	P		P	P	P		P	P
Standard 2. The physically literate individual applies knowledge of concepts, principles, strategies and tactics related to movement and performance.															
Applies the terminology associated with exercise and participation in selected individual-performance activities, dance, net/wall games, target games, aquatics and/or outdoor pursuits appropriately. (S2.H1.L1)	P	P	E		P	P	P	P	P	P	P	P	P	P	
Identifies and discusses the historical and cultural roles of games, sports and dance in society. (S2.H1.L2)		E							P		E		E		
Uses movement concepts and principles (e.g., force, motion, rotation) to analyze and improve performance of self and/or others in a selected skill. (S2.H2.L1)			E	E						E	P	E			
Standard 3. The physically literate individual demonstrates the knowledge and skills to achieve and maintain a health-enhancing level of physical activity and fitness.															
Identifies issues associated with exercising in heat, humidity and cold. (S3.H3.L1)														E	
Evaluates—according to their benefits, social support network and participation requirements—activities that can be pursued in the local environment. (S3.H4.L1)							P								
Applies stress-management strategies (e.g., mental imagery, relaxation techniques, deep breathing, aerobic exercise, meditation) to reduce stress. (S3.H14.L2)											E				
Standard 4. The physically literate individual exhibits responsible personal and social behavior that respects self and others.															
Employs effective self-management skills to analyze barriers and modify physical activity patterns appropriately, as needed. (S4.H1.L1)					E										
Exhibits proper etiquette, respect for others and teamwork while engaging in physical activity and/or social dance. (S4.H2.L1)		P													P
Examines moral and ethical conduct in specific competitive situations (e.g., intentional fouls, performance-enhancing substances, gambling, current events in sport). (S4.H2.L2)									E						
Uses communication skills and strategies that promote team or group dynamics. (S4.H3.L1)		P					E								
Solves problems and thinks critically in physical activity and/or dance settings, both as an individual and in groups. (S4.H4.L1)	E														
Accepts others' ideas, cultural diversity and body types by engaging in cooperative and collaborative movement projects. (S4.H4.L2)						E									
Applies best practices for participating safely in physical activity, exercise and dance (e.g., injury prevention, proper alignment, hydration, use of equipment, implementation of rules, sun protection). (S4.H5.L1)		E											P		
Standard 5. The physically literate individual recognizes the value of physical activity for health, enjoyment, challenge, self-expression and/or social interaction.															
Analyzes the health benefits of a self-selected physical activity. (S5.H1.L1)							E								
Chooses an appropriate level of challenge to experience success and desire to participate in a self-selected physical activity. (S5.H2.L2)															E
Selects and participates in physical activities or dance that meet the need for self-expression and enjoyment. (S5.H3.L1)		E					E								

P = Primary; E = Embedded

INTEGRATED FLY FISHING

LESSON 1: STORYBOARDING THE CAST

Grade-Level Outcomes

Primary Outcomes

Lifetime activities: Demonstrates competency and/or refines activity-specific movement skills in 2 or more lifetime activities (outdoor pursuits, individual-performance activities, aquatics, net/wall games or target games). (S1.H1.L1)

Movement concepts, principles & knowledge: Applies the terminology associated with exercise and participation in selected individual-performance activities, dance, net/wall games, target games, aquatics and/or outdoor pursuits appropriately. (S2.H1.L1)

Embedded Outcome

Working with others: Solves problems and thinks critically in physical activity or dance settings, both as an individual and in groups. (S4.H4.L1)

Lesson Objectives

The learner will:

- draw a diagram that identifies the components of a basic cast correctly after reading Norman Maclean's *A River Runs Through It*, pages 2-4.
- apply fly fishing terminology appropriately.

Equipment and Materials

- Copy of the relevant excerpt from *A River Runs Through It,* by Norman Maclean
- Storyboard
- Task sheet
- Pencil
- Fly rod

Introduction

Today, we will start learning about fly fishing from multiple perspectives through an interdisciplinary module. We will integrate your literature and biology classes with physical education to do this. So, while you are learning to fly fish, you also will learn about the environment and biology of fly fishing. You also will learn about the traditions and meaning of fly fishing through the novella A River Runs Through It. *We'll start off thinking about how to cast by using cues from the story.*

Instructional Task: Learn the Basics of Casting

■ PRACTICE TASK

Alone or in groups of two, students engage in a close reading of Norman Maclean's description of how to cast a fly rod in his novella *A River Runs Through It* (pages 2-4).

- Read carefully,
- re-read,
- decipher difficult language,
- visualize what he's explaining, and
- answer the reading questions on the worksheet in your fly fishing journals.

Student Choices/Differentiation

An audio version can take the place of, or support, the reading of the material.

What to Look For

- Students are actively reading and processing the material.
- Students are using the fly rod to engage in the material and think through what the author is saying.
- Students are on task and supporting one another's learning.

Instructional Task:
Draw the Basic Cast in Storyboard Form

■ PRACTICE TASK

As if you were diagramming in preparation for an instructional video on basic casting, storyboard the process of fly casting using the six storyboard boxes. Draw the caster using a side profile, casting arm to the visible side (see accompanying worksheet).

Refinement

Remind students about the clock references in the book passage to help them use the correct rod positioning.

EMBEDDED OUTCOME: S4.H4.L1. The worksheet leads students through a problem-solving task, first analyzing the reading and then applying that analysis to create the storyboard.

Student Choices/Differentiation

- Break down the movement pattern and identify critical features.
- Students may view a video clip of casting if they need a visual.
- Students may work with a partner to complete the task.

What to Look For

- Students are engaged in the activity and supporting one another's learning.
- The quality of their work reflects their focus and work ethic.
- The storyboards replicate the steps in the reading closely.
- Students understand what they are reading.

Formal and Informal Assessments

- Student storyboard, student talk during closure, and class discussion

Closure

- How are "a little beat in time" and the forward cast interrelated?
- Why do you think Maclean describes the back cast as "an art that ends at two o'clock"?
- Why do you think he goes on to say that it's closer to "twelve than two"?
- Take a moment to describe to a partner the relationship between power and grace in fly casting, according to Maclean.
- As we return for our next lesson on fly casting, I want you to think about how you will use your knowledge of Maclean's voice in the book to develop your own basic fly cast. In particular, focus on this idea of power versus grace and how to "transfer the little fly."

Reflection

- Are students able to pick up on the basic components of the cast from the excerpt?
- Are they able to communicate the components of the basic cast through their diagrams?

Homework

- Read through page 15 in *A River Runs Through It,* by Norman Maclean.
- What does this reading tell you about the culture of fly fishing?
- Be prepared to discuss how the fly fishing culture compares to other cultures you have experience with.

Resources

Maclean, N. (2004). *A river runs through it.* Chicago: University of Chicago Press.

CLOSE READING OF THE FLY CAST TASK SHEET

Name: _____

Introduction

Alone or in a group of two, engage in a close reading of Norman Maclean's description of how to cast a fly rod in his novella *A River Runs Through It*. Read carefully, re-read, decipher difficult language, visualize what he's explaining, and then answer the reading questions on your task sheet. Finally, as if you were diagramming in preparation for an instructional video on basic casting, storyboard the process of fly casting using the six story board boxes.

Norman Maclean, *A river runs through it* (Chicago: University of Chicago Press, 2001), 2-4.

Reading Questions

1. In what order are the fly line, leader, and fly taken from the water at the beginning of the cast? In what order are they placed back upon the water at the end of the cast?

2. What is the most common "natural" mistake made during the cast?

3. How far back should one take the rod during the back cast?

4. What sound should one *not* hear as long as the line speed is controlled? When the cast is not performed correctly in at least two ways, with what object does Maclean so colorfully compare the end result?

5. How many "counts," or basic stages, are there to the cast?

Task Directions

In the boxes provided, storyboard the process of casting as Norman Maclean describes it. Be precise with your illustrations, labels, and descriptions. *Note: The illustrations of the initial position and ending position should be identical.*

- Draw the caster using a side profile, casting arm to the visible side.

- Wherever appropriate, label the following aspects of your drawings: rod, line, leader, fly, casting loop, back cast, and forward cast, as well as each of Maclean's "counts," "a little beat of time," and "check-cast."

- In the smaller boxes along the right side, describe in your own words what is supposed to happen at/in each position/stage.

Address position	Describe the initial position in your own words:
First stage	Describe the first stage in your own words:
Second stage	Describe the second stage in your own words:
Third stage	Describe the third stage in your own words:
Fourth stage	Describe the fourth stage in your own words:
Letdown position	Describe the ending position in your own words:

Rubric: Close Reading of the Fly Cast

Name: _____

Exceeds expectations (3)	Meets expectations (2)	Needs improvement (1)	Incomplete (0)
Neatness and care are evident in detailed and helpful illustrations at each stage. The student goes above and beyond.	Adequate neatness and care are evident. Some aspects may be vague or confusing.	Illustrations are *somewhat* sloppy and unclear because of lack of care and/or using classroom time efficiently.	Illustrations are sloppy and unclear because of lack of care and/or using classroom time efficiently.
The positions of the caster and the stages of the casting are accurately depicted as Maclean describes them.	The positions of the caster and the stages of the casting are *mostly* depicted as Maclean describes them.	The positions of the caster and the stages of the casting are *not entirely* depicted as Maclean describes them.	Illustrations do not evidence a thorough understanding of Maclean's text.
All requested labels are applied clearly and accurately. The student includes additional terms and labels.	All requested labels are applied, but the labels may not always be applied correctly or at the most appropriate places.	Labels are missing and/or inaccurate.	Labels are mostly missing.
Storyboard descriptions are written in the student's own words and are helpful in describing the illustrations.	Storyboard descriptions are *mostly* written in the student's own words and are *mostly* helpful in describing the illustrations.	Storyboard descriptions are too brief, vague, unclear, and/or copied directly from the text.	Descriptions are mostly missing.

Total score: _____

Comments:

From L.C. MacDonald, R.J. Doan, and S. Chepko, eds., 2018, *Lesson planning for high school physical education* (Reston, VA: SHAPE America; Champaign, IL: Human Kinetics).

LESSON 2: ASSEMBLING THE ROD AND BASIC CASTING

Grade-Level Outcomes

Primary Outcomes

Lifetime activities: Demonstrates competency and/or refines activity-specific movement skills in 2 or more lifetime activities (outdoor pursuits, individual-performance activities, aquatics, net/wall games or target games). (S1.H1.L1)

Rules & etiquette: Exhibits proper etiquette, respect for others and teamwork while engaging in physical activity and/or social dance. (S4.H2.L1)

Movement concepts, principles & knowledge: Applies the terminology associated with exercise and participation in selected individual-performance activities, dance, net/wall games, target games, aquatics and/or outdoor pursuits appropriately. (S2.H1.L1)

Embedded Outcomes

Safety: Applies best practices for participating safely in physical activity, exercise and dance (e.g., injury prevention, proper alignment, hydration, use of equipment, implementation of rules, sun protection). (S4.H5.L1)

Movement concepts, principles & knowledge: Identifies and discusses the historical and cultural roles of games, sports and dance in society. (S2.H1.L2)

Self-expression & enjoyment: Selects and participates in physical activities or dance that meet the need for self-expression and enjoyment. (S5.H3.L1)

Lesson Objectives

The learner will:

- identify six components of a fly rod.
- identify the components of a successful basic cast.
- explain the rules of using fly fishing equipment.
- successfully complete a basic fly cast.
- create a fly fishing journal that will be used to support student learning and connect students to the fly fishing culture.

Equipment and Materials

- 15 fly rods, reels, lines
- 15 rod tubes
- 15 targets (Hula-Hoops work well)
- Journal
- Writing implement
- "The Testament of a Fisherman," by Robert Traver

Introduction

What did you learn about the culture of fly fishing from your reading? Today, we will become part of that culture by learning about the fly rod and how to make a basic cast.

Introduce the fly rod, basic cast, and equipment expectations, and then students will make a basic cast with the fly rod. At the end of the lesson, introduce a fly fishing journal assignment and expectations by reviewing the rubric with students.

Instructional Task: Components of the Fly Rod

■ PRACTICE TASK

Introduce the fly rod (tip section, butt section, guides, ferrules, cork, reel seat) and teach students how to put the rod together. Students will follow along with you, assembling their own rods.

Guiding questions for students:

- How do you know what weight rod you are using?
- How does the weight of the rod relate to the type of fishing you are doing?
- How does the weight of the line relate to the rod weight?

Student Choices/Differentiation

Students may review a video clip of assembling a rod.

What to Look For

Students are on task and engaged.

Instructional Task: Equipment Expectations

■ PRACTICE TASK

Discuss the rules related to using the fly rod safely and successfully in class.

EMBEDDED OUTCOME: S4.H5.L1. Review safety guidelines for using a fly rod.

1. Fly rod is always in your hand (never on the ground or leaning against something).
2. Tip at 12 o'clock when not in use.
3. Put rod together and take it down at the casting station only.
4. Maintain a safe distance from others.

Student Choices/Differentiation

Provide a handout or hang a poster with rules.

What to Look For

Students are on task and engaged.

Instructional Task: Basic Cast

■ PRACTICE TASK

Demonstrate a basic cast (no line hand), emphasizing the four components of a successful basic cast (pick up, back cast, forward cast, lay down).

Students perform the basic cast for 10 repetitions with a partner at casting stations designated by cones, while you move from group to group to give feedback. The casting partner observes and gives feedback specific to the four key concepts.

Key Concepts

- Loading the rod
- Casting loop
- Wait time
- Turnover

Extension

Vary the distance of the cast.

Refinement

A common error is bringing the rod back too far so that it doesn't load properly. Students can practice stopping at the end of the back cast so they can see the position of the rod.

Student Choices/Differentiation

- Students choose their partners.
- Students practice at their own pace.
- Proficient students can practice aiming at a target.
- Students may review a video clip of the basic cast.

What to Look For

- Students are engaged.
- Students are applying the components of a basic cast.
- Students are keeping the back cast and forward cast motion within the recommended range (10 - 2).
- Students are getting the feel of loading the rod on the back cast.

Instructional Task: Fly Fishing Journal

■ PRACTICE TASK

Most days throughout the Fly Fishing Module, you will be asked to make entries in your fly fishing journals.

Hand out Robert Traver's "The Testament of a Fisherman" and the journal assignment. Share the rubric with students. Have students begin working on a journal entry.

Extension

If time allows, have students complete their journal entries in class and share their responses.

Student Choices/Differentiation

- Use an audio version of Traver's text, or you may read aloud.
- Provide a sample journal entry.
- Students work at their own pace.

What to Look For

- Quality work that connects student learning with the content.
- Students are making connections between the resource and fly fishing culture.

Formal and Informal Assessments

- Teacher feedback and group feedback on individual casting
- Journal entry

Closure

After equipment is put away, the class will meet to review the rod components and expectations, as well as the key concepts.

- Why is it important to "load the rod"?
- What happens to the line if you don't load it properly?
- Challenge question: In what ways can the fly-caster manipulate the casting loop?
- Next class, we will continue to work on our casting.

Reflection

- Are students getting a feel for the cast?
- Where are they still making mistakes?
- Are they getting a sense of fly fishing culture?

Homework

- Watch the video of a basic cast and assembling a rod on the school's physical education website.
- Fly fishing journal entry.

EMBEDDED OUTCOMES: S2.H1.L2; S5.H3.L1. Students should recognize the special culture of fly fishing and be able to identify elements that make fly fishing enjoyable in responding to the journal questions.

Resources

Traver, R. (1964). "The testament of a fisherman." *The Ozark Fly Fisher Journal.*

Internet keyword search: "fly rod components," "casting a fly rod," "The Testament of a Fisherman, Robert Traver"

FLY FISHING JOURNAL: "TIGHT LINES!"

If you walk into any sizable and reputable book store, you wouldn't be surprised to see an entire section of books on, say, football. You might be surprised, though, to see an entire section on not merely fishing but *fly* fishing. In fact, the number of books devoted to fly fishing is large; fly fishing, for a host of reasons, is a strong lure for those who value personal reflection and writing. Robert Traver, John Gierach, Norman Maclean, and Steve Raymond are just some of the writing talents who have been drawn to fly fishing above all other pursuits. What is it that they are drawn to? What, exactly, are the beauty and the art that they write about? These are just two of the questions we will be trying to answer through your own personal reflection and writing using this journal.

Furthermore, there is the practical side, the scientific side, and the mechanical side of understanding how to fly fish; you need not be a literary giant or even a fan of one to find enjoyment in fly fishing. For everyone, including Traver and Gierach, it is safe to say that it all boils down to the water swirling around our waders, the dancing reflections of light off a moving river, and all the sounds and smells of the natural world around us. Notice that there is no mention of fish. . . .

Task

Throughout the fly fishing unit, you will be asked to make entries in your fly fishing journal. Some of the tasks include the following:

- Reflective responses
- Reading responses
- Peer and self-evaluations of casting and other skills
- Notes and diagrams concerning invertebrate life cycles and so on

Assessment

Grading will be based on completeness, accuracy, neatness, and thoroughness. Include the date and title of the journal entry at the top of each page.

Exceeds expectations (3)	Meets expectations (2)	Needs improvement (1)	Incomplete (0)
Neatness and care are evident in all journal responses. The date and entry title are included with each entry.	Adequate neatness and care are evident. Some entries appear brief. The date and entry title are included with each entry.	Many entries are brief and/or rushed. Neatness and care are not often evident in responses. Dates and titles are sometimes missing.	Many entries are missing.
All responses are thorough and reveal much thought and reflection.	Almost all responses are thorough and reveal much thought and reflection.	Only some responses are thorough and reveal thought and reflection.	Most entries do not reveal thought and reflection.

From L.C. MacDonald, R.J. Doan, and S. Chepko, eds., 2018, *Lesson planning for high school physical education* (Reston, VA: SHAPE America; Champaign, IL: Human Kinetics).

FLY FISHING JOURNAL ENTRY 1: TRAVER'S TESTAMENT

Task

Read Robert Traver's famous "The Testament of a Fisherman" and answer the reading questions in your fly fishing journals for discussion. Most questions are open-ended and require reflection more than analysis, so there is no single "correct" answers.

Testament of a Fisherman, by Robert Traver

I fish because I love to: because I love the environs where trout are found, which are invariably beautiful, and hate the environs where crowds of people are found, which are invariably ugly; because of all the television commercials, cocktail parties, and assorted social posturing I thus escape; because, in a world where most men seem to spend their lives doing things they hate, my fishing is at once an endless source of delight and an act of small rebellion; because trout do not lie or cheat and cannot be bought or bribed or impressed by power, but respond only to quietude and humility and endless patience; because I suspect that men are going along this way for the last time, and I for one don't want to waste the trip; because mercifully there are no telephones on trout waters; because only in the woods can I find solitude without loneliness; because bourbon out of an old tin cup always tastes better out there; because maybe one day I will catch a mermaid; and, finally, not because I regard fishing as being so terribly important but because I suspect that so many of the other concerns of men are equally unimportant—and not nearly so much fun.

Reading Questions

1. Fly fishing has a culture apart from that of other modes of fishing. According to Robert Traver, describe in your own words what beliefs, values, and actions make up the spirit of this unique culture.

2. What are anglers drawn to, and how are they drawn?

3. What is the *goal* of fly fishing? What, in particular, is *not* the goal of fly fishing?

From L.C. MacDonald, R.J. Doan, and S. Chepko, eds., 2018, *Lesson planning for high school physical education* (Reston, VA: SHAPE America; Champaign, IL: Human Kinetics).

LESSON 3: CASTING EVALUATION

Grade-Level Outcomes

Primary Outcomes

Lifetime activities: Demonstrates competency and/or refines activity-specific movement skills in 2 or more lifetime activities (outdoor pursuits, individual-performance activities, aquatics, net/wall games or target games). (S1.H1.L1)

Working with others: Uses communication skills and strategies that promote team or group dynamics. (S4.H3.L1)

Embedded Outcomes

Movement concepts, principles & knowledge: Applies the terminology associated with exercise and participation in selected individual-performance activities, dance, net/wall games, target games, aquatics and/or outdoor pursuits appropriately. (S2.H1.L1)

Movement concepts, principles & knowledge: Uses movement concepts and principles (e.g., force, motion, rotation) to analyze and improve performance of self and/or others in a selected skill. (S2.H2.L1)

Lesson Objectives

The learner will:
- demonstrate a successful basic fly cast 7 out of 10 times.
- describe two ways to manipulate the casting loop.
- evaluate a peer and provide feedback in a supportive manner.

Equipment and Materials

- Fly rods
- Fly reels
- Cones
- Targets
- Data sheet
- Pencils and clipboard

Introduction

Today, you will continue practicing your basic casting technique and complete a peer evaluation so that you'll have a good idea of how you are progressing.

Instructional Task:
Review of Fly Rod Components and Setup

■ **PRACTICE TASK**

Show the various parts of the fly rod and ask students to identify them (tip section, butt section, guides, ferrules, cork, and reel seat).

Guide students once again through the assembly of the rod.

Guiding questions for students:
- How do you know what weight rod you are using?
- How does the weight of the rod relate to the type of fishing you are doing?
- How does the weight of the line relate to the rod weight?

Student Choices/Differentiation

- Use a poster on the wall to remind students about the names of the components.
- Students may review a video clip on setting up the rod.

What to Look For

- Students are engaged and responding to the guiding questions.
- Students need only a few reminders about how to put the rod together.

Instructional Task: Basic Casting Practice

■ PRACTICE TASK

Review the basic cast, emphasizing the four components of a successful basic cast (pick up, back cast, forward cast, lay down) and the key concepts (loading the rod, casting loop, wait time, turnover) Students perform the basic cast for 10 repetitions with a partner at casting stations designated by cones, while you move from group to group to give feedback.

Extension

Change the target for the cast.

Refinements

- Students often release the line early. Remind them to wait until the rod is stopped at the end of the forward cast and let the loop roll out from the tip. Use the cues "stop, shoot" to help correct the problem (Federation of Fly Fishers).
- Remind students that the rod should accelerate smoothly. Tell them to flick the wrist and stop or bend and stop, bend and stop.

Student Choices/Differentiation

- Students choose their partners.
- Students practice at their own pace.
- Proficient students can practice aiming at a more challenging target.

What to Look For

- Students are keeping the back cast and forward cast motion within the recommended range (10 - 2).
- Students are getting the feel of loading the rod on the back cast.
- The rod tip is moving along a straight path.
- Students are accelerating the rod smoothly and flicking the wrist to a stop.

Instructional Task: Peer Evaluation of Basic Cast

■ PRACTICE TASK

Explain the evaluation process that students will use during the lesson. Students provide both spoken and written feedback to each other, emphasizing the information from the previous lesson. Data collected during the process will be used to assess the students' ability to complete the basic cast successfully.

Key Concepts

- Loading the rod
- Casting loop
- Wait time
- Turnover

Students move to a station with a partner. The casting stations, which are designated by cones, include the following:

- Target
- Fly rod
- Reel
- Clipboard
- Pencil
- Data sheet

Students practice casting, alternating with their partners, for 10 minutes. If space permits, all students can practice at the same time. Students then complete the evaluation of their partners' casts (20 minutes each student). Evaluators stand on the line-hand side of the casters. Additional group members (if needed) can help evaluate the caster for their group.

Extensions

- After both partners have casted and evaluated each other, they share their feedback verbally and through the written assessment.
- Students could use video of their casts to complete the evaluation outside of class time.

Guiding questions for students:

- What role does acceleration play in manipulating the casting loop?
- What role does the back cast play in manipulating the casting loop?

EMBEDDED OUTCOMES: S2.H2.L1; S2.H1.L1. During the feedback, partners use correct terminology and application of casting concepts, which are provided on the rubric.

Student Choices/Differentiation

- The length of the rod can vary, from 6 to 9 feet (1.8 to 2.7 m).
- Students may volunteer to demonstrate.
- Students choose their partners.

What to Look For

- Students are actively participating in the activity.
- Student talk is evident, with two-way verbal communication.
- Evaluators are giving written feedback as well as verbal.

Formal and Informal Assessments

- Peer assessment of the cast
- Journal entry

Closure

After equipment is put away, the class will meet to discuss the evaluation.

- What were the common successes related to the casting at your station?
- What aspects of the cast did your group have questions about?
- What did a group member say that helped you find success with your basic cast?
- Name two ways the caster can manipulate the casting loop.
- Next class, you'll learn more about how your non-dominant hand contributes to the cast.

Reflection

- Were students able to make a basic cast?
- Were they able to use the cues from the rubric effectively?
- Were they able to transfer their knowledge as evaluators to their own casting?
- Collect data sheets from peer assessments and review them to determine the progress of the class.

Homework: Fly Fishing Journal Entry

- How does the length of the back cast affect the casting loop?
- Applying what you know about the basic cast, how do you think you could lengthen the casting distance effectively?

Resources

International Federation of Fly Fishers: fedflyfishers.org

Internet keyword search: "fly casting," "fly casting errors"

ASSESSING THE BASIC FLY CAST

Introduction

With your partner, answer the following questions in your fly fishing journals. Then, take turns observing each other performing basic casts and filling out the peer assessment rubrics.

Questions

1. Name two ways to make the casting loop smaller.
2. What is the name of the first guide on the fly rod?
3. What should you always do with your fly rod when not casting it?
4. What is the term for when your line lies completely out in front of you above the water?
5. How can you determine the "weight" of your fly rod?
6. What is one question about fly casting that you have for your teacher?

Task Directions

Watch your partner perform a basic cast 10 times, and assess his or her success each time by marking in the appropriate boxes on the last page of the assessment rubric. You will be giving more detailed feedback on the first 5 casts. After using the rubric to watch specific portions of each of the first 5 casts, you should pause and share your observations with the caster.

Cast 1: The Address and the Pick-up

*Circle the appropriate assessment in each column.

THE ADDRESS							
Feet are straddling the target line, with the foot opposite of the casting arm positioned forward toward the target.			Thumb is on top of the rod grip, pointing toward the target.		The elbow is resting at the caster's side just above the hip.		
Yes	No: opposite foot is not forward	No: feet are not straddling the target line	Yes	No: thumb is not positioned on top or pointed toward target	Yes	No: the elbow is back, out front, or out to the side too much	
THE PICK-UP							
The caster lifts the line appropriately from the water.			The line is accelerated up and back.		During the cast, the elbow stays relatively stationary at the hip. The wrist stays relatively straight through the pick-up.		
Yes	No: too weakly, needs to accelerate	No: too strongly, overpowers the rod	Yes	No: the line drifts down behind the caster because of a weak pick-up	Yes	No: the elbow is lifted during the cast	No: the wrist "cocks" early and/or is too loose

Cast 2: The Pick-up, Back Cast to Stop, and Wait 1

THE PICK-UP								
The caster lifts the line appropriately from the water.			The line is accelerated up and back.			During the cast, the elbow stays relatively stationary at the hip. The wrist stays relatively straight through the pick-up.		
Yes	No: too weakly, needs to accelerate	No: too strongly, overpowers the rod	Yes	No: the line drifts down behind the caster because of a weak pick-up		Yes	No: the elbow is lifted during the cast	No: the wrist "cocks" early and/or is too loose

BACK CAST TO STOP AND WAIT 1					
The rod is stopped abruptly overhead with a wrist flick.			The caster allows the line and leader to straighten behind while the rod, elbow, and wrist are stopped.		
Yes	No: the rod goes too far back	No: the rod is stopped too soon, with no wrist flick	Yes	No: either rod, elbow, or wrist moved during wait 1	No: the rod waits too long and the line drifts down toward the ground

Cast 3: The Pick-up, Back Cast to Stop, and Wait 1

THE PICK-UP								
The caster lifts the line appropriately from the water.			The line is accelerated up and back.			During the cast, the elbow stays relatively stationary at the hip. The wrist stays relatively straight through the pick-up.		
Yes	No: too weakly, needs to accelerate	No: too strongly, overpowers the rod	Yes	No: the line drifts down behind the caster because of a weak pick-up		Yes	No: the elbow is lifted during the cast	No: the wrist "cocks" early and/or is too loose

BACK CAST TO STOP AND WAIT 1					
The rod is stopped abruptly overhead with a wrist flick.			The caster allows the line and leader to straighten behind while the rod, elbow, and wrist are stopped.		
Yes	No: the rod goes too far back	No: the rod is stopped too soon, with no wrist flick	Yes	No: either rod, elbow, or wrist moved during wait 1	No: the rod waits too long and the line drifts down toward the ground

Cast 4: Back Cast to Stop, Wait 1, and Forward Cast to Stop

BACK CAST TO STOP AND WAIT 1					
The rod is stopped abruptly overhead with a wrist flick.			The caster allows the line and leader to straighten behind while the rod, elbow, and wrist are stopped.		
Yes	No: the rod goes too far back	No: the rod is stopped too soon, with no wrist flick	Yes	No: either rod, elbow, or wrist moved during wait 1	No: the rod waits too long and the line drifts down toward the ground

FORWARD CAST TO STOP								
The caster accelerates the line forward, keeping the elbow relatively stationary.			The fly is led forward by a tight casting loop.			The rod motion ends its forward motion with an abrupt stop (10 o'clock).		
Yes	No: too weakly	No: too strongly	Yes	No: the fly dips below the casting loop	No: the casting loop is too large and doesn't create turnover	Yes	No: the rod is stopped beyond 10 o'clock, and the belly of line lands on the ground before the fly	

Cast 5: Back Cast to Stop, Wait 1, Forward Cast to Stop, and Turnover/Letdown

BACK CAST TO STOP AND WAIT 1					
The rod is stopped abruptly overhead with a wrist flick.			The caster allows the line and leader to straighten behind while the rod, elbow, and wrist are stopped.		
Yes	**No:** the rod goes too far back	**No:** the rod is stopped too soon, with no wrist flick	**Yes**	**No:** either rod, elbow, or wrist moved during wait 1	**No:** the rod waits too long and the line drifts down toward the ground

FORWARD CAST TO STOP							
The caster accelerates the line forward, keeping the elbow relatively stationary.			The fly is led forward by a tight casting loop.			The rod motion ends its forward motion with an abrupt stop (10 o'clock).	
Yes	**No:** too weakly	**No:** too strongly	**Yes**	**No:** the fly dips below the casting loop	**No:** the casting loop is too large and doesn't create turnover	**Yes**	**No:** the rod is stopped beyond 10 o'clock, and the belly of line lands on the ground before the fly

TURNOVER/LETDOWN							
The line "turns over" itself above the caster after the rod is checked.		After the line has straightened, the caster slowly lets the rod tip fall in a line toward the target.			After the letdown, the caster places the line beneath the index finger of the rod hand.		
Yes	**No:** the line drifts down because of a weak forward cast or soft check	**Yes**	**No:** the rod stays checked until after the line and leader reach the ground	**No:** the rod descends too soon—before the line turns over itself	**Yes**	**No**	

Task

After each of the 10 casts, mark the appropriate box with an X, meaning no success, or a circle, meaning a successful cast. **Success** = The line, leader, and fly land softly and in a relatively straight line from the caster.

3

Example: On cast 3, the caster does not create turnover and so the line does not land straightened in front of the caster. This is an unsuccessful cast, and so the assessor makes an X through box 3.

1	2	3 ×	4	5	6	7	8	9	10

Describe the ending position in your own words:
Ending Position

TOTAL # OF BOXES CIRCLED: _____

From L.C. MacDonald, R.J. Doan, and S. Chepko, eds., 2018, *Lesson planning for high school physical education* (Reston, VA: SHAPE America; Champaign, IL: Human Kinetics).

LESSON 4: LINE HAND AND REACH CAST

Grade-Level Outcomes

Primary Outcome

Lifetime activities: Demonstrates competency and/or refines activity-specific movement skills in 2 or more lifetime activities (outdoor pursuits, individual-performance activities, aquatics, net/wall games or target games). (S1.H1.L1)

Embedded Outcome

Movement concepts, principles & knowledge: Uses movement concepts and principles (e.g., force, motion, rotation) to analyze and improve performance of self and/or others in a selected skill. (S2.H2.L1)

Lesson Objectives

The learner will:

- use the line hand while making a basic cast.
- complete a successful reach cast in both directions.

Equipment and Materials

- Fly rods
- Reels
- Targets
- Cones

Introduction

You were asked to think about how you might be able to lengthen the distance of your cast. What ideas did you come up with in your journals? Today, we will focus on the line hand (non-dominant hand), which when used effectively, can help you lengthen your cast, as you'll see in future lessons. We'll also work on a reach cast that will allow you to land the fly in a more natural way.

Review the concepts of the casting loop and loading the fly rod. Ask students to share how to safely move behind other casting groups. Introduce the line hand to the basic cast, and add the reach cast.

Instructional Task: Using the Line Hand

■ **PRACTICE TASK**

Explain and demonstrate using the line hand (controls the line) with the basic cast.

- Hold the line (at hip) to create tension during the back cast so the rod will load.
- Loosen to allow the amount of line to lengthen after each stroke (when false casting).
- Strip the line.
- Feather the line.

EMBEDDED OUTCOME: S2.H2.L1 Use the line-hand discussion to emphasize the importance of tension in transferring power from rod to line when casting. Students pair off at cones and practice casting to targets, focusing on the feel of the line hand. One student takes 10 practice casts while the partner keeps track of how many were successful. Students switch roles.

Extension

Repeat, challenging students to use false casting to let more line out.

Refinement

If students are losing tension when releasing the line, watch the line hand. Reinforce the importance of keeping tension with the line hand.

Student Choices/Differentiation

- Vary the length of the line used during casting.
- Use a video clip to illustrate the line hand.
- Students choose their partners.

What to Look For

- Students are using the line hand correctly to keep tension in the line.
- Students are still using proper form for the casting stroke with the dominant hand.

Instructional Task: Reach Cast

■ PRACTICE TASK

Introduce the concepts needed for a successful reach cast.

Key Concepts

- Rod tip control
- Timing
- Water speed
- Fly relative to fly line
- Presentation of fly (more natural)

Students pair off at cones and practice reach casting to targets. One student takes 10 practice casts while the partner keeps track of how many were successful. Students switch roles. Repeat.

Extension

Have students attempt to make 10 reach casts in each direction. Partners will keep track of how many they were able to complete successfully. Switch roles.

Refinement

Keep an eye on the location of the line hand. Students typically raise the line hand with the rod instead of keeping it next to the hip.

Student Choices/Differentiation

- Vary the length of the rod and the distance to the targets.
- Students choose their partners.
- Use a video clip to illustrate the reach cast.

What to Look For

- Students are using the line hand correctly to keep tension in the line.
- Students are hitting the target with their reach casts.

Formal and Informal Assessments

- Peer assessment (how many successful casts out of 10 on each side)
- Journal entry

Closure

- What circumstances might require a fly caster to use the strategy of a reach cast?
- What role does the line hand play in casting?

Reflection

- Were students able to complete reach casts consistently and effectively?
- Were they able to coordinate the line hand with the forward and back casts correctly?

Homework: Fly Fishing Journal Entry

- Why is it important to have more strategies to draw from than the basic cast?
- Why is striving for accuracy important for catching fish?
- What role does fly presentation play in your success as a fly fisher?

Resources

MidCurrent: www.midcurrent.com

Scientific Anglers: www.scientificanglers.com

Fly Fishermen: www.flyfisherman.com

LESSON 5: TROUT FOOD SOURCES

Grade-Level Outcomes

Primary Outcomes

Movement concepts, principles & knowledge: Applies the terminology associated with exercise and participation in selected individual-performance activities, dance, net/wall games, target games, aquatics and/or outdoor pursuits appropriately. (S2.H1.L1)

Lifetime activities: Demonstrates competency and/or refines activity-specific movement skills in 2 or more lifetime activities (outdoor pursuits, individual-performance activities, aquatics, net/wall games or target games). (S1.H1.L1)

Embedded Outcome

Personal responsibility: Employs effective self-management skills to analyze barriers and modify physical activity patterns appropriately, as needed. (S4.H1.L1)

Lesson Objectives

The learner will:

- identify three common invertebrates.
- compare and contrast the three common invertebrates.
- infer where (above or below the surface) an invertebrate is found based on its structure.
- make an accurate cast to a target.

Equipment and Materials

- Fly rods
- Fly reels
- Cones
- Bug targets
- PowerPoint
- Aquatic invertebrate handout

Introduction

Today, you will learn about the types of insects that fish eat. Because a fly mimics an insect, it's important to match the fly to the types of insects that fish feed on.

Show a short clip of fish taking an adult caddis off the top of the water. Ask leading questions to draw students' attention and check understanding of previous knowledge. Introduce the idea of the fly imitating a common trout food source (caddis, mayfly, stone fly).

Instructional Task: Introduction of Aquatic Invertebrates

■ PRACTICE TASK

Introduce invertebrates with the aquatic entomology PowerPoint or with the aquatic entomology handout.

Key Concepts

- Mayfly adults have a sail wing.
- Caddis fly adults have a tent wing.
- Stone fly adults have a flat wing.
- Mayfly nymphs can be differentiated from stone fly nymphs because they are typically much smaller and have three tails (usually).
- Caddis fly nymphs typically have long, trailing legs.

Students work to complete the aquatic entomology handout.

Refinement

A check for understanding will confirm whether or not students understand the task or are on the right track in completing the task.

Student Choices/Differentiation

Provide both the PowerPoint presentation and handout to support student learning.

What to Look For

Student engagement and student talk centered around fish food sources.

Instructional Task: Casting to Targets

■ PRACTICE TASK

Once students have completed the handout, they will move to the casting stations to reinforce invertebrate identification.

Students will:

- cast to laminated picture targets of the big three food sources.
- identify the fly correctly after hitting the target or pass the fly rod to a partner.
- make at least three effective basic casts and identify three different insects correctly in a row.

Refinements

- The distance of the target from the casting group can be manipulated for each group, depending on students' ability level.
- Partners will want to pay particular attention to the casting loop during this activity to monitor the caster's turnover.

EMBEDDED OUTCOME: S4.H1.L1. Students must apply the correct strategies of the basic cast in order to complete the task. This may require a high level of persistence. Provide encouragement and positive feedback about persistence and effort as students practice.

Student Choices/Differentiation

- Vary the length of the rod and the distance to the targets.
- Students choose their partners.

What to Look For

- Students are engaged in the activity and using the correct technique for a basic cast.
- Students are engaging their line hands correctly.
- Students are letting the line load.
- Student talk is centered on correct technique and positive identification of the aquatic invertebrates.

Formal and Informal Assessments

- Completed handouts
- Success in hitting targets
- Journal entry

Closure

- What is a distinguishing characteristic of the mayfly adult? The caddis fly adult? The stone fly adult?
- How are the three common invertebrates similar and different?
- What characteristics can be used to identify an invertebrate as a nymph or an adult?
- How was your basic cast affected as a result of the additional learning today?
- Next class, you'll learn about different fish species and refine your casting.

Reflection

- Were students able to focus on their basic casting technique while at the same time applying the additional learning of the life cycle of aquatic invertebrates?
- Were they able to hit the targets?
- Do they need to adjust their direction or distance?

Homework: Fly Fishing Journal Entry

- Communicate through your writing how to differentiate between the adult and nymph versions of the three common aquatic invertebrates.
- You will be turning in your journals next class.

Resources

Troutnut: www.troutnut.com

AQUATIC ENTOMOLOGY

ADULT MAYFLY.   **ADULT CADDIS FLY.**   **ADULT STONE FLY.**

1. Closely observe the wings on each invertebrate.

   a. Which invertebrate wing is flat on the insect's back?

   b. Which invertebrate wing is like a pup tent (an upside down V)?

   c. Which invertebrate wing is like the sail of a sailboat?

2. What are two characteristics that they all have in common?

   a. _____

   b. _____

3. Based on the structures these invertebrates have, are they likely to live above or below the surface?

Use the handout from the textbook *School of Fly Fishing* (page 145) to compare and contrast the mayfly nymph, the stone fly nymph, and the caddis fly nymph in the following diagram. The outer triangles should have one distinguishing characteristic for each invertebrate. The central triangle should be a characteristic they all have in common.

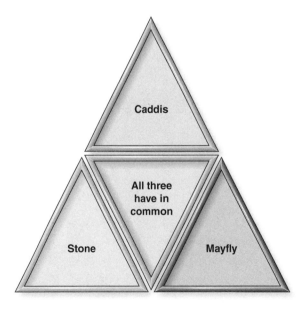

From L.C. MacDonald, R.J. Doan, and S. Chepko, eds., 2018, *Lesson planning for high school physical education* (Reston, VA: SHAPE America; Champaign, IL: Human Kinetics).

LESSON 6: KNOWING YOUR FISH SPECIES

Grade-Level Outcomes

Primary Outcomes

Movement concepts, principles & knowledge: Applies the terminology associated with exercise and participation in selected individual-performance activities, dance, net/wall games, target games, aquatics and/or outdoor pursuits appropriately. (S2.H1.L1)

Lifetime activities: Demonstrates competency and/or refines activity-specific movement skills in 2 or more lifetime activities (outdoor pursuits, individual-performance activities, aquatics, net/wall games or target games). (S1.H1.L1)

Embedded Outcome

Working with others: Accepts others' ideas, cultural diversity and body types by engaging in cooperative and collaborative movement projects. (S4.H4.L2)

Lesson Objectives

The learner will:

- identify all local fish species.
- think interdependently by working together to identify distinguishing characteristics.
- refine casting skills by casting to different targets.

Equipment and Materials

- Fly rods
- Fly reels
- Cones
- Targets with local fish species
- Handouts

Introduction

Last class, you learned about different insects that are part of the fish diet. Today, you will learn about different fish species in the local area and work on refining your casting technique.

Show slides of different staff members or community members with fish they have caught as an attention-getter. Ask students to work with a table partner to write down as many local fish species as possible.

Instructional Task: Fish Identification

■ **PRACTICE TASK**

Hand out copies of a local fish species handout. Students work in small groups to complete the task.

Journal Question

- What are the distinguishing characteristics of local fish species?

Key Concepts

- Key concepts vary by region.
- The key concepts are the characteristics that allow students to differentiate between the local fish species (e.g., coloring, patterns, lifestyle, habitat, size).
- Teachers must determine characteristics for the local fish species.

Student Choices/Differentiation

Students can view video clips of fish in their habitats.

What to Look For

- Students are engaged.
- Students are offering suggestions for distinguishing features of the fish species.

Instructional Task: Casting to Fish Targets

■ PRACTICE TASK

Direct students to the casting stations. In groups, students work together to complete the local fish species handout.

Students alternate casting to the targets. The first student makes a cast. Whichever fish the student strikes (or is closest to) is removed from the target board. Groups make a detailed list of at least three distinguishing characteristics of that species. The next student will then cast, and the procedure is repeated until all local species have been documented on the local fish species handout.

Refinement

Students may find it difficult to distinguish between two similar species (e.g., rainbow trout vs. steelhead). You may need to focus on one subtle difference and look for students to make that connection during the activity.

Student Choices/Differentiation

- Vary the length of the rod and the distance to the targets.
- Students choose their partners.

What to Look For

- Student collaboration.
- Student talk related to fish species.

Instructional Task: Casting to the Correct Fish Species

■ PRACTICE TASK

Collect the handouts and call out a species for the groups to cast to. Students alternate casting to the target until that species is hit. Students keep track of how many casts it takes to hit the target species. Call out a second species, and students repeat the process.

Collect the equipment and debrief the lesson by asking each group to share a characteristic of a particular species. Groups also share how many casts it took to "catch" the identified species.

Guiding questions for students:

- Why is it important to know the species of fish when actively fishing?
- How might knowing the fish species increase your confidence as a fly fisher?

EMBEDDED OUTCOME: S4.H4.L2. Students must work together to produce a list of distinguishing characteristics. Emphasize the importance of accepting the ideas of others and collaborating to make the list.

Extension

Ask students to complete a more difficult cast to the targets. For example, set up an obstacle that requires a roll cast for success.

Student Choices/Differentiation

- Vary the length of the rod and the distance to the targets.
- Students choose their partners.
- Hang posters with fish pictures.

What to Look For

- Student collaboration.
- Correct casting form.
- Students are engaged and supporting one another's learning.

Formal and Informal Assessments

- Success rate on hitting target species
- Local species handouts
- Journal entry

Closure

- Collect the equipment and debrief the lesson by asking each group to share a characteristic of a particular species.
- Groups share how many casts it took to "catch" the identified species.
- Next time, you'll learn more about what fish need in order to survive.

Reflection

- Were students able to identify specific species characteristics?
- Were they able to apply a correct basic cast?
- Where do students still need help?
- Review journal entries.

Homework: Fly Fishing Journal Entry

- Explain how each member of your group was able to add to your list of distinguishing characteristics in a way you did not initially see.
- How does thinking interdependently help a group work better together?

Resources

Local Department of Fish and Wildlife

Local fly fishing business or guide

LOCAL FISH SPECIES

Use this worksheet to identify the distinguishing characteristics of each fish species. Use key concepts, such as size, color, patterns, habitat, and lifestyle.

[Teacher places picture of local fish species #1 here (e.g., rainbow trout, cutthroat trout, brook trout, steelhead salmon)]

What species is this fish?

Identify three distinguishing characteristics:

1.

2.

3.

[Teacher places picture of local fish species #2 here (e.g., rainbow trout, cutthroat trout, brook trout, steelhead salmon)]

What species is this fish?

Identify three distinguishing characteristics:

1.

2.

3.

[Teacher places picture of local fish species #3 here (e.g., rainbow trout, cutthroat trout, brook trout, steelhead salmon)]

What species is this fish?

Identify three distinguishing characteristics:

1.

2.

3.

From L.C. MacDonald, R.J. Doan, and S. Chepko, eds., 2018, *Lesson planning for high school physical education* (Reston, VA: SHAPE America; Champaign, IL: Human Kinetics).

LESSON 7: FISH REQUIREMENTS

Grade-Level Outcomes

Primary Outcomes

Movement concepts, principles & knowledge: Applies the terminology associated with exercise and participation in selected individual-performance activities, dance, net/wall games, target games, aquatics and/or outdoor pursuits appropriately. (S2.H1.L1)

Lifetime activities: Demonstrates competency and/or refines activity-specific movement skills in 2 or more lifetime activities (outdoor pursuits, individual-performance activities, aquatics, net/wall games or target games). (S1.H1.L1)

Physical activity knowledge: Evaluates—according to their benefits, social support network and participation requirements—activities that can be pursued in the local environment. (S3.H4.L1)

Embedded Outcomes

Health: Analyzes the health benefits of a self-selected physical activity. (S5.H1.L1)

Self-expression & enjoyment: Selects and participates in physical activities or dance that meet the need for self-expression and enjoyment. (S5.H3.L1)

Lesson Objectives

The learner will:

- identify where fish are found in both lotic and lentic water environments.
- identify all local fish species.
- identify three common invertebrates.
- refine casting skills to a target.
- discuss the benefits of fly fishing in a physically active lifestyle.

Equipment and Materials

- Fly rods
- Fly reels
- Cones
- Bug targets
- Fish targets
- Assessment handout

Introduction

What do fish need to survive? Why is that important to know as a fly fisher? We will make that connection in this lesson. We'll also talk about how fly fishing contributes to a physically active lifestyle.

Today's casting lesson presents an opportunity for students to demonstrate knowledge of macro invertebrates and their life cycles, as well as local fish species.

Instructional Task: What Fish Need to Survive

■ PRACTICE TASK

Introduce what fish need to survive with several PowerPoint slides and the fish requirements handout.

Key Concepts

- Food
- Shelter
- Oxygen
- Lotic and lentic ecosystems (compare and contrast)

Guiding questions for students:

- What do we need to survive?
- How can we apply what we know about ourselves to what fish need to survive?
- Compare and contrast the needs of fish and humans.

Extension

Make a trip to a pond or water source on campus and have students identify in a drawing as many of the available survival needs as possible.

Student Choices/Differentiation

Provide a handout on ecosystem concepts to support student learning.

What to Look For

- Students are engaged.
- Students are contributing to the discussion.
- Students are able to identify differences in the ecosystems.

Instructional Task: Bug and Fish Assessment

■ PRACTICE TASK

Students make 20 casts to laminated picture targets of local fish species and their food sources. When they hit a target, they must identify the fish or insect correctly on the assessment handout. Their goal is to make an effective basic cast and identify as many bugs and fish correctly in 20 casts.

Extension

Challenge students with more difficult casts.

Refinement

For students who are finding it difficult to hit the targets, have them pay particular attention to their thumbs on the spine of the rod cork. Often, they will let the thumb slip to the side, which affects accuracy.

Student Choices/Differentiation

- Vary the length of the rod and the distance from the targets.
- The assessment can be completed individually or in small groups.

What to Look For

- Students are using correct casting technique.
- Students are actively engaged in the assignment.

Instructional Task: Fly Fishing as Physical Activity

■ PRACTICE TASK

Lead a discussion about the benefits of fly fishing, what's needed in terms of resources and gear, and nearby areas where people can participate.

Guiding questions for students:

- Where can people fly fish within an hour or two of our school?
- How would your gear differ for different types of water (streams, rivers, flat water, salt water)?
- What are the potential benefits of fly fishing?

EMBEDDED OUTCOMES: S5.H1.L1; S5.H3.L1. Use the guiding questions to help students think specifically about the health and enjoyment benefits of fly fishing.

Student Choices/Differentiation

- Provide maps of local bodies of water to support student engagement.
- Students can use devices to search for gear suggestions.

What to Look For

- All students are contributing to the discussion.
- Students are offering meaningful suggestions.

Formal and Informal Assessments

- Student handouts
- Casting assessment
- Exit slip: How can fly fishing be part of a physically active lifestyle?
- Journal entry

Closure

- During the debriefing, ask students to provide examples of where to find fish in both lotic and lentic environments.
- Next class, you'll learn about tying the line so you'll be able to set it up yourselves and be prepared when you break it or lose a fly.

Reflection

- Were students able to make a connection between what fish need and where we might find them in their natural environments?
- Were they able to articulate the benefits of fly fishing for a physically active lifestyle? Review exit slips.

Homework: Fly Fishing Journal Entry

- Research the common flies for a nearby river.
- What fly would you expect to imitate in July, and what fly pattern is popular?
- Choose one other body of water that you have a connection to and repeat the research.

Resources

Online research for the journal entry specific to the river and local area

Troutnut: www.troutnut.com

FISH REQUIREMENTS

Fish try to expend as little energy as possible while being both close to their food source and acquiring plenty of oxygen. They have three basic requirements:

Food

Fish eat invertebrates, small fish, and crustaceans. Fish want to be close to their food source.

Shelter

Fish need protection from predators and from strong currents (but want to be close to feeding lanes so they expend little energy getting food).

Oxygen

Temperature affects oxygen levels in the water. Colder water has more oxygen. Riffled water has more dissolved oxygen. Shade cools the water, allowing higher oxygen levels.

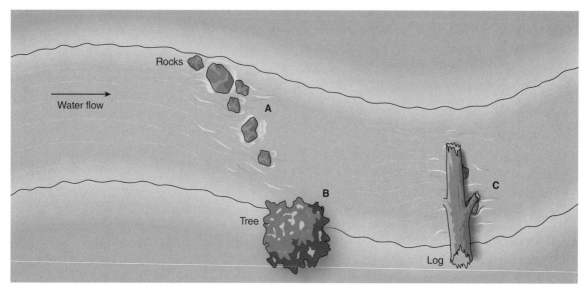

LOTIC (FLOWING) WATER

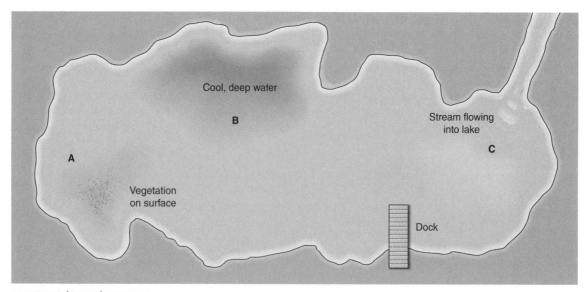

LENTHIC (STILL) WATER

From L.C. MacDonald, R.J. Doan, and S. Chepko, eds., 2018, *Lesson planning for high school physical education* (Reston, VA: SHAPE America; Champaign, IL: Human Kinetics).

LESSON 8: KNOT TYING FOR FLY FISHING

Grade-Level Outcomes

Primary Outcomes

Movement concepts, principles & knowledge: Applies the terminology associated with exercise and participation in selected individual-performance activities, dance, net/wall games, target games, aquatics and/or outdoor pursuits appropriately. (S2.H1.L1)

Lifetime activities: Demonstrates competency and/or refines activity-specific movement skills in 2 or more lifetime activities (outdoor pursuits, individual-performance activities, aquatics, net/wall games and target games). (S1.H1.L1)

Embedded Outcome

Working with others: Uses communication skills and strategies that promote team or group dynamics. (S4.H3.L1)

Lesson Objectives

The learner will:

- tie a fly line to leader connection knot.
- tie a leader to tippet connection knot.
- tie a leader to fly connection knot.
- produce a video on relevant knots for fly fishing.
- apply terminology related to tying flies appropriately.

Equipment and Materials

- Climbing ropes of different sizes
- 10-foot (3 m) chunks of fly line
- Leader material
- Tippet material
- Flies (with hook cut off)
- Access to the Internet
- Video camera or device

Introduction

For homework, you researched the types of flies used in given month or season on a nearby river. What did you find out? Today, you will learn about the critical knots you need for fly fishing.

Start with a story about hooking a big fish. The story grabs students' attention and ends, after a long battle, with the fish breaking off the leader and getting away. The angler, after winding in the line to tie on another fly, realizes that the fly came untied during the battle, which only adds to the frustration. Ask students to recall knot-tying lessons from previous experience (e.g., camping, rock climbing) and the importance of tying the correct knots accurately.

Instructional Task:
Fly Line to Leader, Leader to Tippet, Tippet to Hook

■ **PRACTICE TASK**

Students access the website Animated Knots by Grog: www.animatedknots.com.

Students research one knot for each of the following connections categories:

- Leader to fly line
- Leader to tippet
- Leader or tippet to hook

Extension

Students tie the knots using leader material multiple times and then turn them in to you as evidence of their mastery.

Student Choices/Differentiation

- Students can work with partners.
- Guide students to specific websites to support their focus on this task.

What to Look For

Students are doing research and using materials to develop their instructional videos.

Instructional Task: Student Video

■ PRACTICE TASK

In groups of three or four, students create an instructional video for each of the three knots they chose (there are several ways to tie each connection). Students tie the knots using climbing rope so they are easy to see on the video. Students submit their videos for your review.

Extension

If time is available, students can present their videos to the class.

EMBEDDED OUTCOME: S4.H3.L1. If students work in groups, they will need to work together to make decisions about which knots to tie and how to produce the video. Provide feedback on effective communication skills during the project.

Refinement

For students with limited video skills, provide a video template for them to use (e.g., an iMovie movie trailer).

Student Choices/Differentiation

- Students choose their groups.
- Students choose their knots.

What to Look For

- Students are working together effectively.
- Quality student talk is focused on the learning target.

Formal and Informal Assessments

- Teacher review of video products
- Check of knots tied by students
- Journal entry

Closure

- Why is it important to be fluent in knot tying?
- How might an authentic fly fishing environment affect your ability to tie the correct knot?
- Next time, you'll learn about the catch-and-release philosophy practiced by many fly fishers.

Reflection

- Were students able to use the Internet resource effectively?
- Do they need to spend more time practicing the knots?
- Review student videos and provide feedback.

Homework: Fly Fishing Journal Entry

- Write a short fishing story (three to five paragraphs long) about how your knowledge of tying knots helped land a big fish or how your lack of knowledge in this area lost a big fish.
- If you haven't fished before, you can create a fictional story.

Resources

Internet keyword search: "fly fishing leader," "fly fishing tippet," "fly fishing knots"

LESSON 9: CATCH AND RELEASE

Grade-Level Outcomes

Primary Outcomes

Movement concepts, principles & knowledge: Applies the terminology associated with exercise and participation in selected individual-performance activities, dance, net/wall games, target games, aquatics and/or outdoor pursuits appropriately. (S2.H1.L1)

Movement concepts, principles & knowledge: Identifies and discusses the historical and cultural roles of games, sports and dance in society. (S2.H1.L2)

Embedded Outcome

Rules & etiquette: Examines moral and ethical conduct in specific competitive situations (e.g., intentional fouls, performance-enhancing substances, gambling, current events in sport). (S4. H2.L2)

Lesson Objectives

The learner will:

- discuss the catch-and-release philosophy and conservation issues.

Equipment and Materials

- Fly fishing journals
- "A Choice of Method" by Steve Raymond

Introduction

In your journals, you were asked to write a fish story. Who would like to share the story they wrote with the rest of the class? Today, you will learn about the catch-and-release philosophy and how that interacts with conservation.

Instructional Task: Pre-Reading Questions

■ PRACTICE TASK

Hand out the journal assignment. Have students answer the pre-reading questions in their fly fishing journals before reading Steve Raymond's "A Choice of Method."

Extension

After completing the journal questions, students share their answers with a partner.

Student Choices/Differentiation

Give the questions to the students in the previous class so they have more time to respond.

What to Look For

- Students are answering questions in their fly fishing journals.

Instructional Task: Reading Assignment and Post-Reading Questions

■ PRACTICE TASK

Have students read Steve Raymond's "A Choice of Method" and answer the post-reading questions in their fly fishing journals.

Extension

Provide opportunities for students to share their responses in small groups or with partners, focusing on the learning from Raymond's writing.

EMBEDDED OUTCOME: S4.H2.L2. Use this discussion to draw out the ethics of the catch-and-release philosophy and the conduct of the fly fishers who practice it.

Student Choices/Differentiation

- An audio version can take the place of, or support, the reading of the material.
- Allow students to work in pairs to answer the questions.

What to Look For

- Students are actively answering questions in their fly fishing journals.
- Students are being thoughtful in the discussion responses.
- Everyone is contributing.

Formal and Informal Assessments

Journal entry

Closure

- What is catch and release, and what are the reasons that support it?
- How does this philosophy affect our own community?
- Can you make a connection between catch and release and your previous learning in science?
- Next class, you'll learn how to shoot the line when casting. You also need to turn in your journals for review.

Reflection

- Were students able to connect their learning to our community and their personal story?
- Were students able to connect the catch-and-release philosophy to their environmental science knowledge?

Homework: Fly Fishing Journal Entry

If students haven't completed "A Choice of Method" handout, have them finish as homework.

Resources

Raymond, S. (2005). *The year of the angler and the year of the trout.* Guildford, CT: Lyons Press, 41-45.

FLY FISHING JOURNAL ENTRY: "A CHOICE OF METHOD"

Name: _____

Task

Read Steve Raymond's "A Choice of Method" and answer the questions in your fly fishing journals in preparation for a discussion on philosophy, ethics, and conservation in fly fishing.

Pre-Reading Questions

1. Describe a typical fishing trip that you've been on, heard about, or seen on TV or in a movie. What is the goal of a fisher? Describe the relationship between a fisher and the natural world (water, fish, bug life).

2. Describe what you know about the practice of catch-and-release fishing. Why would someone fish if he is not going to keep the fish?

Post-Reading Questions

1. On page 42, Raymond discusses relationships between such things as plants and insects. Describe at least two *specific* facets of the fly fishing realm and in what way(s) they share a relationship.

2. Explain: "The true nature of the man-fish relationship is one of cooperation, not competition." (page 42)

3. Most officials view hatcheries as completely beneficial to the health of fish populations and water systems. Although there are numerous benefits to using hatcheries, Raymond points out a key drawback. What is this drawback, and how does "the whole [species suffer] as a result"? (page 42)

4. Why are native species of fish so valuable? (page 43)

5. Where else in human history or in modern events have people not "given much thought" to the consequences their actions had or have on the natural world?

6. After reading Raymond's article, revisit your response to pre-reading question 2. How has what he has written informed your knowledge of the reasons supporting the catch-and-release philosophy? How else can success be measured when fishing?

7. Explain: "Killing the fish is an incongruous act." (page 44)

8. What separates the culture of fly fishing from those of other modes of fishing (spinning, deep sea, and so on)?

9. What are Raymond's most convincing reasons that support conservation of fly fishing habitat?

Raymond, S. (2005). *The year of the angler and the year of the trout.* Guildford, CT: Lyons Press, 41-45.

From L.C. MacDonald, R.J. Doan, and S. Chepko, eds., 2018, *Lesson planning for high school physical education* (Reston, VA: SHAPE America; Champaign, IL: Human Kinetics).

LESSON 10: SHOOTING LINE

Grade-Level Outcomes

Primary Outcomes

Movement concepts, principles & knowledge: Applies the terminology associated with exercise and participation in selected individual-performance activities, dance, net/wall games, target games, aquatics and/or outdoor pursuits appropriately. (S2.H1.L1)

Lifetime activities: Demonstrates competency and/or refines activity-specific movement skills in 2 or more lifetime activities (outdoor pursuits, individual-performance activities, aquatics, net/wall games or target games). (S1.H1.L1)

Embedded Outcomes

Movement concepts, principles & knowledge: Uses movement concepts and principles (e.g., force, motion, rotation) to analyze and improve performance of self and/or others in a selected skill. (S2.H2.L1)

Stress management: Identifies stress-management strategies (e.g., mental imagery, relaxation techniques, deep breathing, aerobic exercise, meditation) to reduce stress. (S3.H14.L1)

Lesson Objectives

The learner will:

- "shoot line" an additional 5 feet (1.5 m) beyond the basic cast.
- apply the terminology appropriately.

Equipment and Materials

- Fly rods
- Reels
- Targets
- Cones

Introduction

Today, you will learn how to "shoot the line." This is an important casting technique that helps you transfer the load from the rod to the line. Think about what you've learned about the fly cast. Do you have any ideas about how you can reach fish that are farther away than a basic cast can reach?

Instructional Task: Shooting the Line

■ PRACTICE TASK

Demonstrate shooting the line and introduce concepts needed for a successful cast.

Key Concepts

- Tight casting loop
- Line hand
- Line release
- Timing

Students pair off at cones and practice casting to targets at basic cast length. Once they have warmed up they will "shoot line" to targets that are 5 to 10 feet (1.5 to 3 m) farther away. One student takes 10 practice casts while the partner keeps track of how many were successful. Students switch roles. Repeat as needed.

Extension

Near the end of the lesson, students attempt to shoot line 10 times and keep track of how many times they were able to successfully complete the task.

Refinements

- Students will often let the line go from the line hand too early. Have them focus on letting go of the line as the casting loop passes the caster.
- Line should slide through the fingers of the line hand rather than being let go completely.

EMBEDDED OUTCOME: S2.H2.L1. Use this task to discuss the movement principles that allow longer casts (shooting the line).

Student Choices/Differentiation

- Vary the weight of the fly rod (6-weight rods or higher are more effective for students new to shooting line). More advanced students can vary the weight of the line as well as the rod. Students choose their partners.
- Supply a handout with key concepts or hang posters on the wall.

What to Look For

- Students are using the line hand correctly.
- Students have adjusted their timing to increase the length of the cast.
- The point of release is correct.
- The loop is tight.
- Students are offering suggestions for increasing distance.

Instructional Task: Stress Management

■ **PRACTICE TASK**

Show a video clip from *A River Runs Through It* of the character Paul shooting line and catching a fish. If this clip is not available, use an instructional video clip.

EMBEDDED OUTCOME: S3.H14.L1. Ask students why the characters in the book (or movie) fly fish. Prompt them to think about the rhythmic nature of the activity and the natural setting and how those factors can be important for stress management.

Formal and Informal Assessments

- Student self-assessment (how many successful out of 10 casts)
- Journal entry

Closure

- What circumstances might require a fly caster to use the strategy of shooting line?
- Were you able to shoot the line at least 50 percent of the time?
- What are the key concepts for shooting the line?
- What characteristics of fly fishing might be stress relievers?
- Review for a quiz next class, and get ready to tie your own flies.

Reflection

- Were students able to reach the targets beyond the basic cast distance?
- Were students able to adjust their timing and release point to facilitate a longer cast?
- Review journal entries.

Homework: Fly Fishing Journal Entry

Today, you learned how to cast to fish beyond the reach of a basic cast. What other fishing scenarios would you anticipate needing a strategy to solve? Consider water movement and speed, obstacles, wind, and back cast in your thinking.

Resources

Clip from the movie *A River Runs Through It* or other instructional video clip

LESSON 11: FLY TYING

Grade-Level Outcomes

Primary Outcomes

Movement concepts, principles & knowledge: Applies the terminology associated with exercise and participation in selected individual-performance activities, dance, net/wall games, target games, aquatics and/or outdoor pursuits appropriately. (S2.H1.L1)

Movement concepts, principles & knowledge: Uses movement concepts and principles (e.g., force, motion, rotation) to analyze and improve performance of self and/or others in a selected skill. (S2.H2.L1)

Lifetime activities: Demonstrates competency and/or refines activity-specific movement skills in 2 or more lifetime activities (outdoor pursuits, individual-performance activities, aquatics, net/wall games or target games). (S1.H1.L1)

Embedded Outcome

Movement concepts, principles & knowledge: Identifies and discusses the historical and cultural roles of games, sports and dance in society. (S2.H1.L2)

Lesson Objectives

The learner will:

- tie an elk hair caddis that imitates an adult caddis fly.
- use a rubric to evaluate the fly for quality and proportion.

Equipment and Materials

- Document camera
- Fly tying vise
- #14 hooks
- Bobbin
- Finishing tool
- Thread
- Dubbing
- Elk hair
- Wire
- Fly box for finished flies
- Quizzes, pens

Introduction

For homework, you had to think about times where you might need a casting strategy. What examples did you come up with? Sometimes challenging casting conditions can cause you to lose your fly! There are lots of flies available in stores, but it's a longstanding tradition in fly fishing culture to tie your own flies. Today, you will try tying an elk hair caddis fly. Fly tying can be challenging at first and it takes a lot of patience, so don't get frustrated! Let's take the quiz and then we can start tying flies.

Instructional Task: Quiz

■ PRACTICE TASK

Students take a teacher-generated quiz on terminology and concepts.

Student Choices/Differentiation

Allow extra time if needed, or give a take-home version.

Instructional Task: Fly Tying Demo

■ PRACTICE TASK

Pass around hand-tied flies (or share photos of flies) that imitate caddis, mayfly, and stone fly hatches. Position the document camera over the fly tying vise so students, working in pairs, can see the demonstration on the screen at the front of the class.

Tie an elk hair caddis while students follow along with their own vices and tools. Students create one caddis during the demo.

Key Concepts
- Tying skills (locking on thread, dubbing, wings, whip finish)
- Proportion

Refinement
Students may struggle with proportion while making their flies. Draw attention to the length of the wings relative to the hook.

Student Choices/Differentiation
- Provide a handout with step-by-step instructions and/or pictures.
- Give students access to step-by-step instructions in video form.

What to Look For
- Students are on task.
- Student talk is focused on fly tying techniques and key concepts.

Instructional Task: Tying the Elk Hair Caddis

■ PRACTICE TASK

Students access the teacher-created instructional video from the class website. They will then tie several elk hair caddis flies, using the instructional video to support their learning, paying particular attention to correct proportion.

Key Concepts (Proportion)
- Body shape
- Body length
- Body segments
- Wing size
- Wing length

Refinement
Students will often tie the wings too loosely and they will fall off to the side. Make sure they pull the thread snug on each turn around the wings to ensure a secure hold on top of the fly.

EMBEDDED OUTCOME: S2.H1.L2. Point out that this aspect of the fly fishing culture has its foundation in creativity and imagination. Explain how fly tiers examine real flies in order to imitate them, and the quality of the fly is the difference between catching a fish and not catching one.

Student Choices/Differentiation
Students have access to the teacher-created instructional video and can pause, rewind, or fast forward to fit their own personal tying needs.

What to Look For

- Are students struggling with the fine motor aspect of the skill?
- Are they getting the proportions right?
- Do their flies resemble the real thing?

Instructional Task: Student Self-Evaluation of Fly Tying

■ PRACTICE TASK

Students choose their best elk hair caddis (based on a teacher-generated rubric which focuses on correct proportion and quality) and evaluate it. Students provide evidence for their evaluation scores.

Student Choices/Differentiation

Students choose the fly they think best meets the criteria.

What to Look For

A true reflective process, with evidence that supports students' thinking.

Formal and Informal Assessments

- Quiz
- Student self-evaluations
- Journal entry

Closure

- Why is proportion such an important aspect of fly tying?
- What does it mean to "match the hatch"?
- Next class, I will evaluate your casting technique and we'll work on three specialty casts you can use. Be sure to review the casting rubric for the evaluation for the next lesson on the school's physical education website.

Reflection

- Were students able to use the instructional video to support their learning?
- Was the document camera an efficient way to demonstrate fly tying?
- Review student self-assessments and quizzes.

Homework: Fly Fishing Journal Entry

- Explain how you think you might feel if you were to catch a fish on a fly that you tied personally.
- Make a connection to a previous experience where you had that same feeling and share why.

Resources

Internet keyword search: "Goldenstone Fly Fishing elk hair caddis"

LESSON 12: SPECIALTY CASTS

Grade-Level Outcomes

Primary Outcomes

Lifetime activities: Demonstrates competency and/or refines activity-specific movement skills in 2 or more lifetime activities (outdoor pursuits, individual-performance activities, aquatics, net/wall games or target games). (S1.H1.L1)

Movement concepts, principles & knowledge: Applies the terminology associated with exercise and participation in selected individual-performance activities, dance, net/wall games, target games, aquatics and/or outdoor pursuits appropriately. (S2.H1.L1)

Embedded Outcome

Movement concepts, principles & knowledge: Uses movement concepts and principles (e.g., force, motion, rotation) to analyze and improve performance of self and/or others in a selected skill. (S2.H2.L1)

Lesson Objectives

The learner will:
- execute three specialized casts (roll cast, quartering upstream, reach cast).
- discuss what circumstances require each of the three specialized casts.
- apply terminology associated with casting appropriately.

Equipment and Materials

- Fly rods
- Reels
- Targets
- Cones

Introduction

Review common errors from quizzes, if applicable.

Today, you will practice three specialty casts—the reach cast, which you have practiced already, the roll cast, and quartering upstream. You'll also learn about the situations where you use them. I will evaluate your casting technique while you are practicing.

Instructional Task: Introduction to Specialty Casts

■ PRACTICE TASK

Show a short video clip of a fly fisher making specialized casts to a rising fish. Ask students to recall the reach cast demo and the discussion about how to best present the fly for these water conditions. Explain mending the line.

Guiding questions for students:
- How do I present the fly in the most realistic way possible?
- How can I reduce drag on the fly?

Student Choices/Differentiation

Repeat the video clips, and stop to illustrate key differences in the casts.

What to Look For
- Students are engaged.
- Students are applying past knowledge during the questioning phase.

Instructional Task: Roll Cast

■ PRACTICE TASK

Demonstrate the roll cast, which is used when there is some kind of obstacle behind the caster.

Key Concepts

- No room for back cast
- Water tension
- Anchor point
- D loop
- Forward cast
- Presentation of fly

Set up casting stations so there is an obstacle behind the caster. In pairs, have students practice the motion of the roll cast 10 times.

Extension

Students may add shooting the line to each of the specialty casts.

Refinement

Students often try to overpower the roll cast. Have them pay particular attention to accelerating to a stop on the forward cast.

Student Choices/Differentiation

- Provide a handout or posters with the key concepts.
- Students may review a video clip of the roll cast.

What to Look For

- Line drags across the water to anchor point as rod is lifted.
- Rod comes up to ear.
- Line forms a D loop behind caster.
- Students flick the wrist on forward cast to roll line out.

Instructional Task: Quartering Upstream

■ PRACTICE TASK

Demonstrate quartering upstream, and introduce the concepts needed for successful presentation of the fly.

Key Concepts

- Caster position relative to the fish
- Line hand
- Drag
- Stripping line

Set up the casting stations to indicate the direction of the upstream current (e.g., mark with an arrow). In pairs, one student takes 10 practice casts while the partner keeps track of how many were successful. Students switch roles.

Refinement

Have students practice stripping the line after the "drift" to mimic insect movement and reduce slack line in the water.

Guiding questions for students:

- Why might you want to cast at an angle instead of directly upstream?
- What should you do with the rod while the line is drifting? (Answer: Follow with the tip.)
- How does drag affect the presentation of the fly?
- How can you reduce the amount of drag?

EMBEDDED OUTCOME: S2.H2.L1. Use students' responses about drag to get them to think more broadly about this movement concept. Ask them for examples of drag in other physical activities and how it is reduced or increased.

Student Choices/Differentiation

Provide a handout or posters with the key concepts.

What to Look For

- Students are casting at a 45-degree angle to the upstream current.
- Students are maintaining good casting technique.

Instructional Task: Student Casting and Evaluation

■ PRACTICE TASK

- Students pair off at cones and take turns casting to targets at basic cast length. One student takes five practice casts while the partner keeps track of how many were successful. Students switch roles.
- Evaluate student casting technique using a rubric during practice.
- Repeat, making a reach cast to the targets.
- Repeat, using a roll cast.
- Repeat, quartering upstream.

Extensions

- Students can try to put three casts together (quartering upstream with a roll cast and a reach finish).
- Students attempt to make 10 roll casts, and partners will keep track of how many they were able to successfully complete to the target.

Refinement

Remember, accuracy is critical here. Remind students to focus on a very small landing spot when making the cast.

Student Choices/Differentiation

- Students choose their partners.
- Students choose length and weight of rod.

What to Look For

- Students can distinguish between the different types of casts.
- Students are able to execute the different casts successfully to the targets.
- Students can combine the skills.

Formal and Informal Assessments

- Teacher evaluation
- Peer assessment of number of times caster hit the targets (out of 10) with the roll cast
- Journal entry

Closure

- How does the type of cast, and the water conditions (speed and direction), affect the presentation of the fly?
- What are the key concepts of a successful roll cast?
- When would you want to use a roll cast?
- What are the advantages of quartering upstream?
- Next time, a guest speaker will talk to us about sport fishing regulations and wildlife management careers.

Reflection

- At this point, are students able to put multiple casts together?
- Are they able to identify when to use each cast?

Homework: Fly Fishing Journal Entry

- Draw a stream scene in your journal that includes stream characteristics, cover, oxygen, potential food sources, fish, and a fly caster.
- Provide information about why the caster is positioned where she is and what type of cast he or she will use to catch the fish.

Resources

Fly-Fishing Learning Center: www.orvis.com

Internet keyword search: "roll cast," "quartering upstream," "mending the line"

LESSON 13: FISHING REGULATIONS

Grade-Level Outcomes

Primary Outcomes

Movement concepts, principles & knowledge: Applies the terminology associated with exercise and participation in selected individual-performance activities, dance, net/wall games, target games, aquatics and/or outdoor pursuits appropriately. (S2.H1.L1)

Safety: Applies best practices for participating safely in physical activity, exercise and dance (e.g., injury prevention, proper alignment, hydration, use of equipment, implementation of rules, sun protection). (S4.H5.L1)

Embedded Outcome

Movement concepts, principles & knowledge: Identifies and discusses the historical and cultural roles of games, sports and dance in society. (S2.H1.L2)

Lesson Objectives

The learner will:

- research the local fishing regulations and participate lawfully in recreation.
- apply terminology related to regulations appropriately.
- successfully plan for a fly fishing trip.

Equipment and Materials

Computer access

Introduction

Community guest speaker: Invite a fish and wildlife officer to share experiences and address students about sport fishing regulations. Speaker also leads students in a discussion about potential occupations in the fish and wildlife management field.

Instructional Task: Guest Speaker

■ PRACTICE TASK

Class listens to presentation from guest speaker (fish and wildlife officer) on regulations and potential careers in the field.

EMBEDDED OUTCOME: S2.H1.L2. Use the regulations as a springboard to discuss the relationship of regulations to fly fishing behavior and culture.

Student Choices/Differentiation

Students can ask questions verbally or write them down.

What to Look For

Students are attentive and practicing the skills of SPACE (silence, paraphrasing, accepting language, clarifying questions, evidence) during the presentation.

Instructional Task: Regulations Research

■ PRACTICE TASK

Students access the fish and wildlife website and, in pairs, research a local river you have assigned. They report their findings in a short presentation to three other groups. The presentations should include information about the following:

- River name
- Location
- Season (open, closed)
- Permitting
- Species
- Limits
- Hatch chart
- Access
- Resource bibliography

Share a teacher-generated rubric for the evaluation of the presentation with students.

Student Choices/Differentiation

- Pairs present to small groups. If time permits, one pair from each of the small groups presents to the entire class.
- Students can give an oral presentation or make a poster-type presentation.

What to Look For

Students are actively researching and developing a presentation that includes all of the components.

Instructional Task: Trip Planning

■ PRACTICE TASK

Lead a discussion about the importance of planning when leaving for a fly fishing trip to the river in preparation for the homework assignment.

Guiding questions for students:
- What kinds of gear should you bring and why?
- What safety precautions should you consider?
- How will you manage environmental conditions? (e.g., bugs, sun, wind)
- What regulations do you need to factor in?

Student Choices/Differentiation

- Provide a list of what students should include in planning.
- Allow students to work with partners.

What to Look For

- Students are contributing good ideas for planning the trip.
- Students are including safety considerations.
- Students are engaged in the conversation.

Formal and Informal Assessments

- Teacher evaluation of presentations
- Journal entry

Closure

- How are fishing regulations and the concept of conservation related?
- What can we do individually to contribute to fishing as a sustainable resource? Collectively?
- Next class, you'll learn how to cast long distances and prepare for your trip. Bring your journals in for a check.

Reflection

- Was the guest speaker an effective way to introduce students to fishing regulations?
- Did students seem interested in potential careers in this area? What kind of follow-up should be provided to them?
- Do they have a grasp of the importance of planning?

Homework: Fly Fishing Journal Entry

Students plan a fly fishing trip, covering what to pack, how to get there, communication with other stakeholders, permits, and so on.

Resources

Department of Fish and Wildlife: www.fws.gov and local representative

LESSON 14:
SINGLE- AND DOUBLE-HAUL CASTS

Grade-Level Outcomes

Primary Outcomes

Lifetime activities: Demonstrates competency and/or refines activity-specific movement skills in 2 or more lifetime activities (outdoor pursuits, individual-performance activities, aquatics, net/wall games or target games). (S1.H1.L1)

Movement concepts, principles & knowledge: Applies the terminology associated with exercise and participation in selected individual-performance activities, dance, net/wall games, target games, aquatics and/or outdoor pursuits appropriately. (S2.H1.L1)

Embedded Outcome

Physical activity knowledge: Identifies issues associated with exercising in heat, humidity and cold. (S3.H3.L1)

Lesson Objectives

The learner will:

- add distance and line speed to the cast with a single haul.
- add distance and line speed to the cast with a double haul.
- complete trip planning for a fishing excursion.
- apply casting language appropriately.

Equipment and Materials

- Fly rods
- Reels
- Cones
- Targets

Introduction

Today, you will learn a casting technique that will allow you to cast long distances and limit your fatigue. You'll also complete your trip plans to get ready for the last class.

Instructional Task: Single Haul Introduction

■ PRACTICE TASK

Begin the class by asking students how they can add distance to their casts (shooting line). Ask if they have developed a strategy for casting into the wind. Demonstrate the single haul in the forward cast and separately in the back cast.

Extension

Students use rods to mimic the hauling action (no cast).

Student Choices/Differentiation

- Students have a chance to ask questions.
- Students may review a video clip of the technique.

What to Look For

- Students are attentive and engaged in the discussion.
- Students are getting a feel for tugging the line away from the rod with the line hand.

Instructional Task: Single Haul

■ PRACTICE TASK

Students accelerate the line speed in the forward cast by using a single-haul technique.

Key Concepts
- Great basic cast technique
- Tight casting loop
- Line-hand pull
- Timing

Students practice in pairs at casting stations. One student takes 10 practice casts while the partner keeps track of how many were successful. Students switch roles. Repeat until students are comfortable with the hauling motion.

Extensions
- Repeat, adding shooting the line to the cast.
- Repeat, adding shooting the line and a reach cast to the single haul.

Refinement

Watch that students make short, quick pulls with the line hand. Students often make the motion too long (a full arm's length).

Student Choices/Differentiation
- Students choose their partners.
- Students choose rod length and weight.

What to Look For
- Students are tugging away from the rod during the lift.
- Students are repositioning the line hand level with the reel on the flick.

Instructional Task: Double Haul Instruction

■ PRACTICE TASK

Lead a short discussion about the double haul, and provide a demonstration while students are in their casting pairs at their casting stations. This way they can go right to the double haul on their own.

Refinement

Be sure students follow the line with their line hands all the way to the cork after the single haul before making the quick pull during the forward cast for the double haul.

Guiding questions for students:
- Describe a scenario when you would use a single-haul cast.
- Describe a scenario when you would use a double-haul cast.
- How do these techniques differ from shooting the line?

Student Choices/Differentiation
- Students choose their partners.
- Students choose rod length and weight.

What to Look For
- Students are challenging their comfort levels by working to combine several casts into one.
- Students are able to use correct timing while double hauling.
- Students are able to create turnover at the end of the cast.

Instructional Task: Trip Preparation

■ PRACTICE TASK

Prep students for the upcoming fly fishing field experience. Have students write down their plans.

EMBEDDED OUTCOME: S3.H3.L1. Lead a discussion on how weather (heat, humidity, cold, wind) can affect the fishing experience. Ask students to consider this in their trip preparations.

Student Choices/Differentiation

Provide a checklist for students.

What to Look For

- All students are contributing to the discussion.
- Students are realistic in thinking about the impact of conditions on fishing.

Formal and Informal Assessments

- Trip plans
- Journal entry

Closure

- What are several ways you can add distance to your cast?
- What is the connection between hauling line and effectively casting in the wind?
- What other strategies could you use when casting into the wind?
- Next class will be our field trip. Make sure you come prepared.

Reflection

- Were students able to get the timing needed to effectively haul line?
- Will they need more practice to be successful?
- Review trip plans and journal entries.

Homework: Fly Fishing Journal Entry

- We will be making a fly fishing trip to the river next class. Explain how you will contribute to the success of the class and what being successful means.
- What will you need to bring to be prepared?
- How does attitude play a role in your success?
- How will your attitude affect others?
- Also, read "Chief Seattle's Letter to All the People" and be ready to discuss it on the fishing trip, along with other readings we've done. You can find the reading on the school's physical education website, or just look it up online. Write down a couple of questions for discussion, and bring them with you on the trip.

Resources

Fly-Fishing Learning Center: www.orvis.com

Internet keyword search: "Chief Seattle's Letter to All the People," "single-haul cast," "double-haul cast," "casting into the wind," "casting for distance"

LESSON 15: FISHING TRIP

Grade-Level Outcomes

Primary Outcomes

Lifetime activities: Demonstrates competency and/or refines activity-specific movement skills in 2 or more lifetime activities (outdoor pursuits, individual-performance activities, aquatics, net/wall games or target games). (S1.H1.L1)

Rules & etiquette: Exhibits proper etiquette, respect for others and teamwork while engaging in physical activity and/or social dance. (S4.H2.L1)

Embedded Outcome

Challenge: Chooses an appropriate level of challenge to experience success and desire to participate in a self-selected physical activity. (S5.H2.L2)

Lesson Objectives

The learner will:

- review preparations for a fishing trip.
- apply fly fishing knowledge and skills on the water.
- refine casting to adjust to environmental conditions.
- observe proper fishing etiquette.

Equipment and Materials

- Fly rods
- Reels
- Fly boxes
- Wading boots or other shoes appropriate for a water environment

Introduction

Here we go—it's our big day on the water! Here are your trip plans with my comments. Please review them to make sure you have everything you need before we head out. We'll review safety rules and etiquette once we get to the water. We'll split into two groups at the site. One group will fish while the other discusses the readings we've done. We'll switch halfway through.

Instructional Task: On-site Review

■ PRACTICE TASK

Review safety precautions for fishing in general and any precautions specific to the site. For example:

- Rules for wading (wading may not be allowed by school policy)
- Using the buddy system
- Staying in sight of the teacher
- Appropriate distance between fishers

Review how to land a fish and release it.

Student Choices/Differentiation

Provide handouts with reminders that students can carry with them.

What to Look For

- Students are attentive.
- Students are asking appropriate questions.

Instructional Task: Fishing

■ PRACTICE TASK

- Split into two groups. One group will have a student-led discussion on the readings, while the other students select a spot to fish with a buddy, assemble their rods, choose flies, and fish.
- Students switch roles halfway through the class.

EMBEDDED OUTCOME: S5.H2.L2 Students should select fishing spots that provide an appropriate level of challenge for their ability.

Refinement

Circulate among the students, providing feedback about appropriate casting and fly choices.

Student Choices/Differentiation

- Students choose their buddies.
- Students choose rod length and weight.

What to Look For

- Students are applying the appropriate techniques for the conditions.
- Students are making good choices about places to fish from and to.
- Students are selecting flies appropriate to the expected fish species and insect hatches.

Formal and Informal Assessments

Journal entry

Closure

- How was the trip different from what you imagined?
- In what ways did you feel successful? What part was the most challenging?
- I hope you enjoyed your time on the water today and that you will stick with this great lifetime activity!
- Don't forget we'll be starting a new module next time. Check the school's physical education website for your choices, and be ready to select one.

Reflection

- How well did students do on the water?
- Did they seem well prepared for the fishing conditions?
- What can I do better next time I teach this module?

Homework: Fly Fishing Journal Entry

- Reflect on the trip today.
- What was hard for you? What did you enjoy the most?
- Review your choices for the next module, and be ready to make a selection.

HIKING MODULE

Lessons in this module were contributed by **Tracy Krause**, a physical education teacher at Tahoma High School in Maple Valley, WA.

Grade-Level Outcomes Addressed, by Lesson	Lessons												
	1	2	3	4	5	6	7	8	9	10	11	12	13
Standard 1. The physically literate individual demonstrates competency in a variety of motor skills and movement patterns.													
Demonstrates competency and/or refines activity-specific movement skills in 2 or more lifetime activities (outdoor pursuits, individual-performance activities, aquatics, net/wall games or target games). (S1.H1.L1)	P	P	P	P		P	P	P	P	P	P	P	P
Standard 2. The physically literate individual applies knowledge of concepts, principles, strategies and tactics related to movement and performance.													
Applies the terminology associated with exercise and participation in selected individual-performance activities, dance, net/wall games, target games, aquatics and/or outdoor pursuits appropriately. (S2.H1.L1)	P	P	P						P	P	P		
Identifies and discusses the historical and cultural roles of games, sports and dance in a society. (S2.H1.L2)						E		P		E			
Standard 3. The physically literate individual demonstrates the knowledge and skills to achieve and maintain a health-enhancing level of physical activity and fitness.													
Identifies issues associated with exercising in heat, humidity and cold. (S3.H3.L1)					E						E		
Evaluates—according to their benefits, social support network and participation requirements—activities that can be pursued in the local environment. (S3.H4.L1)					P								
Participates several times a week in a self-selected lifetime activity, dance or fitness activity outside of the school day. (S3.H6.L1)	E							E					
Relates physiological responses to individual levels of fitness and nutritional balance. (S3.H8.L1)			E										
Applies stress-management strategies (e.g., mental imagery, relaxation techniques, deep breathing, aerobic exercise, meditation) to reduce stress. (S3.H14.L2)													E
Standard 4. The physically literate individual exhibits responsible personal and social behavior that respects self and others.													
Exhibits proper etiquette, respect for others and teamwork while engaging in physical activity and/or social dance. (S4.H2.L1)	P		E						P	E			P
Examines moral and ethical conduct in specific competitive situations (e.g., intentional fouls, performance-enhancing substances, gambling, current events in sport). (S4.H2.L2)									E		E		
Uses communication skills and strategies that promote team or group dynamics. (S4.H3.L1)	E	E	E						E			E	
Solves problems and thinks critically in physical activity and/or dance settings, both as an individual and in groups. (S4.H4.L1)		E	E	E			E	P					
Applies best practices for participating safely in physical activity, exercise and dance (e.g., injury prevention, proper alignment, hydration, use of equipment, implementation of rules, sun protection). (S4.H5.L1)						E							P
Standard 5. The physically literate individual recognizes the value of physical activity for health, enjoyment, challenge, self-expression and/or social interaction.													
Analyzes the health benefits of a self-selected physical activity. (S5.H1.L1)										E			
Chooses an appropriate level of challenge to experience success and desire to participate in a self-selected physical activity. (S5.H2.L2)													E
Selects and participates in physical activities or dance that meet the need for self-expression and enjoyment. (S5.H3.L1)													E

P= Primary; E = Embedded

LESSON 1: LEAVE NO TRACE

Grade-Level Outcomes

Primary Outcomes

Movement concepts, principles & knowledge: Applies the terminology associated with exercise and participation in selected individual-performance activities, dance, net/wall games, target games, aquatics and/or outdoor pursuits appropriately. (S2.H1.L1)

Rules & etiquette: Exhibits proper etiquette, respect for others and teamwork while engaging in a physical activity and/or social dance. (S4.H2.L1)

Lifetime activities: Demonstrates competency and/or refines activity-specific movement skills in 2 or more lifetime activities (outdoor pursuits, individual-performance activities, aquatics, net/wall games or target games). (S1.H1.L1)

Embedded Outcomes

Working with others: Uses communication skills and strategies that promote team or group dynamics. (S4.H3.L1)

Engages in physical activity: Participates several times a week in a self-selected lifetime activity, dance or fitness activity outside of the school day. (S3.H6.L1)

Lesson Objectives

The learner will:

- discuss the ethics of Leave No Trace.
- apply the seven principles of Leave No Trace.
- walk a route around the school.

Equipment and Materials

- Leave No Trace cards with definitions (6 sets of 7)
- Index cards and pencils
- Quizzes or surveys

Introduction

Today, we'll start the Hiking Module. Hiking is a great activity for your health and for getting you into the outdoors. We'll introduce the Leave No Trace principles, which are ethical guidelines that support conservation of the environment. The goal is to enjoy the outdoors while hiking as well as to have a minimal impact on the environment so others can enjoy it too. We'll finish up with a short walk to begin working on our hiking fitness. First, let's take a brief pre-assessment of your hiking knowledge.

Instructional Task: Pre-assessment

■ PRACTICE TASK

Students take a teacher-generated quiz or survey about their hiking knowledge.

Student Choices/Differentiation

Allow extra time if needed, or give a take-home version—it could be administered online before the module begins.

What to Look For

- What do students already know about hiking?
- What kinds of hiking experiences have they had?

Instructional Task: Leave No Trace Introduction

■ PRACTICE TASK

Use a personal story to bring attention to the need for "treading lightly" when using our natural resources, and introduce the seven principles of Leave No Trace (LNT).

- Plan ahead and prepare.
- Travel and camp on durable surfaces.
- Dispose of waste properly.
- Leave what you find.
- Minimize campfire impacts.
- Respect wildlife.
- Be considerate of other visitors.

Extension

Students share a specific outdoor experience where they witnessed someone using LNT principles or someone who wasn't.

Guiding questions for students:

- How did this affect your experience positively or negatively?
- How might we use these principles here at school? At home?

Student Choices/Differentiation

- Supply a handout of the principles.
- Students can partner-share and then pick a few principles to share with the whole group.

What to Look For

- Students are engaged.
- All students are contributing to the discussion.
- Students are able to provide good examples.

Instructional Task: LNT Charades

■ PRACTICE TASK

Students split into groups of seven. Give each student an LNT card with one principle written on it. Students take turns, using universal charades rules, acting out their LNT principles. The other students in the group try to guess the principles. The student who guesses correctly gets the card. The student with the most cards at the end gets to choose one person from her group to perform her principle for the whole group.

EMBEDDED OUTCOME: S4.H3.L1. Provide positive feedback to students and groups that are applying effective communication skills.

What to Look For

- Students are engaged.
- Student talk is on task.
- The environment is respectful.

Instructional Task: Walk Around the School Grounds

■ PRACTICE TASK

Distribute index cards and pencils to the students. As a group, take a walk around the school grounds (or a nearby park); students write down their observations during the walk.

Extension

Have students wear a pedometer or use a device to count steps. Use step count to reflect on daily step guidelines.

Guiding questions for students:

- What do you think the difference is between walking and hiking?
- Did you see any examples of Leave No Trace principles during the walk?
- Did you observe anything during the walk that you don't normally notice?

Student Choices/Differentiation

Students can walk at their own pace or with a partner.

What to Look For

- Students are looking closely at their surroundings during the walk.
- Students can apply the principles to a simple walk.
- Are students engaged with others in the group or reflecting on their own?

Formal and Informal Assessments

- Pre-assessment of hiking knowledge
- Student presentations during the game
- Index cards from walk

Closure

- Did you see any examples of LNT during the walk?
- Why is practicing LNT principles an important component of outdoor ethics?
- What do you think will be the most difficult principle to follow? Why?
- What should you do if you observe someone who is not following the LNT principles?
- For the duration of this module, you will need to track your physical activity outside of class. We are trying to see if you are participating in enough physical activity outside of school to meet the recommended guidelines of at least 60 minutes a day. This physical activity will also prepare you for hiking. You can track your physical activity by recording the type of activity and for how long, or you can use a device such as a pedometer, physical activity monitor, or cell phone app. Feel free to offer observations and reflections about physical activity—don't feel limited to just recording steps or time. No matter how you do it, you will need to record your activity in a log or in a web-based program. You can also do this in a blog. We'll check periodically to see how you are doing. (Embedded outcome: S3.H6.L1)

Reflection

- Are students engaged in the activity?
- As a result of the lesson and the closure, do I have evidence that my students understand the seven LNT principles?
- Review observations on student index cards.
- Review pre-assessment results to aid in planning lesson content.

Homework

- As you walk around school between now and next class, focus on how students and staff are using or not using the LNT principles on our campus. Be prepared to share some of your observations.

- Start tracking your physical activity outside of class.

Resources

Leave No Trace: www.LNT.org

LESSON 2: 10 ESSENTIALS OF HIKING

Grade-Level Outcomes

Primary Outcomes

Movement concepts, principles & knowledge: Applies the terminology associated with exercise and participation in selected individual-performance activities, dance, net/wall games, target games, aquatics and/or outdoor pursuits appropriately. (S2.H1.L1)

Lifetime activities: Demonstrates competency and/or refines activity-specific movement skills in 2 or more lifetime activities (outdoor pursuits, individual-performance activities, aquatics, net/wall games or target games). (S1.H1.L1)

Embedded Outcomes

Working with others: Solves problems and thinks critically in physical activity and/or dance settings, both as an individual and in groups. (S4.H4.L1)

Working with others: Uses communication skills and strategies that promote team or group dynamics. (S4.H3.L1)

Lesson Objectives

The learner will:

- identify the 10 essentials for hiking in the backcountry (including day hikes).
- apply the 10 essentials for hiking to an authentic outdoor experience.
- walk a route around the school.

Equipment and Materials

- Paper and pencils
- 10 essentials handout

Introduction

The homework for this class was to record examples of people using (or not using) Leave No Trace principles. Can anyone share something they saw? Today, you'll expand your hiking knowledge by working together to develop the 10 essentials for hiking in the backcountry (including day hikes). We'll finish class with another short walk to help get our physical activity in for the day.

Instructional Task: 10 Essentials

■ PRACTICE TASK

Students read an article from the local media about a lost hiker. Lead a discussion about the importance of preparedness and what can happen to someone who is not prepared.

Extension

Students work together in groups of four to develop their list of 10 essentials.

EMBEDDED OUTCOME: S4.H3.L1 Provide feedback for groups on collaboration and group dynamics.

Student Choices/Differentiation

- Provide the groups with 15 cards, and students choose the 10 essentials from those cards rather than starting from scratch, depending on the background or experience of the group.
- Students choose their groups.

What to Look For

- Students are engaged.
- Group dynamics are positive.

Instructional Task: 10 Essentials Synthesis

■ PRACTICE TASK

Choose one group to share their 10 essentials. Lead a discussion on those items and whether there is group consensus on the 10. Then share the universally accepted 10 essentials (see handout), and students compare and contrast the two lists.

Extension

Groups share their best two additions to the 10 essentials, and they provide a rationale for the additions. Class decides on the best two.

EMBEDDED OUTCOME: S4.H4.L1. Use this task to reinforce problem-solving strategies through questioning.

Guiding questions for students:

- How did your group generate ideas for the 10 essentials?
- What kinds of strategies did you use to decide which 10 to put forward?

Student Choices/Differentiation

Have students write down essentials on a flip chart or whiteboard so everyone can see them for discussion.

What to Look For

Students are talking to each other and practicing the skills of SPACE (silence, paraphrasing, accepting language, clarifying questions, evidence).

Instructional Task: Walk Around the School

■ PRACTICE TASK

With the time remaining in class, organize a walk around the school or neighborhood. If possible, include some hills or uneven terrain. If trails are available, such as a cross country course, that would be ideal.

Guiding questions for students:

- Is there anything from the 10 essentials list that we should take on a walk like this?
- What sorts of wildlife or plant life do you expect to see while walking?

Extension

Students wear pedometers or other activity tracking devices to count their steps on the walk.

Student Choices/Differentiation

- Students can volunteer to lead the group.
- Students can suggest the walking route.

What to Look For

- Students are interacting on the walk.
- Students are maintaining a comfortable pace.

Formal and Informal Assessments

Student lists of essentials

Closure

- Why do we use the word *essential* to describe the 10 items?
- What role does planning play in making certain you have what you need to be successful on a hike?
- What does *successful* mean in this context?
- What is the one thing you should do, beyond packing the 10 essentials, so you can be successful? (Answer: Make your plans known to someone.)
- What did you do well in terms of using SPACE? What were some challenges?

Reflection

- Has every student in each group had a voice in the conversation?
- Were students able to identify most of the 10 essentials?
- Review the lists of essentials produced by student groups for misconceptions.

Homework

- Be prepared next class to share one story about how you properly prepared for a trip or hike, or a story about how you wish you had prepared better for a trip or hike.
- Continue tracking your physical activity outside of school, and set a personal goal for your physical activity levels.

Resources

The Mountaineers: www.mountaineers.org

American Hiking Society: www.americanhiking.org

Washington Trails Association: www.wta.org

THE 10 ESSENTIALS OF HIKING

Ten things you should bring on *every* hike.

1. **Appropriate footwear.** For a short day hike that doesn't involve a heavy pack or technical terrain, trail shoes are great. For longer hikes, carrying heavier loads, or more technical terrain, hiking boots offer more support.

2. **Map and compass/GPS.** A map and compass not only tell you where you are and how far you have to go, it can help you find campsites, water, and an emergency exit route in case of an accident. While GPS units are very useful, always carry a map and compass as a backup.

3. **Extra water and a way to purify it.** Without enough water, your body's muscles and organs simply can't perform as well. Consuming too little water will not only make you thirsty, but susceptible to hypothermia and altitude sickness.

4. **Extra food.** Any number of things could keep you out longer than expected: getting lost, enjoying time by a stream, an injury, or difficult terrain. Extra food will help keep up energy and morale.

5. **Rain gear and extra clothing.** Because the weatherman is not always right. Dressing in layers allows you to adjust to changing weather and activity levels. Two rules: Avoid cotton (it keeps moisture close to your skin), and always carry a hat.

6. **Safety items: fire, light, and a whistle.** The warmth of a fire and a hot drink can help prevent hypothermia. Fires are also a great way to signal for help if you get lost. If lost, you'll also want the whistle as it is more effective than using your voice to call for help (use 3 short bursts). And just in case you're out later than planned, a flashlight/headlamp is a must-have item to see your map and where you're walking.

7. **First aid kit.** Prepackaged first aid kits for hikers are available at any outfitter. Double your effectiveness with knowledge: Take a first aid class with the American Red Cross or a Wilderness First Aid class.

8. **Knife or multi-purpose tool.** These enable you to cut strips of cloth into bandages, remove splinters, fix broken eyeglasses, and perform a whole host of repairs on malfunctioning gear.

9. **Sunscreen and sunglasses.** Especially above tree line when there is a skin-scorching combination of sun and snow, you'll need sunglasses to prevent snow blindness and sunscreen to prevent sunburn.

10. **Daypack/backpack.** You'll want something you can carry comfortably and has the features designed to keep you hiking smartly. Don't forget the rain cover; some packs come with one built-in. Keep the other Essentials in the pack and you'll always be ready to hit the trail safely.

From L.C. MacDonald, R.J. Doan, and S. Chepko, eds., 2018, *Lesson planning for high school physical education* (Reston, VA: SHAPE America; Champaign, IL: Human Kinetics). Reprinted, by permission, from American Hiking Society, 2013, *The 10 essentials of hiking* (Silver Springs, MD: American Hiking Society). Available: https://americanhiking.org/resources/10essentials/

LESSON 3: 10 ESSENTIALS ASSESSMENT

Grade-Level Outcomes

Primary Outcomes

Movement concepts, principles & knowledge: Applies the terminology associated with exercise and participation in selected individual-performance activities, dance, net/wall games, target games, aquatics and/or outdoor pursuits appropriately. (S2.H1.L1)

Lifetime activities: Demonstrates competency and/or refines activity-specific movement skills in 2 or more lifetime activities (outdoor pursuits, individual-performance activities, aquatics, net/wall games or target games). (S1.H1.L1)

Embedded Outcomes

Rules & etiquette: Exhibits proper etiquette, respect for others and teamwork while engaging in physical activity and/or social dance. (S4.H2.L1)

Working with others: Solves problems and thinks critically in physical activity and/or dance settings, both as an individual and in groups. (S4.H4.L1)

Working with others: Uses communication skills and strategies that promote team or group dynamics. (S4.H3.L1)

Lesson Objectives

The learner will:

- apply the LNT principles and the 10 essentials.
- participate in a walking activity around the school.

Equipment and Materials

- Group activity sheet (10)
- Color-coded team materials/folders (10)
- 10-foot (3 m) sections of climbing rope (10)
- Cones (10)
- Exercise cards (10)
- Backpack
- Hiking gear laid out on gym floor (including 10 essentials)

Introduction

Who is willing to share a story from their homework about Leave No Trace? Today, we will continue to work on the 10 essentials and Leave No Trace Principles with a hiking activity and assessment.

Instructional Task: 10 Essentials and LNT Activity

■ PRACTICE TASK

In groups of four, students participate in the 10 essentials and LNT activity. Group members must hold onto the rope throughout the activity and work together to complete the task. This activity requires students to walk or hike around school grounds using a map to find 10 caches. (See "Leave No Trace and the 10 Essentials" task sheet at the end of the lesson.)

EMBEDDED OUTCOME: S4.H2.L1. Reinforce the importance of teamwork in using the map and finding all the caches. Provide positive feedback to groups who are on task and working together to find the caches.

Extension

Students complete a physical or cognitive challenge once they arrive at the cache before they receive the information for the activity.

Guiding questions for students:

- How do you anticipate working in a group of four will make this activity more difficult?
- What will you do to support your team's success?

Student Choices/Differentiation

- Students choose their groups.
- Students work at their own pace.

What to Look For

- Students are engaged.
- Students are collaborating and managing impulsivity.

Instructional Task: 10 Essentials Assessment

■ PRACTICE TASK

After the activity is complete, students sit in their groups of four. A backpack and many hiking items are laid out on the floor. Each group comes forward, and selects one item that is part of the universal 10 essentials and connects that choice to a specific priority.

Guiding questions for students:

- What are the most important survival items in an emergency situation?
- What are some factors that may change your survival priorities?

EMBEDDED OUTCOMES: S4.H4.L1; S4.H3.L1. Students must apply their knowledge of the principles, think critically about which item to choose, and come to some consensus. Provide positive feedback to groups that are making good decisions in a constructive manner.

What to Look For

- Groups are working together and using positive communication skills.
- Students are encouraging each other.

Formal and Informal Assessments

10 essentials assessment

Closure

- What was one success your group had as they worked together to finish the task?
- When you observed the items from the backpack, what was your initial reaction?
- How might weight, such as a heavier backpack, play a role in your enjoyment of a backpacking trip?
- Next time, you'll learn how to pack your backpacks.

Reflection

- Were students working together and including all the group members?
- How well do the students know the 10 essentials?

Homework

- Write down the seven Leave No Trace principles, and provide one specific example of what that might look like on a hike with this class.
- Continue to track your physical activity outside of school.

Resources

Leave No Trace: www.LNT.org

The Mountaineers: www.mountaineers.org

LEAVE NO TRACE AND THE 10 ESSENTIALS

Instructions

- Each team will have a map of the school grounds, instructions, 10 feet of rope, and a team color.
- The goal is to collect a card from all 10 of the "caches" found outside by using the map.
- After all cards are collected, return to the gym.
- Return the cards to the correct folder found at the numbered cones (for cards 1-10), and complete the exercises found on those cones as a group. Repeat this process until all the cards are deposited in sequence and the exercises have been completed.
- Read the information related to the 10 essentials of hiking in the back-country and the Leave No Trace principles at each "cache."
- There will be an assessment at the end of the activity!

Remember

- Stay together as a group!
- Be safe.
- Be respectful of other classes and other teams.
- Take only the card that matches your team color.
- Support one another.
- Do your best.
- Raise the trust meter during this activity.

Essential Questions

Team Color : _____

What role do I play in Leave No Trace?

What is essential about the 10 essentials?

Start at station # _____   Group # _____

From L.C. MacDonald, R.J. Doan, and S. Chepko, eds., 2018, *Lesson planning for high school physical education* (Reston, VA: SHAPE America; Champaign, IL: Human Kinetics).

LESSON 4: PACKING A BACKPACK

Grade-Level Outcomes

Primary Outcome

Lifetime activities: Demonstrates competency and/or refines activity-specific movement skills in 2 or more lifetime activities (outdoor pursuits, individual-performance activities, aquatics, net/wall games or target games). (S1.H1.L1)

Embedded Outcomes

Working with others: Uses communication skills and strategies that promote team or group dynamics. (S4.H3.L1)

Fitness knowledge: Relates physiological responses to individual levels of fitness and nutritional balance. (S3.H8.L1)

Lesson Objectives

The learner will:

- correctly pack both an external and internal framed backpack.
- complete an obstacle course while wearing a backpack.

Equipment and Materials

- Internet access
- Backpacks
- Backpacking items (e.g., sleeping bag, clothes, tent, food, 10 essentials)
- Trekking poles
- Obstacle course items (e.g., stairs, log, ladder)

Introduction

Today, you will research how to pack both an internal and external framed backpack and complete a hiking obstacle course. Most of the time, you need only a small backpack for day hikes, but if you take an extended hike with one or more overnights, you would need a more substantial pack to allow you to carry additional items such as tents, sleeping bags, and meals. That's where internal and external frame packs come in. Some backpackers like to take a minimalist approach and go light or ultralight, where they carry only the most essential items to lighten their packs. That's a more advanced style that should be undertaken only by experienced backpackers. Let's get started!

Instructional Task: Packing

■ PRACTICE TASK

In groups of three or four members of similar size and weight, students access the Internet to research the correct way to pack both internal and external framed backpacks. Students take notes (to be turned in later).

Extensions

- Students correctly pack essential items into their backpacks (some internal and some external).
- After packing, students review a packing checklist and mark each step they successfully completed.

Student Choices/Differentiation

- Group students by size and weight.
- Group students by experience levels.
- Provide suggestions for relevant websites.
- Students choose the type of pack.

What to Look For

- Students are on task and sharing ideas.
- Students are engaged in packing and contributing to the discussion of how to do it correctly.

Instructional Task: Obstacle Course

■ PRACTICE TASK

All students complete, with the support of their team members, the obstacle course while wearing the backpack they packed. The course is intended to simulate some hiking conditions. Course includes the following:

- Stairs
- Logs
- Large tires
- Water
- Cones

EMBEDDED OUTCOME: S3.H8.L1. Use the guiding questions to lead a discussion about how fitness and nutritional balance interact in physical activity.

Guiding questions for students:

- Were you surprised by the level of effort required to do the course with a pack on?
- How did your body react to the effort?
- How does fitness play a role in your ability (or effort) to participate in a hiking or backpacking activity as an adult?
- What types of fitness do you need for hiking and backpacking?
- How does energy balance factor into your ability to participate in hiking or backpacking?

EMBEDDED OUTCOME: S4.H3.L1. Reinforce the need to support others on the course. Provide positive feedback to students and teams that provide support to others.

Refinement

If students are struggling with balance, check to see that pack straps are adjusted appropriately and encourage the use of trekking poles.

Student Choices/Differentiation

- Students can adjust the challenge by adding weight to the pack or removing it.
- Students choose the type of pack.
- Students can use trekking poles for better balance.

What to Look For

- Students are supporting one another's success and positive interactions.
- Students are carrying the packs over the obstacles without struggling.

Formal and Informal Assessments

- Review of student notes
- Review of packing checklist

Closure

- What is one key to packing your backpack?
- What is a common mistake? What role would a checklist play in making a good decision?
- How would a scale support your success?
- When crossing a river on a log or bridge, what should you do with your pack belt?
- How did you feel about using the trekking poles with the pack?

Reflection

- Were students making good decisions about packing?
- Were they moving through the obstacle course with balance and control?
- Review student notes and packing checklists to look for knowledge gaps.

Homework

- We're going to start planning a trip next class, so for homework, come up with some suggestions for locations by talking with family and friends or checking the web or area maps.
- Continue tracking your physical activity outside of school.

Resources

Outdoor clothing and gear from top brands: www.rei.com

Wild Backpacker: www.wildbackpacker.com

LESSON 5: TRIP PLANNING

Grade-Level Outcomes

Primary Outcome

Physical activity knowledge: Evaluates—according to their benefits, social support network and participation requirements—activities that can be pursued in the local environment. (S3.H4.L1)

Embedded Outcomes

Safety: Applies best practices for participating safely in physical activity, exercise and dance (e.g., injury prevention, proper alignment, hydration, use of equipment, implementation of rules, sun protection). (S4.H5.L1)

Physical activity knowledge: Identifies issues associated with exercising in heat, humidity and cold. (S3.H3.L1)

Lesson Objectives

The learner will:

- research and select a local hike.
- create a trip plan.
- determine appropriate items to pack.

Equipment and Materials

- Internet access
- Hiking resources and maps

Introduction

For homework, you were asked to come up with some suggestions for a local day hike. What ideas do you have? These will be good starting points for selecting and planning a hike in today's class.

Instructional Task: Research

■ PRACTICE TASK

Students research and select a local hike using the Internet and/or written resources. The selected hike must fit the following criteria:

- Between 4 and 8 miles (6.4 to 12.8 km) round trip
- Trailhead accessible by car
- Map available
- Trail safe and marked
- Within 50 miles (80 km) of school

Student Choices/Differentiation

- Provide a handout with instructions or a poster or PowerPoint slide.
- Provide a checklist with the criteria for students to use during the research phase.

What to Look For

- Students are engaged in the activity.
- Students are considering all the criteria when evaluating ideas.

Instructional Task: Planning

■ PRACTICE TASK

Students include the following in developing their hike plans for a presentation:

- Route or hike chosen
- Passes and permits
- Creating and leaving a trip plan
- Map
- Gear
- Backpack
- First aid
- Water and food
- Pictures from the trail

Refinement

Provide written and electronic resources for students to choose from. You might schedule a visit from the school librarian for support in acquiring resources to support the research.

Note: This task could be presented as a homework assignment or span two lessons if needed to complete all tasks.

EMBEDDED OUTCOME: S4.H5.L1. The assignment requires and reinforces that students plan for safety aspects, such as hydration, making a trip plan, and first aid. A review of first aid situations that commonly occur out on the trail may be warranted, including extreme weather (e.g., lightning, hypothermia).

Student Choices/Differentiation

Students may use PowerPoint, Prezi, or another presentation software.

What to Look For

- Students are working individually to complete the assignment and are staying on task.
- Students are asking good questions as they progress through the assignment.

Instructional Task: Presentation

■ PRACTICE TASK

Students present their hike plans.

Extension

Students may opt to take the hike on the weekend or at the end of the module, under supervision.

Student Choices/Differentiation

The assignment can be presented in front of the class, presented in small groups, or turned in to you.

What to Look For

Students present quality work as evaluated on the scoring guide or checklist.

Formal and Informal Assessments

- Checklist or rubric (your choice)
- Student presentation evaluation

Closure

- What is important about the planning process?
- How can planning support a successful hike?
- What role does communication play in the planning process?
- What challenges did you find in developing your presentation?
- How did you overcome those challenges?
- Next time, you'll learn how to use a compass while in the outdoors.

Reflection

- Were students on task and following the instructions?
- Were they able to use technology to effectively make their presentation?

Homework

- Research how to deal with severe conditions (heat, cold, humidity) when out on the trail. Write up a summary of your findings, due in lesson 8. (Embedded outcome: S3.H3.L1)
- Continue to track physical activity outside of school. Bring your logs to the next class.

Resources

Washington Trails Association: www.wta.org

LESSON 6: USING A COMPASS

Grade-Level Outcomes

Primary Outcome

Lifetime activities: Demonstrates competency and/or refines activity-specific movement skills in 2 or more lifetime activities (outdoor pursuits, individual-performance activities, aquatics, net/wall games or target games). (S1.H1.L1)

Embedded Outcome

Movement concepts, principles & knowledge: Identifies and discusses the historical and cultural roles of games, sports and dance in a society. (S2.H1.L2)

Lesson Objectives

The learner will:

- identify the basic components of a compass.
- take a bearing using a compass.
- plan and follow a short route using compass bearings.

Equipment and Materials

- Compass (1/student)
- Pencil (1/student)
- Index card (1/student)

Introduction

Last class, we focused on trip planning for a day hike. Today, you will learn how to use a compass, one of the 10 essentials, and create a walking route. Then, I'll test your skills to see if you can follow the route successfully.

Instructional Task:
Compass Introduction and Taking a Bearing

■ PRACTICE TASK

Introduce the basic components of the compass:

- Base
- Azimuth ring
- Magnetic needle
- Orienting arrow
- Travel arrow

Extensions

- Demonstrate how to take a bearing, with students following along on their compasses.
- Practice with a variety of bearings.

Guiding questions for students:

- What types of landmarks should you use to develop a route? (For example: Objects that move or can be moved should be avoided.)
- How can you increase understanding when giving directions to a partner?
- How are clarity and confidence related to one another?

EMBEDDED OUTCOME: S2.H1.L2. Discuss the historical use of the compass and how the technology has changed over time.

Student Choices/Differentiation

- Provide handouts or a poster of a compass with parts labeled.
- Students may review a video clip of taking a bearing.

What to Look For

- Students are engaged.
- Students are taking the bearing correctly.

Instructional Task: Create a Route

■ PRACTICE TASK

Students create a route that includes at least six segments, or legs. They write the route out on an index card. After writing out the route, they follow it to make sure they can take bearings correctly. Students turn their cards in at the end of the lesson.

Extension

Repeat, but specify at least one location students must include in the route.

Refinement

Each student can create a route and exchange cards with a partner. The partner will then follow the directions to complete the route and provide feedback.

Student Choices/Differentiation

This activity can be completed indoors or outdoors depending on the circumstances.

What to Look For

- Students are making responsible decisions and staying on task.
- Students are able to use the bearings and compass correctly.

Formal and Informal Assessments

- Student route cards
- Physical activity logs

Closure

- Why is it important to have a compass as part of your 10 essentials?
- When creating a route, why should you choose permanent objects?
- How can you use North, South, East, and West to differentiate objects and landmarks?

Reflection

- Review student routes. Were students able to create routes successfully?
- Were they able to use a compass correctly?
- Which students may need more practice with this skill?
- Review physical activity logs to see if students are meeting guidelines and personal goals.

Homework

- Continue working on the severe conditions assignment.
- Continue tracking your physical activity outside the school day.

Resources

Brunton Outdoor: www.brunton.com

LESSON 7: FOLLOWING BEARINGS

Grade-Level Outcomes

Primary Outcome

Lifetime activities: Demonstrates competency and/or refines activity-specific movement skills in 2 or more lifetime activities (outdoor pursuits, individual-performance activities, aquatics, net/wall games or target games). (S1.H1.L1)

Embedded Outcomes

Working with others: Solves problems and thinks critically in physical activity and/or dance settings, both as an individual and in groups. (S4.H4.L1)

Engages in physical activity: Participates several times a week in a self-selected lifetime activity, dance or fitness activity outside of the school day. (S3.H6.L1)

Lesson Objectives

The learner will:

- enter a given bearing and find a location.
- follow a route given compass bearings.
- complete an assessment of compass skills.

Equipment and Materials

- Compass (1/student)
- Pencil (1/student)
- Index card with a route developed from previous lesson (1/student)

Introduction

Here are your physical activity logs. I've made some comments with regard to how well you are meeting physical activity guidelines, so be sure to look them over to see if you should be making any adjustments. Last class, you learned how to take a bearing with a compass and use it to create a route. Today, you will build on these skills by following a given route and bearings. This will be a good check on how well you can use the compass.

Instructional Task: Review

■ PRACTICE TASK

Review the parts of a compass and how to take a bearing. Students practice taking bearings.

Student Choices/Differentiation

- Students may review a video clip.
- Use a poster to show names of compass parts.

What to Look For

- Students are using the compass confidently.
- Do students still have questions about how to take a bearing?

Instructional Task: Using a Given Bearing to Find a Location and Follow a Route

■ PRACTICE TASK

Demonstrate how to input a given bearing, and have students follow along. Emphasize the importance of accuracy. Repeat with different bearings.

Extensions

- Students check a route created by another group in the previous lesson. They write their findings, including a map of the route, on the index card they were given. They turn their cards in at the end of the lesson.
- Repeat with a different group's card.

EMBEDDED OUTCOME: S4.H4.L1. Students need to analyze the route and apply their knowledge of bearings to be successful. Debrief about the challenges of following someone else's route.

Student Choices/Differentiation

This activity can be completed indoors or outdoors, depending on the circumstances of the previous lesson.

What to Look For

Students are making responsible decisions and staying on task.

Instructional Task: Compass Assessment

■ PRACTICE TASK

Give students index cards with a brief route to follow. Leave a note or symbol at the end of each route, and ask students to record what they found to ensure they got to the end.

Student Choices/Differentiation

Students could work in pairs or small groups.

What to Look For

- Students are completing the routes successfully.
- Students are correctly following the bearings on the first try.

Formal and Informal Assessments

- Compass assessment
- Physical activity log comments

Closure

- Why is accuracy so important?
- How might accuracy affect the safety of a hiker or hiking group?
- Next class, we will participate in a race. How might you and your partner work together to be fast yet accurate?

Reflection

- Were students able to check the routes successfully?
- Were they using their compasses more confidently after practicing a few times?
- What are they still having trouble with?

Homework

- Review the comments in your physical activity logs, and continue tracking your physical activity outside of school. (Embedded outcome: S3.H6.L1)

- Continue working on your severe conditions assignment.

- Next time, we'll try orienteering. Use the library or look up orienteering online so you have an idea of what it's all about.

- Practice using a compass at home, and try teaching someone to use it. You can use a compass or a device with a compass app on it.

Resources

Bruton Outdoor: www.brunton.com

LESSON 8: ORIENTEERING

Grade-Level Outcomes

Primary Outcomes

Lifetime activities: Demonstrates competency and/or refines activity-specific movement skills in 2 or more lifetime activities (outdoor pursuits, individual-performance activities, aquatics, net/wall games or target games). (S1.H1.L1)

Working with others: Solves problems and thinks critically in physical activity and/or dance settings, both as an individual and in groups. (S4.H4.L1)

Embedded Outcome

Health: Analyzes the health benefits of a self-selected physical activity. (S5.H1.L1).

Lesson Objectives

The learner will:

- apply basic skills from compass lessons to complete an orienteering course.
- work with others to plan a strategy to navigate the course.

Equipment and Materials

- Map
- Compass
- Pencil

Introduction

Today, you will participate in an orienteering course. When you looked up orienteering for homework, what did you learn about this activity? Orienteering is an activity where you navigate from point to point in a sequence, usually as quickly as you can, using a map and compass. Do you know how to prove you were at each site? You'll use punch cards at each site, just like in official competitions. All right, let's get started.

Instructional Task: Orienteering Course

■ PRACTICE TASK

Students form groups of two. Provide instructions regarding the map and compass course (on the school grounds).

Groups of two leave from the starting point every 30 seconds (they write the starting time on their cards). The cards will have a list of 12 coordinates. Groups run along the given coordinate until they reach the destination (there will be a unique card punch at each destination) and punch their cards. Groups continue until they reach the 12th destination (finish line). Course takes about 30 minutes to complete depending on the how well the group members work together.

Students should engage in a discussion about how they can work together to complete the course as efficiently as possible and share their plans on an index card. Then at the end of the lesson, they summarize their experiences related to their goals.

After completing the course, groups write down their finishing times, subtract their start times to find their final times, and turn their cards in.

EMBEDDED OUTCOME: S5.H1.L1 After completing the course, ask students to identify the potential health benefits of hiking and/or orienteering.

Student Choices/Differentiation

- Students choose their partners.
- Students complete the course at their own pace.

What to Look For

- Students are working together to complete the task.
- Students are able to navigate the course using the compass.
- Students are moving directly from one destination to another (i.e., not having to make corrections).

Formal and Informal Assessments

- Student cards (a clear indicator of whether or not students understand the basic concepts in the compass lessons)
- Assessment of severe conditions assignment

Closure

- What was the biggest challenge your group encountered?
- How did you overcome the challenge?
- What was one success your group had relative to communication?
- Be sure to turn in your summaries of what to do when hiking in extreme weather.

Reflection

- Were students able to complete the course correctly?
- Are students seeing how orienteering and hiking can contribute to a physically active lifestyle?

Homework

- Research the term *geocaching*, and be ready to explain it for next class.
- Continue to track physical activity outside of school.

Resources

Orienteering USA: www.us.orienteering.org

LESSON 9: INTRODUCTION TO GPS

Grade-Level Outcomes

Primary Outcomes

Movement concepts, principles & knowledge: Applies the terminology associated with exercise and participation in selected individual-performance activities, dance, net/wall games, target games, aquatics and/or outdoor pursuits appropriately. (S2.H1.L1)

Movement concepts, principles & knowledge: Identifies and discusses the historical and cultural roles of games, sports and dance in society. (S2.H1.L2)

Rules & etiquette: Exhibits proper etiquette, respect for others and teamwork while engaging in physical activity and/or social dance. (S4.H2.L1)

Lifetime activities: Demonstrates competency and/or refines activity-specific movement skills in 2 or more lifetime activities (outdoor pursuits, individual-performance activities, aquatics, net/wall games or target games). (S1.H1.L1)

Embedded Outcomes

Working with others: Uses communication skills and strategies that promote team or group dynamics. (S4.H3.L1)

Rules & etiquette: Examines moral and ethical conduct in specific competitive situations (e.g., intentional fouls, performance-enhancing substances, gambling, current events in sport). (S4.H2.L2)

Lesson Objectives

The learner will:

- use a GPS to find the longitude and latitude of a specific spot on the planet.
- accurately place a cache on campus.
- describe the history and etiquette involved in geocaching.
- use GPS terminology correctly.

Equipment and Materials

- Global positioning system (GPS)
- Cache (small mint container)
- Colored paper clips
- Index card
- Pencil

Introduction

Can anyone tell me what geocaching is? Have any of you ever tried it? (Begin with a personal story of a geocaching experience, and have students share personal stories.) *Geocaching is like a treasure hunt. You use GPS coordinates to find a cache, then you check out the contents and put the cache back for the next person. Most people use geocaching websites to learn about caches in the area and track their finds. Today, we will have an introduction to using a GPS and place caches on campus.*

Instructional Task: Geocaching Introduction

■ PRACTICE TASK

Lead a discussion about the history and etiquette involved in geocaching.

Look at the cache before moving or opening it so you can put it back the same way.

Never remove an object from the cache unless you are replacing it with one of equal or greater value.

Record your visit in the logbook.

Guiding questions for students:

- Why would accuracy be important for setting up a geocache?
- What role does integrity play in the role of a geocache?
- What examples can you give of ethical behavior in geocaching?

EMBEDDED OUTCOME: S4.H2.L2. Use the questions to prompt students to consider ethical conduct in this activity.

Student Choices/Differentiation

Use a poster or other visual aid to list key etiquette points.

What to Look For

- Students are engaged.
- Students are asking good questions.
- Students are offering relevant examples.

Instructional Task: Using a GPS Unit

■ PRACTICE TASK

Provide instructions on how to use a GPS to find the longitude and latitude of a specific point on the planet. Students follow along with their GPS units.

Extension

Students practice using the GPS to find a cache or caches that you placed before class.

Student Choices/Differentiation

- Students may use a variety of devices to find geocaches, including a handheld GPS unit or apps on their cell phones or tablets.
- Students may review a video clip showing the procedure for using GPS units.

What to Look For

- Students are using the technology correctly.
- Students are able to locate the cache without redirecting.

Instructional Task: Placing a Cache

■ PRACTICE TASK

Students work with a partner to hide a cache on campus. You assign a specific area for each group, but students choose the specific location, write down the longitude and latitude, and provide a clue for the cache.

Student Choices/Differentiation

- Students may use a GPS or cell phone app.
- Students choose their partners.

What to Look For

- Students are on task and making good decisions as they maneuver around campus.
- Students are collaborating on the cache placement.

Instructional Task: Student Group Debrief

■ PRACTICE TASK

Collect the cards from the student groups, and lead a conversation about any problems students encountered during the activity.

Guiding questions for students:

- What are some challenges your group faced during the activity?
- Share one specific experience from the activity that demonstrates how you successfully worked together to overcome a challenge.

EMBEDDED OUTCOME: S4.H3.L1. As students share an experience that challenged them in the activity, point out how good communication skills contributed to success.

What to Look For

- Students are engaged.
- Students are sharing relevant examples.
- Students provide sufficient detail on their cards.

Formal and Informal Assessments

Student cards with longitude, latitude, and clues

Closure

- Why is it important to place the cache out of plain sight?
- What do you think will happen if a cache is not replaced in exactly the same spot after it is found?
- How might you feel if someone sabotaged your cache?

Reflection

- Were students engaged in the activity?
- Did they act appropriately around campus?
- Do they need more practice with the GPS unit or are they pretty confident in using it?

Homework

- Research geocaching in the local area, and provide the name of one geocache near your home or school, along with the coordinates. Optional: Provide a picture of yourself or your family along with the cache.
- Continue tracking your physical activity outside of school.

Resources

Geocaching: www.geocaching.com

Internet keyword search: "geocaching," "GPS"

LESSON 10: GEOCACHING

Grade-Level Outcomes

Primary Outcomes

Lifetime activities: Demonstrates competency and/or refines activity-specific movement skills in 2 or more lifetime activities (outdoor pursuits, individual-performance activities, aquatics, net/wall games or target games). (S1.H1.L1)

Movement concepts, principles & knowledge: Applies the terminology associated with exercise and participation in selected individual-performance activities, dance, net/wall games, target games, aquatics and/or outdoor pursuits appropriately. (S2.H1.L1)

Embedded Outcome

Rules & etiquette: Exhibits proper etiquette, respect for others and teamwork while engaging in physical activity and/or social dance. (S4.H2.L1)

Lesson Objectives

The learner will:

- create a mark in a GPS unit.
- apply the "go to" function to find a specific cache.
- use geocaching terminology correctly.

Equipment and Materials

- Global positioning system (GPS)
- Cache (small mint container)
- Colored paper clips
- Index card
- Pencil

Introduction

To reinforce etiquette, begin with a personal story of a geocaching experience related to a cache not being put back appropriately.

Today, you will learn some new GPS skills and then use the GPS to locate caches on campus.

Instructional Task: Using a GPS Unit

■ PRACTICE TASK

Review how to find the longitude and latitude of a specific point on the planet from the previous class. Provide instructions on how to use the GPS to find a cache using the given longitude and latitude of a specific point on the planet. Students follow along on their devices.

Extension

Lead students through the following:

- Creating a mark
- Finding the mark on the GPS
- Selecting the mark
- Using the compass on the GPS to find the cache

Students practice creating a mark and finding the mark on the GPS.

Guiding questions for students:

- How might this skill contribute to the safety of a hiker?
- How would moving a cache affect another student's experience?

EMBEDDED OUTCOME: S4.H2.L1. Use the discussion questions and the introductory story to reinforce the importance of observing proper etiquette to ensure a good geocaching experience for everyone.

Student Choices/Differentiation

Students could use an app on their phones.

What to Look For

- Students are engaged.
- Students are asking good questions.

Instructional Task: Finding Caches and Proof of Find

■ PRACTICE TASK

Students work with a partner to find as many caches as they can in the time permitted. Assign a specific starting spot for each group, and students choose the subsequent caches.

Students take a colored paper clip from each cache they find and write the location on the card next to the number of the cache (proof of find).

Student Choices/Differentiation

- Students choose their partners.
- Students choose caches to locate.

What to Look For

- Students are on task and making good decisions as they maneuver around campus.
- Students are locating the caches efficiently.
- Students are replacing the containers correctly.
- Students are confident in their use of the GPS unit.

Instructional Task: Debrief

■ PRACTICE TASK

Use questioning to help students process their experience.

Guiding questions for students:

- How was today's experience with a GPS different from last class?
- Why is it important to put the cache back exactly as it was found?
- What strategies did you and your partner use to find as many caches as possible?
- How do activities such as geocaching and orienteering contribute to fitness and to a physically active lifestyle?

What to Look For

- Students are enthusiastic about geocaching.
- Students are articulating the importance of etiquette to the experience.

Formal and Informal Assessments

Student cards with cache locations

Closure

- Which cache was placed in the most creative way?
- What made a particular cache fun or interesting to find?
- As you think about hiking, how might a GPS come in handy?
- How can a GPS be considered an 11th essential? Why?
- Next class, we'll be doing some trail maintenance to give back to the environment. Come prepared to work outside.

Reflection

- Were students engaged in the activity?
- Did they act appropriately around campus and return the geocaches to the correct locations?
- Were they observing proper etiquette?

Homework

- Choose a dream destination, and find one geocache you would like to locate on that visit.
- Provide the name of the cache, the coordinates, and what item you would leave in the cache and why. Turn this in next class.
- Continue to track your physical activity outside of school.

Resources

Geocaching: www.geocaching.com

LESSON 11: TRAIL MAINTENANCE

Grade-Level Outcomes

Primary Outcomes

Lifetime activities: Demonstrates competency and/or refines activity-specific movement skills in 2 or more lifetime activities (outdoor pursuits, individual-performance activities, aquatics, net/wall games or target games). (S1.H1.L1)

Movement concepts, principles & knowledge: Applies the terminology associated with exercise and participation in selected individual-performance activities, dance, net/wall games, target games, aquatics and/or outdoor pursuits appropriately. (S2.H1.L1)

Embedded Outcome

Rules & etiquette: Examines moral and ethical conduct in specific competitive situations (e.g., intentional fouls, performance-enhancing substances, gambling, current events in sport). (S4.H2.L2)

Lesson Objectives

The learner will:

- discuss the concept of stewardship.
- make a connection between stewardship and using a natural resource appropriately.
- begin to develop an outdoor ethic.

Equipment and Materials

- Partnership with local parks department
- Parks department supplies tools, gloves, equipment

Introduction

Would anyone like to share their dream destination and the name of the cache? (Students share their destinations and caches.) Those all sound like great places to check out! Today, we're going to switch gears a bit and learn about the outdoor ethic of stewardship. Then we'll participate in trail maintenance for a local trail system as a way of giving back to the hiking community and the local area.

Instructional Task: Stewardship Introduction

■ PRACTICE TASK

Introduce the idea of stewardship, talk about the project site, and have students define the idea of an outdoor ethic through a group discussion.

Guiding questions for students:

- What does stewardship of the environment mean to you? (Possible answers: conservation, protection, sustainable practices, responsible use, and so on)
- Why is stewardship important?
- How does the concept of stewardship connect with ethics in the outdoors?

EMBEDDED OUTCOME: S4.H2.L2 Use the discussion to examine the ethical issues surrounding environmental impact and stewardship.

Refinement

Students could write an advocacy letter to a local policy maker about the impacts of stewardship in your community.

- School superintendent
- Member of Congress
- Principal
- Parks official

Student Choices/Differentiation

List key points of stewardship on a flip chart or handout.

What to Look For

Students are asking questions about the topic and are engaged in the discussion.

Instructional Task: Trail Maintenance

■ PRACTICE TASK

Introduce the parks department representative, who leads a discussion about the instructions and expectations for the event.

Students participate in trail maintenance under the guidance of the local parks department.

Extension

Students may look for opportunities to contribute to the stewardship of their own campus.

Student Choices/Differentiation

- Students select from different maintenance activities.
- Students choose to work independently or in groups.

What to Look For

- Student have been prepped for questions about the site and are involved in the discussion.
- Students are actively working together on the trail project.

Formal and Informal Assessments

- Student talk on task

Closure

- What challenges did you encounter? How did you overcome them?
- What are you most proud of from this activity?
- How did this experience influence your thinking about using a trail system?
- How might this affect your decision making while using our resources?
- What would you do if you saw someone using a resource inappropriately?

Reflection

- Did students interact with the parks department staff in a positive way?
- Did everyone get involved?
- Were they able to make a meaningful contribution?

Homework

- Create a summary of the experience, and use one picture as evidence of your work. Discuss how it feels to be a community contributor and what you expect future hikers to gain from your efforts. Due lesson 13.
- Continue tracking your physical activity outside of school.
- Prepare for a quiz next class.

Resources

Partnership with local parks department

LESSON 12: PREPARING FOR A LOCAL HIKE

Grade-Level Outcomes

Primary Outcomes

Lifetime activities: Demonstrates competency and/or refines activity-specific movement skills in 2 or more lifetime activities (outdoor pursuits, individual-performance activities, aquatics, net/wall games or target games). (S1.H1.L1)

Movement concepts, principles & knowledge: Applies the terminology associated with exercise and participation in selected individual-performance activities, dance, net/wall games, target games, aquatics and/or outdoor pursuits appropriately. (S2.H1.L1)

Embedded Outcomes

Physical activity knowledge: Identifies issues associated with exercising in heat, humidity and cold. (S3.H3.L1)

Working with others: Uses communication skills and strategies that promote team or group dynamics. (S4.H3.L1)

Lesson Objectives

The learner will:

- plan for, prepare for, and pack for a hike on a local trail.
- apply the terminology associated with hiking appropriately during planning.

Equipment and Materials

- Backpack
- 10 essentials

Introduction

Today, you will prepare for a hike at a local trail system, using the trip planning skills you practiced in lesson 5. We'll take that hike in our next class, so make sure to consider the 10 essentials and the weather as you prepare. Once we've finished our preparations, we'll take a short hike around the school grounds with our packs on to be sure they are comfortable and ready for the hike. We'll finish with a quiz.

Instructional Task: Plan

■ PRACTICE TASK

Give students the following instructions:

- Destination
- Date
- Departure time
- Return time

Students form hiking groups of four and make a plan for the hike that matches the instructions.

EMBEDDED OUTCOME: S3.H3.L1. Students are required to share information learned in their severe conditions assignment with others in the group as part of their trip planning.

EMBEDDED OUTCOME: S4.H3.L1. Provide feedback about positive communication strategies to students as they work together on their plans.

Student Choices/Differentiation

Students choose their groups.

What to Look For

- Students are working together to form the hiking plan.
- Each student is contributing.

Instructional Task: Prepare

■ **PRACTICE TASK**

Students gather all the necessary gear and complete a gear checklist for the trip.

What to Look For

Checklist is being completed.

Instructional Task: Pack

■ **PRACTICE TASK**

Students pack the gear correctly into their backpacks. Each backpack must be evaluated by the group members to make sure it is ready for the hike.

Student Choices/Differentiation

- Students choose their packs.
- Students choose the weight of their packs.

What to Look For

- Hiking groups are checking each other's bags.
- Check at least one bag from each hiking group yourself.

Instructional Task: Practice Hike

■ **PRACTICE TASK**

Have students wear backpacks on a short hike around the school grounds or neighborhood. Students walk in their groups of four.

Student Choices/Differentiation

- Students choose their packs.
- Students choose the weight of their packs.

What to Look For

- Students are interacting on the hike.
- Students make adjustments to their packs as needed to be comfortable.

Instructional Task:
Summative Assessment of Hiking Knowledge

■ **PRACTICE TASK**

Administer the quiz, which can be the same as the pre-assessment quiz. If not, be sure to include the pre-assessment questions and compare the results.

Student Choices/Differentiation

Allow extra time if needed, or give a take-home version.

What to Look For

Students show changes in knowledge levels since the pre-assessment.

Formal and Informal Assessments

- Gear checklist
- Peer and teacher backpack check
- Hiking plans
- Quiz

Closure

- Great job on your preparations today. In our next class, we'll take the hike, so come with your bags ready.
- We'll have one final check of your gear before we leave.
- Be sure to wear sturdy, comfortable shoes and be prepared for the weather.

Reflection

- How well did students work together on planning?
- Have they internalized the 10 essentials?
- Review the gear checklists and hiking plans. Are students thinking about safety as they make their plans and preparations?

Homework

- Check the school's physical education website for the gear checklist before class.
- Bring your backpacks to the next class—already packed if possible—along with appropriate footwear and clothing for the hike.
- Review your physical activity logs. Write a reflection that addresses how well you are meeting the guidelines and your personal physical activity goals. How can keeping a log help you prepare for hiking or other physical activity events? Turn this in next class.

Resources

Internet keyword search: "packing for a day hike," "10 essentials for hiking"

LESSON 13: LOCAL HIKE

Grade-Level Outcomes

Primary Outcomes

Lifetime activities: Demonstrates competency and/or refines activity-specific movement skills in 2 or more lifetime activities (outdoor pursuits, individual-performance activities, aquatics, net/wall games or target games). (S1.H1.L1)

Rules & etiquette: Exhibits proper etiquette, respect for others and teamwork while engaging in physical activity and/or social dance. (S4.H2.L1)

Safety: Applies best practices for participating safely in physical activity, exercise and dance (e.g., injury prevention, proper alignment, hydration, use of equipment, implementation of rules, sun protection). (S4.H5.L1)

Embedded Outcomes

Self-expression & enjoyment: Selects and participates in physical activities or dance that meet the need for self-expression and enjoyment. (S5.H3.L1)

Stress management: Identifies stress-management strategies (e.g., mental imagery, relaxation techniques, deep breathing, aerobic exercise, meditation) to reduce stress. (S3.H14.L1)

Challenge: Chooses an appropriate level of challenge to experience success and desire to participate in a self-selected physical activity. (S5.H2.L2)

Lesson Objectives

The learner will:
- check own gear.
- hike on a local trail.
- observe Leave No Trace principles.
- apply best practices for safety while hiking.

Equipment and Materials

- Backpack
- 10 essentials

Introduction

Today, we'll take the hike we prepared for in our previous class. When we start hiking the trail, make sure to follow your group's hiking plan and observe proper hiking etiquette. Most of all, enjoy the great outdoors!

Instructional Task: Pack Check

■ **PRACTICE TASK**

Students have a partner check their gear and packing, using the checklist from last class.

Student Choices/Differentiation

- Students choose their packs.
- Students choose the weight of their packs.

What to Look For

Students have included all 10 essentials.

Instructional Task: Participate in Hike

■ PRACTICE TASK

Students complete the supervised hike with their groups of four, applying Leave No Trace principles.

EMBEDDED OUTCOME: S5.H3.L1. During the hike or after the hike, ask students about what aspects of the hike they found most enjoyable and how enjoyment contributes to a physically active lifestyle.

Student Choices/Differentiation

Groups hike at their own pace.

What to Look For

- Students are using the resource appropriately and supporting one another's success.
- Students are following LNT principles.
- Students are enjoying the experience.

Formal and Informal Assessments

- Successful completion of the hike
- Review of physical activity logs

Closure

- What does it mean to have a successful hike?
- What did you find challenging about the hike? (Embedded outcome: S5.H2.L2)
- How can hiking help you manage your stress? (Embedded outcome: S3.H14.L1)
- What is something that you witnessed or did to support another group member?
- What LNT principle did you apply well?
- What LNT principle do you need to improve on?
- How did this experience influence how you will use our natural resources in the future?
- If you really enjoyed hiking, I encourage you to join the Outdoor Club, where you can participate in more hiking.

Reflection

- Were students applying LNT principles?
- Where they supporting their groups?
- Did the groups stay together and support everyone?
- What would I change for the next time I teach this?

Homework

Remember that we will be starting a new module next time. Be sure to check your options, and be ready to choose your new activity.

Resources

Local parks and recreation department

CHAPTER 6

Extending Students' Skills and Knowledge to Individual-Performance Activities

In *National Standards & Grade-Level Outcomes for K-12 Physical Education* (SHAPE America – Society of Health and Physical Educators, 2014), the individual-performance activities category includes a wide variety of options from which to choose when developing your curriculum. Self-defense, martial arts, skating (in-line and ice), multi-sport events, skateboarding, and many others are possibilities. Individual-performance activities also potentially overlap with other categories, such as aquatics and outdoor pursuits, broadening the choices even further. Many of these activities lend themselves to a fitness focus (Standard 3) as well as personal and social responsibility outcomes (Standard 4), both areas of emphasis for high school. Given the broad spectrum of choices, you should select activities that meet student needs and interests; your facilities and equipment; and further student progress toward physical literacy.

This chapter offers two modules in the individual-performance activity category, beginning with aquatics. The Aquatics Module, contributed by Adrienne Koesterer, an instructor in the physical education department at State University of New York College at Cortland, is based on the assumption that high school students already possess some basic swimming skills, so the emphases are on refining those skills, using aquatic activities for fitness, and implementing water safety practices. The Multi-Sport Events Module, contributed by Mary Westkott, professor in the department of health and physical education and associate head swimming and diving coach at the United States Coast Guard Academy in New London, CT, challenges students as they prepare for a community or school triathlon. The module includes predominantly Level 2 outcomes and emphasizes application of fitness principles and concepts (Standard 3). In the lessons, students focus on setting goals and improving their own performance.

For quick reference, each module begins with a block plan chart of the Grade-Level Outcomes that are addressed within the lessons. The modules incorporate outcomes from every standard, but vary in the degree of emphasis. Every module includes a primary outcome from Standard 1, either demonstrating competency in the relevant activity (Outcome S1.H1.L1) or refining it (Outcome S1.H1.L2). The Aquatics and Multi-Sport Events Modules also include specialized skills in health-related fitness (Outcome S1.H3) and multiple physical activity and fitness outcomes. The lessons in the Multi-Sport Events Module include challenge (Outcome S5.H2.L2) as an embedded outcome, in that students must push themselves physically and mentally.

The modules provide great learning experiences and progressions for the content and also can serve as strong models for similar types of individual-performance activities.

AQUATICS MODULE

Lessons in this module were contributed by **Adrienne Koesterer,** an instructor in the physical education department at State University of New York College at Cortland. Previously, she served as aquatics director at Humboldt State University in Arcata, CA, and she has been an American Red Cross instructor since 1987.

Grade-Level Outcomes Addressed, by Lesson	1	2	3	4	5	6	7	8	9	10	11	12	13	14	15	16
Standard 1. The physically literate individual demonstrates competency in a variety of motor skills and movement patterns.																
Demonstrates competency and/or refines activity-specific movement skills in 2 or more lifetime activities (outdoor pursuits, individual-performance activities, aquatics, net/wall games or target games). (S1.H1.L1)							P		P							
Refines activity-specific movement skills in 1 or more lifetime activities (outdoor pursuits, individual-performance activities, aquatics, net/wall games or target games). (S1.H1.L2)	P	P	P	P		P		P	P		P	P		P	P	
Demonstrates competency in 1 or more specialized skills in health-related fitness activities. (S1.H3.L1)		P	P	P	P				P	P	P	P	P	P	P	P
Standard 2. The physically literate individual applies knowledge of concepts, principles, strategies and tactics related to movement and performance.																
Applies the terminology associated with exercise and participation in selected individual-performance activities, dance, net/wall games, target games, aquatics and/or outdoor pursuits appropriately. (S2.H1.L1)		E													P	
Uses movement concepts and principles (e.g., force, motion, rotation) to analyze and improve performance of self and/or others in a selected skill. (S2.H2.L1)	E						E		E							
Standard 3. The physically literate individual demonstrates the knowledge and skills to achieve and maintain a health-enhancing level of physical activity and fitness.																
Discusses the benefits of a physically active lifestyle as it relates to college or career productivity. (S3.H1.L1)										E						
Identifies issues associated with exercising in heat, humidity and cold. (S3.H3.L1)						E										
Applies rates of perceived exertion and pacing. (S3.H3.L2)						E										
Evaluates—according to their benefits, social support network and participation requirements—activities that can be pursued in the local environment. (S3.H4.L1)														E		
Evaluates risks and safety factors that might affect physical activity preferences throughout the life cycle. (S3.H5.L1)															P	
Relates physiological responses to individual levels of fitness and nutritional balance. (S3.H8.L1)													E			
Identifies types of strength exercises (isometric, concentric, eccentric) and stretching exercises (static, proprioceptive neuromuscular facilitation [PNF], dynamic) for personal fitness development (e.g., strength, endurance, range of motion). (S3.H9.L1)									E							
Calculates target heart rate and applies that information to personal fitness plan. (S3.H10.L1)					P											
Adjusts pacing to keep heart rate in the target zone, using available technology (e.g., pedometer, heart rate monitor), to self-monitor aerobic intensity. (S3.H10.L2)					E											

AQUATICS

(continued)

AQUATICS MODULE *(CONTINUED)*

Grade-Level Outcomes Addressed, by Lesson	Lessons															
	1	2	3	4	5	6	7	8	9	10	11	12	13	14	15	16
Standard 3. The physically literate individual demonstrates the knowledge and skills to achieve and maintain a health-enhancing level of physical activity and fitness. *(continued)*																
Designs a fitness program, including all components of health-related fitness, for a college student and an employee in the learner's chosen field of work. (S3.H12.L1)										P						
Identifies stress-management strategies (e.g., mental imagery, relaxation techniques, deep breathing, aerobic exercise, meditation) to reduce stress. (S3.H14.L1)												E				
Standard 4. The physically literate individual exhibits responsible personal and social behavior that respects self and others.																
Accepts differences between personal characteristics and the idealized body images and elite performance levels portrayed in various media. (S4.H1.L2)							E	P								
Exhibits proper etiquette, respect for others and teamwork while engaging in physical activity and/or social dance. (S4.H2.L1)			E	E							E		E			
Uses communication skills and strategies that promote team or group dynamics. (S4.H3.L1)														E		
Assumes a leadership role (e.g., task or group leader, referee, coach) in a physical activity setting. (S4.H3.L2)																E
Solves problems and thinks critically in physical activity or dance settings, both as an individual and in groups (S4.H4.L1).															E	
Applies best practices for participating safely in physical activity, exercise and dance (e.g., injury prevention, proper alignment, hydration, use of equipment, implementation of rules, sun protection). (S4.H5.L1)	P		P													
Standard 5. The physically literate individual recognizes the value of physical activity for health, enjoyment, challenge, self-expression and/or social interaction.																
Analyzes the health benefits of a self-selected physical activity. (S5.H1.L1)										E						

P = Primary; E = Embedded

LESSON 1: AQUATICS REVIEW

Grade-Level Outcomes

Primary Outcomes

Lifetime activities: Refines activity-specific movement skills in 1 or more lifetime activities (outdoor pursuits, individual-performance activities, aquatics, net/wall games or target games). (S1.H1.L2)

Safety: Applies best practices for participating safely in physical activity, exercise and dance (e.g., injury prevention, proper alignment, hydration, use of equipment, implementation of rules, sun protection). (S4.H5.L1)

Embedded Outcome

Movement concepts, principles & knowledge: Uses movement concepts and principles (e.g., force, motion, rotation) to analyze and improve performance of self and/or others in a selected skill. (S2.H2.L1)

Lesson Objectives

The learner will:

- review basic pool safety rules.
- demonstrate basic aquatic skills, such as submersion and floating.
- demonstrate freestyle and backstroke skills.
- review basic hydrodynamic principles, such as buoyancy and drag.

Equipment and Materials

- Kickboards*
- Life jackets or flotation belts*
- Kickbar floats (optional)*

*Make flotation devices available for students to use in all practice tasks.

Introduction

We're starting a new module on aquatics. We will work on water safety, improving your strokes, and using aquatics as a lifetime fitness activity. Today, I will evaluate what swimming knowledge you already have and introduce hydrodynamic principles that will assist with all movement in the water.

Instructional Task: Rules Around the Pool

■ **PRACTICE TASK**

Discuss what rule infractions will not be tolerated (e.g., running on the deck, going into the deep end if not skilled enough).

Student Choices/Differentiation

Encourage students to suggest rules.

What to Look For

Students are able to follow the rules.

Instructional Task: Immersing the Body

■ PRACTICE TASK

Students blow bubbles while bobbing.

Refinements

- Encourage students not to wipe their faces in between bobs.
- Remind students to keep their ears in the water.

Extensions

- Students repeat, allowing the legs to drift so their bodies float on the front. With their faces in the water, students blow out.
- Students repeat, breathing to dominant side.
- Students repeat, breathing to both sides.

Student Choices/Differentiation

- Students choose 0 to 3 bobs or 3 to10 bobs.
- If students aren't comfortable bobbing, use the following progression:
  - Begin by having students submerge up to their mouths (eyes still above water).
  - Repeat, submerging face past eyes with nose plugged.
  - Repeat, submerging face past eyes without plugging nose.
  - Repeat, submerging entire head.

What to Look For

- Assess students' comfort level.
- Students can take a breath immediately upon their face exiting the water.

Instructional Task: Front Float and Glide

■ PRACTICE TASK

Students float with face immersed.

Guiding questions for students:

- What is the most important element to focus on to keep from sinking? (Answer: Keeping the abdominal muscles tight.)
- How do your arms, legs, and head affect floating? (Answer: If you don't keep them in a streamlined position, you will sink.)
- What does a streamlined position look like, and why is it important?

Extensions

- Have students glide with face immersed using proper straight-leg, floppy-ankle kick.
- Repeat. Have students push off wall and glide underwater (no kick). Give students a second chance to improve their length.
- Same activity but add kick.

Guiding questions for students:

- What are important elements to consider when gliding?
- How did you improve your length of glide?
- How did the kick help?

- When using the kick, why is it important to have a tight, fast kick?
- Sometimes, your kick causes more drag (big kick cause more drag). What are things you must still consider? (Answer: Keeping a streamlined position throughout the push-off and glide.)

EMBEDDED OUTCOME: S2.H2.L1. Use this practice task to help students understand how the glide position reduces drag and resistance in the water.

Student Choices/Differentiation
- Students receive support from a noodle, kickboard, another student, or holding onto the wall.
- Challenge students to float for longer than 10 seconds.

What to Look For
- Students are performing independently.
- Students are able to stay submerged for longer than 10 seconds.

Instructional Task: Freestyle

■ PRACTICE TASK
Students swim the length or width of the pool, face in the water, with full arm extension in front and back.

Refinements
- Reinforce elbow high on recovery.
- For more advanced students, encourage S-shaped pull.
- Have students swim several laps, refining their strokes.

Extensions
- Have students count the number of strokes they use to swim across the pool.
- Repeat the activity to see whether students can decrease the number of strokes.

Guiding questions for students:
- How many strokes did it take?
- In what ways can you decrease the number of strokes? (Answers: stronger kick, reach farther with arms, and so on)
- Why is it important to use fewer arm strokes while swimming?

Student Choices/Differentiation
- Students who aren't totally comfortable in deep water may use the shallow end or the lane next to the wall.
- Students swim at their own pace.

What to Look For:
- Students swim with a smooth motion, arms in opposition, with full extension front and back.
- Students are keeping their faces in the water and breathing to the side.
- Students' kicks are fast and tight.
- Students are rotating their bodies by reaching with their arm strokes.

Instructional Task: Back Float and Glide

■ PRACTICE TASK

Students float with ears immersed and feet at surface. Demonstrate how putting the arms above the head, tilting the head back, and keeping the knees bent help increase buoyancy.

Refinement

Make sure that students are driving the hips up to the surface, which will help correct body position.

EMBEDDED OUTCOME: S2.H2.L1. Use this practice task to help students understand the concept of buoyancy.

Student Choices/Differentiation

- Students may choose to have support from another student or use a kickboard against their abdomens.
- Students may float for longer than 10 seconds.

What to Look For:

Students are able to float for longer than 10 seconds.

Instructional Task: Backstroke

■ PRACTICE TASK

Students swim the length or width of the pool, focused on backstroke technique.

Refinements

- Reinforce hip rotation, shoulder out of the water, straight arm recovery, kick at the surface of the water, and tight abdominals.
- Have students swim five or six body lengths, refining their strokes.

Extensions

- Have students count the number of strokes they use to swim across the pool.
- Repeat activity to see whether students can decrease the number of arm strokes.

Student Choices/Differentiation

- Students who aren't totally comfortable in deep water may use the shallow end or the lane next to the wall.
- Students swim at their own pace.
- Students choose number of laps.

What to Look For:

Students swim with a smooth motion, arms in opposition, and shoulder above water on recovery arm.

Instructional Task: Game of Tag

■ PRACTICE TASK

Set up one or more tag games with shallow-end boundaries. During the game, students are required to use freestyle and backstroke to move around the pool and floating techniques when resting.

Extension

Allow students to modify game rules and size of space to maneuver.

Student Choices/Differentiation

- Students may swim underwater to get away.
- Group students by ability, with more skilled students using the deep end.
- Students may hold onto the wall if needed.

What to Look For:

- Students are using their strokes correctly.
- Students are comfortable underwater.
- Students are using their floating techniques when they need to rest.

Formal and Informal Assessments

- Informal assessment or a rubric or checklist for evaluating freestyle and backstroke
- Exit slip: What are the critical elements of the freestyle stroke?

Closure

- What are three key points for freestyle? Backstroke?
- How can you make yourself more buoyant when swimming?
- What positions have the least drag when swimming?
- Recommend goggles for those who have immersion issues.

Reflection

- Which students have the most trouble floating?
- Which students need practice with their stroke technique?
- Who needs more endurance?

Homework

If students have access to a pool, they can practice getting comfortable with their faces in the water, opening their eyes underwater, and breathing to the side in freestyle.

Resources

Internet keyword search: "freestyle," "backstroke," "buoyancy," "drag"

LESSON 2: FREESTYLE AND BACKSTROKE

Grade-Level Outcomes

Primary Outcome

Lifetime activities: Refines activity-specific movement skills 1 or more lifetime activities (outdoor pursuits, individual-performance activities, aquatics, net/wall games or target games). (S1.H1.L2)

Embedded Outcome

Movement concepts, principles & knowledge: Applies the terminology associated with exercise and participation in selected individual-performance activities, dance, net/wall games, target games, aquatics, and/or outdoor pursuits appropriately. (S2.H1.L1)

Lesson Objectives

The learner will:

- refine freestyle and backstroke.
- demonstrate the survival stroke.
- demonstrate an open turn.

Equipment and Materials

- Kickboards*
- Life jackets or flotation belts*

*Make flotation devices available for students to use in all practice tasks.

Introduction

Today, you will work on drills for freestyle and backstroke and learn the survival stroke and open turns for freestyle.

Instructional Task: Freestyle Kick

■ PRACTICE TASK

Working the width of the pool and using a kickboard, swimmers practice the flutter kick with floppy ankles and minimal knee bend.

Extensions

- Students kick with their faces in the water while breathing to the side.
- Students add pulling on the side to which they breathe, one hand on the kickboard and one hand pulling; students move up to arms alternating in the freestyle movement.

Student Choices/Differentiation

- Students perform drills at their own pace.
- Students choose their lanes.
- Students move to next drill only after comfortable with current one.

What to Look For

- Students show fluid movement.
- Students propel themselves efficiently through the water.

Instructional Task: Freestyle

■ **PRACTICE TASK**

Students swim 4 × 25 yards or meters of freestyle.

Extension

Have students add a fingertip drag—dragging the fingertips in the water on recovery.

Refinements

- Students practice breathing every three strokes to emphasize balance in the stroke.
- Have students extend their arms fully during entry.
- Students may try using a six-beat kick.

Student Choices/Differentiation

- Students swim at their own pace.
- Students choose their lanes.

What to Look For

- Students are using the fingertip drag.
- Students have high elbows and a narrow path through the water.

Instructional Task: Backstroke Kick

■ **PRACTICE TASK**

Using the width of the pool, swimmers kick on their backs in a streamlined position, using similar movement to the freestyle.

Student Choices/Differentiation

- Students swim at their own pace.
- Students choose their lanes.
- Students can use kickboards.

What to Look For

- Students' chins are up, their ears in the water.
- Students' hips are up.
- Splash is minimal.
- Propulsion is smooth.

Instructional Task: Backstroke

■ **PRACTICE TASK**

Students swim 4 × 25 yards or meters of backstroke.

Refinements

- Help students increase shoulder rotation by telling them to think about the pinkie finger entering the water first.
- Students repeat backstroke laps with a focus on pushing the water with the hand all the way to the thighs.

Student Choices/Differentiation

- Students swim at their own pace.
- Students choose their lanes.

What to Look For

- Students' ears are in the water.
- Arm movement is oppositional.
- Propulsion is smooth.

Instructional Task: Survival Stroke

▣ PRACTICE TASK

In at least shoulder-depth water, students float with their arms and legs dangling down like a jellyfish. When they need to take a breath, they first exhale all the way and then using their arms and legs (scissor kick), lift their faces out of the water to inhale.

Extension

Set a goal of a certain number of repetitions or minutes for students to do the survival stroke.

Guiding questions for students:

- When would you use this skill?
- Why is it important to remain calm and relaxed?

Student Choices/Differentiation

- Students can choose to work in pairs for support if they are uncomfortable with the skill.
- Proficient students can perform the skill in the deep end.

What to Look For

- Students are relaxed and calm while performing the stroke.
- Students are able to perform the skill for several minutes.

Instructional Task: Freestyle Open Turn

▣ PRACTICE TASK

Students start near the wall. They touch the wall with one hand, turn around, push off the wall in a streamlined position, and resume swimming.

Extensions

- Students can start in the middle of the pool, swim to the wall, perform the turn, and resume swimming back to the starting point.
- Students repeat and swim to the opposite end, performing another open turn.

Refinements

- Students practice a longer underwater streamline off the wall.
- Students emphasize kicking hard after pushing off the wall.

EMBEDDED OUTCOME: S2.H1.L1. Use the first refinement to the practice task to reinforce terminology such as streamline, drag, and resistance.

Student Choices/Differentiation

- Beginners may practice touch and go on a wall outside the pool.
- More advanced students may focus on a faster touch and go.

What to Look For

- Students are moving smoothly and comfortably.
- Students are pushing off the wall as quickly as possible.

Formal and Informal Assessments

- Informal assessment or a rubric or checklist for evaluating stroke technique
- Exit slip: What are the critical elements of the backstroke?

Closure

- Describe two cues for the backstroke and freestyle.
- Remember, you can be safe in deep water, but if you're unsure, use your survival float.

Reflection

- How long were students able to perform the survival stroke? Do they need more practice?
- Are they ready to move on to a flip turn?
- Which elements of the freestyle and backstroke still need refinement?

Homework

Review videos of the freestyle and backstroke on the school's physical education website.

Resources

Internet keyword search: "freestyle," "backstroke," "swim open turn," "survival stroke"

LESSON 3: ELEMENTARY BACKSTROKE AND RESCUES

Grade-Level Outcomes

Primary Outcomes

Lifetime activities: Refines activity-specific movement skills 1 or more lifetime activities (outdoor pursuits, individual-performance activities, aquatics, net/wall games or target games). (S1.H1.L2)

Fitness activities: Demonstrates competency in 1 or more specialized skills in health-related fitness activities. (S1.H3.L1)

Safety: Applies best practices for participating safely in physical activity, exercise and dance (e.g., injury prevention, proper alignment, hydration, use of equipment, implementation of rules, sun protection). (S4.H5.L1)

Embedded Outcome

Rules & etiquette: Exhibits proper etiquette, respect for others and teamwork while engaging in physical activity and/or social dance. (S4.H2.L1)

Lesson Objectives

The learner will:

- demonstrate the elementary backstroke.
- increase endurance in the freestyle and backstroke.
- demonstrate basic rescue skills.

Equipment and Materials

- Kickboards*
- Life jackets or flotation belts*
- Kickbar floats (optional)*
- Peer assessments and pencils

*Make flotation devices available for students to use in all practice tasks.

Introduction

Today, you will increase swimming distance of the freestyle and backstroke. You also will learn the elementary backstroke, treading water, and rescue skills.

Instructional Task:
Increase Endurance for Freestyle and Backstroke

■ PRACTICE TASK

Students swim 3 × 50 yards or meters each of freestyle and backstroke.

Refinements

- Make sure students do not sacrifice stroke technique for distance.
- Make sure students are still using their kick and arm extensions.

Student Choices/Differentiation

Learners who are more comfortable can do 5 × 50 yards or meters.

What to Look For

- Students maintain correct technique while swimming longer distances.
- Students are increasingly comfortable with swimming longer distances.

Instructional Task: Elementary Backstroke–Kick

■ PRACTICE TASK

While hugging a kickboard and lying on their backs, students kick the width of the pool two times.

Refinement

Remind students to use a strong whip kick and a glide.

Student Choices/Differentiation

- Students swim at their own pace.
- Students choose their lanes.

What to Look For

- Feet are dorsiflexed.
- Knees are closer together than feet.
- Glide is noticeable.

Instructional Task: Elementary Backstroke

■ PRACTICE TASK

Students swim 4 × 25 yards or meters of elementary backstroke. Give students the chicken, airplane, and rocket cues for the three parts of the stroke.

Extension

In pairs, one student evaluates the other's stroke using a checklist or rubric.

Refinement

Coordinating the arm motion and the kick can be challenging. Have students focus on the rhythm of the stroke and how everything comes together in the glide portion. Arms and legs curl, spread, and then snap together.

Student Choices/Differentiation

- Students can choose fewer or more lengths (up to six).
- Students may review video clips to help with timing.
- Students having difficulty with timing may practice arms and legs together on the pool deck.

What to Look For

- Movement is synchronized; arms and hands move at the same pace.
- Glide is noticeable.

Instructional Task: Treading Water

■ PRACTICE TASK

In water at least shoulder depth, swimmers use their hands and elementary backstroke kick to keep their heads above water for 30 seconds.

Extension

Repeat with students using a different type of kick (e.g., flutter, egg beater, butterfly).

Guiding questions for students:

- Which type of kick is most efficient for survival swimming?
- Why?

Student Choices/Differentiation

Students can tread longer, use no hands (just kick), and use other kicks. For a real challenge, they can try to keep their navels out of the water.

What to Look For

- Students are calm.
- Students can keep their heads above water for at least 30 seconds.

Instructional Task: Rescuing a Swimmer in Distress

■ PRACTICE TASK

"Reach or throw but don't go" means that the rescuer reaches out and grabs the victim and pulls him or her in.

Using an extension (e.g., rescue tube, towel, or pole), the rescuer reaches out to the victim, who grabs the object and is pulled in by the rescuer.

EMBEDDED OUTCOME: S4.H2.L1. To build rescuers' confidence, victims should play the role respectfully and not try to pull rescuers into the water on initial attempts.

Extension

Students throw a flotation device out to the victim and pull her or him in with the attached rope.

Guiding questions for students:

- What should you do when you see someone in distress in the water?
- Why would you use an extension instead of jumping in?

Student Choices/Differentiation

- Students choose their partners.
- Students choose the shallow or deep end of the pool.
- Victims who aren't confident treading water may use a flotation device.

What to Look For

- Rescuers are keeping their weight low while pulling in the victims.
- Rescuers are talking to the victims to keep them calm.
- Students are working together to practice the rescue technique.

Formal and Informal Assessments

- Peer assessments
- Exit slip: What are the key points for rescuing a swimmer in distress?

Closure

- Today, you started building your endurance for fitness swimming, and you will continue to work on that.
- You also worked on a basic rescue skill.
- Remember, realize your limitations when seeing a swimmer in distress.
- Do not risk your own life; instead, use equipment to extend your reach and be safe.

Reflection

- Were students fatigued after increasing the number of laps?
- Where did they struggle with the new stroke?
- Review peer assessments for common themes.

Homework

Review videos of the backstroke open turn to get ready for next class.

Resources

American Red Cross: www.redcross.org

LESSON 4: ENDURANCE AND BACKSTROKE OPEN TURNS

Grade-Level Outcomes

Primary Outcomes

Lifetime activities: Refines activity-specific movement skills in 1 or more lifetime activities (outdoor pursuits, individual-performance activities, aquatics, net/wall games or target games). (S1.H1.L2)

Fitness activities: Demonstrates competency in 1 or more specialized skills in health-related fitness activities. (S1.H3.L1)

Embedded Outcome

Rules & etiquette: Exhibits proper etiquette, respect for others and teamwork while engaging in physical activity and/or social dance. (S4.H2.L1)

Lesson Objectives

The learner will:

- perform additional pool lengths in each stroke.
- demonstrate rolling over from freestyle to backstroke and the reverse.
- demonstrate backstroke open turns.

Equipment and Materials

- Stopwatch or timer
- Kickboards*
- Life jackets or flotation belts*
- Kickbar floats*

*Make flotation devices available for students to use in all practice tasks.

Introduction

Today, you will increase distances in all strokes learned, work on rolling over from freestyle to backstroke and back, and practice backstroke open turns.

Instructional Task: Increasing Endurance

■ PRACTICE TASK

Students swim 6 × 50 yards or meters each of freestyle and backstroke.

Students swim 4 × 50 yards or meters of elementary backstroke.

Extension

Have students combine strokes in sets (e.g., one length backstroke followed by freestyle).

EMBEDDED OUTCOME: S4.H2.L1. Discuss lane swimming etiquette (e.g., up and back, circle swimming) with students before they swim laps.

Student Choices/Differentiation

- Students may choose alternate lap lengths, such as 3 × 100 freestyle and backstroke, 2 × 100 elementary backstroke.
- Group students in lanes by ability.
- Challenge more experienced swimmers by timing the laps.

What to Look For

- Students are increasingly more comfortable in the water and able to swim continuously for a longer period of time.
- Students are able to maintain correct technique throughout their laps.

Instructional Task:
Rolling Over From Front to Back and Back to Front

■ PRACTICE TASK

Students swim 2 × 25 yards or meters, swimming half of the length freestyle, then turning over and completing the length with the backstroke.

Students reverse the order on the way back.

Refinement

Have students focus on the purpose of the arms (using a strong pull to turn the body over).

Extension

Have partners observe the turns and provide feedback to the swimmers. Have swimmers focus on making tight turns.

Student Choices/Differentiation

Students swim at their own pace.

What to Look For

- Students are making smooth transitions and maintaining speed.
- Students are making tight turns.

Instructional Task: Backstroke Open Turn

■ PRACTICE TASK

Backstroke flags are 5 meters from the wall. Students start at the middle of the pool and swim toward the wall; when swimmers see the flags, they count the number of arm pulls until they hit the wall.

Extensions

- Repeat, and when students hit the wall, they rotate their bodies, put their feet on the wall, and push off in a streamlined position.
- Students use the dolphin kick for propulsion while underwater.

Refinement

Use this task to practice a longer streamline off the wall.

Student Choices/Differentiation

Students may start at half speed and work up to full speed gradually.

What to Look For

- Students recognize when they are close to the wall so that they don't hit their heads.
- Students take smooth turns and a long streamline off the wall on their backs.

Instructional Task: Timed 100 Yards

■ **PRACTICE TASK**

Students swim a timed 100 yards or meters of freestyle.

Guiding questions for students:

- When should you exhale and why?
- What are some ways to save energy during the event?
- Faster movements do not always equal better results. Who knows why?

Student Choices/Differentiation

Adjust the distance to 25 or 50 yards for students who cannot complete 100 yards.

What to Look For

- Students can maintain correct form throughout the timed swim.
- Students are maintaining a constant speed for each length.
- Students are fatigued at the end.

Formal and Informal Assessment

100-yard timed swim (can serve as a baseline measure of current fitness for building future workouts)

Closure

- Remember to exhale when your face is in the water. That way, when you turn to take a breath, it is much quicker if you don't have to exhale first.
- What type of kick should you use when you're swimming underwater after the turn?
- Try to practice your swimming outside of class to improve faster.
- Next class, we'll try a water aerobics workout.

Reflection

- Were students able to roll over front to back and back to front in a smooth motion?
- Did students use the arm-pull count effectively to anticipate the wall before the turn?
- Are some students ready to move on to the flip turn?

Homework

Do an online search for water aerobics to see what these workouts look like before next class.

Resources

Internet keyword search: "backstroke," "freestyle," "backstroke open turns"

LESSON 5: WATER AEROBICS

Grade-Level Outcomes

Primary Outcomes

Fitness activities: Demonstrates competency in 1 or more specialized skills in health-related fitness activities. (S1.H3.L1)

Fitness knowledge: Calculates target heart rate and applies that information to personal fitness plan. (S3.H10.L1)

Embedded Outcome

Fitness knowledge: Adjusts pacing to keep heart rate in the target zone, using available technology (e.g., pedometer, heart rate monitor), to self-monitor aerobic intensity. (S3.H10.L2)

Lesson Objectives

The learner will:

- demonstrate basic water aerobics exercises.
- calculate target heart rate (THR) and monitor it during a workout.

Equipment and Materials

- Barbell floats
- Music for workout

Introduction

Today, we will explore the many potential exercises available in a water aerobics class. Water aerobics is a great way to use your aquatic skills to keep fit. First, you will learn how to calculate a target heart rate for water exercises.

Instructional Task: Target Heart Rate

■ PRACTICE TASK

Review how to calculate target heart rate. Have students calculate and record their target heart rates.

Student Choices/Differentiation

- Students may work with partners.
- Provide worksheets for students that guide the calculation.

What to Look For

- Students are calculating heart rate correctly.
- Students are asking questions when appropriate.

Instructional Task: Water Aerobics

■ PRACTICE TASK

Warm up in the water, using easy movements or swimming at half speed.

Main set: Use a combination of movements to keep students active throughout the workout. Fast-paced music will make the activity more enjoyable.

Sample exercises: Walking in a circle, jogging in a circle, jumping like a frog, lunges, and grapevines, which all can be done going in one direction and then switching the direction. This adds an additional level of intensity.

Have students take their heart rates at pre-determined points during the main set.

EMBEDDED OUTCOME: S3.H10.L2. Have students adjust their intensity to keep their heart rates in the target zone.

Cool down for 5 minutes with easy movements. Students take their heart rates at the beginning and end of the cool-down.

Extensions

- Repeat, adding some additional in-place movements, such as squat jumps, Russian kicks, mule kicks, and punching underwater.
- Ask students what sports they play, and have them incorporate some of those movements in the water.
- Synchronize movements to music.

Student Choices/Differentiation

- Students can use flotation devices or aqua belts if needed.
- Students move at their own pace.

What to Look For

- Students become winded.
- Students are putting in effort for each movement.
- Students are able to stay within their target heart rate zones for the set time.
- Students are able to perform all the movements.

Formal and Informal Assessments

Students' resting heart rates and target heart rate zone calculations

Closure

- Water aerobics is a wonderful way to customize a water workout based on your interests.
- You can replicate movements from the sport you play, giving you a good workout and training for that sport.
- We will have another water aerobics day later in this module, and I would like you to come up with an exercise we can all do in that lesson.

Reflection

- Review THR calculations. Were students doing them correctly? Do we need to revisit next class?
- Were students challenging themselves to keep their heart rates up?

Homework

Develop a water aerobics exercise that you can demonstrate to the class. You will share this exercise at the end of the module. Feel free to draw from other activities or sports that you engage in. Walking and running in a circle will be covered in class, so come up with something different. Your exercise should last from 3 to 5 minutes.

Resources

Internet keyword search: "water aerobics," "water exercise," "water walking," "deep water running"

LESSON 6: ENDURANCE AND BREASTSTROKE

Grade-Level Outcomes

Primary Outcomes

Lifetime activities: Refines activity-specific movement skills in 1 or more lifetime activities (outdoor pursuits, individual-performance activities, aquatics, net/wall games or target games). (S1.H1.L2)

Fitness activities: Demonstrates competency in 1 or more specialized skills in health-related fitness activities. (S1.H3.L1)

Embedded Outcomes

Physical activity knowledge: Identifies issues associated with exercising in the heat, humidity and cold. (S3.H3.L1)

Physical activity knowledge: Applies rates of perceived exertion and pacing. (S3.H3.L2)

Lesson Objectives

The learner will:

- refine previously learned strokes (freestyle, backstroke, and elementary backstroke).
- demonstrate correct technique for the breaststroke.

Equipment and Materials

- Kickboards*
- Life jackets or flotation belts*

*Make flotation devices available for students to use in all practice tasks.

Introduction

Today, you will increase the distances in your strokes and review the breaststroke.

Instructional Task: Endurance Training

■ PRACTICE TASK

Students swim 3 × 100 yards or meters each of freestyle, backstroke, and elementary backstroke. Students calculate their heart rates.

Refinement

Ask students to swim at a comfortable pace and focus on their technique for the first 100 yards or meters of each stroke.

EMBEDDED OUTCOME: S3.H3.L1 After the workout, discuss how the environment (heat, cold, humidity) can affect exercise and the advantages of swimming in a pool on a very hot or humid day. Remind students of the need to hydrate while in the water.

Student Choices/Differentiation

- Include open turns and flip turns if students are familiar with them.
- Students may adjust distances to accommodate higher or lower fitness levels.
- Students swim at their own pace.

What to Look For

- Students' technique is improving.
- Students are resting less at the walls and can swim at a faster pace.

Instructional Task: Breaststroke Kick

▒ PRACTICE TASK

Students kick four widths of the pool using the whip kick and a kickboard.

Extensions

- Students kick four widths beginning with a glide with the face in the water, breathe, kick, and glide.
- Students progress to lengths of the pool with the breaststroke kick.

Refinement

Have students glide for 3 seconds before the next kick. This forces students to have a strong whip kick and to glide to prevent sinking.

Student Choices/Differentiation

- Students may sit on the side or hold onto the wall, and then progress to using a kickboard.
- Students swim at their own pace.
- Students may adjust distances as needed.

What to Look For

- Toes are up.
- Feet are wider than knees.
- Students are kicking the feet together.
- Glide is noticeable.

Instructional Task: Breaststroke

▒ PRACTICE TASK

Review the phases of the stroke: pull, breathe, kick, glide.

Students swim 4 × 25 yards or meters of breaststroke.

Refinement

Make sure that students are performing the stroke with a natural, flowing rhythm.

Extension

Have students add open turns for breaststroke (using a two-hand touch).

Student Choices/Differentiation

- If a student has knee issues, allow sidestroke kick instead of whip kick.
- Students swim at their own pace.
- Students may adjust distances as needed.
- If students have difficulty with timing, have them practice the kick and the arms together while lying on the pool deck.

What to Look For

- The stroke has distinct segments: pull, breathe, kick, and glide.
- Hands are not going past upper chest level.
- Students glide with arms straight above head and feet together.

Instructional Task: Relay Races to Increase Speed

■ PRACTICE TASK

Using the strokes taught in the module, create relay races. Have students give their RPE or heart rate at the end of each leg that they swim.

Extension

Repeat with kicking only.

EMBEDDED OUTCOME: S3.H3.L2. At the start of the relay races, review RPE and ask students to give their RPE assessment after they swim their legs. After the first relay, they can choose to give heart rate or RPE.

Guiding questions for students:

- What happens to your heart rate when you increase your speed? Why?
- Would you expect the type of relay to affect your heart rate or RPE? Why or why not?

Student Choices/Differentiation

Students choose their own relay strokes.

What to Look For

- Students are swimming faster than in the endurance set at the start of class.
- Students are using RPE or heart rate correctly.
- Students maintain correct technique in their strokes.

Formal and Informal Assessments

- Informal assessment or a rubric or checklist for evaluating stroke technique
- Exit slip: How do the temperature and humidity affect exercise?

Closure

- Today, you worked on improving your endurance as well as your speed in the water.
- You also worked on your breaststroke.
- Who can tell me three important cues of the stroke?

Reflection

- Were students comfortable using RPE?
- What areas of the breaststroke need additional practice?

Homework

Watch a video clip of the dolphin kick on the school's physical education website before next class.

Resources

Internet keyword search: "breaststroke," "hydration," "swimming in heat," "swimming in cold"

LESSON 7: SURFACE DIVES AND DOLPHIN KICK

Grade-Level Outcomes

Primary Outcome

Lifetime activities: Demonstrates competency and/or refines activity-specific movement skills in 2 or more lifetime activities (outdoor pursuits, individual-performance activities, aquatics, net/wall games or target games). (S1.H1.L1)

Embedded Outcomes

Movement concepts, principles & knowledge: Uses movement concepts and principles (e.g., force, motion, rotation) to analyze and improve performance of self and/or others of a selected skill. (S2.H2.L1)

Personal responsibility: Accepts differences between personal characteristics and the idealized body images and elite performance levels portrayed in various media. (S4.H1.L2)

Lesson Objectives

The learner will:

- select and fit life jackets.
- execute surface dives at various depths.
- perform the dolphin kick while swimming underwater.

Equipment and Materials

- Kickboards*
- Life jackets or flotation belts*
- Diving toys (weighted)
- Hula-Hoops (weighted)

*Make flotation devices available for students to use in all practice tasks.

Introduction

Today, you will learn what to look for when picking out a life jacket, how to perform surface dives, and how to swim underwater with a variety of kicks.

Instructional Task: Fitting Life Jackets

■ PRACTICE TASK

Review Type II and Type III life jackets and how to fit them. Tell students to look for a Coast Guard–approved stamp.

Type II are designed for calm inland water, and many will turn an unconscious person faceup in the water.

Type III life jackets are considered to be the most comfortable, but they will not turn an unconscious person faceup.

Students jump in the water with life jackets on and practice the heat escape lessening position (HELP) and huddle positions in case of cold water immersion.

Guiding questions for students:

- What are the advantages and disadvantages of the two types of life jackets?
- Why are inflatables not considered flotation devices?
- How does the HELP relate to what you know about exercising in different temperatures?

Extension

Have students practice swimming different strokes to see which they prefer while wearing a life jacket.

Student Choices/Differentiation

Students may choose the shallow or deep end.

What to Look For

- Students are calm while practicing the HELP.
- Students are able to swim strokes with the life jacket on.
- Students can differentiate between the two types of jackets.

Instructional Task: Surface Dives

■ PRACTICE TASK

Swimmers swim out using the stroke of choice and then perform either a tuck (curled like a ball) or pike (knees straight) surface dive.

Refinement

Make sure that students know how to clear their ears (plug nose and blow gently to release pressure in the ears) if they are diving more than 6 feet (1.8 m) deep.

Extensions

- Throw diving toys 20 yards or meters out from the starting side of the pool. Repeat with students diving to pick up the toys.
- Have students use a surface dive for when they cannot see what is below the water. Students submerge feet first and push the water above their heads so that their bodies go feet first to the bottom.

EMBEDDED OUTCOME: S2.H2.L1. Use this practice task and questioning to review movement concepts such as buoyancy (how to decrease), lever length (long: pike; short: tuck), and rotation.

Student Choices/Differentiation

Students may dive in shallower or deeper water depending on comfort level.

What to Look For

- Students can get down to the bottom of the pool.
- Students are letting out air while descending.

Instructional Task: Dolphin Kick

■ PRACTICE TASK

Students kick 15 feet (4.6 m) underwater with feet together using an undulating body motion (can also be called a mermaid kick), with the body in a streamlined position.

Refinement

Have students focus on the idea of creating a wave of power by pressing down with the chest, which pushes the hips up. Remind them it's more about the core than the legs.

Student Choices/Differentiation

- Students may increase or decrease the distance according to comfort level.
- Have students use fins to accentuate the feel of the kick.

What to Look For

- Students perform a smooth, undulating motion.
- Feet are staying together.
- Students' bodies show flexibility.

Instructional Task: Swimming Underwater

■ PRACTICE TASK

Place weighted hoops around the pool, and have groups of students go underwater and swim through the hoops.

Extension

Repeat, with students using a variety of kicks and bigger breaststroke arm pulls.

Guiding questions for students:

- Why is it important to minimize your effort while swimming underwater? (Answer: To conserve energy.)
- What types of kicks are most efficient underwater?
- How does using bigger arm pulls help you?

Student Choices/Differentiation

Students may choose how many hoops to go through and how far to swim underwater.

What to Look For

- Students are comfortable underwater.
- Students are able to use several kicks in their efforts.

Formal and Informal Assessments

The number of hoops that students are able to navigate (students keep track)

Closure

- Today, we focused on life jackets and underwater swimming. What style of kicking is used most frequently when completely underwater?
- What kinds of fitness are involved in surface diving and swimming underwater?

Reflection

- Were any students really struggling with the dives in deeper water?
- What kinds of activities can they do to be more comfortable?
- Were students able to use the dolphin kick effectively?

Homework

Search online or in magazines or catalogs for images of people in bathing suits. Write a reflection about how these idealized images affect you or your peers, and turn it in next class. (Embedded outcome: S4.H1.L2)

Resources

Internet keyword search: "Type II life jackets," "Type III life jackets," "surface diving," "dolphin kick"

LESSON 8: SIDESTROKE

Grade-Level Outcomes

Primary Outcomes

Lifetime activities: Refines activity-specific movement skills in 1 or more lifetime activities (outdoor pursuits, individual-performance activities, aquatics, net/wall games or target games). (S1.H1.L2)

Personal responsibility: Accepts differences between personal characteristics and the idealized body images and elite performance levels portrayed in various media. (S4.H1.L2)

Embedded Outcome

Fitness knowledge: Identifies types of strength exercises (isometric, concentric, eccentric) and stretching exercises (static, proprioceptive neuromuscular facilitation [PNF], dynamic) for personal fitness development (e.g., strength, endurance, range of motion). (S3.H9.L1)

Lesson Objectives

The learner will:

- refine the sidestroke.
- execute turns for the sidestroke.
- discuss and reflect on idealized body images in the media.

Equipment and Materials

- Kickboards*
- Life jackets or flotation belts*

*Make flotation devices available for all students to use in all practice tasks.

Introduction

Today, you will break down the sidestroke and work on the timing. In addition, you will learn the two different types of turns for the sidestroke. First, though, let's talk about your homework assignment.

Instructional Task: Homework Discussion

■ PRACTICE TASK

Present some media images of idealized body types. Ask if any students are willing to share their reflections from the homework. Describe and discuss healthy body image.

Guiding questions for students:

- How do various media represent men and women in aquatic settings? Elite swimmers?
- How do advertisers use images to sell apparel such as bathing suits?
- How are images altered for consumption, and how realistic are they?

Student Choices/Differentiation

Students can volunteer to share their reflections, but don't require them to do so.

What to Look For

- Responses are thoughtful.
- Students recognize the unrealistic expectations portrayed in the media.

Instructional Task: Sidestroke Kick (Scissor Kick)

■ PRACTICE TASK

Students kick two widths of the pool, holding the kickboard like a violin and resting their ears on the board. The motion is as follows: Bend knees together, bring top leg forward and back leg back, and then scissor legs together.

Extension

Repeat on opposite side.

Student Choices/Differentiation

Students practice at their own pace.

What to Look For

- Legs are staying horizontal in the water.
- The kick provides good propulsion.
- Feet are not going past each other at the finish of the kick.

Instructional Task: Sidestroke

■ PRACTICE TASK

Students swim 4 × 25 yards or meters of sidestroke, with one hand holding the kickboard and one hand pushing from chin to thigh.

Refinement

Have students emphasize the long glide, with arms and kick finishing at the same time.

Extension

Without a kickboard, students use both arms in opposition.

EMBEDDED OUTCOME: S3.H9.L1. Have students identify the type of muscle contraction involved in the sidestroke.

Student Choices/Differentiation

- Students may adjust lengths as needed (e.g., 2 × 25 or 4 × 50 of sidestroke).
- Students swim at their own pace.

What to Look For

- Students use a long glide, arms and kick finishing simultaneously.
- When the bottom arm is above the head, the arm at the surface is on the side of the thigh.
- Hands come together at the shoulder.
- The upper hand pushes the water toward the feet as it comes away from the shoulder.

Instructional Task: Sidestroke Open Turn

■ PRACTICE TASK

Students swim 4 × 25 yards or meters of sidestroke. As they come into the wall, if the right hand is above the head they do an open turn by spinning around. When they push off the wall, the right hand should again be above the head.

Refinement

Repeat, but if the right hand is above the head when they come to the wall, students touch with the right hand, and when they push off, the left hand is above the head. In this case students don't spin—they will face the same direction.

Student Choices/Differentiation

- Students swim at their own pace.
- Students stay on the same side after the turn instead of switching.

What to Look For

- The arm is extended fully when the hand touches the wall.
- The turn is smooth.
- The lead arm is straight overhead when students push off the wall.

Formal and Informal Assessments

- Informal assessment or a rubric or checklist for evaluating stroke technique
- Reflections on media images

Closure

- All swimming strokes use concentric movement.
- Typically, swimmers do not get the soreness you may get from other activities. Fatigue, yes; soreness, no.
- Today, you practiced the sidestroke. If you feel comfortable on only one side, you should focus on the other side when you use this stroke.

Reflection

- Were students successful in identifying the type of muscle contraction, or do we need to review more?
- Were they competent on at least one side of the sidestroke, or do I need to go back and make more refinements?
- Review reflections on media images and comment as appropriate.

Homework

Have students create a stretching plan for swimming that includes dynamic and PNF stretches. (Embedded outcome: S3.H9.L1)

Resources

Internet keyword search: "sidestroke," "concentric," "eccentric"

LESSON 9: ENDURANCE AND BUTTERFLY

Grade-Level Outcomes

Primary Outcomes

Lifetime activities: Refines activity-specific movement skills in 1 or more lifetime activities (outdoor pursuits, individual-performance activities, aquatics, net/wall games or target games). (S1.H1.L2)

Fitness activities: Demonstrates competency in 1 or more specialized skills in health-related fitness activities. (S1.H3.L1)

Embedded Outcomes

Physical activity knowledge: Discusses the benefits of a physically active lifestyle as it relates to college or career productivity. (S3.H1.L1)

Health: Analyzes the health benefits of a self-selected physical activity. (S5.H1.L1)

Movement concepts, principles & knowledge: Uses movement concepts and principles (e.g., force, motion, rotation) to analyze and improve performance of self and/or others in a selected skill. (S2.H2.L1)

Lesson Objectives

The learner will:

- increase endurance in previously learned strokes.
- demonstrate the butterfly stroke.

Equipment and Materials

- Kickboards*
- Life jackets or flotation belts*
- iPads or devices with video apps

*Make flotation devices available for students to use in all practice tasks.

Introduction

Today, you will work on swimming endurance and on the butterfly stroke. In addition, you will partner up and record a video of your partners in order to analyze each stroke according to the standard.

Instructional Task: Butterfly Kick

■ PRACTICE TASK

Students swim two widths of the pool using the butterfly (dolphin) kick and a kickboard.

Refinement

Students attempt to increase the number of kicks per breath.

Extension

Students practice without the kickboard and with the face in the water.

Student Choices/Differentiation

- Students swim at their own pace.
- Students choose their lanes.

What to Look For

Students perform a smooth, undulating movement with flexible feet.

Instructional Task: Butterfly

■ PRACTICE TASK

To practice the arm pull, have students stand in chest-deep water with their hands behind them. Students fling the arms forward over the water and enter at shoulder width. The pull should be an elongated S shape down to the legs.

Extensions

- Students swim the butterfly the width of the pool using the arm pull and fins. The fins give them more power and make it easier to learn the arm pull. Students should kick once as hands enter the water and again as hands are getting ready to leave the water.
- Repeat without fins.

Refinement

Students practice two stroke cycles per breath, not breathing on every arm pull.

Student Choices/Differentiation

- Students swim at their own pace.
- Students choose their lanes.

What to Look For

- Students perform an undulating movement, with hips popping out of the water after hand entry.
- Students use a full arm push to the thighs.
- Recovery is smooth with arms just clearing the water.
- Students take two kicks per arm pull.

Instructional Task: Stroke Endurance

■ PRACTICE TASK

Students swim 5 × 100 yards or meters each of freestyle, backstroke, elementary backstroke, breaststroke, and sidestroke.

EMBEDDED OUTCOMES: S5.H1.L1; S3.H1.L1. After the workout, use guiding questions to help students analyze how swimming can be a part of a physically active lifestyle.

Guiding questions for students:

In the next five years or so, you probably will be working at a job or going to school. Most schools or communities have pools.
- How can aquatics help you be healthy?
- How can aquatics help you maintain fitness?

Student Choices/Differentiation

- Students may adjust rest time between 100s.
- Students may adjust the number of repetitions or the distance as needed.

What to Look For

- Students are maintaining correct technique for each stroke, with correct breathing throughout the set.
- Students are able to complete 100 yards or meters of each stroke.

Instructional Task: Video Analysis

■ PRACTICE TASK

Using each student's smartphone or recording device (or school video camera or iPad), record each student in the six strokes learned (6 × 25 yards or meters of each stroke).

Each student will evaluate his own strokes against the standard (watch video clip of correct performance or use a scoring guide) to see how they compare.

EMBEDDED OUTCOME: S2.H2.L1. Students should apply movement concepts to correct errors. Provide a worksheet to guide their analysis.

Student Choices/Differentiation

- Students can choose a partner and record one another.
- Provide a checklist of cues.

What to Look For

- Students' analyses were accurate.
- Students could make corrections based on movement principles.

Formal and Informal Assessments

Video analysis

Closure

- Did you find the butterfly challenging?
- What are some key points to remember when swimming that stroke?
- What did you learn from seeing yourself on the video?

Reflection

- Review worksheets to get a grasp of student understanding of their stroke performance.
- Use the information to guide decision making for next class.

Homework

- If you didn't complete your stroke analysis today, work on it at home and bring it to the next class.
- Remember, you will lead a water aerobics exercise on the last day. Review what you have researched and planned.

Resources

Internet keyword search: "lap swim workouts," "butterfly"

LESSON 10: WATER POLO

Grade-Level Outcomes

Primary Outcomes

Lifetime activities: Demonstrates competency and/or refines activity-specific movement skills in 2 or more lifetime activities (outdoor pursuits, individual-performance activities, aquatics, net/wall games or target games). (S1.H1.L1)

Fitness activities: Demonstrates competency in 1 or more specialized skills in health-related fitness activities. (S1.H3.L1)

Assessment & program planning: Designs a fitness program, including all components of health-related fitness, for a college student and an employee in the learner's chosen field of work. (S3.H12.L1)

Embedded Outcome

Rules & etiquette: Exhibits proper etiquette, respect for others and teamwork while engaging in physical activity and/or social dance. (S4.H2.L1)

Lesson Objectives

The learner will:

- demonstrate basic water polo skills.
- execute basic water polo tactics.
- design a swim workout.

Equipment and Materials

- Kickboards
- Water polo balls or modified balls
- Whistle and a clock

Introduction

Today, you will learn how to play water polo and play a game. Water polo is a very demanding game in terms of skill and fitness, and it's a great way to help you stay fit. In addition, you will start to design a workout for a 25-year-old college student and a 45-year-old worker in a field you are interested in. You can add this workout to your fitness program.

Instructional Task: Water Polo Skill Practice

■ PRACTICE TASK

Hand out one ball per group of four or five students. Have them practice throwing the ball and catching it with one hand only. Practice can start on the deck, if space permits, or in the shallow end.

Extension

Have students do a relay, swimming heads-up freestyle with the ball in front of them, keeping control of the ball at all times.

Student Choices/Differentiation

- Experienced students should use the non-dominant hand only.
- Students may use two hands to catch if using one hand is too difficult.
- Experienced students may practice in the deep end.

What to Look For

- Students are able to throw and catch the ball with one hand.
- Students can control the ball while swimming.

Instructional Task: Water Polo Modified Game

■ PRACTICE TASK

Students play four 8-minute quarters with 5-minute breaks. Set up multiple playing areas going width-wise. Some courts should be set up in the shallow end and others in the deep end. Use two kickboards leaning together on the deck for goals.

Review the rules:

- No dunking opposing players.
- Play the ball, not the person.
- Catch and throw with only one hand (if all students are capable; otherwise permit two hands).
- Teams must make three or more passes before a shot on goal, or everyone must touch the ball before a shot on goal.
- No contact is allowed.
- A goal is credited when the team knocks down the opposing kickboards.

Extension

Students measure their heart rates or give RPE at the end of each quarter.

EMBEDDED OUTCOME: S4.H2.L1. Review proper etiquette along with the rules. Emphasize the importance of respecting others and safety in the game.

Guiding questions for students:

- What other games are like water polo?
- How are the tactics similar to other invasion games?
- How did you display teamwork in the game?

Student Choices/Differentiation

- Students may use two hands to catch if one hand is too difficult.
- Group teams by ability so that students are playing against others at the same level.
- Adjust the number of quarters or playing time as needed.
- Students choose the shallow or deep end. Those who play in the deep end should review treading water.

What to Look For

Offense

- Everyone is getting a chance to touch the ball.
- Students are swimming to open space to receive a pass.
- Students are shooting on the target (with accuracy).

Defense

- Students are playing the ball and not the opposing player.
- Students are trying to intercept passes.
- Students are marking offensive players so they do not have a clear shot on goal.

Fitness

Everyone is engaged and keeping their heart rates up. If not, do the rules need to be modified further to make that happen?

Instructional Task: Design a Swim Workout

■ PRACTICE TASK

Drawing on what you've learned about aquatic fitness, create a complete workout for both a 25-year-old college student and a 45-year-old worker in the field you are interested in.

Guiding questions for students:

- What should you consider when making workout plans? (Answers: rest, goals, mixing up strokes, sufficient task length to elevate heart rate, warm-up, cool-down, and so on)
- What might need to be adjusted for the two age groups?

Student Choices/Differentiation

- Students may choose activities from class or their experiences to make an exciting workout.
- Provide a checklist of requirements to help structure the workout.

What to Look For

- Workout includes a warm-up, main set, and cool-down.
- Heart rate or RPE is taken.
- Students design a complete body workout.

Formal and Informal Assessments

Student workout plans

Closure

- What kinds of fitness do you need in order to succeed at water polo?
- Were you able to keep your heart rate elevated throughout?
- What did you find the hardest about planning workouts?

Reflection

- Were students able to transfer their game tactics to the game?
- Did students make the connection between the game and fitness?
- Review workout plans to determine where gaps in knowledge may be.

Homework

- If you did not complete your workout plan, finish it as homework and bring it to our next class.
- Practice the water aerobics exercise you will lead.

Resources

Internet keyword search: "water polo," "water polo fitness," "water polo rules," "water polo techniques"

LESSON 11: RACING STARTS AND FLIP TURNS

Grade-Level Outcomes

Primary Outcomes

Lifetime activities: Refines activity-specific movement skills in 1 or more lifetime activities (outdoor pursuits, individual-performance activities, aquatics, net/wall games or target games). (S1.H1.L2)

Fitness activities: Demonstrates competency in 1 or more specialized skills in health-related fitness activities. (S1.H3.L1)

Embedded Outcome

Stress management: Identifies stress-management strategies (e.g., mental imagery, relaxation techniques, deep breathing, aerobic exercise, meditation) to reduce stress. (S3.H14.L1)

Lesson Objectives

The learner will:

- demonstrate a racing start.
- execute flip turns.
- increase endurance in the freestyle, backstroke, and breaststroke.

Equipment and Materials

Kickboards

Introduction

Today, I will introduce racing starts and flip turns while you continue to work on conditioning. We'll also discuss how aquatic activities can help with stress management.

Instructional Task: Warm-Up

■ PRACTICE TASK

Students swim 2 × 50 yards or meters each of sidestroke and elementary backstroke at an easy pace. Students check their heart rates after completing each set.

Student Choices/Differentiation

- Students may swim 2 × 100 of each stroke.
- Students may swim 2 × 25 of just the kick.

What to Look For

- Students are using correct technique.
- Students' movements are smooth.
- Students are building up their heart rates gradually.

Instructional Task: Main Set

■ PRACTICE TASK

Students swim the following:

- 3 × 100 yards or meters of freestyle, with 20 seconds' rest in between
- 4 × 25 yards or meters of backstroke sprint, with 30 seconds' rest in between
- 3 × 50 yards or meters of breaststroke, with 15 seconds' rest in between.

Students measure heart rate or RPE.

Refinement

Stop the class and remind students to make quick turns (quick touch and turn, streamline off wall, fast and strong kick).

EMBEDDED OUTCOME: S3.H14.L1. After the workout, discuss the potential of aerobic exercise, such as swimming, for stress management. Ask students to identify other stress-reduction techniques they could use.

Student Choices/Differentiation

Students may adjust distances or the rest time as needed.

What to Look For

- Students are able to swim the complete distances with the rest time allowed.
- Students are maintaining correct technique throughout.

Instructional Task: Flip Turns

■ PRACTICE TASK

Students stand in chest-deep water and do a forward somersault, putting their heads between their knees and using their arms to help rotate around. Instruct students to blow air out through the nose.

Extensions

- Students take a few strokes and then do the somersault. Repeat until comfortable.
- Students move to a wall in the deeper section of the pool and perform the somersault from a distance that allows the feet to touch the wall mid-somersault. Repeat until they can make the turn consistently. [Note: This often requires trial and error and is based on how fast students swim into the wall.]
- Students swim 100 yards or meters of freestyle, with a flip turn at each wall.

Refinement

Have students focus on underwater movement after the turn using the dolphin kick.

Student Choices/Differentiation

- Students practice at their own pace.
- Students may work in pairs, with one standing at the wall to help the other flip. This will help students get the feel of the turn.

What to Look For

- Students are not lifting the head for a breath before performing the somersault.
- Feet touch the wall with a slight bend at the knees.
- After pushing off the wall, students perform a half turn so that they are facedown, in position for the freestyle.

Instructional Task: Basic Dive

■ PRACTICE TASK

In water at least 9 feet (2.7 m) deep, students begin seated on the side of the pool, chin on chest (or looking at navel) throughout dive, and just roll in.

Extensions

- Change to a kneeling dive, toes over the edge of the pool.
- Change to a standing dive. Both feet have toes curled over the edge. Students bend at the waist and fall in.

Refinement

Remind students to keep chin on chest so they don't pick their heads up as they enter the water.

Student Choices/Differentiation

- One rep at each level is adequate, but many students will require more reps to feel at ease.
- Students do not move to the next position until comfortable and performing correctly.

What to Look For

- Chin is down.
- Students make a head-first entry.

Instructional Task: Racing Dives

■ PRACTICE TASK

Where the water is deep, students stand on the deck in a track-type stance, with one foot at the edge of the pool and one foot back, fingers resting on the edge. Entry angle into the water should be between 30 and 45 degrees.

Refinement

Emphasize the shallowness of the dive in order to be able to begin the stroke quickly. Students repeat the dive and then swim five strokes.

Extension

Use a device to record the dives so students can view their entry angles and make adjustments.

Student Choices/Differentiation

Allow students to stay on the previous task until comfortable with the entry.

What to Look For

- Chin is down.
- Entry is shallow.
- Students are kicking once completely submerged.

Formal and Informal Assessments

Feedback on the two workouts students submitted

Closure

- Remember, whether you are swimming laps or participating in one of the other types of aquatic exercise, swimming can help reduce stress. Moving through the water tends to be relaxing for most people.
- Today, I introduced the flip turn and racing dives. What are three key points to remember for each of these?
- Emphasize the importance of a smooth turn for competition and enjoyable lap swimming.

Reflection

- Which students need extra practice on the dive and the flip turns?

Homework

- Watch a video clip of a swim meet on the school's physical education website, focusing on the racing start and flip turns.
- Practice the water aerobics exercise you will lead.

Resources

Internet keyword search: "flip turns," "racing starts"

LESSON 12: MINI SWIM MEET

Grade-Level Outcomes

Primary Outcomes

Lifetime activities: Refines activity-specific movement skills in 1 or more lifetime activities (outdoor pursuits, individual-performance activities, aquatics, net/wall games or target games). (S1.H1.L2)

Fitness activities: Demonstrates competency in 1 or more specialized skills in health-related fitness activities. (S1.H3.L1)

Embedded Outcome

Rules & etiquette: Exhibits proper etiquette, respect for others and teamwork while engaging in physical activity and/or social dance. (S4.H2.L1)

Lesson Objectives

The learner will:

- demonstrate a variety of strokes while participating in a mini swim meet.
- demonstrate knowledge of rules and etiquette while officiating and participating in the meet.

Equipment and Materials

Kickboards

Introduction

Today, we will hold a mini swim meet to show off the skills that you have learned. The emphasis will be on how much you have improved since the start of this section, not necessarily where you finish.

Instructional Task: Swim Meet Warm-Up

■ PRACTICE TASK

Students swim 3 × 50 yards or meters each of freestyle, backstroke, butterfly, and breaststroke.

Students measure their heart rates or RPE after completing each set.

Student Choices/Differentiation

- Students can perform flip turns or open turns on freestyle.
- Students swim at their own pace.

What to Look For

- Students are building up their heart rates slowly.
- Students are using correct technique.

Instructional Task: Timing a Race

■ PRACTICE TASK

Start a stopwatch on the whistle; students stop when a body part hits the wall at the end of the assigned distance.

On a whistle, students practice timing a partner for a short distance.

Student Choices/Differentiation

Students choose their partners.

What to Look For

- Students are paying attention.
- Students are using the watch correctly.

Instructional Task: Officiating a Swim Meet

■ PRACTICE TASK

Review rules etiquette:

- You may not walk on the bottom or pull on the lane line.
- You must use the specified stroke.
- Fairness: If a game official has any doubt about whether a swimmer violated a rule, the swimmer is not disqualified.
- Flip turns and open turns are permitted.

EMBEDDED OUTCOME: S4.H2.L1 Discuss etiquette and respect beyond the basic rules. Ask for examples of showing respect and support for teammates and opponents.

Student Choices/Differentiation

Make a poster of rules for students to review.

What to Look For

- Students are engaged in the discussion.
- Students provide appropriate examples.

Instructional Task: Mini Swim Meet

Practice Task

Match up swimmers of similar skills or speed, as many as there are lanes in the pool.

- Beginner swimmers: 25-yard races in freestyle, backstroke, and breaststroke
- Intermediate swimmers: 50-yard races in same strokes
- Advanced swimmers: 100-yard races in same strokes

Race order: beginner freestyle, intermediate freestyle, advanced freestyle, beginner backstroke, intermediate backstroke, advanced backstroke, beginner breaststroke, intermediate breaststroke, advanced breaststroke

Students measure heart rate or RPE after each race.

When students are not racing, they are to practice officiating by watching for false starts and timing the finish for their assigned lanes.

Record the mini-meet so students can view it later.

Students engage in all roles: swimmer, lane judge, and timer.

Student Choices/Differentiation

Students may select distances to race.

What to Look For

- Students show sportsmanship and support for teammates.
- Students use correct stroke technique.

Formal and Informal Assessments

Race times

Closure

- So how are you feeling after racing?
- Do you think your strokes and turns have improved?
- Make sure you drink water even though you may not feel thirsty. Hydration is important in all physical activity, and swimming is no exception.
- Next class we'll be repeating the 100-yard timed swim. Set a personal goal that you think is challenging but achievable.

Reflection

- How did the meet go?
- Were students actively engaged in officiating when not racing?
- Did they use the flip turn effectively?

Homework

- Watch our mini-meet on the school's physical education website, and identify one point of improvement for two of your races.
- Practice the water aerobics exercise you will lead.

Resources

Officiating Swimming: www.officiatingswimming.com

USA Swimming: www.usaswimming.org

LESSON 13: AQUA JOGGING

Grade-Level Outcomes

Primary Outcome

Fitness activities: Demonstrates competency in 1 or more specialized skills in health-related fitness activities. (S1.H3.L1)

Embedded Outcome

Fitness knowledge: Relates physiological responses to individual levels of fitness and nutritional balance. (S3.H8.L1)

Lesson Objectives

The learner will:

- increase conditioning with lap swimming.
- demonstrate basic aqua jogging skills.

Equipment and Materials

- Kickboards*
- Life jackets or flotation belts*
- Foot floats (optional)*

*Make flotation devices available for students to use in all practice tasks.

Introduction

Today, you will continue working on conditioning, and I'll be introducing aqua jogging. Aqua jogging is a great workout and is sometimes used by athletes to keep in shape when they are injured. Before we start the aqua jogging, you'll complete a timed 100-yard swim to gauge your progress so far. I'd like you all to write down your goals for the swim, and then we'll begin the warm-up.

Instructional Task: Warm-Up

■ PRACTICE TASK

Have students walk back and forth across the width of the pool, starting slowly and building up speed.

Student Choices/Differentiation

Students move at their own pace.

What to Look For

Students are out of breath.

Instructional Task: Timed 100

■ PRACTICE TASK

Students swim 100 yards or meters of freestyle.

Guiding questions for students:

- How does your time compare with your time at the beginning of the module?
- Did you achieve your goal?
- What do you think you need to continue to improve?

Student Choices/Differentiation

- Students can swim 25 or 50 yards or meters if they cannot complete 100.
- Students who swam only 25 yards or meters the first time may choose to swim farther or faster the next time.

What to Look For

Students are showing signs of improved conditioning, such as ability to swim longer or faster.

Instructional Task: Aqua Jogging

■ PRACTICE TASK

Lead students in an aqua jogging workout, in both shallow and deep water if students are comfortable.

Shallow water skill options: Simulate running through tires, lunges, karaoke, high knees.

Deep water skill options: Take small steps, longer strides. Jogging belts or life jackets are recommended in the deep end.

Students measure heart rate or RPE.

Student Choices/Differentiation

- Students can perform skills in the shallow end or the deep end.
- Students may choose jogging belts or life jackets in the deep end.
- Students move at their own speed.

What to Look For

- Students' respiration rates are increasing.
- Students' faces are becoming flushed.

Instructional Task: Conditioning Workout

■ PRACTICE TASK

Students swim the following:

- 4 × 50 yards or meters of freestyle
- 1st 50, kick only
- 2nd 50, pull only
- 3rd 50, kick only
- 4th 50, pull only
- 4 × 25 yards or meters of freestyle sprint, with 30 seconds' rest in between
- 100 yards or meters of sidestroke or elementary backstroke
- 4 × 50 yards or meters of breaststroke, with 20 seconds' rest in between

Students measure heart rate or RPE.

EMBEDDED OUTCOME: S3.H8.L1. After the workout, question students about their heart rates, respiration, and level of effort during the workout. Discuss how fitness level and nutrition (energy intake) influence the physiological response.

Student Choices/Differentiation

- Students may adjust the number of repetitions at each distance or the distances per rep.
- Students may alter the rest interval if needed.

What to Look For

- Students are showing signs of improved conditioning.
- Students are maintaining form throughout the intervals.

Formal and Informal Assessments

Comparison against 100-yard time from earlier in the module

Closure

- You've probably noticed that we use a variety of strokes when doing our workouts.
- Swimming relies heavily on the chest muscles, so it's important to include backstroke or other back workouts to keep in balance.
- How did aqua jogging compare with lap swimming in terms of your effort?

Reflection

- Were students working hard during aqua jogging?
- Review 100-yard times for level of improvement.
- Use data to plan future workouts.

Homework

- Considering your 100-yard time today, set a goal for time for the end of the module.
- Write down your goal and bring it to our next class to place in your fitness portfolio.
- Practice the water aerobics exercise that you will lead in front of someone else.

Resources

Internet keyword search: "aqua jogging," "water fitness exercises"

LESSON 14: STROKE ASSESSMENT

Grade-Level Outcomes

Primary Outcomes

Lifetime activities: Refines activity-specific movement skills in 1 or more lifetime activities (outdoor pursuits, individual-performance activities, aquatics, net/wall games or target games). (S1.H1.L2)

Fitness activities: Demonstrates competency in 1 or more specialized skills in health-related fitness activities. (S1.H3.L1)

Physical activity knowledge: Evaluates—according to their benefits, social support network and participation requirements—activities that can be pursued in the local environment. (S3.H4.L1)

Embedded Outcome

Working with others: Uses communication skills and strategies that promote team or group dynamics. (S4.H3.L1)

Lesson Objectives

The learner will:

- improve conditioning through lap swimming.
- perform strokes while being assessed.
- evaluate local aquatic opportunities.

Equipment and Materials

- Grading sheets and pen
- Kickboards

Introduction

Today, we will begin final stroke assessments and continue with conditioning swimming. We will spread the assessments over two classes. We will end class by talking about aquatic opportunities outside of school.

Instructional Task: Stroke Assessment Warm-Up

■ **PRACTICE TASK**

Students swim 5 × 50 yards or meters of each stroke:

- First – freestyle
- Second – backstroke
- Third – breaststroke
- Fourth – sidestroke
- Fifth – elementary backstroke

Students check heart rates after completing each stroke.

Student Choices/Differentiation

- Students may use flip turns on freestyle.
- Students swim at their own pace.

What to Look For

- Students are building up their heart rates slowly.
- Students are using correct technique.

Instructional Task: Stroke Assessments

■ PRACTICE TASK

Students perform each of the strokes while you assess their technique using a rubric. If possible, record each student.

Share results with students individually.

Extension

Have students work in pairs. One uses a device to record the other's strokes. They share the video and their analysis of their partner's strokes, which is guided by the rubric.

Student Choices/Differentiation

Students swim at their own pace.

What to Look For

Students are using correct technique. Use a rubric to evaluate their strokes. Share the rubric with students early in the module.

Instructional Task: Conditioning Swimming

■ PRACTICE TASK

While one student is being assessed, the others should be doing the conditioning workout.

- Freestyle pyramid swim: 25, 50, 75, 100, 75, 50, 25 yards or meters, with 30 seconds' rest between each segment (students measure heart rate or RPE at rest intervals)
- 50 yards or meters of breaststroke kick
- 100 yards or meters of backstroke

Refinement

Backstroke: Students emphasize shoulder rotation by focusing on the pinkie finger entering the water first.

Student Choices/Differentiation

- Students may use flip turns on freestyle.
- Racing starts on freestyle from deep end only.
- Students swim at their own pace.

What to Look For

- Students are pushing themselves in the conditioning.
- Students are maintaining correct form.

Instructional Task:
Evaluating Community Aquatics Opportunities

■ PRACTICE TASK

Think, pair, share: In pairs (or small groups), students discuss the types of aquatic opportunities that exist locally. Have students analyze their benefits and participation requirements.

EMBEDDED OUTCOME: S4.H3.L1. Use this task to encourage students to communicate in constructive and positive ways

Student Choices/Differentiation

Students choose their partners.

What to Look For

- Students are engaged in the task.
- Both students are contributing.

Formal and Informal Assessments

Formal stroke assessment and peer assessment (share results with students)

Closure

- Great job on the stroke assessment today.
- How did you like the pyramid workout?
- What was the hardest part for you?

Reflection

- Did the assessments run smoothly?
- Were students working hard at the pyramid while others were being tested?
- What strokes still need work?

Homework

- Think about the different factors that might affect your ability to participate in aquatics across the life span. It might help to talk to your parents or grandparents about how their activities have changed over time and why.
- Review for a quiz in the next lesson.
- Practice the water aerobics exercise you will lead. Bring a copy for me to review in our next class.

Resources

Internet keyword search: "swimming rubrics," "swimming skills analysis"

LESSON 15: STROKE EVALUATION AND LIFETIME PARTICIPATION

Grade-Level Outcomes

Primary Outcomes

Lifetime activities: Refines activity-specific movement skills in 1 or more lifetime activities (outdoor pursuits, individual-performance activities, aquatics, net/wall games or target games). (S1.H1.L2)

Fitness activities: Demonstrates competency in 1 or more specialized skills in health-related fitness activities. (S1.H3.L1)

Physical activity knowledge: Evaluates risks and safety factors that might affect physical activity preferences throughout the life cycle. (S3.H5.L1)

Movement concepts, principles & knowledge: Applies the terminology associated with exercise and participation in individual-performance activities, dance, net/wall games, target games, aquatics and/or outdoor pursuits appropriately. (S2.H1.L1)

Embedded Outcome

Working with others: Solves problems and thinks critically in physical activity and/or dance settings, both as an individual and in groups. (S4.H4.L1)

Lesson Objectives

The learner will:

- increase endurance through lap swimming.
- evaluate factors that may affect swimming as a physical activity throughout adulthood.

Equipment and Materials

- Kickboards
- Grading sheets and pen
- Quizzes and pens or pencils

Introduction

Today, we will conclude stroke evaluations, continue with conditioning, and analyze how participation in aquatic activities may change throughout your lives. You'll take the quiz on your aquatics knowledge first and then begin the warm-up. Turn in your water aerobics exercises so that I can review them before next class.

Instructional Task: Quiz

■ PRACTICE TASK

Have students complete a quiz on their aquatics knowledge.

Student Choices/Differentiation

Allow extra time if needed, or give in a take-home format.

What to Look For

Students are knowledgeable about concepts, skills, and terminology.

Instructional Task: Warm-Up

▧ PRACTICE TASK

Students swim 2 × 50 yards or meters of freestyle:

- kick only (may use kickboard) 50 yds.
- swim freestyle 50 yds.

Students swim 2 × 50 yards or meters of the stroke of their choice:

- kick only (may use kickboard) 50 yds.
- swim stroke of choice 50 yds.

Student Choices/Differentiation

Students can choose which stroke they would like to do.

What to Look For

- Students' respiration rates are increasing.
- Students are swimming with correct form.

Instructional Task: Stroke Assessments

▧ PRACTICE TASK

Students perform each of the strokes while you assess them using a rubric.

Share the results with students individually.

Extension

In pairs, have students record each other and analyze their partners' strokes using the rubric.

Student Choices/Differentiation

Students swim at their own pace.

What to Look For

Students are using proper technique. Use a rubric to evaluate strokes. The rubric should be shared with students early in the module.

Instructional Task: Conditioning

▧ PRACTICE TASK

Students swim the following:

- 200 yards or meters of freestyle
- 100 yards or meters of breaststroke
- 100 yards or meters of backstroke
- 50 yards or meters of elementary backstroke
- 50 yards or meters of sidestroke

Students measure heart rate or RPE between sets – recovery period coincides with time to measure heart rate.

Student Choices/Differentiation

- Students may swim the strokes in any order desired.
- Students may use flip turns or open turns on freestyle.

What to Look For

- Students are using good technique.
- Students are maintaining target heart rate.

Instructional Task:
Evaluating Factors That Affect Physical Activity

■ PRACTICE TASK

Think, pair, share: In pairs, students analyze and discuss factors that may positively or negatively affect their participation in aquatic activities throughout adulthood.

EMBEDDED OUTCOME: S4.H4.L1. Encourage students to look beyond the superficial aspects of aging to analyze factors that might affect participation in physical activity. Consider presenting scenarios that create obstacles to participation and have students generate possible solutions.

Student Choices/Differentiation

Students choose their partners.

What to Look For

- Both students are contributing.
- Students are thinking long term.

Formal and Informal Assessments

Formal assessment of strokes (share results with students)

Closure

- You have now been introduced to the world of fitness swimming. It can be relaxing or challenging depending on the workout of the day.
- Swimming is an exercise that most people can do, whether old or young, thin or big, injured or healthy.
- I encourage you to explore the options available at your local pool and continue with some form of swimming for your lifetime.

Reflection

- Are students still putting forth effort in the workouts?
- Was there enough variety?
- How can we put it all together for the last class?

Homework

- In Lesson 5, I asked each of you to come up with an exercise that we could perform on the next water aerobics day. That day will come in our next class.
- I encourage you to make your exercise fun and different from what we have done so far.
- Think about how you will lead your classmates. You will need to project your voice, provide a demonstration, and give cues.
- Remember, your exercise should be 3 to 5 minutes long.

Resources

Internet keyword search: "swimming rubric," "swimming skills analysis"

LESSON 16: STUDENT-LED WATER AEROBICS

Grade-Level Outcomes

Primary Outcome

Fitness activities: Demonstrates competency in 1 or more specialized skills in health-related fitness activities. (S1.H3.L1)

Embedded Outcome

Working with others: Assumes a leadership role (e.g., task or group leader, referee, coach) in a physical activity setting. (S4.H3.L2)

Lesson Objectives

The learner will:

- demonstrate and teach peers a new movement for water aerobics.

Equipment and Materials

- Kickboards
- Life jackets or flotation belts
- Kickbar floats (optional)
- Music
- Ankle floats

*Make flotation devices available for students to use in all practice tasks.

Introduction

Today is our final day in the water, and we will practice water aerobics. In Lesson 5, I tasked you with coming up with an exercise that we could perform in class. Today is your chance to share it with us. As you share it, be sure to project your voice and provide demonstrations and cues.

Instructional Task: Water Aerobics

■ PRACTICE TASK

Each student will have 3 to 5 minutes for her or his exercise. Group the exercises by warm-up, main set, or cool-down; whether they should be done in shallow or deep water; and what equipment is necessary.

Students stay within their target heart rates during the main set.

EMBEDDED OUTCOME: S4.H3.L2. Use this task to highlight the important qualities of leading a group in physical activities.

Student Choices/Differentiation

- Students can work in pairs.
- Students may use visual aids when describing their exercises.

What to Look For

- Students are enthusiastic when sharing their exercises.
- Students are attentive while their classmates lead exercises.
- Students are creative in their selections.

Formal and Informal Assessments

Checklist or scoring guide for evaluating student-led exercises

Closure

- I hope you enjoyed learning about fitness swimming, water aerobics, and water polo.
- Next time you watch the Olympics, you may have a new appreciation for the skills of the swimmers.

Reflection

- How did peers respond when students taught exercises?
- Did they enjoy trying new movements? Were they respectful?
- What changes would I make to this module for the next time it's taught?

Homework

Check out the activities available in the next modules, and be ready to make a selection.

Resources

Internet keyword search: "water aerobics routines," "water aerobics sequences," "water exercise routines"

MULTI-SPORT EVENTS MODULE

Lessons in this module were contributed by **Mary Westkott**, a professor in the Department of Health and Physical Education and associate head swimming and diving coach at the United States Coast Guard Academy in New London, CT.

MULTI-SPORT EVENTS

Grade-Level Outcomes Addressed, by Lesson	1	2	3	4	5	6	7	8	9	10	11	12	13	14	15	16
Standard 1. The physically literate individual demonstrates competency in a variety of motor skills and movement patterns.																
Demonstrates competency and/or refines activity-specific movement skills in 2 or more lifetime activities (outdoor pursuits, individual-performance activities, aquatics, net/wall games or target games). (S1.H1.L1)						P	P	P	P		P	P	P		P	
Demonstrates competency in 1 or more specialized skills in health-related fitness activities. (S1.H3.L1)														P		
Demonstrates competency in 2or more specialized skills in health-related fitness activities. (S1.H3.L2)			P	P	P	P	P	P	P		P	P	P		P	
Standard 2. The physically literate individual applies knowledge of concepts, principles, strategies and tactics related to movement and performance.																
Applies the terminology associated with exercise and participation in selected individual-performance activities, dance, net/wall games, target games, aquatics and/or outdoor pursuits appropriately. (S2.H1.L1)		E				P		P		P						
Uses movement concepts and principles (e.g., force, motion, rotation) to analyze and improve performance of self and/or others in a selected skill. (S2.H2.L1)					E			P								
Creates a practice plan to improve performance for a self-selected skill. (S2.H3.L1)			P													
Standard 3. The physically literate individual demonstrates the knowledge and skills to achieve and maintain a health-enhancing level of physical activity and fitness.																
Identifies issues associated with exercising in heat, humidity and cold. (S3.H3.L1)														E		
Evaluates—according to their benefits, social support network and participation requirements—activities that can be pursued in the local environment. (S3.H4.L1)	P															
Creates a plan, trains for and participates in a community event with a focus on physical activity (e.g., 5K, triathlon, tournament, dance performance, cycling event). (S3.H6.L2)			P			E	P	P	E	P	E	P	P	P	E	P
Designs and implements a strength and conditioning program that develops balance in opposing muscle groups (agonist/antagonist) and supports a healthy, active lifestyle. (S3.H7.L2)			P													
Identifies the different energy systems used in a selected physical activity (e.g., adenosine triphosphate and phosphocreatine, anaerobic glycolysis, aerobic). (S3.H8.L2)		P														
Develops and maintains a fitness portfolio (e.g., assessment scores, goals for improvement, plan of activities for improvement, log of activities being done to reach goals, timeline for improvement). (S3.H11.L2)			E													
Creates a snack plan for before, during and after exercise that addresses nutrition needs for each phase. (S3.H13.L2)														P		
Applies stress-management strategies (e.g., mental imagery, relaxation techniques, deep breathing, aerobic exercise, meditation) to reduce stress. (S3.H14.L2)														P		

Standard 4. The physically literate individual exhibits responsible personal and social behavior that respects self and others.								
Employs effective self-management skills to analyze barriers and modify physical activity patterns appropriately, as needed. (S4.H1.L1)						E		
Exhibits proper etiquette, respect for others and teamwork while engaging in physical activity and/or social dance. (S4.H2.L1)			P	P				
Uses communication skills and strategies that promote team or group dynamics. (S4.H3.L1)			P		E			
Solves problems and thinks critically in physical activity or dance settings, both as an individual and in groups. (S4.H4.L1)		E						
Applies best practices for participating safely in physical activity, exercise and dance (e.g., injury prevention, proper alignment, hydration, use of equipment, implementation of rules, sun protection). (S4.H5.L1)		P		E				
Standard 5. The physically literate individual recognizes the value of physical activity for health, enjoyment, challenge, self-expression and/or social interaction.								
Analyzes the health benefits of a self-selected physical activity. (S5.H1.L1)	E							
Chooses an appropriate level of challenge to experience success and desire to participate in a self-selected physical activity. (S5.H2.L2)				E	E	E	E	
Identifies the opportunity for social support in a self-selected physical activity or dance. (S5.H4.L1)								E

P = Primary; E = Embedded

LESSON 1: ABOUT MULTI-SPORT EVENTS

Grade-Level Outcomes

Primary Outcome

Physical activity knowledge: Evaluates—according to their benefits, social support network and participation requirements—activities that can be pursued in the local environment. (S3.H4.L1)

Embedded Outcome

Health: Analyzes the health benefits of a self-selected physical activity. (S5.H1.L1)

Lesson Objectives

The learner will:

- discuss the history of multi-sport events.
- describe the benefits of participating in a multi-sport event.
- locate a variety of multi-sport events offered in the community.
- identify different types of multi-sport events.
- describe equipment needed for participation.

Equipment and Materials

- Computer projector
- The history of triathlon: https://vimeo.com/31365051.
- The story of Julie Moss: www.youtube.com/watch?v=VbWsQMabczM.
- Motivational triathlon video: www.youtube.com/watch?v=X4A4n1T0fg0.

Introduction

Today, you are going to learn about the different types of multi-sport events and begin to plan for our own.

Instructional Task: History of the Triathlon

■ PRACTICE TASK

Watch videos on the history of the triathlon.

Extension

Students could view videos of duathlon or aquabike events.

Guiding questions for students:

- What surprised you about the history of triathlons?
- What challenges did the early organizers and competitors face?
- How have multi-sport events evolved since they have become more mainstream?
- What new types of events are offered? Answers: Tough Mudder, obstacle courses, etc.

Student Choices/Differentiation

Students may answer questions in pairs.

What to Look For

- Students are engaged in the videos.
- Students can link the history of the first events to the events of today, including variety of distances and variety of multi-sport events (e.g., duathlon, aquabike, Tough Mudder and other popular obstacle races).

Instructional Task:
Getting Started in Multi-Sport Events

■ PRACTICE TASK

After watching selected videos, students fill out a worksheet that covers pioneers, history questions, governing bodies, and types and distances of events in the videos.

Identify types of multi-sport events, including triathlons, duathlons, and aquabike, and discuss or show the equipment needed for participation (e.g., types of bikes, shoes, swim gear).

Discuss the benefits of participating in multi-sport events.

EMBEDDED OUTCOME: S5.H1.L1. This is a good opportunity to have students analyze the potential health benefits of multi-sport events. Students could work with partners to analyze one multi-sport event and then share their findings with the class.

Student Choices/Differentiation

Make different equipment available for show, such as goggles, tri goggles, road bike, bike shoes, bike shorts, bike pedals, bike helmet, different types of sunglasses, biking jersey, running shoes, and bib belt.

What to Look For

- Students can identify multiple benefits of these types of events.
- All students are participating in the discussion.

Instructional Task: Planning a Multi-Sport Event

■ PRACTICE TASK

Divide the class into groups. Students design a multi-sport event in which they'll participate in the final class of the module.

Students can use the Internet to locate different websites and find races in the community they can use as ideas or examples.

Students share websites they found helpful.

Each group presents their options to the class.

Students vote on the option to train for and do as the final project for the module.

Note: You could also consider having the class participate in a community event instead of designing your own.

Guiding questions for students:

- Besides the Internet, where else might you find information regarding events in your community?
- What factors should you consider in selecting possible events?

What to Look For

- Students are using multiple websites.
- All students are participating in searching.
- All students are involved in identifying different events.

Formal and Informal Assessments

Exit slip: Of the multi-sports events, which is your favorite type of event? Why?

Closure

- What are the benefits of multi-sport events?
- Discuss goal for the end of the module event.
- We'll be learning how to train for the event throughout our module so everyone is prepared.

Reflection

- Did this lesson spark students' interest?
- Does the final project reflect the abilities of all students in the class?
- Were there productive discussions going on?

Homework

Choose an article related to training (e.g., nutrition, training techniques, strength training). You will need to prepare a one-page abstract on your chosen article to share with the rest of the class later in the module.

Resources

USA Triathlon: www.usatriathlon.org

Tri Find: The American Triathlon Calendar: www.trifind.net

Race 360: www.race360.com/triathlon/races

Triathlon Training for Beginners: www.beginnertriathlete.com/races

Internet keyword search: "parks and recreation," "triathlons," "local races"

LESSON 2: TRAINING PRINCIPLES

Grade-Level Outcomes

Primary Outcome

Fitness knowledge: Identifies the different energy systems used in a selected physical activity (e.g., adenosine triphosphate and phosphocreatine, anaerobic glycolysis, aerobic). (S3.H8.L2)

Embedded Outcome

Movement concepts, principles & knowledge: Applies the terminology associated with exercise and participation in selected individual-performance activities, dance, net/wall games, target games, aquatics and/or outdoor pursuits appropriately. (S2.H1.L1)

Lesson Objectives

The learner will:

- review and apply the seven principles of exercise and sport training to selected multi-sport events.
- describe energy systems and their role in training for the triathlon.
- complete an activity to illustrate the use of the anaerobic energy system.
- complete an activity to illustrate the use of the aerobic energy system.

Equipment and Materials

- Chart paper or whiteboards
- Markers
- Gym gear
- Stopwatch

Introduction

Today, we will review essential training principles and energy systems for multi-sport events. We also will test what our bodies do and feel like when using different energy systems. Who can give an example of a training principle?

Instructional Task: Seven Training Principles

■ PRACTICE TASK

Divide the class into seven groups; assign one principle to each group. Have each group come up with their own definitions of what their principle means as applied to training for a multi-sport event.

1. Individuality
2. Specificity
3. Progression
4. Overload
5. Adaptation
6. Recovery
7. Reversibility

EMBEDDED OUTCOME: S2.H1.L1. This task is a good opportunity to review the terminology as well as the training principles. Have students write their descriptions on chart paper or whiteboards. Lead discussions on student responses. Create a form listing all principles of training. Students can fill in the characteristics and definitions of each principle during presentations.

Guiding questions for students:

- What examples can you give of the different principles as they apply to training for a multi-sport event?
- Does each of these principles play an equal role during training?
- Which of these principles plays a larger role than another when training for a triathlon?

Student Choices/Differentiation

Allow students to use a device to search for information if they need it.

What to Look For

- All students are contributing to the group activity.
- Students are able to define the principles correctly.
- Students are applying the principles appropriately to the selected multi-sport event.

Instructional Task:
Anaerobic and Aerobic Energy Systems and Their Role in Training Programs

■ PRACTICE TASK

Have students perform two or three anaerobic activities.

Have students perform one aerobic activity.

Provide an overview of energy systems used in physical activity.

Guiding questions for students:

- How did you feel completing each of the activities?
- What roles do the heart, lungs, and muscles play during training?
- Does anaerobic training have a place in our multi-sport training plan?
- How does aerobic training fit into our event?

Student Choices/Differentiation

Provide examples of appropriate activities if students are struggling for ideas:
- Anaerobic activity:
  - 100-meter sprint or equivalent activity (swimming, spin bike, elliptical)
  - 200-meter sprint or equivalent activity (swimming, spin bike, elliptical)
  - 400-meter sprint or equivalent activity (swimming, spin bike, elliptical)
- Aerobic activity:
  - 800-meter run or equivalent activity (swimming, spin biking, elliptical training)
  - 1500-meter run or equivalent activity (swimming, spin bike, elliptical)

What to Look For

- Students are engaging in productive conversations.
- Students are asking questions and giving correct examples.
- Students are selecting appropriate activities for the energy systems identified.

Formal and Informal Assessments

Principles of training definitions form

Closure

- Training for an event involves many different training principles and understanding your energy systems. You need to use this knowledge to gain maximal results.
- What are the primary energy systems?
- What are the seven training principles?
- In our next class, we will start developing our training plans and perform a sub-max test to assess your current levels of cardiorespiratory endurance, which will influence your plans.

Reflection

- Was I effective in communicating the importance of all the principles of training?
- Through class discussions, did students grasp the concepts of the principles and how to apply them to a program?
- Did the science challenge students to think of their own bodies during exercise?

Homework

Continue working on the abstract of the research article on training that you have selected.

Resources

National Strength and Conditioning Association: www.nsca.com

American College of Sports Medicine: www.ACSM.org

The Cooper Institute: www.cooperinstitute.org

LESSON 3: CREATING A TRAINING PLAN

Grade-Level Outcomes

Primary Outcomes

Movement concepts, principles & knowledge: Creates a practice plan to improve performance for a self-selected skill. (S2.H3.L1)

Engages in physical activity: Creates a plan, trains for and participates in a community event with a focus on physical activity (e.g., 5K, triathlon, tournament, dance performance, cycling event). (S3.H6.L2)

Fitness knowledge: Designs and implements a strength and conditioning program that develops balance in opposing muscle groups (agonist/antagonist) and supports a healthy, active lifestyle. (S3.H7.L2)

Embedded Outcome

Assessment & program planning: Develops and maintains a fitness portfolio (e.g., assessment scores, goals for improvement, plan of activities for improvement, log of activities being done to reach goals, timeline for improvement). (S3.H11.L2)

Lesson Objectives

The learner will:

- complete a sub-max test.
- create a personal eight-week training plan using applied training principles.
- incorporate one day of strength training per week into the training plan.
- begin a training journal to be updated after each training session.

Equipment and Materials

- Projector
- Monthly or weekly calendar planning sheets
- Equipment for selected mode of sub-max test
- Stopwatch

Introduction

Today, we will start with a $\dot{V}O_2$ sub-max test that will allow you to assess your current level of cardiorespiratory endurance and then apply it to your training plan. I'll review the training principles and energy systems covered in our previous class and introduce how to create a training program. Remember, if you really want to improve, you will have to complete the workouts outside of class.

Instructional Task: $\dot{V}O_2$ Sub-maximal Testing

■ PRACTICE TASK

Students perform a sub-max test to determine baseline aerobic fitness levels.

Guiding questions for students:

- What components of fitness does a sub-max test measure?
- What does a sub-max test predict?

EMBEDDED OUTCOME: S3.H11.L2. Discuss the sub-max test results. Test results will become part of students' fitness portfolios and provide the foundation for their training plans.

Student Choices/Differentiation

Students can choose the mode of sub-max test (e.g., stationary bike, swim, or run).

What to Look For

- Students are following the protocol correctly.
- Students are working at the appropriate intensity level.

Instructional Task: Phases of Event Preparation

■ PRACTICE TASK

Review the energy systems and the seven training principles.

Discuss key points of the five phases of preparing for an event.

1. General preparation (30% of the event training period): low intensity, building foundations, preparation for more difficult efforts, technique,
2. Targeted preparation (40% of the event training period): increase intensity slightly, strength training
3. Pre-competition (20% of the event training period): increase intensity to max levels, decreasing in volume
4. Competition (10% of the training period): very specific, low volume
5. Transition (post-competition): active rest and recovery

Show an example of a weekly block plan for training.

Guiding questions for students:

- How long should each phase last if you designed a six-month training plan?
- What other factors should you consider when making a plan? (Answers: Where are we each starting [individuality]? Do we have a base? When is our event? And so on.)
- What is available for training? (Answers: pool, open water, track, and so on)

Student Choices/Differentiation

Provide posters or other visual aids with key points for each phase.

What to Look For

- Students are engaged in the discussion.
- Students are asking good questions.
- Students can give simple examples of how they would adjust their training for one of the disciplines when they move to a new phase.

Instructional Task: Block Training Plan

■ PRACTICE TASK

Review the phases of event preparation (general preparation, targeted preparation, pre-competition, competition, transition) as they relate to sprint triathlon training: double distance and time for Olympic, 1.5 for half, and so on.

In pairs or small groups, students begin filling out an eight-week block training plan, using their sub-max scores as a starting point. Students will break up their plans as follows:

Three weeks of general prep

Four weeks of targeted prep

One week of competition

Lead a discussion on appropriate activities for each phase as students begin to develop their plans:

General Prep

Long, slow distance running: 1.5 to 2 times event distance or time

Long endurance biking: 1.5 to 2 times event distance or time

Long interval swimming: focus on endurance

Targeted Prep

Strength training: multi-joint (compound) moves to work the whole body; three or four sets of 8 to 12 for both strength and endurance

Running: long intervals on track, speed work, hill repeats

Biking: hill repeats, 1-mile (1.6 km) repeats, interval work

Swimming: increase speed, decrease rest intervals, decrease distance intervals, open water swimming

Pre-competition Prep

Running: 800-meter repeats on track

Biking: mile repeats, hill repeats

Swimming: decrease distance, increase rest intervals

Competition Prep

Strength training: none

Running: long, slow recovery; speed work on track (400 to 600 meters)

Biking: long, slow recovery; incorporate 1-mile (1.6 km) speed work into one bike workout

Swimming: long, slow distance; open water, one max-500-meter swim for time

Transition

Post-race workouts are long and slow in nature.

Cycling, running or swimming workouts should feel easy.

Refinements

- Observe students filling out block plans and provide feedback.
- During the general prep phase, check to see whether they are performing weekly workouts that are 1.5 to 2 times the race distances: 5-mile (8 km) runs, 20-mile (32 km) bike rides, 1500-meter swims.
- During the targeted prep phase, check to see whether students are incorporating the following:
    Track workouts
    Pace workouts in pool
    Repeats on bike
    Strength training
- During the race prep phase, check to see whether students are doing the following:
    Decreasing mileage, time, yardage
    Increasing rest intervals
    Increasing intensity

Extensions

- Students exchange drafts of their plans after each section for peer feedback. Provide a checklist to guide peer review.
- Students could create a 10-week block plan that includes the pre-competition phase (general preparation) (3 weeks), targeted preparation (4 weeks), pre-competition (2 weeks), competition (1 week)

Student Choices/Differentiation

Provide a template to guide students in preparing their plans.

What to Look For

- Students are incorporating all the disciplines (watch for students who are struggling).
- Students are able to adjust workouts based on the phase of training.

Formal and Informal Assessments

- Sub-max $\dot{V}O_2$ tests for baseline assessment
- Detailed weekly training programs in block form
- Training journals: instructor choice of web-based or paper-based

Closure

- We covered a lot of information today regarding creating a training program.
- Using the template, finish creating a simple, easy-to-follow program for yourself based on the training principles and the five phases of event preparation.
- Reflect on your training through journaling. After each workout, write about how you felt. Was the workout difficult? Did you push yourself? I will review your journals each week, as this lets you communicate what you are doing outside of class and allows me to give you feedback on your training.

Reflection

- Did students struggle when creating their block plans?
- Should the block plan be more specific next time? Should I have the workouts planned, and they choose where to place them?

Homework

- Continue working on the draft to create a final individualized workout plan. Turn in a copy next class.
- Start following your plan.
- Start your training journal, completing one entry after each training session. Include class activities and training outside of class.
- Continue working on your research abstracts.

Resources

National Strength and Conditioning Association: www.NSCA.org

American College of Sports Medicine: www.ACSM.org

The Cooper Institute: www.cooperinstitute.org

Internet keyword search: "training phases," "triathlon preparation plans"

LESSON 4: BIKE FITTING AND CHANGING A FLAT

Grade-Level Outcomes

Primary Outcomes

Fitness activities: Demonstrates competency in 2 or more specialized skills in health-related fitness activities. (S1.H3.L2)

Safety: Applies best practices for participating safely in physical activity, exercise and dance (e.g., injury prevention, proper alignment, hydration, use of equipment, implementation of rules, sun protection). (S4.H5.L1)

Embedded Outcome

Working with others: Solves problems and thinks critically in physical activity and/or dance settings, both as an individual and in groups. (S4.H4.L1)

Lesson Objectives

The learner will:

- describe how to fit a bike properly.
- discuss the importance of proper bike fit.
- change a flat tire.

Equipment and Materials

- Personal bikes
- Tire iron and tools for changing a flat
- Wrench or Allen wrench
- Multiple bike pumps
- String
- Measuring tape
- Bike trainers, if possible: 1 trainer per 2 students

Introduction

Until now, we have discussed preparing to train. Now, we will shift focus to the individual physical components of a triathlon to learn more about how to maximize your potential. We'll start today with the bike. It's important to fit the bike to the cyclist properly to reduce injuries and allow for a more efficient ride. You also need to know how to change a tire because a flat tire is one of the most common problems out on the road. Please hand in a copy of your training plan.

Instructional Task: Bike Fit

■ PRACTICE TASK

Show a video or bring in an expert from a local bike shop to give a tutorial on how to fit a bike. You can view a basic bike fit video at www.youtube.com/watch?v=VrZBjOloChg.

Extension

Pair students up. Each pair works together to fit each other on their bikes.

1. Students ride their bikes as is.
2. Students put the bikes on a trainer.
3. Peers fit students on their bikes, completing a checklist for their partners.
4. Students re-ride their bikes after proper fitting.
5. Students use the bike fit checklist to check fit.

Refinements

- Watch for too much extension on the downstroke. Remind students that the toes should not point at six o'clock and knees should have a slight bend at the bottom of the downstroke. If this is not the case, the seat might be too high.
- Hands should rest comfortably on the hoods, with arms bent slightly. Upper body should be relaxed. If students are hunched over, the seat might be too low or too far forward, or the stem might need an extender.
- If students are stretched out too far, arms extended fully, the seat might be too high or too far back, or the stem might need to be shortened.

Guiding questions for students:

- How does the fit of the bike affect movement efficiency?
- How does proper bike fit reduce injury?
- Did you feel a difference between riding before and after being fitted on your bike?

EMBEDDED OUTCOME: S4.H4.L1 This is a good opportunity for students to use problem-solving skills to fit the bike to a partner, using guidelines for proper fit.

Student Choices/Differentiation

Allow students to use a device to replay the video, or provide a list of fit guidelines.

What to Look For

- Students are making appropriate adjustments to the bikes.
- Students are working cooperatively to measure bike fit.
- Students are able to apply the guidelines to achieve a comfortable fit.

Instructional Task: Practice Ride

■ PRACTICE TASK

Have students take their bikes on a short ride around the school grounds or a closed parking lot to test out their fit and comfort level. Before mounting the bikes, review key points of shifting gears and braking.

Student Choices/Differentiation

Students may vary hand position from the bars to the drops (road bike).

What to Look For

- Students appear comfortable on their bikes and relaxed in the upper body.
- Knees are bent slightly on the downstroke.
- Students are shifting at the appropriate time.

Instructional Task: Change a Flat Tire

■ **PRACTICE TASK**

Watch a video on how to change a flat tire, such as the video found at www.youtube.com/watch?v=-ZbeR0mJBkk.

Extensions

- Students flip the front-wheel quick-release lever, take off the front wheel, let out any air that remains, remove the flat inner tube and replace it with a new inner tube. After re-inflating the tire, now complete with a new inner tube, place wheel back on the bike and tighten the quick-release lever.
- Students change a flat on the rear tire (more difficult because it involves disengaging the bike chain from the gear wheels, then re-engaging it).

Guiding questions for students:

- Was it more difficult to change the front tire or back?
- Why?
- What equipment do you need to have with you when you ride? Answer: air pump, spare inner tubes, tire lever.

Student Choices/Differentiation

- Allow students to work in pairs.
- Allow students to use a device to replay the video, or provide instructions for fixing a flat tire.

What to Look For

- Students are able to take the tire off the rim.
- Students are able to use the tools correctly.
- Students put the tire back together fully and filled it with air.

Formal and Informal Assessments

Bike fit checklist

Closure

- The goal today was to fit your bikes individually to increase your efficiency on the bike and decrease your likelihood of injury. As with any motor movement—running, biking, swimming—over time, if we perform the movement incorrectly or inefficiently, our bodies will react: knee pain, hip pain, shoulder pain.
- Our goal is to always have clean movements that allow us to create efficient power as we increase our strength in that movement.
- With our bikes fitting properly and our knowledge of how to fix a flat, we will go for a short group ride in our next class to work on rules of the road and bike etiquette.

Reflection

- Were all students able to adjust their bikes?
- Were students successful in changing a flat? Were they still having difficulties?
- Review training plans and look for common errors and misconceptions.

Homework

- Continue working on your research abstracts.
- Continue your journals. I will collect them next class for feedback.
- Review road rules for cycling on the school's physical education website.

Resources

Local bike shop for instructional help

How to Do a Basic Bike Fit: www.youtube.com/watch?v=VrZBjOloChg

How to Fix a Flat: www.youtube.com/watch?v=-ZbeROmJBkk

Internet keyword search: "how to fit a bike," "how to change a flat bike tire"

LESSON 5: CYCLING SAFETY

Grade-Level Outcomes

Primary Outcomes

Fitness activities: Demonstrates competency in 2 or more specialized skills in health-related fitness activities. (S1.H3.L2)

Rules & etiquette: Exhibits proper etiquette, respect for others and teamwork while engaging in physical activity and/or social dance. (S4.H2.L1)

Working with others: Uses communication skills and strategies that promote team or group dynamics. (S4.H3.L1)

Safety: Applies best practices for participating safely in physical activity, exercise and dance (e.g., injury prevention, proper alignment, hydration, use of equipment, implementation of rules, sun protection). (S4.H5.L1)

Embedded Outcomes

Engages in physical activity: Creates a plan, trains for and participates in a community event with a focus on physical activity (e.g., 5K, triathlon, tournament, dance performance, cycling). (S3.H6.L2)

Movement concepts, principles & knowledge: Uses movement concepts and principles (e.g., force, motion, rotation) to analyze and improve performance of self and/or others in a selected skill. (S2.H2.L1)

Lesson Objectives

The learner will:

- identify different hand signals used when cycling.
- practice different hand signals during a group ride.
- discuss cycling etiquette as it applies to both rider and driver.
- demonstrate proper hand signals and etiquette on a 5- to 10-mile (8 to 16 km) group ride.

Equipment and Materials

- Helmets
- Personal bikes

Introduction

All of you have handed in both your journals and your workout plans, and I hope that you have started following your plans. I am excited to read your journals and provide some feedback. Please review the feedback that I have provided on your training plans and adjust them as necessary. From here on out, we will be pretty active in class, focusing on the different disciplines and improving technique and gaining confidence. Today, we will focus on cycling safety, and we'll start by reviewing the rules that you saw on the school website.

Instructional Task: Biking Rules of the Road

■ PRACTICE TASK

Review the rules of the road, including riding on the right side with traffic and riding single file.

Have students demonstrate hand signals while standing.

- Right turn
- Left turn
- Stopping, slowing down
- Hazard on the road

Discuss appropriate communications for cycling in groups:

- Car up, car back
- On your left
- Stopping, slowing down

Extension

Students practice group communication in small groups in a controlled area.

Student Choices/Differentiation

- Use posters or other visual aids to remind students about the rules of the road.
- Students choose their groups for the ride.
- Students ride at their own pace while practicing communication.

What to Look For

- Students are exhibiting good bike skills consistently.
- Students are signaling early enough.
- Students are riding in single file and communicating correctly when passing.

Instructional Task: Group Road Cycling

■ PRACTICE TASK

As a group, go on a 5- to 10-mile (8 to 16 km) ride, rotating the pace line leader.

EMBEDDED OUTCOME: S3.H6.L2. Use this safety ride as part of the training for the event. Create a riding route before class. It can be a loop or an out and back. Select a halfway point to stop, take accountability, and have a quick discussion about progress.

EMBEDDED OUTCOME: S2.H2.L1. Take advantage of the group line to explain special situations such as drafting, taking a "pull," and pace lines. Note that drafting is not permitted in triathlon competitions.

Refinement

Ask students about the distance between bikes when riding single file. The cyclist who is behind is at fault if wheels touch, which can cause a crash. Remind students to keep a safe distance and to vocalize and signal when slowing or stopping.

Guiding questions for students:

- What did you like most about the ride?
- What was the most difficult signal to remember? To execute?
- When did you feel most unsafe? Safe?
- What are some benefits of riding in a group?
- What are some disadvantages?

Student Choices/Differentiation

Students may ride with others of similar pace.

What to Look For

- Pace leader is using correct hand signals.
- All members of the pace line are using hand and vocal signals when appropriate.

Formal and Informal Assessments

Exit slip: What was the most challenging aspect of the group ride today?

Closure

- Review safety rules of riding and group riding.
- Review road etiquette with other cyclists and motorists.
- Next class, we'll have a short quiz on the seven training principles that we covered.

Reflection

- How well did students use hand signals?
- Did they signal early enough?
- Did they remember to use the vocal signals?
- Were they confident when riding on the road?

Homework

- Continue working on your research abstracts, due for lesson 10.
- Adjust your training plans according to my feedback, and continue your individual workouts.
- Continue journaling.
- Review for the quiz.

Resources

Internet keyword search: "cycling signals," "pace line," "cycling group etiquette"

LESSON 6: SWIM TECHNIQUE

Grade-Level Outcomes

Primary Outcomes

Lifetime activities: Demonstrates competency and/or refines activity-specific movements in 2 or more lifetime activities (outdoor pursuits, individual-performance activities, aquatics, net/wall games or target games). (S1.H1.L1)

Fitness activities: Demonstrates competency in 2 or more specialized skills in health-related fitness activities. (S1.H3.L2)

Movement concepts, principles & knowledge: Applies the terminology associated with exercise and participation in selected individual-performance activities, dance, net/wall games, target games, aquatics and/or outdoor pursuits appropriately. (S2.H1.L1)

Embedded Outcome

Engages in physical activity: Creates a plan, trains for and participates in a community event with a focus on physical activity (e.g., 5K, triathlon, tournament, dance performance, cycling event). (S3.H6.L2)

Lesson Objectives

The learner will:

- demonstrate freestyle technique.
- identify key parts of the freestyle: catch, mid-pull, finish, recovery.
- demonstrate at least one drill for technique improvement on each of the four parts of the stroke.
- demonstrate a rhythmic breathing technique used in distance swimming.

Equipment and Materials

- Pool
- Swim goggles
- Swim caps
- Kickboards
- Quizzes and pencils or pens

Introduction

In our previous two classes, we worked on cycling. Today and next class, we will focus on the swim aspect of a triathlon. We'll work on drills in the water to help improve technique, and in our next class, we'll put those drills into practice in a pool workout. First up is the quiz on the seven training principles.

Instructional Task: Quiz

■ PRACTICE TASK

Administer a short quiz on the seven training principles.

Student Choices/Differentiation

Provide extra time for those who need it.

What to Look For

- Students are able to identify the principles correctly.
- Students can apply them appropriately in examples.

Instructional Task: Technique and Efficiency in Water

■ PRACTICE TASK

Choose 10 to 15 freestyle drills that focus on technique and efficiency. See list below for suggestions:

- Kick with board
- Kick on left side: rifle barrel drill
- Kick on right side: rifle barrel drill
- Six-beat kick drill
- Catch-up drill
- Fists drill
- Fingertip drag drill
- Over-exaggerated finish drill

Have students complete 25 yards or meters of each selected drill. Focus should be on the following elements as you provide feedback:

- Body position
- Catch of stroke
- Mid-pull of stroke
- Recovery of stroke
- Breathing and timing

EMBEDDED OUTCOME: S3.H6.L2. Use this task to contribute to the training for the event.

Refinement

Students select one component of the stroke to work on with a partner and appropriate drills. Partner can use peer assessment to provide feedback or use a device to record performance.

Student Choices/Differentiation

- Students can be grouped in lanes according to ability.
- Students may review video clips of correct stroke technique.

What to Look For

- Students are performing drills correctly in terms of body position and head position.
- Timing is correct in rhythmic breathing.
- Kick is effective in producing power.
- Arm is moving through the key positions of catch, mid-pull, finish, and recovery.

Formal and Informal Assessments

- Quiz
- Peer assessment

Closure

- The goal today was to focus on stroke technique and efficiency in the water. You should incorporate the drills we did today into your swim workouts in some capacity.
- In our next class, we will complete a group swim workout and focus on interval training in the pool as well as some triathlon-specific training.

Reflection

- How is the group as a whole in the water?
- Did I choose appropriate drills for their ability?
- What do I need to review more for next class?
- Review peer assessments of strokes to look for common errors.

Homework

- Continue following your workout schedules and working on your research abstracts.
- Continue your journaling.

Resources

USA Swimming: www.usaswimming.org

United States Masters Swimming: www.usms.org

LESSON 7: INTERVAL SWIM WORKOUT

Grade-Level Outcomes

Primary Outcomes

Lifetime activities: Demonstrates competency and/or refines activity-specific movements in 2 or more lifetime activities (outdoor pursuits, individual-performance activities, aquatics, net/wall games or target games). (S1.H1.L1)

Fitness activities: Demonstrates competency in 2 or more specialized skills in health-related fitness activities. (S1.H3.L2)

Engages in physical activity: Creates a plan, trains for and participates in a community event with a focus on physical activity (e.g., 5K, triathlon, tournament, dance performance, cycling event). (S3.H6.L2)

Rules & etiquette: Exhibits proper etiquette, respect for others and teamwork while engaging in physical activity and/or social dance. (S4.H2.L1)

Embedded Outcome

Safety: Applies best practices for participating safely in physical activity, exercise and dance (e.g., injury prevention, proper alignment, hydration, use of equipment, implementation of rules, sun protection). (S4.H5.L1)

Lesson Objectives

The learner will:

- complete a prescribed interval swim workout.
- demonstrate proper swim etiquette and safety rules when swimming in a group.
- demonstrate sighting techniques used in open water swimming.
- demonstrate personal interval time keeping by reading and analyzing the pace clock.

Equipment and Materials

- Swim goggles
- Pace clock
- Kickboards

Introduction

In our previous class, you worked on your swim technique and form. Today, we will incorporate those drills into our warm-up and then complete a sample interval swim workout that you can incorporate into your personal training.

Instructional Task: Pool Swim Workout

■ **PRACTICE TASK**

Lead students in a dynamic warm-up on the pool deck.

Discuss lane etiquette: circle swimming and splitting lanes.

Students complete a prescribed workout of 800 to 1,000 yards or meters. For example:

- 8 × 25 on :45 (review of drills from previous class)
- 4 × 50 on 1:00-1:15 or 15 seconds' rest
- 6 × 100 on 1:45-2:00 or 20 seconds' rest

Refinement

While students are swimming their laps, observe their stroke mechanics and provide feedback during rest intervals. Reinforce cues given in Lesson 6.

Student Choices/Differentiation

- For intervals, group students into lanes based on ability level.
- Give both time and rest intervals for both sets; adjust as needed.
- Students may change strokes if they can't complete the workout using all freestyle.

What to Look For

- Students are performing the movements during the dynamic warm-up correctly.
- During drills, students are focusing on the drill, not the interval.
- Students are watching the clock for their intervals.
- Interval provides an appropriate challenge.
- The time allows most students to be successful.

Instructional Task: Sighting for Open-Water Swimming

■ PRACTICE TASK

Demonstrate two different ways to "sight," which involves looking straight ahead every now and then while swimming in open water to stay on course.

Students swim 3 × 100 yards or meters of freestyle, with 30 seconds' rest, practicing sighting two times during each length.

Extension

Set out a buoy course in the deep end of the pool, and have students swim the course while sighting the buoys.

Guiding questions for students:

- Did your stroke technique change when you started sighting?
- How did this affect the efficiency of your stroke?
- Did you struggle with the breathing and the timing?

EMBEDDED OUTCOME: S4.H5.L1. Use the sighting task to reinforce the importance of sighting for swimming in open water safely.

Student Choices/Differentiation

- If students are having difficulty, increase the rest interval and decrease the interval length.
- Attempt just one sighting per interval until students are more comfortable with the skill.

What to Look For

- Students' sighting is becoming rhythmic.
- Students incorporate sighting smoothly into their swimming.

Formal and Informal Assessments

Exit slip: What are the benefits of sighting in an open-water swim?

Closure

- This week we focused on the swim portion of the triathlon and developing a more proficient technique. You should incorporate the drills we completed into your own personal swim workouts. Today's workout was a sample pool workout, giving you options of set intervals and rest intervals; this should carry over to your development of your workouts.

- Our triathlon will be in open water, without benefit of the nice black line on the bottom of the pool. So, we worked on sighting, which will be a major component of your comfort in open-water swimming.

- In every one of your pool workouts, try to incorporate a mini-set that focuses on sighting.

- Next time, we will take it to the track and work on our running.

- Then, we will have a quiz on the five phases of training.

Reflection

- Was the pool workout challenging enough?
- Were students able to grasp the concept of sighting?
- Do they need to spend more time on that technique?

Homework

- Continue working on your research abstracts. Your presentations are coming up soon.
- Continue your workouts and journaling.
- Review for the quiz you'll take in our next class.

Resources

USA Triathlon: www.usatriathlon.org

Triathlete: www.triathlete.com

US Masters Swimming: www.USMS.org

Internet keyword search: "sighting for open-water swimming"

LESSON 8: RUNNING ANALYSIS

Grade-Level Outcomes

Primary Outcomes

Lifetime activities: Demonstrates competency and/or refines activity-specific movements in 2 or more lifetime activities (outdoor pursuits, individual-performance activities, aquatics, net/wall games or target games). (S1.H1.L1)

Fitness activities: Demonstrates competency in 2 or more specialized skills in health-related fitness activities. (S1.H3.L2)

Movement concepts, principles & knowledge: Uses movement concepts and principles (e.g., force, motion, rotation) to analyze and improve performance of self and/or others in a selected skill. (S2.H2.L1)

Movement concepts, principles & knowledge: Applies the terminology associated with exercise and participation in selected individual-performance activities, dance, net/wall games, target games, aquatics and/or outdoor pursuits appropriately. (S2.H1.L1)

Embedded Outcome

Engages in physical activity: Creates a plan, trains for and participates in a community event with a focus on physical activity (e.g., 5K, triathlon, tournament, dance performance, cycling event). (S3.H6.L2)

Lesson Objectives

The learner will:

- use video analysis to critique a peer's running form.
- provide corrective feedback to a peer to improve running form.

Equipment and Materials

- Video on running efficiency
- Athletic attire
- Video equipment, including phones and tablets
- Running form handout
- Quizzes and pencils or pens

Introduction

This class and the next will focus on the final leg of our triathlon: running. We will work on a video analysis and then complete an interval workout that you can incorporate into your training. We'll finish with a quiz on the phases of training.

Instructional Task:
Running Gait Observations and Recording

■ PRACTICE TASK

Watch a video on running gait and form.

Distribute the running form handout with cues, and review relevant movement concepts.

Guiding questions for students:

- What important movement concepts did you observe during the video?
- How do efficient runners differ in their gait from inefficient runners?
- How do the mechanics of running change as you run faster? Why?

Extension

Working in pairs, students record each other running. Have them download an app or use slow-motion recording on their devices.

Students take video from three angles: side, front, back.

Student Choices/Differentiation

Students may run on a track or a treadmill.

What to Look For

- Students are able to detect and describe differences in good and poor running form.
- Students are able to use the video app effectively.

Instructional Task: Running Gait Analysis

■ PRACTICE TASK

Working in pairs, students view their videos and give corrective and instructional feedback. Students must apply at least one movement concept in their critiques.

Extension

Students practice running while incorporating the feedback. Partners record again and allow them to compare the two performances.

Refinements

- Reposition students to ensure a clear view of the skill for at least three strides, if necessary.
- If feedback is vague or general, direct students to a cue sheet to help them provide specific corrective feedback.

Student Choices/Differentiation

Students may use a checklist or a rubric to score the running performance.

What to Look For

- Students are able to demonstrate the proper technique to their partners.
- Students are using the handouts and resources to give feedback.
- Students can apply the key elements of running to feedback on their peers' video performance.
- Students can apply one or more movement concepts in their analysis and feedback to their partners.

Instructional Task: Interval Running Set

■ PRACTICE TASK

Have students perform a short interval running set with the focus on form while incorporating speed and interval work.

EMBEDDED OUTCOME: S3.H6.L2. This task allows students to make progress on their training while focusing on their form.

Student Choices/Differentiation

Students can run 4-6 × 100 yards or meters, 3-5 × 200 yards or meters, or 2-4 × 400 yards or meters.

What to Look For

- Students are maintaining form when they focus on speed.
- Students selected an appropriate interval set for their fitness levels.
- Students are applying the feedback they received while doing the workout.

Instructional Task: Quiz

■ PRACTICE TASK

Administer a short quiz on the phases of training.

Student Choices/Differentiation

Allow extra time for those who need it.

What to Look For

- Students can identify the phases correctly.
- Students can apply them appropriately in examples.

Formal and Informal Assessments

- Quiz on phases of training
- Peer assessment of running gait
- Gait analysis worksheets

Closure

- As you worked with your partners today, you should have received some valuable feedback. Video analysis of our physical skills can provide us with a clear picture of what we need to do to improve.
- Now, apply that feedback to your training sessions.

Reflection

- How well were students able to apply concepts and proper mechanics to their own videos?
- Were they able to improve their running form after feedback?
- Were students providing feedback in a constructive way, or do they need more guidance on this?

Homework

- Continue working on your research abstracts. They are due in two classes.
- Continue to do your workouts and journal your training sessions.

Resources

Ubersense app

Coach's Eye app

Dartfish Express app

Eat. Run. Rehabilitate: www.eatrunrehabilitate.com

The Run S.M.A.R.T. Project: www.runsmartproject.com

Internet keyword search: "running form," "running gait"

LESSON 9: RUNNING FORM AND INTERVALS

Grade-Level Outcomes

Primary Outcomes

Lifetime activities: Demonstrates competency and/or refines activity-specific movements in 2 or more lifetime activities (outdoor pursuits, individual-performance activities, aquatics, net/wall games or target games). (S1.H1.L1)

Fitness activities: Demonstrates competency in 2 or more specialized skills in health-related fitness activities. (S1.H3.L2)

Engages in physical activity: Creates a plan, trains for and participates in a community event with a focus on physical activity (e.g., 5K, triathlon, tournament, dance performance, cycling event). (S3.H6.L2)

Embedded Outcome

Challenge: Chooses an appropriate level of challenge to experience success and desire to participate in a self-selected physical activity. (S5.H2.L2)

Lesson Objectives

The learner will:

- practice various running drills to improve running form.
- participate in a running workout that enhances fitness.

Equipment and Materials

Stopwatch or timing device

Introduction

In our previous class, you worked on your running form and gait analysis with your partners. I trust that you received some good feedback. Today, we will incorporate that feedback into our run workout. We will perform a dynamic warm-up, then a few drills that will help improve your running form, and then a brief workout that you can incorporate into your training programs.

Instructional Task: Running Drills

■ PRACTICE TASK

Lead students in five or six running drills (50 to 100 yards or meters) that students can apply to their workouts to improve running form.

Refinement

Use the running drills to focus on form. Provide corrective feedback during rest intervals. Peers can also provide feedback with a rubric or checklist.

Student Choices/Differentiation

- Students work at their own pace.
- Students may adjust recovery time if needed.

What to Look For

- Arms are swinging forward and back without crossing the body.
- Torso is leaning forward slightly.
- Force produced by the contact foot is mostly driving the runner forward rather than up and down.

Instructional Task: Running Track Interval Workout

■ PRACTICE TASK

Create a track workout totaling about 1 mile or 1 km in length, with a focus on tempo. Here are two examples:

- 4 × 200 meters on 2:00 or 4 × 200 with 1:00 minutes' rest
- 4 × 400 meters on 4:00 or 4 × 400 with 2:00 minutes' rest

Refinement

During rest intervals, provide corrective feedback on running form. If available, use a device to record running form, and have students view themselves running during the rest intervals. Use the checklist or rubric from the previous task.

Guiding questions for students:

- What is the primary energy system you are using in these intervals?
- Why is it important to try to maintain the same pace for all the intervals?
- How can you apply the idea of intervals in other activities?

EMBEDDED OUTCOME: S5.H2.L2. This is a good opportunity to teach students about the importance of challenging themselves in interval workouts in order to improve their performance and fitness.

Student Choices/Differentiation

- Students may adjust interval length or rest interval if needed.
- Group students by pace or tempo.

What to Look For

- Students are pushing themselves to run at a faster pace (tempo).
- Students are maintaining the same time for each interval.
- Students are able to sustain correct form at the end of the intervals.

Formal and Informal Assessments

Rubric or checklist for self-assessment

Closure

- We worked on various drills today that focus on improving your running form. Incorporate these into your workouts, just as you would incorporate drills into sports training. Our workout today focused on intervals on the track, allowing you to work on tempo.
- In our next class, we will enjoy classroom presentations from your research abstracts.
- Remember to have a one-page abstract to hand in.

Reflection

- Did students focus on tempo and the concept of a track workout?
- Do some students need to work on pacing?

Homework

- Finish your abstracts, and be prepared to present next class.
- Bring a running workout, or part of a workout, from your training plan to complete in our next class. Be prepared to complete your own 20-minute workout at the end of that class.
- Continue journaling your training and progress in your workouts.

Resources

Active: www.active.com

National Strength and Conditioning Association: www.NSCA.org

USA Track and Field: www.usatf.org

USA Triathlon: www.usatriathlon.org

LESSON 10: ABSTRACT PRESENTATIONS

Grade-Level Outcomes

Primary Outcomes

Movement concepts, principles & knowledge: Applies the terminology associated with exercise and participation in selected individual-performance activities, dance, net/wall games, target games, aquatics and/or outdoor pursuits appropriately. (S2.H1.L1)

Engages in physical activity: Creates a plan, trains for and participates in a community event with a focus on physical activity (e.g., 5K, triathlon, tournament, dance performance, cycling event). (S3.H6.L2)

Embedded Outcome

Working with others: Uses communication skills and strategies that promote team or group dynamics. (S4.H3.L1)

Lesson Objectives

The learner will:

- deliver a 5-minute oral presentation on a research article focusing on one aspect of multi-sport training.

Equipment and Materials

- Paper and pencils

Introduction

A lot of information on training for triathlons is available out there, which will help you improve your performance. You have all chosen a research article that focuses on an aspect of training, from sleep to nutrition to strength training. Today, you will share brief presentations of those abstracts and see what you can take away from one another to improve your training plans. As you listen to each presentation, write down one question or one comment for the presenter. After each presenter, I will call on a few of you to ask questions and share thoughts. We'll complete your 20-minute workouts at the end of class and if we don't get to all the presentations today, we'll finish them in our next class.

Instructional Task: Presentation of Abstracts

■ PRACTICE TASK

Students present their abstracts to the class. Include evaluation of how well students applied terminology in the scoring guide.

Ask three students to share thoughts or ask questions after each presenter.

Guiding questions for students:

- How can you apply this to your training?
- What information have you seen on social media that contradicts what you've heard today?

EMBEDDED OUTCOME: S4.H3.L1. Reinforce the importance of constructive student participation in offering comments or questions.

Extension

Students select one component from the presentations and add it to their training plans.

Student Choices/Differentiation

Students may use visual aids or technology in their presentations.

What to Look For

- Students can articulate how the content of the presentation applies to multi-sport training.
- Students' questions are relevant to the presentations.

Instructional Task: 20-Minute Workout

■ PRACTICE TASK

Students engage in the 20-minute running workout they brought to class as homework.

Student Choices/Differentiation

Students choose the workout and the intensity.

What to Look For

- Students are using correct form during the workout.
- Students are pushing themselves.
- Students included a warm-up and cool-down.

Formal and Informal Assessments

Scoring rubric for oral presentations

Closure

- Our goal today was to examine and share some of the research on training and competing in multi-sport events.
- The science of sport is always being researched, and we are constantly learning new things about how our bodies work. Each of you should have started thinking about how some of this research can help you in your training.
- In our next class, we will focus on specificity of training for triathlons by completing a brick workout.

Reflection

- Did students' abstracts cover a variety of topics?
- Next time, should I assign topics to research? Or assign research articles?
- Did students ask good questions? Should I provide scripted questions next time?

Homework

- Research brick workouts to prepare for our next class.
- Continue to journal your training and progress.

Resources

National Strength and Conditioning Association: www.NSCA.org
USA Triathlon: www.usatriathlon.org

LESSON 11: BRICK TRAINING

Grade-Level Outcomes

Primary Outcomes

Lifetime activities: Demonstrates competency and/or refines activity-specific movements in 2 or more lifetime activities (outdoor pursuits, individual-performance activities, aquatics, net/wall games or target games). (S1.H1.L1)

Fitness activities: Demonstrates competency in 2 or more specialized skills in health-related fitness activities. (S1.H3.L2)

Engages in physical activity: Creates a plan, trains for and participates in a community event with a focus on physical activity (e.g., 5K, triathlon, tournament, dance performance, cycling event). (S3.H6.L2)

Embedded Outcome

Challenge: Chooses an appropriate level of challenge to experience success and a desire to participate in a self-selected activity. (S5.H2.L2)

Lesson Objectives

The learner will:

- describe brick training as it applies to multi-sport events.
- participate in a brick-based workout.

Equipment and Materials

- Bikes and helmets
- Running gear, if applicable
- Old towels

Introduction

Complete the presentations from the previous class, if necessary.

We have focused on three disciplines of triathlon training. We can perform each activity separately, but when we put them together, muscle fatigue can play a huge role in how well we complete them in sequence. Fatiguing our muscles on the swim can affect our biking, and we definitely will feel our legs as we get off our bikes and transition to the run. It is this muscle memory and muscle fatigue that we want to incorporate into our training. Our goal is to teach our bodies to prepare effectively and efficiently for the next discipline's physical demands as we recover from the previous one. We do this by pairing two disciplines in the same workout, one after the other, with minimal or no rest between. This type of workout simulates a race and is called a brick workout. First let's watch this video of a transition to a run in a triathlon.

Show a video clip of transitioning from bike to run.

Instructional Task: Brick Workout–Biking to Running

■ PRACTICE TASK

Students should already be able to bike and ride the distances that you plan for the brick workout (i.e., the brick should reflect their training levels). Incorporate brick workouts into the targeted prep phase of training.

Have students ride their bikes around the parking lot or field to a designated dismount area, where students have laid a towel for their gear. Students dismount, remove their helmets (and other biking gear), and switch to running shoes (if necessary). They run 100 yards or meters and return to the dismount area. The first practice attempt should be at an easy pace so that students can learn the sequence. Students should complete two to three bricks, increasing their speed each time to approximate race pace.

Refinement

After students perform the first brick, debrief with questions. Students complete the next bricks on their own, allowing recovery time between sets.

Extension

After doing the mini brick transition, students complete a 5- to 10-mile (8 to 16 km) bike followed by a 1-mile (1.6 km) run.

Guiding questions for students:

- How do you think you will feel during the transition from biking to running? At the end of the run?
- How do you think you will feel during the transition from swimming to running?
- Which transition do you think will be the most difficult for you?

EMBEDDED OUTCOME: S5.H2.L2. Bricks are inherently challenging. Advise students to use a pace on the bike that will allow them to transition to, and complete, the run without exhausting themselves because they have to add the swim leg.

Student Choices/Differentiation

- Students may choose distances for transitions for the brick. Here is an example:
  - 0.5-mile (.8 km) bike + 400-meter run
  - 1.5-mile (2.4 km) bike + 600-meter run
  - 3-mile (4.8 km) bike + 800-meter run
- Students perform at their own pace.
- Students may adjust the number of repetitions.
- More experienced students can focus on improving their time for the transition.

What to Look For

- Students are reacting well to the transition from biking to running.
- Students are recovering from one discipline to the next.
- Students are maintaining form. If not, take note of where form is deteriorating.

Formal and Informal Assessments

Exit slip: What did you find most challenging about doing a "brick"?

Closure

- When you stopped biking and started running, your legs probably felt very heavy. Hence, the term *brick*, as you feel as if your legs are bricks. But you also can look at bricks as building blocks: putting together two disciplines during a workout.
- We train in bricks to simulate the demands of a triathlon. As our bodies adapt to the demands, our muscles will respond.
- This is a great training tool because it's so specific to the event and trains you for two disciplines in one workout.
- In our next class, we will build on the brick training and work on transitions.
- You will get wet, so bring all your gear for next class.

Reflection

- Was the brick workout too much? Should I adjust the distances after the first attempt?
- Are students growing more comfortable with transitioning their gear?
- Were their movements becoming more efficient?

Homework

- Review the term *transitions* in triathlons, and be ready to give a few tips in the next class.
- Continue journaling your training and progress.

Resources

USA Triathlon: www.usatriathlon.org

Internet keyword search: "brick training," "triathlon transitions"

LESSON 12: BRICK TRAINING WITH SWIM

Grade-Level Outcomes

Primary Outcomes

Lifetime activities: Demonstrates competency and/or refines activity-specific movements in 2 or more lifetime activities (outdoor pursuits, individual-performance activities, aquatics, net/wall games or target games). (S1.H1.L1)

Fitness activities: Demonstrates competency in 2 or more specialized skills in health-related fitness activities. (S1.H3.L2)

Engages in physical activity: Creates a plan, trains for and participates in a community event with a focus on physical activity (e.g., 5K, triathlon, tournament, dance performance, cycling event). (S3.H6.L2)

Embedded Outcome

Personal responsibility: Employs effective self-management skills to analyze barriers and modify physical activity patterns appropriately, as needed. (S4.H1.L1)

Lesson Objectives

The learner will:

- perform efficient transitions from swimming to biking and from biking to running in a simulated exercise.
- refine aspects of a transition to decrease time.

Equipment and Materials

- Hose, if available, or big buckets of water
- Swim gear
- Bike gear
- Running gear
- Clipboard
- Writing material
- Stopwatches or timers

Introduction

In our previous class, we shifted to the specificity of a triathlon with the focus on bricks. Now, we will hone in on the importance of transitions from one discipline to the next: swim to bike and bike to run. Both of those transitions play a key role in your performance in the triathlon as well as a key role in recording personal-best times in the event. Let's look at a transition from swim to bike.

Show a video clip of transitioning from swim to bike.

Instructional Task: Transition From Swim to Bike

■ **PRACTICE TASK**

Create a space to simulate a transition area in a race. Mark off the transition area, with a clear entrance and separate exit.

Each student sets up a personal transition area, with shoes, helmet, towel, food, and so on.

Students work in pairs, completing two full swim-to-bike transitions.

The transition simulation includes the following:

1. Students set up their bikes in a marked transition area, placing their personal gear next to their bikes.

2. Hose down gently or pour water over the students. (If a pool is available, students may start from the pool.) Once soaked, students run to the transition area—this should be a run of about 200 yards or meters through grass, dirt, gravel, and so on.

3. Partner 1 completes the brick as partner 2 times the brick, observes, and gives feedback on how to shave off time and be more efficient. Partner 2 takes notes or uses a checklist. Timing starts as soon as partner 1 enters the transition area to transition into biking gear. Timing ends as soon as partner 1 leaves the transition area and mounts the bike. (Although that is not the case typically, it allows students to practice a faster bike mount under simulated pressure.)

4. Partner 1 then bikes about 400 yards or meters and returns to the transition area.

5. Partner 2 gives feedback.

Partner 2 now prepares to simulate the transition from swim to bike, and partner 1 becomes time-keeper and observer.

Refinement

Students repeat the process, taking into account the feedback given and working to beat their times from trial 1.

Extension

Have the supporting partner record the transition instead of observing.

Guiding questions for students:

- What are you finding the most challenging with the transition? Shoes? Helmet? Socks?
- Were you able to reduce your transition time in the second try? If so, what did you change?

Student Choices/Differentiation

- Students work at their own pace.
- Students focus on the transition time, not the bike leg.
- Students select their partners.
- Students may review a video clip of transitions in a race.

What to Look For

- Students are remembering their bike helmets before leaving the transition area.
- Partners are engaged in observation and providing accurate feedback.
- Students show that they had planned the sequence of gear shifts before they reached their bikes.
- Students are able to move quickly and with control on the second attempt.

Instructional Task: Transition From Bike to Run

■ **PRACTICE TASK**

Using the same transition area and the same format from the previous task, students work with partners to complete two bike-to-run transitions.

The transition simulation includes the following:

1. Partner 1 bikes 400 to 800 yards or meters to approach the transition area.

2. Partner 1 dismounts, brings the bike into the transition area—running or walking—and changes to running gear, if applicable.

3. Partner 1 leaves the transition area and runs 400 yards or meters before returning to the transition area.

4. Partner 2 gives feedback.

Refinement

Students repeat the process, taking into account the feedback given and working to beat their times from trial 1.

Extension

Have the supporting partner record the transition instead of observing.

Guiding questions for students:

- What are you finding the most challenging with the transition? Shoes? Helmet? Dismount? Running bike into transition area?
- Were you able to reduce your transition time in the second try? If so, what did you change?

EMBEDDED OUTCOME: S4.H1.L1. Use those questions to have students analyze their transitions and modify their transition area or sequence to improve performance.

Student Choices/Differentiation

- Students work at their own pace.
- Students focus on the transition time, not the bike or run leg.
- Students select their partners.
- Students may review a video clip of transitions in a race.

What to Look For

- Students are running their bikes into transition smoothly. If not, take note of any struggles.
- Partners are engaged in observation and providing accurate feedback.
- Students show that they are planning their paths through transition before they dismount.
- Students are able to move quickly and with control on the second attempt.

Formal and Informal Assessments

Peer feedback and time sheets

Closure

- Today, you focused on your transitions and tried to work out some kinks. As you gain more experience with racing, you will tend to focus on this area a little more.
- A fast transition can reduce your time by a few minutes and can mean the difference between placing in your age group and not placing.
- How did you feel doing this brick? How does it compare with the run brick that we tried last time?
- Are you ready to try putting it all together?
- In our next class, we will head to an open-water area and practice an actual open-water group swim.

Reflection

- If students used a checklist or video, review it before the next class.
- Did students make the transition more smoothly on the second try?
- What's the best way to put both transitions together?

Homework

Continue your training and journaling.

Resources

USA Triathlon: www.usatriathlon.org

Active: www.active.com

Internet keyword search: "triathlon bricks," "brick training," "triathlon transition areas," "triathlon transitions"

LESSON 13: OPEN-WATER SWIM SIMULATION

Grade-Level Outcomes

Primary Outcomes

Lifetime activities: Refines activity-specific movement skills in 1 or more lifetime activities (outdoor pursuits, individual-performance activities, aquatics, net/wall games or target games). (S1.H1.L2)

Fitness activities: Demonstrates competency in 2 or more specialized skills in health-related fitness activities. (S1.H3.L2)

Engages in physical activity: Creates a plan, trains for and participates in a community event with a focus on physical activity (e.g., 5K, triathlon, tournament, dance performance, cycling event). (S3.H6.L2)

Embedded Outcomes

Physical activity knowledge: Identifies issues associated with exercising in heat, humidity and cold. (S3.H3.L1)

Challenge: Chooses an appropriate level of challenge to experience success and desire to participate in a self-selected physical activity. (S5.H2.L2)

Lesson Objectives

The learner will:

- demonstrate swimming techniques used in open water.
- identify safety concerns when swimming in open water.

Equipment and Materials

- Rescue tubes
- Kayaks or paddleboards (safety boats)
- Swim gear
- Brightly colored swim caps

Introduction

Although we have conducted most of our swim training in the pool, the swim leg of a triathlon usually takes place in an open body of water where the elements are changing constantly. Today, we will conduct a group open-water training swim and discuss safety and strategy.

Instructional Task: Open-Water Swim Safety

■ **PRACTICE TASK**

Hold a question and answer period about open-water swim safety.

Guiding questions for students:

- What should you take into account when swimming in open water and might not think about when you are in the pool?
  - Water temperature?
  - Identification?
  - Lifeguard?
  - Open-water swim conditions (ocean water versus fresh water)—pollutants, tides, current, wind?
  - Safety equipment?

EMBEDDED OUTCOME: S3.H3.L1. Use these questions to help students understand the impact of temperature on performance and the need for hydration and, potentially, wetsuits.

Student Choices/Differentiation

Help students understand open-water swims by showing a video or a slideshow of open-water swimming.

What to Look For

- Students can recognize the differences between open-water swimming and pool swimming.
- Students can identify the differences between open-water lake swimming and ocean swimming.

Instructional Task: Simulated Open-Water Swim

■ PRACTICE TASK

Students participate in a simulated open-water swim:

- Remove lane lines from the pool and have students who are waiting cheer and splash to mimic choppy, noisy race conditions in open water.
- Predetermine a distance or course (e.g., out and back, triangle, loop).
- Give each participant a brightly colored cap for safety.
- Review sighting: Have students warm up in shallow water, practicing their sighting while warming up their bodies.
- Discuss what to do if anyone needs assistance: hand up, yell.
- Simulate a triathlon start. For larger groups, use a wave start.

Note: If an open-water course is available, be sure to have lifeguard coverage on land and in a small craft, such as a kayak.

Guiding questions for students:

- Why do triathletes wear brightly colored caps?
- What do you think will be most difficult?
- What are some of your fears?
- What was most difficult?
- Did you overcome your fears?

EMBEDDED OUTCOME: S5.H2.L2. Open-water swimming can be very unnerving for students because of the conditions and number of people in the water. Use this task to debrief about the challenge aspect.

Student Choices/Differentiation

- Allow for multiple distances in the course to account for students' various skill and training levels.
- Strong swimmers may complete the course twice.

What to Look For

- Students are sighting successfully.
- Students are able to maintain a steady sightline while swimming.
- Students react calmly if they bump into another swimmer.

Formal and Informal Assessments

Exit slip: What was the most challenging aspect of the open-water swim simulation?

Closure

- Open-water swimming is very different from pool swimming. You have no walls for taking a break, and safety becomes front and center during training. You should never swim by yourself in open water. What safety considerations should you remember when swimming in open water?

- Many people are afraid of open-water swimming, especially when the elements are unknown. Like anything, the more you practice race-like situations (open water versus pool), the more comfortable and confident you will become by race day.

- As we approach race day, everyone should be tapering off on his or her training. In class, we will piggyback on where everyone is in their training and will reserve a day for active recovery, with yoga.

Reflection

- Were students afraid?
- Should this lesson occur earlier in the module?
- Did I have enough safety equipment?

Homework

- Continue to train for the race! We are almost in the home stretch.
- Continue your journals.
- Create a snack plan for before, during, and after the triathlon that you can use in the event.

Resources

USA Triathlon: www.usatriathlon.org

USA Swimming: www.usaswimming.org

US Masters Swimming. www.usms.org

Internet keyword search: "open-water swim," "triathlon starts," "triathlon nutrition"

LESSON 14: FINAL RACE PREPARATION

Grade-Level Outcomes

Primary Outcomes

Fitness activities: Demonstrates competency in 1 or more specialized skills in health-related fitness activities. (S1.H3.L1)

Stress management: Applies stress-management strategies (e.g., mental imagery, relaxation techniques, deep breathing, aerobic exercise, meditation) to reduce stress. (S3.H14.L2)

Nutrition: Creates a snack plan for before, during and after exercise that addresses nutrition needs for each phase. (S3.H13.L2)

Embedded Outcome

Engages in physical activity: Creates a plan, trains for and participates in a community event with a focus on physical activity (e.g., 5K, triathlon, tournament, dance performance, cycling event). (S3.H6.L2)

Lesson Objectives

The learner will:

- demonstrate various yoga poses.
- practice controlled breathing.
- develop a snack plan for race day.

Equipment and Materials

- Yoga video
- Yoga cards
- Yoga mats
- Stretch straps or towels

Introduction

As we come closer to race day, you should be into the tapering-off phase of your training plans. Recovery is key to your bodies' ability to adapt to the hard training you have been putting in. Today, we will practice yoga that is designed specifically for triathletes. We will focus on poses and stretches that will help with your swimming, biking, and running. You can incorporate all of these poses and stretches into your training. Yoga also is a great way to reduce your stress and improve your breathing technique. We also will think about fueling our bodies for the event by making a snack plan for before, during, and after the race.

Instructional Task: Yoga for Triathletes

■ PRACTICE TASK

Students follow a yoga video or instructor-led yoga class focused on poses to increase flexibility for swimming, biking, and running.

Refinements

- Observe the quality of the poses. Provide feedback about proper alignment of body segments.
- Provide feedback to improve breathing technique.

Extension

Ask students to demonstrate to their peers poses that they might know from their own practice.

Guiding questions for students:

- Where did you feel most tight?
- What poses did you find most helpful?
- How do you feel after practicing yoga?
- What poses do you think you can incorporate into your training and recovery?
- How can you use the breathing techniques in yoga to manage your stress in other areas?

Student Choices/Differentiation

- Have stretch straps available for students who are less flexible.
- Modify poses for students with low flexibility.

What to Look For

- Students are moving through the poses smoothly.
- Students are using proper form when demonstrating various poses.
- Students are focused and practicing their breathing techniques.

Instructional Task: Snack Plan

■ PRACTICE TASK

Review the nutritional needs for the event, including hydration and post-event refueling.

- Quick energy about an hour before and possibly during the event if over an hour
- Hydration during all phases
- Carbohydrate and protein within 30 minutes after the event

In small groups, have students develop a snack plan for the event and then share their ideas with the class.

Student Choices/Differentiation

- Use a poster or other visual aid for key nutrition points.
- Students choose their groups.

What to Look For

- Students are engaged in the discussion and plan development.
- Students can identify the right type of snacks for each phase.
- Students are including fluids in their plans.

Formal and Informal Assessments

Exit slip: How can yoga improve your performance?

Closure

- We are at the end of our training and race day approaches. What concerns do you still have?
- What are some fears?
- What are you looking forward to most?
- Don't forget to review the triathlon course before our next class.

Reflection

- Review exit slips to see if students understand how yoga can help them.
- What do I need to review about the event to make sure that students are ready?

Homework

- Complete your final workouts and final journaling.
- If the event is a community event, students should review the course online. If it's a class-created event, provide course maps as handouts or on the school's physical education website. (Embedded outcome: S3.H6.L2)
- Set some personal goals for the triathlon, and get ready for race day!

Resources

Local yoga chalet

USA Triathlon: www.usatriathlon.org

Flexible Warrior 1.0: Athletic Yoga for Triathletes DVD set

Internet keyword search: "yoga for athletes," "pre-race snacks," "post-race snacks," "hydration for triathlon"

LESSON 15: RACE DAY

Grade-Level Outcomes

Primary Outcomes

Lifetime activities: Refines activity-specific movement skills in 1 or more lifetime activities (outdoor pursuits, individual-performance activities, aquatics, net/wall games or target games). (S1.H1.L2)

Fitness activities: Demonstrates competency in 2 or more specialized skills in health-related fitness activities. (S1.H3.L2)

Engages in physical activity: Creates a plan, trains for and participates in a community event with a focus on physical activity (e.g., 5K, triathlon, tournament, dance performance, cycling event). (S3.H6.L2)

Embedded Outcome

Challenge: Chooses an appropriate level of challenge to experience success and desire to participate in a self-selected physical activity. (S5.H2.L2)

Lesson Objectives

The learner will:

- complete a triathlon.

Equipment and Materials

- Swim gear
- Bike gear
- Running gear
- Course (if completing a class-created triathlon): signs, markers, registration table, lifeguards, and so on

Introduction

Today is race day! All of you have put in a lot of work preparing for today, both in and outside of the classroom. Believe in the work that you have done and, as a class, what we have learned to prepare us for this day. Put into practice the little things to make your transitions smoother and to make each leg of the triathlon successful. The work is done, and today is the day that you reap the benefits of your training and, most important, have fun and enjoy your success. Good luck to everyone!

Instructional Task:
Registration and Student Transition Set-Up

■ PRACTICE TASK

Students register and get a registration packet.

Go through the registration packet with students. Explain where to place registration numbers on bikes, helmets, and shirts.

Students set up their personal transition areas.

Note: If you set up the course, students can review the course before participating. You will need assistance in running the event, including lifeguards, registration volunteers, volunteers to mark the course and provide directions during the event, and finish line volunteers. You also must provide EMT or first aid personnel.

Guiding questions for students:

- Where do the numbers get placed?
- What color is your swim cap? What does this mean?
- What time does the race start?
- What concerns are you having before the race?

Student Choices/Differentiation

Encourage students to participate within their limits, do their personal best, and focus on their own goals.

What to Look For

- Students placed numbers on their bikes correctly.
- Students placed numbers on their running shirts correctly.
- Everyone found their area to set up for transition.

Instructional Task: Complete Triathlon

■ **PRACTICE TASK**

Students complete the triathlon.

Note: Arrange for videotaping of the event to use in the last class.

EMBEDDED OUTCOME: S5.H2.L2. After the triathlon, ask students if they felt challenged by the event and in what ways.

What to Look For

- Everyone completed the swim.
- Everyone transitioned onto the bike.
- Everyone finished the bike.
- Everyone transitioned into the run.
- Everyone finished the run.

Formal and Informal Assessments

Completion of triathlon

Closure

- After a couple of months of training, you all completed your first triathlon! My hope is that you are all very proud of yourself and your accomplishment today.
- Next class when we meet, we are going to reflect on the race, our journey, and what the future holds for you.
- As the race is fresh in your head, at some point today, write down your thoughts and some notes on the entire day. Write down things that went well, things that didn't go so well, things you felt prepared for, and things you felt unprepared for. Also, come up with one word to describe your feelings after the race.
- I am proud of all of you and I hope that you are feeling proud of yourselves! I am looking forward to hearing your reflections in our next class.

Reflection

- Was the chosen race distance realistic?
- What, if anything, could you add to your teachings to make the students more successful?

Homework

- Write down your reflections on the race. Did you meet your goals?
- What did you do well?
- What could you do better?

LESSON 16: REFLECTION AND POST-RACE CELEBRATION

Grade-Level Outcomes

Primary Outcome

Engages in physical activity: Creates a plan, trains for and participates in a community event with a focus on physical activity (e.g., 5K, triathlon, tournament, dance performance, cycling event). (S3.H6.L2)

Embedded Outcome

Social interaction: Identifies the opportunity for social support in a self-selected physical activity or dance. (S5.H4.L1)

Lesson Objectives

The learner will:

- reflect on the effectiveness of his or her training plan.
- identify his or her strengths and weaknesses in the disciplines.

Equipment and Materials

- Writing material
- Whiteboards or poster board
- Results from triathlon

Introduction

In our previous class, everyone participated in the triathlon that we have been training for. Today, I want you to share your reflections of the event and talk about what you liked, what you didn't like, and maybe what you would do differently going forward or training for your next event. At the end of most triathlons and other endurance events, participants partake in refreshments and a little celebration in which everyone congratulates and supports one another. Because this is the end of our event and the module, we'll have a celebration of our own at the end of class!

Instructional Task: Triathlon Reflection

■ **PRACTICE TASK**

Students discuss their race reflections in small groups.

In the same groups, students discuss the guiding questions that weren't covered in their reflections.

Hand out the triathlon results to each student, with times for each disciple and both transitions, if possible.

Have students calculate the pace for each of the disciplines and reflect on the results.

Students present their reflections to the class.

Guiding questions for students:

- What areas of the race went well?
- What did you struggle with?
- What part was most difficult?
- What part were you most prepared for?
- Did you attain your personal goal?
- What area do you feel that you improved on the most?
- What would you change in your training if you could go back?

- What were your words to describe the event?
- If we did this again, what would you change about the event?

Student Choices/Differentiation

Create a handout with guiding questions for each group to answer.

What to Look For

- Students are engaged in the small groups.
- Students are analyzing their performance accurately.

Instructional Task: Module Celebration

■ PRACTICE TASK

Hold a small party with refreshments. Show video clips of the event and each student who participated. Hand out completion certificates, if desired. Invite other school personnel and families, if feasible.

EMBEDDED OUTCOME: S5.H4.L1. Ask each student to compliment some aspect of at least two other students' performance in the race and share feelings about the event.

What to Look For

- Students are supporting one another genuinely.
- Students are interacting with students who they typically don't interact with.
- Students seem to have a sense of accomplishment.

Formal and Informal Assessments

Student reflections

Closure

- I think this class can have a profound effect on your health today and in the future. My hope is that taking this class has sparked something in each of you that will encourage you to compete in another triathlon or multi-sport event.
- I also hope that you learned something about yourself and what it means to train for an event.
- As you saw when you were searching for an event to compete in, multi-sport events occur just about every weekend, in many places, with many opportunities to be a part of them, from participating to volunteering.
- I hope that you continue to compete and train for races. as this is an opportunity to incorporate fitness into your life!
- It's time to think about your next module, so please review your choices before our next class.

Reflection

- Review the written reflections from students.
- What were the biggest challenges in teaching the module?
- What should I do differently next time? Which aspects went really well?
- Do we need to spend more time on training plans?

Homework

Choose the next module.

Resources

USA Triathlon: www.usatriathlon.org

CHAPTER 7

Extending Students' Skills and Knowledge to Net/Wall Games

Net and wall games play an important part in the Grade-Level Outcomes for high school students because so many of these games can be played throughout one's lifetime. They provide great opportunities for physical activity and social interaction, and they can be as recreational or competitive as the players wish. Fortunately, teachers have a wide variety of net/wall sports from which to choose (e.g., racquetball, squash, badminton, pickleball, tennis, table tennis, speedminton, volleyball, wallyball). In this chapter, the focus is on two racket sports that are easily accessible in school settings—badminton and tennis. Like other racket activities, they have the advantages of needing only one other person to play, a minimal amount of equipment, and ready transfer of skills and strategies to other net/wall games.

This chapter offers three modules of lessons in net/wall games. The Badminton Module, contributed by long-time physical education teacher Charla Tedder Krahnke, begins with a review of the basics that students should have learned in middle school and continues helping them build the skills and learn the strategies for participating at a higher level of performance. The Tennis Module, contributed by Melanie Perreault, assistant professor of motor behavior at the College at Brockport, State University of New York, provides beginners with step-by-step progressions and lots of practice opportunities to help develop their skills while still experiencing success. Tennis requires students to develop their striking skills with a longer and heavier racket than the one used in badminton. Also, the tennis ball is more difficult to control than a shuttlecock, making tennis a challenging activity to learn. The Tennis Doubles Module, contributed by Charlie

Rizzuto, a health and physical education teacher at Oyster Bay High School on Long Island, NY, builds on the fundamentals learned in the Tennis Module but focuses specifically on doubles strategies, communication, and net play. This module is available in the e-book and on the web resource only.

Both the Badminton Module and Tennis Doubles Module are presented through the sports education model (Siedentop, Hastie, & van der Mars, 2011). In sport education, the module (unit) is played out like a sport season, with pre-season, in-season, and post-season activities, as well as a culminating event or festival to celebrate the end of the "season." Throughout the modules, students have opportunities not only to practice the skills and strategies of the sport, but also to practice leadership skills, develop team spirit, and immerse themselves in a sport culture. Students are responsible for particular roles on the team that can include coach, general manager, fitness trainer and publicist, to name just a few. You can decide which roles are most relevant for your students. You might even want to designate someone as social media director to tap into the technology that surrounds sport. Having students take on these roles as they experience the flow of a season can make sport and physical activity more engaging for them as well as provide numerous opportunities for learning experiences under Standards 4 and 5. Of course, you can teach badminton and tennis doubles without the sport education component if you wish. You also can use these modules as examples of how to teach using the sport education model and apply the ideas to completely different activities.

For easy reference, each module begins with a block plan chart of the Grade-Level Outcomes that are addressed within the module. The modules in this chapter address Grade-Level Outcomes under all five standards, but the emphases are on Standards 1, 2, and 4. For tennis, the learning activities are directed at demonstrating competency in tennis skills, while in badminton and tennis doubles, the emphasis is on refining skills already learned. All three modules focus on terminology and concepts (Outcomes S2.H1.L1 and S2.H2.L1) and rules and etiquette (Outcome S4.H2.L1). Using the sport education model, both the Badminton Module and the Tennis Doubles Module also provide students with multiple opportunities to take on leadership responsibilities (Outcome S4.H3. L2). All three modules provide great examples for teaching and refining racket activities for a lifetime of participation. The Tennis Doubles Module is available on the e-book and the web resource only.

BADMINTON MODULE

Lessons in this module were contributed by **Charla Tedder Krahnke**, who taught physical education for 31 years and is a former national and state (North Carolina) teacher of the year.

Grade-Level Outcomes Addressed, by Lesson	Lessons														
	1	2	3	4	5	6	7	8	9	10	11	12	13	14	15
Standard 1. The physically literate individual demonstrates competency in a variety of motor skills and movement patterns.															
Refines activity-specific movement skills in 1 or more lifetime activities (outdoor pursuits, individual-performance activities, aquatics, net/wall games or target games). (S1.H1.L2)	P	P	P	P	P	P	P	P	P	P	P	P	P	P	P
Standard 2. The physically literate individual applies knowledge of concepts, principles, strategies and tactics related to movement and performance.															
Applies the terminology associated with exercise and participation in selected individual-performance activities, dance, net/wall games, target games, aquatics and/or outdoor pursuits appropriately. (S2.H1.L1)	E														
Identifies and discusses the historical and cultural roles of games, sports and dance in a society. (S2.H1.L2)											P				
Uses movement concepts and principles (e.g., force, motion, rotation) to analyze and improve performance of self and/or others in a selected skill. (S2.H2.L1)				P							E				
Describes the speed vs. accuracy trade-off in throwing and striking skills. (S2.H2.L2)								E							
Creates a practice plan to improve performance for a self-selected skill. (S2.H3.L1)											E		E		
Standard 3. The physically literate individual demonstrates the knowledge and skills to achieve and maintain a health-enhancing level of physical activity and fitness.															
Discusses the benefits of a physically active lifestyle as it relates to college or career productivity. (S3.H1.L1)											P				
Investigates the relationships among physical activity, nutrition and body composition. (S3.H1.L2)											P				
Evaluates—according to their benefits, social support network and participation requirements—activities that can be pursued in the local environment. (S3.H4.L1)								E							
Identifies stress-management strategies (e.g., mental imagery, relaxation techniques, deep breathing, aerobic exercise, meditation) to reduce stress. (S3.H14.L1)							E								
Standard 4. The physically literate individual exhibits responsible personal and social behavior that respects self and others.															
Accepts differences between personal characteristics and the idealized body images and elite performance levels portrayed in various media. (S4.H1.L2)											P				
Exhibits proper etiquette, respect for others and teamwork while engaging in physical activity and/or social dance. (S4.H2.L1)				E				E					E		E
Examines moral and ethical conduct in specific competitive situations (e.g., intentional fouls, performance-enhancing substances, gambling, current events in sport). (S4.H2.L2)														E	
Uses communication skills and strategies that promote team or group dynamics. (S4.H3.L1)		E													

(continued)

BADMINTON MODULE *(CONTINUED)*

Grade-Level Outcomes Addressed, by Lesson	Lessons														
	1	2	3	4	5	6	7	8	9	10	11	12	13	14	15
Standard 4. The physically literate individual exhibits responsible personal and social behavior that respects self and others.															
Assumes a leadership role (e.g., task or group leader, referee, coach) in a physical activity setting. (S4.H3.L2)	E							E		E					
Solves problems and thinks critically in physical activity and/or dance settings, both as an individual and in groups. (S4.H4.L1)						E									
Applies best practices for participating safely in physical activity, exercise and dance (e.g., injury prevention, proper alignment, hydration, use of equipment, implementation of rules, sun protection). (S4.H5.L1)								P							
Standard 5. The physically literate individual recognizes the value of physical activity for health, enjoyment, challenge, self-expression and/or social interaction.															
Analyzes the health benefits of a self-selected physical activity. (S5.H1.L1)										P					
Selects and participates in physical activities or dance that meet the need for self-expression and enjoyment. (S5.H3.L1)					E										
Identifies the opportunity for social support in a self-selected physical activity or dance. (S5.H4.L1)			E		E							E			

P = Primary; E = Embedded

LESSON 1: SKILL REVIEW AND PRE-ASSESSMENT

Grade-Level Outcomes

Primary Outcome

Lifetime activities: Refines activity-specific movement skills in 1 or more lifetime activities (outdoor pursuits, individual-performance activities, aquatics, net/wall games or target games). (S1.H1.L2)

Embedded Outcome

Movement concepts, principles & knowledge: Applies the terminology associated with exercise and participation in selected individual-performance activities, dance, net/wall games, target games, aquatics and/or outdoor pursuits appropriately. (S2.H1.L1)

Lesson Objectives

The learner will:

- perform the two basic badminton grips (V-grip and thumb grip).
- perform the basic forehand and backhand shot series.
- demonstrate basic offensive and defensive strategies.
- perform the basic forehand and backhand lift shots.

Equipment and Materials

- Foam balls, large shuttlecocks, and regulation shuttlecocks: 3 to 5 for every 2 students if available
- Regulation and modified badminton rackets: 1 per student
- Tape for targets

Introduction

Our next module is sport education badminton. Today, we will review the basic grips as well as the basic shots and strategies you learned in middle school. I will then introduce a new shot called the lift. This is similar to the clear shot. Throughout the module, you will learn a variety of new shots, badminton terminology and concepts, and effective strategies.

Instructional Task: Team Selection

■ PRACTICE TASK

Captains select their teams while the rest of the students are reviewing the skills presented in the next instructional tasks.

Note: Select team captains using an exit slip from a previous class that asks students who are interested to fill out a captain's application with the prompt "I would be a good badminton captain because . . ."

Give captains a role sheet and index cards. While watching the class participate in the skills review, the captains choose six evenly matched teams without knowing which teams are theirs.

After creating the teams, captains choose from among six cards, each with a team number on it. Captains then join their teams in the skills review.

What to Look For

- Teams are even as far as ability and social skills.
- The captains performed this activity in a respectful manner.
- Students with learning or physical disabilities are on a team with a buddy for assistance and safety.

Instructional Task: Basic Badminton Grips

■ PRACTICE TASK

Review grips with students. Remind students of the benefits of a good grip: more accurate net shots and serves, more powerful smashes, and ready for both sides.

Working in pairs, students practice the grips.

Guiding questions for students:

- Who can tell me what the V-grip looks like when executed properly?
- Who can tell me what the thumb grip looks like when executed properly?

Extension

Have students hand the rackets to one another and call out a grip. Partners must take the rackets using the proper grip. Students provide feedback to one another.

Student Choices/Differentiation

- Students choose their partners.
- Students may choose regulation or modified badminton rackets.

What to Look For

V-Grip

- Students create a V with the thumb and index finger when gripping the racket, rather than grabbing the racket in the palm and wrapping the fist around it.
- Students make a V shape rather than a more rounded U shape.

Thumb Grip

- Students allow the thumb to fall naturally without squeezing the handle rather than flattening the thumb onto the implement.

Instructional Task: Basic Badminton Shots

■ PRACTICE TASK

Review the clear, drop, smash, and block shots. Working in pairs, students hit shots directly to each other when you call them out. Task is executed with no net.

Extensions

- Students work in groups of four, adding a net.
- Repeat, gradually increasing the speed of the calls.
- Repeat, with smash and block shots grouped together after the smash is practiced by itself. For example, you will call, "Smash, block combo."
- Students may use a cues checklist to evaluate their own skills for further improvement, or you may use this as a formal assessment.

Refinements

- If students do not use enough force on the drop shot, have them focus on the follow-through.
- You can use video analysis to refine skill execution.
- Be sure that students pronate and snap the wrist on the smash. That increases power while keeping the shuttlecock in bounds.

EMBEDDED OUTCOME: S2.H1.L1. Students must know the names of the various shots in order to use them correctly on your call.

Guiding questions for students:
- Who can give me one teaching cue for the clear shot?
- Repeat question for other shots as you wish.

Student Choices/Differentiation
- Students may choose regulation badminton rackets or modified badminton rackets.
- Students may choose foam balls, larger shuttlecocks, or regulation shuttlecocks.
- Students choose their partners or groups.

What to Look For

Students are executing all of the critical elements of the skills: foot placement, opposition, torso alignment, transition, and follow-through.

Instructional Task: Modified Game Play, Pre-assessment

■ PRACTICE TASK

Students play modified games with no nets.

Students begin each point with a feed and use rally scoring. Students play for a specified time, then rotate.

Extensions
- Use this task as a pre-assessment. Allow students to play as you take notes on your observations.
- Repeat game using a net.

Student Choices/Differentiation
- Students may choose regulation badminton rackets or modified badminton rackets.
- Students may choose foam balls, larger shuttlecocks, or regulation shuttlecocks.
- Students choose their partners or groups.

What to Look For
- Students remember the basic concepts of strategy and game play from middle school.
- Students return to the defensive home position after a shot.
- Students hit to various spots so that their opponents have to move.
- Students try to place shots strategically based on their opponents' positioning.
- Students use different shots to find success.

Instructional Task: Forehand and Backhand Lift Shot

■ PRACTICE TASK

Demonstrate the forehand and backhand lift shots. After each initial demonstration, students practice the movements on their own for 20 repetitions.

Refinement

Refine skill by displaying pictures or playing a video clip for students to view as you circulate to correct form. If any students execute the movement pattern with 100 percent accuracy (possibly a badminton player), ask them to also circulate and help other students.

Student Choices/Differentiation

Students may choose regulation badminton rackets or modified badminton rackets.

What to Look For

Forehand

- Students are using the V-grip (not necessary but recommended).
- Racket is out in front of the body.
- Hips are rotating.
- Students are using a full underhand swing.
- Wrist bends (breaks) then flicks forward.
- Arm rotates inward after assumed contact.

Backhand

- Students are using the thumb grip (not necessary but recommended).
- Racket is out in front of the body.
- Hips are rotating.
- Students are using a full underhand swing.
- Wrist bends back (breaks) then flicks forward.
- Arm rotates outward after assumed contact.

Instructional Task: Lift Shot Against Wall

■ PRACTICE TASK

Working in pairs, students strike an object against a wall.

Students are positioned about 10 feet (3 m) away from the wall. One student kneels next to the other and tosses the object out in front of her at around shoulder height. Students switch every 10 practice attempts. After each student has practiced the forehand once, they switch to the backhand.

Extension

Students practice over the net. One partner attempts a drop shot or short shot, and the receiver attempts a lift shot to the back of the court. After five hits, students switch roles.

Guiding questions for students:

- Is your swing complete? Did you finish the movement?
- Are you breaking your wrist as you anticipate contact?

Student Choices/Differentiation

- Students may choose regulation badminton rackets or modified badminton rackets.
- Students can choose foam balls, larger shuttlecocks, or regulation shuttlecocks.
- Students choose their partners.

What to Look For

- Same as previous task, but with the addition of object height.
- The object contacts the wall above the line.

Formal and Informal Assessments

- Peer assessments by captains
- Informal pre-assessment of game play

Closure

- What grip is recommended when executing a forehand lift shot?
- What grip is recommended when executing a backhand lift shot?
- When would be a good time to try to execute a lift shot? (Answer: When your opponent brings you to the net with a drop shot.)
- If you simply watched the path of the shuttlecock, what other shot might a lift shot look like? (Answer: clear shot)
- Who can tell me why I chose the lift shot as our first new shot? (Answer: Today we reviewed the clear shot.)
- Now let's announce our teams. (Teams are announced. No trades. Take a few minutes to discuss team names.)

Reflection

- Were students able to transfer previous learning into today's lesson? If not, what do they need to practice?
- Were students able to hit the object high while executing the lift shots?
- How well did students who acted as coaches work with their peers?

Homework

Watch a video clip on the school's physical education website about badminton facts. We'll have a verbal quiz next class.

Resources

Kumar, S. (2010). *Badminton skills and rules*. Darya Ganj, New Delhi: Khel Sahitya Kendra.

Badminton World Federation: www.bwfbadminton.org

World Badminton: www.worldbadminton.com

PRE-SEASON TEACHER ASSESSMENT

Name: _____

1 = Never, 2 = Sometimes, 3 = Most of the time

Team name Students	Hits to the open space	Hits various strokes: Clears Drop shots Smash	Hit various shots to move the opponent	Moves back to home position after shots	Keeps short serves low and high serves deep

Teacher suggestions for team coach:

From L.C. MacDonald, R.J. Doan, and S. Chepko, eds., 2018, *Lesson planning for high school physical education* (Reston, VA: SHAPE America; Champaign, IL: Human Kinetics).

LESSON 2: SPORT EDUCATION ROLES

Grade-Level Outcomes

Primary Outcome

Lifetime activities: Refines activity-specific movement skills in 1 or more lifetime activities (e.g., outdoor pursuits, individual-performance activities, aquatics, net/wall games and target games). (S1.H1.L2)

Embedded Outcomes

Working with others: Uses communication skills and strategies that promote team or group dynamics. (S4.H3.L1)

Working with others: Assumes a leadership role (e.g., task or group leader, referee, coach) in a physical activity setting. (S4.H3.L2)

Lesson Objectives

The learner will:

- perform the short and long serves in a practice drill setting.
- define and demonstrate force and trajectory as they apply to the short and long serve.
- use communication skills with teammates during team practices, health-related fitness activities, and drills.

Equipment and Materials

- Badminton rackets
- Shuttlecocks
- Nets
- Hula-Hoops
- Poly spots
- Cones

Introduction

Today, we will begin our badminton sport education season and also find out what you learned about the sport in your homework. Find a partner and share two interesting facts about badminton. Now, join another group and share. Switch. Each group will choose the most interesting fact shared and share that with the class. Who found out why some shuttlecocks are made of feathers while some are plastic and other materials? How fast can a shuttlecock travel during a professional match? This is quite amazing. Today, we will begin our lesson by establishing teams and reviewing the gym procedures of sport education. Remember, as in the past sport education seasons, fair play points begin now! Our lesson today will be on serving strategy.

Instructional Task: Team Organization

■ **PRACTICE TASK**

Assign teams a home grid. Give captains a team folder with an assigned color and number. Teams discuss and assign roles (captain, coach, manager, exercise specialist, publicist, motivator, head official, head statistician, sports council), and the captain fills out the role sheets.

Include team name, mascot, and names of players (roles and something that they like to do).

Students begin making a team poster.

Students begin working on their roles:

- **Exercise specialist:** Design the warm-up using a variety of health- and skill-related activities.
- **Coach:** Plan a team warm-up in the team's home grid. Review shots.
- **Motivator:** Begin making a team cheer.
- **Captain:** Members of each team read and sign contracts stating that they will:
  - accept the captain's decisions without question;
  - work hard to improve their skills;
  - listen to the captain and coach during practices and games; and
  - perform their roles to the best of their ability when on the duty team.

Guiding questions for students:

- Why is it important for you to warm up before physical activity?
- What warm-up exercises could you use for badminton?

Student Choices/Differentiation

Students choose the roles on the team that fit them best.

What to Look For

- Team members are working together to decide on a team name, mascot, and roles.
- Every team member is contributing.

Instructional Task: Team Warm-Up

■ PRACTICE TASK

The exercise specialist or coach (or both) lead each team in their warm-up.

Guiding questions for students:

- Why are you performing each particular exercise?
- Which exercises are dynamic and which are plyometric?

EMBEDDED OUTCOME: S4.H3.L2. Students in the coach and/or exercise specialist roles lead their teammates in the warm-up. Provide feedback on how they perform in their leadership role.

Student Choices/Differentiation

Students may choose the equipment used and the types of warm-ups.

What to Look For

Using a rubric, assess the team warm-ups for how well they address health- and skill-related components, such as

- increases team members' heart rates gradually,
- includes major muscle groups used in badminton, and
- includes movements used in the game.

Instructional Task: Long and Short Serve

■ PRACTICE TASK

Demonstrate long and short serves. Highlight the force and trajectory for each type of serve. Teams practice serves in their grids, alternating long and short serves. Place poly spots as targets.

Refinement

Students stand as close to the middle of the service box and the short service line as possible. Singles players should move 1 or 2 yards or meters back.

Guiding questions for students:
- What do you need to do to generate more force if your serve is falling short?
- How would you change your movement pattern if your short serves are too long?

Student Choices/Differentiation

Students choose their equipment.

What to Look For

Long Serve
- Students drop the shuttlecock before starting the swing.
- Students drop the shuttlecock in front and to the side.
- Students contact the shuttlecock at knee height and hit the shuttle up and out.

Short Serve
- As noted for long serve, but students push the shuttlecock rather than hit it.
- Students contact the shuttlecock at thigh height and keep it as low and short as possible.

Instructional Task: Team Practice

■ PRACTICE TASK

Half of the teams use a court with a net, and the other half work without one. Teams with a net serve to an opponent five times. Type of serve (long or short) depends on where the opponents are standing, and serve should be hit to a space. Students serve until all feel comfortable and are moving their opponents.

Refinements
- Students focus on hitting the shuttlecock at a higher contact point.
- Students drop the shuttlecock closer to the racket instead of in front of the racket.

Extensions
- The teams without a net serve into a hoop. When the shuttlecock lands in the hoop, students take a step back.
- Place poly spots with points around to represent effective short and long serves. Students serve 10 shuttlecocks each and keep the score. These may be added for team points.

Student Choices/Differentiation

Students choose their equipment.

What to Look For
- Servers are moving their opponents.
- Servers are mixing up their serves.

Instructional Task: Serving Competition

■ PRACTICE TASK

Set one hoop in the short-service area and one hoop in the long-service area. Teams try to be first to hit all shuttlecocks into the hoop. If the shuttlecock is in, it may not be taken out. At end of the set time, teams score 2 points per shuttlecock in a hoop.

Student Choices/Differentiation

Students may choose direction in which to serve as well as long or short serves.

What to Look For

- Most students are using proper technique.
- Most students are hitting the short- or long-service courts successfully.

Instructional Task: Serve Strategy and Practice

■ PRACTICE TASK

Discuss when to use high, low, and flick serves, and the importance of varying your serves.

- High serve: Used in singles only.
- Low serve: Used in singles and doubles.
- Flick serve: Used mostly in doubles.
- Drive serve: Most effective when it is unexpected, because it is hit hard, low, and flat.
- Backhand low serve: Shorter distance to travel and is hit in front of the body. The opponent has less time to react.

In grids, teams practice each type of serve as the coach calls them out. Students who are not practicing complete a peer assessment with a checklist of teaching cues for the serves being practiced. Record the serves. Students switch roles after 10 serves.

Extension

Servers practice the serve and opponents try to return it. Students switch roles after five serves.

Refinement

Teammates should provide feedback from the checklist to help refine skill.

EMBEDDED OUTCOME: S4.H3.L1 Remind students about the importance of how to communicate with one another, including using positive reinforcement and support for teammates. Provide corrective feedback as appropriate.

Student Choices/Differentiation

- Students choose the serve that works best for the situation.
- Students choose their equipment.

What to Look For

- Students are successful at the different types of serves.
- Students are varying their serves when facing an opponent.
- Players are using the checklist and providing feedback effectively.

Instructional Task: Practice Game–Using a Variety of Serves to Defend Space

■ PRACTICE TASK

Teams work at their home courts with a net, first in singles and then doubles. Coaches rotate players in and out. Students serve and play out the point. Server works on using the serve as a defensive shot.

Refinements

- Focus on serving long and high to the opponent's backcourt. The opponent will move back to return the shot, which gives the server an advantage.
- Remind students to mix up the serves to make the opponent move side to side and up and back around the court.

Extension

Captains use stats sheets to record placement of serves and the results of the service return.

Student Choices/Differentiation

- Students choose the serve that works best for their situation.
- Students choose their equipment.

What to Look For

- Students are attempting a variety of serves.
- Students are focused on defending their space.

Formal and Informal Assessments

- Peer assessments
- Teacher assessments of video of students serving
- Exit slip: badminton self-assessment

Closure

- When would you use a short serve? A long serve?
- What is the best type of serve for singles and why?
- Complete your exit slips and place them in the folder.

Reflection

- Students worked with each other and performed the duties of their individual roles.
- Coaches and captains helped players increase their skill performance.
- Teams used the stats sheets to help their team members with their singles and doubles performance strategy when serving.

Homework

Choose a badminton skill and research the correct form on videos posted to the school's physical education website.

Resources

Kumar, S. (2010). *Badminton skills and rules*. Darya Ganj, New Delhi: Khel Sahitya Kendra.

TeachPE.com: www.teachpe.com

Badminton World Federation: www.bwfbadminton.org

World Badminton: www.worldbadminton.com

SPORT EDUCATION SAMPLE LESSON DAY 1

1. **Choose team name and mascot.** (Report these to commissioner [teacher] for approval.) Captains get a team folder. Assign color and number. Place on folder.

2. **Assign roles for the team.** Fill out role sheet. Assign according to number of players on a team.

Roles: captain, coach, manager, exercise specialist, publicist, motivator, head official, head statistician, sports council (any roles needed for the sport season)

3. Team completes the following tasks:
   - **Begin making team poster:** Include team name, mascot, names of players (roles and something that they like to do)
   - **Captain:** Have team members read and sign contracts. (10 points)
   - **Exercise specialist:** Review the designated warm-up for clarity and understanding. **(Option:** Exercise specialist designs the warm-up using a variety of health- and skill-related activities.)
   - **Coach:** Plan a 5-minute team warm-up using skills needed for the day.
   - **Motivator:** Create a team cheer.
   - Put poster on the wall when complete. May work on these again at the beginning of class day 2.

4. At the whistle, perform warm-up exercises as a team. (possible 10 points)

5. At next whistle, go to your assigned court.
   - Manager gets the equipment and pinnies for your team.
   - Warm up with equipment. Led by coach. (possible 10 points)

Note: Team points deducted for conduct violations during warm-ups, practices, and games. Additional points for positive behavior.

In this sport education season:
- There are _____ teams.
- _____ members of each team play at one time.
- If a team has more than _____ players, the team members take turns substituting.
- If a team has fewer than _____ players on a given day, the team plays short.

From L.C. MacDonald, R.J. Doan, and S. Chepko, eds., 2018, *Lesson planning for high school physical education* (Reston, VA: SHAPE America; Champaign, IL: Human Kinetics).

TEAM ROLES

Team name: _____

Role	Student name
Captain • Submits paperwork • Assists team coach • Facilitates responsibilities	
Coach • Plans and executes team practices • Models fair play • Establishes lineup for games	
Manager • Ensures team is on appropriate court or field • Ensures the equipment is available	
Head official • Interprets rules • Mediates conflicts • Reports team scores	
Motivator • Establishes a team cheer • Promotes team spirit during practice, warm-ups, and games	
Publicist • Facilitates development of team poster • Posts team members' profiles • Posts team scores	
Sports board representative • Represents team at all sports board meetings • Handles conflict resolution	
Exercise specialist • Selects appropriate warm-ups • Leads warm-ups • Reports injuries to teacher	

From L.C. MacDonald, R.J. Doan, and S. Chepko, eds., 2018, *Lesson planning for high school physical education* (Reston, VA: SHAPE America; Champaign, IL: Human Kinetics).

SERVING COMPETITION

Team name: _____

Player _____	1 ___	2 ___	3 ___	4 ___	5 ___	6 ___
Player _____	1 ___	2 ___	3 ___	4 ___	5 ___	6 ___
Player _____	1 ___	2 ___	3 ___	4 ___	5 ___	6 ___
Player _____	1 ___	2 ___	3 ___	4 ___	5 ___	6 ___
Player _____	1 ___	2 ___	3 ___	4 ___	5 ___	6 ___
Player _____	1 ___	2 ___	3 ___	4 ___	5 ___	6 ___

Serve

Server must stand behind the service line.

Server must serve underhand.

Shuttlecock must land on opposite side of the court.

Shuttlecock must land behind the black service line.

- Mark 1 point for each successful serve.
- Mark an x for each unsuccessful serve.

Scoring

Serve landing in the correct court = 1 point

Inside the hoop = 3 points

Hitting a poly spot = 5 points

Scored by duty team: _____

From L.C. MacDonald, R.J. Doan, and S. Chepko, eds., 2018, *Lesson planning for high school physical education* (Reston, VA: SHAPE America; Champaign, IL: Human Kinetics).

BADMINTON AFFECTIVE SELF-ASSESSMENT EXIT SLIP

Player name: _____ Team name: _____

1. I was/was not a positive member of my team today because I . . .

2. I noticed that a team member needed help with a skill today and I chose to . . .

3. During a game situation, a shot is called out and I know it is in. The best way to handle this situation is …

4. A member of another team is taunting my partner by laughing when he/she misses a shot. I should…

From L.C. MacDonald, R.J. Doan, and S. Chepko, eds., 2018, *Lesson planning for high school physical education* (Reston, VA: SHAPE America; Champaign, IL: Human Kinetics).

LESSON 3: PRESEASON PRACTICE

Grade-Level Outcomes

Primary Outcome

Lifetime activities: Refines activity-specific movement skills for 1 or more lifetime activities (outdoor pursuits, individual-performance activities, aquatics, net/wall games or target games). (S1.H1.L2)

Embedded Outcome

Social interaction: Identifies the opportunity for social support in a self-selected physical activity or dance. (S5.H4.L1)

Lesson Objectives

The learner will:

- design a drill to practice a series of shots in badminton.
- return a smash and a drop shot to defend against an attack.
- demonstrate the importance of a drop shot to create space.
- work with others to create a dance badminton skill routine that enhances physical activity, team spirit, and social skills.

Equipment and Materials

- Rackets
- Shuttlecocks
- Nets

Introduction

Today, we will review more badminton skills you learned in middle school. We will continue our pre-season with practice tasks utilizing each skill. You will continue working as a team and assisting your teammates to improve. For those of you who love music, you are going to create a routine utilizing badminton skills and music to enhance your team dynamics, physical activity, and social skills.

Instructional Task: Dance Badminton Skill Routine

■ PRACTICE TASK

Teams take 5 minutes to discuss skills. They have two lessons to discuss and work on their routines at the beginning of each class period. The routine will be performed on the fifth day for points. Share the rubric with students. Make sure each dance routine covers the criteria that will be used for evaluation.

EMBEDDED OUTCOME: S5.H4.L1. The dance routine is a team building activity that enhances team spirit. Provide feedback related to students supporting one another in the design and performance of the routine.

Student Choices/Differentiation

- Students may choose any appropriate (inoffensive) music.
- Students determine which skills to include.

What to Look For

- Teams are working together and using the proper form on their chosen skills.
- Students are meeting the expectations as outlined in the rubric.

Instructional Task: Practice Clears and Smashes

■ **PRACTICE TASK**

Partners feed to opposite sides of the net. Partner 1 feeds to Partner 2. Students hit five clears and five smashes back across the net.

Extension

Partner 1 clears the shuttlecock across the net. Partner 2 attempts to smash if the clear is not deep.

Refinement

Remind students that racket preparation is key and should be done as soon as they anticipate a possible smash.

Student Choices/Differentiation

- Students choose their partners.
- Students choose their equipment.

What to Look For

- Clears are long and deep.
- Students are using their legs to help clear the shuttlecock.
- Non-racket arm is extended and pointed at the shuttlecock before contact in the smash.
- Racket is up and back in preparation for the smash.

Instructional Task: Clears and Drop Shots

■ **PRACTICE TASK**

One partner serves high to the other, who tries to mask whether the return will be a clear or drop shot.

Refinement

Drop shot should be hit low over the net so it doesn't set the opponent up to smash. If students are hitting it too high, have a player stand on the other side of the net with the racket up and ready to smash to encourage a low trajectory.

Student Choices/Differentiation

- Students choose their equipment.
- Students choose their partners.

What to Look For

- Students are making their opponents move both to and from the net before executing the desired shot to score a point.
- Clear shot sends opponents deep into their half of the court.
- Drop shot has the desired arc.

Instructional Task: Fast Exchange Drill

■ **PRACTICE TASK**

Partners hit forehand and backhand drives, aiming for the body.

Extension

Doubles fast exchange: Player 1 hits straight to Player 2, Player 2 hits diagonally to Player 3, Player 3 hits straight to Player 4, Player 4 hits diagonally to Player 1. Players rotate after five shots each.

Refinement

Remind students to return to ready position after hitting the shuttlecock.

Student Choices/Differentiation

- Students choose their equipment.
- Students choose their partners.

What to Look For

- Students set their feet properly when alternating between the forehand and the backhand.
- Students focus on executing the skill properly as they are forced to also execute it quickly.
- Students use proper body rotation to execute a cross-court shot.
- Players move their feet to appropriately align their bodies while preparing for the next shot.
- Students can follow the pattern of the drill.

Instructional Task: Run-Clear Drill

■ PRACTICE TASK

Player 1 starts at one service line with a shuttlecock. Player 2 is positioned near the back of the diagonally opposite service box. Player 3 stands near the back of the service box opposite Player 2, and Player 4 should be off the court behind Player 2. Player 1 hits a high serve to Player 2. Player 1 runs around the court and stops behind Player 4. As this happens, Player 2 plays a clear down the line in the direction of Player 3. Player 2 then follows her shot to the same end as Player 3.

Each player in turn hits a clear and follows her shot to the opposite side of the net. The rally keeps going until the shuttlecock is no longer in play.

Extensions

- Students repeat with different shots.
- Students repeat with backhand clear.

Student Choices/Differentiation

Students choose their equipment.

What to Look For

- Players are working hard at moving to their spots.
- Students are able to direct their down-the-line shots accurately.
- Students are hitting effective clears.

Instructional Task: Team Half-Court Singles Practice

■ PRACTICE TASK

Teams play games for practice using rally scoring on a half court. Play 5 minutes each and switch. Players not playing rotate between keeping stats and practicing on the side.

Extensions

- Repeat, awarding extra points for successful drop shots.
- Repeat, awarding extra points for successful use of the smash.

Student Choices/Differentiation

- Students choose their opponents based on ability or comfort.
- Players may alter the boundaries of the court to make their games more or less challenging and ensure early success rates.

What to Look For

Students are mixing up their shots and making correct shot choices. Use the application EasyTag to keep a record of shots used during game situations.

Instructional Task: Create a Practice Drill

■ **PRACTICE TASK**

Each team designs a drill to practice the service return, clears, and drop shots to create space on the opponents' side of the net.

Extension

Perform these practice drills utilizing the entire team.

Refinement

If needed, show videos to help students hone their skills. TeachPE.com is a good resource.

Student Choices/Differentiation

Students choose their equipment.

What to Look For

- Teams are utilizing all skills in their drills.
- All students are engaged.

Formal and Informal Assessments

EasyTag record of shots

Closure

- Is it easier for the opponent to attack you from the front or the back? Why?
- Is it easier to send your opponent back by using an overhead or underhand shot?
- What is the easiest shot to keep a rally going?

Reflection

- Were students appropriately using each shot they have learned to this point?
- Were students focusing on body alignment?
- Review the EasyTag record of shots to see if students are making effective choices and applying strategies.

Homework

Practice your dance routine using the skills chosen. Work on your choice of music.

Resources

Kumar, S. (2010). *Badminton skills and rules*. Darya Ganj, New Delhi: Khel Sahitya Kendra.

TeachPE.com: www.teachpe.com

Badminton World Federation: www.bwfbadminton.org

World Badminton: www.worldbadminton.com

BADMINTON SKILLS DANCE

Criterion 1: Each team will choose three different badminton strokes.

Criterion 2: Each stroke will be done on an 8 count.

Criterion 3: Dance will begin with the ready position for their choice of first stroke.

Criterion 4: After each stroke, students will backpedal or jog to their next ready position in an 8 count.

Criterion 5: Students will work in the ready position for 16 counts and begin the next skill.

Criterion 6: The dance will end with student choice of creativity of the follow-through of a stroke.

Criterion 7: Appropriate music of their choice is put to their dance steps.

Badminton Dance Checklist

Circle Yes or No for each player

Player names	Performs three ready positions with smooth transitions	Performs steps and movement correctly	Performs three different badminton strokes	Performs to the beat of the music	Synchronizes movements with team
	Yes No	Yes No	Yes No	Yes No	Yes No
	Yes No	Yes No	Yes No	Yes No	Yes No
	Yes No	Yes No	Yes No	Yes No	Yes No
	Yes No	Yes No	Yes No	Yes No	Yes No

Team name: _____   **Song choice:** _____

From L.C. MacDonald, R.J. Doan, and S. Chepko, eds., 2018, *Lesson planning for high school physical education* (Reston, VA: SHAPE America; Champaign, IL: Human Kinetics).

LESSON 4: LONG AND SHORT SERVES

Grade-Level Outcomes

Primary Outcomes

Lifetime activities: Refines activity-specific movement skills in 1 or more lifetime activities (outdoor pursuits, individual-performance activities, aquatics, net/wall games or target games). (S1.H1.L2)

Movement concepts, principles & knowledge: Uses movement concepts and principles (e.g., force, motion, rotation) to analyze and improve performance of self and/or others in a selected skill. (S2.H1.L1)

Embedded Outcome

Rules & etiquette: Exhibits proper etiquette, respect for others and teamwork while engaging in physical activity and/or social dance. (S4.H2.L1)

Lesson Objectives

The learner will:

- demonstrate the critical elements of the smash and overhead clears.
- recall concepts of trajectory and force as they relate to long and short serves and clears.
- apply trajectory and force in serving and clears during a peer assessment.
- work cooperatively and demonstrate safe practices and etiquette in diverse groups.
- be responsible for their own learning as well as that of their peers (coaching and teaching each other on their teams).

Equipment and Materials

- Rackets and shuttlecocks: 1 per student
- 4 iPads: 2 for officiating video, 2 for stats keeping

Introduction

Today, we will review long and short serves using different types of force. We will also discuss and demonstrate the use of trajectory on short and long serves. You will practice and assess previous skills by working in stations. You will need to use higher-order thinking skills to decide how much trajectory is needed on each shot.

Instructional Task: Team Role Tasks

■ PRACTICE TASK

Assign the day's duties for each role.

- **Captains:** Get your folders. They contain a peer assessment sheet for a station.
- **Managers:** Get the equipment for your teams: jerseys, rackets, and shuttlecocks.
- **Sport education teams:** Go to your home grids to begin ASAP (as soon as possible) activities for the day.
- **ASAP:** Read the whiteboard for the ASAP activities and other instructions of the day.
  1. Begin hitting shots back and forth.
  2. Rally tally: See how many you can hit without making a mistake.
  3. Serves: Practice serving and focusing on the amount of force needed to get the serves over the net and in the service box.
- **Head official:** Assign each member of your team to a duty for today (two students keeping stats sheets, two students keeping score in the serving competition, one or two students scouting).

- **Sports council:** Assist the captain with duties, and assist in resolving any issues.
- **Motivator:** Pump up your team. Remind them of fair play. Cheer for your team and others.
- **Exercise specialist:** Prepare for the team warm-up. Include some health- and skill-related components of your choice. Each team needs to explain which health- and skill-related components are used and the purpose.

Note: Give each team a possibility of 10 points a day for team warm-ups based on criteria you have provided.

What to Look For

- Students are coming into the gym and putting on their jerseys, reading the whiteboard, going to their home grids, and beginning their ASAPs.
- Exercise specialists have the equipment needed for their team's warm-up.

Instructional Task: Long and Short Serves

■ PRACTICE TASK

Review long and short serves using different types of force. Discuss and demonstrate the use of trajectory on serves.

Guiding questions for students:

- Can someone define trajectory?
- Can someone describe the difference in trajectory used in short and long serves and in clears?

Student Choices/Differentiation

Use video clips or diagrams to illustrate different trajectories to support student understanding or review.

What to Look For

- Students are engaged in the discussion.
- Students can identify different types of trajectories for different shots.

Instructional Task: Station Practice

■ PRACTICE TASK

Discuss station procedures and demonstrate the tasks at stations 1 through 5. Place signs or task cards at each station.

Use the Tabata Pro application to let students know when to change stations. For example, it may be set for 10 minutes of music per station and 1 minute of rest (quiet) in between to move to the next station.

Station 1: Fronton (Winner of Each Rally Stays On) Singles (Lead-up Game)

Purpose: Tactics—return to home base.
Captains divide their teams into two groups. Students begin with a drop bounce self-feed and play out the points. Students work to move their opponents using a variety of clears, drives, and drop shots and get back to the home base (poly spot). Using a court chart, one student records (with an X) each time a player returns to home base.
If Team A wins the point, the winning player stays on the court and the player from Team B switches with a teammate. A point is scored to the winning side.
A player who wins three in a row must switch with a teammate.

Station 2: Team Practice and Peer Assessment

Purpose: Work to move opponent or to delay opponent while recovering to center.
Captains perform the peer assessment.
Teams work in two pairs and rotate extra players in 2 v 2. Feeders on one side set up overhead clears. Players hit overhead clears five times. Pairs switch.

Extension

Add five smashes and five drop shots.

Refinement

Use an iPad application to record the drill for analysis. Analyzing the performance of others and reflecting about themselves helps students focus on the key parts of a skill, reinforcing their learning.

Station 3: Serving Competition (Team Points)

Purpose: Focus on trajectory and force needed for each serve and which serve is best to use.
Two students at a time practice serving into the diagonal courts. Students then serve three from each side, scoring points for their teams. Points: correct court = 1 point; hoop = 3 points; poly spot = 5 points.
Captains may talk to and assist their players. The duty team keeps the score.
Players should think about the trajectory and force needed to be successful on each serve.

Station 4: Doubles

Purpose: Practice doubles score and serve rotation.
Captains divide their teams into teams of three to play doubles (each team has one extra player). Extra players rotate in every 2 points.
Captains are looking for the best doubles combinations for the upcoming competitions. Players call out the score before serving and use proper service rotation. Remind students to call "mine" for safety.

EMBEDDED OUTCOME: S4.H2.L1. Review doubles rules and provide feedback specific to proper etiquette and scoring.

Station 5: Duty Team

The duty team has several tasks:

- Report any positive or negative fair play behaviors. (All players.)
- Keep score on the serving court.
- Scout the teams for future play using the match scouting report sheet.
- Perform an informal assessment of serving and shot placement during the doubles competition. At Station 1, one student keeps stats on returns to home base.

Student Choices/Differentiation

Students choose their equipment.

What to Look For

Station 1

- Students are switching on and off the court quickly when losing a point.
- Students are cooperating with their team leaders.

Other

- Groups are working independently.
- Students on the duty team are getting to stations prepared to keep stats, scout, assess, and keep score. Students who are not participating because of injury or sickness may assist the duty team.
- Students are consistently returning to home base.
- Players are focusing on making good feeds for other students.
- Students are focusing on making proper serves during their practice shots, concentrating on the amount of force needed and the follow-through.

Formal and Informal Assessments

- Peer assessments: overhead clear, scouting, serving station, stats sheet
- Exit slip: What station was the most challenging for you today? Why was it the most challenging?

Closure

- What is an advantage and a disadvantage of a long serve? A short serve?
- How does the use of trajectory play a role in strategy?
- Discuss any successes or problems at the team practice stations.
- Complete the exit slips and place them in the folders.

Reflection

- Were students able to stay on task at each station?
- Was the duty team efficient at working with the teams?
- Are students' skills maturing?
- What cues need to be reinforced?
- Review peer assessment data and share with the captains to determine how to best meet the needs of the students.

Homework

- Watch a video from the school's physical education website and practice analyzing the skills of an opponent.
- Practice your dance routine using the skills chosen. You'll be performing it next time.

Resources

Dougherty, N.J. (ed.). (2010). *Physical activity and sport for the secondary school student*. Reston, VA: NASPE.

The Badminton Bible: www.badmintonbible.com

Internet keyword search: "badminton positioning," "badminton strategy"

BADMINTON OVERHEAD CLEAR PEER ASSESSMENT

Three players of each team form a group. Player 1 is the feeder, Player 2 is the hitter, and Player 3 is the observer. Player 1 feeds five high shots to the forehand side. Player 2 hits overhead clears with no rally. Player 3 records. Students rotate after five shots.

Hitter: _____   Observer: _____

Critical elements	1	2	3	4	5
Racket back					
Side to target					
Contact high, arm extended					
Shift weight back to front					

Hitter: _____   Observer: _____

Critical elements	1	2	3	4	5
Racket back					
Side to target					
Contact high, arm extended					
Shift weight back to front					

Team name: _____

Badminton stat sheet

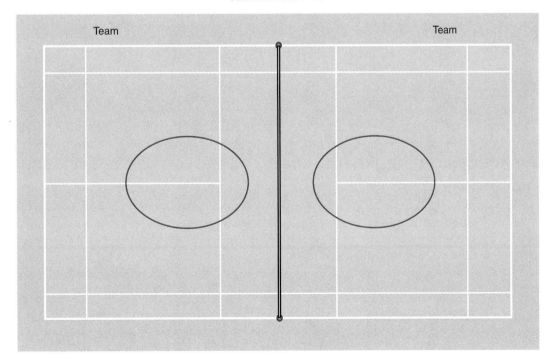

Record: S = shots   X = serves

From L.C. MacDonald, R.J. Doan, and S. Chepko, eds., 2018, *Lesson planning for high school physical education* (Reston, VA: SHAPE America; Champaign, IL: Human Kinetics).

LESSON 5: PRACTICE STATIONS AND BADMINTON DANCE

Grade-Level Outcomes

Primary Outcome

Lifetime activities: Refines activity-specific movement skills in 1 or more lifetime activities (outdoor pursuits, individual-performance activities, aquatics, net/wall games and target games). (S1.H1.L2)

Embedded Outcomes

Self-expression & enjoyment: Selects and participates in physical activities or dance that meet the need for self-expression and enjoyment. (S5.H3.L1)

Social interaction: Identifies the opportunity for social support in a self-selected physical activity or dance. (S5.H4.L1)

Lesson Objectives

The learner will:

- perform a dance created by his or her team to a rhythm of music and badminton skills.
- support the creative dance of other teams by applauding or cheering appropriately.
- work together to improve his or her consistency through direct practice focusing on a series of shots.

Equipment and Materials

- Rackets
- Shuttlecocks
- Nets
- iPad
- Speakers

Introduction

Today's lesson will begin with your badminton dance routines. All teams will receive points based on the rubric. Then you will practice your skills in a station format. Let's get this dance party started!

Instructional Task: Musical Badminton Skills Routine

■ PRACTICE TASK

Teams perform their skill routines to music. Award points based on the rubric (see Lesson 3). Draw for order of performance. Record and post for parents to view.

EMBEDDED OUTCOMES: S5.H3.L1; S5.H4.L1. Use the performance to discuss how physical activity can provide opportunities for self-expression and enjoyment. Ask students to provide examples of how they experienced social support in this dance as well as in other physical activities.

Student Choices/Differentiation

- Students choose their equipment.
- Students choose the music and skills.

What to Look For

Students are meeting the expectations as outlined in the rubric (see Lesson 3).

Instructional Task: Stations for Skill Development

■ PRACTICE TASK

Station 1: Rally Tally

- Students work in pairs.
- Pairs hit over the net as many times as possible without making a mistake.

Extension

Specify particular shots to use during the rally tally.

Refinements

- Remind students to use a variety of shots and go beyond their comfort zones.
- Ask students to focus on the spaces and try not to hit person to person.

Station 2: Around The World

Player 1 hits into the right service court to Player 2 and moves to his or her right to the opposite side of the court. Player 2 returns to Player 3 and moves to the opposite side. Play continues until a point is scored.

Count the number of consecutive hits the team can accumulate. Substitute in a rotation for more than four on a team.

Station 3: Backhand Madness

Partners hit as many backhands as they can in 60 seconds.

Station 4: Target Smash Drill

Place hoops as targets for smashes. Partner feeds with hand or racket from same side as hitter. Score 2 points for landing in each hoop and 1 point for hitting the rim.

Station 5: Royal Rally

Partners rally back and forth, hitting shots that make the opponent move away from home.

Refinement

Students work on running their partners, pushing them back with a clear or lift when they are up, executing a drop shot when they are deep.

Station 6: Badminton Horse

Place different colored spots on the court. Players call a color and serve the shuttlecock to that spot. If it lands on the spot, the next person in line must attempt to hit the same spot. If the player misses, she will receive a letter (H-O-R-S-E). Last player to spell HORSE wins the game.

Student Choices/Differentiation

- Students choose their equipment.
- Students choose their partners.

What to Look For

- Students are showing an understanding of each task by getting started quickly at each station.
- Students work well as a team to make sure their station is run effectively and efficiently.
- Students coach others who may be struggling with a particular skill set.
- Students are appropriately utilizing the skills learned to this point.
- Students are able to execute the skills necessary to implement the strategies.
- Students are using the strategies correctly or are attempting to do so.
- Teams are playing fairly. Remind them they are a team and working to improve skills.

Instructional Task:
Fronton Doubles Round-Robin Tournament

■ PRACTICE TASK

Two pairs face each other for a fronton doubles tournament. High-scoring team stays and low-scoring team goes to the back of the line. Winner of each rally serves. If a doubles pair scores three in a row, they must switch out. Students should call out their scores before beginning the next point. Play for 7 minutes.

Student Choices/Differentiation

- Students choose their partners.
- Students choose their equipment.

What to Look For

- Students are using a variety of shots effectively.
- Students recognize the open spaces for shot location.
- Students communicate with each other while playing doubles.

Formal and Informal Assessments

- Thumbs-up self-check (students show a thumbs-up if they think their skills are improving)
- Dance rubric

Closure

- What was the most difficult part of creating your badminton dance?
- Did everyone contribute to the creation?
- What is the most enjoyable part of sport education thus far?

Reflection

- Are the skills of the students improving with these station activities?
- Were the badminton dance creations successful based on the rubric?

Homework

- Review skills on TeachPE.com and perform shadow drills.
- The exercise specialist on each team will add one or more yoga poses and breathing techniques to their warm-ups as a stress-management technique.

Resources

Mitchell, S.A., Oslin, J.L., & Griffin, L.L. (2013). *Teaching sport concepts and skills: A tactical approach*. Champaign, IL: Human Kinetics.

TeachPE.com: www.teachpe.com

Arizona Badminton Center: www.AZBadmintonCenter.com

LESSON 6: SINGLES STRATEGIES

Grade-Level Outcomes

Primary Outcomes

Lifetime activities: Refines activity-specific movement skills in 1 or more lifetime activities (outdoor pursuits, individual-performance activities, aquatics, net/wall games and target games). (S1.H1.L2)

Stress management: Identifies stress-management strategies (e.g., mental imagery, relaxation techniques, deep breathing, aerobic exercise, meditation) to reduce stress. (S3.H14.L1)

Embedded Outcome

Working with others: Solves problems and thinks critically in physical activity and/or dance settings, both as an individual and in groups. (S4.H4.L1)

Lesson Objectives

The learner will:

- engage in singles play, successfully utilizing both offensive and defensive strategies.
- create space and maintain depth by using underarm clears.
- demonstrate ways yoga and deep breathing may improve performance and relieve stress.

Equipment and Materials

- Badminton rackets
- Shuttlecocks
- Nets
- Hula-Hoops
- Poly spots

Introduction

Today, we will focus on singles strategies. In singles, as in our tennis unit, the basic strategy is to move your opponent. This means you force your opponent to cover distance rapidly and change direction. Once your opponent plays a weak shot, you have the choice between pushing her even farther out of position or attempting to win the rally immediately with a drop or smash. After you play a shot, you should recover toward a central base position. This helps you cover the whole court. Before you start your practice tasks, we're going to talk about some potentially stressful situations in badminton and how you might handle them.

Instructional Task: Stress-Management Role Play

■ PRACTICE TASK

Discuss the role of stress in physical activity and performance.

Each team acts out a stressful badminton match situation (e.g., official making bad calls, opponent is aggressive, score is tied in the championship game). Students offer suggestions on how to handle these situations.

Guiding questions for students:

- Can you give me some examples of elite athletes making mistakes while under stress? (Answer examples: Even professional and college basketball players shoot air balls and golfers miss short putts because of stress.)
- What are some stress-related physical, mental, and social symptoms?
- How does physical activity relieve the body of stress-related symptoms?

Student Choices/Differentiation

Use a video clip of a situation in sport (e.g., a free throw or putt for the win) to illustrate stress and stress-management techniques for students who may not have good examples.

What to Look For

- Teams are using constructive ways to deal with the stressful situations.
- All students on each team are included in their situational activity.

Instructional Task: Team Warm-Up

■ PRACTICE TASK

The exercise specialists add one or more yoga poses and breathing techniques to their teams' warm-up as a stress-management technique.

Monitor all warm-ups and award points as merited (possible 10 points).

Guiding questions for students:

- After trying out some yoga poses, how do you feel?
- What happens when you focus on just your breathing?
- Can you think of some situations in sport where you've seen athletes take a deep breath?

Student Choices/Differentiation

Provide several poses and allow students to select individually.

What to Look For

- Exercise specialists demonstrate the poses correctly.
- Students are taking the warm-up seriously.

Instructional Task: Team Practice and Half-Court Drill

■ PRACTICE TASK

Students focus on creating space on their opponents' side of the court.

One player feeds to the frontcourt while one hits underarm clears to the back of the feeder's court.

Feeder alternates to the forehand and backhand.

Refinement

Students may focus on either the forehand or the backhand for 5 or 10 consecutive repetitions before alternating if they think the progression is moving too quickly.

Student Choices/Differentiation

Students choose their equipment.

What to Look For

- Students are using proper form in the underarm shot.
- Students are able to keep their opponents deep in the court.

Instructional Task:
Attacking Drop Shot and Clear, Clear, Drop

■ PRACTICE TASK

Demonstrate the drill. There are four players on each court, working in two pairs. Partners face each other across the net while standing on the service lines. Player 1 hits a clear to Player 2's forehand.

Player 2 also plays a clear. Player 1 attempts to play a drop shot to Player 1's backhand or forehand. Players repeat five times and switch roles.

Extensions
- Repeat, but change the pattern to clear, drop, drop, clear, smash.
- Players rotate after 2 minutes.

Student Choices/Differentiation
- Students choose their equipment.
- Students choose their partners.

What to Look For
- Students are trying to hit the corners in order to move their opponents.
- Students are hitting the clears deep enough to be effective.

Instructional Task:
Defending Against an Attack and Half-Court Singles

■ PRACTICE TASK

One player feeds a high serve toward the middle and the partner smashes it. Students play out the point.

Refinement

Students work on blocking the smash by keeping a firm wrist.

EMBEDDED OUTCOME: S4.H4.L1. Use the guiding questions to help students think critically and strategically about the game situation and anticipate the opponent's next shot.

Guiding questions for students:
- If you play a shot to one side of the opponent's court, where should you expect the return to come? (Answer: same side)
- If you play a clear or lift deep in the opponent's court, what do you think your opponent will play? (Answer: most likely backcourt)
- If you play a shot at the net (drop or smash), where would you expect the return to come? (Answer: most likely frontcourt)

Student Choices/Differentiation
- Students choose their equipment.
- Students choose their partners.

What to Look For
- Students are anticipating the location of their opponents' next shot.
- Students are having success with the block.

Instructional Task: Attacking the Short Serve

■ PRACTICE TASK

One partner feeds a short serve and the other attacks. Students play out the point.

Refinement

Students try to return the serve flat or downward.

Extension

Follow up with teams playing singles on their courts. Players must use a short serve, while the receiving team tries to attack. Rotate after 2 minutes.

Student Choices/Differentiation

- Students choose their equipment.
- Students choose their partners.

What to Look For

- Students are consistently able to feed a short serve.
- Students are having success with their attacking shots.
- Attacking shots have a flat or downward trajectory.

Instructional Task: Smash Drill

■ PRACTICE TASK

Coach feeds an overhead clear to the net player. Net player smashes toward two other players on the opposite side of the net. These two players try to block the smash (not let the shuttlecock hit the court). Players switch roles after three attempts.

Extension

Repeat, but if the smash is successfully blocked, have the attacking player return the blocked shot.

Refinement

If the smash is not going low and hard, have students focus on snapping their wrists at contact.

Student Choices/Differentiation

Students choose their equipment.

What to Look For

- Players are snapping their wrists when hitting the smash.
- Players are keeping their wrists firm on the block.

Formal and Informal Assessments

Exit slip: Describe one or two tennis skills in which you have improved (or not improved) so far in this module.

Closure

- What is the best way to keep a shot from being returned?
- Which shot from your opponent will give you the best chance at using a smash?
- What is the best shot to use to avoid having a smash returned as a smash?

Reflection

- Did the majority of the class self-report skill improvement via a thumb's-up? If not, why?
- Does 80 percent of the class have an understanding of singles strategies?

Homework

Go to the website www.usabadminton.org. Look up information on camps, clinics, and where to play. Check on any participation requirements, costs, and social opportunities, and be ready to share next class.

Resources

Mitchell, S.A., Oslin, J.L., & Griffin, L.L. (2013). *Teaching sport concepts and skills: A tactical approach*. Champaign, IL: Human Kinetics.

USA Badminton: www.usabadminton.org

Teach PE: www.TeachPE.com

LESSON 7: DOUBLES STRATEGIES

Grade-Level Outcomes

Primary Outcome

Lifetime activities: Refines activity-specific movement in one or more lifetime activities (outdoor pursuits, individual-performance activities, aquatics, net/wall games or target games. (S1.H1.L2)

Embedded Outcome

Physical activity knowledge: Evaluates—according to their benefits, social support network and participation requirements—activities that can be pursued in the local environment. (S3.H4.L1)

Lesson Objectives

The learner will:

- discuss participation opportunities in the local area.
- demonstrate doubles strategies of front–back, side–side, and serve and attack.

Equipment and Materials

- Badminton rackets
- Shuttlecocks
- Nets

Introduction

Today, we will focus on doubles strategies for attacking and defending. Before we start our team warm-ups and practice tasks, we will go over an assignment that each team will work on together.

Instructional Task: Team Assignment

■ PRACTICE TASK

Captains discuss the assignment and assign tasks for homework for their teams (see homework section at the end of the lesson for questions). Distribute the rubric for evaluation. In the next lesson, teams will put together the information collected for homework and prepare to present the information in Lesson 10 of the season. This is for team points.

All students must have a part in the presentation.

EMBEDDED OUTCOME: S3.H4.L1. Have students share the information about local participation opportunities they collected in the Lesson 6 homework with their teams.

Student Choices/Differentiation

- Students may choose which part they will research and also how to present it.
- Students may use posters, PowerPoint, or any technology.
- Provide suggestions for finding the information, if needed.

What to Look For

- All students are taking part in planning the activity.
- Teams are asking good questions.
- Students are taking the initiative to volunteer for tasks.

Instructional Task: Team Warm-Up and Team Practice

■ PRACTICE TASK

Exercise specialists or coaches lead their teams' warm-up.

Students play a modified game (singles or doubles), beginning a point with a low serve.

Defensive players attack the return.

Student Choices/Differentiation

Students choose their equipment.

What to Look For

- Students attack the return instead of merely moving toward it.
- Students can execute a low serve effectively.

Instructional Task: Doubles Strategies

■ PRACTICE TASK

Review doubles positioning strategies.

Serving

When a team is serving, both the server and receiver should be in the up position (and side–side) just behind the service line to gain an attack position.

Receiving

When receiving a high serve, receiver should move to the back of the court to return the serve. The partner should move to the front to prepare to attack.

Rally

Players play side–side unless strengths dictate a front–back setup, such as when one player has greater mobility and can cover more territory (back). Players should always communicate about who is taking the hit and their positioning during the rally.

Play short doubles games, specifying a high serve to begin so the receiving team will practice the front–back position.

Extensions

- Repeat, specifying side–side formation for rallies.
- Repeat, specifying front–back formation for rallies.
- Repeat, with one team playing side–side and defending an attack from a team playing up and back.

Refinement

Stop play to re-position players if they are not sticking with the specified formation.

Guiding questions for students:

- When should you use a front–back formation? Why?
- When should you use a side–side formation? Why?
- What formation works best with your partner?

Student Choices/Differentiation

Students choose their equipment.

What to Look For

- Players are properly aligned and in ready position before the serve.
- Students keep the shuttlecock in front of them as they move back to play a high serve.
- Students anticipate shot locations.
- Students change direction smoothly.
- Students make an effort to return to a neutral court position after each shot.
- Students are choosing appropriate formations for the situation.
- Students are communicating with one another during play.

Instructional Task: Modified Game (1 v 2)

■ PRACTICE TASK

Player A1 hits all clears or drives and stays deep.

Player B1 is at the service line on the opposite side of the net. Player B1 hits all deep shots to Player A1.

Player B2 hits deep cross-court to side A and approaches to play side–side with Player B1. After 5 points, rotate Player B1 to the opposite side to play alone and hit all clears and drives.

Student Choices/Differentiation

Students choose which position to start with.

What to Look For

- Students can control the shuttlecock and hit to the appropriate location.
- Students can hit in a specified sequence.
- Students understand the two types of doubles play. Revisit if necessary.

Instructional Task: Doubles Games

■ PRACTICE TASK

Students play doubles in 2-minute games, working on different strategies.

Teams rotate players on and off.

Refinement

Coaches specify which strategies to practice.

Student Choices/Differentiation

Students choose their equipment.

What to look for

- Students understand the flow of a doubles game.
- Students are implementing the strategies taught.
- Students know how to keep score.

Formal and Informal Assessments

Exit slip: Name two key strategies for doubles play.

Closure

- Which formation gives you the best opportunity to attack?
- Which formation is best to defend an attack?
- Do you think you have enough information to make progress on your assignments?

Reflection

- Was everyone involved in the activity?
- Were all team members able to understand and demonstrate the different types of playing strategies?

Homework

- What are the health benefits of badminton?
- Where can you play outside of school? After graduation?
- What kinds of social opportunities does badminton provide?
- What are the requirements and costs to play?
- What skills are needed to participate in badminton?
- What would be an effective warm-up before playing badminton?
- What muscles are used while playing badminton?
- What would be a good meal to eat before a badminton tournament?
- What are the benefits of a physically active lifestyle for the brain?
- What is the relationship between physical activity, nutrition, and body composition?

Resources

Siedentop, D., Hastie, P., & van der Mars, H. (2011). *Complete guide to sport education.* 2nd ed. Champaign, IL: Human Kinetics.

Badminton World Federation: www.bwfbadminton.org

World Badminton: www.worldbadminton.com

LESSON 8: OFFICIATING AND SCRIMMAGES

Grade-Level Outcomes

Primary Outcomes

Lifetime activities: Refines activity-specific movements in 1 or more lifetime activities (outdoor pursuits, individual-performance activities, aquatics, net/wall games and target games). (S1.H1.L2)

Safety: Applies best practices for participating safely in physical activity, exercise and dance (e.g., injury prevention, proper alignment, hydration, use of equipment, implementation of rules, sun protection). (S4.H5.L1)

Embedded Outcomes

Rules & etiquette: Exhibits proper etiquette, respect for others and teamwork while engaging in physical activity and/or social dance. (S4.H2.L1)

Working with others: Assumes a leadership role (e.g., task or group leader, referee, coach) in a physical activity setting. (S4.H3.L2)

Lesson Objectives

The learner will:

- make decisions as to what part each individual will play on the duty team.
- perform all duties for the scrimmage games.
- demonstrate basic officiating signals.

Equipment and Materials

- Rackets
- Shuttlecocks
- Nets
- iPad
- Speakers

Introduction

Today, we will begin our regular season portion of sport education. First, you'll spend some time working on a team cheer that you can use throughout the season. Then we'll have an officiating clinic so you'll be ready to referee our matches. We'll finish up with doubles matches.

Instructional Task: Team Cheer Competition

■ PRACTICE TASK

Captains lead their teams in developing a cheer (approximately 3 minutes). Students then perform their cheers for the other teams.

Rank teams from 1 to 6 in order of the best cheer or pick the top three.

What to Look For

All students are contributing.

Instructional Task: Officiating Clinic

■ PRACTICE TASK

Hold an officiating clinic to show the duty team their responsibilities and how to officiate a game of badminton for the sport education module. Review the roles of the umpire, line judge and service judge.

Students view a 2-minute video clip that demonstrates the hand signals they will use.

The data team will keep stats sheets, perform scouting, and keep score in each game.

Review the rules of badminton scoring.

Extension

Everyone shows the signals for a serve with contact made above the waist, a foot fault, and misconduct.

Student Choices/Differentiation

Students choose their jobs on the duty team.

What to Look For

- All students know the signals for officiating badminton and when they are used.
- Teams have an understanding of the score and stats sheets.

Instructional Task: Warm-Up and Scrimmages

■ PRACTICE TASK

Play 10-minute scrimmages to allow teams to practice for the duty team. Two teams play each other, and one duty team officiates or plays singles (two doubles games and two singles games).

The scrimmages provide practice for officiating, scoring, and stat keeping.

EMBEDDED OUTCOME: S4.I2.L1. Etiquette, respect, and fair play are important aspects of the module. Fair play points are awarded each class period of the season.

EMBEDDED OUTCOME: S4.H3.L2. Throughout the season, each team member will assume a leadership role with specific duties.

Student Choices/Differentiation

Round 1

Team 1 v 6; duty = 3
Team 2 v 4; duty = 5

Round 2

Team 3 v 2; duty = 1
Team 4 v 5; duty = 6

Round 3

Team 3 v 6; duty = 2
Team 1 v 5; duty = 4

What to Look For

- Duty team members are officiating confidently.
- Players are respectful toward each other and the officials.
- Students are managing the scrimmages fairly independently.

Formal and Informal Assessments

Exit slip: Are you comfortable officiating matches? Why or why not?

Closure

- Can you show me the signal for a shuttlecock hit above the waist? Foot fault? Misconduct?
- What should the duty team do with the serve percentage (stats) sheet?
- What are the responsibilities of the officials?
- Be sure to drop off your exit slips as you leave.

Reflection

- How well did students apply the officiating signals?
- Were students keeping stats correctly?
- Review the exit slips to find out where students may need more practice in officiating.

Homework

- Go to the school's physical education website and review the rules of badminton and officiating signals. Be ready for a quiz in our next class using Plickers (an app that allows a simple, fast check for understanding).
- Continue to work on your presentation on the benefits of badminton.

Resources

Mitchell, S.A., Oslin, J.L., & Griffin, L.L. (2013). *Teaching sport concepts and skills: A tactical approach.* Champaign, IL: Human Kinetics.

Siedentop, D., Hastie, P., & van der Mars, H. (2011). *Complete guide to sport education.* 2nd ed. Champaign, IL: Human Kinetics.

Plickers: www.plickers.com

Badminton Information: www.badminton-information.com

BADMINTON SCORE SHEET

Team name: _____ Player/Players: _____ Court #: ____

Points (circle the points as they are made)

 1   2   3   4   5   6   7   8   9   10   11   12

 13   14   15   16   17   18   19   20   21   22   23   24

Fair play bonus points awarded   1   2   3   Given for _____

Team name: _____ Player/Players: _____ Court #: ____

Points (circle the points as they are made)

 1   2   3   4   5   6   7   8   9   10   11   12

 13   14   15   16   17   18   19   20   21   22   23   24

Fair play bonus points awarded   1   2   3   Given for _____

Game score: _____ Winner: _____

Scorekeeper name (print): _____ Team: _____

From L.C. MacDonald, R.J. Doan, and S. Chepko, eds., 2018, *Lesson planning for high school physical education* (Reston, VA: SHAPE America; Champaign, IL: Human Kinetics).

BADMINTON MATCH TEAM SCORECARD

Singles   Court #

1A _____ v 1B _____   _____

2A _____ v 2B _____   _____

Doubles   Court #

1A _____ v 1B _____   _____

2A _____ v 2B _____   _____

Duty team: _____

From L.C. MacDonald, R.J. Doan, and S. Chepko, eds., 2018, *Lesson planning for high school physical education* (Reston, VA: SHAPE America; Champaign, IL: Human Kinetics).

BADMINTON: SCOUTING THE COMPETITION

Team scouting: _____   Player doing report: _____

Today, you will analyze the strategies of a team you will play. Watch their game. Ask yourself a series of questions that will help you play smarter.

Here are some questions you might want to start with, but feel free to create and answer your own.

- What are their strengths?

- Who is their strongest player? What are his/her strengths? Weaknesses?

- What type of offensive shots or strategies are they using?

- What type of defensive shots or strategies are they using?

- What will be your strategy for defeating this team?

- What lineup will work best for this team?

After playing this team, reflect on the accuracy of your scouting report. How accurate were you? What additional things should you have considered in the report? (Place in folder.)

From L.C. MacDonald, R.J. Doan, and S. Chepko, eds., 2018, *Lesson planning for high school physical education* (Reston, VA: SHAPE America; Champaign, IL: Human Kinetics).

LESSON 9: DOUBLES TEAM PRACTICE

Grade-Level Outcomes

Primary Outcome

Lifetime activities: Refines activity-specific movement skills in 1 or more lifetime activities (outdoor pursuits, individual-performance activities, aquatics, net/wall games and target games). (S1.H1.L2)

Embedded Outcome

Movement concepts, principles & knowledge: Describes the speed vs. accuracy trade-off in throwing and striking skills. (S2.H2.L2)

Lesson Objectives

The learner will:

- demonstrate basic officiating skills.
- correctly use all badminton strokes four out of five times during the team practice and peer assessments.
- practice with a variety of partners to form doubles teams.

Equipment and Materials

- Badminton rackets
- Shuttlecocks
- Nets
- iPads
- Scorecards
- Stats sheets
- Task cards

Introduction

Today, we will begin with our assessment on officiating using Plickers cards. We will then go into our team practices led by your coach and finalize your doubles teams.

Instructional Task: Officiating Assessment

■ PRACTICE TASK

Use Plicker cards to assess officiating knowledge.

Instructional Task: Team Practice

■ PRACTICE TASK

Coaches review strategies to prepare their teams for round-robin singles and doubles tournament play.

1. Hit the shuttlecock consistently high and deep to give yourself time to recover.
2. Aim shots to the opponent's weaker side (usually backhand) to give the advantage of a weak return.
3. For more accuracy, back off on the power.
4. Keep the opponent on the move as much as possible.
5. If you're winning points, keep playing the same way.

6. If you're losing points, change the style of play.

7. Change the speed of play by mixing up shots. For example, hit some slower shots, such as drop shots and net shots, with faster shots in between, such as smashes, and drives.

8. Always play to personal strengths, and try to exploit the opponent's weaknesses.

EMBEDDED OUTCOME: S2.H2.L2. When discussing strategy 3, it's a good opportunity to check for understanding of the speed vs. accuracy trade-off concept from motor learning. Clarify if necessary.

Student Choices/Differentiation

Provide handouts or a poster with strategies for coaches to use and players to review.

What to Look For

- Coach demonstrates strategies if needed.
- Students can describe the speed vs. accuracy trade-off.

Instructional Task: All Shots

■ PRACTICE TASK

Partners take turns feeding and hitting the shuttlecock five times. Coaches call out the shots to use in sequence. Here is a sample sequence:

- High clear, smash
- Lift, drop shot
- Long serve, clear, drop
- Short serve, net shot
- Clear, clear, smash, block

Extension

Coaches spend as much time as they see fit working on each combination of shots. After all, the purpose is to assist all teammates to be the best badminton players possible.

Student Choices/Differentiation

Students choose their partners.

What to Look For

- Students are feeding successfully.
- Students are able to execute the shots on command.
- Watch for shots that students are finding difficult.

Instructional Task: Cross-Court and Down the Line

■ **PRACTICE TASK**

Player 1 is across the net from Players 2 and 3 in a triangle formation.

Player 1 hits a short serve. Player 2 hits a cross-court shot. Player 1 hits down the line to Player 3. Play continues as Player 2 and Player 3 hit cross-court and Player 1 hits all down the line until a mistake is made. Students play five rallies and then switch positions.

Player 1 is working on court movement and down-the-line shots. Player 2 and Player 3 are working on hitting cross-court shots.

Refinement

If Player 1 is having trouble, he or she may stay on one side and work on turning the body to hit down the line.

Student Choices/Differentiation

- Students choose their partners.
- Students choose their equipment.

What to Look For

- Students are cooperating and communicating with each other to maintain proper flow of the game.
- Students are executing the shots appropriately.

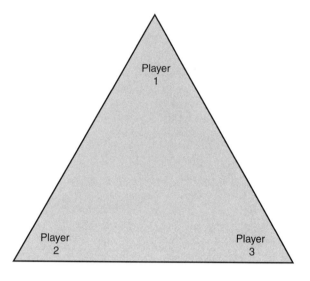

Instructional Task: Task Drill and Situation Cards

■ **PRACTICE TASK**

Play modified doubles games using one or more of the following options:
  Return only cross-court.
  Score is tied.
  Score is ad out.
  Play serve and approach.
  Hit only backhands.

Extension

Teams work longer on a situation based on their effectiveness or lack of effectiveness.

Student Choices/Differentiation

Students choose their partners.

What to Look For

- How do students perform during simulated match points?
- How successful are they when forced to use specific shots in the game?

Instructional Task:
Racket Quickness and Down-the-Line Shots

■ PRACTICE TASK

Working in pairs, one student feeds a shuttlecock to the partner's forehand. Partner returns with a drive down the line. Players switch after five shots.

Extension

Repeat on the backhand side.

Student Choices/Differentiation

- Students choose their partners.
- Feeder may slow the toss.

What to Look For

- Players are successful going down the line.
- Partners are able to feed successfully.

Instructional Task: Lunging for the Shuttlecock

■ PRACTICE TASK

Coach feeds one or two clears deep and then feeds a drop shot, forcing the hitter to lunge for the shuttlecock. Player runs up for the drop shot and then runs off the court and to the back of the line. Next player comes on.

Extensions

- If the drill is too advanced, bring the players in and feed only a drop shot before the players go to the back of the line. Then back the line up to the back line, and players will hit one clear and run up for the drop.
- Add two clears and a drop shot.

Student Choices/Differentiation

Students choose their equipment.

What to Look For

- Students remain balanced while they lunge for the shuttlecock.
- Students get low enough to get their rackets underneath the shuttlecock and execute a return shot.

Instructional Task: 2 v 1 Drill

■ PRACTICE TASK

Students play 2 v 1.

Both players alternately feed 10 shots to the player on the other side of the net. The objective is to move the single player side to side and up and back. Players should focus on moving their feet and anticipating the direction of the shot based on the racket face. If a shuttlecock drops, the count starts over. If a feed is bad, play it again (count is not affected).

Refinement

If a student is unable to get to the shots, ask the feeders to increase the time between shots.

Student Choices/Differentiation

- Students choose their groups.
- Students choose their equipment.

What to Look For

- Teams are taking this drill seriously and not purposely allowing the shuttlecock to drop.
- Feeds are challenging the receivers.

Instructional Task: Doubles Team Practice

■ PRACTICE TASK

Students play doubles games and then rotate positions. Extra players wait on either side of the net to rotate in.

Note: There is no duty team for this activity because all teams are focusing on deciding doubles teams and singles players. Teams are looking for the strongest pairs.

Student Choices/Differentiation

Students choose their partners.

What to Look For

- Students are running the practice efficiently and effectively.
- Students understand their roles and implement them correctly.
- Students respect the roles of their classmates.

Formal and Informal Assessments

Informal assessment of player strengths by team members

Closure

- What is the purpose of hitting the shuttlecock high and deep?
- What usually results when you add more power?
- What is a good strategy if you keep losing points?

Reflection

- Were students hitting the shuttlecock right at their opponents or hitting away to make them move?
- Were the duty teams getting the games going with no problem?
- Were the stats sheets being recorded correctly or should this be revisited at the beginning of class tomorrow?

Homework

- Watch a video of your choice on TeachPE.com. Take notes and tomorrow be prepared to discuss with your team any key points you learned.
- Finish your presentations on the benefits of badminton, and be ready to give them next class.

Resources

Siedentop, D., Hastie, P., & van der Mars, H. (2011). *Complete guide to sport education*. 2nd ed. Champaign, IL: Human Kinetics.

TeachPE.com: www.teachpe.com

LESSON 10: TOURNAMENT ROUND 1

Grade-Level Outcomes

Primary Outcomes

Lifetime activities: Refines activity-specific movement skills in 1 or more lifetime activities (outdoor pursuits, individual-performance activities, aquatics, net/wall games and target games). (S1.H1.L2)

Health: Analyzes the health benefits of a self-selected physical activity. (S5.H1.L1)

Physical activity knowledge: Discusses the benefits of a physically active lifestyle as it relates to college or career productivity. (S3.H1.L1)

Physical activity knowledge: Investigates the relationships among physical activity, nutrition and body composition. (S3.H1.L2)

Personal responsibility: Accepts differences between personal characteristics and the idealized body images and elite performance levels portrayed in various media. (S4.H1.L2)

Embedded Outcome

Working with others: Assumes a leadership role (e.g., task or group leader, referee, coach) in a physical activity setting. (S4.H3.L2)

Lesson Objectives

The learner will:

- present the benefits of badminton with his team.
- engage in game play while successfully utilizing both offensive and defensive strategies.
- actively participate during the round-robin pre-season through playing or serving on the duty team.

Equipment and Materials

- Badminton rackets
- Shuttlecocks
- Nets
- Clipboards and pencils
- Scorecards, stats sheets, scouting sheets

Introduction

Today, we will start with the team presentations on the benefits of badminton and then start our regular season badminton round-robin team tournament. Who is excited? During the presentations, let's be sure to be respectful while we share our information.

Instructional Task: Team Presentations

■ **PRACTICE TASK**

Draw to determine the order of presentations. Award team points and grades based on the rubric.

Guiding questions for students:

Summarize the presentations:

- What are the health benefits of badminton?
- How does being physically active influence college or career productivity?
- What are the relationships between physical activity, nutrition, and body composition?
- What kinds of body images do you see in the media? Are these realistic or healthy?

Student Choices/Differentiation

Students choose the presentation formats.

What to Look For

- Everyone participated in the presentation.
- Teams followed the rubric.
- All parts were included.

Instructional Task: Team Warm-Up and Practice

■ PRACTICE TASK

Exercise specialists lead their teams' warm-up.

Captains check the poster for their teams' court assignments.

Coaches lead their teams' practice. Teams are on the court for 5 minutes and off for 5 minutes, rotating with other teams.

During the team practice, coaches prepare the lineups for each match.

Captains make sure everyone is actively participating.

Head officials assign players to their tasks on the duty team.

Student Choices/Differentiation

Students choose the difficulty of their practice opponent.

What to Look For

- Exercise specialists are running a proper warm-up.
- Students respect the role of the exercise specialists.
- Students are participating fully in the warm-up.

Instructional Task: Tournament Matches

■ PRACTICE TASK

Your team will play two doubles matches to 15 (win by 2) and two singles matches to 15 using rally scoring. A point will be awarded on every serve. You may win, lose, or tie in this competition. A win will count 2 points for your team, a tie 1 point, and a loss 0. Points will be totaled at the end of round-robin play and displayed on the board to be carried over to the next lesson. The publicist will record some of the matches and write up a paragraph about the excitement of the day for the bulletin board. The statistician will record the scores. Officials will place all referee jerseys and whistles at the home station. Duty teams will place stats sheets and score sheets on the clipboards ready for the next round. We will not cheer for teams today, as it will disturb other matches going on at the same time. As a match ends, the next teams will take to the court to begin round two. Let's do this!

Match 1

Court A doubles: 1 v 3

Court B doubles: 1 v 3

Court C singles: 1 v 3

Court D singles: 1 v 3

Match 2

Court A doubles: 4 v 2

Court B doubles: 4 v 2

Court C singles: 4 v 2

Court D singles: 4 v 2

Match 3

Court A doubles: 5 v 6

Court B doubles: 5 v 6

Court C singles: 5 v 6

Court D singles: 5 v 6

Match 4

Court A doubles: 4 v 5

Court B doubles: 4 v 5

Court C singles: 4 v 5

Court D singles: 4 v 5

Match 1 Duty Team

Court A doubles: Team 6

Court B doubles: Team 6

Court C singles: Team 6

Court D singles: Team 6

Match 2 Duty Team

Court A doubles: Team 5

Court B doubles: Team 5

Court C singles: Team 5

Court D singles: Team 5

Match 3 Duty Team

Court A doubles: Team 1

Court B doubles: Team 1

Court C singles: Team 1

Court D singles: Team 1

Match 4 Duty Team

Court A doubles: Team 2

Court B doubles: Team 2

Court C singles: Team 2

Court D singles: Team 2

Refinement

During game play, provide specific feedback about the implementation of strategy and shot selection.

EMBEDDED OUTCOME: S4.H3.L2. Each team member will practice leading others while performing their assigned roles during the matches. Provide feedback to students about how well they are performing their roles.

What to Look For

- Students are performing their roles efficiently.
- Students are able to use the strategies during game play.
- Students who are not involved in these matches or on the duty teams are working on serves on the side if it can be done safely.
- Monitor all aspects of the round-robin as well as students on the side.

Formal and Informal Assessments

- Presentation evaluation
- Tournament play
- Informal assessment during match play

Closure

- What do you think your team needs to work on in order to be a more efficient duty team?
- What was the most challenging about being the duty team?
- What was the most rewarding?

Reflection

- Were teams performing their duties sufficiently during the games?
- Were students showing positive behavior during the competitions?
- Were games being recorded correctly?

Homework

- Search the Internet for the historical and cultural roles of badminton in a society. Write a half page for next class.
- Coaches, based on what you saw in your teams today, create a practice plan for next class.

Resources

Siedentop, D., Hastie, P., & van der Mars, H. (2011). *Complete guide to sport education.* 2nd ed. Champaign, IL: Human Kinetics.

Badminton Culture: www.badmintonculture.com

Most Popular Sports: www.mostpopularsports.net

Internet keyword search: "history of badminton"

LESSON 11: TOURNAMENT ROUND 2

Grade-Level Outcomes

Primary Outcomes

Lifetime activities: Refines activity-specific movement skills in 1 or more lifetime activities (outdoor pursuits, individual-performance activities, aquatics, net/wall games or target games). (S1.H1.L2)

Movement concepts, principles & knowledge: Identifies and discusses the historical and cultural roles of games, sports and dance in a society. (S2.H1.L2)

Embedded Outcomes

Movement concepts, principles & knowledge: Creates a practice plan to improve performance for a self-selected skill. (S2.H3.L1)

Movement concepts, principles & knowledge: Uses movement concepts and principles (e.g., force, motion, rotation) to analyze and improve performance for self and/or others in a selected skill. (S2.H2.L1)

Lesson Objectives

The learner will:

- engage in game play while successfully utilizing both offensive and defensive strategies.
- actively participate during the round-robin pre-season through playing or serving on the duty team.
- Identify cultural and historical roles of badminton on society.

Equipment and Materials

- Badminton rackets
- Shuttlecocks
- Nets
- Clipboards and pencils
- Scorecards, stats sheets, scouting sheets

Introduction

For homework you were to look up the historical and cultural roles of badminton in a society. Discuss with your team what you found. One team member will report to the class. Today, we will continue our round-robin tournament play. Points will be tallied at the end of the round-robin, and seedings for the tournament will be settled. We will begin today with our warm-up and team practice and will get ready for competition. If you had trouble with any skills, let's work on them before we begin.

Instructional Task:
Historical and Cultural Roles of Badminton

■ PRACTICE TASK

Captains meet with their teams and share information gathered from their homework. The group decides what to share. One member from each team reports to the rest of the class.

Guiding questions for students:

- What was the most interesting fact about badminton that you learned?
- Where is badminton most popular in the world?

Student Choices/Differentiation

- Students may volunteer to report to class.
- Students may create posters as an alternative to presenting.

What to Look For

- Students were thorough in gathering information.
- All students brought information to share.

Instructional Task: Team Practice

■ PRACTICE TASK

Exercise specialists lead their teams' warm-up.

Captains check the poster for their teams' court assignments.

Coaches lead their teams' practice. Teams are on the court for 5 minutes and off for 5 minutes, rotating with other teams.

During the team practice, coaches prepare the lineups for each match.

Captains make sure everyone is actively participating.

Head officials assign players to their tasks on the duty team. The student who will be video recording needs to be reminded to get some footage of all the matches.

EMBEDDED OUTCOME: S2.H3.L1. Coaches present practice plans that focus on areas in which their teams need to improve. Players may indicate on an exit slip whether the plan was a good match for their needs.

Student Choices/Differentiation

Students choose their equipment.

What to Look For

- Exercise specialists have added to their routines throughout the module.
- Coaches are implementing appropriate practice plans.
- Students are displaying knowledge of the skills covered thus far in the unit.

Instructional Task: Matches

■ PRACTICE TASK

Match 5
Court A doubles: 3 v 6
Court B doubles: 3 v 6
Court C singles: 3 v 6
Court D singles: 3 v 6

Match 6
Court A doubles: 1 v 2
Court B doubles: 1 v 2
Court C singles: 1 v 2
Court D singles: 1 v 2

Match 7
Court A doubles: 3 v 5
Court B doubles: 3 v 5
Court C singles: 3 v 5
Court D singles: 3 v 5

Match 8
Court A doubles: 4 v 1
Court B doubles: 4 v 1
Court C singles: 4 v 1
Court D singles: 4 v 1

Match 9

Court A doubles: 6 v 2

Court B doubles: 6 v 2

Court C singles: 6 v 2

Court D singles: 6 v 2

Match 5 Duty Team

Court A doubles: Team 4

Court B doubles: Team 4

Court C singles: Team 4

Court D singles: Team 4

Match 6 Duty Team

Court A doubles: Team 3

Court B doubles: Team 3

Court C singles: Team 3

Court D singles: Team 3

Match 7 Duty Team

Court A doubles: Team 6

Court B doubles: Team 6

Court C singles: Team 6

Court D singles: Team 6

Match 8 Duty Team

Court A doubles: Team 2

Court B doubles: Team 2

Court C singles: Team 2

Court D singles: Team 2

Match 9 Duty Team

Court A doubles: Team 5

Court B doubles: Team 5

Court C singles: Team 5

Court D singles: Team 5

Extension

A duty team member records match play. Players analyze the video later for improving skill and strategy.

Refinement

Teams meet with their coaches and captains at the end of round-robin play. Teams discuss positives and negatives about the round-robin, which skills need to be addressed, and whether doubles teams change or singles players switch to doubles.

Student Choices/Differentiation

Students choose the difficulty of their match opponent.

What to Look For

- Student recording the video is getting sufficient footage of each match.
- Team meetings are being taken seriously.
- Go to each team and discuss whatever issues and concerns they may have. Discuss with team coaches what each team needs to work on for the double elimination tournament.

Formal and Informal Assessments

- Tournament play
- Exit slip: Did the coach's practice plan meet your needs?

Closure

- What was your most successful offensive strategy? Defensive?
- What is the importance of the duty teams in the competitions?

Reflection

- Were there any surprises today with student abilities?
- Did the duty teams perform as planned?

Homework

Watch videos of match play, and analyze the players' strengths and weaknesses for next class. (Embedded outcome: S2.H2.L1)

Resources

Siedentop, D., Hastie, P., & van der Mars, H. (2011). *Complete guide to sport education*. 2nd ed. Champaign, IL: Human Kinetics.

LESSON 12: TOURNAMENT ROUND 3

Grade-Level Outcomes

Primary Outcome

Lifetime activities: Refines activity-specific movement skills in 1 or more lifetime activities (outdoor pursuits, individual-performance activities, aquatics, net/wall games or target games). (S1.H1.L2)

Embedded Outcome

Social interaction: Evaluates the opportunity for social interaction and social support in a self-selected physical activity or dance. (S5.H4.L2)

Lesson Objectives

The learner will:

- engage in game play while successfully utilizing both offensive and defensive strategies.
- actively participate during the round-robin pre-season through playing or serving on the duty team.

Equipment and Materials

- Badminton rackets
- Shuttlecocks
- Nets
- Clipboards and pencils
- Scorecards, stats sheets, scouting sheets

Introduction

Thank you so much for all your hard work on this module. I am so impressed with the play of all the teams so far as well as the duty teams. Everyone seems to be on task. This makes the matches much more enjoyable. We want to try to finish the round-robin today. Before getting started, you will vote as a team on awards. You may not vote for your own team. Remember to take voting seriously.

Instructional Task: Awards

■ PRACTICE TASK

Teams vote on awards.

- Best official
- Best duty team
- Most spirited
- Best manager
- Best statistician
- Hustle award
- Best coach
- Best captain
- Best publicist
- Best exercise specialist

EMBEDDED OUTCOME: S5.H4.L2. Use this opportunity to discuss the different ways badminton can offer social support and social interaction. The awards help students support others who perform their duties well.

What to Look For

All students are voting.

Instructional Task: Matches

■ **PRACTICE TASK**

Match 10

Court A doubles: 1 v 6

Court B doubles: 1 v 6

Court C singles: 1 v 6

Court D singles: 1 v 6

Match 11

Court A doubles: 2 v 5

Court B doubles: 2 v 5

Court C singles: 2 v 5

Court D singles: 2 v 5

Match 12

Court A doubles: 3 v 4

Court B doubles: 3 v 4

Court C singles: 3 v 4

Court D singles: 3 v 4

Match 13

Court A doubles: 1 v 5

Court B doubles: 1 v 5

Court C singles: 1 v 5

Court D singles: 1 v 5

Match 14

Court A doubles: 6 v 4

Court B doubles: 6 v 4

Court C singles: 6 v 4

Court D singles: 6 v 4

Match 10 Duty Team

Court A doubles: Team 3

Court B doubles: Team 3

Court C singles: Team 3

Court D singles: Team 3

Match 11 Duty Team

Court A doubles: Team 4

Court B doubles: Team 4

Court C singles: Team 4

Court D singles: Team 4

Match 12 Duty Team

Court A doubles: Team 1

Court B doubles: Team 1

Court C singles: Team 1

Court D singles: Team 1

Match 13 Duty Team

Court A doubles: Team 2

Court B doubles: Team 2

Court C singles: Team 2

Court D singles: Team 2

Match 14 Duty Team

Court A doubles: Team 5

Court B doubles: Team 5

Court C singles: Team 5

Court D singles: Team 5

Refinement

Students should use multiple types of serves. If they are using the same one all the time, remind the coaches to provide feedback about this.

Student Choices/Differentiation

Students choose their equipment.

What to Look For

Perform a game play assessment instrument (GPAI) formal student assessment during match play, reviewing a few students at a time.

Formal and Informal Assessments

Formal assessment of game play

Closure

- What offensive or defensive strategies do you think your team needs to work on before the tournament?
- What is the importance of the duty team in the tournament?

Reflection

- Are there any students who need to have a particular job for the next sport education season based on officiating and stats from today?
- Were students being supportive of each other?

Homework

Work on a practice task for your practice plan for Lesson 13 to be shared with your team.

Resources

Siedentop, D., Hastie, P., & van der Mars, H. (2011). *Complete guide to sport education.* 2nd ed. Champaign, IL: Human Kinetics.

LESSON 13: TOURNAMENT ROUND 4

Grade-Level Outcomes

Primary Outcomes

Lifetime activities: Refines activity-specific movement skills in 1 or more lifetime activities (outdoor pursuits, individual-performance activities, aquatics, net/wall games or target games). (S1.H1.L2)

Movement concepts, principles & knowledge: Creates a practice plan to improve performance for a self-selected skill. (S2.H3.L1)

Embedded Outcome

Rules & etiquette: Exhibits proper etiquette, respect for others and teamwork while engaging in physical activity and/or social dance. (S4.H2.L1)

Lesson Objectives

The learner will:

- create a practice plan to work on weaknesses as a team to prepare for a regular season tournament.
- complete any round-robin games left over from Lesson 12.
- work cooperatively to perform a team cheer for the class.

Equipment and Materials

- Badminton rackets
- Shuttlecocks
- Nets
- Laptop
- Scorecards, stats sheets, scouting sheets

Introduction

We have had a successful end to regular season play with our round-robin tournament. Today, we begin the tournament season play using single elimination. Seeds are based on regular season records. (Set up the tournament using Bracket Maker at the end of round-robin tournament play.) *There will be two doubles matches and two singles matches. Call out all scores regardless of the scoreboard. Any issues should be reported to the officials.*

Instructional Task: Team Practice

■ PRACTICE TASK

Teams develop and implement a practice plan with input from all players.

Exercise specialists lead their teams' warm-up.

Teams perform their cheers.

Student Choices/Differentiation

Each student develops her own practice task for the team practice plan.

What to Look For

- Students selected meaningful practice tasks.
- All students contributed something to the plan.
- Everyone performed the practice tasks to the best of their ability.

Instructional Task:
Complete Single Elimination Matches

■ **PRACTICE TASK**

Match 15

Court A doubles: 2 v 3

Court B doubles: 2 v 3

Court C singles: 2 v 3

Court D singles: 2 v 3

Match 15 Duty Team

Court A doubles: Team 6

Court B doubles: Team 6

Court C singles: Team 6

Court D singles: Team 6

For eliminated teams that are not on duty, a court may be set aside for fronton to accommodate many players.

Refinements

- Have students focus on hitting clears and drop shots.
- Award points for the end of round-robin play.

What to Look For

- Students are using effective strategy in the match.
- Students are communicating with one another.
- Students are remembering to return to ready position.

Instructional Task: Tournament Play

■ **PRACTICE TASK**

Teams re-group to prepare for tournament play.

Coaches make necessary adjustments to their teams.

Teams play based on seeds from the round-robin. Tournament draw is set.

EMBEDDED OUTCOME: S4.H2.L1. Emphasize the importance of proper etiquette, fair play, and respect for officials during the tournament. Students will be asked for examples of fair play on an exit slip.

What to Look For

- Students are engaged in their matches.
- Students are positively supporting each other.

Formal and Informal Assessments

Exit slip: How did you exhibit fair play today?

Closure

- What are some things your team had to do today to be successful?
- What were your goals for your team when on duty and were you successful?
- Were there any celebrations for your team today other than winning a game?

Reflection

- Are students still excited about badminton now that the round-robin has ended? How can I keep them engaged?
- Were students executing skills effectively during game play?
- What do they still need to improve on?
- Were the officials, scorekeepers, and statisticians performing their duties conscientiously?

Homework

Write a reflection on what you learned during this module about playing badminton and from performing your role on the team. What role would you like to take on in the next sport education module and why? This will be placed in your portfolio. Due last class.

Resources

Siedentop, D., Hastie, P., & van der Mars, H. (2011). *Complete guide to sport education.* 2nd ed. Champaign, IL: Human Kinetics.

LESSON 14: TOURNAMENT ROUND 5

Grade-Level Outcomes

Primary Outcome

Lifetime activities: Refines activity-specific movement skills in 1 or more lifetime activities (outdoor pursuits, individual-performance activities, aquatics, net/wall games or target games). (S1.H1.L2)

Embedded Outcome

Rules & etiquette: Examines moral and ethical conduct in specific competitive situations (e.g., intentional fouls, performance-enhancing substances, gambling, current events in sport). (S4.H2.L2)

Lesson Objectives

The learner will:

- celebrate the success of the tournament teams and players by cheering for teammates and other students.
- work cooperatively on a team to participate in competitive tournament play.
- apply skills and strategies in tournament play.
- perform an organizational role to manage the tournament.
- perform duties necessary for the duty team to be successful in smooth transitions during tournament play

Equipment and Materials

- Badminton rackets
- Shuttlecocks
- Nets
- Laptop
- Scorecards, stats sheets, scouting sheets

Introduction

Today, we will complete our badminton team tournament play except for the final match. The best officiating team will perform as the duty team for the final championship game tomorrow unless they are participating in the championship.

Instructional Task: Team Practice

■ PRACTICE TASK

Exercise specialists lead their teams' warm-up.

Coaches repeat their practice plans from Lesson 13.

Teams perform their cheers.

What to Look For

Students are active in their warm-ups and practice plans.

Instructional Task: Tournament Play Continued

■ PRACTICE TASK

Players check the poster on the wall for court assignments.

Complete all but the final match.

For eliminated teams that are not on duty, a court may be set aside for fronton to accommodate many players

Refinement

Emphasize doubles communication and formations during play.

EMBEDDED OUTCOME: S4.H2.L2. After the matches, use guiding questions to discuss the potential impact of competition on fair play and ethical conduct.

Guiding questions for students:

- How can competition affect ethical conduct in badminton?
- Have you seen any examples of this in our tournament?
- Have you seen examples in other sports?
- What happens to the spirit of the game when players do not observe etiquette and fair play or do not respect the opponent?

What to Look For

- Students are playing using appropriate badminton rules, strategies, and skills.
- Students not in a tournament game are engaged on the fronton court.
- Students are still observing etiquette and fair play as the competition heats up.

Formal and Informal Assessments

Exit slip: Offer an example of a decision you made during the tournament that contributed positively to the spirit of the game.

Closure

- What were two things your team had to do today to be successful during competition?
- If you were officiating, how did the tournament pressure affect your role?
- Next class is our last one in this module. Be ready to support the players in the final match and then celebrate your accomplishments in this sport!

Reflection

- Were students able to run the tournament smoothly?
- Were students performing their roles confidently?
- With only our championship game left, what should be implemented differently next time sport education is used for a module?

Homework

Finish your reflection about the badminton module for next class.

Resources

Siedentop, D., Hastie, P., & van der Mars, H. (2011). *Complete guide to sport education.* 2nd ed. Champaign, IL: Human Kinetics.

LESSON 15: FINAL COMPETITION AND CELEBRATION

Grade-Level Outcomes

Primary Outcome

Lifetime activities: Refines activity-specific movement skills in 1 or more lifetime activities (outdoor pursuits, individual-performance activities, aquatics, net/wall games and target games). (S1.H1.L2)

Embedded Outcome

Rules & etiquette: Exhibits proper etiquette, respect for others and teamwork while engaging in physical activity and/or social dance. (S4.H2.L1)

Lesson Objectives

The learner will:

- celebrate the success of the tournament teams and players by cheering for teams in the championship.
- work cooperatively on a team to participate in competitive tournament play.
- perform duties necessary for the duty team to be successful in smooth transitions during tournament play.
- support one another and demonstrate appropriate behavior during the awards ceremony.

Equipment and Materials

- Badminton rackets
- Shuttlecocks
- Nets
- Laptop
- Scorecards, stats sheets, scouting sheets

Introduction

Today, we will have our championship game followed by our awards ceremony. Remember, fair play could make a difference in the final results.

Cheer for all teams and players equally.

Instructional Task: Warm-Up and Team Practice

■ PRACTICE TASK

Exercise specialists lead their teams in a good warm-up for badminton play.

Coaches lead the two teams in a team practice, working on their choice of individual skills, strategies, and teamwork. Teams also discuss specific strategies for play.

Remaining players practice skills of their choosing.

Student Choices/Differentiation

Students choose which individual skills to work on for improvement.

What to Look For

- All members of each team are participating equally.
- Teams are following the coaches' recommendations during their practice session.

Instructional Task: Final Match

■ PRACTICE TASK

Make sure each court has equipment needed, nets tight, and scoring table ready. Decide who will perform duties on each court. Recruit from other teams if necessary.

Final matches will be between the top two singles teams and the top two doubles teams.

Two teams will be assigned as the duty teams. Duty teams prepare the courts for game play—stats sheets ready, scoreboard ready, and laptop at hand.

Other teams will be assigned a side of a court. This will be their team to cheer for in a low key. They will also take notes for this team as to what they need to work on or what they did well. They may also use stats sheets or shot charts.

Extension

Extra teams conduct the GPAI on a team to analyze what they did well and where they made mistakes.

Student Choices/Differentiation

Students choose their duty assignments.

What to Look For

- Duty team is ready to begin the championship game.
- Teams are executing skills effectively.
- Students are employing appropriate tactics for the situation.
- Everyone is engaged in their roles.

Instructional Task: Team Fronton Doubles

■ PRACTICE TASK

Teams participate in a fronton doubles round against other teams.

Tally the final points for teams and finalize awards during this instructional task. You can ask the captains and publicists to assist.

Student Choices/Differentiation

Students choose their partners within their teams.

Instructional Task: Awards Ceremony

■ PRACTICE TASK

All teams receive an award. Award prizes or certificates for individual and team awards.

Take pictures of each team with their team posters to post on the school website.

Publicists write a paragraph (highlights of the season) about their teams to add to their pictures.

EMBEDDED OUTCOME: S4.H2.L1 Students demonstrate respect for each other by supporting award winners with cheers or applause.

What to Look For

- All students are recognized in some way.
- Students are supporting one another with cheers and applause.

Formal and Informal Assessments

- Reflections
- Exit slip: What are three things you would like to change about the season?

Closure

- What skills in badminton did you enjoy learning the most?
- What are three things you liked about the sport education badminton season?
- Did you think the awards voted on by your peers were accurate?
- What do you think the team with the most total points did in order to be successful?
- Be sure to turn in your exit slips and your reflections on the season.
- Check the school website for upcoming modules.

Reflection

- Were the teams supportive of each other during the awards ceremony?
- Did the voting on awards by teams come out the way you thought it should?
- Did the intrinsic awards outweigh the extrinsic?

Homework

Choose a new module for the next class.

Resources

Siedentop, D., Hastie, P., & van der Mars, H. (2011). *Complete guide to sport education*. 2nd ed. Champaign, IL: Human Kinetics.

TENNIS MODULE

Lessons in this module were contributed by **Melanie Perreault**, assistant professor of motor behavior at the College Brockport, State University of New York, where she also teaches tennis.

TENNIS

Grade-Level Outcomes Addressed, by Lesson	Lessons 1	2	3	4	5	6	7	8	9	10	11	12	13	14	15	16
Standard 1. The physically literate individual demonstrates competency in a variety of motor skills and movement patterns.																
Demonstrates competency and/or refines activity-specific movement skills in 2 or more lifetime activities (outdoor pursuits, individual-performance activities, aquatics, net/wall games or target games). (S1.H1.L1)		P	P	P	P	P	P	P	P	P	P	P	P	P	P	P
Standard 2. The physically literate individual applies knowledge of concepts, principles, strategies and tactics related to movement and performance.																
Applies the terminology associated with exercise and participation in selected individual-performance activities, dance, net/wall games, target games, aquatics and/or outdoor pursuits appropriately. (S2.H1.L1)	P	E								P	P					
Uses movement concepts and principles (e.g., force, motion, rotation) to analyze and improve performance of self and/or others in a selected skill. (S2.H2.L1)			E	E	E		E									
Describes the speed vs. accuracy trade-off in throwing and striking skills. (S2.H2.L2)								E								
Creates a practice plan to improve performance for a self-selected skill. (S2.H3.L1)										E		E		E		
Standard 3. The physically literate individual demonstrates the knowledge and skills to achieve and maintain a health-enhancing level of physical activity and fitness.																
Identifies issues associated with exercising in heat, humidity and cold. (S3.H3.L1)									E							
Evaluates—according to their benefits, social support network and participation requirements—activities that can be pursued in the local environment. (S3.H4.L1)													P			
Analyzes the impact of life choices, economics, motivation and accessibility on exercise adherence and participation in physical activity in college or career settings. (S3.H5.L2)													E			
Standard 4. The physically literate individual exhibits responsible personal and social behavior that respects self and others.																
Exhibits proper etiquette, respect for others and teamwork while engaging in physical activity and/or social dance. (S4.H2.L1)	P								E		E					
Uses communication skills and strategies that promote team or group dynamics. (S4.H3.L1)							E				E					
Assumes a leadership role (e.g., task or group leader, referee, coach) in a physical activity setting. (S4.H3.L2)																E
Solves problems and thinks critically in physical activity and/or dance settings, both as an individual and in groups. (S4.H4.L1)								E								
Applies best practices for participating safely in physical activity, exercise and dance (e.g., injury prevention, proper alignment, hydration, use of equipment, implementation of rules, sun protection). (S4.H5.L1)	E															E
Standard 5. The physically literate individual recognizes the value of physical activity for health, enjoyment, challenge, self-expression and/or social interaction.																
Analyzes the health benefits of a self-selected physical activity. (S5.H1.L1)													E			
Selects and participates in physical activities or dance that meet the need for self-expression and enjoyment. (S5.H3.L1)													E			
Identifies the opportunity for social support in a self-selected physical activity or dance. (S5.H4.L1)													E			

P = Primary; E = Embedded

LESSON 1: RULES AND ETIQUETTE

Grade-Level Outcomes

Primary Outcomes

Movement concepts, principles & knowledge: Applies the terminology associated with exercise and participation in selected individual-performance activities, dance, net/wall games, target games, aquatics and/or outdoor pursuits appropriately. (S2.H1.L1)

Rules & etiquette: Exhibits proper etiquette, respect for others and teamwork while engaging in physical activity and/or social dance. (S4.H2.L1)

Embedded Outcome

Safety: Applies best practices for participating safely in physical activity, exercise and dance (e.g., injury prevention, proper alignment, hydration, use of equipment, implementation of rules, sun protection). (S4.H5.L1)

Lesson Objectives

The learner will:

- demonstrate knowledge of a tennis court by correctly labeling its components on a diagram.
- score a tennis game by identifying the correct score in four out of five video scenarios.
- demonstrate knowledge of basic tennis rules by scoring at least 70 percent on a written assessment.

Equipment and Materials

- Multimedia device (TV, laptop, tablet)
- Several video clips of tennis games
- Tennis rackets: 1 per student
- Low-density tennis balls: at least 3 per 4 students
- Tennis rules, etiquette, and scoring assessment
- Printouts of a tennis court (without labels): 1 per student

Introduction

Today, we will be starting our next module on tennis. We will start with an introduction to the rules, scoring, and equipment. Throughout the module, you will learn foundational skills, such as the forehand and backhand, and progress to more advanced skills such as lobs and smashes, as well as learning basic tactics to be successful in game play.

Instructional Task: Learning the Court

■ PRACTICE TASK

Students identify and describe the components of a tennis court using a large tennis court diagram and then progressing onto the court.

Extensions

- Divide the class into two groups: one on each side of the net. Call out locations on the tennis court, and each group must get to the correct location.
- Same task except each group must get to the location as quickly as possible. First group to get all its members to the correct location gets a point. Play until one group reaches a desired point value.
- Hand out tennis court diagrams for students to label.

What to Look For

- Students are getting to the correct locations on the court without much confusion.
- Each student correctly labels all components on the tennis court diagram.

Instructional Task: Game Rules and Etiquette

■ PRACTICE TASK

Explain the basic rules and etiquette for playing a game of tennis.

Extension

Assign scenarios (written or video clips) to groups of students (four or five per group). Students decide what rules or points of etiquette are being followed and which are not being followed. Each group presents to the class for discussion.

Refinement

You may need to review when to switch sides on the court and rules regarding calling balls in and out.

Student Choices/Differentiation

Students volunteer if they would like to present for their groups.

What to Look For

Each group accurately assesses their scenarios in regard to rules and etiquette.

Instructional Task: Scoring

■ PRACTICE TASK

Explain how to score a game of tennis using video clips.

Refinement

You may need to review terms regarding even scores (i.e., deuce) and advantages when closing out a close game.

Extensions

- Show video clips of tennis games without audio or scoring graphics. Students must determine the correct score at random points in the game (as determined by you).
- In groups of four, students explore striking with the racket while attempting to follow rules and etiquette and also keep score.

EMBEDDED OUTCOME: S4.H5.L1. While students are exploring striking, provide feedback related to implementation of rules.

Student Choices/Differentiation

- Students choose their rackets and playing area.
- Students may choose low-density balls.

What to Look For

- Students are able to accurately score the video clips without your input.
- Students are able to keep score on the court.
- Students are following rules and points of etiquette on the court.
- Students are making good contact with the ball.

Instructional Task: Knowledge Quiz

■ PRACTICE TASK

Administer a written assessment on rules, etiquette, and scoring.

Student Choices/Differentiation

Allow extra time if needed or assign for homework.

What to Look For

- Students are able to recall important terminology and etiquette.
- Students are able to score correctly.

Formal and Informal Assessments

- Formal assessment: labeled tennis court diagrams
- Formal written assessment of rules, etiquette, and scoring (benchmark score: 70 percent)
- Informal assessment of striking to determine skill level of students

Closure

- What are some of the areas on the court that you learned today?
- What are some of the rules and points of etiquette that you learned today?
- How are points scored during a game of tennis?
- What was one way you worked well with a classmate today?
- Watch some more videos of tennis matches on your own. Next time you will be learning proper footwork and different types of grips.

Reflection

- Were students able to properly identify the components of a tennis court?
- Were students able to follow all the rules and points of etiquette identified in the lesson?
- Were there differences in the students' skill levels?

Homework

Find video clips of tennis matches and practice keeping score. Notice how the rules and etiquette that you learned today are followed in the videos. (You can use this as an informal talking point at the beginning of the next lesson.)

Resources

Brown, J. (2004). *Tennis: Steps to success*. 3rd ed. Champaign, IL: Human Kinetics.

Tennis court diagram: www.printyourbrackets.com/images/printable-tennis-court-diagram.jpg

Rules of tennis: http://assets.usta.com/assets/1/15/ITF%20-%20RoT%202010.pdf

Internet keyword search: "diagram of a tennis court," "rules of tennis," "etiquette in tennis"

LESSON 2: FOOTWORK

Grade-Level Outcomes

Primary Outcome

Lifetime activities: Demonstrates competency and/or refines activity-specific movement skills in 2 or more lifetime activities (outdoor pursuits, individual-performance activities, aquatics, net/wall games or target games). (S1.H1.L1)

Embedded Outcome

Movement concepts, principles & knowledge: Applies the terminology associated with exercise and participation in selected individual-performance activities, dance, net/wall games, target games, aquatics and/or outdoor pursuits appropriately. (S2.H1.L1)

Lesson Objectives

The learner will:

- perform the ready position, split step, shuffle step, and crossover step, successfully completing three out of five attempts during the shuffle–crossover task.

Equipment and Materials

- Tennis rackets: 1 per student
- Tennis balls: at least 5 per student pair
- Low-density balls

Introduction

Today, you will be learning about footwork. Proper footwork is an essential element of the game of tennis. Even the player with the best strokes will be ineffective if he cannot get to the ball in time to set up for the shot.

Instructional Task: Ready Position and Split Step

■ PRACTICE TASK

Demonstrate the ready position and split step. Students shadow along.

Extensions

- Students pair off and stand at the service line across from each other (four per court). One student shadows a forehand while the other stands in ready position and performs a split step when her partner's racket is in line with her body (i.e., imaginary contact zone). Students trade off after every five attempts.
- Students perform the same task except the partner will drop-hit a ball softly over the net.

Guiding questions for students:

- Why are the ready position and split step important?
- When would you use each?

Refinement

Check the height of the split-step jump and correct if needed. Make sure students are on the balls of their feet in the ready position.

Student Choices/Differentiation

Students may review a video clip of the ready position and split step.

What to Look For

- Ready position: Students are in an athletic stance on the balls of the feet. A common error is for students to be flat-footed.
- Split step: Students jump only a couple of inches off the ground and time it with the opponent's contact with the ball. Common errors include jumping too high and jumping too soon or too late.

Instructional Task: Shuffle Step

■ PRACTICE TASK

Demonstrate the shuffle step. Students pair off: One stands on the baseline center mark and the other on the top of the T facing the baseline (four students on a court). One student rolls ground balls a short distance away from the other student, alternating right and left. The other student "fields" the ground balls using the shuffle step to get into position, then shuffles back to the starting position and performs a split step into ready position (depositing the ball at the center mark). Students alternate after every five attempts.

Extensions

- Students perform the same task except the balls are rolled farther away.
- Students perform the same task except the balls are rolled faster and are sent randomly to the right and left.

Refinement

Reinforce the importance of shuffling, not crossing, the feet while moving to avoid getting tripped up.

Student Choices/Differentiation

- Students may watch a video clip of the shuffle step.
- Students choose their partners.

What to Look For

Students have knees bent and hips low. A common error is crossing the feet.

Instructional Task: Crossover Step

■ PRACTICE TASK

Demonstrate the crossover step. Students pair off and take position on court as in the previous task. One student tosses a ball so that it bounces a short distance from his partner, alternating right and left. The other student uses the crossover step to catch the ball with his outside hand, then returns to the starting position and performs a split step into ready position. Students alternate after every five attempts.

Extensions

- Students perform the same task except the balls are tossed randomly to the right and left.
- Students perform the same task except the balls are placed farther out.
- Students perform the same task except the balls are placed toward the alleys. Students must use a crossover step and then run to catch the ball. To return to the starting position, students must use a shuffle step and split step to return to ready position.
- Students repeat the sequence with a racket in hand.

Refinement

You might need to refine the front crossover if students are crossing behind. Refine the split step and ready position, as needed.

Student Choices/Differentiation

- Students may watch a video clip of the crossover step.
- Students choose their partners.
- Students choose their rackets and balls.

What to Look For

- Students cross in front and with the correct foot.
- Students perform the crossover step before sprinting to catch the ball.
- Students always perform the split step and get into ready position when returning to the starting position.

Formal and Informal Assessments

Exit slip: Why is the split step important and when do you use it?

Closure

- What were the other types of footwork you learned today? (Embedded outcome: S2.H1.L1)
- What was one way you worked well with a classmate today?
- Keep practicing on your own at home. Next class you will be learning the forehand stroke.

Reflection

- Were students able to perform each type of footwork independently?
- Were students able to perform the different types of footwork in combination?
- Were students able to perform the split step with correct timing?

Homework

Practice the different types of footwork at home in front of a mirror.

Resources

Footwork fundamentals: www.fuzzyyellowballs.com/video-tennis-lessons/footwork/footwork-fundamentals/

LESSON 3: FOREHAND

Grade-Level Outcomes

Primary Outcome

Lifetime activities: Demonstrates competency and/or refines activity-specific movement skills in 2 or more lifetime activities (outdoor pursuits, individual-performance activities, aquatics, net/wall games or target games). (S1.H1.L1)

Embedded Outcome

Movement concepts, principles & knowledge: Uses movement concepts and principles (e.g., force, motion, rotation) to analyze and improve performance of self and/or others in a selected skill. (S2.H2.L1)

Lesson Objectives

The learner will:

- perform the eastern forehand grip.
- successfully perform the forehand shot three times in a row with a partner.

Equipment and Materials

- Tennis rackets: 1 per student
- Tennis balls (various densities): at least 3 per student pair

Introduction

Today, you will be learning the forehand shot. This is one of the most common and fundamental shots in tennis. It is used most often during baseline rallies.

Instructional Task: Eastern Forehand Grip

■ PRACTICE TASK

Demonstrate the eastern forehand grip. Students shadow along.

Extension

Have students place their rackets on the ground, and when you say go, students pick up their rackets with the eastern forehand grip.

Refinement

Students refine skill by reviewing pictures of the grip; also, you can post instructional videos of the grip to the school's physical education website.

Student Choices/Differentiation

Students choose their rackets.

What to Look For

Base knuckle (index finger) is on the third bevel of the handle.

Instructional Task: Forehand Strike Movement Pattern

■ PRACTICE TASK

Demonstrate the forehand strike. Students shadow along.

Refinement

Common errors are dropping the racket head or using a flat swing path. Refine skill by having students practice making a U-shaped swing path and keeping the wrist firm throughout the entire stroke. Students may shadow movement with a partner.

Extension

Students peer-assess a partner's striking movement pattern using the critical features. Students use a device to record the movement, if available. Provide a checklist to guide assessment.

EMBEDDED OUTCOME: S2.H2.L1 Students provide feedback based on the assessment to improve partners' striking pattern.

Student Choices/Differentiation

- Students choose their rackets.
- Students may review a video clip of the forehand strike (slow motion).

What to Look For

- Racket is back during preparation.
- Students turn sideways to the net.
- Wrist is firm at contact.
- Swing path is low to high.
- Racket finishes over opposite shoulder.
- Students return to ready position.

Instructional Task: Forehand Strike With Partner

■ PRACTICE TASK

Students pair up and stand across from each other on the service line on one side of the T (four students per court). One partner drop-hits three forehands across the net while the partner uses footwork from the last class to catch the balls. Partners trade roles.

Extensions

- Students perform the same task except they move back to the baseline.
- Students perform the same task except they attempt to keep a rally going while striking with rackets (no catching).
- Students perform the same task except they set a goal for consecutive forehands in a row.

Refinements

- A concern with this task when students are at the service line is that they abbreviate the movement pattern in order to reduce force on the ball. If this is the case, encourage them to use a lower-density ball.
- Another concern is ball control when two rallies are going on at the same time. Encourage students to follow through, pointing their rackets at the target (partner).

Student Choices/Differentiation

- Students may choose to start with lower-density balls.
- Students choose their rackets.
- Students may choke up if having difficulty controlling the racket.
- Students may use a backboard or ball machine, if available.

What to Look For

- Students are swinging through the ball.
- Racket is finishing over the shoulder.
- Wrist is firm at contact.
- Weight transfer is effective.

Instructional Task: Forehand Games

■ PRACTICE TASK

Each group of four students play modified games. The server drop-hits a forehand to the other side, and another player returns the ball using a forehand. Once the ball has been successfully returned, the point is played out and scored like a real game. Server changes after each game. Students must try to use only forehands.

Refinements

- If students are having trouble with placement, remind them to finish the follow-through, with the racket pointing at their intended target.
- Refine student scoring and footwork, if needed.

Student Choices/Differentiation

- Students may choose to change partners.
- Students may decide what type of ball they want to play with.

What to Look For

- Students are correctly keeping score.
- Students are returning to the ready position.
- Students are swinging through on the forehand.

Formal and Informal Assessments

- Peer assessments: striking checklist

Closure

- What grip did you learn today? Can someone demonstrate it for me?
- Can you name three critical features of the forehand?
- How do you create topspin on the ball?
- Can you give some examples of cooperation in today's class?
- Keep practicing the skills at home if you can, and the next lesson you will be learning the one-hand backhand.

Reflection
- Were students hitting the ball with topspin?
- Were students hitting the ball too high or into the net?
- Did students get enough practice with the forehand?
- How well did students remember how to score correctly?
- How well did students demonstrate proper footwork?

Homework
- Practice the forehand striking pattern at home, focusing on the feedback from the peer assessment. You can do that with a racket or another type of long-handled implement.
- Provide students with a handout that shows pictures of the eastern forehand grip.

Resources
Internet keyword search: "tennis grip," "tennis forehand," "tennis forehand grip," "tennis forehand mechanics"

LESSON 4: ONE-HAND BACKHAND

Grade-Level Outcomes

Primary Outcome

Lifetime activities: Demonstrates competency and/or refines activity-specific movement skills in 2 or more lifetime activities (outdoor pursuits, individual-performance activities, aquatics, net/wall games or target games). (S1.H1.L1)

Embedded Outcome

Movement concepts, principles & knowledge: Uses movement concepts and principles (e.g., force, motion, rotation) to analyze and improve performance of self and/or others in a selected skill. (S2.H2.L1)

Lesson Objectives

The learner will:

- perform the eastern backhand grip.
- successfully perform the one-hand backhand shot three times in a row with a partner.

Equipment and Materials

- Tennis rackets: 1 per student
- Tennis balls (various densities): at least 3 per student pair

Introduction

Today, you will be learning the one-hand backhand. Roger Federer and Stan Wawrinka are well known for this shot, and it can be very effective during baseline rallies. Here are a couple of video clips.

Show video clips of Federer's and Wawrinka's backhands.

Instructional Task: Eastern Backhand Grip

■ PRACTICE TASK

Demonstrate the eastern backhand grip. Students shadow along.

Extension

Have students place their rackets on the ground, and when you say go, students pick up their rackets with the eastern backhand grip.

Refinement

Students refine skill by reviewing pictures of the grip; also, you can post instructional videos of the grip to the school's physical education website.

Student Choices/Differentiation

Students choose their rackets.

What to Look For

Base knuckle (index finger) is on the first bevel of the handle.

Instructional Task:
One-Hand Backhand Strike Movement Pattern

■ PRACTICE TASK

Demonstrate the one-hand backhand strike. Students shadow along.

Refinement

Make sure students are using the proper grip. Students refine skill by practicing the follow-through with the racket face out in front. Students shadow swing with a partner.

Extension

Students peer-assess a partner's striking movement pattern using the critical features. Students use a device to record the movement, if available. Provide a checklist to guide assessment.

EMBEDDED OUTCOME: S2.H2.L1. Students use the assessment to provide feedback about partners' performance so that they can improve their stroke.

Student Choices/Differentiation

Students choose their rackets.

What to Look For

- Students use correct backhand grip.
- Arm is bent at contact point (rather than straight).
- Racket does not drop below contact point.
- Racket follows through out front (rather than across body).

Instructional Task: One-Hand Backhand with Partner

■ PRACTICE TASK

Students pair up and stand across from each other on the service line on one side of the T (four students per court). One partner soft-tosses three balls for the other partner to return using the one-hand backhand. The tossing partner uses footwork to catch the balls when they come back over the net. Partners trade roles.

Extensions

- Students perform the same task except they move back to the baseline and the tossing partner feeds balls with a drop-hit forehand.
- Students perform the same task except they attempt to keep a rally going while hitting with their rackets (no catching).
- Students perform the same task except they set a goal for consecutive one-hand backhands in a row.

Refinements

- A concern with this task when students are at the service line is that they abbreviate the movement pattern in order to reduce force on the ball. If this is the case, encourage them to use a lower-density ball.
- Another concern is ball control when two rallies are going on at the same time. Encourage students to follow through with the racket face toward the target (partner).

Student Choices/Differentiation

- Students may choose to start with lower-density balls.
- Students choose their partners.
- Students may review a video clip of the one-hand backhand (slow motion).
- Students may use a backboard or ball machine, if available.

What to Look For

- Students are using the proper grip.
- Students are swinging through the ball.
- Students are following through out front to the target.
- Weight transfer is effective.
- Students are using the crossover step.

Instructional Task: Backhand Games

■ PRACTICE TASK

Each group of four students play modified games. The server drop-hits a forehand to the other side, and another player returns the ball using a one-hand backhand. Once the ball has been successfully returned, the point is played out and scored like a real game. Server changes after each game. Students must try to use only one-hand backhands, except when starting the point.

Refinements

- During modified game play, students may forget about their footwork. Provide feedback to reinforce the shuffle and crossover.
- Students may shorten their swings to gain control. Reinforce the preparation (backswing) and following through to the target.
- Refine student scoring if needed.

Student Choices/Differentiation

- Students may choose to change partners.
- Students may decide what type of ball they want to play with.

What to Look For

- Students are keeping score correctly.
- Students are using correct footwork.
- Students are using the one-hand backhand striking pattern and not running around the ball to hit a forehand.

Formal and Informal Assessments

Informal assessment and peer assessments

Closure

- What grip did you learn today? Who will demonstrate it for me?
- Name three critical features of the one-hand backhand.
- Offer some examples of cooperation in today's class.
- Keep practicing the skills at home if you can, and in our next lesson you will learn the two-hand backhand.

Reflection

- Were students consistently using the proper grip?
- Were students hitting the ball too high or into the net?
- Did students get enough practice with the one-hand backhand?
- How well did students remember how to score correctly?
- How well did students demonstrate proper footwork?

Homework

- Practice the one-hand striking pattern at home, focusing on the feedback from the peer assessment. Use a racket or another type of long-handled implement.
- Provide students with a handout that shows pictures of the eastern backhand grip.

Resources

Internet keyword search: "backhand grip," "tennis backhand," "backhand mechanics"

LESSON 5: TWO-HAND BACKHAND

Grade-Level Outcomes

Primary Outcome

Lifetime activities: Demonstrates competency and/or refines activity-specific movement skills in 2 or more lifetime activities (outdoor pursuits, individual-performance activities, aquatics, net/wall games or target games). (S1.H1.L1)

Embedded Outcome

Movement concepts, principles & knowledge: Uses movement concepts and principles (e.g., force, motion, rotation) to analyze and improve performance of self and/or others in a self-selected skill. (S2.H2.L1)

Lesson Objectives

The learner will:

- perform the two-hand backhand grip.
- successfully perform the two-hand backhand shot three times in a row with a partner.

Equipment and Materials

- Tennis rackets: 1 per student
- Tennis balls (various densities): at least 3 per student pair

Introduction

Today, you will be learning the two-hand backhand. This is the more commonly used version of the backhand and can help you generate a lot of power during baseline rallies.

Instructional Task: Two-Hand Backhand Grip

■ PRACTICE TASK

Demonstrate the two-hand backhand grip. Students shadow along.

Extensions

- Have students place their rackets on the ground, and when you say go, students pick up their rackets with the two-hand backhand grip.
- Extend the task by having students alternate between eastern backhand and two-hand backhand grips.

Refinement

Students refine skill by reviewing pictures of the grip; instructional videos of the grip can also be posted to the school's physical education website.

What to Look For

- Base knuckle (index finger) of the dominant hand is on the second bevel of the handle.
- Non-dominant hand is above the dominant hand, with base knuckle on the sixth bevel.

Instructional Task:
Two-Hand Backhand Strike Movement Pattern

■ **PRACTICE TASK**

Demonstrate the two-hand backhand strike. Students shadow along.

Guiding questions for students:
- How does the two-hand backhand differ from the one-hand backhand?
- What are the advantages of the two-hand backhand?
- What are the advantages of the one-hand backhand?

Refinements
- Reinforce that the primary force comes from the non-dominant hand rather than the dominant in the two-hand backhand.
- Students shadow with a partner.

Extension

Students peer-assess a partner's striking movement pattern using the critical features. Students use a device to record the movement, if available. Provide a checklist to guide assessment.

EMBEDDED OUTCOME: S2.H2.L1. Students provide corrective feedback to partners based on peer assessment.

Student Choices/Differentiation

Students choose their rackets.

What to Look For
- Students are bringing their rackets back with the correct grip.
- Swing pattern is from low to high.
- Students are transferring their weight at the right time.
- Students are following through to the target.

Instructional Task: Two-Handed Backhand With Partner

■ **PRACTICE TASK**

Students pair up and stand across from each other on the service line on one side of the T (four students per court). One partner soft-tosses three balls for the other partner to return using the two-hand backhand. The tossing partner uses footwork to catch the balls when they come back over the net. Partners trade roles.

Extensions
- Students perform the same task except they move back to the baseline and the tossing partner feeds balls with a drop-hit forehand.
- Students perform the same task except they attempt to keep a rally going while hitting with their rackets (no catching).
- Students perform the same task except they set a goal for consecutive two-hand backhands in a row.

Refinements

- If students are abbreviating the movement pattern while at the service line in order to reduce force on the ball, encourage them to swing through and use a lower-density ball.
- If ball control is an issue when two rallies are going on at the same time, encourage students to line up the dominant shoulder with the target (partner) before striking the ball.

Student Choices/Differentiation

- Students may choose to start with lower-density balls.
- Students may use a backboard or ball machine, if available.

What to Look For

Students are making contact at waist level and out front.

Instructional Task: Backhand Games

■ PRACTICE TASK

Each group of four students play modified games. The server drop-hits a forehand to the other side, and another player returns the ball using a two-hand backhand. Once the ball has been successfully returned, the point is played out and scored like a real game. The server changes after each game. Students must try to use only two-hand backhands after the ball is put in play.

Extensions

- Students perform the same task but may use both one-hand and two-hand backhands.
- Students perform the same task but use either the backhand stroke or the forehand as appropriate.

Refinement

Reinforce the importance of the appropriate footwork and early backswing preparation while the ball is approaching.

Student Choices/Differentiation

- Students may choose to change partners.
- Students may decide what type of ball they want to play with.
- Students may decide which style backhand they want to use.

What to Look For

- Students are correctly keeping score.
- Students are performing correct footwork.
- Students are using the two-hand backhand striking pattern.

Formal and Informal Assessments

Informal assessment and peer assessments

Closure

- What grip did you learn today? Can someone demonstrate it for me?
- Can you name three critical features of the two-hand backhand?
- How does the two-hand backhand differ from the one-hand backhand?
- Keep practicing the skills at home if you can, and the next lesson you will be learning some basic tactics for baseline rallies.

Reflection

- Were students consistently using the proper grip?
- Were students hitting the ball too high or into the net?
- Were students generating most of their power from the non-dominant hand?
- Did students get enough practice with the two-hand backhand?

Homework

- Practice the two-hand striking pattern at home. You can do that with a racket or another type of long-handled implement.
- Provide students with a handout that shows pictures of the two-hand backhand grip, or refer them to the school's physical education website for video clips.

Resources

Grip review: https://cdn.shopify.com/s/files/1/0134/9182/files/how_to_grip_a_tennis_racket_large.jpg?225

One-hand versus two-hand backhand: www.youtube.com/watch?v=5gs94l0wKpM

Internet keyword search: "backhand," "one-handed versus two-handed backhand"

LESSON 6: GROUNDSTROKES AND TACTICS

Grade-Level Outcomes

Primary Outcome

Lifetime activities: Demonstrates competency and/or refines activity-specific movement skills in 2or more lifetime activities (outdoor pursuits, individual-performance activities, aquatics, net/wall games or target games). (S1.H1.L1)

Embedded Outcomes

Working with others: Uses communication skills and strategies that promote team or group dynamics. (S4.H3.L1)

Lesson Objectives

The learner will:

- perform baseline rallies using a variety of groundstrokes.
- perform basic tactics (returning home, creating open space) during baseline rallies.

Equipment and Materials

- Tennis rackets: 1 per student
- Tennis balls (various densities): at least 3 per student pair
- Poly spots: at least 2 per court

Introduction

Today, you will be practicing groundstrokes and learning basic tactics used during baseline rallies. Tactics are a way to gain an advantage over an opponent during a game.

Instructional Task: Groundstrokes in Baseline Rally

■ PRACTICE TASK

Students pair up and stand across from each other on the service line on one side of the T (four students per court). Pairs rally cooperatively using forehands and backhands.

Extensions

- Students move back to the baseline and continue to rally cooperatively.
- Students set a goal for consecutive groundstrokes and continue to rally.
- One student on each side of the court stands at the center mark while the other student stands at the fence. The two students at the center mark start a cooperative rally using the whole singles court. After every shot, students at the center mark trade places with students at the fence.
- Students perform the same task but set a goal for consecutive groundstrokes.

EMBEDDED OUTCOME: S4.H3.L1. The extensions for this task present an opportunity to teach students about communicating and cooperating to reach a goal. If they don't, they will not make many consecutive hits.

Refinement

Students may revert to an abbreviated stroke when they try to keep the rally going. Provide corrective feedback to reinforce swinging through the ball. If students are struggling to get to the ball in time to set up, remind them to use proper footwork.

Student Choices/Differentiation

- Students choose a goal for consecutive groundstrokes and modify the goal as needed.
- Students may choose to change partners.
- Students may choose to start with lower-density balls.

What to Look For

- Students show correct form on forehand and backhand strokes.
- Students are bringing the racket back early.
- Wrist and arm are straight at the point of contact.
- Swing path is low to high.

Instructional Task:
Creating Open Space With Shot Selection

■ PRACTICE TASK

Demonstrate cross-court and down-the-line shots.

Students pair up and stand across from each other on the baseline near the alley (four students per court). One student starts a baseline rally with a drop-hit forehand. (Students rotate the server after each rally.) Students on one side of the court may hit only cross-court, and students on the other side may hit only down the line (using forehands or backhands, as appropriate). The rally continues until a student places the ball incorrectly, the ball is hit into the net, or the ball is hit out of bounds. Students change roles (cross-court versus down the line) after every four rallies.

Guiding questions for students:

- How could you win a point during a baseline rally? (Answer: Hit to open space.)
- How can you create open space? (Answer: Pull opponent off the middle of the court.)
- How do you pull the opponent off the middle of the court? (Answer: Hit deep in the corners.)

Extension

Repeat the task except students set a goal for consecutive shots.

Student Choices/Differentiation

- Students may choose to start with lower-density balls.
- Students may choose a goal and modify it as needed.
- Students may review video clips of cross-court and down-the-line shots in match play.

What to Look For

- Students are hitting deep with topspin.
- Students are using proper technique to direct the ball down the line or cross-court.
- Students are preparing early to hit the ball with proper footwork.

Instructional Task: Return Home

■ PRACTICE TASK

On one side of the court ("home" side), position poly spots on each side of the center mark about 2 feet (0.6 m) apart. Students form groups of four: One student on each side of the court stands at the center mark, while the other two students stand at the fence. The student on the home side of the court starts a rally by drop-hitting a forehand. The student on the other side returns the shot to one of the corners of the singles court using a cross-court or down-the-line shot. The home-side student must return the ball and get back to home (between the polyspots) as quickly as possible to recover for the next shot. Once the point is over, the two students who were playing rotate to the other side of the court while the other two students, who were waiting at the fence, take their places and start a new point.

Guiding questions for students:

- How could you defend against an opponent when you are pulled out of position? (Answer: Return "home" [center mark].)
- What should you be looking at as you recover?

Extensions

- Students waiting at the fence count the number of times the hitter returns to home during the point.
- Repeat the task, but students keep individual scores from the points they win.

Refinement

Have students focus on the depth of their shots by placing targets just inside the baseline at the corners of the singles court.

Student Choices/Differentiation

Students may choose to start with lower-density balls.

What to Look For

- Students are getting "home" before the next ball is hit.
- Students are hitting effectively to the corners.
- Students are using appropriate footwork to get to the ball and set up for the shot.
- Students are using appropriate technique for their groundstrokes.

Instructional Task: Groundstroke Games

■ PRACTICE TASK

Groups of four students play modified singles games. On each court, two students play a no-ad game while the other two students perform a peer assessment that focuses on tactics. The server drop-hits a forehand to the other side, and the other player returns the ball using a groundstroke. Once the ball has been successfully returned, the point is played out and scored like a real game. The server rotates after each game, and students trade off after every two games. Students must try to use the tactics practiced earlier in the lesson.

Extension

Students use a device to record the modified games and evaluate the tactics used during play.

Student Choices/Differentiation

- Students may choose to change partners.
- Students may decide what type of ball they want to play with.

What to Look For

- Students are effectively using the tactics of creating open space and returning home.
- Students are able to hit the ball where they want to (e.g., cross-court, down the line, deep).

Formal and Informal Assessments

Informal assessment and peer assessment on tactics

Closure

- What two tactics did you learn today?
- How would you use these tactics in a game?
- What other kinds of tactics do you think might be useful?
- Keep practicing the skills at home if you can, and the next lesson you will be learning the punch serve.

Reflection

- Were students maintaining proper groundstroke technique during baseline rallies?
- Were students able to use the tactics effectively during play?
- Were students using proper footwork to get to the ball, set up, and return to home?

Homework

- Direct students to video clips of tennis matches on the school's physical education website.
- Ask students to identify examples of the two tactics learned in class and any others that they notice.

Resources

One-hand versus two-hand backhand: www.youtube.com/watch?v=5gs94I0wKpM

United States Tennis Association: ww.usta.com

Fuzzy Yellow Balls: www.fuzzyyellowballs.com

Internet search terms: "forehand," "backhand," "cross-court shot," "down-the-line shot," "ready position," "return home"

LESSON 7: PUNCH SERVE

Grade-Level Outcomes

Primary Outcome

Lifetime activities: Demonstrates competency and/or refines activity-specific movement skills in 2 or more lifetime activities (outdoor pursuits, individual-performance activities, aquatics, net/wall games or target games). (S1.H1.L1)

Embedded Outcome

Movement concepts, principles & knowledge: Uses movement concepts and principles (e.g., force, motion, rotation) to analyze and improve performance of self and/or others in a selected skill. (S2.H2.L1)

Lesson Objectives

The learner will:

- perform the continental grip.
- successfully perform three out of five punch serves from the baseline.

Equipment and Materials

- Tennis rackets: 1 per student
- Tennis balls (various densities): at least 5 per student pair

Introduction

Today, you will be learning the punch serve. The serve is a very important shot to have in your repertoire as it starts every point in a tennis match. The punch serve is a simplified version of the full-swing serve, which you will learn next class.

Instructional Task: Continental Grip

■ PRACTICE TASK

Demonstrate the continental grip. Students shadow along.

Extension

Have students place their rackets on the ground, and when you say go, students pick up their rackets with the continental grip.

Refinement

Students refine skill by reviewing pictures of the grip; instructional videos of the grip can also be posted to the school's physical education website.

What to Look For

Base knuckle (index finger) of the dominant hand is on the second bevel of the handle.

Instructional Task: Service Stance and Toss

■ PRACTICE TASK

Demonstrate the service stance and toss. Students shadow along.

Guiding questions for students:

- For singles, where should you stand on the baseline?
- How high should the toss be?
- Where should the toss be positioned and why?

Extensions

- Students pair up and stand on the baseline on the same side of the court (four students per court). One stands to serve in the deuce service box, and the other stands to serve in the ad service box. Students place their rackets on the ground to the dominant side, with the racket head below the baseline. The racket head serves as a target for the toss. Students perform a service toss so that the ball lands on the racket face on the ground. Students switch service positions after 10 tosses.
- Students set a goal for the number of successful tosses.

Refinement

If the toss goes behind the server, have the server focus on lifting the ball (rather than tossing) and keeping her arm fully extended (no bent elbow) as she brings her arm up.

Student Choices/Differentiation

Students may choose what goal to set and modify it as needed.

What to Look For

- Toss should be just in front of the server.
- Students lift the ball rather than throw it (the ball rotates).

Instructional Task: Punch Serve Swing Pattern

■ PRACTICE TASK

Demonstrate the punch serve swing pattern. Students shadow along.

Guiding questions for students:

- Does the swing path resemble another type of skill? (Answer: overhand throw)
- How can you get more power on the ball?

Extensions

- Students pair up and stand on the service line on the same side of the court (four students per court). One pair is positioned to serve: One stands to serve in the deuce service box, and the other stands to serve in the ad service box. The other pair are positioned on the other side of the court to receive the serves. The servers overhand-throw balls to land in the correct service box. The receivers use proper footwork to get to the ball to catch it. Students change roles after every five balls and switch service positions after each full rotation.
- Students perform the same task but move back to the baseline.

Refinement

Reinforce the importance of the weight shift so the server "falls" into the court after releasing with the ball.

Student Choices/Differentiation

Students may choose to switch partners.

What to Look For

- Students are using the correct throwing pattern.
- Students are following through toward the correct service box.
- Students are positioning their feet appropriately.

Instructional Task: Full Punch Serve

■ PRACTICE TASK

Students pair up and stand on the service line on the same side of the court (four students per court). One pair is positioned to serve: One stands to serve in the deuce service box, and the other stands to serve in the ad service box. The other pair are positioned to receive the serves. The servers perform the full punch serve to land in the correct service box. The receivers use proper footwork to get to the ball to catch it. Students change roles after every five balls and switch service positions after each full rotation.

Extensions

- Students perform the same task but move back to the baseline.
- Students perform the same task but the receivers return the ball with a groundstroke.

Refinement

When students are at the service line, they will often truncate the movement pattern in order to reduce force on the ball (serve is long). If this is the case, encourage them to use a lower-density ball.

Student Choices/Differentiation

- Students may choose to change partners.
- Students may decide what type of ball they want to use.
- Students may practice hitting into the fence so they can focus on the motion and not worry about hitting the net.
- Drop the net to allow students to focus on form.

What to Look For

- Students are able to coordinate the toss and swing together.
- Students are following through toward the target.
- Students are hitting down on the ball.

Instructional Task: Peer Assessment

■ PRACTICE TASK

Repeat the full punch serve practice task, but place six students on each court. The extra two students record the servers (using a device with a skill analysis app such as Coach's Eye). After rotating to all positions, students evaluate their serve motion using a rubric or checklist.

EMBEDDED OUTCOME: S2.H2.L1. Students should use the assessment to apply movement concepts to their motion to generate more power on their serves.

Extension

After reviewing their videos, students practice the full punch serve, attempting to integrate corrections.

Student Choices/Differentiation

- Students choose their tennis balls.
- Drop the height of the net to increase success.

What to Look For

- Students are able to use the technology effectively.
- Students are applying the rubric correctly to their video clips.
- Students are able to apply movement concepts to improve their performance.

Formal and Informal Assessments

- Informal assessment
- Peer assessment of serve motion

Closure

- What grip did you learn today? Can someone demonstrate it for me?
- Can you name three critical features of the punch serve?
- What are the most important elements of a good toss?
- Keep practicing the skills at home if you can, and the next lesson you will build on the punch serve to a full-swing serve.

Reflection

- Were students consistently using the proper grip?
- Were students able to consistently serve the ball into the correct service box?
- Were students placing the toss appropriately?
- Did students get enough practice with the punch serve?

Homework

- Practice the punch serve toss and swing pattern at home. Use a mirror, if possible.
- Provide students with a handout that shows pictures of the continental grip and videos of the punch serve on the school's physical education website, in both real time and slow motion.

Resources

United States Tennis Association: www.usta.com

Fuzzy Yellow Balls: www.fuzzyyellowballs.com

Internet search terms: "tennis serve," "punch serve," "serving grip"

LESSON 8: FULL-SWING SERVE

Grade-Level Outcomes

Primary Outcome

Lifetime activities: Demonstrates competency and/or refines activity-specific movement skills in 2 or more lifetime activities (outdoor pursuits, individual-performance activities, aquatics, net/wall games or target games). (S1.H1.L1)

Embedded Outcomes

Working with others: Solves problems and thinks critically in physical activity and/or dance settings, both as an individual and in groups. (S4.H4.L1)

Movement concepts, principles & knowledge: Describes the speed vs. accuracy trade-off in throwing and striking skills. (S2.H2.L2)

Lesson Objectives

The learner will:
- successfully perform the full-swing serve in three out of five attempts from the baseline.

Equipment and Materials

- Tennis rackets: 1 per student
- Tennis balls (various densities): at least 5 per student pair

Introduction

Today, you will be learning the full-swing serve. The full-swing serve builds on the punch serve you learned last class and allows you to generate more power, which will give you an advantage during your service games.

Instructional Task: Full-Swing Movement Pattern

■ PRACTICE TASK

Demonstrate the full-swing serve. Students shadow along.

Guiding questions for students:

- How does the full-swing serve differ from the punch serve?
- How does the full-swing serve allow you to generate more power?

EMBEDDED OUTCOME: S4.H4.L1. Use the guiding questions to help students think critically about force production in the full swing (more body segments and muscles involved, greater rotation, lengthening the preparation, and so on).

Refinements

- Break down the movement pattern and stress critical features, if needed.
- Students shadow with a partner.

Extension

Students peer-assess a partner's full-swing movement pattern using the critical features. Students use a device to record the movement, if available. Provide a checklist to guide assessment.

Student Choices/Differentiation

Students may review a video clip of the full serve in slow motion.

What to Look For

- Students are using the correct grip.
- Students are using the correct starting position.
- Students are timing the racket with the tossing arm.

Instructional Task: Full-Swing Serve

■ PRACTICE TASK

Students pair up and stand on the service line on the same side of the court (four students per court). One pair is positioned to serve: One stands to serve in the deuce service box, and the other stands to serve in the ad service box. The other pair are positioned to receive the serves. The servers perform the full-swing serve with the goal of getting the ball over the net. The receivers use proper footwork to get to the ball to catch it. Students change roles after every five balls and switch service positions after each full rotation.

Extensions

- Students perform the same task but move back to the baseline.
- Students perform the same task but with the goal of serving into the correct service box.
- Students perform the same task but the receivers return the ball with a groundstroke.

Refinements

- The most difficult part is generally the toss. If students can't toss the ball consistently in front, have them go back to the tossing drills from the previous lesson.
- If timing of the swing is off, students may go back to the punch serve, practice the full swing without the ball, or practice against the fence until timing improves.

Student Choices/Differentiation

- Students may decide what type of ball they want to use.
- Students may practice hitting into the fence so they can focus on the motion and not worry about hitting the net.
- Drop the net to allow students to focus on form.

What to Look For

- Toss is just in front of server.
- Timing of racket swing is in synch with the toss.
- Wrist pronates at contact.

Instructional Task: Serve and Return Games

■ PRACTICE TASK

Groups of four students play modified singles games. In each game, two students play a no-ad game while the other two students perform a peer assessment of the serve. As in a real game, the server gets two service attempts. The server rotates after each game, and students trade off after every two games.

Refinement

To provide for more success, allow the server to serve to the same court until he or she can place a ball in the box. That allows the server to focus more on form and less on accuracy. The receiver plays the first ball that is served legally in the box.

EMBEDDED OUTCOME: S2.H2.L2. Use this task to explain how the need for accuracy may impact speed of execution.

Student Choices/Differentiation

- Students may choose to switch partners.
- Students may decide what type of ball they want to play with.
- Students may choose what type of serve to use.

What to Look For

- Students are tossing the ball appropriately.
- Students are following through toward the correct service box.
- Students are positioning their feet appropriately.
- Students are scoring appropriately.
- Students are following the rules and points of etiquette.

Formal and Informal Assessments

- Informal and peer assessments
- Exit slip: What are the rules of serving?

Closure

- Can you name three critical features of the full-swing serve?
- How does the full-swing serve differ from the punch serve?
- Keep practicing the skills at home if you can, and the next lesson you will learn some serve and return tactics that will be helpful in a tennis match.
- Remember to turn in your exit slips.

Reflection

- Were students consistently using the proper grip?
- Were students able to consistently serve the ball into the correct service box?
- Were students placing the toss appropriately?
- Were students able to time the toss and the swing of the racket together?
- Did students get enough practice with the full-swing serve?
- Review exit slips to see where students are still unclear about serving rules.

Homework

Practice the full-swing pattern at home.

Resources

Fuzzy Yellow Balls: www.fuzzyyellowballs.com
United States Tennis Association: www.usta.com
Optimum Tennis: www.optimumtennis.net
Internet search terms: "tennis serve," "serving grip," "serving mechanics"

LESSON 9: SERVE AND RETURN TACTICS

Grade-Level Outcomes

Primary Outcome

Lifetime activities: Demonstrates competency and/or refines activity-specific movement skills in 2 or more lifetime activities (outdoor pursuits, individual-performance activities, aquatics, net/wall games or target games). (S1.H1.L1)

Embedded Outcome

Physical activity knowledge: Identifies issues associated with exercising in heat, humidity and cold. (S3.H3.L1)

Lesson Objectives

The learner will:

- successfully serve inside the correct service box three out of five times.
- successfully return serve three out of five times.
- successfully place a serve to two out of three locations in the service box.

Equipment and Materials

- Tennis rackets: 1 per student
- Tennis balls (various densities): at least 5 per student pair
- Cones: at least 6 per court

Introduction

Tennis is a game that's usually played in the warmer weather. What kinds of issues do you need to think about when it's hot or humid while you are playing? [Answer: hydration, cooling, sun protection (Embedded outcome: S3.H3.L1.)] *Be sure you keep those in mind throughout the module and when you're out playing on your own. Today, you will be learning basic serve and return tactics. Tactics are a way to gain an advantage over an opponent during a game.*

Instructional Task: Serving Consistency

■ PRACTICE TASK

Students pair up and stand on either side of the center mark on the baseline (four students per court). One pair serves five balls to their corresponding service boxes, attempting to get at least three balls in. The other pair stands to receive the serves and collects each ball as it is served. Once one pair has finished serving the other pair serves. Students switch serving locations after each full rotation.

Guiding questions for students:

- What is the difference between a first serve and a second serve?
- What is the best characteristic of a good first serve? (Answer: consistency of at least 70 percent)

Extension

Students set a higher goal for consecutive serves.

Refinement

Challenge students who are consistently getting the serve inside the service box to hit the ball deep in the service court.

Student Choices/Differentiation

- Students choose a goal for consecutive serves after achieving three out of five and modify the goal as needed.
- Students may choose to use the punch serve or full-swing serve.

What to Look For

- Students are getting the ball into the service box.
- Students are using a moderate pace on the ball, or "dinking" it in.
- Students are following through completely.

Instructional Task: Return of Serve

■ PRACTICE TASK

Students pair up and stand on either side of the center mark on the baseline (four students per court). One pair serves four balls to their corresponding service boxes. Students should serve the first two balls hard and the second two balls soft. The other pair stands to receive the serves. For the first two serves, the receivers should try to get the ball in play. For the second two serves, the receivers should try to place the balls deep cross-court. Once one pair has finished serving the other pair serves. Students switch serving and receiving locations after each full rotation.

Guiding questions for students:

- What is the best way to return a hard first serve? (Answer: Block the ball back; get it in.)
- What is the best way to return a softer second serve? (Answer: Attack with best stroke; hit deep to corners.)

Extension

Students perform the same task except they randomize the type of serve (hard versus soft).

Refinement

To block a hard serve successfully, students may need to be reminded not to take a backswing and just use the server's power to get the ball over the net.

Student Choices/Differentiation

- Students may choose to change partners.
- Students may choose to use the punch serve or full-swing serve.
- Students may choose a lower-density ball if having difficulty.

What to Look For

- Students are using an abbreviated backswing for hard serves.
- Students are using a full stroke for soft serves.
- Students are getting the ball back into play.

Instructional Task: Serving Placement

■ PRACTICE TASK

Students pair up, with one pair on each side of the court at the baseline (four students per court). Position three cones (outside corner, center, upper T) in the deuce service box on one side of the court and the ad service box of the opposing side. Each pair takes a turn serving three balls (one to each cone) to the corresponding service box. After a student finishes serving, she walks to the other side of the court to retrieve her balls and serves to the opposing service box. This rotation continues until the task is ended.

Guiding questions for students:
- Where should you try to place your serves?
- What helps determine this? (Answer: position of opponent; strengths and weaknesses of opponent)
- Where should you place the serve if your opponent . . . ? [Describe different scenarios.]

Refinement

Specify a specific order and change it up periodically to encourage greater contextual interference.

Student Choices/Differentiation

Students may choose to use the punch serve or full-swing serve.

What to Look For

- Students are directing the path of the racket toward the target.
- Students are following through completely.
- Students are maintaining a good toss.

Instructional Task: Singles Games

■ PRACTICE TASK

Groups of four students play modified singles games. In each game, two students play a no-ad game while the other two students perform a peer assessment of the serve and return tactics from today's lesson. The server rotates after each game, and students trade off after every two games. Players focus on using the serve and return tactics practiced earlier in the lesson.

Refinement

Once in game play, students may attempt to swing away on the return of serve. Provide feedback to increase use of blocking on hard serves.

Student Choices/Differentiation

- Students may choose to change partners.
- Students may choose to use the punch serve or full-swing serve.
- Students may decide what type of ball they want to play with.

What to Look For

Students are effectively using the tactics of serving consistency, returning serve, and serving placement.

Formal and Informal Assessments

Informal assessment and peer assessments

Closure

- What three tactics did you learn today?
- How would you use these tactics in a game?
- What other kinds of tactics do you think might be useful?
- Keep practicing the skills at home if you can, and the next lesson you will be playing singles. You will also take a knowledge test on the rules, terminology, and strategies of tennis.

Reflection

- Were students maintaining proper serving technique during the practice tasks?
- Were students able to use the tactics effectively during play?
- Were students able to control the placement of the serve?

Homework

- Watch some video clips of tennis matches on the school's physical education website. Determine the first-serve percentage of the players and where they tended to place their serves.
- Review for the knowledge test next class.

Resources

United States Tennis Association: www.usta.com

Fuzzy Yellow Balls: www.fuzzyyellowballs.com

Internet search terms: "serve and return," "serve and return tactics," "serve placement"

LESSON 10: SINGLES PLAY

Grade-Level Outcomes

Primary Outcomes

Lifetime activities: Demonstrates competency and/or refines activity-specific movement skills in 2 or more lifetime activities (outdoor pursuits, individual-performance activities, aquatics, net/wall games or target games). (S1.H1.L1)

Movement concepts, principles & knowledge: Applies the terminology associated with exercise and participation in selected individual-performance activities, dance, net/wall games, target games, aquatics and/or outdoor pursuits appropriately. (S2.H1.L1)

Embedded Outcomes

Rules & etiquette: Exhibits proper etiquette, respect for others and teamwork while engaging in physical activity and/or social dance. (S4.H2.L1)

Movement concepts, principles & knowledge: Creates a practice plan to improve performance for a self-selected skill. (S2.H3.L1)

Lesson Objectives

The learner will:

- demonstrate the following skills effectively in singles play: forehand, backhand, serve, and basic tactics.
- describe strategies, scoring, etiquette, and terminology on a knowledge test.

Equipment and Materials

- Tennis rackets: 1 per student
- Tennis balls (various densities): at least 3 per student pair
- Rubric for forehand, backhand, serve, and tactics: 1 each per student

Introduction

Today, you will be playing singles. This is your opportunity to use all the skills you have learned in real game play. You will also take a test on the rules, strategies, and etiquette of the game at the end of class.

Instructional Task: Singles Play

■ PRACTICE TASK

Group students by fours based on similar skill level. Two students in each group play three games of singles while the other two students evaluate the skills learned so far in class using a rubric you have provided. Students change roles after playing three games. Students change observers after a full rotation.

You will also use the rubric to evaluate each student's performance during the lesson.

Extension

Students change partners after two full rotations.

EMBEDDED OUTCOME: S4.H2.L1 Review etiquette before starting the singles games. Students will self-officiate the matches and observe rules and etiquette.

Student Choices/Differentiation

- Students may choose a lower-density ball if having difficulty.
- Students may choose to use the punch serve or full-swing serve.

What to Look For

- Students are using appropriate form consistently during play.
- Students are using proper etiquette.
- Students are evaluating their peers appropriately and providing constructive feedback.

Instructional Task: Knowledge Test

■ **PRACTICE TASK**

Administer a test that covers rules, terminology, strategy, etiquette, and scoring.

Student Choices/Differentiation

- Allow extra time if needed.
- Give an oral version of the test.

What to Look For

- Students know the rules, terminology, and scoring.
- Students are able to articulate strategy and etiquette.

Formal and Informal Assessments

- Skill assessment (teacher and peer)
- Knowledge test

Closure

- What were some good examples of etiquette you observed today?
- How well were you able to perform the skills you have learned so far during game play?
- What skills are you still struggling with?
- What types of skills did you use today that you have not learned yet?
- Keep practicing the skills at home if you can, and the next lesson you will be learning how to play doubles.

Reflection

- Were students maintaining proper skill technique during play?
- Were students able to use the tactics effectively during play?
- Were students able to evaluate their peers well?
- Review the knowledge tests to determine where students may need clarification.
- Review the skills assessments to see what areas students still need to work on.

Homework

- Teach a sibling or friend how to perform one of the skills or tactics you've learned so far in the module.
- Create a practice plan for two skills in tennis that you would like to improve. Bring it to the next class. (Embedded outcome: S2.H3.L1)

Resources

Sample rubric: http://scahperd.org/wp-content/uploads/2015/04/HS-Notebook-Final-Sept-23.pdf (pp. 133-134)

Internet search terms: "tennis tactics," "tennis strategies," "tennis singles strategies," "tennis etiquette"

LESSON 11: DOUBLES PLAY

Grade-Level Outcomes

Primary Outcomes

Movement concepts, principles & knowledge: Applies the terminology associated with exercise and participation in selected individual-performance activities, dance, net/wall games, target games, aquatics and/or outdoor pursuits appropriately. (S2.H1.L1)

Lifetime activities: Demonstrates competency and/or refines activity-specific movement skills in 2 or more lifetime activities (outdoor pursuits, individual-performance activities, aquatics, net/wall games or target games). (S1.H1.L1)

Embedded Outcome

Working with others: Uses communication skills and strategies that promote team or group dynamics. (S4.H3.L1)

Lesson Objectives

The learner will:

- demonstrate knowledge of tennis doubles rules and basic formations by successfully playing doubles with a partner.
- demonstrate proper communication with a partner during a doubles game by calling ambiguous shots.

Equipment and Materials

- Multimedia device (TV, laptop, tablet)
- Several video clips of tennis doubles games
- Tennis rackets: 1 per student
- Tennis balls (various densities): at least 3 per 4 students

Introduction

Review the results of the knowledge test and skills assessment. Discuss common errors and how to improve.

Today, you will be learning the basic rules and elements of competing in a doubles match. [Show video clips of high-level doubles play to get students excited about the game.] *First, you will warm up by working on the two skills you planned to practice.*

Instructional Task: Student Practice Plans

■ PRACTICE TASK

Students get in pairs and work on the two skills they identified in their practice plans.

Student Choices/Differentiation

- Students design their practice tasks.
- Students choose their partners.

What to Look For

- Students' practice tasks are appropriate for the skills selected.
- Students are putting forth good effort to improve.
- Partners are helping one another.

Instructional Task: Doubles Rules

■ PRACTICE TASK

Lead a discussion on the rules of doubles, highlighting the differences from singles play.

Guiding questions for students:

- What differences did you notice between a doubles and a singles game?
- What are some additional aspects of the game you might consider when playing doubles?

Refinement

Replay the video clips to reinforce the differences identified by students and anything that wasn't identified.

Extension

Students form groups of four and play no-ad doubles games, implementing doubles rules.

Student Choices/Differentiation

- Students may choose to use a lower-density ball.
- Students choose their own partners.

What to Look For

- Students are able to identify differences between singles and doubles play.
- Students are able to use doubles rules during play.

Instructional Task: Basic Doubles Formations

■ PRACTICE TASK

Play the video clips again.

Guiding questions for students:

- What type of formations did you notice in the videos?
- What are some advantages and disadvantages of each?

Refinement

Replay the videos again to reinforce identification of formations.

Extension

Students form groups of four and play doubles games, alternating between different formations.

Guiding questions for students:

- Did you and your partner come up with strategies to use in the different formations?
- Did some formations work better for you and your partner than others? If so, why?

Student Choices/Differentiation

- Students may choose to change partners.
- Students may choose to use a lower-density ball.

What to Look For

- Students are able to identify the different formations.
- Students are able to identify advantages, disadvantages, and strategies for each formation.
- Students rotate through each formation.

Instructional Task: Doubles Communication

■ PRACTICE TASK

Lead a discussion on appropriate communication in doubles play.

Guiding questions for students:

- How essential is good communication between doubles partners?
- What types of things would you want to communicate with your partner?
- What are some ways you can communicate with your partner (verbal and nonverbal)?

Extensions

- Students choose a communication method with their partners and attempt to use it during game play.
- Change partners and practice communication methods.

Refinement

Partners refine type of communication and use of communication as needed.

EMBEDDED OUTCOME: S4.H3.L1. Provide feedback to partners about their communication.

Student Choices/Differentiation

- Students may choose a different partner.
- Students may choose to use a lower-density ball.
- Students may choose their method of communication.

What to Look For

- Students identify situations in which communication would be helpful.
- Students use communication with their partner during game play.

Formal and Informal Assessments

- Informal assessments
- Student practice plans

Closure

- What are some of the rules you learned today?
- What are some of the formations you learned today?
- Why is communication important in doubles?
- What was one way you communicated well with your partner today?
- Next time you will be learning to volley, which is a skill used frequently in doubles.
- Be sure to turn in your practice plans so that I can review them.

Reflection

- Were students able to properly identify the rule differences in doubles?
- Were students able to follow all the rules identified in the lesson?
- How well did students communicate with their partners?
- Review student practice plans and make comments as needed.

Homework

- Find video clips of double matches.
- Identify the formation the players used, what method of communication they used, and how well they communicated.

Resources

Tennis Tips (doubles tennis rules): www.tennistips.org

Internet search terms: "tennis doubles rules," "doubles formations," "doubles strategies"

LESSON 12: FOREHAND AND BACKHAND VOLLEYS

Grade-Level Outcomes

Primary Outcome

Lifetime activities: Demonstrates competency and/or refines activity-specific movement skills in 2 or more lifetime activities (outdoor pursuits, individual-performance activities, aquatics, net/wall games or target games). (S1.H1.L1)

Embedded Outcome

Rules & etiquette: Exhibits proper etiquette, respect for others and teamwork while engaging in physical activity and/or social dance. (S4.H2.L1)

Lesson Objectives

The learner will:
- successfully perform the forehand and backhand volley in three out of five attempts.
- use volleys effectively in game-like situations.

Equipment and Materials

- Tennis rackets: 1 per student
- Tennis balls (various densities): at least 6 per student pair

Introduction

For homework, you were asked to watch doubles matches. Who can tell me formations or communication strategies used in the matches you watched? Today, you will be learning to volley. Volleys are used when you are positioned close to the net. When used effectively, volleys often end a point.

Instructional Task:
Forehand and Backhand Volley Movement Pattern

■ PRACTICE TASK

Demonstrate the forehand and backhand volley. Students shadow along.

Guiding questions for students:
- Where should you be positioned on the court to hit a volley?
- How far do you take the racket back?
- What type of footwork do you use?

Refinements
- Students often try to volley with just their arms. Make sure they are using a crossover step and moving to the ball.
- Students shadow with a partner.

Extension

Students peer-assess a partner's striking movement pattern using the critical features. Students use a device to record the movement, if available. Provide a checklist to guide assessment.

Student Choices/Differentiation

Students may review a video clip of the volley (slow motion).

What to Look For

- Students are stepping forward.
- Students are coming to the ball.

Instructional Task: Volley Backswing

■ PRACTICE TASK

Students pair up. One student stands with his back to the fence and soft-tosses three balls to his partner's forehand side and three balls to the backhand side. The receiver attempts to softly volley the ball back to her partner. Partners switch roles.

Extension

Students perform the same task except the server randomly alternates tosses between forehand and backhand.

Refinement

Students should use a short forward motion without a backswing. Provide feedback to encourage students to use a short punch rather than a backswing.

Student Choices/Differentiation

Students having trouble contacting the ball may choose to start without a ball.

What to Look For

- Students are using the correct grip.
- Students are minimizing their backswing.
- Students are coming toward the ball.
- Students are keeping their wrists firm.

Instructional Task: Volleys With a Partner

■ PRACTICE TASK

Students pair up and stand across from each other on one side of the court (four students per court). One partner stands at the service line, while the other partner stands between the service line and the net. Student at the service line tosses three balls to the volleyer's forehand to return and three to the backhand. Partners trade roles.

Extensions

- Students perform the same task except one partner moves back to the baseline and drop-hits five forehands across the net for the volleyer to return. Partners trade roles.
- Students perform the same task except they try to hit at least three out of five successful volleys.
- Students perform the same task except they increase the goal.

EMBEDDED OUTCOME: S4.H2.L1 Remind students to feed the ball to their partners appropriately so that the volleyers have a good opportunity to return the shot.

Refinement

Suggest a target location for the volley, and have students try to hit the volley to that location.

Student Choices/Differentiation

- Students may choose to change partners.
- Students may choose to start with a lower-density ball.
- Students may choose to modify their goal as needed.

What to Look For

- Students are minimizing their backswing.
- Students are coming toward the ball.
- Students are using appropriate footwork to get in position for the volley.

Instructional Task: Volley Games

■ PRACTICE TASK

Groups of four students play no-ad doubles games. In each game, students play a one up, one back formation. If a player wins a point using a volley, then that team wins the game. The server rotates after each game, and students trade off partners after every four games.

Extension

Repeat the task, but have students focus on hitting to the backhand volley side.

Refinement

If balls are going long on the volley, reinforce the angle of the racket face.

Student Choices/Differentiation

- Students may choose to switch partners.
- Students may decide what type of ball they want to play with.

What to Look For

- Students are minimizing their backswing.
- Students are choosing appropriate times to hit a volley.
- Students are placing the volley well.
- Students are scoring appropriately.
- Students are following the rules and points of etiquette.

Formal and Informal Assessments

- Peer assessments: volley checklist
- Video analysis

Closure

- Can you name three critical features of the forehand and backhand volley?
- What grip do you use for a volley?
- When would you use a volley in a game?
- Keep practicing the skills at home if you can, and the next lesson you will learn how to perform a lob.
- Read the comments I made on your practice plans, and be ready to make any adjustments next class.

Reflection

- Were students consistently using the proper grip?
- Were students consistently minimizing their backswing?
- Were students able to use the volley effectively during a game?
- Did students get enough practice with volleying?

Homework

- Practice volleying at home.
- Research the benefits of playing tennis, where you can play it locally, and what the costs and requirements are.

Resources

Internet keyword search: "tennis volley," "backhand volley"

LESSON 13: LOBS

Grade-Level Outcomes

Primary Outcomes

Lifetime activities: Demonstrates competency and/or refines activity-specific movement skills in 2or more lifetime activities (outdoor pursuits, individual-performance activities, aquatics, net/wall games or target games). (S1.H1.L1)

Physical activity knowledge: Evaluates—according to their benefits, social support network and participation requirements—activities that can be pursued in the local environment. (S3.H4.L1)

Embedded Outcomes

Physical activity knowledge: Analyzes the impact of life choices, economics, motivation and accessibility on exercise adherence and participation in physical activity in college or career settings. (S3.H5.L2)

Health: Analyzes the health benefits of a self-selected physical activity. (S5.H1.L1)

Self-expression & enjoyment: Selects and participates in physical activities or dance that meet the need for self-expression and enjoyment. (S5.H3.L1)

Social interaction: Identifies the opportunity for social support in a self-selected physical activity or dance. (S5.H4.L1)

Lesson Objectives

The learner will:

- successfully perform forehand and backhand lobs three times in a row with a partner.
- perform a lob effectively in game-like situations.
- discuss the benefits of tennis as a lifetime physical activity.

Equipment and Materials

- Tennis rackets: 1 per student
- Tennis balls (various densities): at least 3 per student pair

Introduction

Today, you will be learning the forehand and backhand lob. These shots are very useful when you need to get back into position or when playing against an opponent at the net. First, let's review your homework assignment.

Instructional Task: Homework Discussion

■ PRACTICE TASK

In pairs, students share information about the benefits of tennis as a lifetime physical activity and where they can play. Afterward, ask pairs to share with the whole group.

EMBEDDED OUTCOME: S5.H1.L1; S5.H3.L1; S5.H4.L1. As part of the discussion, students should identify the potential health, enjoyment, and social interaction benefits of tennis. If they do not, prompt them in these areas.

Extension

Ask students to consider other factors that may affect their participation in tennis as they go to college or start a job or career.

Guiding questions for students:

- How might your finances or family situation affect your ability to play?
- What kind of time commitments do you think you might have, and how will that affect your participation?
- Based on where you're planning to live, how accessible do you think courts will be?

EMBEDDED OUTCOME: S3.H5.L2. Use the guiding questions to prompt students to think about how tennis may (or may not) fit into their futures after graduation.

Student Choices/Differentiation

- Students choose their partners.
- Students may volunteer to share with the larger group.

What to Look For

- Students are engaged in the discussion.
- Students identified the health benefits.
- Students identified the physical benefits.
- Students identified the social interaction benefits.

Instructional Task: Student Practice Plans

▥ PRACTICE TASK

Students find a partner and practice the skills in their plans as a warm-up activity. Students should make any adjustments you noted in their plans.

Student Choices/Differentiation

- Students design their practice tasks.
- Students choose their partners.

What to Look For

- Students are putting forth good effort to improve.
- Partners are helping one another.

Instructional Task: Forehand and Backhand Lob Movement Patterns

▥ PRACTICE TASK

Demonstrate the forehand and backhand lob. Students shadow along.

Guiding questions for students:

- How does the forehand lob differ from a regular forehand?
- How does the backhand lob differ from a regular backhand?
- How high does a lob need to be?

Refinements

- Refine skill by breaking down the movement pattern and stressing critical features, if needed.
- Students shadow with a partner.

Extension

Students peer-assess a partner's striking movement pattern using the critical features. Students use a device to record the movement, if available. Provide a checklist to guide assessment.

Student Choices/Differentiation

Students choose their partners.

What to Look For

- Students are opening up the racket face.
- Students are using a higher follow-through.

Instructional Task: Lob With a Partner

■ PRACTICE TASK

Students pair up and stand across from each other on one side of the court (four students per court). One partner stands at the baseline, while the other stands in a volley position. The student in volley position extends his racket as high as possible. The partner at the baseline drop-hits three forehand lobs and three backhand lobs high enough to clear her partner's extended racket. Partners change roles.

Extensions

- All four students use the singles court. One student on each side begins at the center mark on the baseline. The other student on each side stands at the T. Students at the baseline perform a rally using only lobs. They must hit the ball high enough to clear the students in the opposing service box area. Those students at the T must stay in the service box area. If a ball goes out of bounds or is low enough for the student in the service box to hit, the rally is dead. Students change roles after every three rallies.
- Students perform the same task except they try to get at least six consecutive lobs in a row.

Refinement

If students are having trouble clearing the racket, reinforce the importance of opening the face of the racket to help lift the ball.

Student Choices/Differentiation

- Students may choose to start with lower-density balls.
- Students may choose to increase their consecutive lob goal.

What to Look For

- Students are able to consistently clear the partner's extended racket.
- Students are opening up the racket face.

Instructional Task: Lob Games

■ PRACTICE TASK

Groups of four students play no-ad doubles games. In each game, students play a one up, one back formation. If a player wins a point using a lob, then that team wins the game. The server rotates after each game, and students trade off partners after every four games.

Student Choices/Differentiation

- Students may choose to change partners.
- Students may decide what type of ball they want to play with.

What to Look For

- Students are choosing appropriate times to hit a lob.
- Students are placing the lob well.
- Students are scoring appropriately.
- Students are following the rules and points of etiquette.

Formal and Informal Assessments

Informal assessment and peer assessments

Closure

- Can you identify the major differences between a forehand lob and a regular forehand?
- Can you identify the major differences between a backhand lob and a regular backhand?
- How high should a lob be?
- When would you use a lob in a game?
- Keep practicing the skills at home if you can, and the next lesson you will learn how to perform an overhead.

Reflection

- Were students consistently opening up the racket face?
- Were students hitting the ball high enough?
- Did students get enough practice with the lob?
- How well did students use the lob during a game?

Homework

- Practice the lob striking pattern at home.
- Watch a video of lobbing in a doubles game on the school's physical education website. Identify the types of situations where players hit lobs, and critique their effectiveness.

Resources

Internet keyword search: "tennis lob," "forehand lob," "backhand lob"

LESSON 14: OVERHEADS

Grade-Level Outcomes

Primary Outcome

Lifetime activities: Demonstrates competency and/or refines activity-specific movement skills in 2 or more lifetime activities (outdoor pursuits, individual-performance activities, aquatics, net/wall games or target games). (S1.H1.L1)

Embedded Outcome

Movement concepts, principles & knowledge: Creates a practice plan to improve performance for a self-selected skill. (S2.H3.L1)

Lesson Objectives

The learner will:

- successfully perform an overhead in three out of five attempts.
- perform an overhead effectively in game-like situations.

Equipment and Materials

- Tennis rackets: 1 per student
- Tennis balls (various densities): at least 5 per student pair

Introduction

For homework, you watched a video of doubles play where the lob was used. When did players choose to hit the lob? How effective was it? The lob is often used defensively. Today, you will be learning a shot that you can use offensively, the overhead. When used effectively, this shot can end a point during a game.

Instructional Task: Overhead Movement Pattern

■ PRACTICE TASK

Demonstrate the overhead. Students shadow along.

Guiding questions for students:

- How does the overhead differ from the full-swing serve?
- What purpose does pointing at the ball serve?

Refinements

- Refine skill by breaking down the movement pattern and stressing critical features, if needed.
- Students shadow with a partner.

Extension

Students peer-assess a partner's striking movement pattern using the critical features. Students use a device to record the movement, if available. Provide a checklist to guide assessment.

Student Choices/Differentiation

Students may review a video clip of the overhead (slow motion).

What to Look For

- Students are pronating their wrists at contact.
- Students are pointing at the ball.

Instructional Task: Lob With a Partner

■ PRACTICE TASK

Students pair up and stand across from each other on one side of the court (four students per court). One partner stands at the baseline while the other stands near the net. The student at the net holds a racket in a cocked position and self-tosses five balls to hit using an overhead. The partner at the baseline retrieves the balls, and partners change roles.

Extensions

- Students perform the same task except balls are hit off a partner toss. The partner tossing the ball should be positioned off-court to avoid being hit with the ball.
- Students perform the same task except balls are hit off a partner baseline drop-hit lob. The partner at the net starts from a ready position rather than with racket cocked.
- Students perform the same task except they try to hit at least three out of the five balls successfully.

Refinement

If students are having trouble setting up for the overhead, remind them to track the ball by pointing at it and using proper footwork to keep the ball out in front.

Student Choices/Differentiation

Students may choose to increase their goal.

What to Look For

- Students are hitting the ball out in front.
- Students are pronating the wrist at contact.
- Students are tracking the ball with their fingers.
- Students are using proper footwork to position under the ball.

Instructional Task: Overhead Games

■ PRACTICE TASK

Groups of four students play no-ad doubles games. In each game, students play a one up, one back formation. If a player wins a point using an overhead, then that team wins the game. The server rotates after each game, and students trade off partners after every four games.

Student Choices/Differentiation

- Students may choose to change partners.
- Students may decide what type of ball they want to play with.

What to Look For

- Students are choosing appropriate times to hit an overhead.
- Students are placing the overhead well.
- Students are scoring appropriately.
- Students are following the rules and points of etiquette.

Formal and Informal Assessments

Informal assessment and peer assessments

Closure

- Can you identify the major differences between an overhead and a serve?
- When would you use an overhead in a game?
- Keep practicing the skills at home if you can, and the next lesson we will be playing a doubles round-robin tournament.

Reflection

- Were students hitting the ball out front?
- Were students tracking the ball and using proper footwork to get into correct position?
- Did students get enough practice with the overhead?
- How well did students use the overhead during a game?

Homework

- Practice the overhead striking pattern at home.
- Now that you have learned some new skills (overheads, lobs, volleys), adapt your practice plan to include at least one of these skills and bring it to the next class. (Embedded outcome: S2.H3.L1)

Resources

Internet keyword search: "overhead"

LESSON 15: ROUND-ROBIN DOUBLES TOURNAMENT

Grade-Level Outcomes

Primary Outcome

Lifetime activities: Demonstrates competency and/or refines activity-specific movement skills in 2 or more lifetime activities (outdoor pursuits, individual-performance activities, aquatics, net/wall games or target games). (S1.H1.L1)

Embedded Outcome

Movement concepts, principles & knowledge: Creates a practice plan to improve performance for a self-selected skill. (S2.H3.L1)

Lesson Objectives

The learner will:

- use the following skills effectively in doubles play: volley, lob, overhead, and communication.

Equipment and Materials

- Tennis rackets: 1 per student
- Tennis balls (various densities): at least 3 per student pair
- Rubric for forehand, backhand, serve, and tactics: 1 each per student

Introduction

Today, you will be playing in a doubles round-robin tournament while I evaluate the new skills you have learned (volley, lob, and overhead) and your doubles game play (rules, tactics, and etiquette). This is your opportunity to use all the skills you have learned in game play with a variety of opponents. We probably won't get through all the matches or assessments today, so we will finish in the next class. First, you will warm up with your revised practice plans.

Instructional Task: Student Practice Plan

■ PRACTICE TASK

Students find a partner and practice the skills in their plans as a warm-up activity. Students should make any adjustments you noted in their plans.

Student Choices/Differentiation

- Students design their practice tasks.
- Students choose their partners.

What to Look For

- Students are practicing at least one of the new skills (lob, overhead, volley).
- Students are putting forth good effort to improve.
- Partners are helping one another.

Instructional Task: Doubles Round-Robin Tournament

■ PRACTICE TASK

Group students in pairs by skill level. In each round, students play the best of three games. Students rotate opponents after each round (see the resources for an example of a rotation schedule). Assess students' skills and game play. If possible, record matches to complete the evaluation outside of class.

Student Choices/Differentiation

- Students may choose a lower-density ball if having difficulty.
- Students may choose to use the punch serve or full-swing serve.

What to Look For

- Students are consistently using appropriate form during play.
- Students are using proper etiquette.
- Students are communicating and cooperating well with their partners.

Formal and Informal Assessments

Skills and game-play assessment

Closure

- What were some good examples of etiquette you observed today?
- How well were you able to perform the skills you have learned during game play?
- What skills are you still struggling with?
- Next class, we'll finish the tournament and the assessment and finish up by playing some singles matches.

Reflection

- Were students maintaining proper skill technique during play?
- Were students communicating well with their partners?

Homework

Look up the player rating system for the United States Tennis Association. Be ready to share next class.

Resources

Professional Tennis Registry: www.ptrtennis.org/secured/tools/rr/schedules.pdf

Internet search terms: "tournament brackets," "round robin brackets"

LESSON 16: DOUBLES TOURNAMENT AND SINGLES MATCHES

Grade-Level Outcomes

Primary Outcomes

Lifetime activities: Demonstrates competency and/or refines activity-specific movement skills in 2 or more lifetime activities (outdoor pursuits, individual-performance activities, aquatics, net/wall games or target games). (S1.H1.L1)

Working with others: Assumes a leadership role (e.g., task or group leader, referee, coach) in a physical activity setting. (S4.H3.L2)

Embedded Outcome

Safety: Applies best practices for participating safely in physical activity, exercise and dance (e.g., injury prevention, proper alignment, hydration, use of equipment, implementation of rules, sun protection). (S4.H5.L1)

Lesson Objectives

The learner will:

- use the following skills effectively in doubles play: volley, lob, overhead, and communication.
- employ skills and strategies in singles matches.
- officiate a singles match.

Equipment and Materials

- Tennis rackets: 1 per student
- Tennis balls (various densities): at least 3 per student pair
- Rubric for forehand, backhand, serve, and tactics: 1 each per student

Introduction

What did you find out about the player rating system in tennis? What ratings do beginners usually have? Professionals? If you continue to play tennis, you will eventually want to be rated so that you can find other players at your level or join a league. Today is the last day of the Tennis Module, so we will finish our doubles round-robin tournament, and I'll conclude my evaluations of your skills and game play. Then you'll play singles matches and try to officiate a match. Tennis is a game where you usually officiate your own matches and you are on your honor to make the right call. However, officiating is a good test of your ability to implement the rules and show confidence in your knowledge of the game.

Instructional Task: Doubles Round-Robin Tournament

■ **PRACTICE TASK**

Finish the doubles round-robin tournament from the previous class.

Complete your assessment of skills and game play during match play.

Student Choices/Differentiation

- Students may choose a lower-density ball if having difficulty.
- Students may choose to use the punch serve or full-swing serve.

What to Look For

- Students are consistently using appropriate form during play.
- Students are using proper etiquette.
- Students are communicating and cooperating well with their partners.

Instructional Task: Singles Matches

■ PRACTICE TASK

Students play singles in groups of three. While two students play, the third student officiates the match. They play three games, rotating the third player.

EMBEDDED OUTCOME: S4.H5.L1. By officiating games, students demonstrate their ability to implement rules and scoring correctly.

Student Choices/Differentiation

- Students choose their groups.
- Students choose their tennis balls.

What to Look For

- Students are effectively using offensive shots to move the opponent.
- Students are returning to ready position.
- Students are able to apply the rules to officiate during a match.

Formal and Informal Assessments

Skills and game-play assessment

Closure

- What were some good examples of etiquette you observed today?
- How well were you able to perform the skills you have learned during game play?
- What skills are you still struggling with?
- How confident did you feel while you were officiating? Were there any calls you were unsure of?
- Tennis is a lifelong sport, so keep practicing your new skills at home. If you are interested in finding opportunities to play, check out www.USTA.com.
- It's time to think about your next module, so please review your choices before the next class.

Reflection

- Were students maintaining proper skill technique during play?
- Were students showing a good command of scoring and the rules while officiating?
- What may I do the next time we offer tennis to improve the module?

Homework

Go to the school's physical education website and review the next set of module offerings. Be ready for your new selection in the next class.

Resources

United States Tennis Association: www.USTA.com

Professional Tennis Registry: www.ptrtennis.org/secured/tools/rr/schedules.pdf

Internet search terms: "tennis officiating," "tennis tournaments"

CHAPTER 8

Extending Students' Skills and Knowledge to Target Games

Target games are addressed in the Grade-Level Outcomes for high school students because they are lifelong physical activities that everyone can enjoy with family and friends. This category includes activities such as bowling, archery, croquet, shuffleboard, disc golf, and golf. Target games can be very challenging, requiring high levels of accuracy and consistency. Fortunately, there are many terrific resources to help teachers incorporate these activities in their curricula. For example, the National Archery in the Schools Program (NASP) offers instructor training, equipment packages, and a curriculum for trained teachers to use (more information can be found at www.naspschools.org). Bowler's Ed also offers a curriculum and modified equipment for in-school bowling as well as grant opportunities (see www.bowl.com). Teachers can take advantage of these programs, as well as others, to expand their offerings in the target games category.

In this chapter, we have selected beginning golf as the target games module. Golf is an important activity to introduce to students because it's one of the most popular physical activities for adults. Golf requires a great deal of skill, offers many social benefits, and when played without a cart, provides sustained physical activity through walking. When thinking about teaching golf, it's essential to remember that it is a closed skill. A closed skill occurs in an environment that is relatively "constant, predictable, or stationary" (SHAPE America – Society of Health and Physical Educators, 2014, p. 117). The focus in practicing these types of skills is to generate a highly consistent motor pattern because it will lead to greater accuracy in these stable performance environments. Students will need many repetitions to develop this level of consistency in their technique, as well as a great deal of attention to refinements. Because the golfer is hitting while stationary, video analysis is relatively easy to set up and use for self-assessment, peer assessment, and teacher assessment. This module employs video analysis in multiple lessons to help students improve their swings.

Teaching golf does present a number of challenges if you do not have an easily accessible driving range or golf course, and most high schools don't. However, with some creativity, you can practice all the skills of golf in your gym or on your grass field. The lesson plans offer suggestions for simulating a golf environment when one is not available. Until recently, it was difficult to practice golf without a course or range because of the safety risk when hitting real golf balls. Wiffle balls have been used for many years to allow safe practice for the swing, but they don't have the real feel of a golf ball. Fortunately, there are now several options for modified balls (e.g., BirdieBalls) that offer realistic play while minimizing risk of injury.

This Beginning Golf Module, contributed by Brandon Allen, who is an assistant teaching professor in sport management at the University of Southern Mississippi, is aimed at golfers who are new to the game, but it would be great to offer a second level of golf for students who are more experienced. You can modify this module to align with Level 2 outcomes by challenging students to practice the tasks under more difficult circumstances, practicing specialized shots, or approaching it through the lens of fitness training related to golf (e.g., specialized weight training, core strength training). If your school has the facilities to offer playing opportunities, you also might want to consider using the sport education model as a framework. You can pre-assess students, put them in teams based on their ability, and have them work on improving their individual skills. Using the sport education model means that students also could take on sport-related roles such as fitness leader, coach, public relations director, website coordinator, or other interesting positions. The culminating event could be a simulation of a PGA-style tournament with practice rounds, leader boards, caddies, and officials. Leading up to such an event, students could learn about different styles of tournament play and could play qualifying rounds.

For easy reference, we've begun this module with a block plan chart of the Grade-Level Outcomes that are addressed in each lesson. The primary outcomes addressed in the Beginning Golf Module are found under Standards 1, 2, and 4, but you also will see outcomes from under Standards 3 and 5. The main emphases are on developing skill competency (Outcome S1.H1.L1), using appropriate terminology (Outcome S2.H1.L1), and understanding and applying rules and etiquette (Outcome S4.H2.L1). We hope that the Beginning Golf Module provides you with some great ideas for sparking your students' excitement about this lifelong physical activity.

BEGINNING GOLF MODULE

Lessons in this module were contributed by **Brandon Allen**, who is an assistant teaching professor in sport management at the University of Southern Mississippi.

Grade-Level Outcomes Addressed, by Lesson	1	2	3	4	5	6	7	8	9	10	11	12	13	14	15	16
Standard 1. The physically literate individual demonstrates competency in a variety of motor skills and movement patterns.																
Demonstrates competency and/or refines activity-specific movement skills in 2 or more lifetime activities (outdoor pursuits, individual-performance activities, aquatics, net/wall games or target games). (S1.H1.L1)	P	P	P	P	P	P	P	P	P	P	P	P	P	P	P	P
Standard 2. The physically literate individual applies knowledge of concepts, principles, strategies and tactics related to movement and performance.																
Applies the terminology associated with exercise and participation in selected individual-performance activities, dance, net/wall games, target games, aquatics and/or outdoor pursuits. (S2.H1.L1)	E	E		E	P	P	P			P	P		P			
Identifies and discusses the historical and cultural roles of games, sports and dance in a society. (S2.H1.L2)	P															
Uses movement concepts and principles (e.g., force, motion, rotation) to analyze and improve performance of self and/or others in a selected skill. (S2.H2.L1)		E	E		E	E	E			E	E		E			
Describes the speed vs. accuracy trade-off in throwing and striking skills. (S2.H2.L2)													E			
Standard 3. The physically literate individual demonstrates the knowledge and skills to achieve and maintain a health-enhancing level of physical activity and fitness.																
Evaluates—according to their benefits, social support network and participation requirements—activities that can be pursued in the local environment. (S3.H4.L1)									P							
Evaluates risks and safety factors that might affect physical activity preferences throughout the life cycle. (S3.H5.L1)										P						
Standard 4. The physically literate individual exhibits responsible personal and social behavior that respects self and others.																
Exhibits proper etiquette, respect for others and teamwork while engaging in physical activity and/or social dance. (S4.H2.L1)		P	P	P					P				P		P	P
Examines moral and ethical conduct in specific competitive situations (e.g., intentional fouls, performance-enhancing substances, gambling, current events in sports). (S4.H2.L2)														E		
Uses communication skills and strategies that promote team or group dynamics. (S4.H3.L1)		E							E		E					
Solves problems and thinks critically in physical activity or dance settings, both as an individual and in groups. (S4.H4.L1)					E				E							
Applies best practices for participating safely in physical activity, exercise and dance (e.g., injury prevention, proper alignment, hydration, use of equipment, implementation of rules, sun protection). (S4.H5.L1)	E					E	E									E
Standard 5. The physically literate individual recognizes the value of physical activity for health, enjoyment, challenge, self-expression and/or social interaction.																
Analyzes the health benefits of a self-selected physical activity. (S5.H1.L1)					P				E							
Chooses an appropriate level of challenge to experience success and desire to participate in a self-selected physical activity. (S5.H2.L2)															E	
Identifies the opportunity for social support in a self-selected physical activity or dance. (S5.H4.L1)									E							

P = Primary; E = Embedded

BEGINNING GOLF

LESSON 1: INTRODUCTION TO THE GAME

Grade-Level Outcomes

Primary Outcomes

Lifetime activities: Demonstrates competency and/or refines activity-specific movement skills in 2 or more lifetime activities (outdoor pursuits, individual-performance activities, aquatics, net/wall games or target games). (S1.H1.L1)

Movement concepts, principles & knowledge: Identifies and discusses the historical and cultural roles of games, sports and dance in a society. (S2.H1.L2)

Embedded Outcomes

Movement concepts, principles & knowledge: Applies the terminology associated with exercise and participation in selected individual-performance activities, dance, net/wall games, target games, aquatics and/or outdoor pursuits appropriately. (S2.H1.L1)

Safety: Applies best practices for participating safely in physical activity, exercise and dance (e.g., injury prevention, proper alignment, hydration, use of equipment, implementation of rules, sun protection). (S4.H5.L1)

Lesson Objectives

The learner will:

- discuss how the game of golf originated.
- complete a pre-assessment of putting skills.
- perform different drills that will help him or her learn the skill of putting.
- explore ball striking with a putter.

Equipment and Materials

- Putter for each student
- Golf balls or modified golf balls for each student
- Large area for students to spread out
- Full set of golf clubs to demonstrate to students

Introduction

Golf is an activity that you can play throughout your life. Today, I will introduce the game of golf, starting with some history, identifying types of clubs, covering safety practices while participating in groups, and working on putting drills. Throughout the module, you will progress to more advanced motor skills such as chip shots, bunker shots, and, eventually, a full golf swing. Each lesson will build on the previous lesson and might cover particular rules, terminology, safety, equipment, and proper etiquette.

Instructional Task: Golf History

■ PRACTICE TASK

Explain how the game of golf originated, and give a brief overview of the current game.

Use examples of how golf is played today. Explain the benefits of golf as a lifetime sport.

Give students assignments ahead of time, and have them research various aspects of the game. Split research assignments into history, equipment prices, professional golfers, famous golf courses, and so on.

Guiding questions for students:

- Imagine that you are part of a small group of players during the time that golf was invented. What kind of rules and objectives would you have included in the early stages of the game?
- Where do most people say is the birthplace of golf? (Answer: Scotland)
- Do you think that most people accept the idea that Mary, Queen of Scots, was the first woman to play golf in 1567? Why or why not?

Student Choices/Differentiation

- Allow students to choose their topics.
- Students choose how to present their information.

What to Look For

- Ask students how many of them play golf.
- Students are engaged in the discussion.

Instructional Task: Golf Equipment

■ PRACTICE TASK

Introduce the different types of clubs (woods, irons, hybrids, wedges, putters).

EMBEDDED OUTCOME: S2.H1.L1. Have students select clubs based on terminology.

Guiding questions for students:

- When would you use a wood?
- When would you use an iron?
- What clubs are used close to the green?
- What club is used on the green?

What to Look For

- Students are selecting the appropriate club for the shot.
- All students are engaged in the task.

Instructional Task: Pre-assessment Putting

■ PRACTICE TASK

Students stand in a straight line about an arm's length apart, with a specified target area or hole about 5 feet (1.5 m) away. Students putt five times while you assess their strokes using a checklist containing the five critical elements of putting. Students should putt at least five times.

Student Choices/Differentiation

Students choose their putters and balls (standard or modified).

What to Look For

Assess students' use of the five critical elements of putting.

Instructional Task: Exploring Putting

■ PRACTICE TASK

Give each student a set number of balls. Have students putt, making contact with the ball using the lead hand only. After all balls have been hit, students retrieve them.

Extensions

- Repeat with the other hand added to the grip.
- Repeat from a longer distance.
- Have students calculate the number of balls that land within a defined target area.
- Pair up students and play a knock-out game. Students take turns hitting balls into a circle, trying to knock another player's ball out of the circle. If a ball is hit out of the circle, the player whose ball was hit out must follow the ball and play it in from there. Play for a set amount of time. The objective is to have more balls in the circle than your opponent.

Refinement

Remind students to follow through on putts the same distance of their backswing, like a pendulum. That will allow for better control.

Guiding questions for students:

- Is there a particular spot on the club from where the ball tends to release with the least amount of effort?
- What causes the ball to diverge from the target line?
- Can you think of another sport with an element that is similar to the movement of the golf swing?

EMBEDDED OUTCOME: S4.H5.L1 During practice, reinforce the importance of maintaining a safe distance for the swing or stroke. Make sure that students are not being careless with the equipment.

Student Choices/Differentiation

Students choose their putters and balls (standard or modified).

What to Look For

- Students are placing 50 percent of their putts into the target area.
- Note whether students are putting too far or coming up short.
- Students are gripping the club properly.

Formal and Informal Assessments

Pre-assessment in putting

Closure

- Which clubs provide for the most loft?
- What distinguishes woods from irons?
- Who invented the game of golf?
- While putting the ball, did your body position feel awkward? Next lesson will cover setup and alignment techniques for putting.

Reflection

- Did students recognize and demonstrate spatial awareness?
- Were they maintaining a safe distance from one another while hitting?
- Did students adjust their technique after hitting a few times to acquire proper distance?

Homework

- If students have access to equipment at home, have them practice the golf skills and strategies taught throughout the module. If they don't have such access, they can practice their form by using any long implement to imitate the golf club.
- Review the instructional videos for the grip, stance, and approach posted to the school's physical education website. This will be covered in more detail in Lesson 2.

Resources

Heuler, O. (1995). *Perfecting your golf swing: New ways to lower your score.* New York: Serling.

Golf: www.golf.com

United States Golf Association: www.usga.org

Internet keyword search: "putting," "putter," "woods," "irons," "wedges," "hybrid clubs"

LESSON 2: PUTTING

Grade-Level Outcomes

Primary Outcomes

Lifetime activities: Demonstrates competency and/or refines activity-specific movement skills in 2 or more lifetime activities (outdoor pursuits, individual-performance activities, aquatics, net/wall games or target games). (S1.H1.L1)

Rules & etiquette: Exhibits proper etiquette, respect for others and teamwork while engaging in physical activity and/or social dance. (S4.H2.L1)

Embedded Outcomes

Movement concepts, principles & knowledge: Applies the terminology associated with exercise and participation in selected individual-performance activities, dance, net/wall games, target games, aquatics and/or outdoor pursuits appropriately. (S2.H1.L1)

Movement concepts, principles & knowledge: Uses movement concepts and principles (e.g., force, motion, rotation) to analyze and improve performance of self and/or others in a selected skill. (S2.H2.L1)

Working with others: Uses communication skills and strategies that promote team or group dynamics. (S4.H3.L1)

Lesson Objectives

The learner will:

- demonstrate proper putting form, from setup and alignment to ball placement.
- explain ball projection by making contact with an open or closed club face.
- understand the importance of making proper contact with the ball to increase consistent trajectory.
- work with others to discover errors in alignment, setup, grip, and swing.

Equipment and Materials

- Putter or modified putter for each student
- Golf balls or modified balls for each student
- Indoor carpet or putting range
- Ball marker (e.g., coin, sticker) for each pair of students

Introduction

Today, we'll focus on proper technique for putting, emphasizing grip, setup, alignment, and stroke. We'll also talk about etiquette procedures around the green, ball marking, and divot repairs. Let's review our first lesson to get started.

Instructional Task: Preparation for Putting

■ PRACTICE TASK

Students should be aligned in a semi-circle for viewing purposes.

Grip: Demonstrate the proper grip for the putter.

Setup: Students (remaining in a semi-circle) should spread out about arm's length and follow instruction while you demonstrate proper form. Students practice the stance.

Alignment: Demonstrate lining up the ball with the hole. Use railroad tracks an as example.

Refinement

Check students' stance and grips. Emphasize feet shoulder-width apart and Vs on grip pointing toward the shoulders.

Extension

Have students peer-assess and provide verbal feedback to one another on grip, setup, and alignment.

Student Choices/Differentiation

Students may review videos or handouts, if needed.

What to Look For

Grip

- Thumbs of both hands are on top of grip.
- Vs (created by thumb and index finger) of both hands are pointed toward the shoulders or slightly outside.

Setup

- Feet are 12 to 15 inches (30 to 38 cm) apart.
- Hips are thrust out.
- Eyes are plumb with the ball.

Alignment

- Students approach putt from behind before addressing the ball.
- Students place ball mark in line with path toward target.

Instructional Task: Putting Stroke

■ PRACTICE TASK

Demonstrate the proper putting stroke.

On the putting surface, have students spread out and putt toward a target. Each student hits a set number of balls (10, if possible). Balls will be retrieved by all at the same time.

EMBEDDED OUTCOME: S2.H2.L1. During the putting task, ask students what elements of the putting stroke change the speed of the ball. (Answer: degree of backswing and shoulder rotation)

Extension

Have students putt from different distances, or decrease the size of the target.

Refinements

- While students are putting, check to see that the back of the non-dominant hand is facing the target throughout the swing.
- Students might tend to rotate the hips and shoulders. If that seems to be a problem, have students work on putting drills that isolate the hips and shoulders. Students can work on this by holding the putter horizontally. Students should be able to demonstrate the putting stroke with the putter facing the target throughout the swing.

Student Choices/Differentiation

Students choose their putters and balls (standard or modified).

What to Look For

- Students are using a pendulum-type swing.
- Club face is perpendicular to the target line at contact.

- Backswing is the same distance as forward swing.
- There is no breaking of the wrists or arms.

Instructional Task:
Open, Closed, or Squared Club Face "Sweet Spot"

■ PRACTICE TASK

Demonstrate ball trajectory by hitting with an open club face, a closed club face and a squared club face. Demonstrate determining the best area (sweet spot) to make contact with the ball on the putter. Students practice putting in pairs. Partners watch five putts and provide feedback about contact point. Students switch.

EMBEDDED OUTCOME: S4.H3.L1. Reinforce the importance of providing feedback to partners in a supportive manner.

EMBEDDED OUTCOME: S2.H1.L1. Students should use the terms *open club face*, *closed club face*, *square faced*, and *sweet spot* in providing feedback.

Student Choices/Differentiation

Students can practice the swing without the ball, stopping the swing where contact with the ball would be made.

What to Look For

- Note direction the ball comes off the club face.
- Ball should start in the direction of the target.
- Check angle of club face at contact if ball does not go in direction of target.

Instructional Task:
Etiquette, Rules, and Putting Practice

■ PRACTICE TASK

Discuss the honor system in putting: avoid standing on the putting line; avoid talking or moving while others are putting. Demonstrate ball marking as well as the technique of moving ball markers to avoid interfering with another person's line of play.

In pairs, have students putt one after the other to the same target. Have students mark the ball (with coin, sticker, marker) when appropriate and putt again to get closer to the hole or target.

Extension

Discuss golf shoes (soft spikes versus metal) and the type of clothes worn by male and female golfers.

Student Choices/Differentiation

Students may view a video clip of putting in a tournament where the ball had to be marked.

What to Look For

- Students are marking their balls when they lie in another player's line.
- Students are not talking while putting.
- Students are avoiding standing in another player's line.

Instructional Task: Putting Challenge

■ PRACTICE TASK

Set up two holes or two targets for each set of partners or small groups. Students play a game of 21 to practice their putting skills under pressure. Students putt to the target or hole. Closest to the hole gets 1 point; in the hole gets 2 points. Students putt to a second target. They go back and forth until one player gets 21.

Extension

Rotate groups after getting to 21.

Student Choices/Differentiation

- Students choose their partners or groups.
- Students choose their equipment.
- Targets can be placed closer or farther apart to vary the difficulty.

What to Look For

- Students are maintaining good putting form in the game.
- Students are observing proper etiquette.

Formal and Informal Assessments

Student scores on putting challenge

Closure

- Can you name three checkpoints in determining proper setup?
- Can you name two checkpoints in determining proper grip?
- What happens to ball trajectory if a player hits with an open club face? Closed club face?

Reflection

- Were students holding the putter correctly?
- Could students swing the putter with their wrists and arms straight?

Homework

- Practice the golf skills with or without the equipment.
- Review the instructional videos for the grip, setup, and approach on the school's physical education website.

Resources

Heuler, O. (1995). *Perfecting your golf swing: New ways to lower your score.* New York: Serling.

World Golf: www.worldgolf.com

United States Golf Association: www.usga.org

Internet keyword search: "open club face," "closed club face," "squared club face," "honor system"

LESSON 3: READING THE GREENS

Grade-Level Outcomes

Primary Outcomes

Lifetime activities: Demonstrates competency and/or refines activity-specific movement skills in 2 or more lifetime activities (outdoor pursuits, individual-performance activities, aquatics, net/wall games or target games). (S1.H1.L1)

Rules & etiquette: Exhibits proper etiquette, respect for others and teamwork while engaging in physical activity and/or social dance. (S4.H2.L1)

Embedded Outcome

Movement concepts, principles & knowledge: Uses movement concepts and principles (e.g., force, motion, rotation) to analyze and improve performance of self and/or others in a selected skill. (S2.H2.L1)

Lesson Objectives

The learner will:

- analyze a putt to determine slope, speed, and movement.
- demonstrate techniques that assist in consistent putts for slope putts, downhill putts, and 3-foot (0.9 m) putts.
- assist others in skill performance.

Equipment and Materials

- Putters
- Golf balls or modified golf balls (e.g., BirdieBalls, Wiffle balls)
- Indoor carpet or putting range
- Putting targets
- Alignment sticks, if available

Introduction

You've learned the basics of putting, so now you're going to practice more difficult situations such as downhill putts, sloped putts, and 3-foot putts. That means you need to think about how to read the greens.

Instructional Task: Determining Slope

■ PRACTICE TASK

Explain the steps of reading the green and illegal methods of reading the green, such as practice putts or rolling a ball on the surface. Putt on a sloped green to demonstrate ball movement, or show a video of putting on a sloped green.

Extension

In pairs, one student practices reading the green and predicting the ball path. The other student will then putt to test the prediction. After five putts, students switch roles.

Refinement

Students will almost always under-read the slope of a putt. Try to have them draw an imaginary line from the ball to the hole where the ball will fall in on the high side of the hole. If they miss on the high side of the hole, the ball has a chance to still go in, but if they miss on the low side, the ball doesn't have a chance to go in the hole.

Student Choices/Differentiation

- Students may roll a ball on sloped surfaces to determine the severity of the slope.
- Students can use modified clubs.
- Students can use BirdieBalls or Wiffle balls.

What to Look For

- Students are taking the time to read the green.
- Students' predictions are accurate.

Instructional Task: Target Line

■ PRACTICE TASK

Demonstrate techniques for determining the target line. Once the target line is determined, ball markings (such as lines) can be used as a point of reference for aiming toward the target line. Students practice putting in pairs, focusing on the slope and the target line. Students switch after five putts.

Refinement

Use alignment sticks or putting aids, if available, to see if the line of the putter is parallel to the feet line as well as making sure the eyes are either just inside the ball or directly over the ball.

Student Choices/Differentiation

- Students can use modified clubs.
- Students can use BirdieBalls or Wiffle balls.

What to Look For

- Students are looking at the hole from various angles to determine slope.
- Students are placing the ball with markings pointed straight at the target line.

Instructional Task: Three-Foot Putts

■ PRACTICE TASK

Students practice 3-foot (0.9 m) putts from various positions around the hole or target.

Refinements

- Explain the psychological confidence acquired by extending the body closer to the hole after contact.
- Students should strike the ball firmly.

Extension

Repeat in pairs. One student putts while the other uses a device to record the stroke. Students view their own performance and make corrections on next hits. Record feedback and corrections on a worksheet or in a skills journal. Student switch roles after three putts.

EMBEDDED OUTCOME: S2.H2.L1. Use this task to help students apply movement concepts to correct their own performance errors.

Student Choices/Differentiation

- Students can use modified clubs.
- Students can use BirdieBalls or Wiffle balls.

What to Look For

- Feet are shoulder-width apart.
- Students place the ball in front of them in the middle of their stance.
- Students aim for the center of the cup.
- Hips are thrust out.
- Eyes are plumb with the ball.
- Students hit the ball firmly.

Instructional Task: Sloped Putt and Right or Left Break

■ PRACTICE TASK

Students practice the proper putting stroke after adjusting their stance so the ball is in the middle. Students take five putts and switch with a partner.

Refinement

Have students focus on a smooth, pendulum-type swing, where the backswing and forward swing travel the same distance.

Guiding questions for students:

- Why is the location of the golf ball (in relation to the stance) important during the putt?
- Why is it important to keep the backswing and forward swing the same length while putting? (Answer: This will help with overall consistency in putting and prevent putts being missed either extremely short because of deceleration or extremely long because of extreme acceleration through the ball.)

Student Choices/Differentiation

- Students can use modified clubs.
- Students can use BirdieBalls or Wiffle balls.

What to Look For

- Ball is moved back to the middle of the stance.
- Students are using a pendulum-type swing.
- Club face is perpendicular to the target line at contact.
- Backswing is the same distance as forward swing.
- There is no breaking of the wrists or arms.
- Feet are 12 to 15 inches (30 to 38 cm) apart.

Instructional Task: Putting and Etiquette for the Green

■ PRACTICE TASK

Show and explain the different types of putters, based on shape, and discuss etiquette procedures for repairing ball marks on the green, placing bags on the green, dropping clubs or the flagstick on the green, and tending the flagstick.

Student Choices/Differentiation

Students may review a video clip illustrating proper etiquette on the green.

What to Look For

Students are engaged in the discussion.

Formal and Informal Assessments

- Informal and peer assessments
- Worksheets or skills journals

Closure

- What generally happens to the break when a ball is hit firmly? Softly?
- What do the markings on the putters indicate?
- Next class, we'll have a mini putting tournament, so practice your stroke and get ready.

Reflection

- Were students able to control the distance of the putts?
- Were the majority of students consistent in ball placement in regard to a specific target?
- Did they take time to read the green before putting?
- Review worksheets or skills journals to determine what sorts of errors students are working on.

Homework

- Review the instructional videos for putting posted on the school's physical education website.
- Practice your putting stroke.
- Summarize how to read the green and adjust your putt for a sloping green breaking right or left. Bring to next class.

Resources

Heuler, O. (1995). *Perfecting your golf swing: New ways to lower your score.* New York: Serling.

World Golf: www.worldgolf.com

Golf: www.golf.com/instruction

United States Golf Association: www.usga.org

Internet keyword search: "putting etiquette," "tending the flagstick," "reading the green," "marking the ball," "sloping greens"

LESSON 4: CREATING A PUTTING COURSE

Grade-Level Outcomes

Primary Outcomes

Lifetime activities: Demonstrates competency and/or refines activity-specific movement skills in 2 or more lifetime activities (outdoor pursuits, individual-performance activities, aquatics, net/wall games or target games). (S1.H1.L1)

Rules & etiquette: Exhibits proper etiquette, respect for others and teamwork while engaging in physical activity and/or social dance. (S4.H2.L1)

Embedded Outcomes

Working with others: Solves problems and thinks critically in physical activity and/or dance settings, both as an individual and in groups. (S4.H4.L1)

Movement concepts, principles & knowledge: Applies the terminology associated with exercise and participation in selected individual-performance activities, dance, net/wall games, target games, aquatics and/or outdoor pursuits appropriately. (S2.H1.L1)

Lesson Objectives

The learner will:

- demonstrate proper procedures while playing in a modified game.
- recall scoring terms when asked.
- implement rules and etiquette while participating in a mock tournament.
- putt under pressure.
- keep accurate score.

Equipment and Materials

- Putters
- Golf balls or modified balls
- Scorecard for each group (no more than five students per group)
- Putting course with holes or designated area for holes
- Putting targets
- Paper and pencils

Introduction

Today, we'll create a putting course and then hold a mock putting tournament. That way, you can see what it's like to putt under a little pressure. Everything that you've learned so far will be incorporated during this modified game. Before we start, let's review how to read the green and adjust your putt from your homework assignment.

Instructional Task: Creating a Mini Course

■ PRACTICE TASK

Students work in groups to create boundaries and holes for a mini putting course. Each group should be able to create one hole, resulting in three to nine holes for the course. Different areas can be used on the same hole to create more holes for scoring. The design should include par for each hole. Students should sketch their designs.

Refinement

Create a par-2 putting tournament. Students choose the length of the putt for their holes, ranging from 10 to 50 feet (3 to 15 m). The par for each hole, regardless of length, is 2. A one-putt is then a birdie, a two-putt is par, a three-putt is a bogey, and so on.

EMBEDDED OUTCOME: S4.H4.L1. Use this task to reinforce collaboration and problem-solving skills in small groups.

Student Choices/Differentiation

- Students may create obstacles to the hole to make it more challenging.
- Provide examples if students need help creating a course.
- Students choose their own groups.

What to Look For

- Evaluate students' engagement with others when creating the putting holes.
- All students are contributing ideas.
- Everyone is involved in making decisions about the holes.

Instructional Task: Playing and Scoring

■ PRACTICE TASK

Instruct students on keeping score. Students will count the strokes needed to complete the hole and write their scores on a scorecard.

EMBEDDED OUTCOME: S2.H1.L1. Review common scoring terms such as *par*, *birdie*, and *bogey*. Students should play the holes in sequential order and keep track of their scores. If time is a factor, use a shotgun start (groups start at any hole that is open and play in sequential order from there until they complete every hole).

Refinement

Remind students that putting is a closed skill, and consistency in the stroke is the most important. They should feel the pendulum action and have the same distance on the backswing as the extension after contact.

Guiding questions for students:

- How did scoring the hole influence your play?
- How would you alter the design of your putting hole, now that you've had a chance to play it?
- What features of the course did you find the most challenging and why?

Student Choices/Differentiation

Students can be put in pairs and play as a team using a scramble format.

What to Look For

- Students are marking the balls properly.
- Students are following putting etiquette and order of play.
- Students are executing all the critical elements of alignment, grip, and other skills learned in previous lessons.
- Students are scoring correctly.
- Students are trying to read the greens.

Formal and Informal Assessments

- Scorecards
- Sketches of hole designs
- Exit slip: Write down anything about scoring or its terminology that is unclear to you.

Closure

- Was your putting affected by the added pressure of being in a competition?
- Did you catch yourself or another person making a fundamental putting mistake? What was it?
- Next time, we will be moving on to other strokes in golf, but remember that putting is essential for your success once you start playing.

Reflection

- How did the students respond in a group activity?
- Were any students assisting or teaching other students in the group (reading the green, putting stroke, and so on)?
- Review the scorecards from the mini tournament to see how successful students were.
- Check exit slips to determine what aspects of scoring need to be reviewed.

Homework

Review video of three holes of a golf tournament on the school's physical education website, or watch three holes of a tournament on TV or online. Observe and record the sequence of shots, and be ready to discuss next class.

Resources

Heuler, O. (1995). *Perfecting your golf swing: New ways to lower your score*. New York: Serling.

World Golf: www.worldgolf.com

Golf: www.golf.com/instruction

United States Golf Association: www.usga.org

Internet keyword search: "scramble format," "shotgun start," "bogey," "par," "birdie"

LESSON 5: CHIPPING

Grade-Level Outcomes

Primary Outcomes

Lifetime activities: Demonstrates competency and/or refines activity-specific movement skills in 2 or more lifetime activities (outdoor pursuits, individual-performance activities, aquatics, net/wall games or target games). (S1.H1.L1)

Movement concepts, principles & knowledge: Applies the terminology associated with exercise and participation in selected individual-performance activities, dance, net/wall games, target games, aquatics and/or outdoor pursuits appropriately. (S2.H1.L1)

Embedded Outcomes

Safety: Applies best practices for participating safely in physical activity, exercise and dance (e.g., injury prevention, proper alignment, hydration, use of equipment, implementation of rules, sun protection). (S4.H5.L1)

Movement concepts, principles & knowledge: Uses movement concepts and principles (e.g. force, motion, rotation) to analyze and improve performance of self and/or others in a selected skill. (S2.H2.L1)

Lesson Objectives

The learner will:

- demonstrate the proper grip for iron shots.
- explore striking with irons.
- hit chip shots with proper form.
- discuss golf scoring terminology.

Equipment and Materials

- 6, 7, 8, or 9 irons (club for each student) or modified irons
- Golf balls or modified balls
- Putting area or turf suitable for chipping
- Rings or hoops or rope for target practice

Introduction

You have been working on your putting stroke for the past few lessons, so today, you will assess how well you are doing. After that, I will introduce chipping and pitching, covering fundamentals such as grip, setup, and alignment for iron shots. We'll also discuss reading the green and determining which type of shot is needed. Since you watched three holes of a tournament, where do pitching and chipping fit in?

Instructional Task: Putting Assessment

■ PRACTICE TASK

In pairs, students practice their 3-foot (0.9 m) putts to a target or hole. Partners record three putts and then switch roles. Students select one recording for you to evaluate using a checklist or scoring guide.

Student Choices/Differentiation

Students determine which video clip you will evaluate.

What to Look For

Students are executing the critical elements of the putt.

Instructional Task:
Preparation for Chipping and Pitching

■ PRACTICE TASK

Chipping and pitching are used when you are near the green and need to get the ball on so you can putt. Chipping and pitching lift the ball using clubs with angled faces. Chipping is used when you're very close to the green and just need to lift the ball a bit over the fringe and then roll it across the green. Pitching is used when you are farther away and need to land the ball softly or when you need to lift the ball over something, such as a bunker. We'll focus on chipping today.

Demonstrate overlap, interlock, and the 10-finger grip. Students practice their grips.

Demonstrate grip position in relation to body position and proper setup. Have students practice stance and grip.

Extension

Students can peer-assess and provide verbal feedback on the grip and stance.

Refinement

Check the position of each student for knees bent, feet shoulder-width apart, and V of grip pointed to shoulder.

Student Choices/Differentiation

- Students choose the most comfortable grip.
- Students may view a video clip of the stance and grip.

What to Look For

- Checkpoints: V created by the thumb and index finger is pointed toward the same-side shoulder; front two knuckles of the weak hand can be seen; index knuckle of the dominant hand is resting on the same side of the club.
- Arms are hanging loosely, feet are shoulder-width apart, and eyes are over the ball.
- Hips thrust out before knees bend.

Instructional Task: Explore Chipping With an Iron

■ PRACTICE TASK

Assign each student a specified target area or pop-up target. Students attempt to strike the ball toward the target, which is placed at an appropriate distance for chipping. Pattern should resemble a bump and run—a little loft followed by a roll onto the green.

Extensions

- Demonstrate alignment and chipping swing. Have students work in pairs to practice. One student hits chips to the target area while the other one uses a checklist for the swing to provide feedback. Students switch after a set number of hits.
- Students hit to pop-up target and partners count the number of balls that land in the target or target area. Switch roles.

Refinement

Check follow-through position and reinforce weight shift to the front and forward foot pointed to the target.

Guiding questions for students:

- Is there a particular spot on the club (the sweet spot) from where the ball tends to release with the least amount of effort?
- What causes the ball to diverge from the target line?

- What is the relationship of the hands to the face of the club at impact of the ball? (Answer: Grip should always be in front of the club face when chipping.)
- Why is it important to hit down on the ball?

EMBEDDED OUTCOME: S4.H5.L1 During practice, remind students of proper procedures for using an iron. Make sure students are not careless with the equipment. Ensure students are separated far enough apart to prevent injury by club swing. Students should never be in front of another player hitting the ball.

EMBEDDED OUTCOME: S2.H2.L1 Use the same task to have students analyze their partners' skills and apply movement concepts in the feedback.

Student Choices/Differentiation

- Students may use different irons, including modified irons, to explore striking the ball.
- Students may adjust distance to the target.

What to Look For

- Students are getting a feel for the force needed to hit a certain distance.
- Students are swinging smoothly.
- Checkpoints:
  - Hips are open to the target. Forward foot is pointed to the target, club face is squared to the target, and ball position is 2 inches (5 cm) behind the forward heel. Weight shifts to forward side of body.
  - Hands are ahead of the club.
  - Wrists are firm.
  - Club swing stays low to the ground.

Instructional Task: Terminology

■ PRACTICE TASK

Review par, bogey, and birdie, and explain the new terminology: eagle, double eagle, double bogey. Explain the symbols used on the scorecard that correlate with these terms.

Extension

Return students' scorecards from the putting course, and have students identify on the cards if they had any pars, birdies, or bogeys.

Student Choices/Differentiation

- Use posters with words and definitions.
- Provide handouts with terminology.

What to Look For

- Students are engaged in the discussion.
- Students are accurately applying the terminology to their scorecards.

Instructional Task: Chipping Challenge

■ PRACTICE TASK

Place rings around the hole or chipping target at distances of 1 foot (0.3 m), 3 feet (0.9 m), and 6 feet (1.8 m). If rings are not available, use ropes of varying lengths to lay out a circle. Students chip a set number of balls, trying to land the ball in the target. Students receive 5 points for the 1-foot circle, 3 points for the 3-foot circle, and 1 point for the 6-foot circle.

Student Choices/Differentiation

Students choose their equipment and balls.

What to Look For

- Students are able to maintain good swings when under pressure.
- Students are consistently getting inside the 6-foot circle.

Formal and Informal Assessments

- Formal putting assessment
- Informal peer assessment of chipping
- Scorecards (check for correct identification of terminology)

Closure

- What is the term for one stroke under par?
- Under what circumstances should you consider using a chip shot?
- How far should a chip shot go in the air as opposed to roll on the ground?
- What happens if you hit the ball with all your weight on the back foot?

Reflection

- How are students doing on the swing?
- Are they getting a feel for distance?
- Was the ball going straight after contact?
- What do we need to focus on to improve this shot?

Homework

- Review the instructional videos for the grip, stance, and approach on the school's physical education website.
- For next class, think about the ways golf can be part of a physically active lifestyle.

Resources

Heuler, O. (1995). *Perfecting your golf swing: New ways to lower your score.* New York: Serling.

World Golf: www.worldgolf.com

Golf: www.golf.com/instruction

United States Golf Association: www.usga.org

Internet keyword search: "eagle," "chipping," "pitching," "bunkers"

LESSON 6: REFINING THE CHIP SHOT

Grade-Level Outcomes

Primary Outcomes

Lifetime activities: Demonstrates competency and/or refines activity-specific movement skills in 2 or more lifetime activities (outdoor pursuits, individual-performance activities, aquatics, net/wall games or target games). (S1.H1.L1)

Movement concepts, principles & knowledge: Applies terminology associated with exercise and participation in selected individual-performance activities, dance, net/wall games, target games, aquatics and/or outdoor pursuits appropriately. (S2.H1.L1)

Health: Analyzes the health benefits of a self-selected physical activity. (S5.H1.L1)

Embedded Outcomes

Safety: Applies best practices for participating safely in physical activity, exercise and dance (e.g., injury prevention, proper alignment, hydration, use of equipment, implementation of rules, sun protection). (S4.H5.L1)

Movement concepts, principles & knowledge: Uses movement concepts and principles (e.g., force, motion, rotation) to analyze and improve performance of self and/or others in a selected skill. (S2.H2.L1)

Lesson Objectives

The learner will:

- demonstrate the proper technique for chipping the ball.
- control ball flight by adjusting the swing.
- judge approximate location of ball landing area for greater success of distance control to target.
- discuss the health benefits of the game of golf

Equipment and Materials

- 6, 7, 8, or 9 irons
- Golf balls or modified balls (plastic or foam balls may be used for safety)
- Putting area or turf suitable for chipping

Introduction

Today, you will keep working on the chip shot to become more consistent and accurate. You'll review the basics from our previous class and practice hitting to a target. During your practice, you'll see how the loft of ball flight determines the roll of the ball and the distance.

Instructional Task: Chipping Technique

■ PRACTICE TASK

Demonstrate and review the proper technique for chipping. Students practice chipping the ball to a specific target area or pop-up target. Specify a number of practice hits.

Refinements

- Have students control distance with backswing and forward swing rather than with club speed. Have them visualize a clock and relate time to club movement, starting from center (6 o'clock). For example, 7 o'clock in backswing equals 5 o'clock in front swing.
- Students often bend the wrist when making contact with the ball, usually causing poor and inconsistent contact. Have students choke down on the club shaft near the club face and take a practice swing. The top of the club should never hit the side of the body.

EMBEDDED OUTCOME: S4.H5.L1. Explain that chipping and pitching on the green is not permitted. The flagstick can be left in the hole if the player is chipping from the fringe. It cannot be used for putting on the green.

Student Choices/Differentiation

- Students may review a video clip of chipping technique, if needed.
- Students may select the type of club based on personal preference.

What to Look For

- Ball position is near the back of the stance for a typical chip.
- Club head does not pass the grip during the swing.
- Students hit the ball on the downstroke.
- Ball contacts the club on the "sweet spot".
- Hands are forward of the ball at contact.
- There is no scooping (lifting motion of the club head) of the ball.
- Students put appropriate loft on the ball.
- Backswing is the same distance as forward swing.

Instructional Task: Distance Control

■ PRACTICE TASK

Demonstrate distance control by using distance in backswing. Students may need to practice with plastic or foam balls until they get a good feel for making contact. The landing area should be visibly marked so that students can determine success while they practice. Students hit a set number of balls, retrieve, and repeat.

Extensions

- Repeat, varying the distance to the target.
- Repeat, varying the size of the landing area.

Student Choices/Differentiation

- Students may review a video clip of distance control, if needed.
- Students can use modified balls.
- Adjust the target area to allow success.

What to Look For

- Students maintain the same speed in the backswing and forward swing.
- Distance of the backswing equals distance of the forward swing.

Instructional Task: Determining the Iron to Use

■ PRACTICE TASK

Explain the different types of irons and usage including wedges (chipping, pitching, sand). Chipping irons vary, but most players prefer 7, 8, or 9 irons. Each club has a range in degree of loft.

Guiding questions for students:

- Why would you choose a chip shot over a putt or pitch shot? (Answer: Putt when you can, chip when you can't putt, and pitch only if you have to.)
- Which shot would you use if you are very close to the green? (Answer: chip)
- Which shot would you use to hit up and over? (Answer: pitch)

EMBEDDED OUTCOME: S2.H2.L1. Check students' understanding of the relationship between club loft and ball flight (trajectory) and roll after impact.

Student Choices/Differentiation

Students may review a video clip of chipping handout for review.

What to Look For

Students can give different scenarios for using a chip shot versus a pitching wedge. Some reasons for using a chip shot include long distance of green to target; ball is lying in shallow rough; better distance control.

Instructional Task: Chip and Putt

■ PRACTICE TASK

In pairs, have students set up to chip onto a landing area and then putt to a target. Two putts are the maximum. Students score 1 point for hitting the target in two putts and 2 points for hitting the target in one putt. Students take turns and repeat five times.

This will help students start to feel the flow of the game.

Student Choices/Differentiation

- Students choose their partners.
- Students choose their clubs and balls.

What to Look For

- Students are taking their time on the putt.
- Chips are making it to the landing area.
- Note how close to the target students are placing the ball on two putts.

Instructional Task: Terminology

■ PRACTICE TASK

Review terms such as *topping the ball*, *fringe*, *square to the target*, and *addressing the ball*.

Guiding questions for students:

- What causes a golfer to top the ball?
- What shots can you hit from the fringe?

Student Choices/Differentiation

Provide a handout with terminology for review.

What to Look For

- Students are engaged in the discussion.
- Students can apply movement concepts to errors such as topping the ball.
- Students are asking good questions.

Instructional Task: Homework Review

■ PRACTICE TASK

Lead a discussion on how golf can contribute to a healthy lifestyle. Have students share their ideas in small groups and then with the rest of the class.

Student Choices/Differentiation

Students may volunteer to share their lists with the class.

What to Look For

- All students are contributing.
- Students recognize the physical benefits of golf.
- Students can identify the social benefits of golf.

Formal and Informal Assessments

Student responses about healthy lifestyle

Closure

- Where should your hands be in correlation to the club face at ball contact?
- On what side should most of your body weight be before making contact with the ball?
- Next class, we'll focus on pitching.
- Now that you are more aware of the health benefits of the game, you are going to research where you can play in the area.

Reflection

- Were students making solid contact with the ball?
- Could students adjust their swing distance according to the distance of the target?

Homework

Research local golf courses and driving ranges. Find out the costs of playing a round, whether the course is public or private, the requirements for joining (if any), and any other social benefits associated with the course or club. This will be due in Lesson 8.

Resources

Heuler, O. (1995). *Perfecting your golf swing: New ways to lower your score.* New York: Serling.

World Golf: www.worldgolf.com

Golf: www.golf.com/instruction

Golf Info Guide: www.golf-info-guide.com

Internet keyword search: "wedges," "club loft," "fringe"

LESSON 7: PITCHING

Grade-Level Outcomes

Primary Outcomes

Lifetime activities: Demonstrates competency and/or refines activity-specific movement skills in 2 or more lifetime activities (outdoor pursuits, individual-performance activities, aquatics, net/wall games or target games). (S1.H1.L1)

Movement concepts, principles & knowledge: Applies the terminology associated with exercise and participation in selected individual-performance activities, dance, net/wall games, target games, aquatics and/or outdoor pursuits appropriately. (S2.H1.L1)

Embedded Outcome

Movement concepts, principles & knowledge: Uses movement concepts and principles (e.g., force, motion, rotation) to analyze and improve performance of self and/or others in a selected skill. (S2.H2.L1)

Lesson Objectives

The learner will:

- demonstrate the proper technique for pitching the ball.
- control ball flight by adjusting the swing.
- judge approximate location of ball landing area for greater success of distance control to target.

Equipment and Materials

- Pitching wedge or higher degree loft wedges
- Golf balls or modified balls (plastic or foam balls may be used for safety)
- Putting area or turf suitable for pitching
- Swing checklist
- Devices for video analysis

Introduction

Now that you have a good feel for chipping, you will practice pitching from a little farther away from the target.

Show a video of chipping and then pitching so students can see how they differ.

Instructional Task: Pitching Technique

■ PRACTICE TASK

Demonstrate proper technique for pitching. For the pitch, the swing might have a longer backswing, and the wrists will have a hinge action on the backswing instead of being firm. This will create a deeper angle for more height, or loft, on the ball. Students practice pitching the ball to a target area or pop-up target. Specify the number of practice hits.

Refinement

Have students focus on the hinge action to create more loft. Cue students with "hinge," "hold," "and turn through."

Student Choices/Differentiation

- Students may review a video clip of pitching technique, if needed.
- Students may use modified balls.

- Adjust the target area to allow success.
- Students may select the type of club based on personal preference.

What to Look For

- Ball position is in the middle of the stance.
- Hands hinge on the backswing.
- Students hit the ball on the downstroke.
- Ball contacts the club on the sweet spot.
- Hands are forward of the ball at contact.
- There is no scooping of the ball.
- Students put appropriate loft on the ball.
- Backswing and forward swing have a larger arc than for the chip.

Instructional Task: Distance Control

■ PRACTICE TASK

Demonstrate distance control by varying the length of the backswing. Students might need to practice with plastic or foam balls until they develop a feel for making contact. Mark the landing area so that students can determine success while they practice.

Extensions

- Repeat, varying the distance to the target.
- Repeat, varying the size of the landing area.

EMBEDDED OUTCOME: S2.H2.L1. Students record one another with a device while hitting. Students use a checklist to evaluate swing and improve performance by applying movement concepts.

Refinement

Have students control distance with backswing and forward swing rather than with club speed.

Student Choices/Differentiation

- Students may review a video clip of distance control, if needed.
- Students may use modified balls.
- Adjust the target area to allow success.
- Students may select the type of club based on personal preference.

What to Look For

- Students maintain the same speed in the swing.
- Distance in the backswing equals distance in the forward swing.
- Students perform a hinging action on the backswing.

Instructional Task: Wedges

■ PRACTICE TASK

Explain the different types of wedges. Common wedges are pitching, sand, gap, and lob. Each club has a range in degree of loft.

Review components from Lesson 5, and ask students to give reasons for choosing a pitch shot over a putt or chip shot.

Guiding questions for students:

- When would you choose to pitch instead of chip?
- How is ball flight affected by club head loft?
- What clubs would you use if you wanted to reduce the roll on the green?

Student Choices/Differentiation

Students may view a video clip of both shots on a course.

What to Look For

- Students can give different scenarios for using a pitch shot. Some reasons for using a pitch shot include short distance of green to target; ball is lying in deep rough.
- Students understand that higher-lofted wedges produce a higher loft in ball flight, which reduces ball roll on the green surface.

Instructional Task: Pitch and Putt

■ PRACTICE TASK

In pairs, students set up to pitch onto a landing area and then putt to a target. Two putts are the maximum. Students score 1 point for hitting the target in two putts and 2 points for hitting the target in one putt. Students take turns and repeat five times.

Student Choices/Differentiation

- Students choose their partners.
- Students choose their clubs and balls.

What to Look For

- Students are taking their time on the putt.
- Pitches are making it to the landing area.
- Students are incorporating the hinging action on the backswing of the pitch.

Instructional Task: Terminology

■ PRACTICE TASK

Explain the following terms and phrases: *ready golf*, *stroke play*, and *scramble*.

Student Choices/Differentiation

- Use posters with words and definitions.
- Provide handouts with terminology.

What to Look For

- Students are able to explain the differences between standard play and a scramble format.
- Students are asking good questions.

Formal and Informal Assessments

- Peer assessment with video
- Exit slip: When would you pitch and when would you chip?

Closure

- What instruction would you give someone who is hitting on top of the ball when trying to pitch it?
- When should ball contact be made? On the upswing or downswing?
- In our next class, we will play a chipping and pitching game that uses all of the skills that you've learned so far. During the game, I will assess your pitching and chipping skills using a scoring guide, which I'll post on the school's physical education website.

Reflection

- Was the ball coming off the club at an appropriate loft?
- Could students adjust swing distance according to the distance of the target?
- Review exit slips to check for understanding.

Homework

Find an article online or in the library about pitching or chipping technique. Write up a summary of how to improve your stroke, due in Lesson 10.

Resources

Heuler, O. (1995). *Perfecting your golf swing: New ways to lower your score.* New York: Serling.

Golf: www.golf.com

Golf Info Guide: www.golf-info-guide.com

World Golf: www.worldgolf.com

Internet keyword search: "stroke play," "ready golf," "loft"

LESSON 8: MODIFIED CHIPPING AND PUTTING GAME

Grade-Level Outcomes

Primary Outcomes

Lifetime activities: Demonstrates competency and/or refines activity-specific movement skills in 2 or more lifetime activities (outdoor pursuits, individual-performance activities, aquatics, net/wall games or target games). (S1.H1.L1)

Rules & etiquette: Exhibits proper etiquette, respect for others and teamwork while engaging in physical activity and/or social dance. (S4.H2.L1)

Physical activity knowledge: Evaluates—according to their benefits, social support network and participation requirements—activities that can be pursued in the local environment. (S3.H4.L1)

Embedded Outcome

Working with others: Solves problems and thinks critically in physical activity and/or dance settings, both as an individual and in groups. (S4.H4.L1)

Lesson Objectives

The learner will:

- use skills learned in a pressure situation.
- work within a team to determine which shot is the most appropriate given the circumstances.
- implement rules and etiquette techniques while participating in a mock tournament.
- keep correct score.

Equipment and Materials

- High-lofted irons and wedges (7, 8, 9, P, S, W, and so on)
- Golf balls and modified balls
- Putting area or target area
- Paper and pencils

Introduction

Today, you will create your own chipping and putting course and then play a round on it. Playing the course will require you to use all of the skills and knowledge that you've developed so far.

Instructional Task:
Creating a Chipping and Pitching Course

▓ PRACTICE TASK

Students design a chipping and pitching course around a putting green. Explain how this type of course differs from the putting course they already designed. Multiple hitting areas can be designed around one putting green. Determine par for the hole. Students should make a sketch of their designs.

Refinement

Have students consider varying the distances and approaches to the hole (target).

EMBEDDED OUTCOME: S4.H4.L1. In this task, students will think critically and collaborate to design a chipping and pitching course.

Student Choices/Differentiation

Students choose their groups.

What to Look For

- Students are engaging with others to create the course.
- All students are contributing ideas.

Instructional Task: Modified Game

■ PRACTICE TASK

Students play the holes in sequential order and keep track of their scores. If time is a factor, use a shotgun start (groups start at any hole that is open and play in sequential order from there until they complete every hole). Assess students while chipping or putting on one hole using the scoring guide.

Refinement

Students provide feedback on etiquette around the green, such as ball marking, green repair, and flag (in or out of the hole, placement when out).

Student Choices/Differentiation

Students can be put in pairs and play as a team using a scramble format.

What to Look For

- Students are selecting the proper clubs for chipping and pitching.
- Students are marking the balls properly.
- Students are following putting etiquette and order of play.
- Students are executing all the critical elements of alignment, grip, and other skills learned in previous lessons.

Instructional Task: Participation in the Community

■ PRACTICE TASK

Students share their homework assignment on local participation opportunities.

Student Choices/Differentiation

Students can use posters or other visual aids to share what they learned.

What to Look For

- Students identified public and private courses.
- Students included driving ranges.
- Students compared costs.
- Note what benefits they identified.

Formal and Informal Assessments

- Formal assessment on chipping and pitching
- Sketches of hole designs

Closure

- With a pitch or chip shot, where should your hands be in relation to the club face after contact?
- When is a pitch shot preferred over a chip shot?
- Next class, you'll start working with long irons.

Reflection

- Did most students follow the rules of the game?
- Were students conscious of etiquette procedures?
- Did students complete the course in an appropriate number of strokes?

Homework

- Review the checkpoints for the chip and pitch shots, and watch videos online of other golfers.
- Go over the checkpoints with a classmate, and demonstrate the skill by talking through the progression.

Resources

Heuler, O. (1995). *Perfecting your golf swing: New ways to lower your score.* New York: Serling.

Golf: www.golf.com

Golf Info Guide: www.golf-info-guide.com

World Golf: www.worldgolf.com

Internet keyword search: "ready golf," "shotgun start"

LESSON 9: IRONS

Grade-Level Outcomes

Primary Outcomes

Lifetime activities: Demonstrates competency and/or refines activity-specific movement skills in 2 or more lifetime activities (outdoor pursuits, individual-performance activities, aquatics, net/wall games or target games). (S1.H1.L1)

Physical activity knowledge: Evaluates risks and safety factors that might affect physical activity preferences throughout the life cycle. (S3.H5.L1)

Embedded Outcomes

Health: Analyzes the health benefits of a self-selected physical activity. (S5.H1.L1)

Social interaction: Identifies the opportunity for social support in a self-selected physical activity or dance. (S5.H4.L1)

Lesson Objectives

The learner will:

- select the appropriate club for multiple shots.
- identify key checkpoints for the full swing.
- determine ball placement based on club selection.

Equipment and Materials

- Variety of irons
- 2 wedges
- Plastic balls or foam balls
- Area large enough for the group
- Poster paper and markers

Introduction

Today's lesson focuses on the full iron shot, or hitting longer distances with irons. We'll start with GPA, or grip, posture, alignment. These are the three key points you need to check before doing anything else. [Show a video clip of a golfer addressing the ball with an iron, or give a demonstration. Then show addressing the ball and swinging the iron.] Before you practice this shot, let's talk about selecting the right club for the distance from the green.

Instructional Task: Selecting a Club Based on Yardage

■ PRACTICE TASK

Show long irons and point out the angle of the club face compared with wedges or shorter irons. Discuss and demonstrate selecting the proper club based on distance. Let students know they can expect a 10-yard difference between each club. Average yardage distances can be used as a guide for males and females.

Guiding questions for students:

- What club would be a good choice if you are 200 yards from the green?
- If you have 100 yards to the green and you would normally hit a pitching wedge, what club would you hit if you were 120 yards away?
- Which club will go higher—a pitching wedge or a 5 iron? Why?

Student Choices/Differentiation

Create a poster or handout with average distances for males and females.

What to Look For

- Students are engaged.
- Students are suggesting the right clubs.
- Students are applying movement concepts when thinking about distance and trajectory.

Instructional Task: Exploring Striking With an Iron

■ PRACTICE TASK

Review stance, ball position, alignment, and grip. Remind students that ball position will vary slightly based on the length of the club (in the middle of the stance for shorter clubs, closer to the forward heel for longer clubs).

Students should be separated far enough apart to prevent injury by club swing. Students should never be in front of another player hitting the ball. Assign each student a specified target area.

Students hit until all balls are out, then retrieve and repeat.

Refinement

Instead of using the correct club with a full swing, let students use clubs with a lower loft at a three-quarter swing. This generally produces more accurate shots. (Example: Instead of using a full 9 iron, use an 8 or 7 iron with three-quarter swing.)

Extensions

- Repeat, with students hitting with a different iron.
- Repeat, varying the distance to the target or size of the target area.

Guiding questions for students:

- What causes the ball to veer from the target line to the right? To the left?
- If you are topping the ball or not getting any air, what might be the cause?
- What do you think might cause you to hit the ground before the ball?

Student Choices/Differentiation

- Students may use different irons to explore striking.
- Students can use modified balls.

What to Look For

- Check the number of balls that landed within the defined target area to see if students are having success hitting the ball straight.
- Students are able to hit the appropriate distance with the club they are using.
- Ball placement moves forward from the middle of the stance as the club gets longer. For example, a pitching wedge may be played in the middle of the stance, whereas a 5 iron may be played 2 inches (5 cm) inside the forward heel.

Instructional Task: Penalties

■ PRACTICE TASK

Many times, when you hit with long irons, you end up hitting the ball out of bounds or into a hazard, such as sand or water. There are special rules for these situations.

Discuss the differences between the options available after hitting into a hazard versus hitting a ball out of bounds. Review the rules and procedures for taking a drop, as well as the penalties imposed for taking drops and for balls that are out of bounds.

Guiding questions for students:

- If your ball is out of bounds, what are your options?
- If your ball lands in the water, what are your options?
- What can you do if your ball is directly behind a tree in the rough?

Extension

Have students practice taking a drop correctly.

Student Choices/Differentiation

Use photos or video to illustrate these situations.

What to Look For

Students apply the rules correctly to different scenarios.

Instructional Task: Small-Group Activity

■ PRACTICE TASK

In groups, students discuss possible risks and safety factors that can affect physical activity preferences as they get older. They should consider the health and social benefits of golf and how the game might fit into a physically active lifestyle throughout their lifespan. Students write their ideas on poster paper and then share them with the class.

Guiding questions for students:

- What are the risks or safety factors involved in physical activity participation as you get older? Think about your parents or your grandparents to come up with ideas.
- What kinds of physical activities are popular with adults? How might they differ from the choices of young people? Why?
- Why do you think golf is a popular lifetime activity for adults?

EMBEDDED OUTCOMES: S5.H1.L1; S5.H4.L1. In their discussions, students should recognize the health and social interaction potential of golf. If they don't, use prompts to move students toward those ideas.

Student Choices/Differentiation

- Students choose their groups.
- Students decide who will record and who will share with the larger group.

What to Look For

- All students are contributing ideas.
- Students are realistic about the risks and safety factors they will face.
- Students can identify multiple benefits of golf as a lifetime activity.

Formal and Informal Assessments

- Informal assessment of swing
- Group activity sheets

Closure

- Remember: Maintain a smooth swing. Most people tend to swing the club faster when they try to hit for longer distances. Be sure to hit down on the ball. Hold the club just tight enough to keep it secure throughout the swing.
- What differences do you notice from the chip and pitch shots to the full iron shot?
- Why is it necessary to change ball position with different clubs?
- In our next class, you will continue to work with long irons and delve into the finer points of the swing.
- Be sure to turn in your article assignment before you leave class.

Reflection

Review assignments to check for student understanding.

Homework

Review for a quiz on terminology next class.

Resources

Heuler, O. (1995). *Perfecting your golf swing: New ways to lower your score.* New York: Serling.

Golf Info Guide: www.golf-info-guide.com

World Golf: www.worldgolf.com

Golf: www.golf.com

Internet keyword search: "hazards in golf," "out-of-bounds penalties," "long irons," "fairway irons," "club trajectory"

LESSON 10: REFINING THE LONG IRONS

Grade-Level Outcomes

Primary Outcomes

Lifetime activities: Demonstrates competency and/or refines activity-specific movement skills in 2 or more lifetime activities (outdoor pursuits, individual-performance activities, net/wall games or target games). (S1.H1.L1)

Movement concepts, principles & knowledge: Applies the terminology associated with exercise and participation in selected individual-performance activities, dance, net/wall games, target games, aquatics and/or outdoor pursuits. (S2.H1.L1)

Embedded Outcomes

Movement concepts, principles & knowledge: Uses movement concepts and principles (e.g., force, motion, rotation) to analyze and improve performance of self and/or others in a selected skill. (S2.H2.L1)

Working with others: Uses communication skills and strategies that promote team or group dynamics. (S4.H3.L1)

Lesson Objectives

The learner will:

- identify key checkpoints in the backswing.
- demonstrate the backswing.
- identify a hook, slice, draw, and fade.
- recognize the importance of repairing the ground.
- complete a quiz on terminology and concepts.

Equipment and Materials

- Variety of irons
- 2 wedges
- Plastic balls or foam balls
- Area large enough for the group

Introduction

What did you learn from reading your articles on the chip or pitch? Did you find any new tips that you can share with the class? Today, we'll continue working on the full iron shot, breaking it down into two phases: the backswing and the forward swing. I'll focus mainly on the backswing and then identify a few hazards that are common when playing a round of golf. Let's take the quiz first.

Instructional Task: Quiz

■ PRACTICE TASK

Administer a quiz on terminology and concepts used in class to date.

Student Choices/Differentiation

Allow extra time if needed.

What to Look For

Students display a basic understanding of golf terminology and concepts.

Instructional Task: Backswing With an Iron

■ PRACTICE TASK

Demonstrate the proper backswing. Students practice hitting to the target area as in the previous lesson, but have them stop the movement at the top of the backswing before attempting to contact the ball. This will give them a feel for the backswing elements.

Extensions

- Practice the complete swing, with a focus on the backswing.
- Vary the target area.
- Vary the distance to the target.

Refinements

- Students generally pick up the back elbow in the backswing (chicken wing). Place a towel under the back armpit and tell them not to let the towel hit the ground in the backswing.
- Students often pick up their heads to see where the ball went, which affects the ball's trajectory. Have students focus on keeping their heads down and still.

Student Choices/Differentiation

- Students can use modified balls.
- Students select their irons.

What to Look For

- Students are using correct alignment in their stance.
- Students execute the critical elements of the setup, grip, and backswing.
- Students keep their heads down during the swing.
- Students' torsos finish facing the target area (90-degree turn from addressing the ball).

Instructional Task: Detecting Errors

■ PRACTICE TASK

Review the terms *slice, hook, draw, fade, and approach*. Show video clips to illustrate.

Guiding questions for students:

- What causes the ball to slice or hook? Draw or fade?
- What corrections would you suggest to straighten out the flight of the ball? Why?

Extension

In pairs, students hit a series of long-iron shots. Partners use a checklist to provide feedback on the swing and indicate if they see the ball hook, slice, fade, or draw. Students switch roles.

EMBEDDED OUTCOMES: S2.H2.L1; S4.H3.L1 This task allows students to analyze the swing and apply movement concepts to make corrections. It also lets them work on providing their analysis and feedback in a positive, supportive manner.

Student Choices/Differentiation

Students may review the video clips in slow motion.

What to Look For

- Students can identify the types of errors when they see them on the video.
- Students can articulate the movement concepts underlying the flight pattern of the ball.
- Students can detect errors in the swing pattern of the performer.

Formal and Informal Assessments

- Quiz on terminology
- Peer assessment of swing

Closure

- What happens when the arms come off the chest in the backswing?
- What is the difference between bending from the waist first and then bending the knees, as opposed to bending the knees first and then bending at the waist?
- In our next class, we'll spend some time learning about hazards while improving your long-iron shots.

Reflection

- Where are students still struggling with the swing?
- Are students making valid assessments of their peers' swings?
- What do we need to focus on next time?

Homework

Research the term *divot* and explain what it is and what you should do if you make one.

Resources

Heuler, O. (1995). *Perfecting your golf swing: New ways to lower your score*. New York: Serling.

Golf: www.golf.com

Golf Info Guide: www.golf-info-guide.com

World Golf: www.worldgolf.com

Internet keyword search: "fade," "draw," "slice," "hook," "approach"

LESSON 11: SEQUENCING IRONS AND ERROR DETECTION

Grade-Level Outcomes

Primary Outcomes

Lifetime activities: Demonstrates competency and/or refines activity-specific movement skills in 2 or more lifetime activities (outdoor pursuits, individual-performance activities, net/wall games or target games). (S1.H1.L1)

Movement concepts, principles & knowledge: Applies the terminology associated with exercise and participation in selected individual-performance activities, dance, net/wall games, target games, aquatics and/or outdoor pursuits. (S2.H1.L1)

Embedded Outcome

Movement concepts, principles & knowledge: Uses movement concepts and principles (e.g., force, motion, rotation) to analyze and improve performance of self and/or others in a self-selected skill. (S2.H2.L1)

Lesson Objectives

The learner will:

- identify key checkpoints in the forward swing.
- demonstrate the forward swing.
- identify certain hazards.
- demonstrate a strong grip and a weak grip.

Equipment and Materials

- Variety of irons
- 2 wedges
- Driving range with balls
- Plastic balls or foam balls (if driving range is not available)
- Area large enough for the group (if driving range is not available)
- Grass or mats to hit from (if driving range is not available)
- Scorecards and pencils

Introduction

Your homework was to learn about divots. What is a divot? When does it happen? What should you do after hitting a divot? Today, you'll continue to work on your iron shots, focusing on the forward swing instead of the backswing. I will also identify a few hazards that are common while playing a round of golf.

Instructional Task: Forward Swing

■ PRACTICE TASK

Demonstrate the proper forward swing.

Students should focus on transitioning from the backswing to the forward swing. Allow students to take slow and controlled swings while contacting the ball. Give each student a set number of balls. After hitting all the balls, students retrieve them.

Refinements

- Make sure that students' hips are bent out and arms are riding the chest. Many students like to extend their arms to hit the ball, causing poor contact.
- Have students keep the instep of the back foot against the ground as the weight shifts to the back foot during the backswing. Shifting weight to the outside of the back foot drains the shot of power.

Extensions

- Vary the distance to the target.
- Vary the size of the target.

Student Choices/Differentiation

Students may select the type of club based on personal preference.

What to Look For

- Students are using correct alignment in their stance.
- Students are executing the critical elements of the setup and grip.
- Students' leg drive initiates the forward swing.
- Students' weight transfer is distributed to the forward foot at the finish of the swing.

Instructional Task: Error Detection

■ PRACTICE TASK

After demonstrating a strong grip and a weak grip, ask students to describe what they think will happen when a player uses each type of grip. (Answer: With a strong grip, the ball tends to hook; with a weak grip, the ball tends to slice.)

Have students practice hitting with a partner. Students hit 10 balls, and the partner counts how many are slices or hooks.

EMBEDDED OUTCOME: S2.H2.L1. Ask students to think about the mechanisms that create a slice or a hook (grip, club face angle is open or closed, swing is inside-out or outside-in).

Extension

Repeat for any or all of fade, push, pull, and draw.

Refinement

If any students are struggling with slicing the ball or hooking the ball, adjust their grips. This is one factor that could cause them to hit the ball incorrectly.

Student Choices/Differentiation

- Students choose their partners.
- Students choose their equipment.

What to Look For

- Students are identifying slices and hooks accurately.
- Students are able to adjust their grips to correct the errors.

Instructional Task: Stroke Sequence Simulation

■ PRACTICE TASK

Set up a simulated fairway and green (on a grass field or inside a large gym), with students hitting with a long iron at the far end. Students hit modified balls and then take their second shots with another long iron, if necessary. Ideally, they are close enough to the target area after the first shot to chip or pitch on the second shot. Students finish by putting out. Students track their scores.

Extension

Place a special target on the field, and have students try to chip or pitch as close to it as they can. The student who chips or pitches closest to the target may subtract one stroke from his or her score.

Student Choices/Differentiation

Students may play in pairs and hit the best ball.

What to Look For

- Students are choosing an appropriate club for the hit they are making.
- Students are keeping score correctly.
- Students are supporting one another.

Instructional Task: Rules

■ PRACTICE TASK

Review the rules and procedures for taking a drop without penalty. Identify and explain the rules regarding casual water, ground under repair, and ball on or near the cart path.

Extension

In pairs, students practice taking a drop and hitting from the drop.

Student Choices/Differentiation

Show video clips of each situation.

What to Look For

- Students are dropping with the shoulder high and arm extended fully.
- Students adhere to one club length and no closer to the hole.

Formal and Informal Assessments

Scorecards (review to see how students are progressing)

Closure

- If your ball seems to always go left or right of the target, check your grip.
- If you have correctly performed the forward swing, your body weight will be on your forward side.
- In our next class, you'll put together everything you've learned so far to design and play a par-3 course.

Reflection

- Are students grasping the concept of the swing?
- Have they picked up on some of the terminology being used in class?
- Are they able to maintain their form when putting strokes together in a sequence?

Homework

Look up par-3 golf courses to spark ideas for designing your own.

Resources

Heuler, O. (1995). *Perfecting your golf swing: New ways to lower your score.* New York: Serling.

Golf Info Guide: www.golf-info-guide.com

Golf: www.golf.com

World Golf: www.worldgolf.com

Internet keyword search: "golf shot from water," "golf shot from cart path," "golf shot near tree"

LESSON 12: PAR-3 COURSE

Grade-Level Outcomes

Primary Outcomes

Lifetime activities: Demonstrates competency and/or refines activity-specific movement skills in 2 or more lifetime activities (outdoor pursuits, individual-performance activities, aquatics, net/wall games or target games). (S1.H1.L1)

Rules & etiquette: Exhibits proper etiquette, respect for others and teamwork while engaging in physical activity and/or social dance. (S4.H2.L1)

Embedded Outcome

Working with others: Solves problems and thinks critically in physical activity or dance settings, both as an individual and in groups. (S4.H4.L1)

Lesson Objectives

The learner will:

- demonstrate the full iron swing.
- identify faulty techniques in his or her golf swing.
- implement rules and points of etiquette while participating in a mock tournament.
- demonstrate skill under positive pressure situations.

Equipment and Materials

- Variety of irons
- Modified golf balls
- Tees
- Golf course or, if not available, a grass field
- Equipment to simulate hazards
- Scorecards, paper and pencils

Introduction

Today, you'll practice the full golf swing with irons and look at video of your swings to try to improve your form. Then, you'll design a par-3 course. I hope that you have some good ideas from your homework assignment. If time permits, you'll play the course today, and if not, you'll play it in our next lesson.

Instructional Task:
Review All Checkpoints for the Full Swing

■ PRACTICE TASK

Review and demonstrate all the checkpoints for making a proper swing: grip, posture, alignment, same speed for forward swing and backswing, hands lead, and so on.

Students practice the full swing in pairs, each taking five swings without balls followed by five swings with modified balls on tees.

Refinement

Remind students to keep their heads still and to allow rotation so that their navels are facing the target at finish.

Extensions

- Repeat, with each student taking 10 full swings with the ball on the tee.
- Students record their partners' swings using an iPad, phone, or other device. Students identify problems in their own swings and make corrections in the next set of hits.

Student Choices/Differentiation

- Students may review a video clip of the full swing.
- Students may use modified clubs.
- Students may use modified balls.
- Provide a checklist of critical elements of the swing for students to use in self-evaluation.

What to Look For

- Ask questions throughout the review to make sure that students are listening and comprehending.
- Students can identify faulty procedures or technique in the full swing when observing others.

Instructional Task: Designing a Par-3 Course

■ PRACTICE TASK

In small groups, students design a par-3 course. Each group must design one or two holes. Students have the option of creating hazards with equipment, such as cones or mats, or with natural elements. Students must stipulate the boundaries of the fairways. The group with the most creative hole is awarded a mulligan (a do-over).

Once the groups have designed their holes, they must share with the other groups to create a sequence of play.

EMBEDDED OUTCOME: S4.H4.L1. Use this task to review critical thinking and problem-solving skills.

Guiding questions for students:

- How did the requirement to make the course a par 3 affect your design?
- When putting the holes into a sequence, what factors did you consider?
- What ideas did you come up with for hazards using equipment or the natural environment?

Student Choices/Differentiation

Students choose their groups.

What to Look For

Students are engaging with others to create the par-3 course.

Instructional Task: Play the Course

■ PRACTICE TASK

Students play the holes in sequential order and keep their scores. Allow students to tee up their first shot on the created course. If time is a factor, use a shotgun start (groups start at any hole that is open and play in sequential order from there until they complete every hole). Students keep their own scores.

Student Choices/Differentiation

Students can be put in pairs and play as a team using a scramble format.

What to Look For

- Students are selecting the proper clubs.
- Students are marking the balls properly.
- Students are following putting etiquette and order of play.
- Students are executing all the critical elements of alignment, grip, and other skills learned in previous lessons.

Formal and Informal Assessments

- Self-assessments
- Scorecards and sketches of course designs

Closure

- Remember, don't try to kill the ball—an easy, consistent swing will get the job done.
- Your hands should not pass your ear on the backswing.
- Your weight should be on the forward side at the end of the swing.
- Next class, you'll start practicing with the driver—the largest club in the bag.

Reflection

- Are any students frustrated? Spend a little extra time working with them on fundamentals.
- Review scorecards to determine how well students are progressing.

Homework

Research golf gloves and tees, and answer the following questions:

- On which hand should you wear the glove and why?
- Where can you use a tee on the course?
- How high should you tee the ball when using an iron? A driver?

Resources

Heuler, O. (1995). *Perfecting your golf swing: New ways to lower your score.* New York: Serling.

Internet keyword search: "full golf swing," "golf tees," "teeing up the ball"

LESSON 13: USING YOUR DRIVER

Grade-Level Outcomes

Primary Outcomes

Lifetime activities: Demonstrates competency and/or refines activity-specific movement skills in 2 or more lifetime activities (outdoor pursuits, individual-performance activities, aquatics, net/wall games or target games). (S1.H1.L1)

Movement concepts, principles & knowledge: Applies the terminology associated with exercise and participation in selected individual-performance activities, dance, net/wall games, target games, aquatics and/or outdoor pursuits appropriately. (S2.H1.L1)

Embedded Outcomes

Movement concepts, principles & knowledge: Uses movement concepts and principles (e.g., force, motion, rotation) to analyze and improve performance of self and/or others in a selected skill. (S2.H2.L1)

Movement concepts, principles & knowledge: Describes the speed vs. accuracy trade-off in throwing and striking skills. (S2.H2.L2)

Lesson Objectives

The learner will:

- demonstrate the full swing using a driver.
- hit the ball to the approximate location of the desired target.
- identify hole layouts by the appropriate terminology.

Equipment and Materials

- Variety of woods (focus is on the driver)
- Driving range or field
- Range balls or modified balls
- Tees
- Starter bag of clubs for each set of partners

Introduction

So what did you learn about using golf gloves? How about tees? When may you use a tee on a golf course? Why do you want to? Tees are important for hitting with a driver, which is what you are going to work on today. The driver is the longest club in the bag and has the lowest loft. You will need to make a few modifications to your full iron swing, but basically, you will use the same swing with your driver.

Instructional Task: Review All Checkpoints

■ PRACTICE TASK

Review and demonstrate all the checkpoints for making a proper swing, with a few differences in the driver swing:

- Ball position is forward near the front toe.
- The ball is on a tee, at a height that allows about half of it to show above the club head.
- The swing is more of a sweeping motion.

Students practice the full swing in pairs, taking 10 hits. Partner retrieves the balls and the switches roles.

Refinement

Have students focus on smooth rhythm and a sweeping motion.

Extensions

- Repeat, using a smaller target area.
- Repeat, using a different wood.

EMBEDDED OUTCOME: S2.H2.L1; S2.H2.L2 Discuss the advantages and disadvantages of using the driver.

Guiding questions for students:

- What are the advantages of using the driver? (Answer: longer lever, bigger club face leads to more power and distance)
- What are the disadvantages? (Answers: less control, more likely to fade or draw)
- This is called the speed vs. accuracy trade-off. Greater club head speed leads to more power, but unless you're really skilled, your shots probably will be less accurate than with other clubs. In what other physical activities might that be true?

Student Choices/Differentiation

- Students may use modified clubs.
- Students may use modified balls.

What to Look For

- Students are reviewing the checkpoints (alignment, grip, setup, backswing, and forward swing).
- Ball is forward and near the front toe in the stance.
- Students are demonstrating the sweeping motion.

Instructional Task: Shot Sequence

■ PRACTICE TASK

On a field, set up a simulated tee box, fairway, and putting green or target. One student in each pair carries a starter bag with four clubs (wood, middle iron, wedge, and putter), acting as a caddy. The other student hits a wood from a tee, walks up to the ball and hits an iron, then takes a pitch or chip, and finally, a putt. If a student hits the ball out of play, he or she takes a drop. Use modified balls. Students score themselves. Switch roles.

Extension

Repeat, scoring the number of hits to the target.

Refinement

Have partners track slices and hooks, draws or fades, on irons and woods. At the end of the sequence, partners provide the information to the hitters to allow for correction next time.

What to Look For

- Students are setting up correctly for each shot.
- Students are adjusting their swings for the remaining distances.
- Students are executing the critical elements of the swing properly.

Instructional Task: Rules and Terminology

■ PRACTICE TASK

Discuss the different tee box locations and rules and dimensions for teeing the ball up for the first hit. Describe the different types of drivers (degrees of loft, design of club for hook and slice). Explain the terms *dogleg*, *loose impediment*, *obstruction*, and *provisional ball*.

Extension

Show video clips or a course diagram to have students identify doglegs and potential strategies for negotiating them.

Student Choices/Differentiation

- Use photos or videos of a tee box to illustrate.
- Show examples of different types of drivers.

What to Look For

- Students are engaged in the discussion.
- Students are making a connection between the club distance and strategy for dogleg holes.

Formal and Informal Assessments

Peer data on hooks, slices, fades, and draws

Closure

- What are some important things to remember when using your driver? (Answer: Start your backswing in a sweeping motion instead of picking the club straight up; contact with the ball should be right at the beginning of club upswing; and so on).
- Next class, I'll assess your driving form and accuracy, and then you'll start working on special situations, such as hitting out of bunkers.

Reflection

- Were students able to maintain a fair amount of control with the driver?
- Were they comfortable hitting off the tee?
- Were they using the same swing as when they hit the irons?

Homework

Since you'll be working on hitting out of bunkers next class, review the video clips of successful (and unsuccessful) shots on the school's physical education website.

Resources

Heuler, O. (1995). *Perfecting your golf swing: New ways to lower your score.* New York: Serling.

Golf: www.golf.com

World Golf: www.worldgolf.com

Golf Info Guide: www.golf-info-guide.com

Internet keyword search: "dogleg," "tee box etiquette," "tee box markers," "provisional ball"

LESSON 14: BUNKER SHOTS

Grade-Level Outcomes

Primary Outcomes

Lifetime activities: Demonstrates competency and/or refines activity-specific movement skills in 2 or more lifetime activities (outdoor pursuits, individual-performance activities, aquatics, net/wall games or target games). (S1.H1.L1)

Rules & etiquette: Exhibits proper etiquette, respect for others and teamwork while engaging in physical activity and/or social dance. (S4.H2.L1)

Embedded Outcome

Rules & etiquette: Examines moral and ethical conduct in specific competitive situations (e.g., intentional fouls, performance-enhancing substances, gambling, current events in sport). (S4.H2.L2)

Lesson Objectives

The learner will:

- complete a teacher-conducted assessment of the swing using a wood.
- demonstrate how to hit a normal bunker shot.
- demonstrate proper procedures of entering the bunker and leaving the bunker.
- apply appropriate rules of hitting out of the bunker.
- apply appropriate force and technique to hit out of bunker.

Equipment and Materials

- Sand wedges
- Sand bunker or simulated bunker
- Range balls or modified balls
- Woods
- Ethical dilemma handouts

Introduction

After looking at the video clips of bunker shots, what do you think makes the difference between a successful and an unsuccessful one? Today, you will learn how to hit out of the bunker onto the green. We'll focus on what's known as the "fried egg" lie. Before we get to that, I will assess the full swing with a driver.

Instructional Task:
Assessment of the Full Swing With a Wood

■ PRACTICE TASK

Set up the field for students to hit modified balls with woods. In groups of three, one student hits three drives, one takes a video using a device, and the third spots the landing and closeness to the target area. Students rotate roles. You will evaluate the drives with a rubric after class. Award extra points for drives landing within the target area.

Note: This format will save a great deal of class time, but if it's not possible to use video, set the lesson up in stations, with one group warming up, one group being assessed, and two or three groups practicing their bunker shots.

Student Choices/Differentiation

- Students choose their balls.
- Students choose their woods.

What to Look For

Students are executing the key elements of the swing.

Instructional Task: Bunker Shots

■ PRACTICE TASK

Demonstrate proper setup (slightly open stance) and swing. Have students envision the ball as a fried egg. The ball is the yolk, and the sand in the bunker is the white. The goal is to hit the white out from under the yolk. Students take 10 hits out of the sand and then retrieve. Repeat. Focus should be on hitting the ball out of the sand.

Note: If you don't have access to a bunker, you can simulate one by filling some kiddie pools with sand or by working with the track coach to use the long-jump pit. You might want to lay a tarp on the ground in front of the pools or pit to capture the sand and re-use it.

Refinement

Make circles in the sand and have students "blow up" the circle (hit the inside top sand out of the circle).

Extensions

- Repeat, with students aiming for a target beyond the sand.
- Repeat and putt out.

Student Choices/Differentiation

Students choose their wedges.

What to Look For

- Students are using a sand wedge or other appropriate wedge to get the ball out.
- Hips are open 45 degrees left of the target.
- Club face stays fixed throughout the swing, and the face of the club is slightly open.
- Ball placement is about 2 inches (5 cm) inside the forward heel.
- Loft of ball is determined by backswing angle.
- Ball has a high trajectory.
- Club does not dig into the sand.

Instructional Task: Etiquette

■ PRACTICE TASK

Explain how to enter and leave the bunker.

- Enter the bunker at the site closest to the ball, and leave at the same point.
- Make sure you rake the bunker after hitting the shot so the next player doesn't have an undesirable lie.
- Take practice swings outside the bunker so you can't be accused of grounding the club.

Extension

Embedded outcome: S4.H2.L2. Divide students into small groups, and give each group an ethical dilemma (handout) that can occur during tournament play. Have each group discuss the situation and what they think the outcome should be and why. Record on handout.

Student Choices/Differentiation

Students may review a video clip of a player entering and leaving a bunker.

What to Look For

- Students are engaged in the discussion.
- All students are contributing ideas.

Formal and Informal Assessments

- Formal assessment of the swing with a driver
- Ethical dilemma handouts

Closure

- Remember: Envision the ball as a fried egg. The ball is the yolk. Your goal is to hit the white out from under the yolk.
- Do not touch the ground with the club before your forward swing.
- Next class, you'll spend some time refining your shots for special situations.

Reflection

- Review the assessment videos and determine if there are common areas of weakness.
- Review the ethical dilemma handouts to see if students are able to make good choices about application of the rules, etiquette, and the spirit of the game.

Homework

One of the challenges in golf is that the ball is not always lying on flat ground when you need to hit it. For homework, research uphill, downhill, and sidehill lies and how you need to adjust to play the ball in these situations.

Resources

Heuler, O. (1995). *Perfecting your golf swing: New ways to lower your score.* New York: Serling.

Internet search terms: "bunker rules," "bunker shots"

LESSON 15: REFINING YOUR GAME

Grade-Level Outcomes

Primary Outcome

Lifetime activities: Demonstrates competency and/or refines activity-specific movement skills in 2 or more lifetime activities (outdoor pursuits, individual-performance activities, aquatics, net/wall games or target games). (S1.H1.L1)

Embedded Outcome

Challenge: Chooses an appropriate level of challenge to experience success and desire to participate in a self-selected physical activity. (S5.H2.L2)

Lesson Objectives

The learner will:

- Hit a bunker shot from a buried lie.
- Practice hitting an iron on an uphill lie.
- Practice hitting an iron on a downhill lie.
- Practice hitting from a sidehill lie below his or her feet.
- Practice hitting from a sidehill lie above his or her feet.
- Hit a wood from the fairway.

Equipment and Materials

- Wedges
- Variety of irons
- 3 and/or 5 woods
- Sand bunker or simulated bunker
- Modified balls
- Targets
- Station task cards with tasks and cues

Introduction

You've practiced all the basic shots in golf, so today, you will work on how to use these shots under special conditions. For homework, you researched how to adjust to play a ball on different slopes. What are the key points to remember for these types of hits? Also, you'll work on hitting the ball with a wood in the fairway with no tee and on hitting a buried ball in a bunker. We'll divide into six stations so that you can practice all these different shots. You will hit 10 balls at your own pace and then rotate to a new station. If you finish early, you can go back to a station to practice the skill of your choice.

Instructional Task: Stations

■ PRACTICE TASK

Each student hits 10 balls at each station, retrieves the balls after everyone at the station has finished, and then rotates to a new station.

Station 1: Hitting a Buried Ball Out of a Bunker

Set up a simulated bunker or use a bunker. Each student takes 10 practice hits.

Cues for Task Card

- Ball placement is off back foot contact.
- Swing down sharply on the ball to pop it out of the sand.
- Contact back of ball with leading edge of club; club face is slightly closed.
- Club will end up being buried in sand at end of swing. Ball should come out with ease.

Station 2: Hitting From a Downhill Lie

Set up a hitting station where the hitter and ball are positioned on a downhill slope to hit to the target.

Cues for Task Card

- Select a club with a bit more loft.
- Match shoulder angle to the slope (parallel), spine perpendicular.
- Set the ball back a little in your stance.
- Ball will have a tendency to go right, so aim a little left.
- Be sure to stay down through the hit.

Station 3: Hitting From an Uphill Lie

Set up a hitting station where the hitter and ball are positioned on an uphill slope to hit to the target.

Cues for Task Card

- Select a club with a bit less loft.
- Match shoulder angle to the slope (parallel), spine perpendicular.
- Set the ball forward a little in your stance, keeping weight on back foot.
- Ball will have a tendency to go left, so aim a little right.

Station 4: Hitting Fairway Woods

Set up a hitting station on the fairway.

Cues for Task Card

- Stance should be the same as off the tee.
- Swing down sharply on the ball to pop it out of the sand.

Station 5: Hitting From a Sidehill Lie, Ball Below the Feet

Set up a hitting station where the hitter is positioned on a sidehill and the ball is below the feet for the hit to the target.

Cues for Task Card

- Take a slightly longer club, and grip it at the very end.
- Bend deeper in the knees and hips.
- Weight should be more in the heels.
- Ball tends to go right, so aim a little left.

Station 6: Hitting From a Sidehill Lie, Ball Above the Feet

Set up a hitting station where the hitter is positioned on a sidehill and the ball is above the feet for the hit to the target.

Cues for Task Card

- Use a club with a bit more loft.
- Move your grip down a little on the club.
- Weight should be more in the toes.
- Ball tends to go left, so aim a little right.

Student Choices/Differentiation

- Students rotate through the stations at their own pace.
- Leave an iPad at each station that plays a video clip of the specific shot.

What to Look For

- Students are always checking for safety at the stations.
- Students are working independently.
- Students are staying on task.

Formal and Informal Assessments

- Debrief students using assessment of full swing from previous class.
- Exit slip: How can you improve on your full swing?

Closure

- Which of the uneven lies was the most challenging? Why? What adjustments did you make to be more successful? (Embedded outcome: S5.H2.L2)
- When would you use a wood on the fairway?
- Name some differences in the swing for a buried sand lie as opposed to a regular sand lie.
- Next class is our last one for this module. Be ready to put it all together in a tournament.

Reflection

- Were students able to adjust to the different types of lies?
- Were they successful with a buried ball?
- What aspects of the game need to have more focus in the tournament?
- Group students by ability into even teams for the tournament.

Homework

- Review scoring, etiquette, and tournament formats from a handout or the school's physical education website.
- Research handicapping in golf.

Resources

Heuler, O. (1995). *Perfecting your golf swing: New ways to lower your score.* New York: Serling.

Internet keyword search: "uneven lies," "bunker shots," "fairway woods"

LESSON 16: PLAYING A SCRAMBLE

Grade-Level Outcomes

Primary Outcomes

Lifetime activities: Demonstrates competency and/or refines activity-specific movement skills in 2 or more lifetime activities (outdoor pursuits, individual-performance activities, aquatics, net/wall games or target games). (S1.H1.L1)

Rules & etiquette: Exhibits proper etiquette, respect for others and teamwork while engaging in physical activity and/or social dance. (S4.H2.L1)

Embedded Outcome

Safety: Applies best practices for participating safely in physical activity, exercise and dance (e.g., injury prevention, proper alignment, hydration, use of equipment, implementation of rules, sun protection). (S4.H5.L1)

Lesson Objectives

The learner will:

- play a round of golf.

Equipment and Materials

- Starter set of clubs for each student or full set for each group
- Golf balls or modified golf balls
- Tees, ball markers, gloves, and so on
- Scorecards and pencils

Introduction

Today's lesson is the culmination of everything you have learned so far as you play a round of golf. For homework, you learned about handicapping in golf. Can anyone explain what that is? Handicapping is a way of allowing players of different abilities to play on more even terms. Although we won't be using handicaps today, we will make things a little more fair by using a scramble format. Get your clubs and go to a hole with your team for the shotgun start.

Instructional Task: Tournament Play

■ PRACTICE TASK

Group students by ability into equal groups. Assign each group to a certain hole to tee off on; players follow a scramble format. Students use scorecards to track their individual scores. If time or resources are limited, students can play one or two holes.

Note: It would be ideal for students to play on a nine-hole or par-3 course. However, if that is not possible, you can create a modified course and use modified balls for play. Design the holes yourself or use the best ones created by students in previous lessons.

EMBEDDED OUTCOME: S4.H5.L1. Ask students to describe important safety practices while on the course before playing.

Refinement

Select a hole and provide specific corrective feedback on strokes or etiquette to each group as they play the hole.

Student Choices/Differentiation

- Students choose their own teams.
- Students choose which hole to start on.

What to Look For

- Students are selecting appropriate clubs for the shots.
- Students are scoring correctly.
- Students are observing proper etiquette.

Formal and Informal Assessments

- Informal assessment
- Individual scorecards

Closure

- Who had a really great shot today and wants to tell us about it?
- How about a really frustrating moment?
- Golf is a lifetime sport. It is also an ever challenging sport. Don't get discouraged. Keep on practicing and you will get better.
- Don't forget, we will be starting a new module next class. Please check the website for your choices so you'll be ready for a new activity.

Reflection

- Reflect on individual improvements over the course of the module.
- What do I need to work on for next time I teach this module or for students who might want to move on to Level 2 golf?

Homework

Review the next set of modules on the school's physical education website and make a selection before coming to class.

Resources

Heuler, O. (1995). *Perfecting your golf swing: New ways to lower your score.* New York: Serling.

Internet keyword search: "scramble," "best ball," "handicap"

CHAPTER 9

Extending Students' Skills and Knowledge to Dance and Rhythms

Dance is an essential part of the Grade-Level Outcomes for high school students because of the unique opportunities it offers for self-expression and creative movement. Dance also is a valuable skill for social events, such as weddings and parties. Dance is a popular activity choice, particularly among girls, and by offering it in the curriculum, you can help keep girls engaged (Couturier, Chepko, & Coughlin, 2007). Above all, dance is a health-enhancing physical activity for all ages—an enjoyable and simple way to raise anyone's heart rate!

You have many forms of dance from which to choose. You can offer traditional choices (e.g., ballroom, folk, line, ballet, modern) or more current forms (e.g., Latin, hip hop, salsa) or a mixture. Dance modules afford many opportunities to connect with other subject areas (foreign languages, cultural history), the heritage of the community, and student's diverse backgrounds. When making module selections, consider what dance forms will be relevant and meaningful for your students. You may even want to have a dance curriculum pathway (see chapter 4) so that students always have a dance option in the elective program.

This chapter includes two dance modules: choreography and line dance. The Choreography Module, contributed by Lisa Jacob, a physical educator at Maine West High School in Des Plaines, IL, provides students with experiences in moving creatively to different music and readings while applying choreographic tools. The lessons in the module give students opportunities to create movement, sometimes individually and other times in pairs. The module is capped with a performance of student-choreographed movement pieces. Although this chapter doesn't include a traditional social dance module, you can find an example of one in a companion to this book: *Lesson Planning for Middle School Physical Education: Meeting the*

National Standards & Grade-Level Outcomes (Doan, MacDonald, & Chepko and SHAPE America – Society of Health and Physical Educators, Eds., 2017).

Line dance is a popular activity in many parts of the country, and this module, contributed by Patrice Lovdahl, who taught physical education for 30 years before retiring, includes a wide variety of dances to be taught. Students also create their own line dances to share with the rest of the class. This module culminates in a special dance event for families, friends, and other students and school staff. The Line Dance Module appears in the e-book and web resource only.

For easy reference, each module begins with a block plan chart of the Grade-Level Outcomes to be addressed within the module. Both modules rely heavily on outcomes under Standards 1, 4, and 5, but they also address outcomes under Standards 2 and 3. In the Line Dance Module, acquiring competency in a form of dance (Outcome S1.H2.L1), designing and performing a line dance (Outcome S1.H2.L2), and leading dances (Outcome S4.H3.L2) are addressed in multiple lessons. The Choreography Module focuses primarily on choreography and performance (Outcome S1.H2.L2), problem solving (Outcome S4.H4.L1), and dance as a means of expression (Outcome S5.H3.L1). As noted earlier, the Line Dance Module appears in the e-book and web resource only. The Choreography Module also includes numerous instructional tasks that address Level 2 outcomes under Standards 3 and 4. Whether your students are beginners or are more advanced, these dance modules provide opportunities for students to become more proficient at the basics or to take their experience to higher levels.

CHOREOGRAPHY MODULE

Lessons in this module were contributed by **Lisa Jacob**, a physical educator at Maine West High School in Des Plaines, IL, who specializes in dance education.

Grade-Level Outcomes Addressed, by Lesson	Lessons 1	2	3	4	5	6	7	8	9	10	11	12	13	14	15	16
Standard 1. The physically literate individual demonstrates competency in a variety of motor skills and movement patterns.																
Demonstrates competency in a form of dance by choreographing a dance or by giving a performance. (S1.H2.L2)	P	P	P	P	P	P	P		P	P	P	P	P	P	P	P
Standard 2. The physically literate individual applies knowledge of concepts, principles, strategies and tactics related to movement and performance.																
Applies the terminology associated with exercise and participation in selected individual-performance activities, dance, net/wall games, target games, aquatics and/or outdoor pursuits appropriately. (S2.H1.L1)	E	E												P		
Identifies and discusses the historical and cultural roles of games, sports and dance in a society. (S2.H1.L2)							P									
Uses movement concepts and principles (e.g., force, motion, rotation) to analyze and improve performance of self and/or others in a selected skill. (S2.H2.L1)							P								P	
Standard 3. The physically literate individual demonstrates the knowledge and skills to achieve and maintain a health-enhancing level of physical activity and fitness.																
Investigates the relationships among physical activity, nutrition and body composition. (S3.H1.L2)			P													
Analyzes and applies technology and social media as tools for supporting a healthy, active lifestyle. (S3.H2.L2)					E		P				E	E	E	E	E	P
Creates a plan, trains for and participates in a community event with a focus on physical activity (e.g., 5K, triathlon, tournament, dance performance, cycling event). (S3.H6.L2)							P		P	P	P	P	P	P	P	P
Applies stress-management strategies (e.g., mental imagery, relaxation techniques, deep breathing, aerobic exercise, meditation) to reduce stress. (S3.H14.L2)															E	E
Standard 4. The physically literate individual exhibits responsible personal and social behavior that respects self and others.																
Accepts differences between personal characteristics and the idealized body images and elite performance levels portrayed in various media. (S4.H1.L2)			E													
Exhibits proper etiquette, respect for others and teamwork while engaging in physical activity and/or social dance. (S4.H2.L1)	E				P			P	P							
Examines moral and ethical conduct in specific competitive situations (e.g., intentional fouls, performance–enhancing substances, gambling, current events in sport). (S4.H2.H2)								E								
Uses communication skills and strategies that promote team or group dynamics. (S4.H3.L1)													E			
Assumes a leadership role (e.g., task or group leader, referee, coach) in a physical activity setting. (S4.H3.L2)			E												E	
Solves problems and thinks critically in physical activity or dance settings, both as an individual and in groups. (S4.H4.L1)	P	P	P	P	P	P	P		P	P	P	P	P	P		
Accepts others' ideas, cultural diversity and body types by engaging in cooperative and collaborative movement projects. (S4.H4.L2)			P					E		E	E	E		E		

CHOREOGRAPHY MODULE *(CONTINUED)*

Grade-Level Outcomes Addressed, by Lesson	Lessons															
	1	2	3	4	5	6	7	8	9	10	11	12	13	14	15	16
Standard 5. The physically literate individual recognizes the value of physical activity for health, enjoyment, challenge, self-expression and/or social interaction.																
Analyzes the health benefits of a self-selected physical activity. (S5.H1.L1)					E											
Chooses an appropriate level of challenge to experience success and desire to participate in a self-selected physical activity. (S5.H2.L2)				E	E	E						E				
Selects and participates in physical activities or dance that meet the need for self-expression and enjoyment. (S5.H3.L1)				P	P	P			P	P	P	P	P	P	P	P
Identifies the uniqueness of creative dance as a means of self-expression. (S5.H3.L2)		E					P									

P = Primary; E = Embedded

LESSON 1: MOVEMENT MAP

Grade-Level Outcomes

Primary Outcomes

Dance & rhythms: Demonstrates competency in a form of dance by choreographing a dance or by giving a performance. (S1.H2.L2)

Working with others: Solves problems and thinks critically in physical activity and/or dance settings, both as an individual and in groups. (S4.H4.L1)

Embedded Outcomes

Rules & etiquette: Exhibits proper etiquette, respect for others and teamwork while engaging in physical activity and/or social dance. (S4.H2.L1)

Movement concepts, principles & knowledge: Applies the terminology associated with exercise and participation in selected individual-performance activities, dance, net/wall games, target games, aquatics and/or outdoor pursuits appropriately. (S2.H1.L1)

Lesson Objectives

The learner will:

- review basic movement concepts relating to dance.
- create a movement map.
- memorize the movement map by walking it multiple times.
- employ choreographic tools to execute along the journey.
- develop solutions to movement problems.
- discuss choreographic tools and how they help create movement that is interesting and aesthetically intriguing.

Equipment and Materials

- Large open dance space
- Paper and pencil for each student
- Stereo
- Background music of instructor's choice (e.g., "Song of the Caged Bird" or "Crystallize" by Lindsey Stirling, "Moonlight Sonata" by E.S. Posthumus, "Until the Last Moment" by Yanni, African rhythms, African djembe drums)
- Video recording device

Introduction

Today, we're starting a new module on choreography. You have already learned so much about movement, alignment, and dance vocabulary in other modules. You have moved your bodies in many different dance genres, and now you are going to take what you have learned and create something new and wonderful. In the first part of the module, you will learn new choreographic tools and put them into practice. You will study how they can help us create interesting and unique movement with the activities we do each day. At the end of the module, you will choreograph your own dance and perform it for others.

Instructional Task: Review

■ **PRACTICE TASK**

Review movement concepts and terminology that students should have already learned in other modules: travel through the space, level change, tempo change, touch, mirroring, opposition, stillness, fall and recovery, floor work, and so on.

Extension

Have students demonstrate each of the concepts as you review them.

Student Choices/Differentiation

Use a video clip of a dance performance, and stop it when appropriate to illustrate a concept.

What to Look For

- Students are making connections from previously learned dance modules.
- Students are able to demonstrate the concepts.

Instructional Task: Creating a Movement Map

■ **PRACTICE TASK**

Students spread out in the space with paper and pencil. The paper should be oriented horizontally (landscape) in front of them. Students draw a small star anywhere on the page and put the tip of their pencil on that star.

When the music begins, students move their pencils the way the music makes them feel. They can close their eyes if they want, but they should not lift their pencils until the music stops (20 to 30 seconds).

Have students draw a dot where the pencil stopped. They have just created a movement map. The map represents the room. Have them put their pencils away and go stand where the star is on their maps.

Extension

Play the music again and have students walk their maps. When they have all ended on their dots, stop the music and have them return to their stars. They can walk their maps two more times before any choreographic tools are added.

Student Choices/Differentiation

Show samples of movement maps.

What to Look For

Students are not cutting their maps short after they walk it the first time. If it has 48 zigzags, they have to do them!

Instructional Task:
Adding Movement and Choreographic Tools

■ **PRACTICE TASK**

Students follow their movement maps as the verbal directions are changed. Each time the music ends, they go back to stand where their stars were.

Task 1: On your path, you have to execute three turns and one dramatic level change.

Extensions

- Task 2: On your path, you have to execute three turns and one dramatic level change, and you must be still for 10 seconds in an abstract pose.

- Task 3: On your path, you have to execute three turns and one dramatic level change, you must be still for 10 seconds in an abstract pose, and you must fall and recover at least one time.
- Continue to layer new tasks on the dancers every time they return to their stars. The possibilities are endless:
  - Tempo change
  - Touch
  - Interaction
  - Dance movements
  - No use of feet
  - Add arms
  - Begin and end in a pose
- With 15 minutes left in the class, let students know you will be filming the movements they are doing. Find a high vantage point so you can see everyone's movements. Start the music and film.
- Once students have memorized their own personal patterns, they can turn in their maps.

Student Choices/Differentiation

This is a completely free exercise. Students decide exactly what type of movement they want to incorporate into their paths. You can guide them, but they ultimately choose the type of turn, the level change, the pose for stillness, and how they will move their bodies.

What to Look For

- Students are following directions.
- Students are concentrating and not talking at all.

Instructional Task: Cool-Down and Debrief

■ PRACTICE TASK

Have students sit down as you link the camera to the TV or LCD projector (whatever the room provides for watching their work). Ask them to stretch for a cool-down and use the guiding questions for reflection.

Guiding questions for students:

- How did creating the movement map with your pencil make you feel?
- Was it difficult to get all the tasks into your movement map?
- Were you dancing?
- Did you interact with other dancers on your journey? If so, how?
- What did you learn about yourself during this exercise?
- What did you learn about others in the class?

EMBEDDED OUTCOME: S4.H2.L1. Show students the video of their collective movement maps. As they marvel at how cool the "dance" is, remind them that these were just simple tasks put together along with free creative choice to make something amazing. Point out how they had to work together, without talking, and respect each other's paths to move about the space and complete each task.

Student Choices/Differentiation

Students choose their own stretches.

What to Look For

- Students are using their cool-down time effectively.
- Students are excited about the movement maps they created.

Formal and Informal Assessments

- Movement maps
- Video recording of dance

Closure

- What choreographic tools did we use today? (Embedded outcome: S2.H1.L1)
- Choreographic tools help us create interesting movement for the audience members to view.
- When you are working on your own choreography, remember these tools and feel free to use them as you create!

Reflection

- How did my students respond to this lesson?
- What can I do to make this lesson even more effective?
- Review students' movement maps and the video recording of the dance to assess their baseline choreography knowledge.

Homework

Write a brief reflection on your experience with creating a movement map. What was the most difficult part for you? Did you feel as if you were dancing? Why or why not?

Resources

Gilbert, A.G. & SHAPE America – Society of Health and Physical Educators. (2015). *Creative dance for all ages*. 2nd ed. Champaign, IL: Human Kinetics.

Reeve, J. (2011). *Dance improvisations: Warm-ups, games and choreographic tasks*. Champaign, IL: Human Kinetics.

National Dance Educators Organization: www.ndeo.org

Internet keyword search: "dance improvisation," "choreography," "National Core Arts Standards in Dance"

LESSON 2: VERBS

Grade-Level Outcomes

Primary Outcomes

Working with others: Solves problems and thinks critically in physical activity and/or dance settings, both as an individual and in groups. (S4.H4.L1)

Dance & rhythms: Demonstrates competency in a form of dance by choreographing a dance or by giving a performance. (S1.H2.L2)

Embedded Outcomes

Movement concepts, principles & knowledge: Applies the terminology associated with exercise and participation in selected individual-performance activities, dance, net/wall games, target games, aquatics and/or outdoor pursuits appropriately. (S2.H1.L1)

Self-expression & enjoyment: Identifies the uniqueness of creative dance as a means of self-expression. (S5.H3.L2)

Lesson Objectives

The learner will:

- use choreographic tools to improvise movement with specific assignments given.
- think critically and problem-solve about how to move while incorporating specific directions.

Equipment and Materials

- Large open dance space
- Stereo
- 2 bowls, hats, cookie jars, or other object to pull items out of
- Small pieces of paper with verbs written on them in one bowl (e.g., wiggle, burrow, hop, writhe, skip, schlep, roll, slither, jump, slide, undulate, shuffle, gallop, crawl, scooch, convulse, zip, mope, shiver, swim, jog, swivel, and so on)
- Small pieces of paper with directions written on them in the other bowl (up, down, backward, sideways, diagonally, around, reverse, forward, between, above, below, right, left, inside, outside, and so on)
- Enough pieces of paper in each bowl to match the number of students in your class (you can repeat words)
- Background music of instructor's choice: use different songs with different moods for each exercise—it helps to switch the tempo back and forth as their dancing changes and they stretch themselves choreographically (e.g., "Broken America" by Dispatch, "Russian Roulette" by the Pop Heroes, "Let's Get Loud" by JLo, "Jar of Hearts" by Christina Perri, "Limbo" by Daddy Yankee, "The Chain" by Ingrid Michaelson, "Hips Don't Lie" by Shakira, "Let's Go" by Calvin Harris)
- Video recording device

Introduction

Now that you've had some time to reflect, how did you feel about creating a movement map in our previous class? It was really a first step in developing your choreography tools. Today, we will continue our choreography module, using those tools to work on improvisation. Improvisation is a form of movement that is not choreographed. It is movement that you spontaneously create in the moment.

Instructional Task: Discussion of Improvisation

■ PRACTICE TASK

Discuss what improvisation is and what it means to improvise movement. Discuss the ideas of moving before thinking about it and using their entire bodies.

EMBEDDED OUTCOME: S2.H1.L1. Ask students to list and review choreographic tools from the previous lesson: travel through the space, level change, tempo change, touch, mirroring, opposition, stillness, fall and recovery, floor work, and so on.

After the discussion, tell students that they must use travel and interaction in each of their assignments today. Wherever they can use other tools, they should do so.

Then have students take a note from each of the two bowls, read it, return it, and spread out in the space. Tell them they may move only in the direction that they chose, using the verb that they chose. Start the music.

Refinements

- There will be many questions. Do not allow them. Tell students to solve any problems, and when the music starts, they must begin. Giggling is totally acceptable, but talking is not.
- Sometimes turning out the lights helps students drop their insecurities, even though they can see.

Extensions

- When the music stops, yell "freeze." The students will have a laugh, and then you can have them start again with new words. Students can line up and come pick new verbs, or they can find a person next to them and exchange verbs. You can do both of these options during the course of the class.
- Change the music and watch how their movement changes. Continue repeating this exercise until 15 minutes are left in class.
- Feel free to record students' performances toward the end of class when they have shed their insecurities and are really getting into the assignment. Show them their work and laugh together.

Student Choices/Differentiation

This improvisation exercise is completely free, and students choose what movement they will do with just a bit of direction.

What to Look For

- Students are following directions.
- If some students are feeling insecure and not really moving as they could be, stop the class and let students know that everyone is feeling silly about what they are doing. It is out of everyone's comfort zone, but it is the assignment of the day. Embrace the silly and know that everyone in the class is feeling the same way. We are all doing it together to create something new and wonderful.
- Students grow during this task from not having any idea how to execute the verbs that they chose, then they deciding to solve that problem and do the best that they can.

Instructional Task: Discussion

■ PRACTICE TASK

EMBEDDED OUTCOME: S5.H3.L2. Discuss the guiding questions as a class. Prompt students to think about dance as a means of self-expression.

Guiding questions for students:

- What did you learn today about improvisation?
- How did this exercise make you feel, and did that feeling change during the course of the class?
- What did you learn about yourself?
- What did you learn about our class?
- How could you use this activity in your own choreography?
- Can you give examples of how creative dance allows you to express yourself?

Student Choices/Differentiation

Students can write down their ideas or share with a partner.

What to Look For

- Students are responding in a thoughtful manner.
- Students are able to identify qualities that make dance unique in terms of self-expression.

Formal and Informal Assessments

Video recording of movement

Closure

- Today, we did our first improvisation exercise. It required spontaneous creative movement, and you did a great job with guided improvisation today.
- Improvisation can be performed or used as a great tool to help create choreography.
- In our next class, we will work on the choreographic tool of mirroring.
- Be sure to turn in your reflections from our previous class.

Reflection

- How did students respond to this lesson?
- Do I need to work harder to move them out of their comfort zones?
- Do students feel safe enough in my class to improvise movement?
- Is there anything I need to do to make this environment safer?
- Review the video recording of the dance to assess progress.

Homework

- View the dance performance on the school's physical education website. Analyze the movement for choreographic tools. List the tools that you see and turn in the list in our next class.
- Read the paper on dancers and nutrition posted on the school's physical education website before next class.

Resources

Gilbert, A.G. & SHAPE America – Society of Health and Physical Educators. (2015). *Creative dance for all ages*. 2nd ed. Champaign, IL: Human Kinetics.

Reeve, J. (2011). *Dance improvisations: Warm-ups, games and choreographic tasks*. Champaign, IL: Human Kinetics.

National Core Arts Standards: www.nationalartsstandards.org

National Dance Educators Organization: www.ndeo.org

LESSON 3: MIRRORING

Grade-Level Outcomes

Primary Outcomes

Working with others: Solves problems and thinks critically in physical activity and/or dance settings, both as an individual and in groups. (S4.H4.L1)

Working with others: Accepts others' ideas, cultural diversity and body types by engaging in cooperative and collaborative movement projects. (S4.H4.L2)

Dance & rhythms: Demonstrates competency in a form of dance by choreographing a dance or by giving a performance. (S1.H2.L2)

Physical activity knowledge: Investigates the relationships among physical activity, nutrition and body composition. (S3.H1.L2)

Embedded Outcomes

Working with others: Assumes a leadership role (i.e., task or group leader, referee, coach) in a physical activity setting. (S4.H3.L2)

Personal responsibility: Accepts differences between personal characteristics and the idealized body images and elite performance levels portrayed in various media. (S4.H1.L2)

Lesson Objectives

The learner will:

- work on improvisation and use of choreographic tools with a series of different partners.
- think critically to solve movement problems.
- accept the ideas of others by collaborating with a partner to mirror his or her movements.
- discuss the importance of proper nutrition and healthy body composition for dance.

Equipment and Materials

- Large open dance space
- Stereo
- Music of the instructor's choice: a long play that lasts the entire activity is helpful—just background music that students aren't able to sing to or be distracted by (see resource list)
- Any music from Cirque du Soleil for more dynamic accompaniment

Introduction

What choreographic tools did you see in the dance performance you analyzed for homework? Did you see any ways of integrating the tools that surprised you? Today, we are going to use the choreographic tool of mirroring. Mirroring is when you move as a mirror image with another dancer. One dancer will be the leader, and the other will be the mirror image. The goal is not to move so fast that you lose your partner. If someone looks at you and your partner, he should not be able to tell who is leading and who is following. Quickly choose a partner and find a place in the dance space. Face each other and stand about 2 or 3 feet apart.

Instructional Task: Improvisation Exercise

■ PRACTICE TASK

In pairs, students decide who will begin as the leader (e.g., rock, paper, scissors; which partner is older or younger; which partner's birthday is closest).

When the music starts, leaders begin improvising movement with their feet planted. They are free to move everything else. Followers mirror the movements of the leaders.

Call "freeze" after a time, and let the other partner be the leader.

When the music stops and "freeze" is called again, students shake hands and thank their partners.

Extension

Repeat, with students choosing a new partner. They find a place in the space to face each other and decide who will begin as the leader. Students will improvise movement for a time and then switch leadership when you say "freeze."

Student Choices/Differentiation

- This improvisation partner exercise is completely free, and students choose what movement they will do and how they will do it.
- Students choose their partners.

What to Look For

- Do not let students speak or plan their movements. Look for students communicating with words.
- Laughing is always tolerated; talking is not.

Instructional Task: Adding Choreographic Tools

■ PRACTICE TASK

Students find a new partner. With each partner change, add another choreographic tool for students to implement in their mirroring. First, add a level change.

Extension

After both partners have completed that task, have them fist-bump and find new partners. Continue with level change and add tempo change.

Refinement

Remind students not to lose their partners because they are moving too fast. They need to pay attention to how their partners are reacting and adjust movement speed accordingly.

Student Choices/Differentiation

- Students choose their partners.
- Students choose their movements.

What to Look For

- Students are finding new partners. Watch for students trying to pair up with their friends repeatedly.
- Students are able to add the choreographic tools.

Instructional Task: Layering Tools

■ PRACTICE TASK

After two freezes, have students find a new partner. Continue to repeat this process with every choreographic tool you add. Layer them so they are working on multiple tools at the same time.

Refinement

When you decide to add travel as one of the tools, take a break and remind students that if they turn away from the mirror, the mirror image cannot see what they are going to do next. Traveling is tricky and students need to think as they move.

Extensions

Along with level and tempo changes, add travel through the space.

- Change partners and layer on physical touch.
- Repeat, adding group interaction or other choreographic tools.

EMBEDDED OUTCOME: S4.H3.L2. Repeat and layer on intermittent leader change with the tool of stillness. When one partner is done leading, she freezes on his or her own in an interesting pose. When the other partner senses that his leader has stopped, he can hold that stillness as long as he likes and then take over leadership. At this point, you do not have to yell "freeze" anymore. Provide feedback about the importance of being both leaders and followers to successfully complete the task.

Student Choices/Differentiation

- Students choose partners throughout the class.
- Students choose what movements they do for their partners to follow. This lesson is all about the students' choices.

What to Look For

- By the middle of class, the movement gets more real because students are not with their best friends anymore. They have had to venture out to acquaintances in the class, and the movement becomes more about the improvisation and less about the laughter (although there is never anything wrong with laughter!).
- Both partners are comfortable as leaders.
- Students are maintaining their mirroring skills with the layering changes.

Instructional Task: Nutrition Discussion

■ PRACTICE TASK

Improvisation and other forms of dance burn a lot of calories, but dancers are often concerned about their weight, sometimes to an unhealthy degree. Let's discuss the relationships among body composition, nutrition, and physical activity.

Guiding questions for students:

- What are the three macronutrients?
- How do they influence performance?
- How can you maintain a healthy energy balance?
- What is a healthy percentage of body fat?
- What is the physiological importance of body fat?
- What is disordered eating, and what are the dangers of it?
- What are the symptoms?
- Why are dancers at a higher risk for these behaviors?
- What should you do if you suspect someone is engaging in disordered eating?

Student Choices/Differentiation

- Students can work in pairs to answer the questions.
- Show a video about eating disorders.

What to Look For

- Students are engaged in the discussion.
- Students are asking good questions.

Formal and Informal Assessments

Exit slip: What was the most challenging part of the mirroring exercise for you?

Closure

- Mirroring is an excellent choreographic tool. What was the most challenging aspect of using mirroring as a tool?

- Today, you worked with many different partners and had the benefit of seeing and following many different styles of improvisation.

- As you leave today, think about how you can use this in your own choreography.

Reflection

- Are students beginning to open up to the idea of improvisational movement?

- Did they come up with creative ways to lead, or did they do the same thing with each partner?

- What can I do to draw them out if needed?

- Review exit slips to see what students may need more help with.

Homework

- Watch the choreography video clip on the school's physical education website. How was mirroring used in the dance? Be prepared to discuss next class.

- Investigate the body images and performance levels of elite dancers portrayed in the media. Discuss the differences between the idealized images and those of typical teens and adults. How might these idealized images contribute to unhealthy behaviors? What is the potential impact on self-worth? If someone in your family was struggling with these issues, how might you help? Due Lesson 5. (Embedded outcome: S4.H1.L2)

Resources

Gilbert, A.G. & SHAPE America – Society of Health and Physical Educators. (2015). *Creative dance for all ages*. 2nd ed. Champaign, IL: Human Kinetics.

Introduction to choreography: http://choreography09.blogspot.com

Fueling the dancer: http://c.ymcdn.com/sites/www.iadms.org/resource/resmgr/imported/info/dance_nutrition.pdf

National Dance Educators Organization: www.ndeo.org

International Association for Dance Medicine & Science: www.iadms.org

Internet keyword search: "instrumental music," "deep meditation," "relaxing music," "yoga music"

LESSON 4: ACROSS THE FLOOR

Grade-Level Outcomes

Primary Outcomes

Dance & rhythms: Demonstrates competency in a form of dance by choreographing a dance or by giving a performance. (S1.H2.L2)

Self-expression & enjoyment: Selects and participates in physical activities or dance that meet the need for self-expression and enjoyment. (S5.H3.L1)

Working with others: Solves problems and thinks critically in physical activity and/or dance settings, both as an individual and in groups. (S4.H4.L1)

Embedded Outcome

Challenge: Chooses an appropriate level of challenge to experience success and desire to participate in a self-selected physical activity. (S5.H2.L2)

Lesson Objectives

The learner will:

- move through the dance space with random improvisational assignments.
- explore using interplay (using voice along with improvised movement) to express emotions and ideas.
- create movement solutions for interplay.

Equipment and Materials

Large open dance space

Introduction

For homework, you watched a video clip that included some mirroring as a choreographic tool. Where did the dancers use mirroring? Did you find it effective? Why or why not? Our choreography module challenges you to move in new ways. Today, we are going to work on improvisation and interplay. Interplay is improvisation with your voice. It could be words or sounds; it could be loud or soft. It is not planned or pre-determined—it is spontaneous. You will move through the space today using your bodies and your voices. Don't think! Just move!

Instructional Task: Introduction to Interplay

■ PRACTICE TASK

Have all students move to one side of the room. Designate line leaders, and let students know that for each assignment they will select a new line leader. If there is a lot of sufficient space, all students can go at one time.

Students listen to the task given verbally and react individually with their bodies and their voices as they move across the floor. When they get to the other side, they must stand and observe silently. No talking, but giggling is acceptable.

Student Choices/Differentiation

This improvisation and interplay is completely free, and students choose what movement they will do and how they will do it.

What to Look For

- This must be a safe environment. If students think others may be commenting on their movement, it could be detrimental to the lesson.
- Students should use their voice instinctively, not deliberately.

Instructional Task: Across-the-Floor Interplay

■ PRACTICE TASK

Instruct students to "move through the space as if . . ."

Follow this statement with anything you can think up. Students listen to the prompt and react with their bodies and their voices to move across the floor. Be creative and think how you would like your class to discover their voices.

Here are just a few examples: Move through the space as if . . .

- you are made of Jell-O.
- you are flying.
- you are under water.
- you are escaping from bad guys.
- you are in a tunnel and you can hear water coming.
- you are on fire.
- you are blindfolded.
- you don't know what a straight line is.
- you are a principal ballerina.
- you are Katniss Everdeen in the forest.
- you are being pulled against your will.
- you lost your dog.
- you just won the lottery.
- your little brother took your journal and is going to show it to your parents.

Extensions

Move through the space . . .

- leading with your core.
- leading with your extremities.
- while rolling.
- as if there is paper covering the floor and you have colored paint coming out of your toes.
- as fast as you can in slow motion.
- without using your feet.

Refinement

Reinforce the importance of following these instructions in a safe and appropriate manner.

EMBEDDED OUTCOME: S5.H2.L2. Challenge groups of three students to come up with some creative prompts for the class. Have the class try them out with both movements and voice.

Guiding questions for students:

- Which task was the hardest for you? Why?
- How did using interplay change your thinking about the movement?
- How might you use interplay in your choreography?

Student Choices/Differentiation

Students hear and react. They choose how to move and sound as they travel across the floor.

What to Look For

- Any language students use to express ideas is appropriate for school.
- Students are less inhibited using interplay now than at the beginning of class.
- Students' movements and voice are in alignment.

Instructional Task: Cool-Down and Discussion

■ PRACTICE TASK

While stretching, have students respond to the guiding questions.

Guiding questions for students:

- How would you define improvisation?
- How does interplay influence your movements?
- How did you challenge yourself today doing the across-the-floor activity?

Student Choices/Differentiation

Students work with partners.

What to Look For

- Students are engaged in the discussion.
- Students can provide good examples.

Formal and Informal Assessments

Exit slip: What did you learn about movement today in terms of mood?

Closure

- The across-the-floor exercise was a lesson in creativity and mood. Each time you crossed the floor, you made choices on what mood you were going to portray. What were some of the moods that you portrayed today during this activity?
- You also chose how to move your bodies with the prompts given. What choreographic tools did you use today as you crossed the floor?
- How did it feel to incorporate your voice with your movement?
- Please take an exit slip and pencil, and before you leave, thoughtfully answer the question.

Reflection

- Continue to draw students out by asking them guiding questions at the end of class, or even during, if it is appropriate.
- Are students understanding how the exercises are preparing them for choreography?
- We are working toward the student choreography, giving them as many tools in their belt as we can.
- Review exit slips to see if students are grasping the importance of mood to choreography.

Homework

You are going to begin working on a choreography portfolio that will be due at the end of the module. A portfolio is a collection of evidence, or artifacts that demonstrates your proficiency in a particular area, in this case, choreography. Some of you may already have a portfolio, and you will want to update it and revise it to reflect the requirements for this class. Others will need to create one. For homework, you need to view the example of an electronic portfolio I have posted on the school's physical education website. As you navigate through the portfolio, take some notes about what you see as its strengths and weaknesses. We'll discuss these in our next class.

Resources

Green, D. (2010). *Choreographing from within: Developing the habit of inquiry as an artist*. Champaign, IL: Human Kinetics.

McGreevy-Nichols, S., Scheff, H., & Sprague, M. (2004). *Building dances: A guide to putting movements together*. Champaign, IL: Human Kinetics.

Reeve, J. (2011). *Dance improvisations: Warm-ups, games and choreographic tasks*. Champaign, IL: Human Kinetics.

LESSON 5: MOOD EXPLORATION

Grade-Level Outcomes

Primary Outcomes

Self-expression & enjoyment: Selects and participates in physical activities or dance that meet the need for self-expression and enjoyment. (S5.H3.L1)

Dance & rhythms: Demonstrates competency in a form of dance by choreographing a dance or by giving a performance. (S1.H2.L2)

Embedded Outcomes

Challenge: Chooses an appropriate level of challenge to experience success and desire to participate in a self-selected physical activity. (S5.H2.L2)

Health: Analyzes the benefits of a self-selected physical activity. (S5.H1.L1)

Physical activity knowledge: Analyzes and applies technology and social media as tools for supporting a healthy, active lifestyle. (S3.H2.L2)

Lesson Objectives

The learner will:

- listen and react with improvisational movement while interpreting different selections of accompaniment.
- express the emotions of the music while moving.

Equipment and Materials

- Large open dance space
- Stereo
- Many selections of different types of accompaniment (e.g., sounds of whales, African drums, classic rock, classical music, yoga music, sounds of nature, acid rock, pop songs, R&B, love songs and ballads, music from movie soundtracks, music from different eras and decades, foreign music with foreign languages, Broadway musical music, children's music, commercial music)

Introduction

As we continue our choreography module, we will now be exploring mood. The mood of the piece has much to do with the movement you are performing. The accompaniment you choose should enhance your movement and set the tone for the piece. It helps communicate the main idea you are trying to convey in your choreography. Today, you will be experiencing and moving the way the accompaniment or music makes you feel.

Instructional Task: Solo Improvisation

■ PRACTICE TASK

We will be working on solo improvisation today. When the music starts, don't think about it, just move your entire body the way the music makes you feel. Use your choreographic tools in your movement. You will hear all different types of music in the lesson today, and your movements should reflect what you hear.

When the music stops, freeze the pose you happen to be in until the next selection begins. Do not fall out of your pose or talk—just freeze and begin again when you hear the next piece of music start playing.

Once again, giggling is acceptable, talking is not.

Extension

Have students take their heart rates at the completion of the solo improvisation.

Refinements

- Reinforce the importance of focusing on the music as a guide to movement choices. Students' movements should evoke the tone set by the music.
- Remind students to use a variety of choreographic tools in creating their dances.

EMBEDDED OUTCOME: S5.H2.L2. Emphasize the importance of challenging yourself to go beyond your comfort zone in this exercise.

Student Choices/Differentiation

- Students choose their level, their tempo, their travel through the space.
- Students are responsible for making all choices in the way they move in today's lesson.
- Turn out the lights. This makes everyone feel safe and free to move. Try hanging Christmas lights in your studio for lessons such as this as they add the perfect amount of light and fun.

What to Look For

- Students are not staying in the same area or near the same people. Students should be traveling and using all the space.
- Students should move their bodies to reflect the music.
- Students are incorporating a variety of choreographic tools.

Instructional Task: Cool-Down and Discussion

■ PRACTICE TASK

Lead students in a relaxing cool-down. Solo improvisation is usually a workout for all involved. Once students' heart rates are back to resting, have them sit down for a discussion.

Guiding questions for students:

- What type of accompaniment was easiest to move to?
- What type of accompaniment was most difficult to move to?
- What were the moods you portrayed in your movement today?
- Do you see how much the accompaniment you choose can enhance your choreography?
- Can you see that if you just pick your favorite song for your choreography, it might not be the very best choice to convey the idea you are trying to communicate to the audience?

Student Choices/Differentiation

- Students can write down their ideas.
- Students can share their ideas with a partner.

What to Look For

All students are contributing to the discussion. You want every student to have a voice.

Instructional Task: Choreography Portfolio

■ PRACTICE TASK

Discuss the strengths and weaknesses of the portfolio students viewed for homework, then review the requirements for their choreography portfolio. Note: If it's not feasible to do an electronic portfolio, students can always create a traditional paper version or an alternative assignment, such as creating a mixed media collage.

- Create a web-based portfolio that reflects your proficiency in choreography.
- Certain assignments will be identified as required for inclusion in the portfolio as you progress through the module. For example, the portfolio will include preparation for the final choreography performance, and it will include video of the choreography performance.
- The portfolio may include other material from your dance experience, but that is not required.

Extension

Review the rubric for the portfolio with students so they understand the expectations.

Student Choices/Differentiation

Post the requirements to the school's physical education website, or provide a handout for students to take home.

What to Look For

- Students were effective in their critique of the portfolio they viewed for homework.
- Students are asking good questions about the portfolio assignment.

Formal and Informal Assessments

Exit slip: What does your heart rate tell you about the value of dance for health-related fitness? (Embedded outcome: S5.H1.L1)

Closure

- Emphasize how students are growing and stretching themselves creatively and growing more confident in their choreography. Tell them what you saw that was beautiful, poignant, and interesting; what made you laugh; what made you cry.
- Mood is such an important part of creating a piece of choreography. When you get to your final choreography project, you will be challenged to make your movement speak to the audience. Like today, the accompaniment you choose can help you.
- Don't forget to turn in your reflection on dancers and body image.

Reflection

- Were students becoming less inhibited as the class went on?
- Were their movements matching the mood of the music?
- This is usually one of the students' favorite activities. It is also wonderful to behold. Make sure your students feel free to move and enjoy the activity.
- Review exit slips to see if students are making connections to health.

Homework

Review the tutorial for creating an electronic portfolio (Weebly sites are popular and simple to use) on the school's physical education website. Create a simple landing page with your name before the next class. (Embedded outcome: S3.H2.L2)

Resources

Lund, J., & Veal, M. (2013). *Assessment-driven instruction in physical education: A standards-based approach to promoting and documenting learning* [eBook]. Champaign, IL: Human Kinetics.

Melograno, V. (2000). *Portfolio assessment for K-12 physical education.* Reston, VA: American Alliance for Health, Physical Education, Recreation and Dance.

Internet keyword search: "dance improvisation," "e-portfolios," "digital portfolios," "dance portfolios"

LESSON 6: WALL IMPROVISATION

Grade-Level Outcomes

Primary Outcomes

Dance & rhythms: Demonstrates competency in a form of dance by choreographing a dance or by giving a performance. (S1.H2.L2)

Working with others: Solves problems and thinks critically in physical activity and/or dance settings, both as an individual and in groups. (S4.H4.L1)

Working with others: Exhibits proper etiquette, respect for others and teamwork while engaging in physical activity and/or social dance. (S4.H2.L1)

Self-expression & enjoyment: Selects and participates in physical activities or dance that meet the need for self-expression and enjoyment. (S5.H3.L1)

Movement concepts, principles & knowledge: Uses movement concepts and principles (e.g., force, motion, rotation) to analyze and improve performance of self and/or others in a selected skill. (S2.H2.L1)

Embedded Outcome

Challenge: Chooses an appropriate level of challenge to experience success and desire to participate in a self- selected physical activity. (S5.H2.L2)

Lesson Objectives

The learner will:

- work with two other students to create movement solutions to directions as they attach parts or all of their bodies to a wall.
- express the mood of the music while moving.
- evaluate a video recording of group movement using movement and dance concepts.

Equipment and Materials

- Gym, multi-purpose room, or field house (this activity can be done in a dance studio, but you need each dancer to have enough space on the wall—students cannot be too close together)
- Stereo
- Background music: you can use a long play for relaxation, or you can change the music often to see different types of movement and draw out the students' creativity
- Video recording device

Introduction

Hopefully, everyone was able to create a landing page for your e-portfolios. If you had any trouble, please see me after class so we can figure out how to get you on track before we start creating materials for it. Today, you are going to challenge your creativity and your bodies! Please get into groups of three and assign each person in your group one of these three cereals: Wheaties, Cheerios, Corn Flakes. If you are at odds on who should be which, use rock, paper, scissors to choose. Now sit with your trio and listen to the directions. [Feel free to divide your class in any way you choose, or don't divide them at all.] Today, you will need to solve problems without asking for help. You are in charge of your choices and how you will solve the challenges you may face.

Instructional Task: Wall Improvisation Task

■ PRACTICE TASK

We will be doing improvisation today. You will be moving the way the music makes you feel, you will be interacting with others in the class, and you will be attached to a wall. When I give the go-ahead, I want all the trios to spread out around the whole space—do not crowd together – but at least one person in the trio must have a contact point with a wall. Make sure you have space all to yourself and that the three of you can move side to side and up and down. You will listen to the music, and you will listen to the assignments given and react as you think you should. OK, spread out and have fun. No talking!

Let students know they should be in constant movement unless directed otherwise. There is no stillness in this exercise.

If students choose to travel, they must travel in a clockwise manner, unless directed otherwise. Specify whether trios can move throughout the whole space, or must stay in the space surrounding their original contact point with the wall.

Start the music, and give assignments or prompts as the students move.

Video record the students' performance.

Extensions

- All Wheaties must travel counterclockwise.
- All Cheerios must choose a very low level to move in.
- All cereal must use their elbows as their connection to the wall.
- All Wheaties become a piece of art on the wall.
- Other cereals admire the Wheaties' art.
- Corn Flakes interact with another cereal.
- All cereal freeze in an abstract pose for 20 seconds.
- Make the only point in contact with the wall your forehead.
- Change your level back and forth drastically.
- Flatten yourself against a wall while continuing to move.

Refinement

Ask students to exaggerate their movements (over the top) as they respond to the directions.

EMBEDDED OUTCOME: S5.H2.L2. Students will be challenged by obstacles they encounter. They will have to solve problems along the way but must do so without talking. Encourage them to persist in finding a solution.

Student Choices/Differentiation

- Students choose what movements to execute.
- Students choose their groups.

What to Look For

- Students who are not following directions and staying in one spot.
- Students might start off being safe, but will let loose as the class progresses. Challenge them.

Instructional Task: Peer Assessment

■ PRACTICE TASK

Play the video recording on a large screen. Students view their own group's performance and evaluate it using a rubric. Students use the critical discussion questions to reflect on how to improve performance.

Extension

Repeat with students evaluating a different group.

Student Choices/Differentiation

Students choose the group they will evaluate.

What to Look For

- Students are critiquing their movement.
- Students are able to identify how to improve their performance.
- Students are communicating with sensitivity.

Instructional Task: Discussion

■ PRACTICE TASK

With 5 minutes left, pull the students in for a short discussion while stretching.

Guiding questions for students:

- Did you have to solve problems in this activity?
- What were they and how did you overcome them?
- How did it make you feel being attached to the wall? Give me some emotions or adjectives.

Student Choices/Differentiation

- Students can work in pairs.
- Students can write down their responses.
- Students can volunteer to share with the whole group.

What to Look For

All students are contributing to the discussion.

Formal and Informal Assessments

Peer assessments

Closure

- This was a wonderful exercise. What were some things you learned today?
- How might you use a wall or other structure in your own choreography?
- Next class, we're going to spend a lot of time discussing your final choreography project, which also ties into your electronic portfolio. I want to make sure you have plenty of time to do a good job on both.

Reflection

- How did the students behave? Did they all participate?
- As we delve further into the activity of improvisation, are they feeling safe and free to move their bodies without insecurity?
- How can I make sure they all get to this place of freedom?

Homework

Write a reflection based on your group's evaluation of the dance today. Include the elements your group did well and what you can improve on. Identify the choreographic tools you used. Turn it in next class.

Resources

Green, D. (2010). *Choreographing from within: Developing the habit of inquiry as an artist.* Champaign, IL: Human Kinetics.

McGreevy-Nichols, S., Scheff, H., & Sprague, M. (2004). *Building dances: A guide to putting movements together.* Champaign, IL: Human Kinetics.

National Dance Educators Organization: www.ndeo.org

CRITICAL DISCUSSION QUESTIONS

1. Does the choreography solve the problem assigned?
2. Is the intent of the choreography clear?
3. Did you use the space well?
4. Are there contrasts in the choreography?
5. What was most interesting about your piece? Why?

From L.C. MacDonald, R.J. Doan, and S. Chepko, eds., 2018, *Lesson planning for high school physical education* (Reston, VA: SHAPE America; Champaign, IL: Human Kinetics).

LESSON 7: CHOREOGRAPHY PROJECT

Grade-Level Outcomes

Primary Outcomes

Working with others: Solves problems and thinks critically in physical activity and/or dance settings, both as an individual and in groups. (S4.H4.L1)

Dance & rhythms: Demonstrates competency in a form of dance by choreographing a dance or by giving a performance. (S1.H2.L2)

Engages in physical activity: Creates a plan, trains for and participates in a community event with a focus on physical activity (e.g., 5K, triathlon, tournament, dance performance, cycling event). (S3.H6.L2)

Embedded Outcomes

Working with others: Accepts others' ideas, cultural diversity and body types by engaging in cooperative and collaborative movement projects. (S4.H4.L2)

Physical activity knowledge: Analyzes and applies technology and social media as tools for supporting a healthy, active lifestyle. (S3.H2.L2)

Lesson Objectives

The learner will:

- choose a partner and the word for the final choreography project.
- begin research for the final choreography project.
- discuss ideas for dance and event performance.

Equipment and Materials

- Large open dance space
- Paper, pens, and devices for doing research
- Bowl, hat, cookie jar, or basket filled with words written on small pieces of paper: these words should be unfamiliar or unknown to the students; they also must be emotions or states of being, such as the following:

Disconsolateness	Exhaustion	Disconnection
Tempestuousness	Indignancy	Consternation
Insanity	Frustration	Confusion
Serenity	Acrimony	Dread
Flippancy	Betrayal	Distraction
Agony	Grief	Abuse
Jadedness	Sassiness or sass	Disconcertedness
Melancholia	Chaos	Disturbing
Fieriness	Ataraxis	Infatuation

Introduction

Be sure to turn in your reflections on your self-evaluation from last class. Come have a seat in a circle—we are going to talk about your final choreography project. This is a big project, and the more you put into it, the more you will get out of it. All the preparation you do will be part of your portfolio. At the end of the module, you will perform your work at our Choreography Celebration.

Instructional Task: Choreography Project

■ PRACTICE TASK

Choose a partner whom you can work well with. Ask yourself these questions:

- Do I work well with this person?
- Is this person at about the same ability level as I am?
- Will I be able to get together with this person outside of class?
- Is this person willing to work with me on costumes and props?

Your project is to complete a study on an emotion or state of being. You will choose the emotion out of a hat and you will study that emotion. You will create movement that conveys the emotion or makes the audience feel that emotion. Here are the requirements:

- *Your piece must be 1 1/2 to 2 minutes long without repeating.*
- *Your piece must have a designed costume. You need to make it, not just buy matching tops. Use your creativity!*
- *Your piece must be danced, not acted.*
- *Your piece must be your own.*
- *Your piece must have accompaniment that helps convey your emotion. It must be school appropriate.*
- *Your piece must include choreographic tools that you have learned.*

Student Choices/Differentiation

- Provide the instructions as a handout or post to the school's physical education website, so students can review them easily.
- Using video, show an example from a previous year.

What to Look For

- Students are asking good questions.
- Students seem excited about the project.

Instructional Task: Researching Your Emotion

■ PRACTICE TASK

Have each duet choose a word from the hat. Record their names and read the word aloud so that everyone can hear it.

Once everyone has chosen a partner and a word, let students begin their research. Students look up their words together to see what they mean. They must think about what the emotion means to them and a time when they felt that way.

Your first assignment for your final project is to write a paper—one paper per duet, please. You will need to collaborate. Your task is to respond to the guiding questions in paragraph form. Your responses to the questions will be part of your portfolio.

Provide the scoring guide you will be using for the paper.

Students use the remainder of class to start on the project.

Guiding questions for students:

- What does the dictionary say about your word?
- What is your personal definition of your word, and what is your partner's? [Provide an example: "If my word was *happiness*, my definition might be rolling down a grassy hill in the warm sunshine with butterflies."]
- Tell me a story about when you felt this emotion; include your partner's story as well. [Make sure they know that both partners need to contribute their own stories. Give them an example: "If my word was *happiness*, I felt happiness when I was chosen as the lead dancer in a production."]

- How will you tackle this word through movement? [This is tough, so give them examples: "If my word was happiness, I might do a lot of leaps and jumps and turns, and probably no floor work."]
- What type of accompaniment will you use? [This is just to get them thinking. It could be sounds of whales, or classical music, or something by Ed Sheeran.]
- What are you thinking about for a costume? [This is also to get them thinking. Give them examples of cheap and easy costumes: "One pair of dancers wore black old-school turtlenecks with the collar all the way up, black leggings, and socks, and they safety-pinned two huge triangles of black fabric to their sleeves and sides to make wings. Their faces were white, and they had big black circles around their eyes. It was a wonderfully effective look to match their word (melancholy)."]
- Use the remainder of the class to work on the project.

EMBEDDED OUTCOME: S4.H4.L2. This project requires duets to collaborate and respect one another to be successful. Encourage them to be creative and share ideas and experiences to get started.

Student Choices/Differentiation

- Students choose their partners and work with them at their own pace.
- Students begin to create by making choices.

What to Look For

- Everyone has a partner. If not, step in and help connect students.
- Partners are sharing their thoughts and ideas.
- Partners are actively listening to each other.
- Watch for any students who are having trouble.

Formal and Informal Assessments

- Papers on selected emotion
- Reflections on dance performance

Closure

- This is the beginning of a great project. I have such high expectations, and I am never disappointed by what students bring to perform.
- You will work on your project throughout the remainder of the module, but you will also need to do some work on this outside of class to be ready for the Choreography Celebration.
- Since much of what is in your portfolio will be related to your final project, you and your duet partner will have the same basic materials. Make an effort to find a way to individualize yours.
- In the next few classes, you will move to the spoken word. These classes may give you additional ideas for your choreography project.

Reflection

- How did students respond to the assignment?
- Were they asking good questions?
- Where do they need more guidance or practice to be successful?
- Review reflections from last class. Are students using the critical discussion feedback effectively in their self-evaluations?

Homework

- Continue to work on the paper, which is due in Lesson 9.
- Create four links in your portfolio to reflect the main sections of your paper. For example, [your emotion] in Dance; Ideas for Movement; Accompaniment; and Costumes and Props. Due Lesson 10. (Embedded outcome: S3.H2.L2)

Resources

Gilbert, A.G. & SHAPE America – Society of Health and Physical Educators. *(2015). Creative dance for all ages.* 2nd ed. Champaign, IL: Human Kinetics.

Green, D. (2010). *Choreographing from within: Developing the habit of inquiry as an artist.* Champaign, IL: Human Kinetics.

McGreevy-Nichols, S., Scheff, H., & Sprague, M. (2004). *Building dances: A guide to putting movements together.* Champaign, IL: Human Kinetics.

Online dictionary to look up selected emotion

LESSON 8: STRANGE FRUIT

Grade-Level Outcomes

Primary Outcomes

Movement concepts, principles & knowledge: Identifies and discusses the historical and cultural role of games, sports and dance in society. (S2.H1.L2)

Self-expression & enjoyment: Identifies the uniqueness of creative dance as a means of self-expression. (S5.H3.L2)

Embedded Outcome

Rules & etiquette: Examines moral and ethical conduct in specific competitive situations (e.g., intentional fouls, performance–enhancing substances, gambling, current events in sport). (S4. H2.H2)

Lesson Objectives

The learner will:

- recognize the written word as an effective accompaniment.
- appreciate the fact that dance can come from many different ideas, thoughts, and feelings.
- discuss the role of dance in expressing cultural or historical ideas.

Equipment and Materials

- Place for students to watch a film and write down thoughts about it
- Paper and pencil, Chromebooks, or laptops if all students have them
- The poem "Strange Fruit" to read: www.historyisaweapon.com/defcon1/fruitholiday.htm
- The photograph that inspired the poem "Strange Fruit": http://rarehistoricalphotos.com/lynching-thomas-shipp-abram-smith-indiana-1930.
- Video clip of Pearl Primus' dance "Strange Fruit"

Introduction

Today, we will change gears and more deeply explore accompaniment. You have moved to a lot of different music of all styles in our choreography module, but much of today's class will focus on a disturbing topic in our history and how dance was used to convey the emotions around that topic. You will see how a chain of events moved across the country and produced an amazing and moving piece of choreography.

Instructional Task:
Discussion of the Poem "Strange Fruit"

■ PRACTICE TASK

Introduce the students to Abel Meeropol and his background. Read his poem "Strange Fruit."

Have students listen to the poem and write down their interpretation. You may have to read it twice.

Ask some students to share their ideas. Discuss what the students wrote.

Next, let the students know that the photograph they are about to see is real and may be disturbing. Show the photograph of the lynching of Thomas Shipp and Abram Smith. Ask students to describe what they see (e.g., the men hanging, the people assembled).

Guiding questions for students:

- What do you think the onlookers are thinking or saying?
- What are they communicating with their body language?
- What emotions do you think they are experiencing?

Tell the story behind the photograph of Thomas and Abram. Explain that Abel saw this photograph, as did most of the country and beyond. He was so disgusted and saddened that he wrote the poem "Strange Fruit."

Student Choices/Differentiation

- Students share their own ideas and reactions.
- Students may discuss their ideas in pairs or small groups.

What to Look For

- Students are engaged and listening.
- How are they reacting to the poem and the photograph?

Instructional Task:
Discussion of the Dance "Strange Fruit"

■ PRACTICE TASK

Introduce the students to the fascinating and multi-talented Pearl Primus. Tell them a little about his or her background. Then show students his or her dance "Strange Fruit."
In groups of four or five, students discuss how the piece of choreography moved them.

EMBEDDED OUTCOME: S4.H2.L2. Discuss how the dance conveyed the moral and ethical conflict represented by the poem.

Guiding questions for students:

- Was the choreography effective in expressing the idea of the poem?
- Did it help you understand the poem better?
- What choreographic tools did you notice?

Extension

Bring students together and discuss as a class.

Student Choices/Differentiation

- All students are bringing their own thoughts to the group.
- Students choose their groups.
- Students can volunteer to share the ideas of the group with the rest of the class.

What to Look For

- Everyone is being heard.
- Students can identify two or more choreographic tools.

Formal and Informal Assessments

- Reflections from peer assessment last class
- Exit slip: Did you find the dance or the poem more powerful and why?

Closure

- The accompaniment you chose can really help you convey a thought or concept.
- Next class, you will move to the accompaniment of the written word again.
- Before our next class, find a short piece of poetry that speaks to you, one that you want to share and possibly dance to. It should be able to be read in less than a minute, and it must be school-appropriate.
- Be sure to turn in your peer assessment reflections from last class and continue to work on your papers.

Reflection

- This is a somber lesson. Was I sensitive to my students and their feelings?
- Was everyone involved in the discussion?
- Review exit slips to gauge how students are feeling about the assignment.

Homework

- For next class, bring a short poem that can be read in less than a minute and lends itself to movement.
- Finish your choreography papers, due next class.

Resources

American National Biography: www.anb.org

Dance Heritage Coalition: www.danceheritage.org

Rare Historical Photos: http://rarehistoricalphotos.com/lynching-thomas-shipp-abram-smith-indiana-1930

Strange Fruit Poem: www.historyisaweapon.com/defcon1/fruitholiday.htm

LESSON 9: SELECTED POEM

Grade-Level Outcomes

Primary Outcomes

Dance & rhythms: Demonstrates competency in a form of dance by choreographing a dance or by giving a performance. (S1.H2.L2)

Self-expression & enjoyment: Selects and participates in physical activities or dance that meet the need for self-expression and enjoyment. (S5.H3.L1)

Working with others: Exhibits proper etiquette, respect for others and teamwork while engaging in physical activity and/or social dance. (S4.H2.L1)

Working with others: Solves problems and thinks critically in physical activity and/or dance settings, both as an individual and in groups. (S4.H4.L1)

Embedded Outcomes

Working with others: Accepts others' ideas, cultural diversity and body types by engaging in cooperative and collaborative movement projects. (S4.H4.L2)

Engages in physical activity: Creates a plan, trains for and participates in a community event with a focus on physical activity (e.g., 5K, triathlon, tournament, dance performance, cycling event). (S3.H6.L2)

Lesson Objectives

The learner will:

- select a short poem to choreograph with group members.
- express the ideas of the poem in movement.
- collaborate on choreography with the group to perform for their peers.
- demonstrate respect and critical problem-solving skills with group members while collaborating in choreography

Equipment and Materials

Dance space

Introduction

You have all brought in a poem. Get into groups of three [or larger if you have a large class]. Please read your poem to your group and listen carefully to each person's poem. You may need to read through them twice. As you listen to each poem, think of movement that could be done in a group to help illustrate the words you hear. You will discuss and collectively choose one of the three poems to create movement to. All poems will be turned in to me at the end of class. It is important that you are all respectful of each other's ideas. I am looking at how you collaborate, not how one person teaches their ideas to the others. Work together and use everyone's ideas. You will perform your choreography next class.

Instructional Task: Selecting a Poem

■ PRACTICE TASK

Students share their poems and choose one to choreograph.

Refinement

Emphasize that students should select a poem that lends itself to movement and projects some emotion.

Student Choices/Differentiation

Students select the poems that are options for the group.

What to Look For

Make sure natural leaders are not taking over and that the quiet students are not getting left out.

Instructional Task: Choreograph the Poem

■ PRACTICE TASK

After students select their poems, lead a warm-up.
Have students brainstorm ideas for movement and use of choreographic tools.

Refinements

- Students should re-read the poem again and again as they think critically about the poem, collaborate, and choreograph.
- Students may ask you to read the poem for them as they practice moving.

EMBEDDED OUTCOME: S4.H4.L2 Provide feedback and support to groups about what collaboration really means and accepting others' ideas.

Student Choices/Differentiation

- Everyone in each group offers ideas for the choreography.
- Provide a checklist of choreographic tools for students to use.

What to Look For

It is important that this is a collaboration of everyone's ideas.

Instructional Task: Costumes and Props

■ PRACTICE TASK

About halfway through the class, break and discuss the role of costumes and props in choreography and dance.

Refinement

Remind students that costumes and props can be very simple and should enhance the dance, not detract from it.

Extensions

- Have students decide what they will wear for the performance of their poems and if they need any props for their dance. Costumes can be as simple as black pants and matching colored shirts.
- Return to working on choreography. If props are available, students can incorporate them as they practice.

Student Choices/Differentiation

Everyone is bringing ideas to the group.

What to Look For

Everyone is being heard.

Formal and Informal Assessments

Peer assessments of a strength and an area for improvement

Closure

- Did you find it challenging to create movement for your poem?
- Would you consider using a poem for your final choreography project? Why or why not?
- Be sure to turn in your choreography papers and complete your four links in your portfolio, due next class.

Reflection

- Was everyone engaged?
- Was everyone respectful of each other?
- Was there true collaboration going on?
- Review peer assessments. Are students becoming good critics?
- Review choreography papers and provide feedback in writing for next class.

Homework

- Complete the four links for your portfolio, and send me the link so I can check your progress.
- At the end of the module, we will be performing in the Choreography Celebration. We will want to invite students from other classes, teachers, administrators, and family and friends. For homework, make a list of items we will need to think about as we organize this event. (Embedded outcome: S3.H6.L2)

Resources

Green, D. (2010). *Choreographing from within: Developing the habit of inquiry as an artist.* Champaign, IL: Human Kinetics.

McGreevy-Nichols, S., Scheff, H., & Sprague, M. (2004). *Building dances: A guide to putting movements together.* Champaign, IL: Human Kinetics.

Internet keyword search: "dance poems," "choreograph poems"

LESSON 10: POEM PERFORMANCE

Grade-Level Outcomes

Primary Outcomes

Dance & rhythms: Demonstrates competency in a form of dance by choreographing a dance or by giving a performance. (S1.H2.L2)

Self-expression & enjoyment: Selects and participates in physical activities or dance that meet the need for self-expression and enjoyment. (S5.H3.L1)

Working with others: Exhibits proper etiquette, respect for others and teamwork while engaging in physical activity and/or social dance. (S4.H2.L1)

Working with others: Solves problems and thinks critically in physical activity and/or dance settings, both as an individual and in groups. (S4.H4.L1)

Engages in physical activity: Creates a plan, trains for and participates in a community event with a focus on physical activity (e.g., 5K, triathlon, tournament, dance performance, cycling event). (S3.H6.L2)

Embedded Outcome

Working with others: Accepts others' ideas, cultural diversity and body types by engaging in cooperative and collaborative movement projects. (S4.H4.L2)

Lesson Objectives

The learner will:

- collaborate in and refine group choreography for the poem.
- perform as a member of a group for peers at the end of class.
- express the main ideas of the poem through choreography.
- coordinate lists and select tasks to prepare for the choreography event.

Equipment and Materials

- Dance space
- Video camera or phone to record each dance
- Method to post dances for viewing, such as Google Drive, a shared drive, or a private YouTube channel
- Performance notes worksheets and pencils

Introduction

Today, you will continue breathing life into your poem with movement. Continue to work together to put the finishing touches on your creation. When there are 15 minutes left of class, you can go change clothes if you need to and gather your props. Until then you will work to complete your piece of choreography. During the performance, your work will be critiqued as your peers write performance notes. Think of yourself as a critic as well as a dancer!

Instructional Task: Dance Practice

■ PRACTICE TASK

Students continue where they left off and finish their collaborative choreography to their chosen poems.

As they practice, check in with each group and ask the guiding questions.

Guiding questions for students:

- Now that you've had some time to practice, do you think your movements are conveying the intent of the poem? Why or why not?
- Are there ways your group can work together better?
- How can you enhance your movements to make the performance even better?

Student Choices/Differentiation

Everyone in each group offers ideas for refining the choreography.

What to Look For

- Everyone is putting in a good effort.
- All ideas and suggestions are well-received and certain students aren't dominating.
- Movements are expressing the intent of the poem.

Instructional Task: Performance

■ PRACTICE TASK

Let students change clothes if needed and gather props. Seat them all at the front of the room, and give each group a number in order of their performance.

EMBEDDED OUTCOME: S4.H2.L2. Review how to be a respectful and gracious audience member: Watch to learn and comment, and always applaud after a performance.

Distribute the performance notes worksheets. This worksheet includes key points to look for during the performance. Peers will make notes on the sheet to give to the performing group after they dance. Dances will be recorded. Students will watch their dances (provided by you on a shared drive, or emailed in Google Docs, or provided on a private YouTube channel) and critique them.

Each group performs according to assigned numbers. You or a student can be the narrator.

Extension

After each dance, briefly discuss each piece of choreography. This could include the poem they chose, the movements they did, or their collaboration.

Guiding questions for students:

- How did the dance make you feel?
- Did the dancers bring the poem to life?
- Were you able to understand the poem better with their movement?
- Were you moved?
- Was it thought provoking?

Student Choices/Differentiation

Student created the dances.

What to Look For

- Students included a variety of choreographic tools.
- The dances are reflecting the poems.
- All students are contributing to the discussion.
- Focus on questions that will have positive answers. You want everyone to feel good about what they have created.

Instructional Task: Event Organization

▪ PRACTICE TASK

To prepare for Choreography Celebration, have students share their event task lists. Provide feedback about their ideas. Have duets volunteer to take on different responsibilities. Examples include event flyers, event invitations, technical coordinator (lighting and music), event host, event programs, and press release for student paper or school's physical education website. Students select a theme for the materials they will create.

Student Choices/Differentiation

Students can work in small groups.

What to Look For

Students have been thorough in thinking about the tasks associated with hosting an event.

Students are showing initiative in taking on event tasks.

Formal and Informal Assessments

- Peer assessment: performance notes worksheets
- Self-critique of performances

Closure

- Your group work was inspiring today. Thank you so much for your creativity and your healthy collaboration.
- It is not easy to work with a group on choreography, and you did a wonderful job.
- You are learning more and more every day about creating interesting movement. Congratulations to all of you!
- Make sure you talk about your event responsibilities with your partner, and make a plan for getting them done by Lesson 13.

Reflection

- What could I have done to make this lesson segment run more smoothly?
- Should I have chosen their groups for them?
- Did I give them ample time for the assignment?
- Was the discussion fruitful?
- Review performance notes worksheets.

Homework

- Review the feedback on your choreography paper and be ready to start practicing next class.
- Watch your performance and do a self-critique, answering these questions: Are you happy with the finished product your group produced? Why or why not?
- If you could have changed anything, what would you have changed?
- What choreographic tools did you use in your work?
- Who were the people in your group? Did you work well together?
- What did you learn about choreographic collaboration?

Resources

Gilbert, A.G. & SHAPE America – Society of Health and Physical Educators. (2015). *Creative dance for all ages*. 2nd ed. Champaign, IL: Human Kinetics.

Green, D. (2010). *Choreographing from within: Developing the habit of inquiry as an artist*. Champaign, IL: Human Kinetics.

McGreevy-Nichols, S., Scheff, H., & Sprague, M. (2004). *Building dances: A guide to putting movements together*. Champaign, IL: Human Kinetics.

Internet keyword search: "dance self-assessment," "dance collaboration"

LESSON 11: ABSTRACT MOVEMENT

Grade-Level Outcomes

Primary Outcomes

Dance & rhythms: Demonstrates competency in a form of dance by choreographing a dance or by giving a performance. (S1.H2.L2)

Working with others: Solves problems and thinks critically in physical activity and/or dance settings, both as an individual and in groups. (S4.H4.L1)

Self-expression & enjoyment: Selects and participates in physical activities or dance that meet the need for self-expression and enjoyment. (S5.H3.L1)

Engages in physical activity: Creates a plan, trains for and participates in a community event with a focus on physical activity (e.g., 5K, triathlon, tournament, dance performance, cycling event). (S3.H6.L2)

Embedded Outcomes

Working with others: Accepts others' ideas, cultural diversity and body types by engaging in cooperative and collaborative movement projects. (S4.H4.L2)

Physical activity knowledge: Analyzes and applies technology and social media as tools for supporting a healthy, active lifestyle. (S3.H2.L2)

Lesson Objectives

The learner will:

- use random improvisational tasks to create abstracted movements.
- take a mundane task and act it out, then change the acting into dancing using choreographic tools.
- use problem-solving skills to determine how to abstract the movements.
- refine ideas and movements for the choreography project that express the emotion of the selected word.

Equipment and Materials

- Large open dance space
- Different accompaniment for each task: just background, nothing to distract from the task at hand (it helps if the students are not moving around in silence)

Introduction

We will be working on abstract movement today. This is another concept you can use in your choreography project. You will take a recognizable task that should be familiar to everyone and begin by acting it out. Then you will change that acting by creating dance movement. After the task is abstracted into dance, the audience members may not be able to recognize what the original task was unless they are told. Dance is not acting, but we can communicate quite loudly with our movement. There is no such thing as wrong movement today. Choose your own interpretation of the task given and enjoy turning it into dance. We will finish up today with some time to work on your choreography project.

Instructional Task: Abstracting Movement

■ PRACTICE TASK

Today, you will work as a soloist in a group of soloists. Your challenge is to think for yourself and create original movement.

Introduce the idea of taking acting and abstracting it into dance movement. Demonstrate for them so they have an idea.

Note: It helps for them to see it done once. I usually abstract changing the oil in a car (pop the hood, find the lever under the hood, lift the hood, find the dipstick, pull it out, clean it off, put it in, take it out, and inspect it). I usually do it once and ask if any student had any idea what I was doing. They never do. I use a lot of space, and I change direction and level often. Then I talk them through it and the light bulb goes on!

Divide students into three or four groups. Give each group a task (e.g., raking leaves, building a snowman, washing dishes, making a bed—it can be anything) and have them act it out for the rest of the class. Students act the task out by themselves (i.e., there should be a group of soloists executing the task).

Begin the background music and let them start. Tell them to keep doing their task until they are asked to stop. Circulate and give help where needed.

Here are some examples of tasks you can choose:

- Old-fashioned washing with a tub and washboard
- Planting a flower, tree, or garden
- Hand-washing dishes
- Sculpting a life-size figure
- Dressing a child
- Making an apple pie
- Cleaning their room
- Comforting a baby
- Sewing a wedding dress
- Putting up a tent
- Gathering wood and building a fire
- Painting a mural

Extension

Make the groups smaller or keep them the same. Go around and secretly give each group a task so the rest of the class cannot hear, or have them pick a task out of a hat. Remind them not to look at what others are doing, but to just create movement.

Refinement

This is a more advanced concept and may be outside of some students' comfort zones. Let them know there are no wrong answers.

Student Choices/Differentiation

- Each student chooses how to act because this is a solo project within a group.
- Students have complete control over what they do and make choices on what they think is right to do.

What to Look For

- All students are acting.
- All students are doing solo acting. There should be little to no interaction.

Instructional Task: Peer Performance

■ PRACTICE TASK

With 20 minutes left in class (or however much is appropriate for the number of groups you have), ask students to sit down. Groups take turns performing their abstract tasks for their peers.

Number each group so they know what order they will perform in. Have each group perform, and then ask the rest of the class if they can figure out what the task is by the common thread of students abstracting it. Announce the task and have the group perform again. See if the class can now see the creation.

EMBEDDED OUTCOME: S4.H4.L2. Use the peer performance as an opportunity to discuss the importance of accepting ideas as well as the physical and cultural diversity of others when choreographing a dance.

Student Choices/Differentiation

Students perform what they have been working on in class. They made individual choices as they moved their bodies.

What to Look For

- This is a wonderful activity where you really see student growth.
- Watch for kids breaking barriers and becoming more confident than they were at the beginning of the module.

Instructional Task: Choreography Project

Practice Task

Students spend the rest of class working on the movement portion of their projects. Partners discuss and refine their ideas and try some of them out. Provide the final project checklist (see handout) to guide their decisions.

Student Choices/Differentiation

Students choose movements and sequence.

What to Look For

Both students in the duet are contributing ideas.

Formal and Informal Assessments

Exit slip: In what ways did you collaborate with others in abstracting movement?

Closure

- What did you learn about taking a concept and putting it to movement?
- Was it pleasing to you as the audience member?
- Did it make you think? Did you have different thoughts about each task presented?
- What does this tell you about the dance audience?
- What is your goal in dance performance?
- Is it OK if different audience members saw different things?

Reflection

- How did the lesson go? Did students get out of their comfort zones?
- Did they interpret the tasks differently? Did everyone do their own thing, or did all things look similar because students were peeking at each other?
- How could I change the lesson to be even more effective?

Homework

- Finalize your accompaniment (music or spoken word) for your project with your partner before coming to class.
- Begin moving sections of your choreography paper into your portfolio under the relevant links. Use the feedback to make revisions as appropriate. Add a link for the dress rehearsal video (Lesson 15). (Embedded outcome: S3.H2.L2).You should also think about the appearance of your e-portfolio. You may want to add graphics or photos to make it more attractive.

Resources

McGreevy-Nichols, S., Scheff, H., & Sprague, M. (2004). *Building dances: A guide to putting movements together.* Champaign, IL: Human Kinetics.

Reeve, J. (2011). *Dance improvisations: Warm-ups, games and choreographic tasks.* Champaign, IL: Human Kinetics.

Internet keyword search: "choreography," "abstracting movement"

FINAL PROJECT CHECKLIST

Name of duet: _____

Element	Descriptors	Yes/No
Originality	The piece demonstrates creativity in its use of movement and choreographic tools.	
Amount of dance	Both members of the duet are dancing throughout the piece, with only minor stops or pauses.	
Use of choreographic tools	A variety of choreographic tools are incorporated in the performance.	
Accompaniment choice	The movement is well suited to the music (spoken word).	
Performance quality	Performance is confident and fluid.	
Costume/props design	The costumes and/or props enhance the performance rather than distract from it.	
Presentation of emotion	The expressiveness of the movement conveys the intended emotion.	
Time	Performance is within time guidelines.	

From L.C. MacDonald, R.J. Doan, and S. Chepko, eds., 2018, *Lesson planning for high school physical education* (Reston, VA: SHAPE America; Champaign, IL: Human Kinetics).

LESSON 12: TOUCH AND MOVE

Grade-Level Outcomes

Primary Outcomes

Working with others: Solves problems and thinks critically in physical activity and/or dance settings, both as an individual and in groups. (S4.H4.L1)

Self-expression & enjoyment: Selects and participates in physical activities or dance that meet the need for self-expression and enjoyment. (S5.H3.L1)

Dance & rhythms: Demonstrates competency in a form of dance by choreographing a dance or by giving a performance. (S1.H2.L2)

Engages in physical activity: Creates a plan, trains for and participates in a community event with a focus on physical activity (e.g., 5K, triathlon, tournament, dance performance, cycling event). (S3.H6.L2)

Embedded Outcomes

Challenge: Chooses an appropriate level of challenge to experience success and desire to participate in a self- selected physical activity. (S5.H2.L2)

Physical activity knowledge: Analyzes and applies technology and social media as tools for supporting a healthy, active lifestyle. (S3.H2.L2)

Lesson Objectives

The learner will:

- explore the choreographic tool of touch.
- combine touch with other choreographic tools (e.g., travel, change of level, change of tempo).
- continue developing the choreography for the dance event.
- use movement to express emotion in the choreography.

Equipment and Materials

- Large open dance space
- Stereo
- Background music that is just sound, not something recognizable to the students (relaxation music, yoga music, and meditation music all work well)

Introduction

Today, you will be still, move, and be moved, literally! You will be exploring the choreographic tool of touch today along with all other tools already in your tool belt. You will be making physical contact with and moving around each other. You will allow yourself to be manipulated from one fixed position to another, and you will also be doing the manipulating. At the end of class, you will have some time to work on your projects.

Instructional Task: Improvisation With Touch

■ PRACTICE TASK

Have students get into a large circle at arm's-length apart with an agreed-upon facing. You can start them all facing the same direction, or you can ask them to pick a facing (to center, away from center, right, left, or any degree in between). When in the circle, students are still like statues.

Ask for two volunteers, or choose two strong students to begin the improvisation assignment. The two students can start anywhere in the circle they want. When the music starts, they begin moving. They should move as they choose: around, through, under, over, behind, in front of. They also have the option to manipulate the still dancers' bodies. They can move arms, legs, torsos, heads; they can dance with the posed dancers and around them.

When the music stops, whomever the movers are standing closest to will come to the center of the circle. The music begins again, and these two students start dancing, moving, and manipulating. This continues until everyone has had a turn to be a mover.

Note: Placing this lesson near the end of the module gives students time to become comfortable with each other and with manipulating each other's bodies without fear or feelings of judgment.

Extensions

- Change the direction of the dancers in the circle.
- Have students hold their poses until they're manipulated again.

EMBEDDED OUTCOME: S5.H2.L2. Students may feel uncomfortable being manipulated by other dancers. Discuss how this may challenge them and the need to trust one other to be fully engaged in the dance.

Student Choices/Differentiation

Students choose their own path and make choices about the movement they make and how they manipulate each dancer.

What to Look For

- Student appropriateness: Do not allow students to manipulate dancers into obscene poses or to pose dancers touching another dancer inappropriately.
- They are free to touch each other, but in a creative or aesthetic way.
- Dancers must make the task about dancing around the architecture of the still bodies. It is less about the manipulation than the movement they are creating.
- Make sure they are not just moving arms and legs—they need to be dancing.

Instructional Task:
Combining Touch and Other Choreographic Tools

■ PRACTICE TASK

With students in the same circle, give different instructions. For example, have the students take a new facing, or everybody face a new direction and begin again. Watch and see what students need to work on, or what can be added or taken away for each assignment. Here are some examples of instructions:

- You must change level two times.
- You must manipulate each dancer as you come to them.
- You must turn the dancers into architecture.
- You must use attitude, arabesque, and your favorite turns as you travel.
- You must move in slow motion.

Refinement

Remind students about their other choreographic tools (level change, tempo change, travel, touch, and so on), and encourage combinations of these as they follow the instructions.

Student Choices/Differentiation

Students make choices on what they do and how they move.

What to Look For

- Everyone is participating.
- Everyone is being creative and following directions.
- Giggling is permitted; talking is not.

Instructional Task: Choreography Project

■ PRACTICE TASK

Students work on their projects, refining the movements with the music (or spoken word) they have selected.

Refinement

Remind students that they can add tools such as abstracting movement and touch and move to their projects.

Student Choices/Differentiation

- Students choose their movements and music.
- Students use the final project checklist to help refine the movements.

What to Look For

- Students are respectful of partners' ideas.
- Students are making progress on their movement sequences.

Formal and Informal Assessments

Exit slip: What was the most challenging part of this exercise for you?

Closure

- You are getting much better and more comfortable with improvisation.
- When you can be free and uninhibited with your improvisational movement, your creative choreography will take on that same freedom.

Reflection

- Are any students still having issues with shyness or feeling inhibited with their movement?
- What other things can I do to draw them out?
- How are their duet projects progressing? Do I need to provide more class time to work on them?

Homework

- Bring in a draft of your event task (flyers, invitations, and so on) for next class.
- Practice your duet choreography outside of class.
- Send me the link to your portfolio so I can check on your progress. (Embedded outcome: S3.H2.L2)

Resources

Green, D. (2010). *Choreographing from within: Developing the habit of inquiry as an artist.* Champaign, IL: Human Kinetics.

McGreevy-Nichols, S., Scheff, H., & Sprague, M. (2004). *Building dances: A guide to putting movements together.* Champaign, IL: Human Kinetics.

Internet keyword search: "dance improvisation," "dance improvisation with manipulation," "choreography"

LESSON 13: EXCERPT

Grade-Level Outcomes

Primary Outcomes

Self-expression & enjoyment: Selects and participates in physical activities or dance that meets the need for self-expression and enjoyment. (S5.H3.L1)

Dance & rhythms: Demonstrates competency in a form of dance by choreographing a dance or by giving a performance. (S1.H2.L2)

Working with others: Solves problems and thinks critically in physical activity and/or dance settings, both as an individual and in groups. (S4.H4.L1)

Engages in physical activity: Creates a plan, trains for and participates in a community event with a focus on physical activity (e.g., 5K, triathlon, tournament, dance performance, cycling event). (S3.H6.L2)

Embedded Outcomes

Working with others: Uses communication skills or strategies that promote team or group dynamics. (S4.H3.L1)

Physical activity knowledge: Analyzes and applies technology and social media as tools for supporting a healthy, active lifestyle. (S3.H2.L2)

Lesson Objectives

The learner will:

- work with a small group analyzing text to choreograph movement to the excerpt.
- perform choreographed movement for peers.
- evaluate peers' performance.
- practice choreography of emotion in duet to music (or spoken word).
- finalize costumes and/or props for performance.
- finalize event materials and roles.

Equipment and Materials

- Large open dance space
- Rubric for peer evaluation
- Video recording device
- Music selected by each group for their project
- Books with markers in them and highlighted text. This can be a wonderful cross-curricular project using books the students are reading or have read. I have had dance students perform these in person or on tape for English, social science, and drama classes. See suggestions at the end of the lesson.

Introduction

Please get into groups of five. Today, you will be choreographing an excerpt from a book. I have 10 books here. Send a delegate from your group to choose a book from my bag. On the front of the book is a sticky note telling you specifically what you need to read. Read the marked text out loud multiple times, and have more than one person in your group read it. Really study it. You will need to interpret what you have read, solve problems, reach consensus, and create a dance as a group. You will be creating movement to complement the text. There will be no acting today, just dancing! At the end of class, I will read your text while you perform the movement you have created with your group. We will use the remaining time to work on your choreography project and the Choreography Celebration.

Instructional Task: Designing the Dance

■ PRACTICE TASK

Have students get into groups of five. Distribute the rubric for peer evaluation. Call up one delegate to choose a book. You can do a blind choice, or lay the books out and let students choose. Each group reads the passage, interprets it, and creates movement that goes along with it. All these things must be collaborated on as a group. Students practice as they formulate their choreography.

Refinement

Remind students to integrate multiple choreographic tools in their design.

EMBEDDED OUTCOME: S4.H3.L1. Students need to collaborate to create their finished product. Reinforce the importance of constructive feedback and supportive language as students plan and practice their dance.

Student Choices/Differentiation

- Students choose their groups.
- Students collaborate to choose movements and choreographic tools.

What to Look For

- Everyone's ideas are being considered.
- Everyone is bringing ideas to the group.
- Students are being kind to one another as they work on compromise.

Instructional Task: Performance

■ PRACTICE TASK

Groups perform what they have created for their peers while you read the paragraph or passage.

Extension

While one group performs, the other groups conduct a peer critique (see handout). Record the performances so you can evaluate them later. After each performance, groups share their evaluations as a way to provide feedback to the dancers.

Student Choices/Differentiation

- Students choose their groups.
- Students collaborate to choose movements and choreographic tools.

What to Look For

- Students are supporting one another.
- Students are using all the choreographic tools.
- Students are able to use the rubric correctly.

Instructional Task: Choreography Project

■ PRACTICE TASK

Students work on their projects, refining the movements and practicing with the accompaniment they have chosen.

Refinement

Emphasize the transitions between movements and how they represent the music (or spoken word).

Extension

Students finalize costumes and/or props for the performance.

Student Choices/Differentiation

- Students choose their movements and the music or spoken word.
- Students use the final project checklist to guide decisions.

What to Look For

- Students are making progress on their movement sequences.
- Students are working together to finalize their sequences.

Instructional Task: Event Roles and Materials

■ PRACTICE TASK

Each duet shows the work they've done on posters, flyers, press releases, programs, invitations, and so on. The class will approve the final designs, and the information will be distributed electronically. Discuss roles for the dress rehearsal and the celebration. At the dress rehearsal, students will rotate through roles such as tech teams (video recording and music), critics (using the same rubric in this lesson for peer assessment), performers, and audience. At the performance, they will focus solely on performing. Students invite a school official to host the event.

Student Choices/Differentiation

Students create the materials for the event.

What to Look For

- Materials reflect thoughtful preparation and are attractive.
- Students are asking good questions about the event roles.

Formal and Informal Assessments

- Peer assessments
- Teacher evaluation after lesson

Closure

- This was a difficult assignment. I hope you are proud of what you created. I hope you are proud of how you created it.
- Give your group members a high five or a hug. Great work today!
- Are you becoming confident about your choreography project?
- Do you think you'll be ready to perform in three more classes?

Reflection

- This assignment usually exceeds my expectations. The students have done a lot of work with improvisation to this point and love to "dance out" the words from the page.
- Were the students all engaged?
- Was everyone's voice being heard and considered?
- What can I do to help any student who was not participating?
- Are the projects progressing enough to be ready for the performance?
- Assess the video to gauge progress.

Homework

- Review for a quiz next class on concepts and terminology.
- Practice your choreography project with your partner.
- Enhance your portfolio. For example, you could add photos of costumes or props or insert an audio file with your music. (Embedded outcome: S3.H2.L2)

Resources

See the list of suggested excerpts, or select your own book passages.

SUGGESTIONS FOR EXCERPTS FOR LESSON 13

- *The Great Gatsby*
- *The Hobbit*
- *Island of the Blue Dolphins*
- *Of Mice and Men*
- *Odyssey*
- *The Book Thief*

Talk to other teachers to see what students are reading. You also can use books that are popular, such as the Twilight series or Harry Potter series.

You will need to scan the books for a paragraph or two that lend themselves to movement. Here is an example I use:

Of Mice and Men by John Steinbeck

A far rush of wind sounded and a gust drove through the tops of the trees like a wave. The sycamore leaves turned up their silver sides, the brown dry leaves on the ground scudded a few feet. And now on row of tiny wind waves flowed up the pool's green surface. As quickly as it had come, the wind died, and the clearing was quiet again. The heron stood in the shallows, motionless and waiting.

Here is another: *Island of the Blue Dolphins* by Scott O'Dell

Night came and though I was afraid to leave the cliff I knew that I could never stay there until morning, that I would go to sleep and fall. Neither could I find my way home, so I climbed down from the ledge and crouched at the foot of the cliff.

And another: *The Book Thief* by Markus Zusak

Please believe me when I tell you that I picked up each soul that day as if it were newly born. I even kissed a few weary, poisoned cheeks. I listened to their last gasping cries. Their vanishing words. I watched their love visions and freed them from their fear. I took them all away and if ever there was a time I needed a distraction this was it. In complete desolation, I looked at the world above. I watched the sky as it turned from silver to gray to the color of rain. Even the clouds were trying to get away.

From L.C. MacDonald, R.J. Doan, and S. Chepko, eds., 2018, *Lesson planning for high school physical education* (Reston, VA: SHAPE America; Champaign, IL: Human Kinetics).

CHOREOGRAPHY PEER CRITIQUE

Name: _____

Excerpt: _____

1. What about this piece grabbed your attention?

2. What choreographic tools did you recognize?

3. Describe the costumes and props. Did they enhance the piece or detract from it?

4. If the choreographer was going to continue this piece, what suggestions would you offer on what to do?

5. Did the choreography move you? Did it make you think? Did you like the choreography? Why or why not?

From L.C. MacDonald, R.J. Doan, and S. Chepko, eds., 2018, *Lesson planning for high school physical education* (Reston, VA: SHAPE America; Champaign, IL: Human Kinetics).

LESSON 14: INANIMATE OBJECT

Choreography

Grade-Level Outcomes

Primary Outcomes

Working with others: Solves problems and thinks critically in physical activity and/or dance settings, both as an individual and in groups. (S4.H4.L1)

Self-expression & enjoyment: Selects and participates in physical activities or dance that meets the need for self-expression and enjoyment. (S5.H3.L1)

Dance & rhythms: Demonstrates competency in a form of dance by choreographing a dance or by giving a performance. (S1.H2.L2)

Movement concepts, principles & knowledge: Applies the terminology associated with exercise and participation in selected individual-performance activities, dance, net/wall games, target games, aquatics and/or outdoor pursuits appropriately. (S2.H1.L1)

Engages in physical activity: Creates a plan, trains for and participates in a community event with a focus on physical activity (e.g., 5K, triathlon, tournament, dance performance, cycling event). (S3.H6.L2)

Embedded Outcomes

Working with others: Accepts others' ideas, cultural diversity and body types by engaging in cooperative and collaborative movement projects. (S4.H4.L2)

Physical activity knowledge: Analyzes and applies technology and social media as tools for supporting a healthy, active lifestyle. (S3.H2.L2)

Lesson Objectives

The learner will:

- create shapes with a partner and an object (chair) to perform for the class.
- create a movement sequence using shapes and transitions.
- perform in a duet.
- self-assess and refine the choreography project, focusing on expressive elements.
- apply knowledge of choreographic tools and terminology on a written quiz.

Equipment and Materials

- Large open dance space
- Video recording devices
- Background music: whatever you feel like playing; just keep repeating the same song over and over so all students are creating to the same music (instrumental is best)
- A chair or another large object for each pair of students

Introduction

This is your last class working on new choreographic tools. The remainder of the module will be devoted to a dress rehearsal and the Choreographic Celebration. For today, choose a partner different from the one in your duet. One of you go get a chair and the other come and get a handout, and then find some space to work in. You're going to work with a new partner to create movement around an inanimate object—in this case, a chair. Follow the directions on your handout, which will help you try out different shapes and combinations. After you work with the chair, you'll take your quiz and finish up with practice time for your performance.

Write the directions on a whiteboard, put them up on your document camera or LCD projector, or provide a handout.

Instructional Task:
Creating Shapes With an Inanimate Object

■ PRACTICE TASK

You are the instructor today. I will not be available for questions because there are no wrong answers! Work through the instructions and create, revise and, create some more!

1. Choose a partner and get a chair.
2. Place the chair in the space where you will move.
3. Make a curved shape with one body part touching the chair, one touching the floor, and one touching your partner. Memorize this shape (shape #1).

Extensions

- Make a shape containing at least one straight line, with six body parts making contact with the chair, floor, or partner. Memorize this shape (shape #2).
- Make a shape where one partner would lose balance if she were not supported by the hair of his or her partner. Memorize this shape (shape #3).
- Make a shape where both partners need to be supported by the other partner. Memorize this shape (shape #4).

Student Choices/Differentiation

- Students choose their partners.
- Students choose the movements they do to create choreography.
- Use a handout, whiteboard, or projector to give students directions.

What to Look For

- Everyone is participating and collaborating well with a partner.
- Students are finding creative ways to make shapes.

Instructional Task:
Creating Movement With an Inanimate Object

■ PRACTICE TASK

Repeat shapes 1 through 4, adding interesting transitions that can be as long or short as you like. Feel free to move away from the chair during transitions, always returning for the next shape (transitions task).

Extensions

1. Move over, under, around, and across the chair. Choose the order you will do this in.
2. Repeat transitions task but change your tempo.
3. One partner will make a new shape using the chair; the other partner must move away from the chair.
4. Repeat the three tasks above with the other partner completing the action.
5. Repeat shape #3 or #4, creating a new shape.
6. Perform your duet for another duet.

EMBEDDED OUTCOME: S4.H4.L2. Discuss the importance of accepting others' ideas and abilities when working together in creating dance. Students should try to make ideas work rather than dismiss them.

Student Choices/Differentiation

- Students choose their partners.
- Students choose the movements they do to create choreography.

What to Look For

- Everyone is able to remember the shapes as they add transitions.
- Pairs are working together effectively to create sequences.
- Pairs are respecting each other's ideas.

Instructional Task: Quiz

■ PRACTICE TASK

Administer a quiz on choreographic tools and terminology.

Student Choices/Differentiation

Allow extra time if needed, or create a take-home version.

What to Look For

Students are knowledgeable about the tools of choreography.

Instructional Task: Choreography Project

■ PRACTICE TASK

Each pair practices their choreography piece, making final refinements.

Refinement

Suggest that students consider adding an object to their own choreography if they are interested.

Extension

Two pairs work together, with one pair recording the other. Each pair watches their own video to evaluate their own performance and make revisions as desired.

Student Choices/Differentiation

- Students choose their movements and music.
- Students use the final project checklist to guide refinements.

What to Look For

- The sequence looks like a collaborative effort.
- Students have made refinements to their shapes and transitions.
- Students are using their choreographic tools.

Formal and Informal Assessments

- Self-assessments of video
- Quiz

Closure

- You all had the exact same instructions, and yet your pieces were all very different. See how creative you all are.
- It is interesting to see what each group choreographs and how each group interprets the instructions differently.

- Next class, we will focus on practicing for your performance. Please bring your costumes and props for the dress rehearsal.
- Remember, you will be taking turns video recording, running the music (or narrating for spoken word), critiquing, and being a good audience member for each performance. I will use the video recording for evaluating your final choreography project.

Reflection

- How did the students react to dancing with an object (chair)?
- Review quizzes to see if there are common gaps in understanding.
- Review videos to check readiness for performance.

Homework

- Practice your choreography project with your partner.
- Finish your portfolio. Your choreography video from the dress rehearsal will be added after next class. (Embedded outcome: S3.H2.L2)
- Take home invitations to your families, and promote the Choreography Celebration with the flyers and posters you made.

Resources

Gilbert, A.G. & SHAPE America – Society of Health and Physical Educators. (2015). *Creative dance for all ages*. 2nd ed. Champaign, IL: Human Kinetics.

Green, D. (2010). *Choreographing from within: Developing the habit of inquiry as an artist*. Champaign, IL: Human Kinetics.

McGreevy-Nichols, S., Scheff, H., & Sprague, M. (2004). *Building dances: A guide to putting movements together*. Champaign, IL: Human Kinetics.

LESSON 15: DRESS REHEARSAL

Grade-Level Outcomes

Primary Outcomes

Self-expression & enjoyment: Selects and participates in physical activities or dance that meets the need for self-expression and enjoyment. (S5.H3.L1)

Dance & rhythms: Demonstrates competency in a form of dance by choreographing a dance or by giving a performance. (S1.H2.L2)

Engages in physical activity: Creates a plan, trains for and participates in a community event with a focus on physical activity (e.g., 5K, triathlon, tournament, dance performance, cycling event). (S3.H6.L2)

Movement concepts, principles & knowledge: Uses movement concepts and principles (e.g., force, motion, rotation) to analyze and improve performance of self and/or others in a selected activity. (S2.H2.L1)

Embedded Outcomes

Working with others: Assumes a leadership role (e.g., task or group leader, referee, coach) in a physical activity setting. (S4.H3.L2)

Physical activity knowledge: Analyzes and applies technology and social media as tools for supporting a healthy, active lifestyle. (S3.H2.L2)

Stress management: Applies stress management strategies (e.g., mental imagery, relaxation techniques, deep breathing, aerobic exercise, meditation) to reduce stress. (S3.H14.L2)

Lesson Objectives

The learner will:

- rehearse his or her choreography.
- dance his or her choreography for his or her peers.
- support peers during their performances.
- evaluate the performance of another duet.

Equipment and Materials

- Large open dance space
- Music for each group
- Video recording devices
- Copies of peer critique

Introduction

Great job on your quizzes last class. [Review any portions where students did not do well.] Today is our dress rehearsal—I hope everyone remembered their costumes and props! You have 10 minutes to practice your choreography piece with your partner. Then each duet will perform for the rest of class in the same order we will use for the final performance. When you are not dancing, you and your partner will rotate through the roles of audience, tech team, and critics. Time to practice!

Instructional Task: Choreography Project

■ PRACTICE TASK

Duets practice their choreography with music, costumes, and props.

Refinement

Encourage dancers to be expressive in their movements.

Student Choices/Differentiation

Duets practice at their own pace.

What to Look For

- Sequences look polished.
- Duets are working together as a team.

Instructional Task: Dress Rehearsal

■ PRACTICE TASK

The first duet performs, with the second duet "in the wings." Two duets act as the tech team by video recording and taking charge of the music. Two other duets evaluate the performance using the peer critique form (Lesson 13). You will evaluate the performances from the video outside of class. The rest of the duets act as a supportive audience. Rotate roles.

EMBEDDED OUTCOME: S4.H3.L2. During the performance, the other students take on leader roles. Provide feedback about students performing these roles confidently and efficiently.

Refinements

- Remind critics to focus on the critique questions to provide feedback.
- Reinforce the importance of the audience being attentive during the performance and supporting the performers with applause at the end.

Student Choices/Differentiation

- Students choose their partners.
- Students choose the movements they do to create choreography.

What to Look For

- Audience is providing a positive environment for the dress rehearsal.
- Students are managing their roles well.

Formal and Informal Assessments

- Peer assessments
- Formal assessment by teacher of duet performances

Closure

- How did you feel about your performance in the dress rehearsal?
- What gives you the most anxiety about the Choreography Celebration?
- What stress-management techniques can you use before performing to help with this stress? (Embedded outcome: S3.H14.L2)
- Do you have any questions before the final performance or before submitting your portfolio?
- How can the digital portfolio or other technology help you support a healthy lifestyle?
- I have sent out the invitations around the school for the celebration, but you need to remind your family!

Reflection

- Are students excited about the event? Confident?
- Did their performances demonstrate a wide range of choreographic tools?
- View videos and assess performance of duets.

Homework

Your portfolio is due before the next class. Add the video clip from today's dress rehearsal, and make any last changes you might have. Send me your link before the celebration so I can set up some screens to display them for the audience. (Embedded outcome: S3.H2.L2)

Resources

Gilbert, A.G. & SHAPE America – Society of Health and Physical Educators. (2015). *Creative dance for all ages*. 2nd ed. Champaign, IL: Human Kinetics.

Reeve, J. (2011). *Dance improvisations: Warm-ups, games and choreographic tasks*. Champaign, IL: Human Kinetics.

Internet keyword search: "dance recitals," "dance performances," "dance events"

LESSON 16: FINAL PERFORMANCE

Grade-Level Outcomes

Primary Outcomes

Self-expression & enjoyment: Selects and participates in physical activities or dance that meets the need for self-expression and enjoyment. (S5.H3.L1)

Dance & rhythms: Demonstrates competency in a form of dance by choreographing a dance or by giving a performance. (S1.H2.L2)

Engages in physical activity: Creates a plan, trains for and participates in a community event with a focus on physical activity (e.g., 5K, triathlon, tournament, dance performance, cycling event). (S3.H6.L2)

Physical activity knowledge: Analyzes and applies technology and social media as tools for supporting a healthy, active lifestyle. (S3.H2.L2)

Embedded Outcome

Stress management: Applies stress management strategies (e.g., mental imagery, relaxation techniques, deep breathing, aerobic exercise, meditation) to reduce stress. (S3.H14.L2)

Lesson Objectives

The learner will:

- perform the choreography piece with his or her partner in a culminating event.
- use choreography and accompaniment to express his or her selected emotion.
- display his or her individual choreography portfolio.

Equipment and Materials

- Large open dance space
- Music for each group
- Video recording device

Introduction

This is it—it's time to perform your choreography! If you're feeling a little stressed, use your favorite stress-management technique before going out to perform. Thank you for sending me the links to your portfolios. I will be showing them on different screens around the room after your performance. Let's warm up and get ready to dazzle our audience!

Instructional Task: Dance Event

■ PRACTICE TASK

Have students ready with costumes and props after warming up. Duets perform in a pre-determined sequence. The recital manager (you or another school official) will introduce each duet and the name of their piece. Ask another teacher or a parent to record the event so it can be posted on the school's physical education website or used in students' portfolios.

Note: The special event may also be conducted after school or at a dance recital or concert.

EMBEDDED OUTCOME: S3.H14.L2. Students will practice their stress management technique between the warm-up and the performance.

Student Choices/Differentiation

Students may choose the order of performance.

What to Look For

- Students performed confidently.
- The audience responded warmly.
- The costumes and props enhanced the performances.

Instructional Task: Celebration

■ PRACTICE TASK

If possible, have refreshments available for the end of the dance so students and the audience can socialize.

Play a video of the performances in the background.

If some students have done paper portfolios, they can be displayed for the audience members to peruse and enjoy. Digital portfolios can be displayed on laptops or additional screens.

What to Look For

- Students are interacting with families and other students.

Formal and Informal Assessments

Exit slip: What was the most interesting concept you learned in this choreography module?

Closure

- Terrific work out there! All that practice paid off!
- I am very proud of the progress you've made, and I hope you feel great about your performances today.
- You all used the tools in different and interesting ways.
- Remember, next class we start a new module, so be sure to check out the choices before class.

Reflection

- What components of choreography did the students really excel at?
- Which ones were underutilized?
- What would I do differently if I were to teach this again?

Homework

Check out the next modules on the school's physical education website, and be ready to participate in a new one.

Resources

Internet keyword search: "dance performance," "dance recital," "dance event"

Extending Students' Skills and Knowledge to Fitness Activities

The category of fitness activities (SHAPE America – Society of Health and Physical Educators, 2014, p. 61) centers on activities whose main objective is exercising to attain and/or maintain a health-enhancing level of fitness. It's evident that these types of activities are naturally aligned with the Grade-Level Outcomes under Standard 3, which encompass physical activity and fitness knowledge, engaging in physical activity, assessment and program planning, nutrition, and stress management. Classic fitness activities such as running, weight training, and walking are good options as fitness activities, but as this category has evolved, trendy activities such as Zumba, spinning, and cross-training are good choices, as well. As you plan your curriculum, you will want to identify favorite fitness activities in your area (or in the media) and provide students with the opportunity to acquire the skills and knowledge to succeed in them. By selecting activities that capture students' interest, you enhance the potential for student motivation and engagement. Fitness activities—particularly the trendy ones—might seem to come and go quickly, but the knowledge that students gain in one activity can be readily transferred to another one. To facilitate this transfer, you will want to emphasize the concepts and principles that underlie fitness and physical activity.

This chapter includes modules for three fitness activities. The first is a 15-lesson Yoga and Stress Management Module, contributed by Ericka Fangiullo, dean of students at Windsor High School in Windsor, CT. The module's lessons begin with the basics of yoga practice so that students new to the activity can participate comfortably. The yoga poses become more challenging as the lessons progress, but students have choices to allow them to participate at a level that feels comfortable.

By the end of the final lesson, they will have learned how yoga can help them manage stress, and they will have developed their own yoga sequences.

The 16-lesson Resistance Training Module, contributed by Anthony Smith, a visiting professor at the University of Southern Mississippi's School of Kinesiology, introduces students to several different forms of resistance training, including power lifting and resistance training using weight machines and free weights. The lessons also place a strong emphasis on resistance training that students can undertake without heavy weight-training equipment, including body-weight exercises, and using resistance bands and small pieces of apparatus. The lessons also give students opportunities to learn about speed, agility, and plyometric training and to develop a skill-related fitness plan.

Finally, the 16-lesson Pilates Module, contributed by Joni M. Boyd, assistant professor of exercise science at Winthrop University in Rock Hill, SC, provides progressions for beginner and intermediate Pilates sequences. The Pilates Module is available in the web resource and e-book only. By the end of the module, students will be comfortable with a variety of mat and standing exercises, with using an exercise ball, and with adding resistance bands to their routines. Students also will develop a behavior-modification plan that addresses a health or physical activity behavioral change.

For quick reference, each module begins with a block plan chart of the Grade-Level Outcomes that are addressed within each lesson. As you might expect, the lessons here place a heavy emphasis on a wide range of outcomes under Standard 3, which addresses acquiring the knowledge and skills to attain a health-enhancing level of physical activity and fitness. Each module also addresses the development of competency in specialized skills in health-related fitness activities (Outcome S1.H3.L1). Although Standards 1 and 3 are the focus, each module includes outcomes from every standard. The Resistance Training and Pilates Modules make frequent use of the application of terminology and movement concepts (Outcomes S2.H1.L1 and S2.H2.L1). The Pilates and Yoga Modules provide opportunities for students to lead others in physical activity (Outcome S4.H3.L2). All three modules address outcomes related to challenge (Outcome S5.H2.L2) and the health benefits of the respective fitness activities (Outcome S5.H1.L1). Also, each of the modules shows you how to provide an in-depth learning experience in fitness activities for your students that will further their physical literacy. As noted earlier, the Pilates Module is available in the web resource and e-book only.

YOGA AND STRESS MANAGEMENT MODULE

Lessons in this module were contributed by **Ericka Fangiullo**, dean of students at Windsor High School in Windsor, CT, where she taught physical education and health previously for 15 years.

Grade-Level Outcomes Addressed, by Lesson	Lessons														
	1	2	3	4	5	6	7	8	9	10	11	12	13	14	15
Standard 1. The physically literate individual demonstrates competency in a variety of motor skills and movement patterns.															
Refines activity-specific movement skills in 1 or more lifetime activities (outdoor pursuits, individual-performance activities, aquatics, net/wall games or target games). (S1.H1.L2)									P	P	P				
Demonstrates competency in 1 or more specialized skills in health-related fitness activities. (S1.H3.L1)	P	P	P	P	P	P	P	P	P	P	P	P	P	P	P
Standard 2. The physically literate individual applies knowledge of concepts, principles, strategies and tactics to movement and performance.															
Applies the terminology associated with exercise and participation in selected individual-performance activities, dance, net/wall games, target games, aquatics and/or outdoor pursuits appropriately. (S2.H1.L1)				P							P				
Standard 3. The physically literate individual demonstrates the knowledge and skills to achieve a health-enhancing level of physical activity and fitness.															
Discusses the benefits of a physically active lifestyle as it relates to college or career productivity. (S3.H1.L1)											E				
Participates several times a week in a self-selected lifetime activity, dance or fitness activity outside of the school day. (S3.H6.L1)	P				E				E		E				
Relates physiological responses to individual levels of fitness and nutritional balance. (S3.H8.L1)										E					
Identifies stress-management strategies (e.g., mental imagery, relaxation techniques, deep breathing, aerobic exercise, meditation) to reduce stress. (S3.H14.L1)							E	P	P						
Standard 4. The physically literate individual exhibits personal and social behavior that respects self and others.															
Employs effective self-management skills to analyze barriers and modify physical activity patterns appropriately, as needed. (S4.H1.L1)		P	E												
Uses communication skills and strategies that promote team or group dynamics. (S4.H3.L1)									E						
Assumes a leadership role (e.g., task or group leader, referee, coach) in a physical activity setting. (S4.H3.L2)													E	E	E
Solves problems and thinks critically in physical activity or dance settings, both as an individual and in groups. (S4.H4.L1)												E			
Applies best practices for participating safely in physical activity, exercise and dance (e.g., injury prevention, proper alignment, hydration, use of equipment, implementation of rules, sun protection). (S4.H5.L1)								E							
Standard 5. The physically literate individual recognizes the value of physical activity for health, enjoyment, challenge, self-expression and/or social interaction.															
Analyzes the health benefits of a self-selected physical activity. (S5.H1.L1)					E										
Chooses an appropriate level of challenge to experience success and desire to participate in a self-selected physical activity. (S5.H2.L2)	E	E									E				

P = Primary; E = Embedded

LESSON 1: PRINCIPLES OF YOGA

Grade-Level Outcomes

Primary Outcomes

Fitness activities: Demonstrates competency in 1 or more specialized skills in health-related fitness activities. (S1.H3.L1)

Engages in physical activity: Participates several times a week in a self-selected lifetime activity, dance or fitness activity outside of the school day. (S3.H6.L1)

Embedded Outcome

Challenge: Chooses an appropriate level of challenge to experience success and desire to participate in a self-selected physical activity. (S5.H2.L2)

Lesson Objectives

The learner will:

- practice proper yoga and classroom etiquette.
- practice breathing techniques.
- practice the class warm-up.
- track, in a journal, self-selected lifetime activity practiced outside of class.

Equipment and Materials

- Yoga mat for each person
- Appropriate yoga music

Introduction

Today, we start a new module on yoga. In most of your physical education classes, you work in groups and have developed those skills over time. This module is different because you will work on your own. You'll focus on your body, listen to your body, and adjust for what it needs and what it can do. During our lessons in yoga, no one will do something "better" than anyone else; you will just do it differently. Everyone's body is different, and everyone has different strengths and limitations. Let's start by watching a few video clips of yoga in action.

Instructional Task: Introduction to Seated Position

■ PRACTICE TASK

In their own personal space, students place a mat on the floor and perform an easy pose (seated position).

What to Look For

Walk around the room and give feedback on students' positions:

- Are their legs crossed?
- Are their backs straight?
- Are their shoulders relaxed?
- Are their wrists resting on their knees?
- Are their heads in neutral spine position?
- Are their eyes closed (when cued)?

Extension

Students can challenge themselves to have their feet on their thighs when legs are crossed.

Student Choices/Differentiation

Students may have their ankles crossed farther out in front of them, or one leg extended, if they are uncomfortable (back should still be straight regardless of legs).

Instructional Task: Ground Rules and the Five Principles

■ PRACTICE TASK

Review yoga concepts while in a seated position. Then review the ground rules:

- Keep your own space.
- Maintain a quiet classroom.
- Do everything slowly.
- Once you have the move, close your eyes to experience it fully.
- Use introspection (push yourself to your limit; what does your mind do).
- Compare yourself to yourself, never to others.

The Five Principles of Yoga

1. Relaxation
2. Exercise
3. Proper breathing
4. Proper diet
5. Positive thinking and meditation

Guiding questions for students:

Have students give examples of each principle. Ask questions such as the following:

- What similarities and differences do you see with the yoga principles and those of general physical activity?
- You can add to the ground rules and make it a social contract.
- What other ground rules will help make this experience positive?

Student Choices/Differentiation

If students are uncomfortable, have them sit straight, working the core muscles (back/spine, abdominals) and self-assess the core area of their bodies.

What to Look For

- Are students engaged?
- Are they making self-modifications?

Instructional Task: Breathing (Pranayama)

■ PRACTICE TASK

Have students close their eyes while seated and breathe through the nose.

- Breathing is life.
- *Prana* = vital life energy; *yama* = discipline/control.
- We exhale carbon dioxide and expel all toxic waste from our bodies.
- Talk about using breath to control stress.

Extensions

- Through the nose, inhale for 4 counts, exhale for 4 counts. (You count, then students do it on their own.)
- Repeat, inhale for 4, hold for 4, exhale for 4.
- Repeat, inhale for 8, exhale for 8.
- Repeat, inhale for 8, hold for 4, exhale for 12.

Student Choices/Differentiation

- If students have trouble, have them stay on the level where they are comfortable.
- If students cannot keep their eyes closed, you can provide blindfolds.

What to Look For

- Are students keeping their eyes closed (this is very hard for students to do and practice)? Cue or give blindfolds.
- Are students keeping proper seated position? Cue.
- Are students controlling their exhale?

Instructional Task: Warm-Up Asanas

■ PRACTICE TASK

Discuss the importance of warming up the spine. Repeat the exercises on both sides, emphasizing smooth and slow transitions. New poses are in italics in the Practice Task, Refinements, and Extensions sections. If you are not familiar with a pose, look up the skill descriptions online.

- *Seated spinal twist*
- *Neck circles*
- *Cat/Cow*
- *C stretch*
- *Thread the needle*
- *Seated angle*

Refinements

Seated spinal twist:

- Pull navel into back.
- Go as far as it is slightly uncomfortable and hold (do not overtwist).

C stretch:

- Spine should look like a letter C from above.

Thread the needle:

- Encourage students to lift arm a little higher if they are balancing well.

Seated angle:

- Reach forward one more inch.

Extensions

- *Extended spinal twist:* Seated spinal twist with one hand behind the back on the floor to deepen the stretch.
- *Seated angle:* Modify to change stretch—feet pointed or flexed, chin forward or back rounded, eyes closed or eyes open.

Student Choices/Differentiation

Cat/cow:

- Move to breath.
- Start together with cues and then at own pace.
- Encourage eyes closed so that students are not comparing.

Thread the needle:

- If uncomfortable, students may put same-side leg out for balance.
- Arm should be pointing directly up; students may change the angle of the arm if painful.

What to Look For

Spinal twists:

- Are students pulling their shoulders around?
- Are their heads looking behind on the twists?

Neck circles:

- Are students moving slowly through the circles?

Cat/cow:

- Are the hands under the shoulders?
- On the inhale, is the back up and rounded?
- On the exhale, are the head and tailbone up?

C stretch:

- Is the back flat?
- Are students exhaling as they turn to center?
- Are they looking over the shoulder as they form the C?

Thread the needle:

- Are they able to hold their balance while reaching up?

Seated angle:

- Are they holding the stretch, not bouncing?

Instructional Task: Cool-Down

■ PRACTICE TASK

Have students get onto their backs into *corpse pose (savasana)*.

Cue breathing.

Student Choices/Differentiation

If uncomfortable, students may bend the knees and put the feet flat on floor, or put a towel under the lower back.

What to Look For

- Are students eyes' closed?
- How many students had to modify their position?
- Students are relaxing visibly.

Formal and Informal Assessments

- Teacher observation and correction
- Journal assignments (see homework): Students may keep journals on paper or electronically; students could do this in a blog as well.

Closure

Quiet the mind; chime the gong. Have students listen and focus on the sound as long as they can.

Reflection

- Did I use appropriate voice tone?
- Did students have trouble with any poses?

Homework

You will keep a journal throughout this module. You will have some questions to address each time, and you also will record your physical activity outside of class so that we can see how active you are and whether you are meeting the physical activity guidelines. Review the scoring guide for how the journal will be evaluated. Questions:

- How easy/difficult were the breathing techniques for you today? What was easy/difficult?
- How did your body feel after the warm-up?
- Log your physical activity outside of class. Include the type of physical activity and how long you did it.

Resources

Brown, C. (2003). *The yoga bible*. Cincinnati: Walking Stick Press.

Martin, K., Boone, B., & DiTuro, D. (2006). *Hatha yoga illustrated*. Champaign, IL: Human Kinetics.

Stephens, M. (2012). *Yoga sequencing*. Berkeley, CA: North Atlantic Books.

Internet keyword search: "seated spinal twist," "cat/cow," "corpse pose," "c-stretch pose," "thread the needle pose," "seated angle pose"

10-POINT RUBRIC FOR JOURNAL ENTRIES

10 points: answered the questions thoroughly, included personal insight, and showed understanding of topic area by supporting opinions well

7-9 points: answered the questions using some personal insight and showed some understanding of the topic area

5-6 points: answered the questions vaguely, using a little personal insight, and showed they know what the topic area is

3-4 points: put little effort into the questions, answered the minimum, and showed little understanding of the topic area

1-2 points: put no effort into the questions, did only a small part of the questions, did the questions but did not follow directions, did not understand the questions and did not ask for help or clarification

0 points: the questions were not completed or done at all

From L.C. MacDonald, R.J. Doan, and S. Chepko, eds., 2018, *Lesson planning for high school physical education* (Reston, VA: SHAPE America; Champaign, IL: Human Kinetics).

LESSON 2: ASANAS

Grade-Level Outcomes

Primary Outcomes

Personal responsibility: Employs effective self-management skills to analyze barriers and modify physical activity patterns appropriately, as needed. (S4.H1.L1)

Fitness activities: Demonstrates competency in 1 or more specialized skills in health-related fitness activities. (S1.H3.L1)

Embedded Outcome

Challenge: Chooses an appropriate level of challenge to experience success and desire to participate in a self-selected physical activity. (S5.H2.L2)

Lesson Objectives

The learner will:

- practice proper yoga and classroom etiquette.
- practice breathing techniques.
- practice the class warm-up.
- practice new asanas.
- adjust poses to match personal capabilities.

Equipment and Materials

- Yoga mat and block for each person
- Appropriate yoga music

Introduction

Today, we will add asanas into the practice after reviewing the class routine and warm-up. Each lesson will build on prior knowledge. Just focus on yourself, and remember that it's okay if your posture is not exactly the same as the person next to you. Also, be aware of your body, and be conscious of introspection—pushing yourself to your physical limits, without hurting yourself.

Instructional Task: Warm-Up

■ PRACTICE TASK

- Starting in a seated position, everyone focuses on their breath.
- Review the ground rules from Lesson 1.
- Go slowly through the warm-up progression performed in the previous class.
- Add wrist and ankle circles to the warm-up, as students will be transferring weight onto their hands.

Student Choices/Differentiation

As students become more comfortable, once they get into the stretch, have them close their eyes. This will be difficult for some students, but it's the first step in helping students focus on themselves and not on others.

What to Look For

Walk around the room and offer feedback on students' positions.

- Are their backs straight?
- Are their shoulders relaxed?
- Are their heads in neutral spine position?

Instructional Task: New Asanas

■ PRACTICE TASK

Demonstrate new poses.

Have students get on all fours (called *tabletop*).

While holding tabletop, students do the following:
- Extend right arm.
- Extend left arm.
- Extend right leg.
- Extend left leg.
- Extend right arm and left leg.
- Extend left arm and right leg.

Child's pose (a resting pose)

Downward dog

Extensions
- *Downward dog*, right leg lifted, followed by *child's pose*
- *Downward dog*, left leg lifted, followed by *child's pose*

Refinement

Downward dog:
- Arms should be an extension of the back, all in one line.

Guiding questions for students:
- Are you challenging yourself?
- Are you listening to your body?

EMBEDDED OUTCOME: S5.H2.L2. Remind students to perform the poses at a level that challenges them now and throughout the module.

Student Choices/Differentiation

Video clips or posters can help students learn and remember new poses. If students cannot perform an extension, they should stay at the level at which they can perform. This will be the practice throughout the module. It is sometimes difficult for students to accept their level.
- **Child's pose:** Students may put their hands at their sides, palms up, and decide whether they like this expression of child's pose better.
- **Downward dog:** Students may need to bend the knees to push their heels into the mat. Instruct them to lift each leg only as far as is comfortable.

What to Look For
- Tabletop: Students are holding their arms/legs parallel to the ground.
- Students are showing that they know their limits.
- Students are breathing throughout the session.

Instructional Task: Cool-Down

■ PRACTICE TASK

Have students assume a comfortable position on their backs in savasana (corpse pose).
- Cue breathing.
- Cue body awareness.

Refinement

Encourage students to push their lower backs into the floor.

Student Choices/Differentiation

If uncomfortable, students may bend their knees and put their feet flat on the floor, or put a towel under their lower backs.

What to Look For

Students' eyes are closed.

Formal and Informal Assessments

- Teacher observation and correction
- Journal assignments (see homework)

Closure

Quiet the mind; chime the gong. Have students listen and focus on the sound as long as they can.

Reflection

- Were students able to perform all the physical extensions from tabletop?
- Did I give students appropriate skill feedback?

Homework

Journal assignment:
- Reflect on your experience in yoga so far. How does your body feel?
- Log all of your physical activity outside of class. Include the type of physical activity and how long you did it.

Resources

Brown, C. (2003). *The yoga bible*. Cincinnati: Walking Stick Press.

Martin, K., Boone, B., & DiTuro, D. (2006). *Hatha yoga illustrated*. Champaign, IL: Human Kinetics.

Stephens, M. (2012). *Yoga sequencing*. Berkeley, CA: North Atlantic Books.

Internet keyword search: "tabletop pose," "downward dog," "child's pose"

LESSON 3: STANDING PRACTICE

Grade-Level Outcomes

Primary Outcome

Fitness activities: Demonstrates competency in 1 or more specialized skills in health-related fitness activities. (S1.H3.L1)

Embedded Outcome

Personal responsibility: Employs effective self-management skills to analyze barriers and modify physical activity patterns appropriately, as needed. (S4.H1.L1)

Lesson Objectives

The learner will:

- demonstrate class routines, previous asanas, and yoga etiquette.
- demonstrate new asanas.

Equipment and Materials

- Yoga mat for each person
- Appropriate yoga music

Introduction

Today's lesson will continue to build on previous knowledge. As you move toward learning standing postures, daily routines will become more intense and flowing. As you build on past knowledge, your practice will become more challenging both physically and mentally. We'll start with our usual warm-up [see Lessons 1 and 2].

Instructional Task: Guided Practice

■ PRACTICE TASK

Demonstrate new poses.

Have the class move into the following:

- Downward dog
- Child's pose
- *Rag doll*
- *Rag doll* to standing: Roll up to standing to a 10 count.
- *Quiet mountain:* This resting asana is a common way to transition from sitting to standing that maintains flow.

Extensions

- After child's pose, downward dog, right leg up, followed by child's pose
- Downward dog, left leg up, followed by child's pose, then downward dog

Refinements

Downward dog:

- Focus on hamstrings and calves, push heels in, and extend through shoulders.

Rag doll:

- Count to 10 aloud to ensure that students move slowly the first time. Eventually, they will be able to roll up slowly on their own.

Student Choices/Differentiation

Video clips or posters can help students learn and remember new poses.
- Downward dogleg up: Students raise leg only as far as is comfortable.

What to Look For

- Students are performing the asanas correctly.
- Students are breathing correctly.
- Are students' knees locked in rag doll?
- Students are moving to standing slowly.
- Am I cueing breathing?

Instructional Task: Standing Guided Practice

Everything is done on both sides.

■ PRACTICE TASK

Demonstrate new poses.

Triangle sequence right side:

Half pyramid (back knee to floor)

Pyramid
- Curl back toes under and come up off back knee.
- Hold and breathe.

Triangle
- Repeat triangle sequence to the left side.

Refinement

Half pyramid and pyramid: Focus on keeping the front knee as straight as possible. If your knee is bent, come up a little higher so you can keep it straight.

EMBEDDED OUTCOME: S4.H1.L1. This is a good opportunity to scan the room and notice the varying levels and talk about how everyone is using asanas to benefit themselves. Just because some students can stretch farther than others doesn't mean that the benefits are different.

Instructional Task: Standing Transition to Floor

■ PRACTICE TASK

Guide students through standing poses to floor work:
- *Quiet mountain*
- Roll down to *rag doll*
- Low lunge right
- Low lunge left
- *Staff pose*
- *Seated forward bend*

Refinements

Staff pose:
- Body should be at 90 degrees, with legs straight and feet flexed. Bend knees slightly, if necessary, to move body into this position.

Seated forward bend:
- Focus on keeping the back flat while performing the stretch; hinge at the hips.

Student Choices/Differentiation

- Video clips or posters can help students learn and remember new poses.
- **Triangle:** Students may use a block for their hands if they cannot touch the floor.

What to Look For

Triangle:
- Students are keeping their legs straight.
- Students' feet are pointing in the correct direction.

Pyramid:
- Students are able to hold where they are comfortable without bending the front knee.

Low lunge:
- Are students' knees going past the ankles?

Staff:
- Students' bodies are 90 degrees to their legs.

Instructional Task: Cool-Down

Should be no more than 7 minutes.

■ PRACTICE TASK

Savasana (corpse pose)

Cue the following during the posture:

- Focus on your breath.
- Now focus on your heart rate.
- Maintain awareness of your body.

Student Choices/Differentiation

Students may bend their knees or put a rolled towel under the lower back if uncomfortable.

What to Look For

Are students able to stay still?

Formal and Informal Assessments

- Teacher observation and correction
- Journal assignments (see homework)

Closure

Quiet the mind; chime the gong. Have students listen and focus on the sound as long as they can.

Reflection

- Are students able to understand my cues?
- Am I able to demonstrate and cue at the same time?

Homework

Journal assignment: Give students an opportunity to read your responses and respond to questions, if necessary.

- Do you play any sports or participate in regular physical activity outside of school? If so, what? How often?
- What do you like about exercise? What do you dislike?

- What prevents you from exercising?
- How can you address these obstacles?
- Log all your physical activity outside of class. Include the type of physical activity and how long you did it.

Resources

Brown, C. (2003). *The yoga bible*. Cincinnati: Walking Stick Press.

Martin, K., Boone, B., & DiTuro, D. (2006). *Hatha yoga illustrated*. Champaign, IL: Human Kinetics.

Stephens, M. (2012). *Yoga sequencing*. Berkeley, CA: North Atlantic Books.

Internet keyword search: "triangle pose," "pyramid pose," "half pyramid pose," "seated forward bend," "staff pose", "quiet mountain pose," "rag doll pose"

LESSON 4: SUPINE POSTURES

Grade-Level Outcomes

Primary Outcome

Fitness activities: Demonstrates competency in 1 or more specialized skills in health-related fitness activities. (S1.H3.L1)

Embedded Outcome

Health: Analyzes the health benefits of a self-selected physical activity. (S5.H1.L1)

Lesson Objectives

The learner will:

- demonstrate proper breathing techniques while doing asanas.
- demonstrate new asanas and asanas learned previously.

Equipment and Materials

- Yoga mat for each person
- Band or belt
- Appropriate yoga music

Introduction

The focus today will be on supine postures, or postures on your back. We also will work the shoulders a little. Remember to open your mind to new experiences. Corpse pose can include a verbal body scan, so we will leave about 5 extra minutes for that. Let's start our warm-up [see Lessons 1 & 2], which we will extend to be ready for the rest of the lesson.

Instructional Task: Extended Warm-Up

- Warm up hip flexors and hamstrings.
- Hold these poses for about five breaths.

■ PRACTICE TASK

On the back in supine position:
- Right knee to chest, extend leg straight up
- Lying-down spinal twist

Refinements

- Remind students to keep the shoulders on the floor while dropping the knee over the hips across the body.
- Repeat sequence to the left.

Student Choices/Differentiation

- Knee to chest: Pull knee to side to deepen the stretch if knee can touch chest easily.
- Extend leg straight up: Students may wrap a belt around the foot if they cannot reach behind their knee with leg straight.
- Lying-down spinal twist: Students add pressure on the extended arm to further the stretch.

What to Look For

- Students are keeping the opposite leg straight on the ground during knee to chest.
- Students' legs are as straight as possible and foot flexed while extended.
- Students are keeping their shoulders on the ground in lying-down spinal twist.

Instructional Task: New Asanas From Supine Position

■ PRACTICE TASK

Demonstrate the new poses and have students perform the following sequence:

- *Crab*
- *Crab extensions*
- *Egg roll*
- *Bridge*
- *Wind relieving*
- *Bridge*
- *Wind relieving*
- *Bridge*
- *Fish*

Extensions

Crab:

- Crab with right leg extended, followed by egg roll
- Crab with left leg extended, followed by egg roll

Bridge:

- Extend right leg, extend left leg.

Refinements

Crab:
- Tighten abdominal muscles when pulling bottom up.

Egg roll:
- Push the lower back into the floor when the knees are into the chest.

Fish:
- Remind students to keep arms as close together as possible under the body, with palms down.

Student Choices/Differentiation

Video clips or posters can help students learn and remember new poses.

- Crab: May have varying levels of height.
- Crab extensions: If students can't get legs parallel to the ground, they may lift to where it is comfortable for them to hold.
- Bridge: Students may put their hands on the lower back to give support if their core is weak. If comfortable, students may link hands under the back and press palms away from body to stretch shoulders.
- Fish: Students lift to the point at which they are comfortable.

What to Look For

- Are students' hands under their shoulders and feet under their knees in crab?
- Are students rolling softly and staying on their mats in egg roll?
- Are students tightening the core when lifting in crab and bridge?
- Are students keeping their knees aligned when they lift a leg in crab and bridge extensions?

Instructional Task: Cool-Down

Can be a little longer today with a quick body scan.

■ PRACTICE TASK

Have students lie on their backs in savasana (corpse pose).
Cue with breath counting.
Cue a quick head-to-toe scan: Start at the feet and work up, stating each body part, asking students to become aware of the body part, breathe into it, and relax it.

Student Choices/Differentiation

Knees can be up with feet on the floor for those whose lower back is uncomfortable.

What to Look For

- Students have their eyes closed.
- Students seem relaxed.

Formal and Informal Assessments

- Teacher observation and correction
- Journal assignments (see homework)

Closure

Quiet the mind; chime the gong—have students listen and focus on the sound as long as they can.

EMBEDDED OUTCOME: S5.H1.L1. Ask students to consider how yoga can contribute to health. What components of fitness or well-being does yoga help develop?

Reflection

- How did students do with the supine poses? Are they making progress on back bends?
- Are they comfortable with breathing at the right time during the poses?
- Which students are struggling with the new poses?

Homework

Journal assignment:
- Do you find that you have any pain in your back? What was particularly difficult or easy for you today?
- Were you aware of your breathing? Why or why not? What can help you become more aware?
- Respond to any other comments or questions.
- Log all of your physical activity outside of class. Include the type of physical activity and how long you did it.

Resources

Brown, C. (2003). *The yoga bible*. Cincinnati: Walking Stick Press.

Martin, K., Boone, B., & DiTuro, D. (2006). *Hatha yoga illustrated*. Champaign, IL: Human Kinetics.

Stephens, M. (2012). *Yoga sequencing*. Berkeley, CA: North Atlantic Books.

Internet keyword search: "crab pose," "fish pose," "wind relieving pose," "bridge," "egg roll"

LESSON 5: TRANSITIONS

Grade-Level Outcomes

Primary Outcomes

Fitness activities: Demonstrates competency in 1 or more specialized skills in health-related fitness activities. (S1.H3.L1)

Movement concepts, principles & knowledge: Applies the terminology associated with exercise and participation in selected individual-performance activities, dance, net/wall games, target games, aquatics and/or outdoor pursuits appropriately. (S2.H1.L1)

Embedded Outcome

Engages in physical activity: Participates several times a week in a self-selected lifetime activity, dance or fitness activity outside of the school day. (S3.H6.L1)

Lesson Objectives

The learner will:

- demonstrate proper breathing techniques while performing asanas.
- demonstrate asanas learned previously.
- demonstrate moving through postures.
- apply yoga terminology (name of pose) correctly.

Equipment and Materials

- Yoga mat for each person
- Block
- Appropriate yoga music

Introduction

Today, we will add a large number of new poses. As the routines start to include more poses, transitions and flow from asana to asana become more important. Routines also will start to repeat. This is important for the physical part of yoga—the muscle memory. But it's also important for the mental part—remembering postures, repeating them, and holding for longer periods of time. Let's start our warm-up [see Lessons 1 and 2].

Instructional Task: Beginning Asana Sequence

■ PRACTICE TASK

Demonstrate the new poses.

Have students curl their toes under and push up to downward dog.

Rag doll

Hang and hold

Slowly roll up to quiet mountain.

Five-pointed star

Refinement

Students' arms should be parallel to the floor.

- Triangle
- Pyramid
- Quiet mountain
- Rag doll

Repeat on the other side.

Student Choices/Differentiation

Triangle and pyramid: Students can use the block for the hand that is down in order to help them keep the front leg straight

What to Look For

- Students' knees are soft in rag doll.
- Students remember to roll up slowly.
- Students remember how to use the block for triangle and pyramid.

Instructional Task:
Introduction to Moving Through a Posture

■ PRACTICE TASK

Demonstrate the new poses.

From downward dog, have students walk their feet back into a plank position.

Lower to flat on the floor to a 5 count and begin the following sequence:

Cobra
- Lower slowly.

Downward dog
- Drop to knees and pull back.

Caterpillar to *cobra*
Repeat cobra three times.
- Students lie flat on their abdomens, chin on mat.

Half locust
Locust
Half bow (grab one leg at a time behind)
Bow (grab both legs)

Refinements

Cobra:

- Students should be lifting with the lower back, using the arms for balance, pressing the pelvis into the mat.
- Keep the chin close to the floor when moving through.

Half locust:

- Press chin into mat; lock knees.

Extension

Half locust:

- Raise right leg, then left leg; repeat, trying to raise a little higher the second time.

Student Choices/Differentiation

Video clips or posters can help students learn and remember new poses.

- Cobra: Students will have varying levels of height off the mat based on lower-back flexibility and strength. This is OK!
- Caterpillar to cobra: For those students with more upper body strength, have them hover lower to the floor as they move through the posture, and to move very slowly.
- Half and full locust: Again, there will be varying levels of leg height. Encourage students to self-differentiate based on flexibility and strength.
- Half and full bow: Some students will be able to grab just the ankles and that is it; others should pull their upper bodies up as high as possible.

What to Look For

Cobra:

- Students pushing their chins into the mat and lifting with their lower backs.
- Students are keeping their elbows in and using their hands as support.

Half locust:

- Students are pushing their chins into the mat.

Locust:

- Are students keeping their legs straight and knees locked when they lift?
- Students are lifting the chest.

Bow:

- Students are pulling back with their legs to open up and lift the chest.
- Students breathing when holding the asana.

Instructional Task: Cool-Down

■ PRACTICE TASK

Have students lie on their backs in savasana (corpse pose).

Cue with breath counting.

Cue a quick head-to-toe scan: Start at the feet and work up, stating each body part, asking students to become aware of the body part, breathe into it, and relax it.

Student Choices/Differentiation

- Those whose lower backs are uncomfortable may keep knees up with feet on the floor.
- Place a rolled-up towel under the lower back.

What to Look For

- Students have their eyes closed.
- Students seem relaxed.

Instructional Task: Review of Poses

■ PRACTICE TASK

Review the names of the various poses, and ask students to demonstrate the poses as they are called.

Student Choices/Differentiation

Provide flash cards with pictures of poses, and have students identify the names of the poses.

What to Look For

- Students can demonstrate each pose correctly.
- Do any students have to look around to see what others are doing before forming the pose?

Formal and Informal Assessments

- Teacher observation and correction
- Journal assessment and assignment (see homework)

Closure

Quiet the mind; chime the gong. Have students listen and focus on the sound as long as they can.

EMBEDDED OUTCOME: S3.H6.L1. Have students review their journals to see how much physical activity they are putting in outside of class each day. Do they see any patterns?

Reflection

- How is my timing?
- Do I need to spend more time on asanas?
- Was too much planned?

Homework

Journal assignment:

- Write a brief synopsis of today's practice, what you liked, didn't like, had difficulty with, and so on.
- Tell me something about yourself that you want to share. (Purely to get to know your students.)
- Log all your physical activity outside of class. Include the type of physical activity and how long you did it.

Resources

Brown, C. (2003). *The yoga bible*. Cincinnati: Walking Stick Press.

Martin, K., Boone, B., & DiTuro, D. (2006). *Hatha yoga illustrated*. Champaign, IL: Human Kinetics.

Stephens, M. (2012). *Yoga sequencing*. Berkeley, CA: North Atlantic Books.

Internet keyword search: "bow pose," "locust," "caterpillar pose," "cobra pose," "five-pointed star," "triangle," "pyramid"

LESSON 6: LOWER BACK

Grade-Level Outcomes

Primary Outcome

Fitness activities: Demonstrates competency in 1 or more specialized skills in health-related fitness activities. (S1.H3.L1)

Embedded Outcome

Stress management: Identifies stress-management strategies (e.g., mental imagery, relaxation techniques, deep breathing, aerobic exercise, meditation) to reduce stress. (S3.H14.L1)

Lesson Objectives

The learner will:

- demonstrate proper breathing techniques while performing asanas.
- review asanas learned previously.
- demonstrate new standing and lower-back asanas.

Equipment and Materials

- Yoga mat for each person
- Block
- Appropriate yoga music

Introduction

Today, we will add staff pose to our regular warm-up [see lessons 1 and 2]. After that, we will practice some new asanas. Now that you've learned the basics, try to extend your stretch and push your bodies. We also will start to explore stress during the cool-down of this lesson. This will build over the next few lessons.

Instructional Task: Beginning Asana Sequence

■ PRACTICE TASK

Have students curl their toes under and push up to downward dog.
Drop knees into caterpillar.
Cobra
Downward dog
Repeat the flow two times.

Student Choices/Differentiation

Encourage students to get their chins as close to the mat as they can. It requires more upper-body strength.

What to Look For

- Caterpillar: Students putting their chins close to the mat.
- Students are moving under control.

Instructional Task: New Asanas, Lower-Back Focus

■ PRACTICE TASK

Demonstrate the new poses.
From downward dog, have students move onto their knees and begin the following sequence:

- *Gate*
- *Half circle*
- *Camel*
- Child's pose

Repeat sequence on the other side.

Refinements

Half circle:

- Make sure students' support hand is directly under the shoulder. Other arm should extend as far as possible.

Camel:

- Push the shoulder blades together.

Extension

Camel:

- Be sure to progress through camel: Hands on lower back first, one hand on heels at a time (see differentiation).

Student Choices/Differentiation

- Gate and half circle: Remind students to work at their level.
- Camel: If students are not comfortable with the tops of their feet pressed flat against the mat, have them go back to toes curled under, heels up.

What to Look For

- Students are breathing while holding the poses.
- Did students stop at their level or push themselves?
- Students need encouragement to push the limits.
- Are students pushing too hard?

Instructional Task: Standing Asanas Review Sequence

■ PRACTICE TASK

From child's pose, move into downward dog.

Rag doll

Roll up slowly to quiet mountain.

Triangle

Warrior I

Warrior II

Five-pointed star

Repeat on the other side.

Roll down to rag doll.

Hands to floor

Student Choices/Differentiation

- Remind students to use the block in triangle if they need it.
- Remind students to challenge themselves by sitting lower in the warriors and keeping arms straight.

What to Look For

- How are students transitioning between asanas?
- Are they moving with flow?
- Am I still correcting minor mistakes?

Instructional Task: Cool-Down

■ **PRACTICE TASK**

Have students lie on their backs in savasana (corpse pose).

Cue with breath counting.

EMBEDDED OUTCOME: S3.H14.L1 As students are relaxing, their heart rates coming down, ask them to think about stressors in their lives. Cue with examples.

Student Choices/Differentiation

Those whose lower backs are uncomfortable may keep the knees up with feet on the floor.

What to Look For

- Did the class demeanor change when you asked them about their stressors?
- Did you notice physical tension?

Formal and Informal Assessments

- Teacher observation and correction
- Journal assignments (see homework)

Closure

Quiet the mind; chime the gong. Have students listen and focus on the sound as long as they can.

Reflection

- How are students' transitions?
- How are students doing on the new poses?
- Are their movements flowing from one pose to another?

Homework

Journal assignment:

- During savasana, I had you think about stressors. Make a list of the things you were thinking about.
- How did this affect your savasana practice?
- Log all of your physical activity outside of class. Include what you did and how long you did it.

Resources

Brown, C. (2003). *The yoga bible*. Cincinnati: Walking Stick Press.

Martin, K., Boone, B., & DiTuro, D. (2006). *Hatha yoga illustrated*. Champaign, IL: Human Kinetics.

Stephens, M. (2012). *Yoga sequencing*. Berkeley, CA: North Atlantic Books.

Internet keyword search: "warrior 1," "warrior 2," "camel pose," "gate pose," "half circle pose," "child's pose," "five-pointed star pose"

LESSON 7: BALANCE

Grade-Level Outcomes

Primary Outcomes

Stress management: Identifies stress-management strategies (e.g., mental imagery, relaxation techniques, deep breathing, aerobic exercise, meditation) to reduce stress. (S3.H14.L1)

Fitness activities: Demonstrates competency in 1 or more specialized skills in health-related fitness activities. (S1.H3.L1)

Embedded Outcome

Safety: Applies best practices for participating safely in physical activity, exercise and dance (e.g., injury prevention, proper alignment, hydration, use of equipment, implementation of rules, sun protection). (S4.H5.L1)

Lesson Objectives

The learner will:

- demonstrate proper breathing techniques while performing asanas.
- demonstrate new asanas and asanas learned previously.
- demonstrate an understanding of stress, and be able to relate it to his life, as shown in journal entries.

Equipment and Materials

- Yoga mat for each person
- Block
- Appropriate yoga music
- Stress at a Glance sheet

Introduction

Today, we will introduce balance into the practice. The focus and physicality of balance are important parts of yoga practice. Some of you will do this easily, and others will have difficulty, but as with anything in yoga, be sure to work at your own level. The benefits are the same. We also will spend some time before the cool-down, talking about stress, simply defining it and thinking about strategies for managing it. Let's start our warm-up [see Lessons 1 and 2].

Instructional Task: Beginning Asana Sequence

■ PRACTICE TASK

Demonstrate the new poses. Move onto one knee and follow this sequence:

- Half warrior I
- *Half prayer twist*
- Half warrior II
- *Plank*: Repeat on the other side.

Refinement

Half prayer twist

- Be sure to twist to the side of the bent leg.

Student Choices/Differentiation

Video clips or posters can help students learn and remember new poses.

- If the full plank position is too difficult, students may practice on their knees (like a modified push-up).

What to Look For

- Students maintain balance in the half prayer twist.
- Students are holding the plank straight, using their core.

Instructional Task: Standing Balance

■ PRACTICE TASK

Demonstrate the new poses.

From plank, have students jump their feet to their hands and slowly come to standing.

Quiet mountain: While in quiet mountain, talk about balances and the importance of having a focus point, tight core, and controlled body.

Tree: Start with the foot low on the ankle and hands in namaste.

Prayer squat: Repeat two times on each side.

Extension

Tree:
- Students move the foot as close to the groin as possible.

Refinement

Tree:
- Raise hands over head.

EMBEDDED OUTCOME: S4.H5.L1. While working on new poses, especially balancing poses, focus feedback on alignment so that students can perform the poses safely and with better balance.

Student Choices/Differentiation

Video clips or posters can help students learn and remember new poses.
- Tree: Students may choose to keep the foot low or hands in namaste.

What to Look For

- Are students falling over?
- Students are maintaining body control.
- Students remember to stand in quiet mountain when frustrated.

Instructional Task: Introduction to Stress Discussion

■ PRACTICE TASK

Have students move into a circle with their mats and sit in an easy pose. Hold a discussion about stress.

Guiding questions for students:

- What is stress?
- What happens to my body during stress?
- What particular things make me stressed?
- Why do some people get less stressed than others?
- How does stress make me feel?
- What do I do now to handle my stress?
- What else can I do to handle my stress?
- What techniques have we practiced in yoga that can help with stress?

Go over the suggested strategies on the Stress at a Glance handout.

Student Choices/Differentiation

During any kind of discussion, go where the conversation leads, making sure to use students' questions and comments as a springboard to further ideas.

What to Look For

- Students are comfortable sharing.
- Students display a basic understanding of stress.
- Students might be surprised at how many stress-relief strategies they use already.
- Is this a stressed-out class?

Instructional Task: Cool-Down

■ PRACTICE TASK

Have students lie on their backs in savasana (corpse pose).
Cue with breath counting.
Have students recognize a stressor, then cue them to let it go with each exhale.

Student Choices/Differentiation

Knees can be up with feet on the floor for those whose lower back is uncomfortable.

What to Look For

Is my tone of voice relaxing?

Formal and Informal Assessments

- Teacher observation and correction
- Journal assignments (see homework)

Closure

Quiet the mind; chime the gong—have students listen and focus on the sound as long as they can.

Reflection

- Was I able to keep the discussion of stress going?
- Was I able to feed off of student comments?

Homework

Students bring in something that they use to de-stress, such as music, a stress ball, and so on.
Journal assignment:

- What was your overall impression of today's discussion about stress?
- What did you learn? What did you already know?
- What is something specific to you that you do to lower your stress, or to calm you down when you are stressed?
- Log all your physical activity outside of class. Include the type of activity and how long you did it.

Resources

Brown, C. (2003). *The yoga bible*. Cincinnati: Walking Stick Press.

Martin, K., Boone, B., & DiTuro, D. (2006). *Hatha yoga illustrated*. Champaign, IL: Human Kinetics.

Stephens, M. (2012). *Yoga sequencing*. Berkeley, CA: North Atlantic Books.

Internet keyword search: "prayer twist," "plank," "tree pose," "prayer squat pose"

STRESS AT A GLANCE

- Stress is a normal part of life that either can help us learn and grow or can cause us significant problems.
- Stress releases powerful neurochemicals and hormones that prepare us for action (to fight or flee).
- If we don't take action, the stress response can create or worsen health problems.
- Prolonged, uninterrupted, unexpected, and unmanageable stresses are the most damaging types of stress.
- We can manage stress with regular exercise, meditation or other relaxation techniques, structured timeouts, and learning new coping strategies to create predictability in our lives, such as:

    - Identify your triggers.
    - Keep a stress journal.
    - Improve time management skills.
    - Overcome burnout.
    - Do something you enjoy.
    - Learn how to say no.
    - Practice relaxation techniques.
    - Keep a positive attitude.
    - Balance work and play.
    - Talk about your problems.
    - Exercise regularly.
    - Eat a healthy diet.

- Many behaviors that intensify in times of stress and unhealthy ways of coping with stress, such as using pain medicines and other drugs, or alcohol, smoking and overeating, actually worsen the stress and can make us more sensitive to further stress.

While some treatments for stress appear promising, managing one's stress depends largely on his or her willingness to make the changes necessary for adopting a healthy lifestyle.

From L.C. MacDonald, R.J. Doan, and S. Chepko, eds., 2018, *Lesson planning for high school physical education* (Reston, VA: SHAPE America; Champaign, IL: Human Kinetics). Reprinted from MedicineNet.com. Available: http://www.medicinenet.com/stress/article.htm

LESSON 8: RELAXATION

Grade-Level Outcomes

Primary Outcomes

Stress management: Applies stress-management strategies (e.g., mental imagery, relaxation techniques, deep breathing, aerobic exercise, meditation) to reduce stress. (S3.H14.L2)

Fitness activities: Demonstrates competency in 1 or more specialized skills in health-related fitness activities. (S1.H3.L1)

Embedded Outcome

Working with others: Uses communication skills and strategies that promote team or group dynamics. (S4.H3.L1)

Lesson Objectives

The learner will:

- discuss with the class her stress-reducing object and how it helps her.
- demonstrate the ability to relax by participating in a long deep-relaxation practice.

Equipment and Materials

- Yoga mat for each person
- Appropriate yoga music
- Deep-relaxation script

Introduction

Today, we will start by sharing our homework assignments with one another. After that, we will come together to practice a deep-relaxation script. It's important to remember that this is an active relaxation and not a sleep session. [Some students might fall asleep.] At the end of class, you will work on your journaling, which is a skill that requires practice, just like any other.

Instructional Task: Discussion About Homework Object

■ PRACTICE TASK

Have students sit in groups of three or four initially. In their small groups, have them discuss the following:

- What is your object?
- What stresses you out?
- What do you use it for?
- How does it help you?

Have students come together in their own spaces and ask for anyone who wants to share with the large group.

EMBEDDED OUTCOME: S4.H3.L1. Before students share, remind them of the importance of listening skills and respecting different ideas. Provide corrective feedback on communication.

Student Choices/Differentiation

- If any students forgot their stress-relief objects, allow them to answer the questions as if they had brought them.
- Students choose small groups.
- Students choose whether to share with the larger group.

What to Look For

- Students are engaged.
- Students are showing respect toward one another and listening attentively.

Instructional Task: Deep-Relaxation Activity

■ **PRACTICE TASK**

Students lie down on their backs in savasana.

Students will be in this pose for about 45 minutes, so encourage them to get comfortable, yet still on their backs.

Read a deep-relaxation script, or play a pre-recorded one (see Resources).

Student Choices/Differentiation

- Dim the lights in part of the room for students who might have trouble relaxing at first.
- Students think "in" and "out" as they breathe to help them focus on their breath and relax.

What to Look For

- Students are able to be on their backs quietly for the entire activity.
- Students are taking the activity seriously.
- Students appear to be more relaxed at the end of the script.

Formal and Informal Assessments

- Teacher observation and correction
- Journal assignments (see homework)

Closure

Quiet the mind; chime the gong. Have students listen and focus on the sound as long as they can.

Journal questions during class:

- Were you able to be aware during the whole practice? If not, what was the last thing you remember?
- Were you able to keep your body still?
- How do you feel? Both physical and mentally?

Reflection

- Am I reading and responding to students' journals in a timely fashion?
- Are students embracing this form of communication and assessment?

Homework

Have students pinpoint one or more de-stressing techniques that they think might work for them, and urge students to use them going forward.

Journal assignment:

- What was your overall impression of today's discussion about stress?
- What did you learn? What did you already know?
- What do you do to lower your stress or to calm you when you are stressed?
- Log your physical activity outside of school. Include the type of activity and how long you did it.

Resources

iTunes has some pre-recorded scripts: Kelly Howell Guided Relaxation.

Other sites for guided relaxation scripts:

www.innerhealthstudio.com

www.pent.ca.gov/trn/guidedimageryscript.pdf (free basic relaxation script you can use today or shorten to use in any savasana)

www.k-state.edu/counseling/student/biofedbk/guideim.html

Internet search terms: "yoga relaxation," "stress management," "relaxation scripts"

LESSON 9: SUN SALUTATIONS

Grade-Level Outcomes

Primary Outcomes

Fitness activities: Demonstrates competency in 1 or more specialized skills in health-related fitness activities. (S1.H3.L1)

Lifetime activities: Refines activity-specific movement skills in 1 or more lifetime activities (outdoor pursuits, individual-performance activities, aquatics, net/wall games, or target games). (S1.H1.L2)

Embedded Outcomes

Challenge: Chooses an appropriate level of challenge to experience success and desire to participate in a self-selected physical activity. (S5.H2.L2)

Engages in physical activity: Participates several times a week in a self-selected lifetime activity, dance or fitness activity outside of the school day. (S3.H6.L1)

Lesson Objectives

The learner will:

- demonstrate proper breathing techniques while performing asanas.
- refine previous asanas.
- demonstrate new balancing poses.

Equipment and Materials:

- Yoga mat for each person
- Block
- Appropriate yoga music

Introduction

Going forward, practice will begin to flow and repeat more. Today, we'll work on two new balancing poses and sun salutations. We'll start with our usual warm-up and add staff pose [see Lessons 1 and 2].

Instructional Practice: Sun Salutation

There are many, many variations of sun salutations. See the reference section for some detailed website suggestions.

■ PRACTICE TASK

Have students move into downward dog.

Rag doll

Quiet mountain

While students are here, give a brief explanation of the purpose and practice of sun salutation.

Go through sun salutation:

- Head to knees
- Look up
- Head to knees
- Hands to floor, right leg back to lunge
- Plank
- Caterpillar to upward dog

- Downward dog
- Left leg forward to lunge
- Standing forward bend
- Inhale up and back
- Mountain

Cue slowly at first, gradually increasing pace. Do numerous times on both sides.

Guiding questions for students:

- Why is the sun salutation such an important practice in yoga?
- Why, in your estimation, does the sun salutation end with hands in mudra position?

Refinement

Downward dog: Remind students to work on keeping their heels on the ground and butt up in the air.

Student Choices/Differentiation

Allow students to bend their knees slightly on standing forward; bend if straight legs are too uncomfortable.

What to Look For

- Students are breathing correctly.
- Students are keeping the core tight in plank.

Instructional Practice: New Balancing Asanas

■ PRACTICE TASK

Demonstrate the new poses and have students follow the sequence:

Standing head to knee

Dancer

Refinements

- *Standing head to knee*: Keep elbows in and chest forward.
- *Dancer*: Keep hips and shoulders square to the front wall for ultimate balance.

Extensions

- *Standing head to knee:* Pull chest to leg, chin to knee.
- *Dancer*: Use ankle to pull arm back to get back leg parallel to the floor. Repeat on the other side.
- *Note:* YouTube is a great resource if you have the technology available, especially if you cannot demonstrate some of the different extensions of the asanas.

EMBEDDED OUTCOME: S5.H2.L2. This is a good place to see whether students are choosing the appropriate level of challenge, which will be evident by their ability to balance on one leg. Students should bend the leg if they can't balance over the straight leg.

Student Choices/Differentiation

Standing head to knee:

- Students will show varying levels of leg straightness.
- Students can keep the balancing-leg knee slightly bent to help with the balance, but work toward straightening both legs.

Dancer:

- For those struggling with balance, have them keep the knee down and arm up and stay there.
- For those advanced, have them lean and reach as forward as possible.

What to Look For

- Did I remind students about a focal point?
- Are students' bodies under control?
- Are they handling it appropriately if they are having difficulty balancing?

Instructional Practice: Cool-Down

■ PRACTICE TASK

Have students lie on their backs in savasana (corpse pose).

Cue with breath counting.

As your students are relaxing, their heart rates coming down, have them focus on the movement of their abdomens during breathing.

Student Choices/Differentiation

Knees can be up with feet on the floor for those whose lower back is uncomfortable.

What to Look For

- Did the class demeanor change when you asked them to about think about their breathing?
- Can you notice physical tension dissipating?

Formal and Informal Assessments

- Teacher observation and correction
- Journal assessments and assignments (see homework)

Closure

Quiet the mind; chime the gong. Have students listen and focus on the sound as long as they can.

Reflection

- Are students using proper etiquette during their practice?
- Am I aware of differentiating as necessary for each student?
- What can I plan that will challenge them in the next lesson?

Homework

Journal assignment:

- We moved a little faster today during our sun salutation practice. What are your overall feelings on this?
- You challenged yourself with two difficult balances today. Were they easy? Difficult? What specifically?
- What did you do to accommodate? What can I do to help you?
- Log your physical activity outside of school. Include the type of activity and how long you did it.
- On average, how many times per week are you participating in physical activity, including physical education class? Are you meeting Outcome S3.H6.L1?
- Calculate the average number of minutes per week that you were physically active, including in physical education class. Are you meeting the national guidelines for physical activity?

Resources

Great site for everything sun salutation: www.yogajournal.com/category/beginners/how-to/sun-salutations.

Internet keyword search: "dancer yoga pose," "standing knee pose"

LESSON 10: VINYASA

Grade-Level Outcomes

Primary Outcomes

Lifetime Activities

Refines activity-specific movement skills in 1 or more lifetime activities (outdoor pursuits, individual-performance activities, aquatics, net/wall games or target games). (S1.H1.L2)

Fitness activities: Demonstrates competency in 1 or more specialized skills in health-related fitness activities. (S1.H3.L1)

Embedded Outcome

Fitness knowledge: Relates physiological responses to individual levels of fitness and nutritional balance. (S3.H8.L1)

Lesson Objectives

The learner will:

- demonstrate proper breathing techniques while performing asanas.
- refine asanas learned previously.

Equipment and Materials

- Yoga mat for each person
- Block
- Appropriate yoga music
- Video recording device

Introduction

Today, I will introduce the term vinyasa, or yoga flow. In our previous class, I introduced the sun salutation as a beginning to this, and today, we will move through many postures more quickly than we have before, repeating the sequence numerous times. This will help you with muscle memory, as well as keeping the muscles warm and increasing the heart rate more than you have to this point. We'll start with our warm-up sequence [see Lessons 1 and 2] and extend it with sun salutations.

Instructional Task: Warm-Up Extension

■ PRACTICE TASK

Sun salutation (two times on each side)

Extensions

- Have students use a device to record one sun salutation.
- Students review the recording to evaluate the flow and alignment of their movements.
- Ask students to calculate their heart rates after sun salutation and record.

Refinement

Direct students to focus on spine alignment during the sequence.

Student Choices/Differentiation

- Students use a device, if available, to measure heart rate or take the pulse with a 6-second count.
- Provide a checklist or scoring guide for students to use in their self-assessment.

What to Look For

- In the warm-up, students focused on breathing and keeping the spine aligned.
- Students performed sun salutation correctly.

Instructional Task: *Vinyasa*

■ PRACTICE TASK

Downward dog
Rag doll
Mountain
Inhale arms up
Head to knee
Lunge (right leg back)
Upright lunge
Arms up to warrior I
Hands down to lunge
Plank
Plank – lower and hover
Upward dog
Downward dog
Upward dog
Downward dog
Lunge (right leg back)
Straighten leg to triangle
Five-pointed star
Warrior II
Open heart (arms clasped behind back)
Standing seal (head to knees, mudra arms)
Stand up
Lunge (bend right knee)
Standing forward bend
Sweep arms up
Mountain: Repeat three more times for a total of two times on each side.

Refinement

Focus on flow between positions and timing of the breath.

Extension

Ask students to take their heart rates and record.

Student Choices/Differentiation

Students should hold poses and balances at their own level.

What to Look For

- Are students staying with the cues?
- Am I going too fast? Too slow?

Instructional Task: Cool-Down

■ PRACTICE TASK

Have students lie on their backs in savasana (corpse pose).
Cue with breath counting.
As your students are relaxing, their heart rates coming down, have them think about relaxing the face and jaw.

Extension

Ask students to take their heart rates and record.

EMBEDDED OUTCOME: S3.H8.L1. Use the guiding questions to help students understand how the body responds to changing levels of exercise intensity.

Guiding questions for students:

- How did your heart rate change from the sun salutation to vinyasa?
- How does the body respond to flowing, continuous movements such as vinyasa?
- Were you surprised by the intensity of the workout? Why?
- What factors affect your body's response to exercise and in what way? (Answer: fitness level, nutritional balance, and so on)

Student Choices/Differentiation

Allow those whose lower backs are uncomfortable to keep the knees up with feet on the floor.

What to Look For

- Students are staying still.
- Students' breathing is slow and regular.

Formal and Informal Assessments

- Teacher observation and correction
- Journal assignments (see homework)

Closure

- Quiet the mind; chime the gong. Have students listen and focus on the sound as long as they can.
- Next class, we will have a quiz on the terminology and principles you have learned so far in this module.

Reflection

- What am I learning about students from their journals?
- Are they understanding the concepts?
- What do I need to change about my delivery?

Homework

Review for the quiz on yoga next class.
Journal assignment:

- How was today's practice different from what we have done in the past? How was it the same?
- Did you like the vinyasa? What was easy? What was hard?
- Have you been using your de-stressing techniques? What is an example of when and how you used them?
- Log your physical activity outside of school. Include the type of activity and how long you did it.

Resources

Brown, C. (2003). *The yoga bible*. Cincinnati: Walking Stick Press.

Martin, K., Boone, B., & DiTuro, D. (2006). *Hatha yoga illustrated*. Champaign, IL: Human Kinetics.

Stephens, M. (2012). *Yoga sequencing*. Berkeley, CA: North Atlantic Books.

Internet keyword search: "open heart pose," "standing seal pose," "vinyasa"

LESSON 11: SHOULDERS

Grade-Level Outcomes

Primary Outcomes

Lifetime activities: Refines activity-specific movement skills in 1 or more lifetime activities (outdoor pursuits, individual-performance activities, aquatics, net/wall games and target games). (S1.H1.L2)

Fitness activities: Demonstrates competency in 1 or more specialized skills in health-related fitness activities. (S1.H3.L1)

Movement concepts, principles & knowledge: Applies the terminology associated with exercise and participation in selected individual-performance activities, dance, net/wall games, target games, aquatics and/or outdoor pursuits appropriately. (S2.H1.L1)

Embedded Outcomes

Physical activity knowledge: Discusses the benefits of a physically active lifestyle as it relates to college or career productivity. (S3.H1.L1)

Engages in physical activity: Participates several times a week in a self-selected lifetime activity, dance or fitness activity outside of the school day. (S3.H6.L1)

Lesson Objectives

The learner will:

- demonstrate proper breathing techniques while performing asanas.
- refine asanas learned previously.
- demonstrate asanas with focus on the shoulders.
- apply the terminology and principles of yoga during a written assessment.

Equipment and Materials

- Yoga mat for each person
- Block
- Appropriate yoga music

Introduction

Today, we will continue our vinyasa with a guided practice. It will be a review of asanas that we've practiced, along with a few new ones and some extensions. The new focus will be on the shoulders. This will be the last time I lead our practice, as we will transition to student-led routines as a final assessment over the next three classes. We'll start with our regular warm-up sequence [see Lessons 1 and 2] and then extend it with staff and seated angle poses. At the end of class, you'll take the quiz on yoga.

Instructional Task: Warm-Up Extension

■ **PRACTICE TASK**

EMBEDDED OUTCOME: S3.H1.L1 As students complete the warm-up, and before moving on to vinyasa, discuss the value of yoga to a physically active lifestyle.

Guiding questions for students:

- What are the benefits of a physically active lifestyle?
- How does yoga contribute to a physically active lifestyle?
- How can yoga help your productivity in college or a career?

Student Choices/Differentiation

Warm up can include going through some of the spinal twists more than once and holding for less time or for longer time.

What to Look For

Am I cueing students to focus on breathing and keeping the spine aligned?

Instructional Task: Vinyasa

■ PRACTICE TASK

Demonstrate the new poses.

Downward dog

Dolphin (downward dog on elbows)

Downward dog

Extensions

- Lift leg and rotate over body to open and stretch hips.
- Repeat, switching legs in hip opener.
- Rag doll
- Quiet mountain
- Sun salutations four times
- Five-pointed star
- Triangle
- *Extended side angle*
- Pyramid

- Lunge
- Repeat triangle through lunge on other side
- Plank
- Elbow plank
- Plank
- Downward dog
- Hip opener
- Rag doll
- Quiet mountain

Student Choices/Differentiation

Video clips or posters can help students learn and remember new poses.

- Dolphin: Keep knees bent if hamstrings are tight. Keep hips up if comfortable.
- Extended side angle: Wrist can either rest on bent leg or all the way to the floor (depending on comfort level).

What to Look For

- Are students staying with my cues?
- Am I going too fast? Too slow?
- Are they breathing during side angle pose?

Instructional Task: Shoulder Focus

■ PRACTICE TASK

Demonstrate the new poses.

Students should move slowly to a seated position on the mat.

Bridge

Crab

Wheel

Refinement

Cue students to come down slowly.

Student Choices/Differentiation

Video clips or posters can help students learn and remember new poses.
- Wheel: If students are very comfortable, you can have them lift an arm or leg as a challenge.
- If wheel is too difficult, students can stay with bridge.

What to Look For

- Students are pushing through their heels during wheel.
- Students are able to lift their heads off the ground in wheel.

Instructional Task: Cool-Down

■ PRACTICE TASK

Have students lie on their backs in savasana (corpse pose).
Cue with breath counting.

Student Choices/Differentiation

Knees can be up with feet on the floor for those whose lower back is uncomfortable.

What to Look For

- Are students breathing appropriately?
- Are they letting go of any tension?

Instructional Task: Quiz

■ PRACTICE TASK

Administer a quiz on yoga practice and principles.

Student Choices/Differentiation

Allow extra time where needed.

What to Look For

- Are students able to identify the different poses correctly?
- Do they understand the importance of breathing at the proper time?

Formal and Informal Assessments

- Teacher observation and correction
- Cognitive test on yoga terminology and principles
- Journal assignments (see homework)

Closure

- Quiet the mind; chime the gong. Have students listen and focus on the sound as long as they can.

Reflection

- After reading the journal questions, consider how many students would feel comfortable taking a class outside of the school.
- What could I have done differently to make more students feel comfortable? Or does everyone feel comfortable?

Homework

Journal assignment:

- What have you discovered about your body during the past 11 classes?

- How comfortable are you with the postures thus far?

- Would you be able to take a yoga class outside of school? Why or why not?

- This was the last time for logging all your physical activity outside of class.

- Describe the patterns that you found in your log. For example, what days and times are you most active? Least active? Do you like to be active with others or by yourself?

- How active are you outside of physical education class?

- Do you need to change your patterns to meet the guidelines? (Embedded outcome: S3.H6.L1)

Resources

Brown, C. (2003). *The yoga bible.* Cincinnati: Walking Stick Press.

Martin, K., Boone, B., & DiTuro, D. (2006). *Hatha yoga illustrated.* Champaign, IL: Human Kinetics.

Stephens, M. (2012). *Yoga sequencing.* Berkeley, CA: North Atlantic Books.

Internet keyword search: "dolphin pose," "wheel," "side angle pose"

LESSON 12: STUDENT YOGA SEQUENCE

Grade-Level Outcomes

Primary Outcome

Fitness activities: Demonstrates competency in 1 or more specialized skills in health-related fitness activities. (S1.H3.L1)

Embedded Outcome

Working with others: Solves problems and thinks critically in physical activity and/or dance settings, both as an individual and in groups. (S4.H4.L1)

Lesson Objectives

The learner will:

- demonstrate knowledge of asanas and sequencing of a mini routine.
- research a new asana.
- design a routine to teach to the class as outlined in the instructions and rubric.

Equipment and Materials

Chromebook, computer, or other resources for each student or set of partners.

Introduction

In today's class, I will review your quiz results and go over your final assessment. This project includes a set of partners working together to design a 20- to 25-minute yoga practice, based on previous knowledge. You must also research one new asana and teach it to the class. In the next three classes, students will lead the class and fill out evaluations on the process. This is a great way to check overall understanding of your yoga practice.

Note: If classes are large, use small groups instead of partners.

Instructional Task: Working on Presentation

■ PRACTICE TASK

Have students seated throughout the space. Distribute the instructions and scoring guide for the project and review them with students (see handout).

- Students may work together or alone.
- Once they decide what new asana they will teach, have them come tell you so you do not have any repeats.

EMBEDDED OUTCOME: S4.H4.L1 Students have to think about how to put their routines together, using critical components from previous lessons.

Student Choices/Differentiation

Make sure you have a variety of resources available, including websites, books, and music. Have students share if they find a good site as a resource.

What to Look For

- Are students on task?
- Are they having difficulty deciding on a routine?
- How strong is their knowledge of asanas?

Instructional Task: Practicing Routines

■ PRACTICE TASK

Students write down the sequence they want to try. Have them practice the sequence.

Refinement

Students often have a difficult time with the timing of the sequence and how long to hold each position. Have them practice and make adjustments until sequences are smooth and fluid.

Extension

Once students are comfortable with their sequences, have them practice verbal cues for leading the class.

What to Look For

- Will students need more time?
- How is their timing?
- Can they fill the entire time (20 to 25 minutes)?

Formal and Informal Assessments

- Teacher observation and correction
- Journal assessments

Closure

- Quiet the mind; chime the gong. Have students listen and focus on the sound as long as they can.
- We'll start your routines next class, so please be ready. You should try to practice so your movements are smooth and your cues are timed properly.

Reflection

- Do you think this task was easy for them?
- Do they need more time planning?
- Are you confident in your teaching that they learned enough?

Homework

Finish up and finalize your routines for the next three classes.
Journal assignment:

- Do I feel prepared for my routine? Do I need more time?
- Did I have any immediate questions for the new postures?

Resources

Brown, C. (2003). *The yoga bible*. Cincinnati: Walking Stick Press.

Martin, K., Boone, B., & DiTuro, D. (2006). *Hatha yoga illustrated*. Champaign, IL: Human Kinetics.

Stephens, M. (2012). *Yoga sequencing*. Berkeley, CA: North Atlantic Books.

Good websites: www.yoga.com; www.yogajournal.com/category/poses; www.artofliving.org/yoga/yoga-poses/yoga-poses-categories; www.yogabasics.com/practice/yoga-postures.

Internet keyword search: "yoga sequences," "yoga poses," "short yoga routines"

GROUP-LED YOGA SEQUENCE RUBRIC
INSTRUCTIONS AND GUIDELINES

1. Each yoga session must be 20 to 25 minutes in length.

2. You must include one new asana that you have researched.

3. Follow the sequence we have been learning in class: Start with centering, then easy poses (warming up), more challenging poses, less challenging poses (cooling down), and relaxation (corpse pose).

4. Review the rubric carefully so you know how your sequence will be assessed.

5. Practice the sequence and the cue—don't just wing it.

6. Have fun and be creative!

Checklist for Yoga Sequence

Warm-up

_____ Abdominal routine (5 min)

_____ Got the class's attention to focus and quiet the mind

_____ Incorporated breathing into warm-up

_____ Used proper asanas

_____ Reached all body parts

_____ Warmed up the spine

Practice

_____ Chose asanas and pranyamas the class has practiced

_____ Chose at least one new asana

_____ New asana was taught properly

_____ Practice session had flow from one asana to another

_____ Practice was challenging to all levels

_____ Incorporated pranayama in all asanas

_____ Used correct names and instructed asanas correctly

_____ Maintained student focus

_____ Remained on time

Relaxation

_____ Allotted enough time (no more than 5 min)

_____ Maintained focus on clearing mind and pranayama

_____ Brought people into relaxed state

_____ Ended session on time

General

_____ Showed obvious understanding and knowledge of subject matter

_____ Used appropriate tone of voice; all students could hear

_____ Music chosen was appropriate for the routine

_____ Maintained a balance of flow and timing

_____ Did and instructed the asanas and pranyamas correctly

_____ Demonstrated that they were prepared

From L.C. MacDonald, R.J. Doan, and S. Chepko, eds., 2018, *Lesson planning for high school physical education* (Reston, VA: SHAPE America; Champaign, IL: Human Kinetics).

LESSON 13: STUDENT-LED YOGA SEQUENCES

Grade-Level Outcomes

Primary Outcome

Fitness activities: Demonstrates competency in 1 or more specialized skills in health-related fitness activities. (S1.H3.L1)

Embedded Outcome

Working with others: Assumes a leadership role (e.g., task or group leader, referee, coach) in a physical activity setting. (S4.H3.L2)

Lesson Objectives

The learner will:

- demonstrate knowledge of asanas through a sequenced mini routine.
- present the mini routine to the class and lead the class in performing it.
- evaluate classmates.

Equipment and Materials

- Copy of the feedback form for each student for each presentation
- Copy of the class evaluation and reflection sheet for each student
- Copy of the grading rubric for each student
- CDs, music playback devices, and speakers available for students
- Mats and blocks for each student

Introduction

In the remaining lessons, you will perform your final projects as well as evaluate them. I will also be evaluating your routines. I will lead a short warm-up [see Lessons 1 and 2], *which you will end with your new asana. Then we'll get started on the student-led routines.*

Instructional Task: Student Presentations

■ PRACTICE TASK

Have the order of presentations available for students.

- Presentations should be 20 to 25 minutes long, with a 5-minute transition period to switch students and complete the feedback form.
- Keep groups moving. If a group ends early, note that on the rubric. Don't let groups go over the time limit to prevent backup.
- You complete the rubric for each routine as well.

EMBEDDED OUTCOME: S4.H3.L2. During the task, students have the opportunity to lead their classmates in a new routine. Provide feedback about how well they led the class, as well as on the poses themselves.

Student Choices/Differentiation

Allow students to choose the order of presentations.

What to Look For

- How is their timing?
- How is their cueing?
- Was their teaching of the new asana effective?
- Could students follow the sequence?

Formal and Informal Assessments

- Rubric for presentations
- Feedback form
- Final evaluation
- Journal assignments (see homework)

Closure

- How did you feel about the new routines you practiced today?
- Was it difficult to evaluate each other?
- If you led a routine today, what, if anything, would you change for next time?

Reflection

- Did students have trouble leading their classmates for the full time?
- Was there good flow in their routines?
- Did they remember to incorporate good breathing technique?

Homework

Journal assignment:

- How effective were the routines you experienced today?
- Would you change anything?

PEER YOGA LESSON EVALUATION

Name: _____ Block: _____ Date: _____

Please answer all questions in accordance with the yoga routine that just occurred. Please make sure you support your answers and provide details as appropriate.

1. What did you like about your classmates' lesson? Why?

2. What do you think your classmates could have done better? How could they improve the session?

3. How did you feel during the session? What made you feel this way? (Please give details.)

4. On a scale of 1 to 5, I give this lesson a _____ .

5. Additional comments:

From L.C. MacDonald, R.J. Doan, and S. Chepko, eds., 2018, *Lesson planning for high school physical education* (Reston, VA: SHAPE America; Champaign, IL: Human Kinetics).

LESSON 14: STUDENT-LED YOGA SEQUENCES

Grade-Level Outcomes

Primary Outcome

Fitness activities: Demonstrates competency in 1 or more specialized skills in health-related fitness activities. (S1.H3.L1)

Embedded Outcome

Working with Others: Assumes a leadership role (e.g., task or group leader, referee, coach) in a physical activity setting. (S4.H3.L2)

Lesson Objectives

The learner will:

- demonstrate knowledge of asanas through a sequenced mini routine.
- present the mini routine to the class and lead the class in performing it.
- evaluate classmates.

Equipment and Materials

- Copy of the feedback form for each student for each presentation
- Copy of the class evaluation and reflection sheet for each student
- Copy of the grading rubric for each student
- CDs, music playback devices, and speakers available for students
- Mats and blocks for each student

Introduction

Today, we will continue with your final project and your evaluations of them. I will evaluate your projects. I also will lead a short warm-up [see Lessons 1 and 2], which you will end with your new asana. Then we'll continue with the student-led routines.

Instructional Task: Student Presentations

■ PRACTICE TASK

Have the order of presentations available for students.

- Presentations should be 20 to 25 minutes long, with a 5-minute transition period to switch students and complete the feedback form.
- Keep groups moving. If a group ends early, note that on the rubric. Don't let groups go over the time allotment to prevent backup.
- You complete the rubric for each routine as well.

EMBEDDED OUTCOME: S4.H3.L2 During the task, students have the opportunity to lead classmates in a new routine. Provide feedback about how well they led the class, as well as on the poses themselves.

Student Choices/Differentiation

Allow students to choose the order of presentations.

What to Look For

- How is their timing?
- How is their cueing?
- Was their teaching of the new asana effective?
- Could students follow the sequence?

Formal and Informal Assessments

- Rubric for presentations
- Feedback form
- Final evaluation
- Journal assignments (see homework)

Closure

- How did you feel about the new routines you practiced today?
- Was it difficult to evaluate each other?
- If you led a routine today, what, if anything would you change for next time?

Reflection

- Did students have trouble leading their classmates for the full time?
- Was there good flow in their routines?
- Did they remember to incorporate good breathing technique?

Homework

Journal assignment:
- How effective were the routines you experienced today?
- Would you change anything?

LESSON 15: STUDENT SELF-EVALUATION

Grade-Level Outcomes

Primary Outcome

Fitness activities: Demonstrates competency in 1 or more specialized skills in health-related fitness activities. (S1.H3.L1)

Embedded Outcome

Working with others: Assumes a leadership role (e.g., task or group leader, referee, coach) in a physical activity setting. (S4.H3.L2)

Lesson Objectives

The learner will:

- demonstrate knowledge of asanas through a sequenced mini routine.
- present the routine and lead the class in performing it.
- evaluate classmates.

Equipment and Materials

- Copy of the feedback form for each student for each presentation
- Copy of the class evaluation and reflection sheet for each student
- Copy of the grading rubric for each student
- CDs, music playback devices, and speakers available for students
- Mats and blocks for each student

Introduction

Today, we will finish the remaining projects and you will evaluate yourselves, each other, and the class as a whole. We'll finish up the module with a yoga challenge!

Instructional Task:
Complete Student Presentations and Teacher Evaluations

■ PRACTICE TASK

Have the order of presentations available for students.

- Presentations should be 20 to 25 minutes long, with 5-minute transition period to switch students and complete the feedback form.
- Keep groups moving. If a group ends early, note that on the rubric. Don't let groups go over the time allotment to prevent backup.
- You complete the rubric for each routine as well.

EMBEDDED OUTCOME: S4.H3.L2. During the task, students have the opportunity to lead classmates in a new routine. Provide feedback about how well they led the class, as well as on the poses themselves.

Student Choices/Differentiation

Allow students to choose the order of presentations.

What to Look For

- How is their timing?
- How is their cueing?
- Was their teaching of the new asana effective?
- Could students follow the sequence?

Instructional Task: Evaluation

Practice Task

At the end of all the presentations, have students fill out the final evaluation.

Student Choices/Differentiation

Allow students more time to complete evaluations if needed.

Instructional Task: Yoga Challenge

Practice Task

Set up stations with new yoga poses that haven't been introduced yet. Some poses should be advanced and others easy. Students can go in pairs to the stations they are interested in and try the new poses.

Student Choices/Differentiation

- Students can choose the level of pose to try.
- Students can choose to do as many as they would like.

What to Look For

- Are students successful at trying new poses on their own?
- Are they remembering to breathe appropriately?
- Are they challenging themselves?

Formal and Informal Assessments

- Rubric for presentations
- Feedback form
- Final evaluation

Closure

- Have students sit around in a circle and describe their experience in the class in one word.
- Discuss other types of yoga they may want to explore.
- Remind students to be thinking about their next module.

Reflection

- Read through all the evaluations. How could you improve the module for next time?
- Did I offer my students the best possible experience?
- What did they learn?

Homework

Make sure you review the new module outline and critical elements of the first skill by next class.

YOGA SELF-EVALUATION

Name: _____ Period: _____

Evaluation questions: Full credit will be given for answering the questions thoroughly. (5 points each)

Answer the questions in your journal.

1. What physical benefits did you gain from this class?

2. What were the biggest obstacles you had or tried to overcome?

3. What did you like the most? Why? Why was this important to you?

4. What did you like the least? Why?

5. What did you learn about yourself?

6. What did you learn about me?

7. How would you convince a classmate to try yoga?

8. Give me some general comments on your impression. Is the class what you expected? Would you take it again? Were you challenged? Explain.

Rubric for Yoga Self-Evaluation

Excellent–4	Good–3	Fair–2	Poor–1
• All answers are well thought out and thorough. • Evidence of learning is clearly present. • Opinions are well supported. • Subject-area knowledge is apparent by answers given.	• Most answers are well thought out and thorough, with a few vague statements. • Some evidence of learning is present. • Opinions are somewhat supported. • Subject-area knowledge is somewhat apparent.	• Questions are answered, but answers are not well thought out. • Little evidence of learning is present. • Opinions are stated but not supported. • Subject-area knowledge is only vaguely apparent.	• Some questions are answered, but answers are not thorough or well thought out. • Little or no evidence of learning is present. • Opinions are not stated clearly. • Little or no subject area-knowledge is apparent.

Number grade: _____   Letter grade: _____

From L.C. MacDonald, R.J. Doan, and S. Chepko, eds., 2018, *Lesson planning for high school physical education* (Reston, VA: SHAPE America; Champaign, IL: Human Kinetics).

RESISTANCE TRAINING MODULE

Lessons in this module were contributed by **Anthony Smith**, a visiting professor at the University of Southern Mississippi's School of Kinesiology, where he teaches strength and conditioning programming, sport law, and pedagogy methods.

Grade-Level Outcomes Addressed, by Lesson	Lessons															
	1	2	3	4	5	6	7	8	9	10	11	12	13	14	15	16
Standard 1. The physically literate individual demonstrates competency in a variety of motor skills and movement patterns.																
Demonstrates competency in 1 or more specialized skills in health-related fitness activities. (S1.H3.L1)	P		P	P	P	P	P	P		P	P	P	P			P
Standard 2. The physically literate individual applies knowledge of concepts, principles, strategies and tactics related to movement and performance.																
Applies the terminology associated with exercise and participation in selected individual-performance activities, dance, net/wall games, target games, aquatics and/or outdoor pursuits. (S2.H1.L1)					E	P		P	P	P	P		P			
Uses movement concepts and principles (e.g., force, motion, rotation) to analyze and improve performance of self and/or others in a selected skill. (S2.H2.L1)						E						P	P			
Standard 3. The physically literate individual demonstrates the knowledge and skills to achieve and maintain a health-enhancing level of physical activity and fitness.																
Discusses the benefits of a physically active lifestyle as it relates to college or career productivity. (S3.H1.L1)	P														P	
Investigates the relationships among physical activity, nutrition and body composition. (S3.H1.L2)															P	
Evaluates the validity of claims made by commercial products and programs pertaining to fitness and a healthy, active lifestyle. (S3.H2.L1)				P												
Participates several times a week in a self-selected lifetime activity, dance or fitness activity outside of the school day. (S3.H6.L1)		E						E						E		
Demonstrates appropriate technique on resistance-training machines and with free weights. (S3.H7.L1)			P	P	P	P	P	P		P	P	P				
Designs and implements a strength and conditioning program that develops balance in opposing muscle groups (agonist/antagonist) and supports a healthy, active lifestyle. (S3.H7.L2)			P	P	P	P			P							
Identifies the different energy systems used in a selected physical activity (e.g., adenosine triphosphate and phosphocreatine, anaerobic glycolysis, aerobic). (S3.H8.L2)													E	P		
Identifies types of strength exercises (isometric, concentric, eccentric) and stretching exercises (static, proprioceptive neuromuscular facilitation [PNF], dynamic) for personal fitness development (e.g., strength, endurance, range of motion). (S3.H9.L1)	P															
Identifies the structure of skeletal muscle and fiber types as they relate to muscle development. (S3.H9.L2)								E	E							
Calculates target heart rate and applies that information to personal fitness plan. (S3.H10.L1)												E				
Develops and maintains a fitness portfolio (assessment scores, goals for improvement, plan of activities for improvement, log of activities being done to reach goals, timeline for improvement). (S3.H11.L2)		P								P				P	P	
Analyzes the components of skill-related fitness in relation to life and career goals, and designs an appropriate fitness program for those goals. (S3.H12.L2)												E	P			

(continued)

RESISTANCE TRAINING MODULE *(CONTINUED)*

Grade-Level Outcomes Addressed, by Lesson	Lessons															
	1	2	3	4	5	6	7	8	9	10	11	12	13	14	15	16
Standard 3. The physically literate individual demonstrates the knowledge and skills to achieve and maintain a health-enhancing level of physical activity and fitness.																
Designs and implements a nutrition plan to maintain an appropriate energy balance for a healthy, active lifestyle. (S3.H13.L1)															P	
Creates a snack plan for before, during and after exercise that addresses nutrition needs for each phase. (S3.H13.L2)															E	
Standard 4. The physically literate individual exhibits responsible personal and social behavior that respects self and others.																
Employs effective self-management skills to analyze barriers and modify physical activity patterns appropriately, as needed. (S4.H1.L1)		E														
Exhibits proper etiquette, respect for others and teamwork while engaging in physical activity and/or social dance. (S4.H2.L1)					P											
Uses communication skills and strategies that promote team or group dynamics. (S4.H3.L1)	E				E		E									P
Solves problems and thinks critically in physical activity and/or dance settings, both as an individual and in groups. (S4.H4.L1)																E
Accepts others' ideas, cultural diversity and body types by engaging in cooperative and collaborative movement projects. (S4.H4.L2)													E			
Applies best practices for participating safely in physical activity, exercise and dance (e.g., injury prevention, proper alignment, hydration, use of equipment, implementation of rules, sun protection). (S4.H5.L1)	E	P	P	E	P	P	P	P		P	P	P	P			P
Standard 5. The physically literate individual recognizes the value of physical activity for health, enjoyment, challenge, self-expression and/or social interaction.																
Analyzes the health benefits of a self-selected physical activity. (S5.H1.L1)			E													
Chooses an appropriate level of challenge to experience success and desire to participate in a self-selected physical activity. (S5.H2.L2)										E	E					E
Selects and participates in physical activities or dance that meet the need for self-expression and enjoyment. (S5.H3.L1)				E												
Identifies the opportunity for social support in a self-selected physical activity or dance. (S5.H4.L1).			E													

P = Primary; E = Embedded

LESSON 1: INTRODUCTION TO SKILL-RELATED FITNESS AND STRETCHING

Grade-Level Outcomes

Primary Outcomes

Physical activity knowledge: Discusses the benefits of a physically active lifestyle as it relates to college or career productivity. (S3.H1.L1)

Fitness knowledge: Identifies types of strength exercises (isometric, concentric, eccentric) and stretching exercises (static, proprioceptive neuromuscular facilitation [PNF], dynamic) for personal fitness development (e.g., strength, endurance, range of motion). (S3.H9.L1)

Fitness activities: Demonstrates competency in 1 or more specialized skills in health-related fitness activities. (S1.H3.L1)

Embedded Outcomes

Working with others: Uses communication skills and strategies that promote team or group dynamics. (S4.H3.L1)

Safety: Applies best practices for participating safely in physical activity, exercise and dance (e.g., injury prevention, proper alignment, hydration, use of equipment, implementation of rules, sun protection). (S4.H5.L1)

Lesson Objectives

The learner will:

- reflect on and discuss the importance and benefits of living a physically active lifestyle.
- identify the components of health-related fitness and how those components are necessary across a lifetime.
- discuss the importance and benefits of flexibility.
- practice dynamic and static stretching to improve flexibility and range of motion (ROM).
- develop a flexibility training plan for improving flexibility and ROM.

Equipment and Materials

- Whiteboard and markers
- Worksheet for collecting stretch names and pencils
- Flexibility plan template

Introduction

Today, we begin a module on different forms of strength and conditioning. We will concentrate on resistance training and skill-related fitness components. By the end of the module, you will be able to develop a resistance-training plan as well as a plan for skill-related fitness. We will start the module by discussing the benefits of physical activity and compare the components of health-related fitness with skill-related fitness. We also will learn about different types and purposes of stretching exercises. Throughout the module, we will highlight exercises you can perform at home with very little equipment.

Instructional Task:
Discussion on Benefits of Physical Activity

■ PRACTICE TASK

Provide a PowerPoint on the importance of and the benefits of physical activity and exercise.

Guiding questions for students:

- Why do we need to participate in physical activity?
- What are some of the benefits achieved through participation in physical activity?
- What is exercise?
- What are some examples of physical activity and exercise that you have performed?
- Is physical activity the same as exercise?

Extension

The discussion can move into the differences between physical activity and exercise, with examples of popular activities in the past and present.

Student Choices/Differentiation

Provide videos and handouts to reinforce material.

What to Look For

Students are able to define physical activity and exercise accurately and relate appropriate examples of each.

Instructional Task: Quick Write

■ PRACTICE TASK

Ask students the following questions and have them respond first on the paper and then share with the class.

Guiding questions for students:

- Name the five components of health-related fitness.
- Identify at least one test that can be used to measure your individual level of health-related fitness.
- Name the six components of skill-related fitness.
- Choose one skill-related fitness component and identify how it could be tested.

Extension

Add more than one assessment tool for each component (students can access the Internet for more options).

Student Choices/Differentiation

Students can work with a partner.

What to Look For

- Students are able to identify all five components of health-related fitness.
- Students can identify the six components of skill-related fitness.
- Students are able to identify at least one assessment tool for each component.

Instructional Task: Class Discussion on Stretching

■ PRACTICE TASK

Remind students that no single test for flexibility can measure total body flexibility. When warming up, dynamic stretches are more appropriate for most activities; static stretching for improving range of motion is best done after the workout.

Guiding questions for students:

- What are the benefits of stretching?
- How often should a person stretch?
- What types of stretching should a person do?
- Does it matter how long a person stretches?
- When should a person stretch?
- Are there any types of stretching that should be avoided?
- What is the difference between static stretching and dynamic stretching?

Have students work in groups to identify a variety of stretches for each body part. Hand out worksheets for students to list specific stretches by name. Allow group members to write the names of stretches on the board under the category of dynamic stretches and static stretches.

Extension

Show students a video of various types of stretches done properly and stretches that need to be avoided.

Student Choices/Differentiation

Students may choose a group representative to write the stretches on the board.

What to Look For

- Students are aware that some stretches can be performed in a static and a dynamic form.
- Students are able to identify multiple stretches for each major muscle area.

Instructional Task: Dynamic Stretching Activities

■ PRACTICE TASK

Have students move into their own space at one end of the gym floor, facing the opposite end. Demonstrate how to perform dynamic stretching while moving from one side of the gym to the other. Use a pre-selected list of dynamic stretches to start.

Extension

After a few stretches, allow students to rotate, demonstrating and leading the class in additional dynamic stretches.

EMBEDDED OUTCOME: S4.H3.L1. If students choose to participate as a group leader, encourage them to provide positive feedback, not unnecessary criticism about someone's lack of flexibility.

Student Choices/Differentiation

- Students move at their own pace when performing dynamic stretches.
- Students can rotate performing as the leader in specific stretches.

What to Look For

Students are attempting to perform each repetition of the stretch in a full range of motion for the joint.

Instructional Task:
Static and Partner-Assisted Stretches

■ PRACTICE TASK

Demonstrate a variety of stretches that one can do with the aid of a partner (e.g., butterfly groin stretch, supine hamstring stretch, chicken-wing chest stretch). Students pair up and practice the stretches.

Have students find a space in the gym to themselves facing the front. Allow students to rotate, leading specific static stretches listed on the board in front of the class.

Refinement

Provide feedback to students on how much pressure to apply to their partners' joints.

EMBEDDED OUTCOME: S4.H5.L1. Remember not to stretch your partner too far the first time and to begin a static hold once she indicates you have achieved her full range of motion.

Student Choices/Differentiation

- Students choose their partners.
- Students can lead the class in specific stretches.

What to Look For

Students are holding each stretch for at least 10 seconds.

Instructional Task: Flexibility Plan

■ PRACTICE TASK

Hand out the flexibility plan worksheets, and ask students to design a dynamic stretching routine to use as a warm-up and a static stretching routine to improve range of motion after working out. They should be able to perform both routines at home. A basic plan should include at least one primary stretch for each muscle group. Have students complete the plan for homework.

Extension

Have students create a plan that has at least two different stretches for each muscle group.

Refinement

If students struggle with creating separate plans for static and dynamic, have them prepare a plan for just the one version that they feel most comfortable with.

Student Choices/Differentiation

- Students choose which exercises to include in their plans.
- Students may work with partners.
- Provide a list of exercises from which students can choose.

What to Look For

Students are placing each stretch correctly in the appropriate column for static and dynamic.

Formal and Informal Assessments

- Flexibility plans
- Exit slip: What are the components of skill-related fitness?

Closure

- Today, we focused on the importance of physical activity and exercise in our lives. Being able to identify various types of physical activity and exercise, along with performing self-assessments, goes a long way in living a healthy lifestyle.
- I encourage you to find time after school each day to participate in some type of physical activity, on your own or with a group.
- Remember, you will need to learn your flexibility routines to do as warm-ups and cool-downs for each class.

Reflection

- Were students generally knowledgeable about the five components of health-related fitness? Skill-related fitness?
- Were they able to distinguish between the testing methods for each component?
- Did students recognize that some stretches could fit into dynamic, static, and partner categories depending on how quickly they were performed?
- Review flexibility plans. Check to see that students have covered all major muscle groups and that plans are appropriate for their purposes.

Homework

- If plans were not completed, have students finish them for homework.
- Students should practice their plans at home so they will be ready to use them in class.
- Choose a physical activity you enjoy, and write down the components of fitness that you need in order to be successful in doing it (health-related and/or skill-related).

Resources

Bompa, T. (2015). *Conditioning young athletes*. Champaign, IL: Human Kinetics.

Corbin, C., & Lindsey, R. (2007). *Fitness for life*. 5th ed. Champaign, IL: Human Kinetics.

HIGH SCHOOL PHYSICAL EDUCATION FLEXIBILITY PLAN SAMPLE WORKSHEET

For each body part, identify the name of at least one dynamic stretch and one static stretch that you can complete in a total-body flexibility development plan. For this assignment, name at least one stretch in the primary body part category. If you can, identify exercises for each subset of body parts.

Primary body part	Subset body part	Dynamic stretch	Static stretch
Ankles	Calves		
	Shins		
Knees	Quads		
	Hams		
Hips	Abductors		
	Adductors		
	Hip flexors		
	Hip extensors		
Shoulders	Chest		
	Back		
	Deltoids		
	Traps		
Elbows	Biceps		
	Triceps		
Wrists	Forearm flexors		
	Forearm extensors		

From L.C. MacDonald, R.J. Doan, and S. Chepko, eds., 2018, *Lesson planning for high school physical education* (Reston, VA: SHAPE America; Champaign, IL: Human Kinetics).

LESSON 2: ASSESSING SELECTED FITNESS COMPONENTS

Grade-Level Outcomes

Primary Outcomes

Assessment and program planning: Develops and maintains a fitness portfolio (e.g., assessment scores, goals for improvement, plan of activities for improvement, log of activities being done to reach goals, timeline for improvement). (S3.H11.L2)

Safety: Applies best practices for participating safely in physical activity, exercise and dance (e.g., injury prevention, proper alignment, hydration, use of equipment, implementation of rules, sun protection). (S4.H5.L1)

Embedded Outcome

Personal responsibility: Employs effective self-management skills to analyze barriers and modify physical activity patterns appropriately, as needed. (S4.H1.L1)

Lesson Objectives

The learner will:

- discuss the previous homework assignment related to physical activity and the components of health-related fitness.
- use basic field tests using the Internet to measure personal fitness levels for the selected fitness categories in a safe manner.
- self-assess current level of fitness in selected components.
- complete a summary analysis of personal fitness scores by identifying strengths and areas for improvement.

Equipment and Materials

- Body-weight scales
- Stadiometer
- Wall height measurement chart
- Data collection sheets
- Calculators
- Stopwatches
- Measuring tapes
- Cones
- Yardsticks
- Chalk
- Rulers
- Sit-and-reach boxes
- Fitnessgram score sheets

Introduction

Today, we'll discuss your homework assignment to see what kind of activities you chose and what types of fitness they require. We also will perform a series of self-assessments for selected components of fitness we will use throughout the module. Some of these are field tests and don't require a lot of special equipment. For each component, you will be able to compare yourself to a standard for other students of similar age and gender. Remember that although you will perform self-assessments and peer assessments, your scores are for your information only. You don't have to compare your results with those of your classmates unless you want to do so. You'll add your assessments to your fitness portfolios.

Instructional Task: Discussion About Homework

■ PRACTICE TASK

In small groups, students share their selected physical activities and the components of fitness they require. Students should discuss each other's ideas and provide feedback to one another.

Extension

Students can share activities with the whole class.

Student Choices/Differentiation

- Students choose their groups.
- Students can volunteer to share with the whole class.

What to Look For

- Students are able to identify the components of fitness in their favorite physical activities.
- Students are providing feedback in a supportive manner.

Instructional Task: Body Composition

Note: Students could complete these assessments in a station format.

■ PRACTICE TASK

Discuss reasons for assessing body composition and its relationship to health. Point out limitations of using body mass index as a measure.

Guiding questions for students:

- What does body composition tell us, and why is it important?
- What are some good points of using body mass index (BMI)?
- What are some limitations?
- What other methods of measuring body composition are you familiar with?

Demonstrate the appropriate method for using the body-weight scale and the stadiometer for accurately measuring height.

Distribute data collection worksheets to each student, and have them rotate through the body-weight and height stations. Body weight should be measured individually in a location that ensures privacy. Students can work in pairs to measure height.

Students perform BMI calculations by hand and identify their personal levels of BMI based on the guidelines.

Extensions

- Have students input data into selected websites to verify their previous calculations and identify their personal levels of BMI to the standards listed.
- Have students compare results to bio-impedance scores or previous scores from Fitnessgram in their fitness portfolios.

EMBEDDED OUTCOME: S4.H1.L1. Remind students that these initial tests are simply a tool to establish a beginning point for future fitness development. All students will have to overcome some type of barrier, either mental, physical, social, or emotional, during their journey into a healthy lifestyle.

Student Choices/Differentiation

Students choose their partners for height measurement.

What to Look For

- Students are engaged in the discussion.
- Students can identify appropriate uses for BMI.

Instructional Task: Shoulder Flexibility

■ PRACTICE TASK

Discuss the specificity of flexibility. Demonstrate the appropriate way to test shoulder flexibility using the back-scratch method with a partner. Have students warm up.

Hand out data collection sheets for flexibility, and allow students to evaluate their flexibility in both shoulders.

Guiding questions for students:

- Were you equally flexible on both sides?
- If not, what explanation would you give?

Refinement

It's normal for students to feel slight discomfort during the assessment, but make sure they do not push the stretch to the point of pain.

Student Choices/Differentiation

Students choose their partners.

What to Look For

- Students are stretching fully —but not straining—during the assessment.
- Partners are assisting one another.

Instructional Task: Lower Back and Hamstring Flexibility

■ PRACTICE TASK

Demonstrate how to appropriately perform the back-saver sit-and-reach test before allowing students to perform the test on their partners.

Students follow protocol and record scores.

Extensions

- Have students use the Internet to identify additional field-based flexibility and range-of-motion (ROM) assessment tools and write them down on the worksheet.
- Provide students with materials to perform additional tests for measuring flexibility. Students collect that data on themselves with their partners.

Student Choices/Differentiation

Students choose their partners.

What to Look For

- Knees stay straight during the reach.
- Students are reaching and holding the stretch.

Instructional Task: Muscular Strength and Endurance

■ PRACTICE TASK

Review the differences between muscular strength and muscular endurance.

Demonstrate proper technique for a simple wall-sit test (measuring muscular endurance) and the broad jump (muscular strength, power). Remind students to do their dynamic stretching warm-ups before the assessment.

Pass out data collection sheets, and allow students to rotate through each station with a partner. After completing the assessment, students do their static stretching routines as a cool-down.

Guiding questions for students:

- What test does Fitnessgram use to assess muscular strength and endurance of the abdominals?
- What test does Fitnessgram use to assess muscular strength and endurance of the upper body?
- Would you expect to see a relationship between any of your Fitnessgram scores and the tests we did today? Why or why not?

Extension

Allow students to explore the Internet to identify additional field tests for evaluating muscular strength and muscular endurance and write their findings on the worksheet.

Student Choices/Differentiation

Students choose their partners.

What to Look For

- Students can identify appropriate measurement tests for both muscular strength and muscular endurance.
- Students are using proper form and technique during fitness testing.

Formal and Informal Assessments

- Scores for each of the components
- Exit slip: What is body composition, and why is it important?

Closure

- During this portion of the module, we explored various ways to self-assess your fitness level for three components of fitness. You can perform many of these activities without purchasing any major equipment.
- Your assessment scores will become part of your fitness portfolio and can be used as a baseline for developing fitness plans.
- We aren't focusing on cardiorespiratory endurance in this module, but if we wanted to assess that component of health-related fitness, how could we do it?
- Next class, we'll learn about exercises that use your body weight as resistance.

Reflection

- Were students successful in finding additional field tests for each component, or did they need additional guidance?
- Did students comprehend that each area of fitness can be measured in simple terms without expensive tools and equipment?
- Review exit slips to check for understanding.
- Review test scores to determine where each student is in terms of the components.

Homework

- Compare your fitness scores to criteria or standards for each test performed.
- Write a summary of how you performed on each test, what your current fitness level for each component is, and how much you liked or disliked the testing procedure. You will add this summary to your fitness portfolios.
- Now that you have some flexibility scores, modify your flexibility plan as needed.

Resources

Corbin, C., & Lindsey, R. (2007). *Fitness for life*. 5th ed. Champaign, IL: Human Kinetics.

Internet keyword search: "body composition," "flexibility measurement," "muscular strength tests," "muscular endurance tests"

LESSON 3: DESIGNING AN AT-HOME BODY-WEIGHT FITNESS PROGRAM

Grade-Level Outcomes

Primary Outcomes

Fitness knowledge: Designs and implements a strength and conditioning program that develops balance in opposing muscle groups (agonist/antagonist) and supports a healthy, active lifestyle. (S3.H7.L2)

Fitness activities: Demonstrates competency in 1 or more specialized skills in health-related fitness activities. (S1.H3.L1)

Safety: Applies best practices for participating safely in physical activity, exercise and dance (e.g., injury prevention, proper alignment, hydration, use of equipment, implementation of rules, sun protection). (S4.H5.L1)

Embedded Outcomes

Health: Analyzes the health benefits of a self-selected physical activity. (S5.H1.L1)

Social interaction: Identifies the opportunity for social support in a self-selected physical activity or dance. (S5.H4.L1).

Engages in physical activity: Participates several times a week in a self-selected lifetime activity, dance or fitness activity outside of the school day. (S3.H6.L1)

Lesson Objectives

The learner will:

- identify appropriate exercises to stimulate muscular strength and muscular endurance using only body weight.
- recall basic muscle groups in the human body.
- develop a basic workout program that can be performed outside of class.
- supervise and spot peers during workout routines.

Equipment and Materials

- Anatomical chart
- Peer assessment rubrics
- Basic workout program templates
- Muscle group and exercise worksheets
- Clipboards
- Whiteboard easel
- Worksheets for listing exercises

Introduction

Today, we will explore various options of resistance training that you can perform at home with no equipment. You can attain lifetime fitness without going to a gym or spending money on equipment, if you know what do to. First, we will explore the various exercises; then you will be paired with a partner to demonstrate to each other how to perform the exercises. Partners evaluate each other on the proper technique. Then, we'll design a workout plan for one week using only the exercises listed on your worksheets.

Instructional Task:
Discussion on Body Weight as Resistance

▪ PRACTICE TASK

Lead the class in a discussion of basic workout exercises that require only body weight.

Guiding questions for students:

- What activities have you performed that might be considered exercise?
- What are the benefits of performing weight resistance training?
- How often should you perform weight resistance training?

Extension

Discuss the overload and frequency, intensity, time, and type (FITT) principle in relation to resistance training, particularly frequency and intensity. Include the importance of recovery.

Student Choices/Differentiation

Students perform activity examples and explain why they believe this activity can be considered exercise.

What to Look For

- Students are able to come up with the benefits of performing weight resistance exercise.
- Students are able to describe the FITT principle as it applies to weight resistance programming.

Instructional Task: Total-Body Exercise Compilation

▪ PRACTICE TASK

Students work with a partner to identify the muscle groups associated with the lower body and the upper body.

Students identify at least two exercises for each muscle group of the lower body and two for each group of the upper body. They include directions and critical elements.

Extension

Students can use the Internet to research additional exercises for each muscle group.

Refinement

Be sure that students are identifying exercises that are appropriate for each muscle group.

Student Choices/Differentiation

- Students select their partners.
- Students provide additional options for each muscle group.

What to Look For

- Exercises match the muscle group indicated.
- Exercises have directions for performance and cues for evaluation.

Instructional Task: Dynamic Warm-Up

▪ PRACTICE TASK

Students perform the dynamic stretching routines that they planned in Lesson 1.

Refinement

Ask students to adjust their plans if their assessment scores indicated an area of weakness.

Student Choices/Differentiation

- Students have designed their warm-ups.
- Students may use an index card with the exercises on it if they have trouble remembering the exercises.

What to Look For

- Warm-ups are raising students' heart rates and causing them to break a sweat.
- Students are performing the exercises correctly.
- Exercises are addressing all the major muscle groups.

Instructional Task: Peer Evaluation

■ PRACTICE TASK

Discuss how to evaluate another student's performance during an exercise by using the critical elements. For example, for push-ups, hands should be straight under the shoulders and the core.

Allow students to practice body-weight resistance activities while being evaluated by their partners.

EMBEDDED OUTCOME: S5.H4.L1. Remind students to provide positive feedback and encouragement while their "client" is performing each skill.

Student Choices/Differentiation

Students select the exercises.

What to Look For

- Students are using proper form and following the directions for the exercise.
- Peers are providing feedback on form and technique.

Instructional Task: Body-Weight Training Program

■ PRACTICE TASK

Students use the template to create a three-day-a-week at-home body-weight training program using a variety of exercises (stipulate the number of exercises) throughout the week. They use data from Lesson 2 for a baseline, where appropriate. Students must include exercises that develop opposing muscle groups.

Extensions

- Have students select a new partner, and allow them to guide the new partner through the workout listed on their body-weight training program, performing one set of each exercise.
- Students may go through their routines multiple times in one day.
- Students cool down with their static stretching routines.

EMBEDDED OUTCOME: S5.H1.L1. Ask students to analyze and share the health benefits of their selected exercises.

Student Choices/Differentiation

- Have examples of total-body weight resistance plans available for students to view.
- Students decide on the length of their plans (one day or multiple days).
- Students may choose to create a four-day-a-week split routine (two upper-body workouts and two lower-body workouts).

What to Look For

- Programs contain at least one exercise for each muscle group.
- Students are maintaining proper form during exercises.
- Students are giving maximum effort.
- Peers are providing feedback and positive reinforcement while supervising exercises.
- Students are performing exercises with a high level of effort.

Formal and Informal Assessments

- Peer evaluation rubrics for exercise technique
- Basic workout plans for three days of body-weight training

Closure

- You have completed an assignment to add to your fitness portfolio, an at-home body-weight workout program. We have discussed the benefits of a weight resistance program, identified specific exercises for each muscle group, and created a general workout program for use at home.
- Starting today, I want you to keep a log of your body weight exercises as well as any other physical activity you do outside of class.
- Next class, you will learn about using weight-training machines for resistance training.

Reflection

- Did students demonstrate a strong understanding of the connection between the exercises and the specific muscle groups worked during the routine?
- Do students have a general idea about how to create a basic total-body fitness plan?
- Can students effectively evaluate form and technique during exercise?
- Review workout plans to see if students are on track or if they need additional information or clarifications.

Homework

- Continue to practice technique and form for the body-weight exercises in your program.
- Record your repetitions and exercises in a log. Include your other physical activity done outside of class. Remember that although this module doesn't focus on cardio, you should still be getting that component outside of class to meet the physical activity guidelines. (Embedded outcome: S3.H6.L1)

Resources

Haff, G. Gregory, and Triplett, N. Travis. (2017). *Essentials for strength training and conditioning.* 4th ed. Champaign, IL: Human Kinetics.

Internet keyword search: "body-weight workout plan," "body-weight training"

HIGH SCHOOL RESISTANCE-TRAINING TEMPLATE FOR AT-HOME TOTAL-BODY BODY-WEIGHT WORKOUT

Use this template to design an at-home body-weight workout plan for one week, essentially three separate days. Try to list different exercises for each body part on successive days. As before, at a minimum, you can list exercises for the primary body part; including exercises for the subset of muscle groups is considered a bonus.

Primary body part	Subset body parts	Day 1	Day 2	Day 3
Ankle	Calves			
	Shins			
Knees	Quads			
	Hams			
Hips	Abductors			
	Adductors			
	Hip flexors			
	Hip extensors			
Shoulders	Chest			
	Back			
	Deltoids			
	Traps			
Elbows	Biceps			
	Triceps			
Wrists	Forearm flexors			
	Forearm extensors			

From L.C. MacDonald, R.J. Doan, and S. Chepko, eds., 2018, *Lesson planning for high school physical education* (Reston, VA: SHAPE America; Champaign, IL: Human Kinetics).

LESSON 4: SMALL APPARATUSES

Grade-Level Outcomes

Primary Outcomes

Fitness activities: Demonstrates competency in 1 or more specialized skills in health-related fitness activities. (S1.H3.L1)

Fitness knowledge: Designs and implements a strength and conditioning program that develops balance in opposing muscle groups (agonist/antagonist) and supports a healthy, active lifestyle. (S3.H7.L2)

Physical activity knowledge: Evaluates the validity of claims made by commercial products and programs pertaining to fitness and a healthy, active lifestyle. (S3.H2.L2)

Fitness knowledge: Demonstrates appropriate technique on resistance-training machines and with free weights. (S3.H7.L1)

Embedded Outcomes

Self-expression & enjoyment: Selects and participates in physical activities or dance that meet the need for self-expression and enjoyment. (S5.H3.L1)

Safety: Applies best practices for participating safely in physical activity, exercise and dance (e.g., injury prevention, proper alignment, hydration, use of equipment, implementation of rules, sun protection). (S4.H5.L1)

Lesson Objectives

The learner will:

- identify and discuss fads and myths associated with fitness products.
- demonstrate appropriate technique for at least one upper-body and one lower-body exercise using a small apparatus.
- develop a workout plan that addresses opposing muscle groups while using only small apparatus equipment.

Equipment and Materials

- Medicine balls of various weights
- Stability balls of various sizes
- Exercise bands of different resistance
- Dumbbells of various weights
- Body bars of various weights
- Specialty bars for plate-loaded weights
- Jump ropes
- Kettlebells
- BOSU balls
- Balance pods
- Index cards
- Pens
- Small apparatus data collection worksheets
- Small apparatus workout plan templates

Introduction

Today, we're continuing our theme of creating workouts that can be done at home. As you can see from the collection of materials in front of you, you are going to explore different ways you can work out with small equipment that doesn't cost much. Before the physical activity, let's discuss fads and fallacies and myths about working out, trends in fitness equipment, and workout protocol. Once we conclude the discussion, you will join three others in your assigned group and move to the assortment of pre-selected fitness equipment. First, you will identify the names of the equipment and, as a group, determine at least one exercise for each major muscle group that you can work out using that particular piece of equipment. At the end of the day, you will turn in your list of exercises for every station.

Instructional Task: Class Pre-Test and Discussion

■ PRACTICE TASK

Prepare a list of fitness fads and facts, and have students respond on index cards whether each statement is a fad or a fact.

Here are some examples: You can spot-reduce fat; no pain, no gain; weight resistance training does not burn fat; carbohydrates are bad.

Review each statement, and discuss how and why it is a fad or a fact.

Extensions

- Have students identify other concepts they believe to be fad or fact and discuss their implications.
- If time permits, show a brief video on fads and fallacies in fitness.

Student Choices/Differentiation

- Have examples for students to view if needed.
- Students can work in small groups or pairs.

What to Look For

- Students are aware of the fads and fallacies related to fitness products and activities.
- Students can identify the principles behind the fallacies.

Instructional Task: Small Apparatus Stations

■ PRACTICE TASK

After students complete their dynamic warm-ups, have them separate into groups and move to a station where one type of small apparatus is located. Small apparatus equipment can include stability balls, medicine balls, kettlebells, elastic bands, and BOSU balls.

Have students identify at least one exercise for each major muscle group using the selected small apparatus.

Rotate stations after a set time.

Extensions

- Students can identify more than one exercise for a muscle group.
- Students can identify an exercise that engages more than one muscle group.

Refinement

Provide feedback to students about going through the full range of motion in the exercises.

EMBEDDED OUTCOME: S5.H3.L1. Instruct students to be creative when experimenting with the new equipment. See if they can make an exercise that combines two or more body parts. If students enjoy the new exercises, they will be more likely to continue to do them.

Student Choices/Differentiation

Students develop their own combinations.

What to Look For

- All the muscle groups are being used.
- The exercises listed are appropriate for the selected muscle group.

Instructional Task: Small Apparatus Workout Plan

■ PRACTICE TASK

Provide students with index cards, and ask them to create a total-body workout plan using various small apparatus equipment. Plans should address opposing muscle groups.

Extensions

- Have students create a three-day workout plan.
- Have students create a four-day push–pull routine or a five-day split routine using only small apparatus equipment.

Student Choices/Differentiation

- Students can work with a partner.
- Have examples of total-body workout plans available for students to view.

What to Look For

The total-body workouts include all major muscle groups.

Instructional Task: Small Apparatus Workout Practice

■ PRACTICE TASK

After students perform their dynamic warm-ups, have them select an index card from the stack and participate in the workout program on the card.

Students perform one set of 12 to 15 reps of each exercise. Students will cool down with their static stretching routines.

EMBEDDED OUTCOME: S4.H5.L1 Remind students about safety, proper form and technique, and gym etiquette in cleaning the equipment before leaving the station.

Student Choices/Differentiation

Students select the workout card they are interested in.

What to Look For

- Students are using proper form.
- Students are following appropriate safety and etiquette rules.

Formal and Informal Assessments

- Index card responses on fads and fallacies
- Workout plans for small apparatuses
- Exit slip: What were the strengths and weaknesses of the workout plan on the index card?

Closure

- In this lesson, we have discussed how some small apparatus equipment is good while others are more likely a fad.
- Many commercials suggest that their equipment is the best product out there for developing fitness.
- Knowing what pieces of equipment are fads can help you make better decisions when purchasing fitness products.
- Understanding how and when to use various types of equipment can have many benefits, including working out from home, using equipment at the gym, and purchasing appropriate fitness equipment.

Reflection

- Did students perform the same exercises with the small apparatuses or did they try to create new and different exercises?
- Did students have enough time at each station to allow them to explore various exercise options?

Homework

- Take the index card home and review the workout program. Write a paragraph on your experience going through the workout, and describe how it felt.
- Record your body-weight exercise repetitions and exercises in a log. Include your physical activity outside of class.

Resources

Cissik, J., & Dawes, J. (2015). *Maximum interval training.* Champaign, IL: Human Kinetics.

Internet keyword search: "fitness fads," "fitness fallacies"

LESSON 5: LOWER-BODY MACHINES

Grade-Level Outcomes

Primary Outcomes

Fitness activities: Demonstrates competency in 1 or more specialized skills in health-related fitness activities. (S1.H3.L1)

Fitness knowledge: Demonstrates appropriate technique on resistance-training machines and with free weights. (S3.H7.L1)

Fitness knowledge: Designs and implements a strength and conditioning program that develops balance in opposing muscle groups (agonist/antagonist) and supports a healthy, active lifestyle. (S3.H7.L2)

Safety: Applies best practices for participating safely in physical activity, exercise and dance (e.g., injury prevention, proper alignment, hydration, use of equipment, implementation of rules, sun protection). (S4.H5.L1)

Rules & etiquette: Exhibits proper etiquette, respect for others and teamwork while engaging in physical activity and/or social dance. (S4.H2.L1)

Embedded Outcomes

Working with others: Uses communication skills and strategies that promote team or group dynamics. (S4.H3.L1)

Movement concepts, principles & knowledge: Applies the terminology associated with exercise and participation in selected individual-performance activities, dance, net/wall games, target games, aquatics and/or outdoor pursuits appropriately. (S2.H1.L1)

Lesson Objectives

The learner will:

- demonstrate proper safety practices for using machines, spotting during free weights, and moving around the room during physical activity.
- exhibit proper etiquette in the gym.
- demonstrate proper form and technique for two different machines for the lower body.
- calculate the 10-rep-max weight a peer should use.
- identify lower-body exercises with agonist/antagonist pairings.

Equipment and Materials

- Copies of classroom rules and gym etiquette
- Lower-body exercise machines (identified by name)
- Peer assessment grading form and rubrics
- 10-rep-max progression worksheets
- Lifting straps
- Lifting belts

Introduction

How are you doing on your at-home resistance routine? In today's class, we'll start your introduction to the weight room, starting with machines for lower-body exercises. I will review safety procedures, provide directions on how to adjust the machines, give cues for performing the activities correctly, and identify common mistakes you might see along the way. In addition, you will determine your 10-repetition max for selected machines.

Instructional Task: Safety Demonstrations

■ PRACTICE TASK

Review basic safety precautions and spotting technique. Point out where errors in safety can occur. Students should practice spotting for a selected lift.

Refinement

Since not all students will be familiar with the equipment in the weight room, everyone should attempt to pick up the bars and plates so they get a feel for how much they weigh and the amount of effort needed to handle each piece and not drop it.

EMBEDDED OUTCOME: S4.H3.L1. Spotting is essential in lifting. Students should focus on safety and also building trust through clear and supportive communication.

Student Choices/Differentiation

Students choose their partners.

What to Look For

- Students are engaged in the discussion.
- Students are using correct spotting technique.
- Partners are communicating with each other.

Instructional Task:
Gym Etiquette Demonstrations and Group Discussion

■ PRACTICE TASK

Go over the guidelines for etiquette and how they are applied while on the gym floor.

Guiding questions for students:

- What is etiquette?
- What is meant by the term *gym etiquette*?

Student Choices/Differentiation

Have examples ready for students to view.

What to Look For

- Students are identifying gym etiquette events and activities.
- Students are asking good questions.

Instructional Task:
Demonstration of Proper Technique and Adjusting Machines

■ PRACTICE TASK

Demonstrate technique and machine adjustments for selected equipment.

Students rotate from station to station, practicing proper technique on lower-body machines with light resistance. Students should try machines for all major muscle groups. Stations can include leg extension, leg curl, leg press, calf press, hip adduction, hip abduction, hip flexion, and hip extension machines.

Students should focus on aligning their joints with the colored dots on the machines, making sure all adjusted seats and back rests are situated so there is no additional movement or space between the body and the pad.

Partners spot as needed.

Student Choices/Differentiation

- Experienced students may perform the exercises using free weights in place of machines.
- Inexperienced students may perform body-weight exercises if they are uncomfortable on the machines.
- Students choose their partners.

What to Look For

- Students are using proper technique and reviewing the safety components of each exercise.
- Students are adjusting the machines when needed.

Instructional Task: Predicting 10-Rep Max

■ PRACTICE TASK

Discuss the protocol for predicting max weight by using the 10-rep-max format. Students complete their dynamic warm-up routines before starting the 10-max-rep protocol.

Students follow the protocol for establishing a 10-max rep for the leg press and then cool down with their static stretching routines.

Refinement

Instruct students not to increase the weight too much from one set to the next. If the weight changes too much, it result in injury.

Student Choices/Differentiation

Students choose either the leg press or back squat for the test.

What to Look For

- Students supervise their peers and monitor for proper technique.
- Students use the protocol to proceed with the test.
- Students attempt to perform the exercise with maximum effort.

Instructional Task: Lower-Body Exercise Discussion

■ PRACTICE TASK

In pairs, students list all the lower-body machine exercises that might be included in a workout program, naming the exercises and the muscle groups that are worked.

Guiding questions for students:

- What are the benefits of using machines for resistance training as opposed to free weights?
- What are some of the disadvantages of using machines?
- Why is it important to know what your estimated max rep is?
- How can you implement the overload principle using machines?

EMBEDDED OUTCOME: S2.H1.L1. Once students create the list, have them group the exercises into pairs of exercises for opposing muscle groups (agonist/antagonist).

Student Choices/Differentiation

- Students choose their partners.
- Students decide which exercises to include.

What to Look For

- Students can identify the purpose of the different machines.
- Students are able to group agonist/antagonist exercises correctly.

Formal and Informal Assessments

- Discussion of gym etiquette and rules
- Student demonstration of appropriate technique for lower-body exercises
- Assessments of lower-body strength
- Exercise lists

Closure

- Today, we reviewed important safety practices and etiquette for the weight room.
- We examined a variety of lower-body exercises using machines and estimated your maximum strength in a safe manner.
- This process will be repeated using upper-body machines next.
- At the completion of these two lessons, you will have a greater understanding of the types of exercises you will want to include in your workout plans and programs.

Reflection

- Were students comfortable using free-weight exercises as opposed to the machines?
- Did students understand the overall benefit of the 10-rep max-format for safety?

Homework

- Taking your max-rep results into account, write down the exercises you might use for the muscle groups you think you need to strengthen.
- Record your body-weight exercise repetitions and exercises in a log. Include your physical activity outside of class.

Resources

Bompa, T. (2015). *Conditioning young athletes*. Champaign, IL: Human Kinetics.

School rules and policy for student behavior and conduct

Internet keyword search: "top 10 rules of lifting safety," "weight-training and weight-lifting safety"

LESSON 6: UPPER-BODY MACHINES

Grade-Level Outcomes

Primary Outcomes

Fitness activities: Demonstrates competency in 1 or more specialized skills in health-related fitness activities. (S1.H3.L1)

Fitness knowledge: Demonstrates appropriate technique on resistance-training machines and with free weights. (S3.H7.L1)

Fitness knowledge: Designs and implements a strength and conditioning program that develops balance of opposing muscle groups (agonist/antagonist) and supports a healthy, active lifestyle. (S3.H7.L2)

Safety: Applies best practices for participating safely in physical activity, exercise and dance (e.g., injury prevention, proper alignment, hydration, use of equipment, implementation of rules, sun protection). (S4.H5.L1)

Embedded Outcome

Movement concepts, principles & knowledge: Uses movement concepts and principles (e.g., force, motion, rotation) to analyze and improve performance of self and/or others in a selected skill. (S2.H2.L1)

Lesson Objectives

The learner will:

- demonstrate proper form and technique for two different machines for the upper body.
- teach an upper-body machine exercise to a partner and evaluate the partner's movement after practice.
- calculate the 10-rep-max weight a peer should use.
- identify upper-body exercises in agonist/antagonist pairings.

Equipment and Materials

- Upper-body exercise machines (identified by name)
- Peer assessment grading form and rubrics
- 10-rep-max progression worksheets
- Upper-body workout plan templates
- Lifting straps
- Lifting belts

Introduction

Before we start on today's assignment, turn in your workout logs from the lower-body machines workout. For today's activity, I will go over each of the machines for the upper body, providing directions on how to adjust the machines, giving cues for performing the activities correctly, and identifying common mistakes you may experience along the way. In addition, you will help determine the 10-rep max for the bench press machine. Once we have been through all the machines, you will take your partner through a total-body dynamic warm-up and then through an upper-body workout using the machines. Remember, you must describe the machine and what body parts it works, perform a demonstration, and provide instruction of what NOT to do, or what might be incorrect form. Once you feel comfortable, get my attention and I will assess your ability to teach and supervise during your partner's performance.

Instructional Task: Demonstration of Proper Technique

■ **PRACTICE TASK**

Demonstrate proper technique and adjustments on a variety of upper-body machines. The upper-body machines can include chest press and chest fly, lat pull-down, seated row, military press, deltoid flys, seated biceps curl, seated dips, and the hyperextension machine. Students make sure that all body parts are making contact with the pads and that each joint is located in line with the colored dots at each juncture.

Students practice techniques and safety on upper-body machines using light resistance.

Student Choices/Differentiation

- Students select the machines that they want to use.
- Students determine time for testing based on comfort level.
- Experienced students may use free weights in place of machines.
- Inexperienced students may perform body-weight exercises if they are uncomfortable on the machines.

What to Look For

- Students are using proper technique and reviewing the safety components of each exercise.
- Students are adjusting the machines when needed.

Instructional Task: Peer Assessment of Performance in Upper-Body Machines

■ **PRACTICE TASK**

Students perform their dynamic stretching routines. Partners work together to review the correct procedures for each exercise. Students evaluate the technique of a partner on at least one upper-body machine using a rubric.

EMBEDDED OUTCOME: S2.H2.L1. Partners provide feedback on technique to help improve performance on a selected exercise.

Student Choices/Differentiation

Student selects which exercise to assess.

What to Look For

- Students are providing supportive, corrective feedback.
- Students are critiquing technique accurately.

Instructional Task: Predicting Maximum Effort

■ **PRACTICE TASK**

Partners follow protocol for establishing a 10-max rep for the bench press. Students cool down with their static stretching routines.

Extension

Experienced students can use the bench press or machine chest press.

Refinement

Instruct students not to increase the weight too much from one set to the next. If the weight changes too much, it might become a safety issue for the lifter and result in injury.

Student Choices/Differentiation

Students choose their partners.

What to Look For

- Students supervise their peers and monitor for proper technique.
- Students use the protocol to proceed with the test.
- Students attempt to perform the exercise with maximum effort.

Instructional Task: Upper-Body Exercise Discussion

■ PRACTICE TASK

Review overload and the FITT principle. Have students work together to create a list of upper-body machine exercises by name and the muscles they work. Students then pair agonist/antagonist exercises.

Have pairs turn in a list of all the exercises they performed during class. Review the lists at the end of the day so students can add new exercises they haven't performed to their workout lists.

Extension

Have students find additional exercises for the upper body online and include them in their workout plans.

Student Choices/Differentiation

- Students choose their partners.
- Students find alternative exercises online.

What to Look For

- Exercises work just the upper body.
- Students are identifying the machines and exercises correctly.

Formal and Informal Assessments

- Student demonstration of appropriate technique for upper-body exercises
- Peer evaluation of movement technique using supervisor protocol
- Assessment of upper-body strength using the 10-rep-max protocol
- Exercise lists

Closure

- Today, we examined a variety of upper-body exercises using machines.
- You were able to demonstrate proper technique and the ability to effectively evaluate the technique of others.
- Finally, you learned how to estimate your maximum strength in a safe manner.
- Next time, you will learn how to use free weights for resistance training.

Reflection

- Did students follow the 10-rep-max protocol better than with the lower body?
- Are they able to determine opposing muscle groups and how to work them?

Homework

- Taking your assessment results into account, write down which exercises you would use to address upper-body weaknesses.
- Record your body-weight exercise repetitions and exercises in a log. Include your physical activity outside of class.

Resources

Bompa, T. (2015). *Conditioning young athletes*. Champaign, IL: Human Kinetics.

Internet keyword search: "resistance machines," "10 rep max protocol," "upper body conditioning"

LESSON 7: PUSH–PULL METHOD FOR FREE WEIGHTS

Grade-Level Outcomes

Primary Outcomes

Fitness activities: Demonstrates competency in 1 or more specialized skills in health-related fitness activities. (S1.H3.L1)

Fitness knowledge: Demonstrates appropriate technique on resistance-training machines and with free weights. (S3.H7.L1)

Safety: Applies best practices for participating safely in physical activity, exercise and dance (e.g., injury prevention, proper alignment, hydration, use of equipment, implementation of rules, sun protection). (S4.H5.L1)

Movement concepts, principles, & knowledge: Applies the terminology associated with exercise and participation in selected individual-performance activities, dance, net/wall games, target games, aquatics and/or outdoor pursuits). (S2.H1.L1)

Embedded Outcome

Working with others: Uses communication skills and strategies that promote team or group dynamics. (S4.H3.L1)

Lesson Objectives

The learner will:

- discuss why it's important to use a variety of workout systems and know about different types of workout equipment for maintaining one's motivation to exercise.
- review previous material on spotting and identify different techniques for dumbbells.
- use guided discovery with a partner to explore different exercise options for each body part using free weights.
- practice lifting technique with free weights.

Equipment and Materials

- Barbells and collars
- Plate weights
- Bumper plates
- Dumbbells of various sizes

Introduction

Now that you have a foundation of exercises using machines and pin-loaded devices, I will expand your program development. The tools for working out for this lesson are free weights, including the bar and dumbbells. For those of you not ready for true free-weight exercises, you may use bumper plates instead of heavier weights. We also will move toward an advanced workout program called a split routine. The split routine for today is known as the push–pull method. Let's start with a discussion on workout programs and routines.

Instructional Task: Discussion on Workout Methods

■ **PRACTICE TASK**

Lead the class in a discussion about using free weights and the push–pull split system of training.

Guiding questions for students:

- What are the advantages of using free weights over machines?
- What are the disadvantages?
- What is a split routine?
- What are the benefits of using a split routine during weight-training programs?
- How are split systems organized?

Student Choices/Differentiation

Provide examples of a split routine for students to look at.

What to Look For

- Students are able to recall various workout programs.
- Students are asking good questions.

Instructional Task: Safety Demonstrations

■ PRACTICE TASK

Review the basic safety precautions and spotting technique covered earlier in the module. Emphasize the importance of alignment, technique, spotting, and staying within your limits. Students should practice spotting for selected lifts.

EMBEDDED OUTCOME: S4.H3.L1 Spotting is essential in lifting and particularly in using free weights. Students should focus on safety and also building trust through clear and supportive communication.

Student Choices/Differentiation

Students choose their partners.

What to Look For

- Students are engaged in the discussion.
- Students are using correct spotting technique.
- Partners are communicating with each other.

Instructional Task: Guided Discovery for Free Weights

■ PRACTICE TASK

Have students work with a partner to identify three exercises for the lower body and three exercises for the upper body. Students should move from station to station, trying the free-weight exercises.

Have students write the names of the exercises and indicate whether they are push or pull exercises. Push exercises for the lower body include leg press, leg extension, toe press; pull exercises include leg curl, adduction exercises, and hip flexion exercises. Push exercises for the upper body include chest press, military press, incline chest press; pull exercises include lat pulls, seated rows, and upright rows.

Extension

Students can use the Internet to check whether their exercises are push or pull.

Refinement

Stop the class and reinforce any etiquette or safety concerns if needed.

Student Choices/Differentiation

- Students select new partners.
- Students share ideas with other groups.

What to Look For

- Students can correctly identify both lower-body and upper-body exercises.
- Students can distinguish between push and pull exercises.

Instructional Task: Free-Weight Practice

■ PRACTICE TASK

Students perform their dynamic warm-ups. With a partner to spot, have students try one set of 10 repetitions for each of the exercises they selected. Remind students to start with light weights. Students cool down with their static stretching routines.

Guiding questions for students:

- When should you be inhaling? Exhaling?
- Why should you hold or pause slightly at full extension or flexion?

Refinement

Provide feedback about proper alignment while lifting to prevent injury.

Student Choices/Differentiation

- Students choose their partners.
- Students can use dumbbells or the bar without weights if they are not comfortable adding plates.

What to Look For

- Students are attentive spotters.
- Students are using proper technique for each exercise.

Formal and Informal Assessments

Exit slip: Name at least one exercise that is push and one that is pull for the same joint.

Closure

- The push–pull training program is one of many used by experienced weight trainers. It has a few advantages over the basic total-body workout in that you can spend more time working on specific body parts.
- Just remember when doing this type of workout that you have to go a little slower between the sets and exercises since this routine isn't necessarily about muscular endurance or aerobic training.

Reflection

- Are students demonstrating an understanding of how to generate a workout plan and program?
- Is information from the previous programming progressions being demonstrated in the new format?

Homework

- Record your body-weight exercise repetitions and exercises in your log. Include your physical activity outside of class and turn it in next class.
- Look up unilateral lifting exercises on the Internet to be ready for next class.

Resources

Haff, G. Gregory, and Triplett, N. Travis. (2017). *Essentials for strength training and conditioning.* 4th ed. Champaign, IL: Human Kinetics.

Internet keyword search: "push–pull routines," "weightlifting push–pull routines," "upper-body push–pull exercises," "lower-body push–pull exercises"

LESSON 8: UNILATERAL EXERCISES

Grade-Level Outcomes

Primary Outcomes

Movement concepts, principles, & knowledge: Applies the terminology associated with exercise and participation in selected individual-performance activities, dance, net/wall games, target games, aquatics and/or outdoor pursuits). (S2.H1.L1)

Fitness activities: Demonstrates competency in 1 or more specialized skills in health-related fitness activities. (S1.H3.L1)

Fitness knowledge: Demonstrates appropriate technique on resistance-training machines and with free weights. (S3.H7.L1)

Safety: Applies best practices for participating safely in physical activity, exercise and dance (e.g., injury prevention, proper alignment, hydration, use of equipment, implementation of rules, sun protection). (S4.H5.L1)

Embedded Outcome

Fitness knowledge: Identifies the structure of skeletal muscle and fiber types as they relate to muscle development. (S3.H9.L2)

Lesson Objectives

The learner will:

- describe various workout routines that are progressively more difficult.
- identify appropriate exercises for each body part through the use of free-weight equipment.
- apply the terminology associated with exercises and equipment appropriately.
- practice unilateral exercises safely.

Equipment and Materials

- Dumbbells of various weights
- Kettlebells of various weights
- Elastic bands of various strengths
- Pin-loaded machines
- Cable-based machines
- Unilateral upper-body worksheet
- Unilateral lower-body worksheet

Introduction

To keep a workout routine from becoming dull and boring, you should always expand and experiment with how you perform certain exercises. In today's lesson, we will perform unilateral exercises for a change of pace. Unilateral is a term you that looked up for homework. Can anyone tell me what it means? Yes—unilateral exercises are those performed with only one side of the body, as in biceps curls with just the right arm. When you finish your set with the right arm, you perform the same exercise with the left arm. Exercising this way has some advantages over other training methods, and we will start class by discussing those advantages as well as some disadvantages.

Instructional Task: Class Discussion

■ **PRACTICE TASK**

Lead the class in discussing unilateral training.

Guiding questions for students:

- What does the term *unilateral* mean?
- What are some advantages of using a unilateral exercise?
- What are some disadvantages of using unilateral training during a workout?

Extension

The discussion can move into compound exercises and single-joint exercises.

Student Choices/Differentiation

Provide handouts with examples of compound exercises and single-joint exercises.

What to Look For

- Students are able to describe exercises as single joint and compound correctly.
- Students are engaged in the discussion.

Instructional Task: Unilateral Upper Body

■ PRACTICE TASK

Have students complete their dynamic warm-ups. Students then pair up and move around the room to each upper-body station and perform the exercises on one side of the body at a time. For upper-body exercises, the basic repetition range is 8 to 12.

Refinement

Advise students that using only one side of the body during free-weight and machine exercises calls for a reduced amount of weight. Usually this is less than half of what a person can perform when using both sides of the body.

Students record all weights and exercise names on the unilateral upper-body worksheet.

Extension

Students can create an exercise that might include more than one muscle group (compound exercise).

Student Choices/Differentiation

Students choose which exercises to practice.

What to Look For

Students make the appropriate weight selection based on only the one side of the body being used.

Instructional Task: Unilateral Lower Body

■ PRACTICE TASK

Students pair up, move around the room to each lower-body station, and perform the exercises on one side of the body at a time. For lower-body exercises, the basic repetition range is 10 to 15.

Students record all weights and exercise names on the unilateral lower-body worksheet.

Students cool down with their static stretching routines.

Refinement

Remind students that lower-body exercises usually demand more reps than upper-body exercises. Students should select a heavier weight but also keep their form and use proper technique and spotters.

Student Choices/Differentiation

Students choose which exercises to practice.

What to Look For

- Students make the appropriate weight selection based on the side of the body being used.
- Students are using spotters.

Formal and Informal Assessments

- Unilateral worksheets
- Exit slip: Give me an example of a single-joint unilateral exercise for the [insert body part].

Closure

- The workout plan for the day incorporated two new concepts: combining various exercise tools and using unilateral exercises. Let's review your exercise lists and share ideas with other groups.
- Both methods are considered advanced training programs, as they relate to progressions and fitness development.
- As we explore a variety of exercise techniques, equipment, and programs, I expect to see you including these ideas and concepts in your resistance-training program.

Reflection

- Do students identify exercises now by how many joints are involved?
- Are they comfortable using free weights?
- Are they ready to write a resistance-training plan?
- Review physical activity logs. Are students participating in enough physical activity to meet government-recommended guidelines?

Homework

Research the types of muscle fibers and how different fiber types influence muscle development. Summarize your findings for Lesson 9. (Embedded outcome: S3.H9.L2)

Resources

Bompa, T., & Carrera, M. (2015). *Conditioning young athletes*. Champaign, IL: Human Kinetics.

Internet keyword search: "unilateral resistance training," "unilateral upper body exercises," "unilateral lower body exercises"

LESSON 9: PROGRAM DEVELOPMENT

Grade-Level Outcomes

Primary Outcomes

Assessment & program planning: Develops and maintains a fitness portfolio (e.g., assessment scores, goals for improvement, plan of activities for improvement, log of activities being done to reach goals, timeline for improvement. (S3.H11.L2)

Fitness knowledge: Designs and implements a strength and conditioning program that develops balance in opposing muscle groups (agonist/antagonist) and supports a healthy, active lifestyle. (S3.H7.L2)

Movement concepts, principles & knowledge: Applies the terminology associated with exercise and participation in selected individual-performance activities, dance, net/wall games, target games, aquatics and/or outdoor pursuits appropriately. (S2.H1.L1)

Embedded Outcomes

Fitness knowledge: Identifies the structure of skeletal muscle and fiber types as they relate to muscle development. (S3.H9.L2)

Engages in physical activity

Participates several times a week in a self-selected lifetime activity, dance or fitness activity outside of the school day. (S3.H6.L1)

Lesson Objectives

The learner will:

- set SMART goals and objectives throughout the lesson.
- analyze scores from fitness testing for muscular strength and endurance.
- create an activity list of the fitness activities of interest for each of the components.
- compile a workout chart that details progressions leading up to goal completion.
- apply terminology correctly during goal setting and score analysis.

Equipment and Materials

- Specific, measurable, attainable, realistic and timely (SMART) goals worksheets
- Previous fitness scorecards for all fitness tests
- Physical activity worksheets
- Week-long fitness schedule templates
- Pencils

Introduction

For homework, you learned about different muscle fiber types. What types did you find? How do these types influence performance and conditioning? You have tried several types of resistance training. Who can give me some examples? Today, you will develop a draft of a resistance-training plan to include in your fitness portfolio. You will use your testing scores as a baseline, and your plan should enhance those components that you would like to improve. Let's get started.

Instructional Task: Establishing SMART Goals

■ PRACTICE TASK

Provide students with a PowerPoint presentation or handout on specific, measurable, attainable, realistic and timely (SMART) goals, and practice creating objectives.

Guiding questions for students:

- What is the difference between goals and objectives?
- What does SMART stand for?
- What fitness goals might a person create while in high school?

Extension

The discussion can expand into the FITT principle and how those guidelines interact with SMART goals.

Refinement

Remind students that personal goals are just that: personal. Creating goals that are realistic and yet include opportunity for exploration in the fitness realm can lead to a lifetime of fitness participation and enhanced health.

Student Choices/Differentiation

Provide handouts and materials to reinforce subject matter.

What to Look For

- Students' goals are reasonable and can be accomplished.
- The objectives align with the goals.

Instructional Task: Analysis and Evaluations

■ PRACTICE TASK

Students retrieve their scores from their fitness portfolios from all the assessments they have completed.

Have students review their scores and fitness levels and then write SMART goals for muscular strength and endurance.

Extension

Students can create a list of the exercises and activities they enjoy doing and plan to include in their workout plans.

Student Choices/Differentiation

Students select which exercises to include in their workout plans.

What to Look For

- Students are listing exercises that cover the components of health-related fitness.
- Students are including enough exercises for each body part and muscle group.

Instructional Task: Workout Plan

■ PRACTICE TASK

Hand out the fitness schedule templates to all students. Allow students to share ideas with partners or small groups.

Using the FITT principle, students organize a one-week schedule (micro-cycle) of exercises for muscular strength and endurance, with a workout frequency of three times a week.

Students perform two of the workouts in school, using weight machines or free weights, and one at home using body-weight exercises and whatever equipment is available. Students may include exercises they have used in their body-weight programs but should add some small apparatuses as well.

Students should plan for three sets of each exercise. Their goals should indicate whether they are focusing on endurance or strength to determine the appropriate number of reps per set.

Refinement

Remind students that the frequency, intensity, and time concepts relate to the type of exercises performed and the training period they focus on. If powerlifting, the fewer sets they do, the fewer reps and a greater percentage of the max lift they should perform. If in the basic strength period, then lifts should progressively get harder as students do more sets.

Extension

Discuss the concepts of periodization and micro-, meso-, and macro-cycles in resistance training. Have students create three more charts for successive weeks that include progressions in weights, reps, and/or time for one meso-cycle.

Student Choices/Differentiation

- Students choose their partners.
- Students create individualized schedules for resistance exercises.
- Students choose weight machines, free weights, or a combination of both.
- Students choose body-weight exercises, small apparatuses, or a combination of both.

What to Look For

- Students are creating schedules that align with their SMART goals.
- Schedules incorporate time for each component of fitness.

Formal and Informal Assessments

- Week-long schedules of fitness activities
- Muscle fiber type assignment (Embedded outcome: S3.H9.L2)
- SMART goals worksheets
- Exit slip: Tell me one of your SMART goals.

Closure

- The assignment for today was to complete a resistance-training plan for one week based on what you know about resistance training to this point.
- To do that, we have reviewed how to establish SMART goals and how to identify the objectives, or steps, leading to the completion of those goals, and you have outlined a basic workout plan and schedule to help you achieve them.
- I will review your plans before the next class and provide you with some feedback so you can start practicing the plans safely.

Reflection

- Were students able to align their goals with the specific activities relevant to success on a daily basis? For down the road?
- Review SMART goals to make sure students understand how to write them.
- Review week-long fitness plans to ensure students are on the right track.

Homework

- Finish your meso-cycle charts if time ran out in class.
- Review terminology and concepts on the school's physical education website for a test next class.
- Review the comments I made in your logs. Continue to record your physical activity outside of class. (Embedded outcome: S3.H6.L1)

Resources

Corbin, C., & Lindsey, R. (2007). *Fitness for life.* 5th ed. Champaign, IL: Human Kinetics.

National Association for Sport and Physical Education. (2011). *PE metrics: Assessing standards 1-6 in secondary school.* Reston, VA: Author.

Powers, S., Dodd, S., & Jackson, E. (2014). *Total fitness and wellness.* 6th ed. San Francisco: Pearson.

Internet keyword search: "SMART goals," "FITT principle," "micro-cycle," "meso-cycle," "macro-cycle," "periodization"

MUSCULAR STRENGTH AND ENDURANCE
WEEK-LONG ROUTINE

Circle your fitness-level experience: Beginner   Intermediate   Advanced

Decide on the frequency (days per week):

      1   2   3   4   5   6   7

Decide on the time (sets of each exercise):   1-2   3-4   5+

Decide on the intensity (reps in each set): <3 reps   4-6   8-10   >12

Decide on the type of workout routine:
  2 days: skill-related
  3 days: total body
  4 days: split halves
  5 days: body parts

Create a week-long workout routine on the back of this paper that you can follow.

Guidelines:

  If total body: 2 exercises for 6 body parts (12 exercises) × 3 days
  If split halves: 3 exercises for 3 body parts (9 exercises) × 4 days
  If body parts: 6 exercises for 1 body part (6 exercises) × 5 days

Order of operation:

  Legs, back, chest, shoulders, arms, abs
  Quads, hams, calves
  Upper, middle, lower
  Front, lateral, side
  Triceps, biceps, forearms
  Lower, obliques, upper
  Compound or single joint
  Free weights or machines or small equipment or body weight

Muscular Strength and Endurance Week-Long Routine

	Monday	Tuesday	Wednesday	Thursday	Friday
Body parts					
Time					
Intensity					
Exercises 1 2 3 4 5 6 7 8 9 10 11 12					

From L.C. MacDonald, R.J. Doan, and S. Chepko, eds., 2018, *Lesson planning for high school physical education* (Reston, VA: SHAPE America; Champaign, IL: Human Kinetics).

LESSON 10: PROGRAM PRACTICE

Grade-Level Outcomes

Primary Outcomes

Movement concepts, principles & knowledge: Applies the terminology associated with exercise and participation in selected individual-performance activities, dance, net/wall games, target games, aquatics and/or outdoor pursuits appropriately. (S2.H1.L1)

Fitness activities: Demonstrates competency in 1 or more specialized skills in health-related fitness activities. (S1.H3.L1)

Fitness knowledge: Demonstrates appropriate technique on resistance-training machines and with free weights. (S3.H7.L1)

Safety: Applies best practices for participating safely in physical activity, exercise and dance (e.g., injury prevention, proper alignment, hydration, use of equipment, implementation of rules, sun protection). (S4.H5.L1)

Embedded Outcome

Challenge: Chooses an appropriate level of challenge to experience success and desire to participate in a self-selected physical activity. (S5.H2.L2)

Lesson Objectives

The learner will:

- demonstrate knowledge of the terminology, movement concepts, and principles of effective workout components during a cognitive test.
- demonstrate competency in the fitness activities through safe participation and appropriate technique.
- demonstrate fitness knowledge through evaluation of own resistance-training workout plan.

Equipment and Materials

- Cognitive assessment test
- Individual workout plans
- Self-evaluation forms
- Resistance-training equipment
- Resistance-training machines

Introduction

Today, you're going to practice your resistance-training plans and make adjustments if necessary. Be sure to look at the comments I made on your plans before you start. You'll also be taking a knowledge test. To keep everyone as active as possible, groups will rotate between taking the test and practicing their workout plans.

Instructional Task: Written Cognitive Test

■ PRACTICE TASK

Assign students a seat within the gym where they can be supervised while others can participate in a workout and also be supervised.

Student Choices/Differentiation

Students can choose where to sit to take the cognitive test.

What to Look For

Students have a basic grasp of the terminology and concepts.

Instructional Task: Practicing the Workout Plans

■ PRACTICE TASK

Students warm up with their dynamic stretching routines.

Students practice their workout plans with a partner. Partners act as spotters.

At the completion of their plans, students cool down with their static stretching routines.

Refinement

As students are working from their plans, observe their technique. Provide corrective feedback on alignment and form.

Student Choices/Differentiation

- Students choose their partners.
- Students work at their own pace.

What to Look For

- Students are engaged in the workout.
- Technique for each exercise is correct.
- Spotters are communicating and attentive.

Instructional Task: Self-Assessment of Plans

■ PRACTICE TASK

Hand students a workout evaluation worksheet and have them find a place on the gym floor to self-assess their plans.

EMBEDDED OUTCOME: S5.H2.L2. Remind students that the workout should challenge them. Have them comment on this aspect in the self-assessment and what adjustments they may need to make if the plan is too hard or too easy.

Student Choices/Differentiation

Students may complete the assessment for homework if they are unable to complete it in class.

What to Look For

- Students accurately evaluated their workouts.
- Students can identify adjustments that need to be made.

Formal and Informal Assessments

- Self-assessment of plans
- Teacher assessment of plans
- Cognitive test

Closure

- How did you feel about your plan when you tested it out?
- Do you need to make adjustments now that you have tried it out?
- Did you work opposing muscle groups?
- Next class, you will learn about plyometric training.

Reflection

- Were students who were completing the written exam bothered by the noise from students who were working out?
- Review self-assessments of plans. Did students provide a realistic evaluation of their workout plans?
- Do their plans align with their goals?
- Review cognitive test results for patterns and misunderstandings.

Homework

- Practice the at-home resistance-training workout before the next class. This takes the place of your body-weight resistance program. Record the sets and repetitions in a log, and write up how you felt during the workout. Was it challenging? Were the exercises balanced between muscle groups?
- Log any other physical activity you do between now and the next class.

Resources

Corbin, C., & Lindsey, R. *Fitness for life*. 5th ed. (2007). Champaign, IL: Human Kinetics. (cognitive test questions)

SAMPLE POST-WORKOUT SELF-EVALUATION FORM

Rate the following components of the workout program on a scale of 1 to 5, with 1 meaning totally disagree and 5 meaning totally agree.

In my opinion, the workout:

Covered the entire body _____

Had objectives (FITT) that matched the goals (training period) _____

Included sufficient components of warm-up, program, and cool-down _____

Challenged me physically _____

Contained easy-to-follow directions for each exercise _____

Followed the order of operations for exercises _____

From L.C. MacDonald, R.J. Doan, and S. Chepko, eds., 2018, *Lesson planning for high school physical education* (Reston, VA: SHAPE America; Champaign, IL: Human Kinetics).

LESSON 11: PLYOMETRICS FOR ALL

Grade-Level Outcomes

Primary Outcomes

Movement concepts, principles & knowledge: Applies the terminology associated with exercise and participation in selected individual-performance activities, dance, net/wall games, target games, aquatics and/or outdoor pursuits appropriately. (S2.H1.L1)

Fitness activities: Demonstrates competency in 1 one or more specialized skills in health-related fitness activities. (S1.H3.L1)

Fitness knowledge: Demonstrates appropriate technique on resistance-training machines and with free weights. (S3.H7.L1)

Safety: Applies best practices for participating safely in physical activity, exercise and dance (e.g., injury prevention, proper alignment, hydration, use of equipment, implementation of rules, sun protection). (S4.H5.L1)

Embedded Outcomes

Challenge: Chooses an appropriate level of challenge to experience success and desire to participate in a self-selected physical activity. (S5.H2.L2)

Assessment & program planning: Analyzes the components of skill-related fitness in relation to life and career goals, and designs an appropriate fitness program for those goals. (S3.H12.L2)

Lesson Objectives

The learner will:

- discuss the terminology, concepts, and principles of plyometric training and how it may affect overall health.
- demonstrate new plyometric exercises to peer groups and discuss the safety of each movement.
- practice various upper- and lower-body plyometric exercises with a partner.
- design a plyometric workout plan.
- practice upper-body resistance-training exercises.

Equipment and Materials

- Plyometric boxes
- Speed ladders
- Medicine balls of various weights
- Floor pads
- Mini hurdles
- Plyometric worksheets
- Plyometric program design templates

Introduction

Let's review the written test from our previous class to clear up any misconceptions before moving on to new content.

Because you have practiced all the parts of your resistance-training program, you are ready to implement it. From now on, we will use the second half of each class for you to perform a segment of your workout and use the beginning of each class to introduce new concepts. Today, we're going to move on to sport-specific and skill-related fitness concepts, including plyometrics. Plyometrics are a version of training that is often done with athletes. However, we are going to explore how everyone can benefit from some plyometric movements. By the end of the module, you will develop a plan for skill-related fitness related to your career or life goals.

Instructional Task:
Class Discussion on Plyometric Exercises

■ PRACTICE TASK

Lead a class discussion on plyometric exercises and their connection to fitness and health.

Guiding questions for students:

- What does the term *plyometric* mean?
- What are some activities that require you to "explode" during the movement?
- What are the components of skill-related fitness?
- How do these components relate to participation in different sports?
- What careers or professions can you think of where skill-related fitness is important?

Extension

Review a PowerPoint on the six skill-related fitness components.

Student Choices/Differentiation

- Have additional handouts ready for students to view different types of plyometric exercises for beginners and advanced performance.
- Have students view a brief video on plyometric exercises.

What to Look For

Students can identify specific exercises that are considered plyometric.

Instructional Task:
Upper- and Lower-Body Plyometric Exercises

■ PRACTICE TASK

Demonstrate to students a variety of plyometric exercises for each body part. Basic exercises for the lower body include line hops, jumps in place, jumps for height or distance, and speed ladder drills. Basic exercises for the upper body include plyometric push-ups, medicine ball press and catch, and medicine ball throws.

Hand out the plyometric worksheets with the names of several pieces of workout equipment. Have students gather in groups and move from station to station, discussing how to use each piece of equipment for plyometric exercise.

Extension

Create a list of exercises for each muscle group using the desired piece of equipment—and it must be in plyometric format.

Refinement

Encourage students who have little experience in the weight room to participate in exercises on the lower end of the plyometric spectrum, which (e.g., have longer/more ground contact time.

Student Choices/Differentiation

- Students choose which group to work with.
- Students decide which exercises to list on the worksheet.

What to Look For

All students are contributing to the group activity.

Instructional Task: Plyometric Stations

■ PRACTICE TASK

Students work with a partner and move from station to station, practicing the activities discussed previously.

EMBEDDED OUTCOME: S5.H2.L2. The first time that students try a new exercise, they should go through it slowly. Have them practice until they can perform it correctly at the slower speed, and then allow them to challenge themselves to go faster or at full speed.

Student Choices/Differentiation

- Students choose their partners for station work.
- Students attempt activities at their own pace.

What to Look For

- Students are able to align appropriate exercises for the intended muscle groups. The demonstrated exercises actually work the body part indicated by the students.
- Students can perform plyometric exercises with proper form.

Instructional Task: Practicing the Workout Plans

■ PRACTICE TASK

Because students have been practicing plyometric exercises with the lower body, have them focus on the upper-body elements of their workout programs. Partners act as spotters.

After the workout, students cool down with their static stretching routines.

Refinement

As students are working from their plans, observe their technique. Provide corrective feedback on alignment and form.

Student Choices/Differentiation

- Students choose their partners.
- Students work at their own pace.

What to Look For

- Students are engaged in the workout.
- Technique for each exercise is correct.
- Spotters are communicating and attentive.

Formal and Informal Assessments

Observation of proper technique using specialized equipment, e.g., plyometric boxes, speed ladders, medicine balls, mini-hurdles (informal assessment performed by teacher during practice)

Closure

- For some of you, today's program might make you a little more sore than normal.
- The explosive nature of plyometric exercises usually requires more energy and effort, therefore breaking down more muscle.
- As with the other components of strength and conditioning, I hope you can acknowledge the need for and importance of adding some plyometric exercises to your workouts, whether you are playing a competitive sport or not.

Reflection

- Were students able to complete the basic plyometric exercises with enough force to be effective?
- Are students becoming more confident in their lifting programs?

Homework

- Log your physical activity outside of class.
- Think about your career plans and analyze the physical demands that they might involve. List the skill-related components in which you will need to meet the demands of your career. If your career plans don't involve much in the way of physical demands, think about the physical activities that you plan to include in your lifestyle and base your list on that. Due next class. (Embedded outcome: S3.H12.L2)

Resources

Bompa, T. (2015). *Conditioning young athletes*. Champaign, IL: Human Kinetics.

Cissik, J., & Dawes, J. (2015). *Maximum interval training*. Champaign, IL: Human Kinetics.

Internet keyword search: "plyometric exercises," "plyometric equipment," "plyometric training"

PLYOMETRIC WORKSHEET

In groups, discuss and practice using each piece of equipment to design an exercise for the listed body parts.

Body part	Body weight only	Medicine ball	Stability ball	Speed ladder	Mini hurdles	Body bar
Lower body						
Quads						
Hams						
Calves						
Hips: sides						
Hips: front and back						
Upper body						
Chest						
Back						
Shoulders						
Biceps						
Triceps						
Forearms						

From L.C. MacDonald, R.J. Doan, and S. Chepko, eds., 2018, *Lesson planning for high school physical education* (Reston, VA: SHAPE America; Champaign, IL: Human Kinetics).

LESSON 12: SPEED AND AGILITY TRAINING

Grade-Level Outcomes

Primary Outcomes

Assessment & program planning: Analyzes the components of skill-related fitness in relation to life and career goals, and designs an appropriate fitness program for those goals. (S3.H12.L2)

Movement concepts, principles & knowledge: Uses movement concepts and principles (e.g., force, motion, rotation) to analyze and improve performance of self and/or others in a selected skill. (S2.H2.L1)

Fitness activities: Demonstrates competency in 1 or more specialized skills in health-related fitness activities. (S1.H3.L1)

Fitness knowledge: Demonstrates appropriate technique on resistance-training machines and with free weights. (S3.H7.L1)

Safety: Applies best practices for participating safely in physical activity, exercise and dance (e.g., injury prevention, proper alignment, hydration, use of equipment, implementation of rules, sun protection). (S4.H5.L1)

Embedded Outcome

Fitness knowledge: Calculates target heart rate and applies that information to personal fitness plan. (S3.H10.L1)

Lesson Objectives

The learner will:

- discuss sport science principles of force, motion, angles, and rotation as they relate to improved performance on skills tests.
- analyze components of fitness as they relate to career goals and identify the appropriate testing activities relevant to their development.
- demonstrate appropriate testing format and skill technique in a variety of fitness tests.
- implement a total-body workout program with a partner that includes a warm-up, testing, a workout, and a cool-down that covers total-body exercises.
- practice speed and agility training exercises safely.
- practice upper-body resistance-training exercises.

Equipment and Materials

- Speed ladder
- Floor dots
- Floor tape
- Stopwatches
- Chalk
- Speed and agility worksheets

Introduction

For homework, you analyzed the skill-related fitness demands of a possible career or lifestyle activity. I want you to keep these demands in mind as you learn about speed and agility. The process will be a little different in that once we discuss the terms, you will practice several drills and then perform testing on each other. By the end of this module, you will develop a skill-related fitness plan, and these tests will help you understand your baseline for the plan.

Instructional Task:
Discussion on Skill-Related Fitness Components

■ PRACTICE TASK

Lead a discussion on the components of skill-related fitness and how they differ from health-related fitness components.

Guiding questions for students:

- What is the difference between speed and quickness?
- Can you think of some examples of a test for speed?
- How does that differ from a test for agility?
- How are agility and balance related?

Extension

The discussion can move into the benefits of improvement in the skill-related fitness components for sports and careers.

Student Choices/Differentiation

Provide pictures and videos to reinforce content.

What to Look For

Students can identify the differences between the terms and meanings.

Instructional Task: Research and Practice

■ PRACTICE TASK

Have students use the Internet to research activities that measure and develop speed and agility. Students then use the speed and agility worksheet to identify at least one simple field test for each of the components.

Extensions

- For each skill, identify at least three practice activities that can be used to enhance the skill.
- Research tests for other components of skill-related fitness (i.e., balance, coordination, reaction time, power).

Student Choices/Differentiation

- Students choose which activities to list.
- Experienced students can list practice activities.

What to Look For

- Listed activities are appropriate for each component.
- All students are engaged.

Instructional Task: Evaluation and Testing

■ PRACTICE TASK

Establish testing stations for speed and agility. Have students pair up, and hand out a data collection sheet. Students complete their dynamic warm-ups before testing.

Partners alternate performing the skill test at each station and recording the data for each other.

Extensions

- Students can attempt multiple test variations for each component.
- Students can set up tests for other skill-related fitness components.

Refinements

- Remind students to follow the directions for each test as consistently as possible. If initial scores are outside the prescribed parameters, then have students review the steps involved and look for errors.
- Encourage students to use as few movements as possible when changing directions. The fewer times their feet touch the ground, the faster their movements will be, enhancing their test scores.

EMBEDDED OUTCOME: S3.H10.L1. Have students take their heart rates before the test, immediately after the test, and 1 minute later to see which zone they are in immediately after the test and how quickly they recover.

Student Choices/Differentiation

Students choose which specific test to perform for each component.

What to Look For

- Students are practicing the skills tests before being tested.
- Students are performing the tests accurately.
- Students are performing the activities with good form and alignment.
- When counting the pulse using the carotid method, students' hands are not around the esophagus.
- When counting the pulse using the radial method, students are not pressing into the wrist with the thumb.

Instructional Task: Practicing the Workout Plans

■ PRACTICE TASK

Since students have been practicing speed and agility exercises with the lower body, have them focus on the upper-body elements of their workout programs. Partners act as spotters.

After the workout, students cool down with their static stretching routines.

Refinement

As students are doing their plans, observe their technique. Provide corrective feedback on alignment and form.

Student Choices/Differentiation

- Students choose their partners.
- Students work at their own pace.

What to Look For

- Students are engaged in the workout.
- Technique for each exercise is correct.
- Spotters are communicating and attentive.

Formal and Informal Assessments

Speed and agility testing scores

Closure

- Although the development of speed and agility will not always be necessary for every person in the room, both components can enhance your fitness for a variety of activities. Speed and agility may be necessary for some jobs, many recreational activities, and other lifetime actions.
- As with weight resistance, once you stop training for speed and agility you may lose some of your gains, but knowing how to self-test and assess your status, you will be able to create a program to add to your health-related fitness concepts.

Reflection

- Could students verbalize ideas of how they can use these specific training activities for their non-sport life?
- Were they performing the activities with good technique?
- Were they getting enough practice opportunities to perform well?

Homework

- Write a brief paragraph reflecting on your performances in speed and agility testing. How do you think you did? What did you learn about your own abilities? What can you do to enhance any of the scores where you weren't as successful?
- Continue to log your physical activity outside of class, and perform your at-home resistance-training program before the next class.

Resources

Corbin, C., & Lindsey, R. (2007). *Fitness for life*. 5th ed. Champaign, IL: Human Kinetics.

Topend Sports: www.topendsports.com

TeachPE: www.teachpe.com

Internet keyword search: "skill-related fitness testing," "skill testing"

LESSON 13: OLYMPIC TRAINING AND POWERLIFTING

Grade-Level Outcomes

Primary Outcomes

Fitness activities: Demonstrates competency in 1 or more specialized skills in health-related fitness activities. (S1.H3.L1)

Movement concepts, principles & knowledge: Uses movement concepts and principles (e.g., force, motion, rotation) to analyze and improve performance of self and/or others in a selected skill. (S2.H2.L1)

Fitness knowledge: Demonstrates appropriate technique on resistance-training machines and with free weights. (S3.H7.L1)

Safety: Applies best practices for participating safely in physical activity, exercise and dance (e.g., injury prevention, proper alignment, hydration, use of equipment, implementation of rules, sun protection). (S4.H5.L1)

Embedded Outcomes

Working with others: Accepts others' ideas, cultural diversity and body types by engaging in cooperative and collaborative movement projects. (S4.H4.L2)

Fitness knowledge: Identifies the different energy systems used in a selected physical activity (e.g., adenosine triphosphate and phosphocreatine, anaerobic glycolysis, aerobic). (S3.H8.L2)

Lesson Objectives

The learner will:

- discuss the movement concepts and principles of powerlifting and Olympic lifting.
- practice and demonstrate proper technique and safety when working in a group setting in the power cages and during explosive lifting.
- demonstrate proper technique during one specialized skill or portion of a power or Olympic lift.

Equipment and Materials

- Several sections of PVC pipe, 6 feet long, or broom handles 6 feet long
- Weight lifting bar
- Weightlifting straps
- Weightlifting belts

Introduction

We are moving into Olympic and powerlifting events today. Because you are learning new lifting techniques, you will not be spending time on your personal resistance-training workouts. Olympic lifts and power lifts are the universal means to measure strength and conditioning. I have saved these lifts for the end so that those of you who have never participated in this type of exercise have now had several weeks of weight resistance training to prepare you. At the end of this portion of the module, you will have the choice to use the bumper plates to test your technique on three of the lifts, or for those of you more experienced in lifting, you can choose to be evaluated on how well you max out on three of the lifts.

Instructional Task: Class Discussion

■ PRACTICE TASK

Provide a PowerPoint on the differences between powerlifting and Olympic-style lifting.

Guiding questions for students:

- What is meant by the term *powerlifting*?
- How does that differ from Olympic-style lifting?
- How can a person relate powerlifting and Olympic lifting to everyday living?

Extension

The discussion can move into CrossFit and functional lifting exercises.

EMBEDDED OUTCOME: S4.H4.L2. Emphasize that performing the activities in powerlifting isn't always about the highest weight, but about how fast you can move the weight you are working with. Your ability to do that may depend on your experience and body type.

What to Look For

- Can students identify any power lifts?
- Can students identify any CrossFit activities?

Instructional Task: Pre-powerlifting Exercises

■ PRACTICE TASK

Demonstrate the squat and shoulder mobility assessment protocol. All students must pass these tests before weight can be added to any particular exercise.

After a warm-up including dynamic stretching, have students perform the assessments one at a time for pass or fail. The primary assessments for Olympic lifting include the squat and shoulder mobility protocol: overhead wall touch, overhead squat, overhead squat with elevated heel, body-weight squat, hurdle hip assessment, lunge assessment, shoulder mobility assessment 2, active straight-leg raise, trunk stability push-up, and rotary stability. If students cannot complete the assessment successfully, have them perform the flexibility and strengthening exercises associated with each assessment tool.

Extension

Once students pass the assessment, they can begin to practice with a PVC pipe (or broomstick) or bar.

Student Choices/Differentiation

- Students with experience in power lifts can provide peer support to less experienced students on technique.
- Students may review a video clip on protocol.

What to Look For

Students perform the assessments using the pass/fail scoring protocol and notify you if they are not successful.

Instructional Task: Powerlifting and Olympic Lifting Exercises

■ PRACTICE TASK

Briefly review the rules of the gym and gym etiquette when using free weights, including spotting technique.

In groups of four, students practice performing each series on a separate day (this portion of the module may take up to five days to finish). The three major lifts for this section are the clean, jerk, and snatch. Using the guidebook, students must demonstrate each step of each lift before moving to the next step (e.g., the jerk series includes press behind the neck, press, push press from behind the neck, push press, power jerk from behind the neck, power jerk in front of the neck, and split jerk).

Extensions

- Students who master proper technique with full ROM may add weight to each successive set.
- Have students use a device to record their partners' lifting technique. Peers evaluate each other's technique and provide feedback. Provide a checklist of critical features to guide their assessment.
- Students cool down with their static stretching routines.

Student Choices/Differentiation

- Students may choose to use a kettlebell or dumbbell instead.
- Students must stay with the bar or PVC pipe until you observe correct, consistent technique.
- Students choose their groups.

What to Look For

- Students achieve proper technique in each lift stage before moving to the next stage.
- Group members demonstrate proper spotting technique.

Formal and Informal Assessments

- Teacher observation of lifting technique
- Peer evaluations

Closure

- For some of you, this was an intense way to exercise. If you were not familiar with these types of lifts, I hope you can see how they could be useful to you in everyday movements.
- Although some of you will be reluctant to perform these exercises later in life, I still want you to consider implementing them into your workout programs for the year.
- Next class, you will work on a plan for skill-related fitness.

Reflection

- Did the less-experienced students enjoy the total-body lifting movements associated with powerlifting?
- Were students able to provide an accurate assessment of their peers' movements?

Homework

- Log your physical activity outside of class. Include a reflection on how you felt about the powerlifting techniques we tried today.
- Read the summary on the school's physical education website of the different energy systems used in physical activity. Come to class prepared to discuss how these relate to resistance training. (Embedded outcome: S3.H8.L2)

Resources

Randolph, D. (2015). *Ultimate Olympic weightlifting: A complete guide from beginning to gold medal.* Berkeley, CA: Ulysses Press.

Internet keyword search: "CrossFit," "powerlifting techniques," "Olympic lifting techniques"

LESSON 14: DEVELOPING A SKILL-RELATED FITNESS PROGRAM

Grade-Level Outcomes

Primary Outcomes

Assessment & program planning: Develops and maintains a fitness portfolio (e.g., assessment scores, goals for improvement, plan of activities for improvement, log of activities being done to reach goals, timeline for improvement. (S3.H11.L2)

Fitness knowledge: Identifies the different energy systems used in a selected physical activity (e.g., adenosine triphosphate and phosphocreatine, anaerobic glycolysis, aerobic) (S3.H8.L2)

Movement concepts, principles & knowledge: Applies the terminology associated with exercise and participation in selected individual-performance activities, dance, net/wall games, target games, aquatics and/or outdoor pursuits appropriately. (S2.H1.L1)

Embedded Outcome

Engages in physical activity: Participates several times a week in a self-selected lifetime activity, dance or fitness activity outside the school day. (S3.H6.L1)

Lesson Objectives

The learner will:

- set SMART goals and objectives.
- analyze scores from fitness testing for muscular strength and endurance.
- create an activity list of the fitness activities of interest for each of the components.
- compile a workout chart that details progressions leading up to goal completion.
- apply the terminology of skill-related fitness correctly when developing goals and analyzing scores.

Equipment and Materials

- Worksheets on energy systems
- Scores from skill-related fitness tests
- Week-long fitness schedule templates
- Pencils

Introduction

In this module you have tried exercises and lifts that you can use to improve your skill-related fitness. Who can give me some examples? Today, you will develop a draft of a skill-related fitness plan to include in your fitness portfolio. You will use your testing scores as a baseline. You should focus on your skill-related career and life goals as you build your plan. Let's start by reviewing the energy system information that you read for homework.

Instructional Task: Discussion on Energy Systems

■ PRACTICE TASK

Have students work in small groups or pairs to complete a short worksheet on energy systems (see handout). The worksheet should ask students to think of examples of physical activity for each system. After completing the worksheet, review the answers as a group.

Student Choices/Differentiation

Provide posters or visual aids listing the different energy systems.

What to Look For

- All students are contributing to completing the questions on the worksheet.
- Students are asking good questions in the class review.

Instructional Task: Analysis and Evaluations

■ PRACTICE TASK

Students retrieve their scores from their fitness portfolios for all the skill-related tests they have completed. These are the scores from Lesson 2 and any of the 10-rep-max assessments for various exercises and equipment.

Have students review their career or lifestyle skill-related fitness requirements, their scores, and their fitness levels. Students write SMART goals for at least two skill-related fitness components that match their career or lifestyle needs.

Extension

Students can create a list of the exercises and activities they enjoy doing and plan to include in their workout plans.

Student Choices/Differentiation

- Students select which exercises to include in their workout plans.
- Provide handouts and materials to reinforce subject matter.

What to Look For

- Students are listing exercises that cover the skill-related components of fitness.
- Created goals are reasonable and able to be accomplished.

Instructional Task: Workout Plan

■ PRACTICE TASK

Hand out the fitness schedule template to all students (see Lesson 9). Allow students to share ideas of what they want to do with a partner or small group.

Using the FITT principle, students organize a one-week schedule (micro-cycle) of exercises for skill-related fitness, with a workout frequency of two times a week. Students should plan workouts that can be done at school (under supervision). They may include powerlifting if they choose.

Extension

Students create three more charts for successive weeks that include progressions in overload for one meso-cycle.

Student Choices/Differentiation

- Students choose their partners.
- Students create individualized schedules for exercises.

What to Look For

- Students are creating schedules that align with their SMART goals.
- Schedules incorporate time for each component of skill-related fitness.

Formal and Informal Assessments

- Week-long schedules of skill-related fitness activities
- Energy systems worksheets
- Exit slip: Which energy systems are predominantly used in power activities?

Closure

- The assignment for today was to complete a skill-related fitness training plan for one week that relates to your career or life goals.
- I will review your plans before the next class and provide you with some feedback so you can start practicing the plans safely.

Reflection

- Were students able to align their goals with the specific activities relevant to success on a daily basis? For down the road?
- Review week-long fitness plans to ensure students are on the right track.
- Review energy systems worksheets to clarify misconceptions next class.

Homework

Log your physical activity outside of class. Write a reflection on how well you are meeting the physical activity guidelines outside of school. Be prepared to turn it in next class. Begin logging your food intake for at least three days. Use the food intake worksheet to record everything you eat and drink. (Embedded outcome: S3.H6.L1.) We will discuss how to analyze it next class.

Resources

Bompa, T. (2015). *Conditioning young athletes*. Champaign, IL: Human Kinetics.

Cissik, J., & Dawes, J. (2015). *Maximum interval training*. Champaign, IL: Human Kinetics.

Powers, S., Dodd, S., & Jackson, E. (2014). *Total fitness and wellness*. 6th ed. San Francisco: Pearson.

Randolph, D. (2015). *Ultimate Olympic weightlifting: A complete guide from beginning to gold medal*. Berkeley, CA: Ulysses Press.

Internet keyword search: "skill-related fitness," "speed training," "agility training," "powerlifting"

ENERGY SYSTEMS AND PHYSICAL ACTIVITY

Complete the following table related to the three major energy systems of the body.

Energy system	Key concepts	Time	Intensity level	Fitness examples	Sport examples	Daily life examples

From L.C. MacDonald, R.J. Doan, and S. Chepko, eds., 2018, *Lesson planning for high school physical education* (Reston, VA: SHAPE America; Champaign, IL: Human Kinetics).

DIETARY FOOD ANALYSIS

Each student should receive three copies of this form.

Meal or snack	Food item	Protein (g)	× 4 Cals/ gram	Carbohydrate (G)	× 4 Cals/ gram	Fat (G)	× 9 Cals/ gram	Total calories	Category
B L D S									G F V M D O
B L D S									G F V M D O
B L D S									G F V M D O
B L D S									G F V M D O
B L D S									G F V M D O
B L D S									G F V M D O
B L D S									G F V M D O
B L D S									G F V M D O
B L D S									G F V M D O
B L D S									G F V M D O
B L D S									G F V M D O
B L D S									G F V M D O
B L D S									G F V M D O
B L D S									G F V M D O
B L D S									G F V M D O
B L D S									G F V M D O
B L D S									G F V M D O
B L D S									G F V M D O
B L D S									G F V M D O
Totals									

B = breakfast   G = grains   D = dairy

L = lunch   F = fruits   O = other

D = dinner   V = vegetables

S = snack   M = meats, poultry, and fish

Total calories = _____

Total calories from protein = _____   Percentage of calories from protein = _____

Total calories from carbohydrate = _____   Percentage of calories from carbohydrate = _____

Total calories from fat = _____   Percentage of calories from fat = _____

Totals: G _____ F _____ V _____ M _____ D _____ O _____

Circle the number if you made the appropriate number of servings.

From L.C. MacDonald, R.J. Doan, and S. Chepko, eds., 2018, *Lesson planning for high school physical education* (Reston, VA: SHAPE America; Champaign, IL: Human Kinetics).

LESSON 15: NUTRITION

Grade-Level Outcomes

Primary Outcomes

Physical activity knowledge: Discusses the benefits of a physically active lifestyle as it relates to college or career productivity. (S3.H1.L1)

Assessments & program planning: Develops and maintains a fitness portfolio (assessment scores, goals for improvement, plan of activities for improvement, log of activities being done to reach goals, timeline for improvement). (S3.H11.L2)

Nutrition: Designs and implements a nutrition plan to maintain an appropriate energy balance for a healthy, active lifestyle. (S3.H13.L1)

Physical activity knowledge: Investigates the relationships among physical activity, nutrition and body composition. (S3.H1.L2)

Embedded Outcome

Nutrition: Creates a snack plan for before, during and after exercise that addresses nutrition needs for each phase. (S3.H13.L2).

Lesson Objectives

The learner will:

- participate in an open discussion on food, diet fads, and nutrition.
- keep a log of food intake for three days.
- analyze food intake for total calories, fat, protein, and carbohydrate and percentage of diet from fat, protein, and carbohydrate.
- develop a healthy meal plan for one to three days.
- evaluate a peer's meal plan.
- discuss the relationships among body composition, nutrition, and physical activity.

Equipment and Materials

- Three-day food intake logs
- Diet development templates
- Pencils
- Printable materials from ChooseMyPlate.gov: www.choosemyplate.gov/printable-materials
- RDA wall chart
- Assessment rubric for meal planning

Introduction

Today, you will begin the process of evaluating how well you eat. Understanding your food intake can go a long way toward determining how you might meet the fitness, health, and wellness goals you established earlier. To do that, we will review the basic components of nutrition, including protein, carbohydrate, and fat. You have been recording your food intake over three days, and we will use that information to perform a food analysis on your diet. From there, you can make adjustments to better accommodate your fitness and health goals. I'll also return your skill-related fitness plans to you. Please review the feedback and make adjustments as needed.

Instructional Task:
Discuss the Effects of Appropriate Diet

■ PRACTICE TASK

Provide a PowerPoint presentation on the basic principles of diet and nutrition.

Guiding questions for students:

- What is the difference between diet and nutrition?
- What is a calorie?
- What are the three macronutrients?
- What are the characteristics of nutrient-dense foods?
- How can you maintain a good energy balance throughout the day?

Extension

The discussion can move into recommended dietary allowance (RDA) and MyPlate (www.choosemyplate.gov).

Student Choices/Differentiation

Provide handouts and materials to reinforce the information.

What to Look For

- Students can define both diet and nutrition correctly.
- Students recognize the three macronutrients.

Instructional Task: Analyzing Caloric Intake

■ PRACTICE TASK

Students review their food intake data collection sheets and identify the information necessary for each column.
Have students visit various websites that display caloric intake values and find the values for each food item they have listed. Students should determine whether consumed food is one or more servings.

Extension

Have students locate additional supplemental values for food (e.g., sugar, fiber, salt) and record them on the form, as well.

Student Choices/Differentiation

Provide handouts to assist students.

What to Look For

Students can quickly identify caloric values and differentiate them from the percentage of total calories.

Instructional Task: Create Diet Plan

■ PRACTICE TASK

Students use the worksheets to calculate caloric needs based on age, gender, and activity level. Students calculate the percentages of protein, carbohydrate, and fat necessary in daily consumption. They create a daily diet plan for one day with foods that fulfill the daily requirements for protein, carbohydrate, and fat in total calories and percentage of total calories.

EMBEDDED OUTCOME: S3.H13.L2. As students prepare a daily meal plan, ask them to think about trying new snacks. The snacks should address pre-exercise and post-exercise needs for skill-related fitness or resistance training.

Extension

Have students add several days to the diet plan and provide a greater variety of food products.

Student Choices/Differentiation

Students choose which foods to include in their diet plans.

What to Look For

Students are creating meal plans that fall within the guidelines.

Instructional Task: Peer Evaluation

■ PRACTICE TASK

Have students exchange meal plans with someone who hasn't been their partner before. Hand each student a copy of the assessment tool for meal planning. A basic assessment tool (e.g., www.super-tracker.usda.gov) allows peers to check for mathematical errors, evaluate the food intake for each food group, and measure intake adjustments based on goals of adding or losing weight.

Students review the meal plan content for total calories, fat, carbohydrate, and protein based on the initial calculations and check to see if the plan fits.

Student Choices/Differentiation

Students choose their partners.

What to Look For

- Students are making accurate evaluations with the rubric.
- Students are providing feedback in a positive, supportive manner.

Instructional Task: Discussion on Body Composition

■ PRACTICE TASK

At the beginning of the module, you calculated your body mass index (BMI) as a measure of body composition. Now that we have discussed nutrition, let's talk about the relationships among body composition, physical activity, and nutrition.

Guiding questions for students:

- How does physical activity affect your body composition?
- Why is BMI not a good measure of body composition for active people?
- How does the food you eat affect body composition?
- How are excess calories stored in the body?
- How is body composition related to health?

Student Choices/Differentiation

Provide handouts with summaries of information about body composition and nutrition.

What to Look For

Students are engaged in the discussion.

Formal and Informal Assessments

- Meal plans
- Peer assessments of meal plans
- Physical activity logs

Closure

- Gaining an understanding of how food intake affects our ability to become and stay fit is important.
- For this lesson, we examined how to estimate your daily caloric intake and where those calories came from.
- Knowing about foods and the macronutrients they contain helps you maintain your current weight or to gain or lose weight safely.
- Turn in your physical activity logs.
- Have you heard about obstacle courses, such as mud runs? In our next class, we will wrap things up with an obstacle course that will test your skill-related fitness components in a team format. Come to class ready to be challenged!

Reflection

- Are students understanding that what you put into your body makes you who you are?
- Do they understand how to complete a nutritious meal plan?
- Review physical activity logs. Are students completing enough physical activity to meet government recommended guidelines?

Homework

- Share your daily meal plan with your parents and ask whether you can participate in grocery shopping for the week.
- Practice your skill-related fitness plan activities at home.

Resources

Powers, S., Dodd, S., & Jackson, E. (2014). *Total fitness and wellness*. 6th ed. San Francisco: Pearson.

ChooseMyPlate: www.choosemyplate.gov

MyFitnessPal: www.myfitnesspal.com (free calorie counter)

SuperTracker: www.supertracker.usda.gov

LESSON 16: OBSTACLE COURSE CHALLENGE

Grade-Level Outcomes

Primary Outcomes

Fitness activities: Demonstrates competency in 1 or more specialized skills in health-related fitness activities. (S1.H3.L1)

Working with others: Uses communication skills and strategies that promote team or group dynamics. (S4.H3.L1)

Safety: Applies best practices for participating safely in physical activity, exercise and dance (e.g., injury prevention, proper alignment, hydration, use of equipment, implementation of rules, sun protection). (S4.H5.L1)

Embedded Outcomes

Challenge: Chooses an appropriate level of challenge to experience success and desire to participate in a self-selected physical activity. (S5.H2.L2)

Working with others: Solves problems and thinks critically in physical activity and/or dance settings, both as an individual and in groups. (S4.H4.L1)

Lesson Objectives

The learner will:

- participate in an obstacle course that focuses on skill-related fitness components.
- cooperate and coordinate with team members to identify strategies for completing the obstacle course.
- demonstrate competence in specialized skills associated with health-related activities included in the obstacle course.
- participate at an appropriate level of performance, including being aware of unsafe actions and events while completing the obstacle course.

Equipment and Materials

- Obstacles for course
- Worksheets for skill-related fitness components
- Pencils

Introduction

How many of you have seen a Tough Mudder or American Ninja Warrior obstacle course? [Show a video clip to motivate students.] *Well, we're going to cap off this skill-related fitness module with our own version of School Warrior Challenge. I have placed you in teams, and you will complete the course as a group. There will be times when you will need to figure out how to negotiate an obstacle and other times where you will need to work together to get through the course. The objective is to complete the course as a team. Above all, focus on performing safely!*

Instructional Task: Course Walk-Through

■ PRACTICE TASK

Set up a course that includes elements related to skill-related fitness, muscular strength, and endurance. Obstacles can include agility and speed items used earlier in the module as well as stations where students do body-weight exercises. If possible, include a wall climb, upper-body exercises, and jumping. If you have access to a PAR course (jogging trail with fitness stations), you can include those items in the course. Be creative, but keep it safe. You may want to place posters at key points to help students remember the tasks and sequence.

Distribute worksheets. Have students walk through the course as you explain the requirements for each obstacle. For each obstacle, have students record the components of skill-related fitness used. Check for understanding of the course requirements.

Demonstrate the course at half speed, stopping at any obstacle where there are questions.

Student Choices/Differentiation

Students may review a video clip of students doing the course from a previous year.

What to Look For

- Students understand the sequence and tasks.
- Students ask clarifying questions.

Instructional Task: Course Preparation

■ PRACTICE TASK

Students warm up with their dynamic stretching routines. While they are completing their warm-up, call out the names and members of each team (which you have organized in advance based on scores from earlier classes).

After the warm-up, teams get together to discuss strategies for negotiating the course.

Extension

Teams can come up with a name and a cheer for the competition.

EMBEDDED OUTCOME: S4.H4.L1. Team members will need to analyze the best way to get through the course and come up with a strategy to perform well as a group.

Student Choices/Differentiation

- Students complete their own warm-ups.
- Teams are grouped for even ability levels.

What to Look For

- All students are contributing to the proposed strategy.
- Students are supporting each other's ideas.

Instructional Task: Run the Course

■ PRACTICE TASK

Each team takes a half-speed run through the course for practice. Teams may stop and practice obstacles that are more difficult.

When the competition starts, scores are based on a team time. Team members may assist one another at any point in the course. Team members must stick together and may not proceed to the next obstacle until the whole team has completed the previous one. Students should be cheering for other teams during the competition.

As teams complete the course, students cool down with their static stretching routines.

EMBEDDED OUTCOME: S5.H2.L2. Remind students that the course should challenge them, but they should always be under control.

Extensions

- Have a post-course celebration with refreshments and team awards.
- Students complete a brief reflection on the experience of running the course and how the previous lessons contributed to their success.

Student Choices/Differentiation
Students participate at their own levels.

What to Look For
- Students are working hard but participating safely.
- Students are supporting one another.

Formal and Informal Assessments
Self-reflections

Closure
- This was our last class in this module. How did you feel about your performance on the course?
- Which elements were the most challenging?
- Do you think this activity tested the skill-related fitness components we have been practicing?
- Did you like the team format? Why or why not?
- How confident do you feel about your ability to perform resistance training and skill-related fitness?
- In our next class, we will start a new module, so check out your options on the school's physical education website.

Reflection
- Were students able to make connections between the skills and knowledge in the module and the obstacle course?
- Are their fitness portfolios comprehensive? Are there other aspects of fitness we need to address?
- What went well in this module?
- What could I do better the next time I teach it?

Homework
Check out the next modules, and be ready to choose one next class.

Resources
Internet keyword search: "obstacle courses," "adult obstacle courses"

CHAPTER 11

Extending Students' Skills and Knowledge to Designing and Implementing Personal Fitness Plans

For high school students, one of the most important areas to address is Standard 3 of the National Standards for K-12 Physical Education (SHAPE America – Society of Health and Physical Educators, 2014, p. 54). In particular, students need the knowledge and skills to develop and implement a personal fitness or physical activity plan. Reflecting that focus, this chapter contains two modules on designing and implementing personal fitness programs. Both modules illustrate progressions you can use to help students learn these valuable skills, but they take different approaches. The Fitness Assessment and Program Planning Module, contributed by Rebecca Bryan, who teaches fitness education and other physical education courses at State University of New York College at Cortland, emphasizes assessing one's level of fitness, planning a personal fitness program, and monitoring one's progress toward fitness. In the module's lessons, students engage in resistance training and cardiorespiratory activities as a means of improving their personal fitness.

The Fitness Walking Module, also contributed by Rebecca Bryan, emphasizes fitness through walking, but students also learn how to assess and monitor their fitness while engaging in a fitness activity.

You can adapt each module easily to incorporate different activities that are suitable to your students' particular needs and interests. For example, you can use any number of cardiorespiratory or resistance-training exercises in the lessons within the Fitness Assessment and Program Planning Module. As presented in this chapter, the module includes cardio kick and step aerobics, but you could substitute other popular aerobic activities such as Zumba or Spinning.

You can implement lessons from the Fitness Walking Module nearly anywhere, inside or outside. It allows you to take advantage of what your school's surrounding environment has to offer. Those who teach in colder climates, for example, could adapt the module for using snowshoes, providing a geographically relevant alternative. The Fitness Walking Module also prepares students for one of the most popular fitness activities among adults (walking), which will support their participation in lifelong physical activity.

For easy reference, each module begins with a block plan chart of the Grade-Level Outcomes addressed within each lesson. The lessons in each module address outcomes over several National Standards, although most of the primary outcomes reside under Standards 3 and 1.

The main focuses of the Fitness Assessment and Programming Module are designing a personal fitness program (Outcome S3.H12.L1), developing competency in fitness activities (Outcome S1.H3.L1), safety (Outcome S4.H5.L1), and proper technique in resistance training (Outcome S3.H7.L1). The Fitness Walking Module, also contributed by Rebecca Bryan, focuses on competency in fitness activities (Outcome S1.H3.L1). The module also includes many lessons that teach students how to calculate and use target heart rate (Outcome S3.H10.L1) and to self-monitor their physical activity (Outcome S4.H1.L1). These modules provide great examples for implementing critical fitness and physical activity outcomes in your curriculum.

FITNESS ASSESSMENT AND PROGRAM PLANNING MODULE

Lessons in this module were contributed by **Rebecca Bryan**, assistant professor in the department of physical education at the State University New York College at Cortland, where she teaches undergraduate- and graduate-level courses in fitness education; curriculum, instruction and assessment; adapted physical education; and physical education leadership.

Grade-Level Outcomes Addressed, by Lesson	Lessons															
	1	2	3	4	5	6	7	8	9	10	11	12	13	14	15	16
Standard 1. The physically literate individual demonstrates competency in a variety of motor skills and movement patterns.																
Demonstrates competency in 1 or more specialized skills in health-related fitness activities. (S1.H3.L1)				P	P	P	P	P	P	P	P	P	P			
Standard 3. The physically literate individual demonstrates the knowledge and skills to achieve a health-enhancing level of physical activity and fitness.																
Discusses the benefits of a physically active lifestyle as it relates to college or career productivity. (S3.H1.L1)								E				E	P			
Evaluates risks and safety factors that might affect physical activity preferences throughout the life cycle. (S3.H5.L1)											E		E			
Demonstrates appropriate technique on resistance-training machines and with free weights. (S3.H7.L1)				P	P		P		P			P		P		
Identifies types of strength exercises (isometric, concentric, eccentric) and stretching exercises (static, proprioceptive neuromuscular facilitation [PNF], dynamic) for personal fitness development (e.g., strength, endurance, range of motion). (S3.H9.L1)				E	E		E		E					E		
Calculates target heart rate and applies that information to personal fitness plan. (S3.H10.L1)	E					P		P		P	P		P			
Designs a fitness program, including all components of health-related fitness, for a college student and an employee in the learner's chosen field of work. (S3.H12.L1)	P	P	P	P	P	P	P	P	P	P	P	P	P	P	P	P
Analyzes the components of skill-related fitness in relation to life and career goals and designs an appropriate fitness program for those goals. (S3.H12.L2)																P
Standard 4. The physically literate individual exhibits responsible personal and social behavior that respects self and others.																
Employs effective self-management skills to analyze barriers and modify physical activity patterns appropriately, as needed. (S4.H1.L1)												E				
Exhibits proper etiquette, respect for others and teamwork while engaging in physical activity and/or social dance. (S4.H2.L1)					P											
Solves problems and thinks critically in physical activity and/or dance settings, both as an individual and in groups (S4.H4.L1)															E	E
Applies best practices for participating safely in physical activity, exercise and dance (e.g., injury prevention, proper alignment, hydration, use of equipment, implementation of rules, sun protection). (S4.H5.L1)	P	P	P	P	P	E	P		P			P		P		
Standard 5. The physically literate individual recognizes the value of physical activity for health, enjoyment, challenge, self-expression and/or social interaction.																
Analyzes the health benefits of a self-selected physical activity. (S5.H1.L1)															E	

P = Primary; E = Embedded

LESSON 1: REVIEW OF FITNESS PRINCIPLES

Grade-Level Outcomes

Primary Outcomes

Assessment & program planning: Designs a fitness program, including all components of health-related fitness, for a college student and an employee in the learner's chosen field of work. (S3.H12.L1)

Safety: Applies best practices for participating safely in physical activity, exercise and dance (e.g., injury prevention, proper alignment, hydration, use of equipment, implementation of rules, sun protection). (S4.H5.L1)

Embedded Outcome

Fitness knowledge: Calculates target heart rate and applies that information to personal fitness plan. (S3.H10.L1)

Lesson Objectives

The learner will:

- review vocabulary and provide examples of activities and exercises for each definition.
- identify and differentiate between the components of health-related and skill-related fitness concepts.
- connect heart rate to exercise intensity.

Equipment and Materials

- Vocabulary index cards
- Heart rate sheets and pencils/pens (1 per student)
- Music
- 2 agility ladders
- 4 dot mats
- 40 small or medium cones
- 5 jump ropes

Introduction

Today, we will start our review of health-related fitness and the FITT principle. We will begin with a review and self-assessment of the health-related fitness components. This self-assessment is a review of your last Fitnessgram. After you self-assess, you will use the FITT and training principles and target heart rate to develop a cardio and weight-training program. By the end of the learning segment, you will be able to use the FITT principle to design a health-related fitness plan for a college student and a career professional in the field of work of your choice. After we review vocabulary terms, you will take a curl-up test and then perform some activities at fitness stations.

Instructional Task: Vocabulary Task

■ PRACTICE TASK

Have students get into small groups (two to four). Give each group an index card with a vocabulary word and definition (see the list of potential vocabulary words). Each group reads a vocabulary word and its definition to the class and then performs an example of an exercise or activity that includes the vocabulary term. Groups have 3 minutes to read over the definition and come up with an example to share with the class. Have the whole class participate.

Refinement

If students are giving examples from only one type of activity, prompt them to consider a greater variety.

Guiding questions for students:

- In what are other activities we can participate for health-related fitness or skill-related fitness?
- In what activities do you participate now?

Student Choices/Differentiation

Give students a list of exercises to match with the correct vocabulary.

What to Look For

Students can provide examples to explain or demonstrate their vocabulary terms.

Instructional Task: Curl-Up Test

■ PRACTICE TASK

Today, you will take the curl-up test from Fitnessgram. You took this test earlier in the year, so it should be familiar. You will use your results to determine your progress and also for fitness planning purposes.

Have students pair up.

Partner A performs the curl-up test while Partner B watches for form. Once the Partner A students have completed the test, the Partner B students perform curl-ups while Partner A students watch for form.

Students record their scores.

Refinement

Make sure students do not do the following:

- Lift their feet
- Let the head touch the ground between trials
- Use their elbows to push off the ground
- Have partners hold their feet

Student Choices/Differentiation

Perform the assessment within stations.

What to Look For

Students can identify proper and improper curl-up form.

Curl-Up Form

- Head is down (touching floor or mat) and fingertips are touching strip.
- Knees are bent, heels touching ground.
- Finger pads slide across the strip and back as body curls up (shoulder blades off floor) and back down.
- Movement is in time with the CD cadence.

Instructional Task: Fitness Station Review

■ PRACTICE TASK

Students gather in small groups and go to assigned stations to begin working. All groups rotate clockwise. The stations include activities for components of health-related and skill-related fitness. Students take their heart rates at each station.

Embed questions within the stations and at the end of the lesson to check for students' understanding of the fitness concepts.

This activity can be used as a pre-assessment of students' health-related and skill-related fitness knowledge.

Health-Related Stations
- Jogging around the gym
- Jumping rope
- Push-ups or planks
- Walking lunges with a twist

Skill-Related Stations
- Agility ladders
- Dot mat drills
- Sideways jumps
- Standing long jump

Music plays for 1 minute and 30 seconds and then pauses for 30 seconds. During the pause, students take and record their 15-second heart rates and rotate clockwise to the next station.

After rotating through the stations, students walk one lap around the station area to cool down. Then bring students in to stretch both the upper body and lower body (static stretching).

Guiding questions for students:
- What health-related or skill-related fitness concepts are you working on at each station?
- What are the similarities and differences between health-related and skill-related fitness concepts?

EMBEDDED OUTCOME: S3.H10.L1. *Be sure to take and record your heart rate at each station.*

Student Choices/Differentiation
- Some stations include choices (e.g., push-ups or modified push-ups; curl-ups or dead bugs; Pilates twists or medicine ball twists; lunges, body squats, or wall sits; rope jumping, jumping jacks, lap running, or running lines).
- All stations are for time at students' selected pace.

What to Look For
- Students recognize the differences between health-related and skill-related fitness.
- Students can match the concepts and the exercises.

Formal and Informal Assessments
- Heart-rate sheets
- Vocabulary sheets
- Curl-up test

Closure
- Today, we reviewed health-related and skill-related fitness concepts and some fitness vocabulary. What did we assess when you took the curl-up test?
- What stations were more skill related than health related?
- You will continue to add to your fitness vocabulary. In the lessons that follow, you will assess fitness in a variety of ways as a check-in from your previous fitness testing and to create a good cardio and weight program for yourself using the FITT principle.
- Who can tell me what the acronym *FITT* stands for? We will be talking much more about it.

Reflection

- Can students differentiate between fitness concepts?
- Can students provide examples of particular concepts (vocabulary)?
- Review curl-up tests results.

Homework

Fill in the vocabulary sheet in the fitness section of the physical education binder.

Resources

Virgilio, S.J. (2012). *Fitness education for children*. 2nd ed. Champaign, IL: Human Kinetics.

Internet keyword search: "FITT principle," "health-related fitness components," "Fitnessgram," "target heart rate"

POSSIBLE VOCABULARY FOR VOCABULARY TASK

1. Cardiorespiratory endurance
2. Muscular strength
3. Muscular endurance
4. Body composition
5. Agility
6. Speed
7. Power
8. Balance
9. Coordination
10. Dynamic stretching
11. Static stretching
12. Aerobic
13. Anaerobic
14. Reaction time
15. Concentric action
16. Eccentric action
17. Fitness

From L.C. MacDonald, R.J. Doan, and S. Chepko, eds., 2018, *Lesson planning for high school physical education* (Reston, VA: SHAPE America; Champaign, IL: Human Kinetics).

LESSON 2: PHYSICAL ACTIVITY LOG

Grade-Level Outcomes

Primary Outcomes

Assessment and program planning: Designs a fitness program, including all components of health-related fitness, for a college student and an employee in the learner's chosen field of work. (S3.H12.L1)

Safety: Applies best practices for participating safely in physical activity, exercise and dance (e.g., injury prevention, proper alignment, hydration, use of equipment, implementation of rules, sun protection). (S4.H5.L1)

Embedded Outcome

Fitness knowledge: Identifies types of strength exercises (isometric, concentric, eccentric) and stretching exercises (static, proprioceptive neuromuscular facilitation [PNF], dynamic) for personal fitness development (e.g., strength, endurance, range of motion). (S3.H9.L1)

Lesson Objectives

The learner will:

- log his physical activity over three days using Activitygram.
- perform proper curl-ups and push-ups during the assessment.
- identify breaks in form (the cues) of curl-ups and push-ups when assessing partners.

Equipment and Materials

- Mat and curl-up strips (1 per pair)
- 3 sit-and-reach boxes
- 3 tape measures (taped to wall for height)
- 3 scales (for weight)
- 3 yardsticks for trunk lift
- Fitnessgram cadence CD
- Fitness test score sheet (1 per student)
- 3-day Activitygram sheet (1 per student)

Introduction

In our previous class, we reviewed vocabulary and health-related and skill-related fitness concepts. Today, you will begin logging your daily activity with the Activitygram Physical Activity Recall. This will provide you with feedback on how active you are each day. You also will complete some check-in fitness assessments for you to document information about your own fitness as well as how to measure and program for others using the FITT and training principles. After assessing your health-related fitness using the Fitnessgram assessments, you will do some weight-training assessments. After this week, you will be able to establish a weekly weight and cardio plan.

Instructional Task: Activitygram Instructions

■ PRACTICE TASK

Hand out the Activitygram three-day log. Students are to log two weekdays and one weekend day and then turn in the log.

Review the log with the class and explain how to fill it out. The Fitnessgram and Activitygram book and CD offer teacher resources with a sample Activitygram. Use it to show students how to log their activity.

Student Choices/Differentiation

- Create or use a different physical activity log to have students capture their weekday and week-end day physical activity behavior.
- Allow students to use a device, app, or website to log their activity.

What to Look For

- Students know how to use and fill in the Activitygram assessment.
- Students understand that they are to fill in two weekdays and one weekend day.

Instructional Task:
Upper-Body Strength and Endurance Testing

■ PRACTICE TASK

Have students complete a number of assessments to see whether they can assess their own fitness and use the assessments for programming purposes. The first task is the Fitnessgram push-up test, which should be a review.

Have students pair up.

Partner A performs the push-up test while Partner B watches for form. Once the Partner A students have completed the test, the Partner B students perform push-ups while Partner A students watch for form.

Students record their scores.

Refinement

Remind students to stay on cadence.

Guiding questions for students:

- What do the push-up and curl-up tests measure?
- What are other ways to measure muscular strength and endurance?
- Are these health-related or skill-related fitness assessments?
- What are the primary muscles you use while doing push-ups?
- What type of contractions are you using for each movement?
- If you wanted to improve your push-up score, what are some alternative activities you could do to work on increasing upper-body strength and endurance? Be sure you are thinking of the same muscle groups.

EMBEDDED OUTCOME: S3.H9.L1. Use these guiding questions to engage students about muscular strength and endurance concepts.

Student Choices/Differentiation

- Perform the assessment within stations.
- Students choose their partners.

What to Look For

Students can identify proper and improper push-up form.

Push-Up Form

- Hands are shoulder-width apart.
- Back is flat (no hills or valleys).
- Elbows lower to 90 degrees.
- Elbows return to straight, locked position.
- Movement is in time with the CD cadence.

Instructional Task: Fitness Station Self-Assessment

■ PRACTICE TASK

Perform this task if time permits; otherwise, carry it over to the next lesson.

Groups of three partners are assigned a station. They rotate through the stations to self-assess the following fitness concepts:

- Sit and reach (flexibility)
- Trunk lift (strength and flexibility)
- Shoulder stretch (flexibility)
- Height and weight

Have students work on vocabulary while waiting to perform station activities.

Sit and Reach Form

- Shoes are off; one leg is straight with the sole of the foot against the box; the other leg is bent with the heel flat on the ground.
- Arms are out, hands together (one on top of the other).
- Student reaches slowly three times and holds the fourth.

Refinements

- Sit and reach: Be sure that the knee does not leave the floor.
- Sit and reach: Watch that hands stay together and students reach slowly and hold the fourth time.

Guiding questions for students:

- What other ways can we measure flexibility?
- How might flexibility affect you as you age? Why is flexibility important?

Student Choices/Differentiation

Students choose their groups.

What to Look For

- Students are assessing properly.
- Students are using appropriate form.

Formal and Informal Assessments

- Push-up test results
- Flexibility assessment results
- Activitygram logs

Closure

- Today, we discussed the Activitygram and you started your self-assessment using the Fitnessgram.
- Tomorrow, you will continue your self-assessment and will work on your vocabulary in preparation for developing fitness programs for college students and working professionals.
- Be prepared to complete a one-mile run. What will that help you measure?

Reflection

- Do students know what each of the tests is testing?
- Do students know how to assess themselves properly?
- Did students understand the Activitygram assessment enough to complete it on their own for three days?

Homework

Complete your Activitygram assessment over three days (two weekdays and a weekend day). This will be due in Lesson 6.

Resources

Meredith, M.D., & Welk, G.J., eds. (2010). *Fitnessgram & Activitygram test administration manual.* 4th ed. Champaign, IL: Human Kinetics.

LESSON 3: HEALTH-RELATED FITNESS ASSESSMENT

Grade-Level Outcomes

Primary Outcomes

Assessment and program planning: Designs a fitness program, including all components of health-related fitness, for a college student and an employee in the learner's chosen field of work. (S3.H12.L1)

Safety: Applies best practices for participating safely in physical activity, exercise and dance (e.g., injury prevention, proper alignment, hydration, use of equipment, implementation of rules, sun protection). (S4.H5.L1)

Lesson Objectives

The learner will:

- perform the dynamic warm-up with correct form.
- define and provide examples of the elements of the FITT principle.
- examine how he or she runs the mile (1.6 km) with his or her lap time splits.

Equipment and Materials

- 1 or 2 stopwatches
- Vocabulary cards (1 set per 2 students)
- 3 sit-and-reach boxes
- 3 tape measures (taped to wall for height)
- 3 scales (for weight)
- Mats and 3 yardsticks for trunk lift

Introduction

Today, you will continue working on your fitness assessments. You will run the mile to measure aerobic capacity (or cardiorespiratory endurance) and finish any other tests you need to finish. Cardiorespiratory endurance is considered the most important area of a fitness program. Who can tell me why? Research shows that acceptable levels of cardiorespiratory endurance are associated with a reduced risk of many health problems. Cardiorespiratory exercise and physical activity, overall, yield the greatest health-related benefits. This does not mean that muscular fitness and flexibility are not important. It just means that cardiorespiratory endurance is very important to health-related fitness.

Instructional Task: Dynamic Warm-Up With FITT Vocabulary

■ PRACTICE TASK

Students pair up and line up one behind the other. The first partner starts the task and when halfway down to the cone or line, the second partner follows.

After the first set of exercises, students pick up one card. They discuss the FITT principle on the card and give an example for both a cardiorespiratory and a strength exercise. See the FITT principle guidelines website in the Resources section of this lesson for the text to create the card.

- Jog down and back
- High knees down and back
- Card one
- Butt kickers down and back
- Card two

- Lunge and twist halfway and jog out down and back
- Card three
- Carioca down and back
- Card four

Collect cards and ask students to share an example for both cardio and strength that includes all four principles.

Guiding questions for students:

- When setting up a fitness plan, what is frequency?
- What are some ways to measure intensity?
- What is time?
- Explain type.

Extension

Provide exercise programs and have students identify each FITT principle.

Student Choices/Differentiation

- Students can take notes and write out definitions and provide an example for homework.
- Students choose different exercises for the dynamic warm-up from a list.
- Let students warm up on their own from a selected list of exercises.
- Students choose their partners.

What to Look For

- Students are performing the warm-up using correct form.
- Students can provide examples for both cardiorespiratory and strength activities.
- Students understand the FITT principle.
- Students' examples are aligned with the concept.

Instructional Task: 1-Mile Run

■ PRACTICE TASK

Students stay with their partners for the 1-mile (1.6 km) run. Partner A runs the mile first while Partner B logs Partner B's lap times. This allows students to see their splits. Once Partner A students have completed their mile, Partner B students line up to run theirs, with Partner A students recording lap times.

If the class is large, prevent congestion by staggering the start using two stopwatches.

As students finish their mile, encourage them to walk around to cool down and to stretch out on their own.

Guiding questions for students:

- Looking at your lap times and your splits, what do you notice about how you run the mile? Is there anything you would like to change or work on?
- Do you think you are in the Healthy Fitness Zone? Looking at your results what can you do to maintain or improve your cardiorespiratory endurance?
- Why is cardiorespiratory endurance considered the most important health-related fitness component?
- How might you assess cardiorespiratory endurance in older adults? What type of lifetime activities do many older adults participate in for cardiorespiratory endurance?

Student Choices/Differentiation

- Students perform the PACER Fitness Test.
- Students perform a walk test.
- Students choose their partners.

What to Look For
- Students are trying their best.
- Students can find their lap split times.
- Students are in the Healthy Fitness Zone.
- Students know why cardiorespiratory endurance is so important.

Instructional Task: Fitness Assessment

■ **PRACTICE TASK**

Students rotate through the assessments that they need to finish.
- Sit and reach
- Trunk lift
- Shoulder stretch
- Height and weight

Extension

Students who are finished can work on vocabulary or walk laps.

Student Choices/Differentiation

Students choose the order in which to complete the assessments.

What to Look For
- Students have completed their fitness assessments.
- Students' fitness logs are complete.

Formal and Informal Assessments
- 1-mile run results
- Vocabulary sheets

Closure
- What did we measure today?
- Why is cardiorespiratory endurance, or aerobic capacity, considered the most important component of any health-related fitness program?
- In what activities can you participate that help build your cardiorespiratory endurance?
- Look over your mile lap times and see how you ran the mile. Also think about how you can maintain or improve your cardiorespiratory endurance. In our next class, we will meet in the weight room to review safety and etiquette and complete more assessments.

Reflection
- Can students provide an example using the FITT principle?
- Are students in the Healthy Fitness Zone?
- Have students completed their fitness assessment logs?

Homework
- Be sure to fill in your vocabulary words in your binder and provide examples for the FITT principle.
- Also using the FITT principle, develop a draft of a three-days-a-week plan for improving or maintaining both your cardiorespiratory endurance and your flexibility. Due two classes from now.

Resources

Meredith, M.D., & Welk, G.J., eds. (2010). *Fitnessgram & Activitygram test administration manual.* 4th ed. Champaign, IL: Human Kinetics.

The Cooper Institute: www.cooperinstitute.org

FITT Principle Guidelines: https:www.verywell.com/f-i-t-t-principle-what-you-need-for-great-work-outs-1231593

LESSON 4: RESISTANCE TRAINING

Grade-Level Outcomes

Primary Outcomes

Assessment and program planning: Designs a fitness program, including all components of health-related fitness, for a college student and an employee in the learner's chosen field of work. (S3.H12.L1)

Safety: Applies best practices for participating safely in physical activity, exercise and dance (e.g., injury prevention, proper alignment, hydration, use of equipment, implementation of rules, sun protection). (S4.H5.L1)

Rules & etiquette: Exhibits proper etiquette, respect for others and teamwork while engaging in physical activity and/or social dance. (S4.H2.L1)

Fitness knowledge: Demonstrates appropriate technique on resistance-training machines and with free weights. (S3.H7.L1)

Fitness activities: Demonstrates competency in 1 or more specialized skills in health-related fitness activities. (S1.H3.L1)

Embedded Outcome

Fitness knowledge: Identifies types of strength exercises (isometric, concentric, eccentric) and stretching exercises (static, proprioceptive neuromuscular facilitation [PNF], dynamic) for personal fitness development (e.g., strength, endurance, range of motion). (S3.H9.L1)

Lesson Objectives

The learner will:

- discuss the importance of the weight room rules and abide by them.
- properly demonstrate the stations and discuss the muscle groups being exercised.
- demonstrate correct form and alignment.

Equipment and Materials

- Station cards
- Notes (or PowerPoint)
- Weight room: all you have available for resistance training (bands, free weights, medicine balls, machines, and so on)

Introduction

Now that you have assessed your health-related fitness, we will discuss how to set up a resistance training plan for muscle fitness based on your goals and data from Fitnessgram and Activitygram. At the end of the module, you will be able to develop a plan for yourself as a college student as well as a plan for an individual in your choice career. Before you can do that, we must review the benefits of resistance training and different exercises that we can do. Today, we will review safety and etiquette in the weight room and the different stations available to you for working on muscular fitness.

Note: The focus of this module is not on weight training. It's a good module for scaffolding on previous learning. The best time to conduct this learning segment is after students have learned about resistance training and the weight room. Still, this lesson reviews safety, etiquette, and how to use equipment properly.

Instructional Task:
Weight Room Etiquette and Safety Reminders

■ PRACTICE TASK

Have students take notes in their binders on the benefits of resistance training:

- Easier performance of daily activities
- Increased lean body mass
- Increased metabolism
- Stronger muscles, tendons, and ligaments
- Stronger bones and reduced risk of osteoporosis
- Decreased risk of injury
- Decreased risk of low-back pain
- Enhanced feelings of well-being and self-confidence

Give students the vocabulary words for the lesson. They can fill in the definitions.

Review safety and weight room rules:

- No horseplay at any time.
- No food, drink, or gum in the weight room.
- Do not sit on equipment during your rest interval.
- Wear proper clothes.
- Wear shoes at all times (no sandals or open-toe shoes).
- Do not slam the weights on the weight machines.
- Use a spotter with all free-lifting stations (bench press, incline press, squats, and so on).
- Return all free weights to the correct weight racks.
- Report any injury to the teacher immediately.
- Never lift weights without a teacher present in the room.
- Always wipe down stations after use and at the end of class with proper cleaning materials.

Demonstrate correct technique for each lift, including proper hand and foot placement and spine alignment.

Refinement

Remind students to lift weights at a slow, steady pace (do not lift too fast).

Guiding questions for students:

- Why is proper alignment so important?
- Why should you lift at a consistent, slow-to-moderate rate and not fast?

Student Choices/Differentiation

- Provide handouts to go over with the class.
- Have students read sections aloud.

What to Look For

- Students can identify the importance of the weight room rules.
- Students are engaged in the discussion and are taking notes.

Instructional Task: Station Review

■ PRACTICE TASK

Show students how to spot properly on stations where spotting is required. At other stations, partners are responsible for double-checking that the machine is set up appropriately for their partners to use correct form and alignment.

Place students in groups of two to four (depends on the number of stations). Give them a cue card for a particular machine or station. The card will show how to adjust the machine weights (e.g., pins, seats) and the proper alignment and movement. The cards also identify what muscles are being worked. Students go to the appropriate station and learn how to use that machine and how to adjust it appropriately.

Refinement

Provide feedback specific to using the equipment safely.

Extension

Groups share and demonstrate their stations to the rest of the class, showing how to use the station and what muscle groups it works.

EMBEDDED OUTCOME: S3.H9.L1. As groups share their stations, they should indicate the type of exercise (e.g., isometric, concentric, eccentric).

Guiding questions for students:

- When you are not lifting, what are you doing for your partner?
- If you want to increase your leg strength, what stations work on leg strength?

Student Choices/Differentiation

- Offer basic instruction on more difficult stations, and then let students explore stations safely with a guided discovery sheet.
- Students may use a self-check test (Darst & Pangrazi, 2009).

What to Look For

- Students can demonstrate their assigned station properly.
- Students can identify what muscle groups are being targeted by specific exercises.
- Students can perform resistance exercises at stations with proper cues and alignment.

Instructional Task: Station Review

■ PRACTICE TASK

After all groups have presented their station, groups rotate to the next one. If time permits, groups will rotate through all the stations before class ends to become familiar with what equipment is available and how to use it properly.

Refinements

- Remind students to lift in a slow, controlled manner.
- Ensure time is used effectively at each station with rest and sets.

Student Choices/Differentiation

Students choose the amount of weight and the number of sets and reps, so long as they are safe.

What to Look For

- Students can identify the muscle groups being targeted without looking at the station card.
- Students can perform the exercises safely and properly.
- Partners are spotting when necessary.

Formal and Informal Assessments

Exit slip: List three weight room rules and protocols.

Closure

- Today, you learned about the weight room and resistance training. Do we need machines or special equipment to work on muscle fitness?
- What other things could we do to work on muscle fitness?
- What are the benefits of resistance training?
- Tonight, think about a goal for your resistance training. Do you want to build strength? Do you want to be more toned? Do you want to work more on muscular endurance or a combination?
- Depending on your goals, the amount of weight and the number of sets and reps will be different. We will discuss this more in our next class. Be sure to complete the vocabulary in your binder. Also, remember that your Activitygram is due in Lesson 6. Be sure you log two weekdays and one weekend day. Your cardio and flexibility plan is due next time.

Reflection

- Can students set up the equipment properly?
- Do students know which stations work on which muscle groups?
- Are students using correct form and proper alignment?
- Are students being safe and responsible?

Homework

Write down whether you want to work on building strength, toning your body, building muscular endurance, or working toward a combination of those. Give reasons for your answer. Please bring your answer to our next class, when we will be in the weight room.

Resources

Dale, D., McConnell, K., & Corbin C. (2007). *Fitness for life: Wraparound teacher's edition and resources kit*. 5th ed. Champaign, IL: Human Kinetics.

Darst, P.W., & Pangrazi, R.P. (2009). *Dynamic physical education for secondary school students*. 6th ed. San Francisco: Pearson Benjamin Cummings.

Faigenbaum, A., & Westcott, W. (2009). *Youth strength training programs for health, fitness, and sport*. Champaign, IL: Human Kinetics.

Very Well: https:www.verywell.com/the-principle-of-overload-definition-3120362

Very Well: https://www.verywell.com/principle-of-specificity-definition-3120375

Internet keyword search: "weight room safety," "weight room protocols," "weight lifting technique"

RESISTANCE TRAINING VOCABULARY

Specificity[1]—Students must select exercises that mimic the skill patterns used in the sport and that involve only the muscle groups used to perform a technical skill.

Overload—Using an excessive load to attain improvement in training.

Progression[2]—An increase in work being completed over time. This usually is represented by an increase in volume or intensity during a training program.

Repetition[3]—One complete movement of an exercise.

Set[3]—A group of repetitions performed continuously without resting.

Strength[3]—The maximal amount of force a muscle or muscle group can generate.

Strength training[3]—Also called resistance training. A specialized method of conditioning that includes the progressive use of a wide variety of resistive loads and a variety of training modalities designed to enhance muscular fitness.

[1]-Reprinted from Bompa and Carrera 2015.

[2]-Reprinted from NSCA & Brown (ed) 2017.

[3]-Reprinted from Faigenbaum and Westcott 2009.

From L.C. MacDonald, R.J. Doan, and S. Chepko, eds., 2018, *Lesson planning for high school physical education* (Reston, VA: SHAPE America; Champaign, IL: Human Kinetics).

LESSON 5: MODIFIED 1 REPETITION MAXIMUM

Grade-Level Outcomes

Primary Outcomes

Assessment & program planning: Designs a fitness program, including all components of health-related fitness, for a college student and an employee in the learner's chosen field of work. (S3.H12.L1)

Safety: Applies best practices for participating safely in physical activity, exercise and dance (e.g., injury prevention, proper alignment, hydration, use of equipment, implementation of rules, sun protection). (S4.H5.L1)

Fitness knowledge: Demonstrates appropriate technique on resistance-training machines and with free weights. (S3.H7.L1)

Fitness activities: Demonstrates competency in 1 or more specialized skills in health-related fitness activities. (S1.H3.L1)

Embedded Outcome

Fitness knowledge: Identifies types of strength exercises (isometric, concentric, eccentric) and stretching exercises (static, proprioceptive neuromuscular facilitation [PNF], dynamic) for personal fitness development (e.g., strength, endurance, range of motion). (S3.H9.L1)

Lesson Objectives

The learner will:

- determine her or his modified 1 repetition maximum (1 RM) for selected exercises.
- perform weight training activities using correct form and proper alignment.
- spot her or his peers properly to ensure safety.

Equipment and Materials

- Modified 1RM task sheet with table (1 per student; look up the table online if you don't have access to one)
- Weight room

Introduction

Last lesson, we reviewed the weight room and all it has to offer. Today, we will focus on how to set up an appropriate muscle fitness training program for a two-days-a-week plan depending on your goals. First, you will determine your modified 1 repetition max, which will help you determine how much weight you should be lifting for particular exercises based on your goals and sets and reps. This will help you apply the FITT and overload principles to the muscular fitness portion of your plan.

Instructional Task: Warm-Up

■ PRACTICE TASK

Before grouping students for the modified 1RM activity, run them through a 5- to 7-minute warm-up of light cardio, range-of-motion (ROM) exercises, and light stretches.

Guiding questions for students:

- Why is it important to warm up before lifting weights?
- What are some ways you can warm up before lifting?

Student Choices/Differentiation

- Students may jog a lap and then perform some dynamic stretches.
- Students may go through a dynamic stretching routine.

What to Look For

Students are participating in the warm-up activities.

Instructional Task:
Finding Modified 1 Repetition Max (1RM)

■ PRACTICE TASK

Hand out the modified 1RM instructions and task sheet and review them with students.

Have students pair up and start at a station. Review proper spotting. There are a total of 16 stations (you can make more or fewer as desired). Nine stations are modified 1RM stations, and the others are not.

The modified 1RM stations are as follows:

- Shoulder press
- Leg press
- Bench press
- Knee extension
- Hamstring curl
- Biceps curl
- Heel raise
- Lat pull-down
- Triceps press

Other stations include the following:

- Planks
- Curl-ups or V-sits
- Side planks
- Dead bugs
- Medicine ball twists, seated or standing
- Opposite arm/leg extensions on hands and knees
- Medicine ball partner twists, seated or standing

Number the stations so that about every other station measures a modified 1RM. Rotate students through the stations.

EMBEDDED OUTCOME: S3.H9.L1. Have students review muscle groups and types of exercises at each station.

Refinements

- Be sure the weight is not too heavy and can be lifted at least five times.
- Be sure students are lifting in a slow and controlled manner.
- Be sure students are lifting through the full and appropriate range of motion.
- Be sure equipment is adjusted appropriately and peers are spotting.

Guiding questions for students:

- Who can tell me what 1RM is?
- What does it measure?
- When you are not lifting, what are you doing for your partner?

Student Choices/Differentiation

- At the non-1RM stations, students have the option of doing flexibility exercises or yoga poses.
- Students choose their partners.

What to Look For

- Students can lift with correct form and technique.
- Students can find their estimated 1RM.

Formal and Informal Assessments

- 1RM task sheets
- Cardio and flexibility plans

Closure

- Today, you found your estimated 1RM. Why is finding your 1RM helpful when planning a fitness program?
- When determining how much weight you will lift, what part of the FITT principle are you using?
- What other principle does it cover?
- Now using your Fitnessgram and estimated 1RM, develop the muscle fitness portion of your fitness plan. You should end up with a five-days-a-week plan that includes all the health-related fitness components with two days of muscle fitness and three days of cardio each week.
- Turn in your cardio and flexibility plans, so I can review them.

Reflection

- How well did students do in finding the estimated 1RM for the different muscle groups?
- Were they putting in a good effort?
- Were they able to use the table correctly? Did partners spot attentively?
- Review cardio and flexibility plans.

Homework

- Using your modified 1RM and your overall goals for muscular fitness, develop a resistance-training routine that you can complete two days a week that includes upper- and lower-body and core exercises. This should be in addition to your cardio and flexibility plan draft.
- Remember you can work on muscle fitness without a weight room, so don't just plan on using machines. You can use body weight, bands, medicine balls, free weights, and so on.
- Be sure to include the actual exercises you will perform and the FITT principles.
- Note: If you want to work on increasing strength, you will do fewer reps and sets at a higher percentage of your estimated 1RM (heavier weight). To work on toning and muscular endurance, then you would use lighter weight (a lower percentage of estimated 1RM) with higher reps and sets. Your draft plan is due next class.

Resources

Dale, D., McConnell, K., & Corbin C. (2007). *Fitness for life: Wraparound teacher's edition and resources kit*. 5th ed. Champaign, IL: Human Kinetics.

Faigenbaum, A., & Westcott, W. (2009). *Youth strength training programs for health, fitness, and sport*. Champaign, IL: Human Kinetics.

National Academy of Sports Medicine: www.nasm.org

Built Lean: www.builtlean.com

Internet keyword search: "1-Rep Max," "modified 1-Rep Max," "FITT principle"

DETERMINING MODIFIED 1RM

1. Choose a weight that you think you can lift between 5 and 10 times. Do not use a weight that you can lift fewer than five times.

2. Using the proper technique and alignment, lift the weight as many times as possible. Count the number of lifts and write the number on your task sheet. If you were able to do more than 10, rest while your partner goes, and then try again after adjusting the weight.

3. If you can tell that you will not be able to lift the weight at least 5 times, stop and adjust the weight. Partners should be watching and helping for safety.

If you were able to find the appropriate weight for lifting it 5 to 10 times, but no more, then refer to the table posted on the wall (or school's physical education web site). Find the weight that you lifted in the left-hand column. Now find the number of reps that you completed in the top row. Your estimated 1RM score is the number in the box where the column and row intersect. Record that on your task sheet.

From L.C. MacDonald, R.J. Doan, and S. Chepko, eds., 2018, *Lesson planning for high school physical education* (Reston, VA: SHAPE America; Champaign, IL: Human Kinetics). Adapted from: Dale, D., McConnell, K., & Corbin C. (2007). *Fitness for life: Wraparound teacher's edition and resources kit*. 5th ed. Champaign, IL: Human Kinetics; Faigenbaum, A., & Westcott, W. (2009). *Youth strength training programs for health, fitness, and sport*. Champaign, IL: Human Kinetics.

TASK SHEET

Exercise	Weight	Number of reps	Estimated 1RM
Shoulder press			
Leg press			
Bench press			
Knee extension			
Hamstring curl			
Biceps curl			
Heel raise			
Lat pull-down			
Triceps press			

From L.C. MacDonald, R.J. Doan, and S. Chepko, eds., 2018, *Lesson planning for high school physical education* (Reston, VA: SHAPE America; Champaign, IL: Human Kinetics).

LESSON 6: STEP AEROBICS WORKOUT 1 AND TARGET HEART RATE ZONE

Grade-Level Outcomes

Primary Outcomes

Assessment & program planning: Designs a fitness program, including all components of health-related fitness, for a college student and an employee in the learner's chosen field of work. (S3.H12.L1)

Fitness knowledge: Calculates target heart rate and applies that information to personal fitness plan. (S3.H10.L1)

Fitness activities: Demonstrates competency in 1 or more specialized skills in health-related fitness activities. (S1.H3.L1)

Embedded Outcome

Safety: Applies best practices for participating safely in physical activity, exercise and dance (e.g., injury prevention, proper alignment, hydration, use of equipment, implementation of rules, sun protection). (S4.H5.L1)

Lesson Objectives

The learner will:

- perform the step aerobics routine with correct form and alignment.
- perform the step aerobics routine within his or her target heart rate zone.
- participate safely in the routine by monitoring heart rate and slowing down or modifying activity as needed.

Equipment and Materials

- 1 stepper per student
- Upbeat music (step aerobics) or video

Introduction

Let's talk about your cardio/flexibility plans (share common feedback). For the next several lessons, we will participate in muscle fitness activities two days a week and in cardiorespiratory activities three days a week. You will be given a variety of activities to participate in related to maintaining or improving your health-related fitness. You will continue to use the FITT principles in class. You also will create a plan for yourself as a college student based on your own Fitnessgram and Activitygram scores. Today, we will focus on cardio. We will be doing a step aerobics routine. The goal during the step aerobics is to stay within your target heart rate zone.

Instructional Task: Determining Target Heart Rate Zone

■ PRACTICE TASK

Students lie quietly for 2 minutes and then take their resting heart rates. Students use the Karvonen formula to find their moderate target heart rate zone (50 percent to 70 percent) and their vigorous target heart rate zone (70 percent to 85 percent).

Extension

Students find their 10-second target heart rate zones by dividing lower and upper limits by 6.

Guiding questions for students:

- What does heart rate tell us?
- Why do we want a low resting heart rate?
- Target heart rate can be used to measure what part of the FITT principles for exercise?

Student Choices/Differentiation

Students may work with a partner when using the formula to calculate moderate target heart rate zone.

What to Look For

- Student calculations are correct.
- Students can articulate why knowing resting and target heart rates are important.

Instructional Task: Step Aerobics

■ PRACTICE TASK

Have students sit at the steppers.

Discuss safety and possible modifications.

Students participate in a beginning step aerobics routine that includes a warm-up, a combo-move workout phase, and a cool-down. Use a DVD or play a routine from YouTube that has good basic moves and simple workout combos that are easy to learn (45 minutes). You could also create your own routine for students to follow.

EMBEDDED OUTCOME: S4.H5.L1. Reinforce safe practices when engaging in aerobic activity and specifically step aerobics.

After the basic warm-up phase, pause and have students take a 15-second heart rate and record it.

After each of the three combos, pause and have students take a 15-second heart rate and record it on their target heart rate (THR) zone sheet.

After the cool-down, have students take a 15-second heart rate and record it.

Note: You can create and teach your own routine with a good warm-up, workout phase, and cool-down. Be sure you have appropriate step music and know how to cue.

Using a link or video is helpful because then you can participate (model) with students as well as move around and help students individually and provide feedback and prompts.

If you are using a video, make sure you know the routine and have at least watched or gone through it once.

Refinement

Watch for foot placement and body alignment on the stepper.

Guiding questions for students:

- Are you in your target heart rate zone?
- Do you feel as if you are getting a good aerobic workout?
- Why is cooling down important?

Student Choices/Differentiation

- Students may perform the exercises on the floor without using the stepper.
- Students may use heart rate monitors, if available.
- Students may add height to the stepper.
- Students may perform more or fewer arm movements.
- Students may choose their routines from a list.
- Students can perform at a slower rate.

What to Look For

- Students are able to stay on beat.
- Students are working within their target heart rate zones.
- Students are performing the moves properly with correct form and alignment.

Formal and Informal Assessments

- Resistance training plan
- Activitygram
- Exit slip: List three other activities you could complete for a good cardio workout.

Closure

- What did you like about today's cardio activity?
- What are some other group exercise activities that might be available to you in the community?
- How about at your choice college?
- How can staying physically active help you in college?
- What are some of the benefits of physical activity for college students?
- Make sure you turn in your Activitygram and resistance training assignments.
- For homework, you will create a plan for you as a college student in your choice of college.

Reflection

- Were students engaged in the routine?
- Did students stay moderately active for the duration of the step aerobics activity? Were students able to monitor their heart rate and stay within their THR zones during the activity?
- Review Activitygram and resistance training assignments to check student understanding.

Homework

- You are a student at the college of your choice, taking 15 or 16 credit hours. Using your Fitnessgram and Activitygram results and your draft plans, develop a fitness program for yourself at college.
- You must include the components of health-related fitness and use the FITT and training principles.
- Be sure to look up your choice college to see what that school and the local community have to offer for physical activity participation.
- Make yourself a realistic plan using the college's resources.
- Use your class notes and refer to the scoring rubric for guidance.

Resources

Kennedy-Armbruster, C., & Yoke, M. (2009). *Methods of group exercise instruction*. 2nd ed. Champaign, IL: Human Kinetics.

Jenny Ford step aerobics workout: She has various workouts, so select one that works best for you. Workouts can be downloaded for a small fee if this will work better than using Wi-Fi in the gymnasium.

Internet keyword search: "step aerobics"

SCORING GUIDE FOR COLLEGE STUDENT FITNESS PLAN

Student: _____

College: _____

Principle applied	Not included or vague; need to revise	Level 1 C– to C+	Level 2 B– to B+	Level 3 A
Overload	0/3	1/3	2/3	3/3
Progression	0/3	1/3	2/3	3/3
FITT aerobic	0-1/4	2/4	3/4	4/4
FITT muscular	0-1/4	2/4	3/4	4/4
FITT flexibility	0-1/4	2/4	3/4	4/4
Personal goals for the health-related fitness concepts are outlined and addressed within plan	No goals stated	One goal stated but not explained	A few goals stated and identifiable throughout plan	A few goals stated and shown clearly in plan
Activities outlined and described and specificity addressed	No	Stated activities	Described activities	Activities are specific to goals and plan
Final score:	Comments:			

Note: Plan should be for 30 days minimum. Please place goals at top of the plan. The fitness plan must be typed. Points will be taken away accordingly.

From L.C. MacDonald, R.J. Doan, and S. Chepko, eds., 2018, *Lesson planning for high school physical education* (Reston, VA: SHAPE America; Champaign, IL: Human Kinetics).

LESSON 7: MUSCLE FITNESS WORKOUT 1

Grade-Level Outcomes

Primary Outcomes

Assessment & program planning: Designs a fitness program, including all components of health-related fitness, for a college student and an employee in the learner's chosen field of work. (S3.H12.L1)

Safety: Applies best practices for participating safely in physical activity, exercise and dance (e.g., injury prevention, proper alignment, hydration, use of equipment, implementation of rules, sun protection). (S4.H5.L1)

Fitness activities: Demonstrates competency in 1 or more specialized skills in health-related fitness activities. (S1.H3.L1)

Fitness knowledge: Demonstrates appropriate technique on resistance-training machines and with free weights. (S3.H7.L1)

Embedded Outcome

Fitness knowledge: Identifies types of strength exercises (isometric, concentric, eccentric) and stretching exercises (static, proprioceptive neuromuscular facilitation [PNF], dynamic) for personal fitness development (e.g., strength, endurance, range of motion). (S3.H9.L1)

Lesson Objectives

The learner will:

- execute appropriate sets and reps for his or her weight-training goals.
- lift the appropriate percentage of his or her modified 1RM based on his goals.
- participate safely in the weight room using proper amount of weight, form, alignment, technique, and spotting.

Equipment and Materials

- Jump ropes (1 per pair)
- Weight-training log sheets (1 per student)
- Pencils (1 per pair)
- Weight room (station task cards)

Introduction

I was really pleased with your resistance training plans and your Activitygram logs. Please look over the notes I made on your papers. Last class was a cardio day. Today is our muscle fitness day. After we warm up, you will be in the weight room working on your muscle fitness goals. Remember, if you are working on developing more strength, then you will do fewer sets and reps at a higher weight. Does this mean you are lifting your max weight? No! But you are lifting a greater percentage of your modified 1RM. If your goal is overall muscle fitness toning or endurance, then you will do more sets and reps at a lower percentage of your modified 1RM. Regardless of your goal, you should be lifting with slow, smooth, controlled movements. Remember to take adequate rest between sets, and partners should be watching and spotting as necessary to keep everyone safe. Remember that the weight room is a quiet space . . . low whisper voices only.

Instructional Task: Warm-Up (8-10 Minutes)

■ PRACTICE TASK

Have students pair up. Each pair will have one jump rope.

One partner will start with the jump rope and jump for 45 seconds while the other partner does one of the following:

- Mountain climbers
- High knee skips
- Lunge and twist
- Butt kickers

Partners switch every 45 seconds and go down the list of non-jump-rope activities until they have each completed them all.

Extension

Switch between jump rope and dynamic stretches in place of other activities.

Refinement

Remind students that form is more important than speed when doing the dynamic stretches.

Guiding questions for students:

- Why is warming up before lifting weights important?
- What kind of warm-up is best for weight training?

Student Choices/Differentiation

- All students may participate in jump rope intervals at the same time.
- Students may choose to do a dynamic warm-up.
- Students choose their partners.

What to Look For

- Students are performing activities safely and correctly.
- Students are using correct form.

Instructional Task: Weight Room Workout

■ PRACTICE TASK

Assign partner groups to stations as they enter the weight room and grab a log sheet and a pencil. Students adjust the equipment as necessary and begin their first set. Partners rotate each set to provide rest in between sets as they each do their reps. If students finish before they are to rotate to the next station, then they wait patiently and quietly. Remind students about safety and spotting.

Rotate students through with a timer or by using low but upbeat music with breaks.

Following is a list of possible stations of machines, medicine balls, and free weights that you could set up in the weight room. With mats, you can also do body-weight work.

Resistance Machine Stations

- Leg press
- Leg extension
- Leg curl
- Hip adduction
- Hip abduction
- Chest press
- Seated row
- Overhead press
- Biceps curl
- Triceps extension

- Weight-assisted pull-up
- Weight-assisted bar dip
- Low-back extensions
- Abdominal curl

Free-Weight Stations
- Barbell squat
- Dumbbell step-up
- Barbell chest press
- Dumbbell chest fly
- Dumbbell one-arm row
- Dumbbell overhead press
- Dumbbell biceps curl
- Dumbbell triceps extension

Medicine Ball Stations
- Medicine ball squat toss
- Medicine ball lunge pass
- Medicine ball chest pass
- Medicine ball overhead throw
- Medicine ball backward throw
- Medicine ball side pass
- Medicine ball overhead squat
- Medicine ball single-leg dip and reach
- Medicine ball push-up
- Medicine ball lower-back lift
- Medicine ball V-sit
- Medicine ball twist and turn

Body-Weight Stations
- Push-ups
- Plank
- Curl-ups or another abdominal exercise
- Prone back raise
- Trunk curl
- Triceps dips

Set up enough stations that vary upper body, lower body, and core for all students to participate in during the class period. You can number the stations so that students rotate through a mix of exercises. Students should mark on their log sheets what stations they finished. This will help you place students back into the correct stations because it will likely take two class periods to get through the weight circuit. Remind students about safe spotting practices.

If you do not have access to the weight room, provide body-weight, free-weight, resistance band, stabilizer ball, and medicine ball weight-training tasks in a station format.

Refinements
- Students adjust form and alignment as needed.
- Students adjust weight and number of sets and reps based on goals and safety.
- Have students breathe in for 3 or 4 seconds as they lift and breathe out for 3 or 4 seconds as they lower for both concentric and eccentric work. This helps ensure controlled movement.
- Make sure students are moving through the full range of motion on each exercise.

EMBEDDED OUTCOME: S3.H9.L1. As students go through the stations, have them identify what type of exercises they are performing (i.e., isometric, concentric, eccentric).

Guiding questions for students:

- What percentage of your 1RM max are you working at? Do you need to make any adjustments?
- How did you determine the weight for the other exercises you did not have a 1RM for?
- What muscle groups are you working on at each station?

Student Choices/Differentiation

- Students choose their partners.

What to Look For

- Students are performing exercises with correct form and technique.
- Students are going through the full ROM with slow, controlled, smooth movement.
- Students are lifting the appropriate weight for their goals.
- Students are spotting and keeping partners safe.

Instructional Task: Stretching

■ PRACTICE TASK

Students find an open space to stretch. They go through the following flexibility routine:

- Chest stretch
- Triceps and lat stretch
- Upper-back stretch
- Hamstring stretch
- Low-back and hip stretch
- Inner-thigh stretch
- Quad stretch
- Calf stretch

Refinements

- Remind students not to bounce.
- Students stretch to slight discomfort and hold the position in proper alignment for 20 seconds. They should feel the stretch, but it should not be painful.

Student Choices/Differentiation

- Students may stretch with a partner.
- Students may choose to do the upper- and lower-body stretches in their plans.

What to Look For

- Students are stretching with good alignment.
- Students are holding the stretches for the full count.
- Students checked their heart rates during cool-down.

Formal and Informal Assessments

- Station log sheets

Closure

- Today was the first day of your resistance training. How do you feel?
- Do you need to adjust any weight or sets and reps? It is okay to do so, just be sure to put it in your log.

- Be sure to make note of what station you finished so you can start there next time we're in the weight room. Why is this important? The stations are designed to give you each an overall body workout. They rotate from upper body, lower body, and core so no matter where you leave off each day, you should have worked a variety of muscle groups.
- If you were lifting more often, how might you set up your routine? Next time, we will meet in the gym for step aerobics.

Reflection

- Did students log their sets and reps?
- Were students moving through the resistance exercises at a good rate and with correct form?
- Were the stations adequate?
- Do any stations need to be adjusted for the next weight-training lesson?

Homework

Continue to work on your college student fitness plan.

Resources

Faigenbaum, A., & Westcott, W. (2009). *Youth strength training programs for health, fitness, and sport.* Champaign, IL: Human Kinetics.

Internet keyword search: "resistance training exercises," "strength training," "weight room spotting"

LESSON 8: STEP AEROBICS WORKOUT 2

Grade-Level Outcomes

Primary Outcomes

Assessment & program planning: Designs a fitness program, including all components of health-related fitness, for a college student and an employee in the learner's chosen field of work. (S3.H12.L1)

Fitness knowledge: Calculates target heart rate and applies that information to personal fitness plan. (S3.H10.L1)

Fitness activities: Demonstrates competency in 1 or more specialized skills in health-related fitness activities. (S1.H3.L1)

Embedded Outcome

Physical activity knowledge: Discusses the benefits of a physically active lifestyle as it relates to college or career productivity. (S3.H1.L1)

Lesson Objectives

The learner will:
- perform the step aerobics routine with correct form and alignment.
- perform the step aerobics routine within her THR zone.
- participate safely in the routine by monitoring her heart rate and slowing down or modifying activity as needed.

Equipment and Materials
- 1 stepper per student
- Upbeat music (step aerobics) or video

Introduction

Today is our second cardio day. We will continue with step aerobics this week and start kickboxing next week. Remember, it is important to work continuously at a moderate level to get the aerobic benefits from the activity. You will pause to take your heart rate to see if you are working in your target heart rate zone. Tomorrow, we are back in the weight room. Remember to participate safely, slow down as needed, and drink plenty of water.

Instructional Task: Step Aerobics

■ PRACTICE TASK

Students sit at a stepper for quick safety reminders.

Students then participate in the same routine as the first aerobics lesson or a new routine on DVD, from YouTube, or that you created (45 minutes).

You can find many more routines on YouTube.

Intermittently pause and have students take a 15-second heart rate.

Refinements
- Check form, foot alignment, and pace.

EMBEDDED OUTCOME: S3.H1.L1 After the workout, lead a discussion with students on the benefits of an active lifestyle:
- What are the benefits of a healthy, active lifestyle?
- How about more specifically to a college student?
- How might an active lifestyle affect your performance at college or at work?

Guiding questions for students:

- Are you in your target heart rate zone?
- Do you feel as if you are getting a good aerobic workout?
- At what intensity are you working? At what frequency and for what amount of time are you participating in step aerobics this week?

Student Choices/Differentiation

- Students may perform the exercises on the floor without using the stepper.
- Students may perform at a slower rate.
- Students may exercise near a wall if they need some help with balance.
- Adjust step height if needed.
- Add or remove arm movements.
- Students may use heart rate monitors, if available.
- Students may choose their routine.

What to Look For

- Students are able to stay on beat.
- Students are working at a moderate level.
- Students are performing the moves properly with correct form and alignment.

Formal and Informal Assessments

Exit slip: Give two examples of how aerobic activities contribute to a healthy lifestyle.

Closure

- What did you like about today's cardio activity?
- Are you feeling more comfortable with the movements?
- Next time, we'll be working on muscle fitness and we'll have a quiz on resistance training concepts. Be sure to review before class.

Reflection

- Were students engaged in the routine?
- Did students stay moderately active for the duration of the step aerobics activity?
- Were students able to monitor their heart rates and stay within their THR zones during activity?

Homework

- Continue to work on your fitness plan as a college student.
- Evaluate what resources are available to you while at your choice college, and consider time and scheduling.
- Review for the quiz on resistance training.

Resources

Kennedy-Armbruster, C., & Yoke, M. (2009). *Methods of group exercise instruction*. 2nd ed. Champaign, IL: Human Kinetics.

Jenny Ford step aerobics workout: She has various workouts, so select one that works best for you. Workouts can be downloaded for a small fee if this will work better than using Wi-Fi in the gymnasium.

Internet keyword search: "step aerobics"

LESSON 9: MUSCLE FITNESS WORKOUT 2

Grade-Level Outcomes

Primary Outcomes

Assessment & program planning: Designs a fitness program, including all components of health-related fitness, for a college student and an employee in the learner's chosen field of work. (S3.H12.L1)

Fitness knowledge: Demonstrates appropriate technique on resistance-training machines and with free weights. (S3.H7.L1)

Safety: Applies best practices for participating safely in physical activity, exercise and dance (e.g., injury prevention, proper alignment, hydration, use of equipment, implementation of rules, sun protection). (S4.H5.L1)

Fitness activities: Demonstrates competency in 1 or more specialized skills in health-related fitness activities. (S1.H3.L1)

Embedded Outcome

Fitness knowledge: Identifies types of strength exercises (isometric, concentric, eccentric) and stretching exercises (static, proprioceptive neuromuscular facilitation [PNF], dynamic) for personal fitness development (e.g., strength, endurance, range of motion). (S3.H9.L1)

Lesson Objectives

The learner will:

- lift weights using correct form and alignment.
- lift the appropriate amount of weight based on her goals and modified 1RM.
- monitor and spot her partner to keep each other safe.

Equipment and Materials

Weight room

Introduction

Today is day two of your resistance workout. Be sure to adjust the weights or your sets and reps as needed to meet your goals. Remember, do not lift too heavy or too fast. The best gains come from correct form and slow, controlled movement. Be sure you are adjusting the equipment to keep in proper alignment. Partners should be checking and spotting. Keep each other safe. Be sure to start at the station you left off on in the previous class. It should be marked on your log.

Instructional Task: Warm-Up

■ **PRACTICE TASK**

Students spread out and do the following warm-up:

- Jumping jacks (25)
- Ski jumps (20)
- Elbow-to-knee march (20)
- Frankensteins in place (10)
- Squat jumps (10)
- Lunge and twist (10)
- In-place butt kickers (20)

Repeat if needed.

Guiding questions for students:

- Why is warming up important?
- How is warming up for weight training different from warming up for other activities such as cardio activities?

Student Choices/Differentiation

- Students can complete each activity for a certain number of reps and sets.
- Students may warm up with jump rope intervals.

What to Look For

- Students are warming up.
- Students can explain why warming up before lifting weights is important.
- Students are performing activities safely and properly.

Instructional Task: Weight Room Workout

■ PRACTICE TASK

Remind students to start at the station after the last station they finished in the previous muscle fitness lesson. Ask them to grab a log sheet and a pencil. Students adjust the equipment as necessary and begin their first set. Partners rotate each set to provide rest in between sets. If students finish before they are to rotate to the next station, they wait patiently and quietly.

Rotate students through with a timer or by using low but upbeat music with breaks. Remind students about safety and spotting.

Refinements

- Make sure students are moving through their full ROM.
- Students should move through the exercises at a slow and controlled pace.
- Students adjust weight and equipment for safety, form, and alignment.

EMBEDDED OUTCOME: S3.H9.L1. As students go through the stations, have them identify what type of exercises they are performing (i.e., isometric, concentric, eccentric).

Guiding questions for students:

- Do you need to adjust any of your weights or 1RM percentages? Be sure to use the correct weight for the sets and reps that you want to do.
- Is your resistance training plan balanced across the muscle groups?

Student Choices/Differentiation

Students choose their partners.

What to Look For

- Students are performing exercises with correct form and technique.
- Students are going through the full ROM with slow, controlled, smooth movement.
- Students are lifting the appropriate weight for their goals.
- Students are spotting and keeping partners safe.
- Students are logging the weight and sets and reps of each station in their logs.

Instructional Task: Cool-Down and Stretching

■ PRACTICE TASK

Students find an open space to stretch. They go through the following flexibility routine:

- Chest stretch
- Triceps and lat stretch
- Upper-back stretch
- Hamstring stretch
- Low-back and hip stretch
- Inner-thigh stretch
- Quad stretch
- Calf stretch

Refinements

- Remind students not to bounce.
- Students stretch to slight discomfort and hold the position in proper alignment for 20 seconds. They should feel the stretch, but it should not be painful.

Student Choices/Differentiation

- Students can stretch with a partner.
- Students may choose to do the upper- and lower-body stretches in their plans.

What to Look For

- Students are stretching with good alignment.
- Students are holding the stretches for the full count.

Instructional Task: Weight-Training Test

■ PRACTICE TASK

Administer a quiz on resistance training concepts (e.g., what exercises work what muscles, how to lift for toning versus strength, analysis of correct form and alignment).

Student Choices/Differentiation

Quiz could be given as a take home assignment to allow more time.

Formal and Informal Assessments

- Resistance training quiz
- Station log sheets

Closure

- Today was day two of your resistance training program.
- Imagine it is day 20 of your program and some of the lifts are becoming easier. What might you need to do to your program?
- What training principles should you examine? (Answer: overload and progression)
- Think of how you might change your workout to address each principle.
- Nice work today. Tomorrow, we will be back in the gym for cardio step aerobics.

Reflection

- How are students doing with their logs?
- Are students lifting weights with good technique and form?
- Do students understand the overload and progression principles?

Homework

Bring your college fitness programs to class next time. You will be sharing it with a peer.

Resources

Faigenbaum, A., & Westcott, W. (2009). *Youth strength training programs for health, fitness, and sport*. Champaign, IL: Human Kinetics.

LESSON 10: STEP AEROBICS WORKOUT 3

Grade-Level Outcomes

Primary Outcomes

Assessment & program planning: Designs a fitness program, including all components of health-related fitness, for a college student and an employee in the learner's chosen field of work. (S3.H12.L1)

Fitness knowledge: Calculates target heart rate and applies that information to personal fitness plan. (S3.H10.L1)

Fitness activities: Demonstrates competency in 1 or more specialized skills in health-related fitness activities. (S1.H3.L1)

Embedded Outcome

Physical activity knowledge: Evaluates risks and safety factors that might affect physical activity preferences throughout the life cycle. (S3.H5.L1)

Lesson Objectives

The learner will:

- perform the step aerobics routine with correct form and alignment.
- perform the step aerobics routine within his or her THR zone.
- participate safely in the aerobic routine by monitoring his or her heart rate and slowing down or modifying activity as needed.
- review FITT principles and plan development.

Equipment and Materials

- 1 stepper per student
- Upbeat music (step aerobics) or video

Introduction

Overall, you did well on the resistance training quiz. Let's review a few points that need clarification. Today is another day of cardio. After we review the fitness plans you created for yourself as a college student, you will participate in your third day of step aerobics. Next week you will be doing cardio kickboxing on your cardio days. These are group exercise activities. What other group exercise activities are available? What types of classes are offered at your college or in the community? If you don't want to do group exercise, what else can you do for aerobic activity? Let's discuss your plans based on your college selection.

Instructional Task: Homework Review

■ PRACTICE TASK

Students get into small groups and share with each other their college fitness plans. Have them look at what was similar, what was different, and what they liked about others' plans that they had not thought of. Each group then shares briefly with the class.

Collect the fitness plans.

Refinement

Different groups could share what they did for one of the health-related fitness concepts. For example, a few groups would discuss what they planned for cardio, a few groups for muscle fitness, a few for flexibility, and so on.

Student Choices/Differentiation

Students choose groups.

What to Look For

- Students are able to use the FITT principle for each health-related fitness concept.
- Students are aware of other ways to become or stay fit besides going to the gym.
- Students looked up the physical activity opportunities at their selected colleges.

Instructional Task: Step Aerobics

■ PRACTICE TASK

Today is a new cardio stepper routine. It has many of the same moves, but it is slightly shorter. We have less time today because of the class discussion.

Again, this routine can be one you created, or you can use a routine from a DVD or YouTube.

Pause and have students take a 15-second heart rate at different points in the routine.

Refinements

- Check foot placement on the step, and remind students to step in the center.
- Posture should be upright during the routine.

EMBEDDED OUTCOME: S3.H5.L1. Lead a discussion on risks and safety factors that may affect physical activity throughout the lifespan:

- How might age affect a person's preference to participate in a group exercise activity such as step aerobics?
- What other factors may contribute to participation in group exercise such as step aerobics?

Guiding questions for students:

- Are you getting a good aerobic workout?
- Are you in your target heart rate zone?
- If you are not, what do you need to do?

Student Choices/Differentiation

- Students may perform the exercises on the floor without using the stepper.
- Students may perform at a slower rate.
- Students may use a wall for stability.

What to Look For

- Students are able to stay on beat.
- Students are working at a moderate level.
- Students are performing the moves properly with correct form and alignment.

Formal and Informal Assessments

College fitness plans

Closure

- What did you like so far about the activities in cardio and muscle fitness?
- What would you like to try in the future?
- Do you think you are getting more fit?
- Do you think you are working on all your health-related fitness concepts?
- Next class, we will be starting kickboxing and will be back in the weight room after that. What are other ways you can work on your health-related fitness without having to go to a gym or group exercise class?

Reflection

- Did students complete their fitness plans?
- Do they understand the FITT and training principles?
- Did students monitor their heart rates to stay in their target heart rate zones?
- Can students think of other ways to stay physically active outside the gym?

Homework

For next class, think about and write up the following:

- What is your dream job?
- What are your career plans?
- For the career you have chosen, what are the physical requirements to perform the job well?
- Is the job mostly sedentary (desk job) or is it active? Explain.
- What type of skills do you need?
- How can maintaining a healthy lifestyle benefit you in your chosen career?

Resources

Kennedy-Armbruster, C., & Yoke, M. (2009). *Methods of group exercise instruction.* 2nd ed. Champaign, IL: Human Kinetics.

Jenny Ford Fitness: http://jennyford.com. There are many other step aerobics instructors and videos out there. This is just one suggestion of many.

Internet keyword search: "step aerobics," "step aerobic routines"

LESSON 11: CARDIO KICKBOXING WORKOUT 1

Grade-Level Outcomes

Primary Outcomes

Assessment & program planning: Designs a fitness program, including all components of health-related fitness, for a college student and an employee in the learner's chosen field of work. (S3.H12.L1)

Fitness knowledge: Calculates target heart rate and applies that information to personal fitness plan. (S3.H10.L1)

Fitness activities: Demonstrates competency in 1 or more specialized skills in health-related fitness activities. (S1.H3.L1)

Embedded Outcome

Personal responsibility: Employs effective self-management skills to analyze barriers and modify physical activity patterns appropriately, as needed. (S4.H1.L1)

Lesson Objectives

The learner will:

- perform the basic moves of a cardio kickboxing routine.
- maintain moderate to vigorous physical activity (MVPA) throughout the routine by checking heart rate.
- participate safely by moving with correct form and in self-space.

Equipment and Materials

- Upbeat music or video

Introduction

Today is a cardio day. Last week, you did step aerobics. This week, you will get to participate in cardio kickboxing. There are many ways you can get aerobic exercise. These are just two group exercise types for you to sample. You can find many routines online to do at home. Remember, the physical activity guidelines suggest that people get at least 60 minutes of moderate to vigorous physical activity (MVPA) on most days. We can accumulate this activity through walking, running, cycling, swimming, and so on. Remember, you do not need to have access to a gym in order to stay physically active. Thinking about the career you hope to have, what are some of the physical activity requirements? How might you include physical activity throughout your day or stay physically active to be more productive in your life and career? You have planned out a fitness routine for yourself as a college student. Next, you will think about how to keep active and healthy as a professional. First, let's learn some basic kickboxing moves.

Instructional Task: Kickboxing Intro

■ PRACTICE TASK

Have students spread out across the gym in rows with windows (as in teaching dance). Make sure you can see everyone and everyone can see you.

Slowly go through a series of basic moves (see list below). This teaches students the moves and slowly warms them up.

First get into your fighting stance: Stand with feet staggered, knees slightly bent, rear heel lifted.

Bring fists to chin, elbows near ribs, palms facing each other.

Punches

- **Jab:** A short, straight forward punch. Feet are staggered in fighting stance. Strike with same fist as forward stance foot (i.e., left foot forward, punch with left hand).
- **Cross:** A punch thrown from the back hand. Feet are staggered in fighting stance. Throw punch from back hand (i.e., left foot forward, punch with right fist) with slight hip rotation.
- **Hook:** A short punch with a circular motion while the elbow remains bent. Lead with same foot as forward foot (i.e., left foot forward in fighting stance, punch with left fist).
- **Uppercut:** An upward punch. Elbow bent and fist to sky in quick sharp motion; can be with lead or back fist in staggered fighting stance.

Kicks

- **Front kick:** A forward leg strike. Lead with front leg in staggered fighting stance. Pull the knee up and kick forward with foot flexed to strike target with the heel.
- **Side kick:** A diagonal kick. Fighting stance, turn body sideways, pull up knee, and kick leg outward diagonally across body. Extend the leg toward target; strike with heel and with toes slightly down.
- **Roundhouse kick:** A rotational kick. Fighting stance, come to ball of foot of non-kicking leg and rotate toes to side as kicking (back) leg comes around to strike target with shin or top of instep of foot. Can kick at different levels (low, medium, high).

Refinements

- **Jabs:** Quick punches. Can alternate fists or combine with other punches. Punch with speed and control.
- **Cross:** Use core and hips for power. Combine with jabs and other punches.
- **Hook:** Pivot on ball of back foot. Keep arm bent and make fast strong motion. Combine with other punches.
- **Uppercut:** Use legs and hips to drive punch up for more power. Keep punch just below eye level.
- **Front kick:** Drive knee and foot forward, push through heel.
- **Side kick:** Turn body sideways, extend leg and kick through target with heel.
- **Roundhouse kick:** Drive kicking knee forward, pivot hip, and retreat leg back to stance. Hit target with shin or instep. Change level of kick.

Student Choices/Differentiation

- Students may do a video warm-up and learn as they go.
- Students may complete a dynamic warm-up first.
- Students may perform moves at their own pace.
- Students may do the exercises near a wall if they need to use it to balance.

What to Look For

Students are performing the moves with correct form.

Instructional Task: Kickboxing Routine

■ PRACTICE TASK

Prepare students to participate in a kickboxing routine. Again, there are many DVDs or routines on YouTube, and some can be downloaded. Using video allows you to move around the class and provide cues and feedback as well as model for students. You can create your own routine as well—just be sure you include a warm-up, workout phase, and cool-down.

Be sure to stop the class a few times for students to check their heart rates, or prompt students to check if they are in their THR zones.

Include a cool-down at the end of the workout.

Refinements

- When using kicks, be sure to provide different levels as options for correct form and balance needs of students.

- For punches, watch that students do not overextend at the joints.
- Provide alternative pacing and moves for more complex movements and combinations.
- Watch balance and moves that require counterbalance.

Guiding questions for students:

- Are you in your target heart rate zone?
- What is your heart rate like during this activity compared with step aerobics (same, higher, lower)?
- Is it more difficult to find your zone? Easier?

EMBEDDED OUTCOME: S4.H1.L1 During the routine, ask students to self-adjust based on their target heart rates and their level of perceived skill proficiency. Can students manage themselves during the routine to choose the level they work at?

Student Choices/Differentiation

- Students may choose step aerobics, Tae Bo, cardio HITT routines, or circuit training.
- Students may perform moves at a slower rate.
- Students may perform kicks at lower levels or make other needed adjustments to the moves.

What to Look For

- Students are participating safely.
- Students are using correct form.
- Students are working in their target heart rate zones.
- Students can adjust the intensity level of their workouts.

Formal and Informal Assessments

Exit slip: What parts of cardio kickboxing were the hardest for you?

Closure

- Today, you participated in a different cardio workout. There are many ways to get a good cardio workout. What are some other ways that interest you?
- What do you think you will do for cardio when you're an adult?
- What about the other health-related fitness concepts?
- Next time, we're back in the weight room for a weight workout. Be sure to have your activity logs in your binders. I will be checking them.

Reflection

- Were students using correct form during activity?
- Were students working at a moderate to vigorous level?
- Were students able to adjust or modify their intensity level based on their heart rates?
- Review exit slips for feedback on activity.

Homework

- In your binder with your vocabulary, please write about what you like and dislike about step aerobics.
- What do you like and dislike about cardio kickboxing?
- If you were to do one of these activities outside of class, which would you choose and why?
- What other type of cardio activities would you like to try that you have not? Explain.

Resources

Internet keyword search: "cardio kickboxing workout," "cardio kick"

LESSON 12: MUSCLE FITNESS WORKOUT 3

Grade-Level Outcomes

Primary Outcomes

Assessment & program planning: Designs a fitness program, including all components of health-related fitness, for a college student and an employee in the learner's chosen field of work. (S3.H12.L1)

Safety: Applies best practices for participating safely in physical activity, exercise and dance (e.g., injury prevention, proper alignment, hydration, use of equipment, implementation of rules, sun protection). (S4.H5.L1)

Fitness knowledge: Demonstrates appropriate technique on resistance-training machines and with free weights. (S3.H7.L1)

Fitness activities: Demonstrates competency in 1 or more specialized skills in health-related fitness activities. (S1.H3.L1)

Embedded Outcome

Physical activity knowledge: Discusses the benefits of a physically active lifestyle as it relates to college and or career productivity. (S3.H1.L1)

Lesson Objectives

The learner will:
- evaluate a partner's form during Fitnessgram assessments.
- use proper weight room and assessment etiquette to keep all students safe.
- lift weights using correct form and alignment.

Equipment and Materials

- Curl-up mats and strips (1 per pair of students)
- Music and Fitnessgram cadence CD
- 3 sit-and-reach boxes
- 3 yardsticks
- Weight room

Introduction

Today is a muscle fitness day. You will be performing a curl-up test before heading into the weight room. You will start at the same station where you started on the first muscle fitness day. I have added three sit-and-reach stations and three trunk-lift stations. You will need to complete these two assessments during your weight room workout either today or during the next muscle fitness lesson. Remember to use correct form and alignment and to perform your lifts in a slow and controlled manner. You will be stretching on your own in the weight room today. Be sure to stretch your upper and lower body.

Instructional Task: Curl-Up Test

■ PRACTICE TASK

Have students pair up.

Partner A performs the curl-up test while Partner B watches for form. Once the Partner A students have completed the test, the Partner B students perform curl-ups while Partner A students watch for form.

Students record their scores.

Refinements
- Remind students to stay on cadence and to have fingertips cross the strip.
- Check to see that heels stay in contact with the ground.

EMBEDDED OUTCOME: S3.H1.L1. Lead a discussion about the benefits of a physically active lifestyle for college and career productivity:
- How might muscular strength and endurance affect your productivity in your career?
- How might flexibility affect your productivity in your career?

Guiding questions for students:
- Have you improved? If not, why might that be?
- Have you done resistance training long enough to see any gains?
- Do you think you need to adjust your plan or give yourself more time?

Student Choices/Differentiation
- Have students self-assess at stations.
- Provide a checklist to use for evaluating form.
- Students may review video clips of form.
- Students choose their partners.

What to Look For

Students can identify correct and incorrect form.

Curl-Up Form
- Head is down (touching floor or mat) and fingertips are touching strip.
- Knees are bent, heels touching ground.
- Finger pads slide across the strip and back as the body curls up (shoulder blades off floor) and back down.
- Movement is in time with the CD cadence.

Instructional Task: Resistance Workout

■ PRACTICE TASK

With their workout partners, students go to a station and adjust the equipment as necessary to begin their first set. Partners rotate each set to provide rest in between sets as they each do their reps. If students finish before they are to rotate to the next station, then they wait patiently and quietly. Remind students to be attentive spotters.

Rotate students through with a timer or by using low, but upbeat music with breaks.

Mixed in with today's stations are three sit-and-reach boxes and three trunk-lift stations for students to self-assess.

Refinements
- Students adjust weight and equipment for goals, safety, and correct form.
- Have students count 3 or 4 seconds on the inhale and exhale. Check to see that they are breathing when they lift.

Guiding questions for students:
- Do you need to adjust any of your weight? Be sure you have the correct weight for the sets and reps you want to do.
- Is your resistance training plan balanced across the muscle groups?

Student Choices/Differentiation

Students choose their partners.

What to Look For

- Students are performing exercises with correct form and technique.
- Students are going through the full ROM with slow, controlled, smooth movement.
- Students are lifting the appropriate weight for their goals.
- Students are spotting and keeping partners safe.
- Students are logging the weight and sets and reps of each station in their logs.

Formal and Informal Assessments

- Curl-up test results
- Station logs

Closure

- Today, you performed the curl-up test again and worked more on muscle fitness. If you did not see any improvement on your curl-up or other tests, why might that be?
- What do think you should do?
- Tomorrow is our last day of cardio kickboxing. Be ready for your workout.
- Be sure to turn in your binders before you leave class.

Reflection

- Are students able to identify breaks in form?
- Are students lifting weights properly?
- Review binders and provide feedback.

Homework

- Be sure your logs are up to date.

Resources

Faigenbaum, A., & Westcott, W. (2009). *Youth strength training programs for health, fitness, and sport*. Champaign, IL: Human Kinetics.

Meredith, M.D., & Welk, G.J., eds. (2010). *Fitnessgram & Activitygram test administration manual*. 4th ed. Champaign, IL: Human Kinetics.

LESSON 13: CARDIO KICKBOXING WORKOUT 2

Grade-Level Outcomes

Primary Outcomes

Assessment & program planning: Designs a fitness program, including all components of health-related fitness, for a college student and an employee in the learner's chosen field of work. (S3.H12.L1)

Fitness knowledge: Calculates target heart rate and applies that information to personal fitness plan. (S3.H10.L1)

Fitness activities: Demonstrates competency in 1 or more specialized health-related fitness activities. (S1.H3.L1)

Embedded Outcome

Physical activity knowledge: Evaluates risks and safety factors that might affect physical activity preferences throughout the life cycle. (S3.H5.L1)

Lesson Objectives

The learner will:
- maintain MVPA throughout the cardio kickboxing routine by checking heart rate.
- participate safely by moving with correct form and in self-space.
- discuss the benefits of group exercise.

Equipment and Materials

Upbeat music or video

Introduction

Nice work on your binders so far. I have made comments for you and you can pick them up after class. Today is our last group fitness cardio day. You will do the mile for cardio assessment two classes from now. You will be checking in again on your health-related fitness to see if you have maintained or improved any of your scores. It has been a short unit, but you can use the Fitnessgram as a good self-check. Now back to cardio kickboxing. What are some of the basic moves you learned last class?

Instructional Task: Quick Review and Vocabulary

■ PRACTICE TASK

Students sit with their binders and review what they have learned about the FITT principles and how to use them when designing a fitness plan. One student in each group takes notes on the discussion.

EMBEDDED OUTCOME: S3.H5.L1 Discuss the differences in how working adults often stay active versus high school and college students. Factors to consider include life choices, accessibility, and finances.

Guiding questions for students:
- Why might our choice in physical activities change as we age?
- What are some of the changes in barriers and resources? Physiological changes? Other changes?

Following the discussion, review the homework assignment that will be due at the end of module.

What to Look For
- Students are engaged in the discussion.
- Students are providing appropriate examples.

Instructional Task: Kickboxing Routine

■ PRACTICE TASK

Prepare students to participate in a kickboxing routine. Again, there are many DVDs or routines on YouTube, and some can be downloaded. Using video allows you to move around the class and provide cues and feedback as well as model for students. You can create your own routine as well—just be sure you include a warm-up, workout phase, and cool-down.

Be sure to stop the class a few times for students to check their heart rates, or prompt students to check if they are in their THR zones.

Refinements
- Check the height of the kick and adjust if needed.
- Remind students to restrain jabs and punches (not overextending joints) for safety.
- Perform kicks and punches in a controlled manner—tighten muscles.

Guiding questions for students:
- Are you in your target heart rate zone?
- Are you working at a moderate or vigorous rate?
- How does your heart rate change during different segments of the routine?

Student Choices/Differentiation
- Students may choose step aerobics, Tae Bo, cardio HITT routines, or circuit training.
- Students may move at a slower rate.
- Students may perform kicks at lower levels or make other needed adjustments to the moves.

What to Look For
- Students are participating safely.
- Students are using correct form.
- Students are working in their target heart rate zones.
- Students can adjust the intensity level of their workouts.

Formal and Informal Assessments
- Task 1 discussion notes

Closure
- Think about the importance of health-related fitness across your lifespan. You have thought about it as a college student and developed a fitness plan. The next step is to think about it as a professional in your career.
- How can you stay healthy and physically active as an adult working full time?
- What are the benefits of group exercise?
- What other types of group exercise would interest you? Be sure to think critically about your homework.
- What will a typical work day look like for you?
- When will you work out or otherwise be physically active?
- What type of physical activity do you think you will participate in as an adult?

Reflection
- Could students differentiate between how adults typically stay active and how teenagers and college students stay active?
- Were students able to adjust the intensity of their workouts to stay within their target heart rate zones?
- Do students understand how heart rate can be used for intensity and overload?

Homework

- Students create a fitness program for an employee in their chosen field. If the student isn't sure of that field yet, offer a couple of real-life career scenarios. They select one scenario and create a plan to help that person be physically active based on information given, such as what the person likes, how much time is available for exercise, and what resources are available.

- Students must consider the physical activity guidelines and FITT principles for this assignment.

- Homework is due at the end of the module.

Resources

Internet keyboard search: "cardio kickboxing workout," "cardio kickboxing"

LESSON 14: MUSCLE FITNESS WORKOUT 4

Grade-Level Outcomes

Primary Outcomes

Assessment & program planning: Designs a fitness program, including all components of health-related fitness, for a college student and an employee in the learner's chosen field of work. (S3.H12.L1)

Safety: Applies best practices for participating safely in physical activity, exercise and dance (e.g., injury prevention, proper alignment, hydration, use of equipment, implementation of rules, sun protection). (S4.H5.L1)

Fitness knowledge: Demonstrates appropriate technique on resistance-training machines and with free weights. (S3.H7.L1)

Fitness activities: Demonstrates competency in 1 or more specialized skills in health-related fitness activities. (S1.H3.L1)

Embedded Outcome

Fitness knowledge: Identifies types of strength exercises (isometric, concentric, eccentric) and stretching exercises (static, proprioceptive neuromuscular facilitation [PNF], dynamic) for personal fitness development (e.g., strength, endurance, range of motion). (S3.H9.L1)

Lesson Objectives

The learner will:

- evaluate a partner's form during Fitnessgram assessments.
- lift weights with proper alignment in a slow, controlled manner.
- use proper weight room and assessment etiquette to keep all students safe.

Equipment and Materials

- Fitnessgram cadence CD
- 3 sit-and-reach boxes
- 3 yardsticks
- Weight room

Introduction

Today is the final muscle fitness day in the weight room. First, you will complete the push-up and shoulder stretch test. Then in the weight room, you and your workout partner will start where you left off in the last workout. Be sure that you complete the sit-and-reach and trunk-lift tests today if you have not already. Be sure to stretch today. In our next lesson, we'll be back to cardio and running the mile, so come prepared.

Instructional Task: Push-Up and Shoulder Stretch Test

■ PRACTICE TASK

Review the assessment. Then students pair up.

Partner A performs the push-up test while partner B watches for form. Once the Partner A students have completed the test, the Partner B students perform push-ups while the Partner A students watch for form.

Students record their scores.

Next have students do the shoulder stretch and mark whether their fingers can touch or not.

Refinements

- Remind students to stay on cadence.
- Make sure their elbows are getting to 90 degrees.

Guiding questions for students:

- Have you improved? If not, why might that be?
- Have you done resistance training long enough to see any gains?
- Do you think you need to adjust your plan or give yourself more time?
- What about exercise specificity—have you practiced push-ups?

Student Choices/Differentiation

- Have students self-assess at stations.
- Provide a checklist to use for evaluating form.
- Students may review video clips of form.
- Students choose their partners.

What to Look For

Students can identify correct and incorrect form.

Push-Up Form

- Hands are shoulder-width apart.
- Back is flat (no hills or valleys).
- Elbows lower to 90 degrees.
- Elbows return to straight, locked position.
- Movement is in time with the CD cadence.

Instructional Task: Resistance Workout

■ PRACTICE TASK

With the same partners, students go to the station where they left off in the last muscle fitness class. Students adjust the equipment as necessary and begin their first set. Partners rotate each set to provide rest in between sets as they each do their reps. If students finish before they are to rotate to the next station, then they wait patiently and quietly. Remind students to be attentive in spotting.

Rotate students through with a timer or by using low but upbeat music with breaks.

Mixed in with today's stations are three sit-and-reach boxes and three trunk-lift stations for students to self-assess. They need to complete these assessments today if they did not complete them before.

Refinements

- Students adjust form and alignment as needed.
- Students adjust weight and number of sets and reps based on goals and safety.

EMBEDDED OUTCOME: S3.H9.L1. Have students review their fitness plans and identify the types of stretching and the types of strength exercises they have included.

Guiding questions for students:

- Do you need to adjust any of your weight? Be sure you have the correct weight for the sets and reps you want to do.
- Is your resistance training plan balanced across the muscle groups?

Student Choices/Differentiation

Students choose partners.

What to Look For

- Students are performing exercises with correct form and technique.
- Students are going through the full ROM with slow, controlled, smooth movement.
- Students are lifting the appropriate weight for their goals.
- Students are spotting and keeping partners safe.
- Students are logging the weight and sets and reps of each station in their logs.

Formal and Informal Assessments

- Station log sheets
- Flexibility assessment

Closure

- Today concludes our resistance training in the weight room. How can you keep up a good resistance training plan outside of class?
- If you do not use modified 1RM for determining your baseline, what else can you use?
- What did you like about being in the weight room?
- Remember, we were in the weight room to learn different ways to resistance train. Depending on your goals, you will have to set up a plan using the training and FITT principles that work best for you.
- I will do a binder check next class, and you should be prepared to run the mile.

Reflection

- What did students learn about resistance training?
- Can students recognize ways to work on muscle fitness outside the gym?
- Do students know proper weight room etiquette and safety?

Homework

Work on the scenarios due at the end of the learning segment. Remember there is a binder check next class.

Resources

Faigenbaum, A., & Westcott, W. (2009). *Youth strength training programs for health, fitness, and sport*. Champaign, IL: Human Kinetics.

Meredith, M.D., & Welk, G.J. (2010). *Fitnessgram & Activitygram test administration manual*. 4th ed. Champaign, IL: Human Kinetics.

LESSON 15: 1-MILE RUN

Grade-Level Outcomes

Primary Outcome

Assessment & program planning: Designs a fitness program, including all components of health-related fitness, for a college student and an employee in the learner's chosen field of work. (S3.H12.L1)

Embedded Outcome

Health: Analyzes the health benefits of a self-selected physical activity. (S5.H1.L1)

Lesson Objectives

The learner will:
- assess his or her cardiorespiratory endurance by running the mile as best he can.
- compare and reflect on his or her mile scores and lap time splits.

Equipment and Materials

1 or 2 stopwatches

Introduction

Were you surprised by your flexibility scores in our previous lesson? What changes did you see? Why might you not have seen improvements in your fitness scores? Thinking about the training principles you have learned, what things might affect your progress? Today, we'll complete a mile run. Let's see if your mile time has changed. Remember, this is about doing your best for you. Have a great run.

Instructional Task: Dynamic Warm-Up

■ PRACTICE TASK

Collect binders from students.

Students go through a dynamic warm-up, then pair up and line up one behind the other. The first partner starts the task and when halfway down to the cone or line, the second partner follows.

Dynamic tasks are as follows:
- Jog down and back
- High knees down and back
- Butt kickers down and back
- Lunge and twist halfway and jog out down and back
- Carioca down and back
- Athletic-slide down and back
- Jog down and back

Student Choices/Differentiation

- Let students warm up on their own from a selected list of exercises.
- Students choose their partners.

What to Look For

Students are performing the warm-up using correct form.

Instructional Task: 1-Mile Run

■ PRACTICE TASK

Students stay with their partners for the 1-mile (1.6 km) run. Partner A runs the mile first while Partner B logs her lap times. This allows students to see their splits. Once the Partner A students have completed their mile, the Partner B students line up to run theirs while Partner A students record the lap times to find their splits. As students finish the mile, encourage them to walk around to cool down and to stretch on their own.

EMBEDDED OUTCOME: S5.H1.L1. Discuss the health benefits of physical activity. What affect does cardiorespiratory endurance have on overall health and well-being?

Guiding questions for students:

- Looking at your lap times and splits, did they change? How?
- Did your overall mile time improve? Why do you think that is?
- In what other ways could you test your aerobic fitness?
- How might specificity of training influence your mile run results?

Student Choices/Differentiation

- Students may perform the PACER test.
- Students may perform a walk test.
- The entire class may run at the same time. Students choose their partners.

What to Look For

- Students are trying their best.
- Students showed improvement.
- Students are in the healthy fitness zone.
- Students see the advantage of training using the same type of exercise as the test.

Instructional Task: Cool-Down Stretches

■ PRACTICE TASK

Students cool down and stretch the major muscle groups on their own while you call small groups of students up for their binder checks.

Go through the checklist and hand back the binders.

Refinement

Students hold static stretches for 20 seconds.

Student Choices/Differentiation

A couple of students may lead the class through a cool-down.

What to Look For

- Students are analyzing the skill during the practice task.
- Students are performing both upper- and lower-body stretches.

Formal and Informal Assessments

- 1-mile run results
- Binder checklists

Closure

- Did you see any change in your mile run?
- The cardio and muscle fitness lessons taught you how to develop a good fitness plan using all the health-related fitness concepts and the FITT principles.
- You had to take information you had about yourself and use it to develop a plan for you as a college student.
- These are skills that you can take with you outside of school and throughout life to stay healthy and active. Remember, your final assignment on the career fitness plan is due next class.

Reflection

- Do students see the value in knowing how to develop a fitness plan?
- Did students see any difference in two weeks?
- Do students know that they might need more time to see larger gains in their fitness?

Homework

Your career scenario homework is due in our next class.

Resources

Meredith, M.D., & Welk, G.J., eds. (2010). *Fitnessgram & Activitygram test administration manual.* 4th ed. Champaign, IL: Human Kinetics.

LESSON 16: PEER EVALUATION OF FITNESS PLAN

Grade-Level Outcomes

Primary Outcomes

Assessment & program planning: Designs a fitness program, including all components of health-related fitness, for a college student and an employee in the learner's chosen field of work. (S3.H12.L1)

Assessment & program planning: Analyzes the components of skill-related fitness in relation to life and career goals, and designs an appropriate fitness program for those goals. (S3.H12.L2)

Embedded Outcome

Working with others: Solves problems and thinks critically in physical activity and/or dance settings, both as an individual or in groups. (S4.H4.L1)

Lesson Objectives

The learner will:
- evaluate a peer's fitness program.
- provide feedback to a partner about her plan.
- share strengths and unique features of his or her partner's plan with the class.

Equipment and Materials

- Scoring guides or rubrics for peer assessments
- Pencils or pens
- Flip charts and markers

Introduction

Today, you will peer-assess your partner's career fitness plan using a scoring guide I will provide. It's the same scoring guide I will use to evaluate your fitness plan.

Instructional Task: Review Career Fitness Plan

■ PRACTICE TASK

In pairs, students score each other's fitness plans using the scoring guide. Students should read the scoring guide before doing their reviews. After scoring the plans, students discuss areas of strengths as well as areas that could be improved with their partners.

EMBEDDED OUTCOME: S4.H4.L1. In scoring the plans, students need to think critically about the assessment criteria and apply their knowledge to provide relevant feedback.

Extension

Students identify one or more strengths or unique aspects of the career fitness plan they reviewed and share it with the class.

Guiding questions for students:
- What were the most challenging aspects of developing a career fitness plan?
- Was it more or less difficult than your college fitness plan? Why?
- What did you learn by scoring your partner's plan?

Student Choices/Differentiation

- Students choose their partners.
- Students use flip charts to record their responses.

What to Look For

- Students are taking the time to review each item in the scoring guide carefully.
- Students are communicating areas for improvements with sensitivity.

Formal and Informal Assessments

Peer assessments

Closure

- This module gave you the opportunity to create fitness plans for college and career settings.
- You designed and implemented these plans by applying your knowledge of health-related and skill-related fitness concepts, principles, and activities.
- You should be able to develop fitness plans that you can use at any stage of your life.
- It's time to think about your next module, so please review your choices before the next class.

Reflection

- Did students struggle with any concepts or ideas at the end of the module?
- Were students able to apply their knowledge from the college fitness plan to develop a career fitness plan?
- What could I do better the next time this module is offered?
- Review peer assessments for a better understanding of student's knowledge about planning.

Homework

- Keep adapting and refining your fitness program while we move on to the next module.
- Review the new modules on the school's physical education website so you'll be ready for the next class.

FITNESS WALKING MODULE

Lessons in this module were contributed by **Rebecca Bryan**, an assistant professor in the department of physical education at the State University of New York College at Cortland, where she teaches undergraduate- and graduate-level courses in fitness education, curriculum, instruction and assessment, adapted physical education, and physical education leadership.

FITNESS WALKING

Grade-Level Outcomes Addressed, by Lesson	1	2	3	4	5	6	7	8	9	10	11	12	13	14	15	16
Standard 1. The physically literate individual demonstrates competency in a variety of motor skills and movement patterns.																
Demonstrates competency in 1 or more specialized skills in health-related fitness activities. (S1.H3.L1)	P	P	P	P	P	P	P	P	P	P	P	P	P	P	P	P
Standard 2. The physically literate individual applies knowledge of concepts, principles, strategies and tactics related to movement and performance.																
Uses movement concepts and principles (e.g., force, motion, rotation) to analyze and improve performance for a self-selected skill. (S2.H2.L1)				E												
Standard 3. The physically literate individual demonstrates the knowledge and skills to achieve and maintain a health-enhancing level of physical activity and fitness.																
Discusses the benefits of a physically active lifestyle as it relates to college or career productivity. (S3.H1.L1)	P						P	P								P
Identifies issues associated with heat, humidity and cold. (S3.H3.L1)												E			P	P
Evaluates – according to their benefits, social support network and participation requirements–activities that can be pursued in the local environment. (S3.H4.L1)														E		P
Evaluates risks and safety factors that might affect physical activity preferences throughout the life cycle. (S3.H5.L1)													E			P
Analyzes the impact of life choices, economics, motivation and accessibility on exercise adherence and participation in physical activity in college or career setting. (S3.H5.L2)					E	E					P					P
Identifies types of strength exercises (isometric, concentric, eccentric) and stretching exercises (static, proprioceptive neuromuscular facilitation [PNF], dynamic) for personal fitness development (e.g., strength, endurance, range of motion). (S3.H9.L1)		E														
Calculates target heart rate and applies that information to personal fitness plan. (S3.H10.L1)		P	P	P	P	P	P	P	P	P	P	P	P	P	P	
Adjusts pacing to keep heart rate in target zone, using available technology (e.g., pedometer, heart rate monitor), to self-monitor aerobic intensity. (S3.H10.L2)		P	P			E			E							
Standard 4. The physically literate individual exhibits responsible personal and social behavior that respects self and others.																
Employs effective self-management skills to analyze barriers and modify physical activity patterns appropriately, as needed. (S4.H1.L1)	E							E	E	E	E				E	P
Uses communication skills and strategies that promote team or group dynamics. (S4.H3.L1)																E
Standard 5. The physically literate individual recognizes the value of physical activity for health, enjoyment, challenge, self-expression and/or social interaction.																
Analyzes the health benefits of a self-selected physical activity. (S5.H1.L1)								E								P
Identifies the opportunity for social support in a self-selected physical activity or dance. (S5.H4.L1)									E	E						P

P = Primary; E = Embedded

LESSON 1: INTRODUCTION TO FITNESS WALKING

Grade-Level Outcomes

Primary Outcomes

Physical activity knowledge: Discusses the benefits of a physically active lifestyle as it relates to college or career productivity. (S3.H1.L1)

Fitness activities: Demonstrates competency in 1 or more specialized skills in health-related fitness activities. (S1.H3.L1)

Embedded Outcome

Personal responsibility: Employs effective self-management skills to analyze barriers and modify physical activity patterns appropriately, as needed. (S4.H1.L1)

Lesson Objectives

The learner will:

- demonstrate good walking technique.
- discuss the benefits of walking.
- estimate number of steps per mile.

Equipment and Materials

- Pedometers (1 per student)
- Task sheets (1 per student)
- Stopwatch

Introduction

Today, we begin our walking unit. You will learn about the benefits of walking and how to keep track of your steps and your daily moderate-to-vigorous physical activity through heart rate. We also will evaluate the local environment for walking and hiking access. The goal of this unit is for you not only to accumulate physical activity during class but also to use technology and heart rate to set goals and modify your daily step and physical activity totals.

Instructional Task: Discussion and Walking Technique

■ PRACTICE TASK

Prompt students with questions and trivia about the benefits of walking.

Describe correct walking technique and why it is important.

Preparation Phase

- Stand tall (head to ankle alignment).
- Pull shoulders back.
- Tighten abdominal muscles.

Execution

- Step forward.
- Heel strikes first (45 degrees).
- Toe pushes off.

Follow-Through

- Swing arms in opposition to legs.

Have students pair up and walk for 25 steps, analyzing each other's technique for two or three trials using the walking technique checklist.

Extensions

- Provide scenarios of various technique and gait issues, and have partners describe missing elements or those that need refinement.
- Have students walk at a slow pace, normal moderate pace, and fast pace to see if their technique changes

EMBEDDED OUTCOME: S4.H1.L1. Students use the partner analysis feedback to modify walking pattern as appropriate.

Guiding questions for students:

- What do many adults do for physical activity?
- Why do you think walking is a popular lifetime activity for adults?
- What are at least three health benefits of walking moderately 30 minutes a day?
- What are some possible barriers to walking for physical activity?
- How can you add walking activities to your day to increase your overall physical activity outside of PE class?

Student Choices/Differentiation

Students choose partners.

What to Look For

- Students are using proper technique.
- Students are aware of the benefits of walking as a physical activity:
  - Noncompetitive
  - Does not require a lot of skill
  - Good way to increase heart rate and maintain target heart rate
  - Does not cause much impact on joints
  - Reduces stress
  - Can help prevent injuries

Instructional Task: Introduction to Pedometers

Note: If pedometers are not available, you can tie walking directly to heart rate and design the module to work on keeping within a moderate target heart rate zone (50 to 70 percent).

■ PRACTICE TASK

Practice reading the pedometers and resetting them.

Students put their pedometers on and reset them. They perform the tasks on the guided discovery pedometer task sheet.

Refinements

- Students should position the pedometer between the hip and navel. They may need to adjust alignment and experiment with counting their steps to find the most accurate spot to clip and wear the pedometer.
- Remind students to walk at typical pace and stride.

Guiding questions for students:

- How does the pedometer register steps?
- Why might the pedometer register more or fewer steps than the number taken?

Student Choices/Differentiation

Students may walk 25, 50, or 100 steps and then check the pedometer.

What to Look For

- Students are checking the placement of their pedometers.
- Students are getting accurate step counts.

Instructional Task: Estimating Steps and Time

■ PRACTICE TASK

Have students guess how many steps and how many minutes it will take them to walk a mile (four laps). Students reset their pedometers to zero and walk four laps (roughly 1 mile) to get their actual step counts and times.

If you have no pedometers, have students take their heart rates at the end of each lap and estimate time and pace.

Extension

Students walk one lap and record steps and time, using results to estimate four-lap steps and time. Then, they reset pedometers and walk four laps, and compare the four-lap step count and time to their estimates. Students note how accurate their estimates were and discuss why the estimates were off, if they were.

Refinements

- Remind students that the pedometer must be placed properly and not tilted to get the most accurate count.
- Emphasize walking at a natural pace and stride.

Guiding questions for students:

- How many steps do you think you take in a day?
- How could you increase the number of steps you take daily?

Student Choices/Differentiation

Students may choose to walk one, two, or three laps (or change to yards on a football field) and then multiply as necessary for steps and time to estimate approximately 1 mile (four laps).

What to Look For

Students can estimate step and time counts for 1 mile fairly accurately.

Formal and Informal Assessments

- Informal walking technique checklists
- Pedometer task sheets

Closure

- What are the health benefits of walking for physical activity?
- Describe the phases of good walking technique.
- How can pedometers help promote walking or change physical activity behavior?
- How many miles or kilometers would you need to walk to complete 10,000 steps a day?
- How can you increase your walking activity outside of school?
- Nice work today. We will continue to work on walking and add in heart rate to measure physical activity levels.

Reflection

- Did students know the benefits of moderate walking?
- Did students understand how pedometers work?
- Did students know how to estimate steps, mileage, and time?
- Review pedometer task sheets and walking checklists.

Homework

- Look up and describe the information about taking 10,000 steps a day.
- Is this different depending on your age? Gender? How so? Explain.
- Due next class period.

Resources

Pangrazi, R.P., Beighle, A., & Sidman, C.L. (2007). *Pedometer power: Using pedometers in school and community.* 2nd ed. Champaign, IL: Human Kinetics.

Walking Connection: walkingconnection.com/fitness-walking-technique-and-form/

SparkPeople: www.sparkpeople.com/resource/fitness_articles.asp?id=1220

Health and Style: healthandstyle.com/fitness/how-to-walk-with-good-posture/

Internet keyword search: "pedometers," "step count," "proper walking technique"

WALKING TECHNIQUE CHECKLIST

Name: _____ Partner: _____

Technique	Trial 1		Trial 2		Trial 3	
	Y	N	Y	N	Y	N
Preparation phase:						
Stand tall (head-to-ankle alignment)	__	__	__	__	__	__
Shoulders back	__	__	__	__	__	__
Abdominals tight	__	__	__	__	__	__
Execution:						
Step forward	__	__	__	__	__	__
Heel strikes first (45 degree)	__	__	__	__	__	__
Toe pushes off	__	__	__	__	__	__
Follow-through:						
Arms swing in opposition to legs	__	__	__	__	__	__

Feedback for partner: _____

_____

_____

_____

_____

_____

From L.C. MacDonald, R.J. Doan, and S. Chepko, eds., 2018, *Lesson planning for high school physical education* (Reston, VA: SHAPE America; Champaign, IL: Human Kinetics). Based on Pangrazi, Beighle, and Sidman 2007.

PEDOMETER TASK SHEET

Put your pedometer on, and be sure to reset it to zero. Check to see that you have placed the pedometer correctly and closed it securely.

1. Walk (be sure to count to yourself) 50 steps at your normal pace in a straight line. Try not to let your counting change your normal gait or pace. After the 50 steps, open the pedometer carefully and record how many steps it registered on the line below. Repeat two more times.

2. Number of steps recorded: 1) _____   2) _____   3) _____

3. Did your pedometer record more, fewer, or the exact number of steps across the trials? Explain: _____
_____

4. Why might the pedometer have registered a different number of steps than you counted (50)? _____

_____

_____

_____

_____

5. Now think about walking a mile on the track. Estimate how many steps and how long you think it will take you to walk four laps (roughly 1 mile) at a moderate pace.

   a. 1-mile step-count estimate: _____

   b. 1-mile walk-time estimate: _____

6. Be sure that your pedometer is reset at zero and close it securely. Now, walk four laps for time and for actual step count. Once you finish your mile, step off the track and record your final step count and walk time.

   a. Actual 1-mile step count: _____

   b. Actual 1-mile walk time: _____

7. Did you overestimate or underestimate your step count? _____

   Your time? _____

8. What was your step-count difference? _____   Time difference? _____

9. Please reflect on this activity. Were you surprised by how close or how far off your estimates were? What factors might have played a role in your actual step count or mile time? What did you learn from this activity?

_____

_____

_____

_____

_____

_____

10. Add up all the steps you took in class today. How many total steps did you record? _____

11. Now estimate how many miles you would walk if you completed 10,000 steps. _____

12. Homework: Look up information about taking 10,000 steps a day. Does it differ depending on your age? Gender? Explain.

_____

_____

_____

_____

_____

_____

From L.C. MacDonald, R.J. Doan, and S. Chepko, eds., 2018, *Lesson planning for high school physical education* (Reston, VA: SHAPE America; Champaign, IL: Human Kinetics). Based on Pangrazi, Beighle, and Sidman 2007.

LESSON 2: WALKING PACE

Grade-Level Outcomes

Primary Outcome

Fitness activities: Demonstrates competency in 1 or more specialized skills in health-related fitness activities. (S1.H3.L1)

Embedded Outcome

Fitness knowledge: Identifies types of strength exercises (isometric, concentric, eccentric) and stretching exercises (static, proprioceptive neuromuscular facilitation [PNF], dynamic) for personal fitness development (e.g., strength, endurance, range of motion). (S3.H9.L1)

Lesson Objectives

The learner will:

- perform good walking technique at different paces.
- estimate step counts for particular paces (17-minute mile, 15-minute mile, 13-minute mile).
- evaluate the effects of different walking paces on step counts.

Equipment and Materials

- Pedometers (1 per student)
- Task sheets (1 per student)
- Stopwatch

Introduction

We will continue our walking unit today. First, let's review: What are some of the health benefits of walking? Describe correct walking technique. About how many steps did you take in a mile? Approximately how many miles would you walk in 10,000 steps? From your homework, can you tell me why 10,000 steps is considered a good daily goal? Today, you will see how different walking paces can affect your step count. In following lessons we will discuss pace relative to heart rate to maximize the health benefits of walking at a moderate pace.

Instructional Task:
Warm-Up (Slow, Medium, and Fast Pace)

Note: If pedometers are not available, you can tie walking directly to heart rate and design the unit to work on keeping within a moderate target heart rate zone (50 percent to 70 percent). This lesson demonstrates how pace affects heart rate.

■ PRACTICE TASK

Students put on their pedometers and reset them to zero. When the music begins, they walk at a slow pace for 60 seconds using correct walking technique. When the music pauses, they stop, look at the step count, and reset. When the slightly faster music begins, students walk around at a moderate pace for 60 seconds. When the music pauses, they look at their pedometers and reset. When fast-beat music begins, students walk at their fastest power-walk speed for 60 seconds, then stop, check step count, and reset.

Repeat one or two times.

Preparation Phase

- Stand tall (head to ankle alignment).
- Pull shoulders back.
- Tighten abdominal muscles.

Execution

- Step forward.
- Heel strikes first (45 degrees).
- Toe pushes off.

Follow-Through

- Swing arms in opposition to legs.

Extension

Repeat with different movements (e.g., lunges, butt kickers, carioca).

Guiding questions for students:

- Did you notice what happens to your heart rate when you power-walk or when you pick up the pace?
- Why does this matter?
- Did your step count or heart rate change doing different movements? How?

Refinement

Watch for changes in walking technique. Remind students to pick up the pace but keep proper technique.

Extensions

- Students walk with a partner and compare their steps with each other at different paces.
- Alter the walking direction or the time.
- Have students do each pace for a particular distance (e.g., 20 yards or meters).
- Change to slow-, moderate-, and fast-paced intervals for 2 minutes each. Repeat two times, and have students look at differences in step count for each 2-minute interval.

Student Choices/Differentiation

Students may choose to use poles (Nordic walking) or walking stick.

What to Look For

- Students are using good walking technique at all three paces.
- Students have their pedometers on appropriately and are resetting and closing them properly.

Instructional Task: Lap Pacing

■ PRACTICE TASK

Students walk laps at different paces and record their step counts after each lap.

- For the first lap, students walk a 17-minute-mile pace.
- Students walk a second lap at a 15-minute-mile pace.
- Students walk the third lap at a 13-minute-mile pace.
- For the fourth lap, students may choose any pace and record both lap time and step count.

At the end, students calculate their estimated steps for a mile at each pace. See the task sheet.

Guiding questions for students:

- How did each pace feel?
- What did your heart rate feel like at each pace?
- If you wanted to get more benefit from walking and still enjoy it, what pace do you think would be most beneficial for you?

Student Choices/Differentiation
- Students may choose lap paces.
- Students may walk one lap very slowly, one lap at a typical pace, and one lap at a very fast pace and time each, and then estimate mile times and steps from each lap's pace.

What to Look For
- Students can pace themselves while walking.
- Students can estimate their steps for a mile at each pace based on one-lap step counts.
- Students can describe what happens to their step counts at different paces and why.
- Students can describe what happens to their heart rates at different walking paces.

Instructional Task: Cool-Down Stretches

■ PRACTICE TASK

Cooling down and stretching are important after walking. Have students put their pedometers away and come together as a class for a flexibility cool-down routine. Students hold each stretch for 15 to 20 seconds on both sides of the body.
- Calf stretch
- Achilles stretch
- Hamstring stretch
- Glute stretch
- Shoulder stretch
- Chest stretch
- Triceps stretch

EMBEDDED OUTCOME: S3.H9.L1. While stretching, students identify the types of stretching they are doing and what the purpose is.

Guiding questions for students?
- Why is flexibility important?
- Why is it good to stretch after walking?

Student Choices/Differentiation
Students may stretch on their own or with a partner (upper and lower body).

What to Look For
- Students can perform the flexibility routine with correct form and technique.
- Students can discuss why stretching after physical activity is important.

Formal and Informal Assessments

Exit slip: Describe three ways to incorporate more stretching into your everyday life.

Closure
- Today, we looked at how pacing can affect step count. What happened to your step count as your pace increased?
- How did the walking pace affect your heart rate? Why does this matter?
- How can you include more walking in your daily routine?
- How might wearing a pedometer affect your walking behavior?

Reflection

- Could students adequately pace?
- Could students estimate their steps per mile?
- Should I add heart rate and calculating target heart rate in our next class?

Homework

- Think about all the walking you do. How many steps do you believe you take throughout the day?
- By next class, log your total steps for one day.

Resources

Darst, P.W. & Pangrazi, R.P. (2009). *Lesson plans: Dynamic physical education for secondary school students*. 6th ed. San Francisco: Pearson Benjamin Cummings.

Pangrazi, R.P., Beighle, A., & Sidman, C.L. (2007). *Pedometer power: Using pedometers in school and community*. 2nd ed. Champaign, IL: Human Kinetics.

PACING TASK SHEET

Estimated 17-minute-mile step count: _____

    Lap 1: 17-minute-mile step count _____

Estimated 15-minute-mile step count: _____

    Lap 2: 15-minute-mile step count _____

Estimated 13-minute-mile step count: _____

    Lap 3: 13-minute-mile step count _____

Lap 4: your choice.   Lap time _____   Step count _____

    Estimated mile step count at this pace _____

Total steps taken today in class: _____

What pace did you prefer? Why? _____

_____

_____

What happened to your step count when your pace increased? Did it change? How?
Why do you think that is? Explain. _____

_____

_____

From L.C. MacDonald, R.J. Doan, and S. Chepko, eds., 2018, *Lesson planning for high school physical education* (Reston, VA: SHAPE America; Champaign, IL: Human Kinetics).

LESSON 3: WALKING AND HEART RATE

Grade-Level Outcomes

Primary Outcomes

Fitness knowledge: Calculates target heart rate and applies that information to personal fitness plan. (S3.H10.L1)

Fitness activities: Demonstrates competency in 1 or more specialized skills in health-related fitness activities. (S1.H3.L1)

Fitness knowledge: Adjusts pacing to keep heart rate in the target zone, using available technology (e.g., pedometer, heart rate monitor), to self-monitor aerobic intensity. (S3.H10.L2)

Equipment and Materials

- Task sheets (1 per student)
- Pedometers (1 per student)
- Some calculators
- Stopwatches

Lesson Objectives

The learner will:
- calculate her or his moderate and vigorous target heart rate zones (using Karvonen formula).
- explore pace and heart rate related to walking intensity.
- self-regulate by working within her or his target heart rate zone.

Introduction

Who wants to share the number of steps he or she took from the log? In our previous class, you learned how pacing affects your step count and what happens to your heart rate as you increase your pace. You will continue to explore heart rate today while counting your steps and considering how you can get the most benefit from your walking. First, to find your personalized target heart rate zone, you must find your resting heart rate. Who can tell me when the best time is to find your resting heart rate? (Answer: in the morning when you wake before getting out of bed) *That's right, but since you did not do that today, I want you all to rest for a few minutes and then take your resting heart rate.*

Instructional Task:
Resting Heart Rate and Calculating Target Heart Rate (THR)

■ PRACTICE TASK

Show students how to take their heart rates either at the wrist or neck. Have them practice for 30 seconds.

Next, students spread out and lie down on their backs for 2 to 4 minutes. When time is up, students take their 30-second resting heart rate, record it, and multiply by 2. (It is more accurate to take a longer heart rate than it is to take it for 6 seconds and multiply by 10.)

Show students the Karvonen equation for finding their THR zones. Go through a practice equation together. See the task sheet.

After reviewing the formula, students find both their moderate and vigorous THR zones.

Refinements

- Students use heart rate monitors.
- Students take their heart rates for a full 60 seconds.

The Karvonen formula is the most accurate, but you could calculate a percentage of the maximal heart rate to estimate target heart rate range. This simpler equation is less accurate.

Guiding questions for students:

- How can you use heart rate when out for a walk?
- What else might affect your heart rate when you are walking besides pace? (Answer: terrain, hills, heat, and so on)
- Why should you consider your heart rate when walking for physical activity?

Student Choices/Differentiation

- Students may take their heart rates at the neck or wrist.
- Give students a completed sample equation before finding their own so they have an example to go by.

What to Look For

- Students can find their pulse to take their heart rates.
- Students can find their 60-second resting heart rates by multiplying by 2 or taking their heart rates for 60 seconds.

Instructional Task:
Moderate and Vigorous Laps for Heart Rate and Steps

■ PRACTICE TASK

Have students walk one lap at a moderate pace and take a 15-second or 30-second heart rate at the end of the lap. They should record their heart rates and the steps. Remind students to reset their pedometers before starting each lap.

For the second lap, students run one lap at their own running pace and then record heart rate and steps. Repeat, with students walking another lap and then running another lap to compare heart rate, lap time, and steps.

After logging heart rate, time, and steps after completing the fourth lap, students take a cool-down lap at their own pace. They will again time the lap, take a step count, and measure heart rate at the conclusion of the cool-down lap.

Refinement

Check for changes in walking technique. Encourage students to maintain good technique regardless of pace.

Guiding questions for students:

- What happened to your step count when you ran compared to when you walked? Why might this be?
- Do you think the pedometer is accurate when you run? Why or why not?
- When walking at a moderate pace, were you within your moderate target heart rate zone? If you were not, how can you get there?
- How about running? Where were you in your target heart rate zone?

Student Choices/Differentiation

- Students may do more laps of either walking or running.
- Students may walk for 4 minutes, run for 4 minutes, and repeat, or select another time interval.
- Students may walk two, run one, walk two, run one, or walk two, run two, and so on.
- Students may use walking poles or sticks.

What to Look For

- Students can use their heart rates to pace.
- Students can change their pace to stay within their THR zones or recognize how it feels to be in their THR zones.

Instructional Task: Cool-Down Stretches

■ **PRACTICE TASK**

Have students put their pedometers away and come together as a class for a flexibility cool-down routine. Students hold each stretch for 15 to 20 seconds on both sides of the body.

- Quad stretch
- Calf stretch
- Achilles stretch
- Hamstring stretch
- Glute stretch
- Shoulder stretch
- Chest stretch
- Triceps stretch

Students record their heart rates at the conclusion of the stretching.

Refinements

- Make sure students hold their static stretches and do not bounce.
- Remind students about the importance of alignment and to stretch all major muscle groups.

Guiding questions for students:

- During your flexibility cool-down, what did your heart rate do?
- Why are you stretching after this walking activity?

Student Choices/Differentiation

Students can stretch on their own or with a partner.

What to Look For

- Students are doing the stretches with correct form and holding for an adequate amount of time.
- Students recognize the type of stretching they are doing (e.g., static, dynamic).

Formal and Informal Assessments

- Task sheets – heart rate
- Exit slip: compare your walking heart rate with your stretching heart rate.

Closure

- Today, you used both pedometers and target heart rate while walking. Can anyone tell me what the daily physical activity recommendations are for adults?
- How can you use target heart rate to gauge your daily physical activity?
- Do you know what your moderate heart rate feels like? Vigorous heart rate?
- Keep thinking about how you could use a pedometer or your target heart rate while walking to accumulate your daily physical activity minutes or steps.

Reflection

- Were students able to calculate the lower and upper limits of their target heart rate zones?
- Did students maintain technique regardless of pace?
- Do students understand heart rate and the effects of physical activity on heart rate?

Homework

- Now that you have used both pedometers and heart rate, think of how you can use both to increase your daily moderate to vigorous physical activity and daily step counts.
- Create a list of five places where you could walk outside of school to increase your daily steps and daily moderate physical activity.

Resources

Calculating target heart rates

CALCULATING HEART RATE

Find estimated max heart rate:

> 220 − your age

Find heart rate reserve (HRR):

> Max heart rate (MHR) − resting heart rate (RHR) = heart rate reserve (HRR)

Find lower limit (50 percent) of moderate THR:

> HRR × .50 + RHR = lower limit of target heart rate zone

Find upper limit (70 percent) of moderate THR:

> HRR × .70 + RHR = upper limit of target heart rate zone

National Association for Sport and Physical Education. (2011). The physical best teacher's guide: Physical education for lifelong fitness. 3rd ed. Ayers, S.F., Sariscsany, M.J., eds. Champaign, IL: Human Kinetics, p. 83.

Tell students to round up or down.

Example: Joe is 15 and has a resting heart rate of 60.

Max heart rate: 220 − 15 = 205

HRR: 205 − 60 = 145

50% = 145 × .5 = 72.5 (73) + 60 = **133** (lower limit)

70% = 145 × .7 = 101.5 (102) + 60 = **162** (upper limit)

Moderate target heart rate zone is 133 to 162.

Now, students find Joe's vigorous THR zone (70 to 85 percent) and then do their own THR zones for both a moderate range and vigorous range.

Log Sheet

Lap 1 Heart rate: _____   Step count: _____

Lap 2 Heart rate: _____   Step count: _____

Lap 3 Heart rate: _____   Step count: _____

Lap 4 Heart rate: _____   Step count: _____

Total step count: _____

From L.C. MacDonald, R.J. Doan, and S. Chepko, eds., 2018, *Lesson planning for high school physical education* (Reston, VA: SHAPE America; Champaign, IL: Human Kinetics). Reprinted, by permission, from S.F. Ayers and M.J. Sarsiscsany, 2011, *The physical best teacher's guide: Physical education for lifelong fitness,* 3rd ed. (Champaign, IL: Human Kinetics), 83.

LESSON 4: LANE LAP COMPARISONS

Grade-Level Outcomes

Primary Outcomes

Fitness knowledge: Calculates target heart rate and applies that information to personal fitness plan. (S3.H10.L1)

Fitness knowledge: Adjusts pacing to keep heart rate in target zone, using available technology (e.g., pedometer, heart rate monitor), to self-monitor aerobic intensity. (S3.H10.L2)

Fitness activities: Demonstrates competency in 1 or more specialized skills in health-related fitness activities. (S1.H3.L1)

Embedded Outcome

Movement concepts, principles & knowledge: Uses movement concepts and principles (e.g., force, motion, rotation) to analyze and improve performance of self and/or others for a self-selected skill. (S2.H2.L1)

Lesson Objectives

The learner will:

- perform the tasks at a moderate-to-vigorous physical activity (MVPA) level.
- track his heart rate during each task and modify his intensity level as needed to stay in his or her target heart rate (THR) zone.

Equipment and Materials

- Pedometers (1 per student)
- Jump ropes (6 to 8)
- Steppers (6 to 8)
- Depending on space, mats for curl-ups
- Cones
- Stopwatches
- Task sheets

Introduction

You have been working on staying in your target heart rate zone while walking. You have also been seeing how many steps you can accumulate during class. Thinking about the 10,000-step goal, how many more steps do you think you could get if you parked at the far end of the parking lot instead of right in front of the store? Today, we will see how many more steps you get depending on what lane you walk in on the track. You will still be checking your heart rate to stay within your moderate target heart rate zone. Why do you want to work at a moderate pace? What are other tools you could use to check if you are being moderately physically active?

Instructional Task: Warm-Up Stations and THR Review

■ PRACTICE TASK

Students put on their pedometers and get into groups of five or six. Direct groups to a one of the six stations. Each station is 1 minute in length. When the music stops, students find their pulse, count for 15 seconds, and record their heart rates on their sheets after multiplying by 4. Students record the number of steps registered on their pedometers and rotate to the next station.

Stations can include the following activities (or create your own):
1. Push-ups and/or planks
2. Aerobic steps (step-ups on steppers)
3. Power walking
4. Lunges, wall sits, or body-weight squats
5. Curl-ups or V-sits
6. Jumping rope or ski jumps

Refinements
- Check the form for each activity (e.g., flat backs for push-ups and planks, walking form for power walk, safe knees [90 degrees] for lunges, wall sits, and squats).
- Choose the percentage of the THR zone for students to stay within.

Guiding questions for students:
- Are you learning what it feels like to be working at a moderate or vigorous level according to your heart rate?
- At which stations were you in the target heart rate zone? What station was your heart rate the highest? The lowest?
- How could you adjust if you were not in the zone (too low, too high)?
- How could you incorporate a quick warm-up like this at home?
- How many steps did you accumulate during the warm-up?
- What type of health-related fitness were you working on during this activity?

Student Choices/Differentiation
- Students may choose to work at a moderate or vigorous level.
- Students may perform modified push-ups or wall push-ups.
- On ground marching, or high-knee step-ups, or step-ups onto a higher step, and so on, students may increase or decrease the pace.
- Students may perform medicine ball twists or dead bugs.

What to Look For
- Students are in their target heart rate zones.
- Students can modify their intensity level to stay in their target heart rate zones.
- Students are performing at the stations continuously for 1 minute with correct form.

Instructional Task: Partner Lap Comparisons by Lane

■ PRACTICE TASK

Students jog or power walk out to the track. Today, students will see the step-count differences of the track lanes. With a partner, students walk laps in the different lanes to see how many steps they take in each one. Eight lanes are standard on a track. Four sets of partners begin in lanes 1 and 2, 3 and 4, 5 and 6, and 7 and 8 (i.e., one partner walks the odd lanes and the other the even). Students should walk at a pace that keeps them in their moderate heart rate zones. Students rotate lanes after each lap—if they started in 1 and 2, they move to 3 and 4, and so on. Lanes 7 and 8 would move to 1 and 2. Have cones set up with staggered starts to provide adequate spacing or stagger the start. Faster walkers should move to the front to prevent congestion. Students measure heart rate throughout to see if they are staying in their zones.

Refinements
- Vary the length of time students take their heart rates (10, 15, 30 seconds).
- Watch for consistency in heart rate over the laps—challenge students to keep their heart rates as close to the same as possible for all four laps.
- Reinforce proper walking form.

Guiding questions for students:
- How different were step totals from one lane to another?
- Were you able to stay within your target heart rate goal? Why or why not?
- What can you change to stay in the zone if you were not?

EMBEDDED OUTCOME: S2.H2.L1 Use questioning to apply movement concepts to walking technique:
- How are you feeling about your walking technique?
- Does pacing affect your technique?
- Do you feel you have to concentrate more on technique when walking at a faster (more vigorous) pace?
- How might technique change as pace changes?
- Do you notice any changes in your stride length or frequency?
- How can technique play a role in injury prevention?

Student Choices/Differentiation
- Students may choose to work at a moderate or vigorous level
- Student may jog or run the laps.
- Students may use walking poles or sticks.

What to Look For
- Students are using good walking technique.
- Students are setting a goal and staying in their target heart rate zones.

Instructional Task: Cool-Down Stretches

■ PRACTICE TASK

Have students put their pedometers away and come together as a class for a flexibility cool-down routine. Students hold each stretch for 15 to 20 seconds on both sides of the body.
- Quad stretch
- Calf stretch
- Achilles stretch
- Hamstring stretch
- Glute stretch
- Shoulder stretch
- Chest stretch
- Triceps stretch

Students record their heart rates at the conclusion of the stretching.

Refinement

Ask students to breathe through their stretches, deep inhales and exhales, pushing a little further each time while staying in proper alignment.

Guiding questions for students:
- During your flexibility cool-down, what did your heart rate do?
- Why are you stretching after this walking activity?

Student Choices/Differentiation

Students may stretch on their own or with a partner.

What to Look For
- Students are performing the stretches with correct form.
- Students are holding the stretches and not bouncing.

Formal and Informal Assessments

Students' ability to measure heart rate

Closure
- How much moderate to vigorous physical activity did you get during class today?
- How much more do you need to do outside of class to meet the daily recommendations?
- How many total steps did you take?
- What can you do to meet the 10,000-step guideline?
- From your homework, what examples did you find of places for physical activity in the community?
- Tomorrow you will review your daily step and physical activity totals for the week and set some goals.

Reflection
- Were students able to take accurate heart rate measures consistently?
- Were they able to gauge their MVPA levels (e.g., what a moderate pace in their moderate target heart rate zone feels like)?
- Did students maintain correct walking form regardless of pace?

Homework
- Reflect on the week's walking activities. What can you do at home to increase your daily steps and your moderate to vigorous physical activity levels?
- Where are some places you would like to walk?
- What are the barriers you might face related to walking outside of school?
- How might you remediate these barriers?
- How might tools such as pedometers, heart rate monitors, and other physical activity monitors or apps help you manage your daily physical activity?

Resources

Internet keyword search: "walking to relieve back pain," "walking technique"

LESSON 5: GOAL SETTING

Grade-Level Outcomes

Primary Objectives

Fitness knowledge: Calculates target heart rate and applies that information to personal fitness plan. (S3.H10.L1)

Fitness activities: Demonstrates competency in 1 or more specialized skills in health-related fitness activities. (S1.H3.L1)

Embedded Outcome

Physical activity knowledge: Analyzes the impact of life choices, economics, motivation and accessibility on exercise adherence and participation in physical activity in college or career settings. (S3.H5.L2)

Lesson Objectives

The learner will:

- set individual goals for increasing daily step totals and time spent in moderate-to-vigorous physical activity (MVPA).
- estimate step totals accumulated throughout the school day by walking out her schedule.

Equipment and Materials

- Goal sheets (1 per student)
- Campus walk sheets (1 per student)
- Pedometers (1 per student)

Introduction

This week, you estimated your step counts toward meeting the 10,000-step goal and used heart rate to accumulate moderate to vigorous physical activity, or MVPA. What did you learn about your activity level from your reflection? Today, you will set goals related to daily steps or daily moderate to vigorous physical activity. You will be able to choose what type of goal you want to work on. Setting goals will be important for you as you transition into college or the workplace. What do you know about physical activity levels after high school? What are some ways you can stay active? Why walking?

Instructional Task: Review Task Sheets and Set Goals

■ PRACTICE TASK

Hand back the students' task sheets from the first four lessons (physical activity logs, step logs, and heart rates). Students look over their step counts and heart rates. Next, review how to set SMART (specific, measurable, attainable, realistic, and timely) goals.

Have students set goals in class and outside of class for walking and accumulating either more steps or more time throughout the day in MVPA. See the goal sheet.

EMBEDDED OUTCOME: S3.H5.L2. This assignment focuses students on thinking about the barriers to engaging in physical activity in college and career settings.

Extension

Have students set both daily step and heart rate goals (MVPA).

Guiding questions for students:

- Are your goals realistic?
- Are they SMART goals?
- Have you considered the barriers you may face in increasing your step count or your daily moderate to vigorous physical activity?
- How will you use target heart rate?

Student Choices/Differentiation

Provide examples of goals for students to use.

What to Look For

- Students can set one or two SMART goals.
- Students can answer the questions on the task sheet.
- Students can set realistic goals considering some of the barriers they may face.

Instructional Task: Campus Walk

■ PRACTICE TASK

Students put on their pedometers and reset them. They then estimate how many steps they accumulate around campus.

Students either walk out their daily schedules, or you create routes from buildings, lunch areas, fields, and so on, for students to walk out to determine the number of steps it takes them to get from point to point.

Extension

Discuss with the science teacher different activities or content that students could do or look for during their walk to match what they are learning in that class.

Guiding questions for students:

- After the campus walk, do your goals need to be adjusted?

Student Choices/Differentiation

- Students may walk out their schedule or follow a route in small groups (e.g., from the office to each building, classroom, or other designated areas; the PE facilities: locker room to gym to track to pool).
- Students may use walking poles or sticks.

What to Look For

- Students can maintain a moderate heart rate during the campus walk.
- Students get a rough estimate of their daily steps for a school day.

Instructional Task: Strength Exercises and Cool-Down

■ PRACTICE TASK

Students perform abdominal and upper- and lower-body strength exercises and then stretch out and cool down.

They monitor their heart rates during the activity to see what level they are working at. This will reinforce how students feel when they are working at particular levels.

Students do the following for time or a specific number:

- Regular push-ups or modified push-ups
- Curl-ups or dead bugs
- Lunges or ski jumps

Students hold each stretch for 15 to 20 seconds on both sides of the body.

- Quad stretch
- Calf stretch
- Achilles stretch
- Hamstring stretch
- Glute stretch
- Shoulder stretch
- Chest stretch
- Triceps stretch

Refinements

- Watch for correct form. Remind students to get their elbows to 90 degrees for push-ups.
- Are lunges in safe alignment? Have students step backward if struggling with knees over toes.
- Remind students to breathe throughout their exercises and stretches.

Student Choices/Differentiation

- Students may perform the exercises on their own as they finish their campus walk.
- Students may do the exercises and cool down with partners or in small groups.
- Students may modify the number of repetitions or length of time for the exercises.

What to Look For

- Students are performing the fitness activities with correct form.
- Students are stretching with correct form.
- Students can discuss why muscle strength and flexibility are important.

Formal and Informal Assessments

- Goal sheets
- Task sheets
- Homework questions

Closure

- Today, you worked on setting goals to increase your daily step totals and your time spent in moderate to vigorous physical activity. Why is this important for your health?
- How can setting goals help you now and in the future to maintain a healthy lifestyle?
- How might tools such as pedometers, heart rate monitors, activity monitors, and apps support your goals or motivate you to meet certain physical activity goals?
- We will continue our walking module next class. For homework, please answer the questions on the back of your goal sheet. They are due next class meeting.

Reflection

- Were students' goals realistic for their circumstances?
- Did students' goals include all the elements of a SMART goal?

Homework

Answer the questions on your goal sheet, and adjust your goals if needed after estimating your daily campus steps. Complete the homework questions.

Resources

Pangrazi, R.P., Beighle, A., & Sidman, C.L. (2007). *Pedometer power: Using pedometers in school and community.* 2nd ed. Champaign, IL: Human Kinetics.

GOAL SHEET

How many total steps did you take in class this week? _____

How much walking do you do outside of class?_____

Approximately how much time did you spend in your target heart rate zone?_____

How can you use walking to increase your MVPA daily? _____

Considering your average number of steps taken during class, how might you increase them? _____

Come up with one or two goals. Your goals should include one of the following: increasing average daily steps by a certain increment (e.g., 2,000 steps); increasing daily steps by a certain percentage (e.g., up by 10 percent); a time goal (e.g., walking for a certain amount of time); or a mileage goal. Remember, all walking should be in your target heart rate zone. Decide what type of goals you want to set and determine how you will work toward your goals. Your goals should be SMART (specific, measurable, attainable, realistic, and time sensitive). _____

_____

Next, describe how you plan to meet your goals, both in class and outside of class.

_____

What barriers might you have to meeting your goals?_____

How can you work around these possible barriers? _____

Now create a log sheet for yourself. For the next two weeks, you will need to log your class and daily step totals as well as the time you spend in MVPA. This log sheet will help you see your progression toward your goals.

Homework

As a college student or professional in your choice career, what barriers might you face related to getting your daily steps or time spent in MVPA?

_____

_____

Are the barriers you currently face (those you wrote about while setting goals in class) similar to those you may face in college or in your career? Explain.

_____

_____

What strategies might help eliminate or minimize these possible barriers?

_____

_____

What types of tools might you use to help you manage your goals and daily physical activity now, in college, and as a professional?

_____

_____

From L.C. MacDonald, R.J. Doan, and S. Chepko, eds., 2018, *Lesson planning for high school physical education* (Reston, VA: SHAPE America; Champaign, IL: Human Kinetics).

CAMPUS WALK TASK SHEET

School parking lot or drop-off zone to quad/entrance:

School entrance to your first-period class (room # _____):

1st per. (room # _____) to 2nd per. (room # _____):

2nd per. (room # _____) to 3rd per. (room # _____):

3rd per. (room # _____) to 4th per. (room # _____):

4th per. (room # _____) to 5th per. (room # _____):

5th per. (room # _____) to 6th per. (room # _____):

6th per. (room # _____) to 7th per. (room # _____):

Locker room to gym: _____

Locker room to fields: _____

Gym to track: _____

Considering your step totals from your schedule (what you just walked), approximately how many steps a day do you think you take at school?

From L.C. MacDonald, R.J. Doan, and S. Chepko, eds., 2018, *Lesson planning for high school physical education* (Reston, VA: SHAPE America; Champaign, IL: Human Kinetics).

LESSON 6: STEP COUNT

Grade-Level Outcomes

Primary Outcomes

Fitness knowledge: Calculates target heart rate and applies that information to personal fitness plan. (S3.H10.L1)

Fitness activities: Demonstrates competency in 1 or more specialized skills in health-related fitness activities. (S1.H3.L1)

Embedded Outcomes

Physical activity knowledge: Analyzes the impact of life choices, economics, motivation and accessibility on exercise adherence and participation in physical activity in college or career settings. (S3.H5.L2)

Fitness knowledge: Adjusts pacing to keep heart rate in target zone, using available technology (e.g., pedometer, heart rate monitor), to self-monitor aerobic intensity. (S3.H10.L2)

Lesson Objectives

The learner will:

- evaluate SMART goals.
- walk for 30 minutes and track his or her heart rate on his or her own.
- modify his walking pace to meet his or her goals and maintain a moderate THR.

Equipment and Materials

- Pedometers (1 per student)
- Stopwatches (5) for students who do not have watches to take heart rate, or set up a station where students can check heart rate
- Students' log sheets

Introduction

Today, you will continue walking and review your step and physical activity goals. Please get out your homework to discuss. What are some of the common barriers high school students might face related to obtaining their daily moderate to vigorous physical activity? What are some ideas you have for overcoming those barriers? Do you think some of these barriers are the same for college students and career professionals? Now think about your goals and your plan for meeting your goals. You will share these with a partner so you can evaluate each other's goals and provide constructive feedback. Make sure your partner has SMART goals. What are SMART goals again?

Instructional Task: Review of Goals

■ PRACTICE TASK

Have students pair up or get into small groups. They should have their homework and their goals. Students switch goals with a partner for review; they discuss whether the goals are SMART, why they set the goals they did, how they plan to meet them, and some of the barriers they may face and how they hope to overcome them.

EMBEDDED OUTCOME: S3.H5.L2. Have students think about a variety of factors, such as financial, family commitments, and accessibility, when identifying barriers.

Guiding questions for students:

- What are the elements of SMART goals?
- Does your partner's plan match her goals? Are her goals realistic?

Student Choices/Differentiation

Put students with similar goals in the same group.

What to Look For

- Students can pick out the elements of SMART in their partners' goals.
- Students can evaluate goals critically.

Instructional Task: Warm-Up

■ PRACTICE TASK

Students put on a pedometer and participate in a dynamic warm-up. All movements are to a cone or line.

EMBEDDED OUTCOME: S3.H10.L2. Prompt students to check their heart rates at one or more points during the warm-up to check if they are working at a moderate or vigorous pace (self-management).

- Light jog down and back
- 50 percent run halfway, sprint for second half, repeat on the way back
- High knees down and butt kickers back
- Carioca down and back (both sides)
- Light jog down and back

Extension

Repeat or change up the warm-up activities to include sumo squats, lunges, more sprints, and so on.

Guiding questions for students:

- When should we do dynamic warm-ups in place of static stretching? Why?
- If you were working on increasing flexibility, what type of flexibility would be best to do daily?
- When should we perform flexibility tasks?

Student Choices/Differentiation

Students may choose dynamic warm-up exercises from a list.

What to Look For

- Students are performing the dynamic warm-up with correct form.
- Students can evaluate their heart rates on their own during the warm-up.

Instructional Task: 30-Minute Walk

■ PRACTICE TASK

Students participate in a 30-minute walk to see how many steps they can accumulate. They should be checking their heart rates on their own throughout the activity to be sure they are working at a moderate rate. Students can work toward some of their goals by increasing steps or trying to do so many laps within the 30 minutes.

The timed walk can be on the track if need be, or a large lap area can be created on campus in field space to change it up.

Be sure students are logging all their daily steps in class and outside of class on the logs they created.

Extensions

- Ask students to count how many of certain types of trees, plants, birds, and so on they see during their walk. Or have them count cars, people, teachers, and friends.
- Create a walk bingo card.

Guiding questions for students:

- Are you better able to feel when you are in your target heart rate zone?
- What other activities can you do at home to help you meet your goals?

Student Choices/Differentiation

- Students may walk or run.
- Students may use walking poles or sticks.
- Students may choose to walk on a track or another course instead.

What to Look For

- Students can stay in their THR zones for the entire 30 minutes.
- Students can self-manage the time to work on goals.

Instructional Task: Strength Activities and Cool-Down

■ PRACTICE TASK

Students do the following for a specific time or a specific number:

- Planks (elbows or straight arm) or side planks
- Mountain climbers or burpees
- Body-weight squats or wall sits or lunges

Students hold each stretch for 15 to 20 seconds on both sides of the body:

- Quad stretch
- Calf stretch
- Achilles stretch
- Hamstring stretch
- Glute stretch
- Shoulder stretch
- Chest stretch
- Triceps stretch

Refinement

Have students set goals for strength exercises and flexibility to work toward.

Extension

Have students create their own cool-down with strength and flexibility criteria in small groups, and then each day students lead each other through the cool-downs they developed.

Guiding questions for students:

- What type of stretching are we doing?
- When is static stretching most beneficial?

Student Choices/Differentiation

- Students may modify the number of repetitions if needed.

What to Look For

Students are performing both strength activities and stretches with correct form and proper alignment.

Formal and Informal Assessments

- Daily step logs
- Goal sheets

Closure

- Today, you reviewed your SMART goals and also worked on accumulating steps and moderate to vigorous physical activity during your 30-minute walk.
- How many steps did you get today during class?
- How will this help with your daily goals?
- What are some things you have planned for your goals outside of PE class?
- What is the difference between the warm-up stretches we did and the cool-down stretches?

Reflection

- Were students able to evaluate SMART goals and plans?
- Could students manage taking and logging their heart rates on their own without being prompted?
- Could students recall the different types of stretching and when and why to use each?

Homework

- Physical activity decreases significantly as we get older. The first large decrease in physical activity occurs after high school. What are some of the reasons physical activity behavior decreases after high school and during college?
- Explain the benefits of walking at a moderate level (THR zone) and how as a college student you could use walking to accumulate the daily MVPA recommendations.
- What technologies and other resources might support or motivate you to be physically active in college? Explain. Due in lesson 8.

Resources

Internet keyword search: "fitness walking," "MVPA," "target heart rate"

LESSON 7: DIRECTIONS CHALLENGE 1

Grade-Level Outcomes

Primary Outcomes

Physical activity knowledge: Discusses the benefits of a physically active lifestyle as it relates to college or career productivity. (S3.H1.L1)

Fitness knowledge: Calculates target heart rate and applies that information to personal fitness plan. (S3.H10.L1)

Fitness activities: Demonstrates competency in 1 or more specialized skills in health-related fitness activities. (S1.H3.L1)

Embedded Outcomes

Fitness knowledge: Adjusts pacing to keep heart rate in target zone, using available technology (e.g., pedometer, heart rate monitor), to self-monitor aerobic intensity. (S3.H10.L2)

Health: Analyzes the health benefits of a self-selected physical activity. (S5.H1.L1)

Lesson Objectives

The learner will:

- complete the challenge tasks in a group.
- monitor her or his heart rate and steps to adjust pace as needed.
- discuss and answer challenge trivia related to the benefits of a physically active lifestyle as it relates to college or career productivity.

Equipment and Materials

- 1 pedometer per student
- 6 challenge cards (1 per group of 5)
- 1 pencil per group
- 5 stopwatches
- Question cards and cones for stations (number depends on how many you set up)
- 5 tennis rackets and balls
- 10 soccer balls
- 5 basketballs

Introduction

Today, you will be walking in groups for a directions challenge. The goal is to accumulate steps and work at a moderate heart rate to help you accumulate more time in moderate to vigorous physical activity. The directions challenge walk will have clues, trivia, and activities to complete. Remember to walk at a good pace and to periodically check your heart rate for your log. You will also need to log your steps at the end of class.

Instructional Task: Dynamic Warm-Up

■ PRACTICE TASK

Students put on a pedometer and participate in a dynamic warm-up. All movements are to a specific cone or line.

EMBEDDED OUTCOME: S3.H10.L2. Prompt students to check their heart rates at one or more points during the warm-up to check if they are working at a moderate or vigorous pace (self-management).

- Light jog down and back (at least 24 yards)
- 10 push-ups
- 50-percent run to halfway down, sprint for second half, repeat on the way back
- 10 push-ups
- High knees down and butt kickers back
- 10 push-ups
- Carioca down and back (both sides)
- Light jog down and back

Extension

Repeat or change up the warm-up activities to include sumo squats, lunges, more sprints, and so on.

Refinement

Have students see if they can use their heart rates to track from very moderate to moderate to vigorous intensity.

Guiding questions for students:

What other ways can you warm up before physical activity?

Student Choices/Differentiation

Students may choose alternate exercises from a list.

What to Look For

Students are performing the warm-up with correct form.

Instructional Task: Directions Challenge

■ PRACTICE TASK

Place students into groups of five and give each group a directions challenge card (see example). The goal of the challenge is to follow the map and clues and accumulate as many steps as possible.

Everyone starts from the same place, but the cards are ordered differently so that each group goes to different first clues to prevent congestion.

Refinements

- Create the challenge to have shortcuts (fewer steps) and longer routes to see what choices students make (i.e., do they work on accumulating more steps or completing the tasks?). You could also add roadblocks—if students choose to do a shortcut more than once, they must complete a task before getting their next clue.
- Emphasize working as a team to complete the scavenger hunt. Add some teamwork challenges at each stop.

Extensions

- Set up the course like an orienteering race or a geocaching activity.
- Students create their own directions challenge.

EMBEDDED OUTCOME: S5.H1.L1. The directions challenge cards can prompt students to think about the health benefits of walking. Cards can include questions to answer.

Student Choices/Differentiation

Students may practice reading compasses and maps.

What to Look For

- Students are working together to complete the challenge.
- Students are monitoring their heart rates and steps and modifying their pace as needed.
- Students can answer questions about the importance of a physically active lifestyle.

Instructional Task: Cool-Down Stretches

■ **PRACTICE TASK**

Have students put their pedometers away and come together as a class for a flexibility cool-down routine. Students hold each stretch for 15 to 20 seconds on both sides of the body.

- Quad stretch
- Calf stretch
- Achilles stretch
- Hamstring stretch
- Glute stretch
- Shoulder stretch
- Chest stretch
- Triceps stretch

Extensions

- Students lead the cool-down stretching.
- Have students come to class with a new cool-down stretch or activity to share during cool-down.

Student Choices/Differentiation

- Students may cool-down with partners or in small groups.
- Students can modify the number of repetitions as needed.

What to Look For

- Students are performing the flexibility exercises with correct form.
- Students can discuss ways to include strength and flexibility in their daily physical activity.

Formal and Informal Assessments

- Daily step logs
- Directions challenge cards

Closure

- Today, you worked as a group in the directions challenge walk. As an individual and group, you should have monitored your THR and step totals. Be sure to include those in your logs for today.
- What could you do outside of class to make your walks more interesting?
- What other types of activities are available in the community that include walking and could have you accumulate many steps?

Reflection

- Did students answer the questions correctly?
- Did students monitor and log their steps and check their heart rates on their own?

Homework

Complete the homework question assigned last class. It is due next lesson.

Resources

Darst, P.W. & Pangrazi, R.P. (2009). *Dynamic physical education for secondary school students.* 6th ed. San Francisco: Pearson Benjamin Cummings.

DIRECTIONS CHALLENGE CARD EXAMPLE

Create a directions challenge based on the space and equipment available. Order the activities differently for each group so students are spread out and areas do not get congested.

Start: Write down your warm-up steps and reset your pedometer.

1. Exit the gym and walk to the tennis courts; log your steps. At the tennis courts, use the equipment provided and rally with your group for 2 minutes. Log your steps and put the equipment back as you found it.

2. Leave the tennis courts and walk halfway around the track to the far goal post. Complete 25 jumping jacks and log your steps.

3. Now get back on the track and finish your lap at the next goal post. Log your steps and as a group answer the question posted on the pole.

4. From the goal post, walk to the 50-yard line and perform 25 mountain climbers; log your steps.

5. From the 50-yard line, jog or run to the end zone. Do your best touchdown dance and log your steps.

6. From the end zone, walk up the sideline back to the end zone where you started. At the cone, log your steps and answer the question posted on the cone.

7. Now walk to the soccer field. At the orange cones, grab a ball and dribble the ball alone or with a partner down the field and back. Log your steps.

8. Now walk to the far soccer goal on the field and see how many times in a row you can volley a soccer ball on your body. Try this three times and then log your steps. Be sure to write down your answer to the question posted on the goal.

9. Walk from the soccer goal to the outside basketball courts. At court one, grab a ball and dribble down and do a layup from the foul line. Get your rebound, dribble back to the foul line, and do another layup; log your steps.

10. Walk to court five and do six sprints (half court). Then take one walking lap around the outside of the court back to the basket. Log your steps and answer the question.

11. End: Meet on court three for a class cool-down. What were your individual total steps? What were your group total steps? Be sure to log your total class steps and time in MVPA in your personal log. Were you able to stay in your THR zone? Did you check? When? If you were not in your zone, what could you do next time?

From L.C. MacDonald, R.J. Doan, and S. Chepko, eds., 2018, *Lesson planning for high school physical education* (Reston, VA: SHAPE America; Champaign, IL: Human Kinetics).

LESSON 8: DIRECTIONS CHALLENGE 2

Grade-Level Outcomes

Primary Outcomes

Physical activity knowledge: Discusses the benefits of a physically active lifestyle as it relates to college or career productivity. (S3.H1.L1)

Fitness knowledge: Calculates target heart rate and applies that information to personal fitness plan. (S3.H10.L1)

Fitness activities: Demonstrates competency in 1 or more specialized skills in health-related fitness activities. (S1.H3.L1)

Embedded Outcome

Social interaction: Identifies the opportunity for social support in a self-selected physical activity or dance. (S5.H4.L1)

Lesson Objectives

The learner will:

- complete the directions challenge hunt activities with correct form.
- self-monitor and adjust his or her physical activity level to stay in his or her THR zone.
- log and keep track of his or her daily step totals and identify his or her progress or what barriers he faces.

Equipment and Materials

- 1 pedometer per student
- 6 scavenger hunt cards (1 per group of 5 or 6)
- 3 cones
- 5 jump ropes
- 5 stopwatches
- 1 bench or use bleachers or have 5 steppers
- Optional: Music can be used if available outside

Introduction

Let's review your homework. What happens to physical activity levels as we age? Why? What are some strategies you came up with to get your steps while you're at college? Would they be different if you were working? How can you use technology to help you stay active? Today, you will do another directions challenge. I've planned a lot of physical activity and steps. Keep working toward your goals and with your groups. Be sure to monitor your heart rate to see if you are accumulating moderate to vigorous physical activity. Keep logging your daily step and physical activity totals inside and outside of class. We'll start with our usual dynamic warm-up.

Instructional Task: Directions Challenge 2

■ PRACTICE TASK

Students put on a pedometer and get into groups of five or six. Give each group a directions challenge card with a list of activities to complete. This directions challenge takes place on a track and football field (see example). Students work on accumulating steps and time in MVPA. They will log their class time total at the end of class in their personal logs.

Extensions

- Have students create their own directions challenge in small groups, bring them to class, and switch with different groups to complete each other's.
- Add trivia questions to each task related to walking technique, barriers to physical activity, benefits of physical activity, and so on.

Guiding questions for students:

- What other activities might you be able to do while out on a walk?
- When looking over your logs, how are you doing meeting your goals in class?
- What challenges are you facing outside of class?
- How might you overcome any challenges?

Student Choices/Differentiation

- Students can change the space, the activities, and so on.
- Students choose the challenge card.

What to Look For

- Students are working at a moderate to vigorous pace.
- Students are completing activities with correct form.
- Students are monitoring their steps and MVPA with heart rate.

Instructional Task: Cool-Down Stretches

■ PRACTICE TASK

Have students put their pedometers away and come together as a class for a flexibility cool-down routine. Students hold each stretch for 15 to 20 seconds on both sides of the body.

- Quad stretch
- Calf stretch
- Achilles stretch
- Hamstring stretch
- Glute stretch
- Shoulder stretch
- Chest stretch
- Triceps stretch

EMBEDDED OUTCOME: S5.H4.L1. Use the stretching time to lead a discussion about how walking provides opportunities for social interaction and support. Ask students to provide examples from the walking activities they have been doing.

Refinements

- Create partner stretch routines for students.
- Remind students to focus on breathing.

Student Choices/Differentiation

- Students may cool-down with partners or in small groups.
- Students can modify number of repetitions of the exercises as needed.

What to Look For

- Students are performing the flexibility exercises with correct form.
- Students can discuss ways to include flexibility in their daily physical activity.

Formal and Informal Assessments

- Daily step logs
- Exit slip: What difficulties did you face in following the route?

Closure

- Be sure to log your class total steps and your average heart rate for today's activities. How many of you think you were doing moderate to vigorous physical activity (MVPA) for the majority of class time?
- How many steps did you take?
- How could you include some of these activities in your day outside of school?
- Could you do something similar to this when out for a walk? Explain.
- Great work today and great effort. I hope you are logging both your daily class and total daily steps and your time in MVPA. Keep tracking your progress toward your goals. Next class, we will be doing a poker walk, and in two classes, a team challenge timed walk for steps.

Reflection

- How well were groups working together to complete the scavenger hunt?
- How engaging were the tasks?
- Would you change any tasks or add any in the future?
- Are students still logging their steps and heart rates both in class and outside of class?
- Review homework sheets to evaluate for any misconceptions.

Homework

Continue to complete step and time logs.

Resources

Darst, P.W. & Pangrazi, R.P. (2009). *Dynamic physical education for secondary school students.* 6th ed. San Francisco: Pearson Benjamin Cummings.

DIRECTIONS CHALLENGE 2

1. Walk two laps in the first two lanes of the track.

2. Go to the end zone and perform three sets of 10 push-ups or modified push-ups.

3. From the end zone, jog to the 50-yard line and perform 25 curl-ups or dead bugs.

4. Jog from the 50-yard line to the other end zone and perform three sets of 20- to 30-second planks, or challenge yourself for longer or with side planks.

5. From the end zone, go to the sideline and walk up the sideline, across the back of the end zone, down the other sideline, and across the second end zone (walk the perimeter of the field) at a moderate pace.

6. At the goal post, perform 30 to 50 step-ups on the step or bench provided, or do high knee marches in place.

7. Walk two laps around the track in the outside two lanes.

8. Walk to the second goal post and jump rope for 1 minute at your own pace, or do ski jumps for 1 minute.

9. End: Meet on the 20-yard line marked with three cones for a class cool-down.

Note: Again, change the order of activities on each card so the whole class is not doing the same activities at the same time.

From L.C. MacDonald, R.J. Doan, and S. Chepko, eds., 2018, *Lesson planning for high school physical education* (Reston, VA: SHAPE America; Champaign, IL: Human Kinetics).

LESSON 9: FITNESS WALKING

Grade-Level Outcomes

Primary Outcomes

Fitness knowledge: Calculates target heart rate and applies that information to personal fitness plan. (S3.H10.L1)

Fitness activities: Demonstrates competence in 1 or more specialized health-related fitness activities. (S1.H3.L1)

Embedded Outcomes

Fitness knowledge: Adjusts pacing to keep heart rate in target zone, using available technology (e.g., pedometer, heart rate monitor), to self-monitor aerobic intensity. (S3.H10.L2)

Self-expression & enjoyment: Selects and participates in physical activities or dance that meet the need for self-expression and enjoyment. (S5.H3.L1)

Lesson Objectives

The learner will:

- walk at a moderate pace during the poker walk.
- monitor and log her or his daily step totals.
- follow the rules of the poker walk.

Equipment and Materials

- 1 pedometer per student
- 1 envelope per pair
- 6 to 10 decks of cards
- Poker score sheets
- 5 cones

Introduction

After the warm-up today, you will be doing a poker walk with a partner. The goal is to walk at a moderate rate and accumulate steps. As you walk, you will draw cards at different stations, trying to draw the best hand. We will play a few rounds of poker walk with different poker goals, such as low score and high score.

Instructional Task: Warm-Up

■ PRACTICE TASK

Students put on a pedometer and participate in a dynamic warm-up. All movements are to a specified cone or line.

EMBEDDED OUTCOME: S3.H10.L2 Prompt students to check their heart rates at one or more times during the warm-up to check if they are working at a moderate or vigorous pace (self-management).

- Light jog down and back
- 10 push-ups
- 50 percent run to halfway down, sprint for second half, repeat on the way back
- 10 burpees
- High knees down and butt kickers back
- 10 curl-ups
- Carioca down and back (both sides)
- 10 curl-ups
- Light jog down and back
- 10 lunges

Extension

Repeat or change up the warm-up activities to include sumo squats, lunges, more sprints, and so on.

Student Choices/Differentiation

Students may choose to do push-ups or curl-ups at the end.

What to Look For

Students are performing the warm-up activities properly.

Instructional Task: Poker Walk

■ PRACTICE TASK

Students walk in a designated area (a track or create a large walking area for students). Set out cones throughout the walking area where students pick up a card without looking at it and put it in their envelope for their poker hand. Students pick up only one card at each stop.

Round 1: Look for the high poker hand.

Note: Have different decks at each stop so you know students picked up cards at each area and not just one, or mark the cards to distinguish which stop they came from. If you are worried about students looking for cards they want, wait until all cards are drawn to state what the goal is for the round (e.g., high poker hand).

Extensions

- Round 2: Look for the low poker hand.
- Round 3: Add a wild card.
- Round 4: Add a draw at the end (students can look at their hand and choose whether to discard and draw one card).

EMBEDDED OUTCOME: S5.H3.L1. Have students discuss whether they found walking more enjoyable when they added the poker game to it. Ask them to think of other things that make walking enjoyable.

Student Choices/Differentiation

Students may complete this activity in small groups, as a team, or individually.

What to Look For

- Students are walking at a moderate pace between poker stops.
- Students are choosing just one card.

Instructional Task: Cool-Down

■ PRACTICE TASK

As students come in with their poker hands, prompt them to stretch on their own. Remind them to stretch the major muscle groups and to breathe and hold stretches for 15 to 20 seconds.

Extensions

- From a list of muscular strength and endurance and flexibility activities, allow students to choose two of each to do.
- Provide a list and allow students to work independently (or with a partner) on the list.

Formal and Informal Assessments

Daily step logs

Closure

- Today, you continued accumulating steps and moderate to vigorous physical activity in our walking module. Be sure your logs are complete and up to date.
- Bring your logs to class next time for a check-in on your progress toward your goals. Be sure your logs include class physical activity and overall daily physical activity.

Reflection

- Did students walk at a moderate pace during the poker walk?
- Were students able to manage not looking at their cards?
- Were students logging their daily steps and MVPA?

Homework

Make sure your daily logs are up to date and bring them with you next class.

Resources

Darst, P.W. & Pangrazi, R.P. (2009). *Lesson plans: Dynamic physical education for secondary school students.* 6th ed. San Francisco: Pearson Benjamin Cummings.

LESSON 10: TEAM CHALLENGE WALK

Grade-Level Outcomes

Primary Outcomes

Fitness knowledge: Calculates target heart rate and applies that information to personal fitness plan. (S3.H10.L1)

Fitness activities: Demonstrates competency in 1 or more specialized skills in health-related fitness activities. (S1.H3.L1)

Embedded Outcome

Social interaction: Identifies the opportunity for social support in a self-selected physical activity or dance. (S5.H4.L1)

Lesson Objectives

The learner will:

- evaluate his or her goals and adjust as needed.
- manage his or her own steps and heart rate during the team challenge while also supporting teammates.
- strategize how to overcome barriers he or she may face in meeting physical activity goals.

Equipment and Materials

- 1 pedometer per student
- 12 hoops
- 12 poly spots
- 4 hurdles
- 20 small cones
- 6 tires (if available)
- Stopwatch
- 1 index card per team to record and add up steps

Introduction

Today, we will see how you are all doing in meeting your class and daily goals. How many of you are meeting your goals? If you are struggling meeting your goals, why might that be? After you reflect and warm up, you will be walking in a team challenge. You will want to accumulate your own personal steps and moderate to vigorous physical activity, but your totals will count as a team.

Instructional Task: Review of Goals

■ PRACTICE TASK

Students take out their logs and discuss with a partner how they are doing in meeting their goals.

Student Choices/Differentiation

Students may to choose to write a reflection on the questions during class in place of discussion.

What to Look For

Students are critically reflecting on their goals and progress to date.

Guiding questions for students:

- Are you meeting your goals? If not, why?
- What barriers have you faced?

- How have you overcome some barriers?
- If you were to set new goals, what would you change and why?
- How might setting goals help you stay physically active in college or your career?

Refinement

Remind students to go beyond reviewing their goals to critically reflecting on them.

Instructional Task: Warm-Up

■ PRACTICE TASK

Students put on pedometers. Place students into their teams for the team challenge walk and do a dynamic warm-up to a pre-determined cone or line. Students take heart rate prior to starting the warm-up.

- Light jog down and back
- High knees down and butt kickers back (repeat)
- Carioca down and back (both sides)
- Light jog down and back

Student Choices/Differentiation

Students may select warm-up exercises from a list.

What to Look For

- Students are performing the warm-up properly.
- Students are working hard enough to get their heart rates up.

Instructional Task: Team Challenge Walk

■ PRACTICE TASK

Place students into teams of four. In their teams, they will complete a 25-minute timed walk on the course, which includes some simple obstacles. The goal of the team challenge is to finish as many laps as possible and accumulate steps. Students log their own steps and MVPA and add up their team's steps to see how they did as a team. They do not have to walk as a team, just score as a team.
  Possible obstacles:

- Step though tires or hoops.
- Go through cones.
- Jump over low hurdles.
- Play hopscotch (poly spots).
- Go through set-up hoops.

Extensions

- Extend the length (time) of the walk.
- Vary the obstacles based on equipment available.

EMBEDDED OUTCOME: S5.I4.L1. Use the guiding questions to discuss and reinforce the opportunities for social support in walking.

Refinements

- Set up the activity as a team race. Time all groups for a specified number of laps or steps.
- Create a team challenge. Groups must stay together to meet goals and complete the course.

Guiding questions for students:
- How can you work toward your goals while also supporting your teammates?
- How might working with others support physical activity behavior?
- Do you prefer to work out with friends or alone?
- How do you know if you are working at a moderate pace?

Student Choices/Differentiation
- Students choose their groups.
- Students may choose to work within their moderate or vigorous target heart rate zones for the lesson. Or they may vary between the two by checking heart rate if wanting to create an interval effect.

What to Look For
- Students are moving at a moderate pace.
- Students are working toward their goals individually and as a team.
- Students can check their heart rates on their own.

Instructional Task: Cool-Down Stretches

■ PRACTICE TASK

As each team completes the timed walk, students add up their team steps and log their individual steps. They then perform a flexibility cool-down routine as a team. Students hold each stretch for 15 to 20 seconds on both sides of the body.
- Quad stretch
- Calf stretch
- Achilles stretch
- Hamstring stretch
- Glute stretch
- Shoulder stretch
- Chest stretch
- Triceps stretch

Extensions
- Team leaders lead the group through the cool-down.
- Teams select from a list the cool-down activities they will do together as a team.

Guiding questions for students:
- Why is it important to include flexibility work in your daily physical activity?
- How does flexibility help us as we age?
- How does it help with injury prevention?

Student Choices/Differentiation
- Students may stretch on their own.
- Students may stretch as a class.

What to Look For
Students are using correct form in their stretches.

Formal and Informal Assessments

Daily step logs

Closure

- Today, you continued to work on your goals and support team goals. How might working with others support physical activity behavior?
- Do you prefer to work out with friends or alone?
- How could social support help you stay physically active in college or your career?

Reflection

- Were students working toward their goals?
- Could students work on their individual goals and also support classmates (team) in their goals?
- Review step log to check student progress and return.

Homework

- Review your logs and write a short reflection. Are you meeting or working toward your goals?
- Have you faced any barriers toward meeting your goals? Explain.
- What are some strategies you can use to overcome these barriers?
- How might you modify your behavior to meet your physical activity goals?
- Have you exceeded your goals? If so, what might that tell you about the goals you made?
- Discuss how setting goals might help you stay physically active in college or in your career.

LESSON 11: TIMED WALK

Grade-Level Outcomes

Primary Outcomes

Fitness knowledge: Calculates target heart rate and applies that information to personal fitness plan. (S3.H10.L1)

Fitness activities: Demonstrates competency in 1 or more specialized skills in health-related fitness activities. (S1.H3.L1)

Physical activity knowledge: Analyzes the impact of life choices, economics, motivation and accessibility on exercise adherence and participation in physical activity in college or career settings. (S3.H5.L2)

Embedded Outcomes

Personal responsibility: Employs effective self-management skills to analyze barriers and modify physical activity patterns appropriately, as needed. (S4.H1.L1)

Fitness knowledge: Adjusts pacing to keep heart rate in the target zone, using available technology (e.g., pedometer, heart rate monitor), to self-monitor aerobic intensity. (S3.H10.L2)

Lesson Objectives

The learner will:

- walk for 30 minutes and manage to track his or her heart rate on his or her own.
- modify his or her walking pace to meet his or her goals and maintain a moderate THR.
- discuss strategies for overcoming barriers to participating in physical activity outside of class.

Equipment and Materials

- 1 pedometer per student
- Stopwatches (5) for students who do not have watches to take heart rate, or set up a station where students can check heart rate
- Students' log sheets

Introduction

Today, we are checking in again on goals and step totals. You will complete a 30-minute timed walk on a course set up on campus. You will walk for 30 minutes at either a moderate or vigorous pace. Remember, you are working on your step goals and daily moderate to vigorous physical activity goals. Don't forget to check whether you are in your target heart rate zone. You can walk or run. Be sure your logs are up to date with your reflections. I will be collecting your homework.

Instructional Task: Review and Warm-Up

■ PRACTICE TASK

Have students sit with a partner and review their homework. Then bring everyone together to discuss the reflection questions as a class.

EMBEDDED OUTCOME: S4.H1.L1 Discuss common barriers to participating in physical activity and how to modify behavior to overcome barriers.

Guiding questions for students:

- What barriers did you and your partner both list?
- What barriers did your partner have that you did not think of?
- What suggestions did you come up with for how to eliminate or minimize barriers?
- Why is it important to understand the barriers we might face when living and participating in a healthy, physically active lifestyle?

Instructional Task: Warm-Up

■ PRACTICE TASK

Students put on a pedometer and participate in a dynamic warm-up. All movements are to a specified cone or line.

- Light jog down and back
- 15 push-ups
- 50-percent run to halfway down, sprint for second half, repeat on the way back
- High knees down and butt kickers back
- 20 curl-ups
- Carioca down and back (both sides)
- Light jog down and back

EMBEDDED OUTCOME: S3.H10.L2. Prompt students to check their heart rates at one or more points during the warm-up to check if they are working at a moderate or vigorous pace (self-management).

Extension

Repeat or change up the warm-up activities to include sumo squats, lunges, more sprints, and so on.

Student Choices/Differentiation

Students can volunteer to lead the warm-up.

What to Look For

- Students completed their reflections.
- Students are completing activities properly.
- Students can evaluate their heart rates on their own during the warm-up.

Instructional Task: 30-Minute Timed Walk

■ PRACTICE TASK

Students participate in a 30-minute walk to see how many steps they can accumulate. They should be checking their heart rates on their own throughout the activity to be sure they are working at a moderate rate. Students can work toward some of their goals by increasing steps or trying to do so many laps within the 30 minutes.

The timed walk will be on a large lap area on campus to change it up.

Be sure students are logging all their daily steps in class and outside of class on the logs they created.

Extension

If there is a local park nearby, have a walk at the park or a community walk.

Student Choices/Differentiation

Students may choose to complete the timed walk on the track.

What to Look For

- Students are walking at a moderate pace.
- Students are checking heart rate to stay in their THR zone.
- Students are working toward their goals.

Instructional Task: Cool-Down Stretches

■ **PRACTICE TASK**

Have students come in from the 30-minute walk and stretch out. Students hold each stretch for 15 to 20 seconds on both sides of the body.

- Quad stretch
- Calf stretch
- Achilles stretch
- Hamstring stretch
- Glute stretch
- Shoulder stretch
- Chest stretch
- Triceps stretch

Guiding questions for students:

- What is the difference between the warm-up stretches we did and the cool-down stretches?
- What other activities are you doing at home to help you meet your physical activity goals?
- Do they include strength and flexibility?

Student Choices/Differentiation

- Students may stretch on their own.
- Students may change up the stretches.
- A student volunteer can lead the cool-down.

What to Look For

Students are stretching properly.

Formal and Informal Assessments

Logs and reflection questions

Closure

- Today, we discussed your reflections of your goals so far and some barriers to physical activity. You continued accumulating steps and MVPA during your 30-minute walk. How many steps did get today during class?
- How will this help with your goals?
- What are some things you have planned for your goals outside of PE class?
- What are some strategies for overcoming some of the barriers we discussed?
- What strategies might be effective if motivation is one of your barriers? (Depending where the discussion goes, you can also prompt about social support and different technologies that might enhance motivation.)
- I am handing out a homework question that is due Lesson 15. Be sure to answer the questions completely and thoughtfully.

Reflection

Are students making progress toward their goals? Review logs and reflections to assess student progress.

Homework

- Scaffold questions (due Lesson 15): Describe what career you plan to have in the future. How much physical activity do you think you will acquire during your work day (i.e., are you mostly sitting in a desk job or moving a lot on your feet)?
- What are the benefits of living a physically-active lifestyle for college or career productivity and for your overall well-being?
- Describe the benefits of walking and why many adults choose walking as their main form of physical activity.
- Discuss how you could use a pedometer and THR to plan for and accumulate the daily physical activity recommendations for adults. Are there other technologies that might help you with your walking or physical activity behavior?
- Decide on a walking plan or other mode of physical activity to maintain your health (describe). Explain how you will use walking or your choice exercise to meet the daily physical activity recommendations and how your plan will keep you healthy and productive for college or your career.

Resources

Internet keyword search: "fitness walking," "step count," "MVPA"

LESSON 12: PARCOURSE WALK 1

Grade-Level Outcomes

Primary Outcomes

Fitness knowledge: Calculates target heart rate and applies that information to personal fitness plan. (S3.H10.L1)

Fitness activities: Demonstrates competency in 1or more specialized skills in health-related fitness activities. (S1.H3.L1)

Embedded Outcome

Physical activity knowledge: Identifies issues associated with exercising in heat, humidity and cold. (S3.H3.L1)

Lesson Objectives

The learner will:

- participate in MVPA by completing a parcourse.
- adjust her or his pace or physical activity level by checking her or his heart rate.
- perform activities with correct form.

Equipment and Materials

- 1 pedometer per student
- 15 cones
- 10 steppers
- Stopwatch

Introduction

Today and tomorrow, you will see how many steps you take by walking a par course. Can anyone tell me what a parcourse is? Has anyone ever seen a parcourse at a park or in the community? They are often on walking trails and include areas to do specific exercises such as pull-ups, push-ups, step-ups, and curl-ups. We have created a parcourse for you to participate in. Be sure to keep your goals in mind, and don't forget to check if you are in your target heart rate zone.

Instructional Task: Warm-Up Lap

■ PRACTICE TASK

Have students put on pedometers.

Walk a lap with the class to show the route and the activities.

Student Choices/Differentiation

Students may walk with a partner.

What to Look For

- Students know how to complete the activities at each par course station properly.
- Students are getting their heart rates up.

Instructional Task: Parcourse Walk I

■ PRACTICE TASK

Have students get into groups of three or four. Assign groups either red or blue stations. Students start the parcourse at different stations and complete only the stations whose color matches the color they were assigned for the day. Set up the par course as a large lap that includes the fields, track, and blacktop. If a local park is close by, check to see whether it has a parcourse.

Students complete their five color stations and repeat if time remains. Students are working on staying within their personal THR zone goals (moderate or vigorous).

The stations are as follows:

Red Stations
- Pull-ups
- Lunges
- Curl-ups
- Triceps dips
- Step-ups

Blue Stations
- Jump-ups
- Push-ups
- Trunk twists
- Cone hops (log hops)
- V-sits

Extension

Students could complete all stations each lap.

Refinement

On lunges, forward knee should be aligned with the ankle, not in front of the ankle or over the foot.

Student Choices/Differentiation
- Students choose their groups.
- Students may choose to complete one set of at least 8 reps for each lap of the course.
- Students choose a number of stations to complete each lap.
- Students choose what stations to complete every other lap.

What to Look For
- Students are working at a moderate or vigorous pace.
- Students are using correct form at the parcourse stations.
- Students are checking their heart rates during the walk.

Instructional Task: Cool-Down Stretches

■ **PRACTICE TASK**

Have students put their pedometers away and come together as a class for a flexibility cool-down routine. Students hold each stretch for 15 to 20 seconds on both sides of the body.
- Quad stretch
- Calf stretch
- Achilles stretch
- Hamstring stretch
- Glute stretch
- Shoulder stretch
- Chest stretch
- Triceps stretch

Guiding questions for students:

- Have you been stretching outside of class? If not, try to add stretching to your daily physical activity.
- What kinds of stretching are you doing?
- What muscle groups are you targeting?

EMBEDDED OUTCOME: S3.H3.L1. Use the cool-down time to discuss how the weather can impact the physical activity experience. Ask students about how their bodies react in the heat, the cold, and the humidity. Relate their responses to the weather during this lesson.

Student Choices/Differentiation

- Students may stretch individually or do partner stretches
- Students may change up the stretches.
- A student volunteer leads the cool-down.

What to Look For

- Students are properly stretching.
- Students are holding the stretch (not bouncing).

Formal and Informal Assessments

Exit slip: What did you like or dislike about using the parcourse?

Closure

- Today, you acquired more steps and moderate to vigorous physical activity by participating in a par course walk. Next time you are at a park, check to see if it has a parcourse. What benefits do parcourses and fitness trails provide?
- Consider accessibility. How might the accessibility to trails and parcourses affect one's adherence to physical activity?
- Be sure to log your steps and MVPA for today. Next class, we will participate in the second half of the course activities.
- Let's review your homework question, which is due in Lesson 15.

Reflection

- Did students work at a moderate level?
- Did students work at the par course stations appropriately?

Homework

Look up some local parks to check for parcourses or fitness trails near your home or the school.

Resources

Internet keyword search: "par course," "fitness trails," "fitness paths," "outdoor exercise stations"

LESSON 13: PARCOUSE WALK 2

Grade-Level Outcomes

Primary Outcomes

Fitness knowledge: Calculates target heart rate and applies that information to personal fitness plan. (S3.H10.L1)

Fitness activities: Demonstrates competency in 1 or more specialized skills in health-related fitness activities. (S1.H3.L1)

Embedded Outcome

Physical activity knowledge: Evaluates risk and safety factors that might affect physical activity preferences throughout the life cycle. (S3.H5.L1)

Lesson Objectives

The learner will:
- participate in MVPA during the parcourse.
- adjust his pace or physical activity level by checking his heart rate.
- perform activities with correct form.

Equipment and Materials
- 1 pedometer per student
- 15 cones
- 10 steppers
- Stopwatch

Introduction

Today, you will continue to walk the parcourse. Did anyone find a parcourse near your neighborhood? If you did the red stations yesterday, you will do the blue stations today. Again, be sure to keep your goals in mind, and don't forget to check whether you are in your target heart rate zone. Let's start with a warm-up lap. Put on your pedometers.

Instructional Task: Parcourse Walk II

■ PRACTICE TASK

Students get into the same groups of three or four as the previous lesson. Today, the red group is the blue group, and the blue group is the red group. Students start the parcourse at different stations and complete only the stations whose colors they were assigned for the day. The parcourse is set up on a large lap that includes the fields, track, and blacktop. If a course exists nearby, take advantage of it for the lesson.

Students complete their five color stations and repeat if time remains. Students work on staying within their personal THR zone goals (moderate or vigorous).

The stations are as follows:

Red Stations
- Pull-ups
- Lunges
- Curl-ups
- Triceps dips
- Step-ups

Blue Stations

- Jump-ups
- Push-ups
- Trunk twists
- Cone hops (log hops)
- V-sits

Extension

Have students design a parcourse challenge of their own.

Refinement

Create a course for a moderate heart rate goal and a course for a more vigorous heart rate goal.

Student Choices/Differentiation

- Students may work alone or in groups.
- Students may complete all the stations each lap.
- Students may choose three stations to do during their walk.
- Students may choose the number of reps they do at each station.

What to Look For

- Students are working at a moderate or vigorous pace.
- Students are using correct form at the parcourse stations.
- Students are checking their heart rates during the walk.

Instructional Task: Cool-Down Stretches

▪ PRACTICE TASK

Have students put their pedometers away and come together as a class for a flexibility cool-down routine. Students hold each stretch for 15 to 20 seconds on both sides of the body.

- Quad stretch
- Calf stretch
- Achilles stretch
- Hamstring stretch
- Glute stretch
- Shoulder stretch
- Chest stretch
- Triceps stretch

Refinement

Add yoga poses to the cool-down.

Student Choices/Differentiation

- Students may add stretches into the parcourse.
- Students may stretch individually or with a partner.
- Students may change up the stretches.
- A student volunteer leads the cool-down.

What to Look For

- Students are stretching properly.
- Students are holding the stretch (not bouncing).

Formal and Informal Assessments

Exit slip: Which parcourse stations did you prefer and why?

Closure

- Today, you finished the parcourse activities and accumulated more steps and moderate to vigorous physical activity. Be sure to log your information. What other activities might you see in a parcourse?
- Many courses include flexibility exercises. Parcourses often give you a well-rounded workout that includes all the health-related fitness concepts.
- What might be some of the risks or safety considerations you need to consider before and during the use of a parcourse? If you do not have a parcourse near you or the nearby course is in poor condition, how could you add some of the other health-related fitness concepts to your walk? (Embedded outcome: S3.H5.L1)
- Nice work today. Keep working on your goals outside of class. In our next lesson, you will be getting your steps walking a golf course.

Reflection

- Could students manage their physical activity behavior?
- Could students participate in the parcourse at a moderate level or just the walk?
- Did students check their heart rates to see if they were in the zone?

Homework

Continue to work on questions from Lesson 11, which are due in Lesson 15.

Resources

Internet keyword search: "parcourse," "fitness trails," "fitness paths," "outdoor exercise stations"

LESSON 14: DISC GOLF

Grade-Level Outcomes

Primary Outcomes

Fitness knowledge: Calculates target heart rate and applies that information to personal fitness plan. (S3.H10.L1)

Fitness activities: Demonstrates competency in 1 or more specialized skills in health-related fitness activities. (S1.H3.L1)

Embedded Outcome

Physical activity knowledge: Evaluates—according to their benefits, social support network and participation requirements—activities that can be pursued in the local environment. (S3.H4.L1)

Lesson Objectives

The learner will:

- walk at a moderate pace between disc golf holes.
- focus on accumulating MVPA and steps during a disc golf tournament.

Equipment and Materials

- 1 pedometer per student
- Music
- 12 cones
- 18 disc golf holes or hoops or cones
- 1 disc per student (or 1 per 2 students if you do not have enough)
- 1 course map and score sheet per group

Introduction

Today, we will change up our walking module by working on accumulating steps and moderate to vigorous physical activity during a disc golf match. What other activities can you participate in that include walking and can add to your daily MVPA goals? There is a large disc golf course set up. You and your partner will walk the 18-hole course at a moderate to vigorous pace between holes. Remember to log your class steps and daily MVPA.

Instructional Task: Warm-Up–Racetrack Fitness

■ PRACTICE TASK

Students pair up and put on pedometers. One partner starts on the inside of the coned area. The second partner starts on the outside of the area. When the music starts, the partners each do the first activity listed on the inside and outside task cards. When the music pauses, the partners switch to the next cone and again do the first activity listed. They continue to switch when the music pauses, until all tasks are completed on the inside and outside of the coned area (the racetrack).

Inside Tasks

- Push-ups or modified push-ups
- Curl-ups or V-sits
- Mountain climbers or burpees
- Lunges
- Student choice

Outside Tasks
- Light jog
- High knees
- Butt kickers
- Carioca
- Student choice

Students check their heart rates.

Refinement
Create breaks in activity for students to check heart rate, or have students check heart rate on two occasions inside the track and two occasions outside the track, or provide enough time for students to check heart rate each rotation.

Guiding questions for students:
- What areas of health-related fitness did you work on?
- What was missing? (Answer: flexibility)

Student Choices/Differentiation
- Student choice is built in through pace, number, and activity modifications.

What to Look For
- Students are working at a moderate to vigorous pace.
- Students are checking their heart rates.
- Students are performing the fitness activities with correct form.

Instructional Task: Disc Golf Course

■ PRACTICE TASK

With your same partner, you will walk and participate in a disc golf tournament. Student pairs all start at different holes. You are still working on accumulating steps and moderate to vigorous physical activity for your daily totals. Walk at a moderate pace between holes.

You will have three shots to score on the hole. If you do not score in your three shots, then you will score a four.

Send groups of students to begin at all 18 holes. Students at hole 18 proceed to hole 1, and so on.

EMBEDDED OUTCOME: S3.H4.L1. Use the guiding questions to help students identify options in the local environment related to walking or other physical activities.

Guiding questions for students:
- Are there any disc golf courses in the community where you could play?
- What other activities can you do for fun in the community that will keep you active?
- How about at the college you want to attend or where you plan to live when you work?

Student Choices/Differentiation
- Students may choose what throws to use.
- Students may choose the pace to walk between holes.

What to Look For
- Students are walking at a moderate pace between holes.
- Students are logging their class step totals.

Formal and Informal Assessments

- Step logs
- Exit slip: How did your steps in disc golf compare to your parcourse steps last class? What is your reaction?

Closure

- Today, you participated in another activity that included walking. What other activities are available in the community?
- Remember to always look at what your community offers. Are there golf or disc golf courses? Are there parks with walking and hiking trails or parcourses?
- Consider what is available to you on or near your college campus or future work environment that you can access to maintain a physically active lifestyle.
- Our next class is the last day of our walking unit. Be sure your logs are complete and you have your homework that is due tomorrow.

Reflection

- Were students moving at a moderate pace?
- Were they logging their daily steps and MVPA?
- Could students identify activities they can pursue in the community, in college, and as a professional?

Homework

Continue to work on your homework from Lesson 11, due next class.

Resources

Darst, P.W. & Pangrazi, R.P. (2009). *Lesson plans: Dynamic physical education for secondary school students*. 6th ed. San Francisco: Pearson Benjamin Cummings.

LESSON 15: COMPARING STEP TOTALS

Grade-Level Outcomes

Primary Outcomes

Physical activity knowledge: Discusses the benefits of a physically active lifestyle as it relates to college or career productivity. (S3.H1.L1)

Fitness knowledge: Calculates target heart rate and applies that information to personal fitness plan. (S3.H10.L1)

Fitness activities: Demonstrates competency in 1 or more specialized skills in health-related fitness activities. (S1.H3.L1)

Embedded Outcome

Personal responsibility: Employs effective self-management skills to analyze barriers and modify physical activity patterns appropriately, as needed. (S4.H1.L1)

Lesson Objectives

The learner will:

- maintain a moderate to vigorous pace for the entire 30-minute walk.
- adjust the pace adequately depending on goals and heart rate.
- reflect on the benefits of daily physical activity for college and career productivity.

Equipment and Materials

- 1 pedometer per student
- Stop watches

Introduction

This is the last day you will need to log your class and daily step totals. What are the benefits of walking? Did your moderate to vigorous physical activity behavior change throughout this module? Did you meet your goals? Today, you will participate in a 30-minute timed walk. This walk will be used to compare your step totals from Lessons 6 and 11 to this lesson. You will then reflect on the module and your goals as a whole. Remember to check your heart rate to stay in your target heart rate zone. You may walk or run.

Instructional Task: Review and Warm-Up

■ PRACTICE TASK

Ask students to think about their goals and how their physical activity behavior may have changed during this unit. Have them think about the step totals they had in Lesson 6 and how many they hope they have today.

Then students put on a pedometer and participate in a dynamic warm-up.

EMBEDDED OUTCOME: S4.H1.L1 Prompt students to check their heart rates at one or more points during the warm-up to check if they are working at a moderate or vigorous pace (self-management).

- Light jog down and back
- 10 push-ups
- High knees down and butt kickers back
- 10 push-ups
- Carioca down and back (both sides)
- Light jog down and back
- 25 curl-ups

Guiding questions for students:

- Do you do any strength activities outside of class?
- What types of activities do you do?
- Any flexibility activities?

Student Choices/Differentiation

- A student volunteer can lead the warm-up.
- Students may change up the activities.
- Students may change the number of repetitions.

What to Look For

- Students are critically reflecting.
- Students are performing the warm-up with correct form.

Instructional Task: 30-Minute Walk

■ PRACTICE TASK

Students participate in a 30-minute walk to see how many steps they can accumulate. They should be checking their heart rates on their own throughout the activity to be sure they are working at a moderate rate. This is the final walk to address the students' goals. Students will be able to compare their 30-minute walk step totals and mileage from Lessons 6 and 11 to this lesson.

The timed walk could take place on the track, if need be, or create a large lap area on campus in field space to change it up. If a park is nearby, you can complete a community walk.

Be sure students log their final class and daily steps on the logs they created. They will hand them in with their reflection questions next class.

Guiding questions for students:

- In what other ways will you use your target heart rate zone to participate in moderate to vigorous physical activity?
- How can you continue to track your daily physical activity levels?
- What type of new goals will you set to maintain an active lifestyle?

Student Choices/Differentiation

- Students may walk or run.
- Students may choose to complete the walk on the track or another course.

What to Look For

- Students are using their THR zones to adjust their pace.
- Students can walk with a good pace for the entire 30 minutes.

Instructional Task: Cool-Down Stretches

■ PRACTICE TASK

Have students come in from the 30-minute walk and stretch out. Students hold each stretch for 15 to 20 seconds on both sides of the body.

- Quad stretch
- Calf stretch
- Achilles stretch
- Hamstring stretch
- Glute stretch

- Shoulder stretch
- Chest stretch
- Triceps stretch

Guiding questions for students:
- When creating physical activity goals, how can you include flexibility?
- What type of flexibility will benefit you most and why?

Student Choices/Differentiation

Students select the order of stretches.

What to Look For
- Students are performing the stretches with proper alignment.
- Students are holding the stretches.
- Students' range of motion has improved over the course of the module.

Formal and Informal Assessments

Step logs with reflections

Closure
- Today concludes our walking module. How many of you had higher step totals today compared with Lesson 6 or Lesson 11? Both?
- Why do you think that is?
- What are the health benefits of walking?
- Remember that as we age, many adults get their physical activity from walking.
- How can you participate in physical activity by walking in your community?
- What is available? (Answer: hiking, golfing, parks, and so on)
- You have homework questions to reflect on the module and your goals, daily steps, and physical activity. Your homework is due next class. We will also have a test on the knowledge you have learned during this module.

Reflection
- Did students know the benefits of walking?
- Did students know what activities are available in their communities?

Homework

For next class, review your walking unit and step logs to answer the following questions.

1. What day did you have the highest step counts in class? Why do you think that is?
2. What day did you have the lowest step counts in class? Why do you think that is?
3. What were your highest and lowest step-count days outside of class? Are these the same as the in-class days?
4. Add up your weekly step totals. Approximately how many miles or kilometers did you walk during this module?
5. Overall, were you able to increase your daily MVPA? Explain.
6. If we were to do this module again and set new goals, what would you change and why?
7. What technologies and strategies will you use to stay physically active in college and/or your career?

LESSON 16: WALKING TEST AND REFLECTION

Grade-Level Outcomes

Primary Outcomes

See block plan chart for outcomes to be assessed on test.

Physical activity knowledge: Discusses the benefits of a physically active lifestyle as it related to college or career productivity. (S3.H1.L1)

Physical activity knowledge: Identifies issues associated with exercising in heat, humidity and cold. (S3.H3.L1)

Physical activity knowledge: Evaluates—according to their benefits, social support network and participation requirements—activities that can be pursued in the local environment. (S3.H4.L1)

Physical activity knowledge: Evaluates risks and safety factors that might affect physical activity preferences throughout the life cycle. (S3.H5.L1)

Physical activity knowledge: Analyzes the impact of life choices, economics, motivation and accessibility on exercise adherence and participation in physical activity in college or career settings. (S3.H5.L2)

Personal responsibility: Employs effective self-management skills to analyze barriers and modify physical activity patterns appropriately, as needed. (S4.H1.L1)

Health: Analyzes the health benefits of a self-selected physical activity. (S5.H1.L1)

Social interaction: Identifies the opportunity for social support in a self-selected physical activity or dance. (S5.H4.L1)

Embedded Outcome

Working with others: Uses communication skills and strategies that promote team or group dynamics. (S4.H3.L1)

Lesson Objectives

The learner will:
- describe and apply fitness and physical activity knowledge on a written exam.
- share personal experiences from daily logs and homework assignments.

Equipment and Materials
- Exams
- Pencils
- Flip charts and easels

Introduction

We're starting today's class with a knowledge test on the module. Once you have completed that, we will move on to review the homework from our last class.

Instructional Task: Knowledge Test

■ PRACTICE TASK

Administer a knowledge test on the concepts and principles taught during the module.

Student Choices/Differentiation

Allow extra time if needed.

Instructional Task:
Review of Homework Assignment From Lesson 15

■ PRACTICE TASK

In small groups, have students share their answers from the homework. Ask one member of each group to share her responses with the whole class.

EMBEDDED OUTCOME: S4.H3.L1 Use this group task to reinforce the importance of good listening and communication skills. Provide specific feedback related to appropriate communication.

Student Choices/Differentiation
- Students choose their groups.
- Students may choose to be the recorder.
- Small groups may choose to report out to the whole class.
- Students may use flip charts to record responses.

What to Look For
- All students are contributing to the group discussion.
- Group members are listening to and supporting each other.

Formal and Informal Assessments

Knowledge tests

Closure
- I am impressed by the progress you made in this walking module and how well you are able to apply the fitness and physical activity knowledge you have learned. You can use that knowledge in any fitness activity you choose to do, not just walking.
- Walking is very versatile—you can do it anywhere. It's a popular activity for adults and families and something you can do throughout your lives for health, enjoyment, and social interaction.
- It's time to think about your next module, so please review your choices before the next class.

Reflection
- Were there any concepts or ideas students still struggled with at the end of the module?
- What could I do better the next time this module is offered?

Homework
- Keep working on improving and monitoring your fitness while you get ready for your next module.
- Check the school's physical education website for a list of upcoming modules so you will be prepared to choose next class.

Glossary

affective domain—The learning domain in which the focus is on personal-social development, attitudes, values, feelings, motivation and emotions (SHAPE America – Society of Health and Physical Educators, 2014, p.115).

applying—A level of competency at which learners can demonstrate the critical elements of the motor skills or knowledge components of the Grade-Level Outcomes in a variety of physical activity environments.

assessment—The gathering of evidence about student learning and making inferences on student progress and growth based on that evidence (adapted from SHAPE America, 2014, p. 90).

cognitive domain—The learning domain in which the focus is on knowledge and information (facts and concepts), with an emphasis on the understanding and application of knowledge and information through higher-order thinking skills (SHAPE America, 2014, p. 115).

competency—Sufficient ability, skill, and knowledge for meeting the demands of a task or activity. In this book, competency is defined as the ability to participate with skill and ability at the recreational level in self-selected activities (SHAPE America, 2014, p. 115).

deliberate practice—A highly structured activity, the explicit goal of which is to improve performance. Tasks are created to overcome the learner's weaknesses, and performance is monitored carefully to provide cues for ways to improve further (Ericsson et al., 1993, p. 368).

differentiated instruction—Instruction that is varied to address the needs of students and their various levels of skill or knowledge.

embedded outcomes—Grade-Level Outcomes that are related to the primary content of a lesson and that give students opportunities to meet more than one outcome during the learning or practice task (Holt/Hale, Hall, 2016, p. 18; SHAPE America, 2014, p. 116).

emerging— A level of competency at which learners are in the beginning stages of acquiring motor skills and knowledge. Mastery of the skills and knowledge is emerging through deliberate practice tasks, and, at this stage, learners are developing competency.

etiquette—Expectations regarding behavior and social norms associated with particular games or activities, including rules of behavior that define and provide parameters for participating appropriately in the activity or game (SHAPE America, 2014, p. 116).

fitness activities—Activities with a focus on improving or maintaining fitness, which might include yoga, Pilates, resistance training, spinning, running, fitness walking, fitness swimming, kickboxing, cardio kick, Zumba, and exergaming (SHAPE America, 2014, p. 116).

FITT—An acronym that stands for frequency, intensity, time, and type of exercise, each of which can be manipulated to create an overload on the body to force it to adapt, or become more fit (SHAPE America, 2014, p. 116). (See *overload principle*.)

formative assessment—Assessment that is ongoing during instruction, allowing teachers to track student progress and adapt instruction accordingly (SHAPE America, 2014, p. 90).

fundamental motor skills—The locomotor, non-locomotor or stability, and manipulative skills that provide the foundation for the more complex movement patterns of games and sports, gymnastics, and dance (SHAPE America, 2014, p. 116).

individual interest—Relatively consistent attraction to an activity based on one's traits and experiences.

individual-performance activities—Activities that one can perform alone. Examples include gymnastics, figure skating, track and field, multi-sport events, in-line skating, wrestling, self-defense, and skateboarding (SHAPE America, 2014, p. 116).

Level 1 outcomes—Grade-Level Outcomes for high school students that reflect the fitness knowledge and skills that students must acquire and attain by the time they graduate to be considered prepared to maintain a healthy fitness level in college or in a career (SHAPE America, 2014, p. 117).

Level 2 outcomes—Grade-Level Outcomes for high school students that build on Level 1 competencies by augmenting the fitness knowledge and skills considered desirable for college or career readiness (SHAPE America, 2014, p. 117).

lifetime activities—Activities that are suitable for participation across one's life span and that one can pursue alone or with a partner, as opposed to only with a team. As used in this book, lifetime activities include the categories of outdoor pursuits, selected individual-performance activities, aquatics, net and wall games, and target games (SHAPE America, 2014, p. 117).

maturing—A level of competency at which learners demonstrate the critical elements of the motor skills and knowledge components of the Grade-Level Outcomes, which they will continue to refine with practice. As the environment context changes, a maturing pattern might fluctuate, reflecting more maturity in familiar contexts and less maturity in unfamiliar or new contexts, thus the term *maturing* (SHAPE America, 2014, p. 117).

modified games—Games (usually small-sided) in which the rules have been modified to emphasize the skills taught in class (e.g., creating a penalty for dribbling to emphasize teaching students to pass rather than dribble) (SHAPE America, 2014, p. 117).

movement concepts—Concepts related to the skillful performance of movement and fitness activities. Movement concepts include spatial awareness, effort, tactics, strategies, and principles related to movement efficiency and health-enhancing fitness.

net/wall games—Games in which "teams or individual players score by hitting a ball into a court space with sufficient accuracy and power so that opponents cannot hit it back before it bounces once (as in badminton or volleyball) or twice (as in tennis or racquetball) (Mitchell et al., 2006, p. 21). Generally, opponents are separated by a net, although in some cases, they share a court, and the walls are in play (squash, racquetball).

outcomes—Statements that specify what learners should know or be able to do as the result of a learning experience (SHAPE America, 2014, p. 117).

outdoor pursuits—Activities that are performed in the outdoors, including boating (e.g., kayaking, canoeing, sailing, rowing), hiking, backpacking, fishing, orienteering and geocaching, ice skating, skateboarding, snow or water skiing, snowboarding, snowshoeing, surfing, bouldering/traversing/climbing, mountain biking, adventure activities, and ropes courses. The outdoor pursuits that one selects often depend on the environment-related opportunities within the geographical region (SHAPE America, 2014, p. 117).

overload principle—The principle of placing progressively greater stress or demands on the body during exercise to cause it to adapt, or become more fit. One does that by manipulating the frequency, intensity, time (duration), and type (FITT) of activity (SHAPE America, 2014, p. 117).

physically literate individuals—Those who have learned the skills and acquired the knowledge necessary for participating in a variety of physical activities. A physically literate individual knows the implications and the benefits of involvement in various types of physical activities, participates regularly in physical activity, is physically fit, and values physical activity and its contributions to a healthy lifestyle (SHAPE America, 2014, p. 11).

psychomotor domain—The learning domain in which focus is on motor skills (SHAPE America, 2014, p. 117).

relatedness—A sense of being connected or supported by others (Zhang et al., 2011, p. 53).

situational interest—Attraction to an activity based on the interaction of factors such as newness, challenge, and pleasure (Chen, Darst, & Pangrazi, 1999).

summative assessment—Assessment that occurs at the close of a unit of instructional sequence, providing teachers with a comprehensive summary of each student's progress and growth (SHAPE America, 2014, p. 90).

target games—Games in which "players score by throwing or striking an object to a target" (Mitchell et al., 2006, p. 21). Accuracy is a primary focus of the activity, and competitors make no physical contact with one another (Haibach et al., 2011, p. 369). Strategies and tactics are based on movement and consistency.

technology—Software, websites, devices, and applications used in a physical education setting to enhance teaching and learning (SHAPE America, 2014, p. 118).

References and Resources

Preface

SHAPE America – Society of Health and Physical Educators. (2014). *National Standards & Grade-Level Outcomes for K-12 physical education*. Champaign, IL: Human Kinetics.

Chapter 1

Barnett, L.M., van Beurden, E., Morgan, P.J., Brooks, L.O., & Beard, J.R. (2008a). Childhood motor skill proficiency as a predictor of adolescent physical activity. *Journal of Adolescent Health, 44*, 252-259.

Barnett, L.M., van Beurden, E., Morgan, P.J., Brooks, L.O., & Beard, J.R. (2008b). Does childhood motor skill proficiency predict adolescent fitness? *Medicine & Science in Sports & Exercise, 40*, 2137-2144.

Bernstein, E., Phillips, S.R., & Silverman, S. (2011). Attitudes and perceptions of middle school students toward competitive activities in physical education. *Journal of Teaching in Physical Education, 30*, 69-83.

Bryan, C., Sims, S., Hester, D., & Dunaway, D. (2013). Fifteen years after the Surgeon General's report: Challenges, changes, and future directions in physical education. *Quest, 65*, 139-150.

Chen, A., & Darst, P.W. (2001). Situational interest in physical education: A function of learning task design. *Research Quarterly for Exercise and Sport, 72* (2), 150-164.

Chen, A., Darst, P. W., & Pangrazi, R. P. (1999). What constitutes situational interest? Validating a construct in physical education. *Measurement in Physical Education and Exercise Science, 3* (3), 157-180.

Couturier, L.E., Chepko, S., & Coughlin, M. (2007). Whose gym is it? Gendered perspectives on middle and secondary school physical education. *The Physical Educator, 64* (3), 152-157.

Duckworth, A., Peterson, C., Matthews, M., & Kelly, D. (2007). Grit: Perseverance and passion for long-term goals. *Journal of Personality and Social Psychology, 92* (6), 1087-1101.

Ennis, C. (2011). Physical education curriculum priorities: Evidence for education and skillfulness. *Quest, 63*, 5-18.

Ericsson, K. (2006). The influence of experience and deliberate practice on the development of superior performance. In K. Ericsson, N. Chamness, P. Feltovich, & R. Hoffman (Eds.), *The Cambridge handbook of expertise and expert performance* (pp. 685-705). Cambridge, UK: Cambridge University Press.

Garn, A.C., Cothran, D.J., & Jenkins, J.M. (2011). A qualitative analysis of individual interest in middle school physical education: Perspective of early adolescents. *Physical Education & Sport Pedagogy, 16* (3), 223-236.

Garn, A.C., Ware, D.R., & Solmon, M.A. (2011). Student engagement in high school physical education: Do social motivation orientations matter? *Journal of Teaching in Physical Education, 30*, 84-98.

Grieser, M., Vu, M.B., Bedimo-Rung, A.L., Neumark-Sztainer, D., Moody, J., Young, D.R., & Moe, S.G. (2006). Physical activities attitudes, preferences, and practices in African American, Hispanic, and Caucasian girls. *Health Education & Behavior, 33* (1), 40-51.

Hannon, J.C., & Ratcliffe, T. (2005). Physical activity levels in coeducational and single-gender high school physical education settings. *Journal of Teaching in Physical Education, 24*, 149-164.

Hill, G., & Hannon, J.C. (2008). An analysis of middle school students' physical education physical activity preferences. *Physical Educator, 65* (4), 180-194.

Kambas, A., Michalopoulou, M., Fatouros, I., Christoforidis, C., Manthou, E., Giannakidou, D., Venetsanou, F., Haberer, E., Chatzinikolaou, A., Gourgoulis, V., & Zimmer, R. (2012). The relationship between motor proficiency and pedometer-determined physical activity in young children. *Pediatric Exercise Science, 24*, 34-44.

Ntoumanis, N., Pensgaard, A., Martin, C., & Pipe, K. (2004). An idiographic analysis of amotivation in compulsory school physical education. *Journal of Sport & Exercise Science, 26*, 197-214.

Ommundsen, Y. (2006). Pupils' self-regulation in physical education: The role of motivational climates and differential achievement goals.

European Physical Education Review, 12 (3), 289-315.

Placek, J.H. (1983). Conceptions of success in teaching: Busy, happy, and good? In T. Templin & J. Olsen (Eds.). *Teaching in physical education* (pp. 46-56). Champaign, IL: Human Kinetics.

Portman, P. (2003). Are physical education classes encouraging students to be physically active?: Experiences of ninth graders in their last semester of required physical education. *The Physical Educator, 63* (3), 150-161.

SHAPE America – Society of Health and Physical Educators. (2014). *National Standards & Grade-Level Outcomes for K-12 physical education.* Champaign, IL: Human Kinetics.

Smith, M.A., & St. Pierre, P. (2009). Secondary students' perceptions of enjoyment in physical education: An American and English perspective. *The Physical Educator, 66* (4), 209-221.

Stodden, D.F., Goodway, J.L., Langendorfer, S.J., Roberton, M., Rudisill, M.E., Garcia, C., & Garcia, L.E. (2008). A developmental perspective on the role of motor skill competence in physical activity: An emergent relationship. *Quest, 60*, 290-306.

Stodden, D., Langendorfer, S., & Roberton, M. (2009). The association between motor skill competence and physical fitness in young adults. *Research Quarterly for Exercise and Sport, 80* (2), 223-229.

Strong, W.B., Malina, R.M., Blimkie, C.J., Daniels, S.R., Dishman, R.K., Gutin, B., Hergenroeder, A.C., Must, A., Nixon, P., Pivarnik, J.M., Rowland, T., Trost, S., & Trudeau, F. (2005). Evidence based physical activity for school-age youth. *Journal of Pediatrics, 146*, 732- 737.

Stuart, J.H., Biddle, S.H., O'Donovan, T.M., & Nevill, M.E. (2005). Correlates of participation in physical activity for adolescent girls: A systematic review of recent literature. *Journal of Physical Activity and Health, 2*, 423-434.

Subramaniam, P.R. (2009). Motivational effects of interest on student engagement and learning in physical education. *International Journal of Physical Education, 46* (2), 11-19.

Xu, F., & Liu, W. (2013). A review of middle school students' attitudes toward physical activity. In L.E. Ciccomascolo & E.C. Sullivan (Eds.), *The dimensions of physical education* (pp. 286-295). Burlington, MA: Jones & Bartlett Learning.

Zhang, T., Solmon, M., Kosma, M., Carson, R.L., & Gu, X. (2011). Need support, need satisfaction, intrinsic motivation, and physical activity participation among middle school students. *Journal of Teaching in Physical Education, 30*, 51-68.

Having the Skills to Succeed

Barnett, L.M., van Beurden, E., Morgan, P.J., Brooks, L.O., & Beard, J.R. (2008a). Childhood motor skill proficiency as a predictor of adolescent physical activity. *Journal of Adolescent Health, 44*, 252-259.

Barnett, L.M., van Beurden, E., Morgan, P.J., Brooks, L.O., & Beard, J.R. (2008b). Does childhood motor skill proficiency predict adolescent fitness? *Medicine & Science in Sports & Exercise, 40*, 2137-2144.

Bernstein, E., Phillips, S.R., & Silverman, S. (2011). Attitudes and perceptions of middle school students toward competitive activities in physical education. *Journal of Teaching in Physical Education, 30*, 69-83.

Bevans, K., Fitzpatrick, L., Sanchez, B., & Forest, C.B. (2010). Individual and instructional determinants of student engagement in physical education. *Journal of Teaching in Physical Education, 29*, 399-416.

Castelli, D.M., & Valley, J.A. (2007). Chapter three: The relationship of physical fitness and motor competence to physical activity. *Journal of Teaching in Physical Education, 26*, 358-374.

Duckworth, A., Peterson, C., Matthews, M., & Kelly, D. (2007). Grit: Perseverance and passion for long-term goals. *Journal of Personality and Social Psychology, 92* (6), 1087-1101.

Faigenbaum, A., Lloyd, R., Sheehan, D., & Myer, G. (2013). The role of the pediatric exercise specialist in treating exercise deficit disorder in youth. *Strength & Conditioning Journal, 35* (3), 34-38.

Hamilton, K., & White, K.M. (2008). Extending the theory of planned behavior: The role of self and social influences in predicting adolescent regular moderate-to-vigorous physical activity. *Journal of Sport & Exercise Science, 30*, 56-74.

Hands, B., Larkin, D., Parker, H., Straker, L., & Perry, M. (2009). The relationship among physical activity, motor competence and health-related fitness in

14-year-old adolescents. *Scandinavian Journal of Medicine & Science in Sports, 19*, 655-663.

Hardy, L., Reinten-Reynolds, T., Espinel, P., Zask, A., & Okely, A. (2012). Prevalence and correlates of low fundamental movement skill competency in children. *Pediatrics, 130* (2), e390-e398.

Kambas, A., Michalopoulou, M., Fatouros, I., Christoforidis, C., Manthou, E., Giannakidou, D., Venetsanou, F., Haberer, E., Chatzinikolaou, A., Gourgoulis, V., & Zimmer, R. (2012). The relationship between motor proficiency and pedometer-determined physical activity in young children. *Pediatric Exercise Science, 24*, 34-44.

Luban, D., Morgan, P., Cliff, D., Barnett, L., & Okely, A. (2010). Fundamental movement skills in children and adolescents. *Sports Medicine, 40* (12), 1019-1035.

Standage, M., Duda, J., & Ntoumanis, N. (2003). Predicting motivational regulations in physical education: The interplay between dispositional goal orientations, motivational climate, and perceived competence. *Journal of Sport Sciences, 21*, 631-647.

Stodden, D.F., Goodway, J.L., Langendorfer, S.J., Roberton, M., Rudisill, M.E., Garcia, C., & Garcia, L.E. (2008). A developmental perspective on the role of motor skill competence in physical activity: An emergent relationship. *Quest, 60*, 290-306.

Stodden, D., Langendorfer, S., & Roberton, M. (2009). The association between motor skill competence and physical fitness in young adults. *Research Quarterly for Exercise and Sport, 80* (2), 223-229.

van Beurden, E., Barnett, L.M., Zask, A., Dietrich, U.C., Brooks, L.O., & Beard, J. (2003). Can we skill and activate children through primary school physical education lessons? "Move It Groove It"—a collaborative health promotion intervention. *Preventive Medicine, 36*, 493-501.

The Learning Activity Is Interesting

Bryan, C., Sims, S., Hester, D., & Dunaway, D. (2013). Fifteen years after the Surgeon General's Report: Challenges, changes, and future directions in physical education. *Quest, 65*, 139-150.

Chen, S., Chen, A., & Zhu, X. (2012). Are k-12 learners motivated in physical education? A meta-analysis. *Research Quarterly for Exercise and Sport, 83* (1), 36-48.

Chen, A., & Darst, P.W. (2001). Situational interest in physical education: A function of learning task design. *Research Quarterly for Exercise and Sport, 72* (2), 150-164.

Gao, Z., Lee, A.M., Ping, X., & Kosam, M. (2011). Effect of learning activity on students' motivation, physical activity levels and effort/persistence. *ICHPER-SD Journal of Research in Health, Physical Education, Recreation, Sport & Dance, 6* (1), 27-33.

Prusak, K.A., Treasure, D.C., Darst, P.W., & Pangrazi, R. (2004). The effects of choice on the motivation of adolescent girls in physical education. *Journal of Teaching in Physical Education, 23*, 19-29.

Smith, M.A., & St. Pierre, P. (2009). Secondary students' perceptions of enjoyment in physical education: An American and English perspective. *The Physical Educator, 66* (4), 209-221.

Stuart, J.H., Biddle, S.H., O'Donovan, T.M., & Nevill, M.E. (2005). Correlates of participation in physical activity for adolescent girls: A systematic review of recent literature. *Journal of Physical Activity and Health, 2*, 423-434.

Subramaniam, P.R. (2009). Motivational effects of interest on student engagement and learning in physical education. *International Journal of Physical Education, 46* (2), 11-19.

Treasure, D.C., & Roberts, G.C. (2001). Students' perceptions of the motivational climate, achievement beliefs, and satisfaction in physical education. *Research Quarterly for Exercise and Sport, 72* (2), 165-175.

Wilkinson, C., & Bretzing, R. (2011). High school girls' perceptions of selected physical activities. *The Physical Educator, 68* (2), 58-65.

Zhang, T., Solmon, M., Kosma, M., Carson, R.L., & Gu, X. (2011). Need support, need satisfaction, intrinsic motivation, and physical activity participation among middle school students. *Journal of Teaching in Physical Education, 30*, 51-68.

The Learning Experience Provides a Socially Supportive and Inclusive Climate

Cockburn, C. (2001). Year 9 girls and physical education: A survey of pupil perception. *The Bulletin of Physical Education, 37* (1), 5-24.

Cockburn, C., & Clarke, G. (2002). "Everybody's looking at you!": Girls negotiating the "femininity deficit" they incur in physical education. *Women's Studies Forum, 25* (6), 651-665.

Couturier, L.E., Chepko, S., & Coughlin, M. (2007). Whose gym is it? Gendered perspectives on middle and secondary school physical education. *The Physical Educator, 64* (3), 152-157.

Eime, R., Harvey, J., Sawyer, N., Craike, M., Symons, C., Polman, R., & Payne, W. (2013). Understanding contexts of adolescent female participation in sport and physical activity. *Research Quarterly for Exercise and Sport, 84,* 157-166.

Fagrell, B., Larsson, H., & Redelus, K. (2012). The game with the game: Girls' position in physical education. *Gender and Education, 24* (1), 101-118.

Garn, A.C., Cothran, D.J., & Jenkins, J.M. (2011). A qualitative analysis of individual interest in middle school physical education: Perspective of early adolescents. *Physical Education & Sport Pedagogy, 16* (3), 223-236.

Garn, A.C., Ware, D.R., & Solmon, M.A. (2011). Student engagement in high school physical education: Do social motivation orientations matter? *Journal of Teaching in Physical Education, 30,* 84-98.

Grieser, M., Vu, M.B., Bedimo-Rung, A.L., Neumark-Sztainer, D., Moody, J., Young, D.R., & Moe, S.G. (2006). Physical activities attitudes, preferences, and practices in African American, Hispanic, and Caucasian girls. *Health Education & Behavior, 33* (1), 40-51.

Haerens, L., Kirk, D., Cardon, G., De Bourdeauhuij, I., & Vansteenkiste, M. (2010). Motivation profiles for secondary school physical education and its relationship to the adoption of a physically active lifestyle among university students. *European Physical Education Review, 16* (2), 117-139.

Hannon, J.C., & Ratcliffe, T. (2005). Physical activity levels in coeducational and single-gender high school physical education settings. *Journal of Teaching in Physical Education, 24,* 149-164.

Hill, G., & Hannon, J.C. (2008). An analysis of middle school students' physical education physical activity preferences. *The Physical Educator, 65* (4), 180-194.

Hills, L. (2006). Playing the field(s): An exploration of change, conformity and conflict in girls' understandings of gendered physicality in physical education. *Gender and Education, 18* (5), 539-556.

Kahan, D., & Graham, K. (2013). Quantitative analysis of students' reasons for nonsuiting and support of policy change at one middle school. *Research Quarterly for Exercise and Sport, 84,* 512-521.

McKenzie, T.L., Prochaska, J.J., Sallis, J.F., & LaMaster, K.J. (2004). Coeducational and single-sex physical education in middle schools: Impact on physical activity. *Research Quarterly for Exercise and Sport, 75* (4), 446-449.

Ntoumanis, N., Pensgaard, A., Martin, C., & Pipe, K. (2004). An idiographic analysis of amotivation in compulsory school physical education. *Journal of Sport & Exercise Science, 26,* 197-214.

Ommundsen, Y. (2006). Pupils' self-regulation in physical education: The role of motivational climates and differential achievement goals. *European Physical Education Review, 12* (3), 289-315.

O'Neill, J.R., Pate, R.R., & Liese, A.D. (2011). Descriptive epidemiology of dance participation in adolescents. *Research Quarterly for Exercise and Sport, 82* (3), 373-380.

Patnode, C.D., Lytle, L.A., Erickson, D.J., Sirard, J.R., Barr-Anderson, D.J., & Story, M. (2011). Physical activity and sedentary activity patterns among children and adolescents: A latent class analysis approach. *Journal of Physical Activity and Health, 8,* 457-467.

Portman, P. (2003). Are physical education classes encouraging students to be physically active?: Experiences of ninth grades in their last semester of required physical education. *The Physical Educator, 63* (3), 150-161.

Taylor, W., Yancey, A., Leslie, J., Murray, N., Cummings, S., Sharkey, S., Wert, C., James, J., Miles, O., & McCarthy, W. (1999). Physical activity among African American and Latino middle school girls: Consistent beliefs, expectations, and experience across two sites. *Women & Health, 30* (2), 67-82.

Velija, P., & Kumar, G. (2009). GCSE physical education and the embodiment of gender. *Sport, Education and Society, 14* (4), 383-399.

Xu, F., & Liu, W. (2013). A review of middle school students' attitudes toward physical activity. In L.E. Ciccomascolo & E.C. Sullivan (Eds.), *The dimensions of physical education* (pp. 286-295). Burlington, MA: Jones & Bartlett Learning.

Yli-Piipari, S., Leskinen, E., Jaakkola, T., & Liukkonen, J. (2012). Predictive role of physical education motivation: The developmental trajectories of physical activity during grades 7-9. *Research Quarterly for Exercise and Sport, 83* (4), 560-569.

Chapter 2

Holt/Hale, S., & Hall, T. (2016). *Lesson planning for elementary physical education: Meeting the National Standards & Grade-Level Outcomes.* Reston, VA: SHAPE America; Champaign, IL: Human Kinetics.

SHAPE America – Society of Health and Physical Educators. (2014). *National Standards & Grade-Level Outcomes for K-12 physical education.* Champaign, IL: Human Kinetics.

Chapter 3

Cockburn, C. (2001). Year 9 girls and physical education: A survey of pupil perception. *The Bulletin of Physical Education, 37* (1), 5-24.

Corbin, C.B. (2002). Physical activity for everyone: What every physical educator should know about promoting lifelong physical activity. *Journal of Teaching Physical Education, 21,* 128-144.

Couturier, L., Chepko, S., & Coughlin, M. (2007). Whose gym is it? Gendered perspectives on middle and secondary school physical education. *The Physical Educator, 64* (3), 152-157.

Derry, J.A. (2002). Single-sex and coeducation physical education: Perspectives of adolescent girls and female physical education teachers. *Melpomene Journal, 21* (3), 21-27.

Gallahue, D.L., Ozmun, J., & Goodway, J. (2012). *Understanding motor development: Infants, children, adolescents, adults.* New York: McGraw-Hill.

Gao, Z., Lee, A., & Harrison, L. (2012). Understanding students' motivation in sport and physical education: From expectancy-value model and self-efficacy theory perspectives. *Quest, 60,* 236-254.

Garn, A., Ware, D., & Solmon, M. (2011). Student engagement in high school physical education: Do social motivation orientations matter? *Journal of Teaching in Physical Education, 30,* 84-98.

Hannon, J., & Ratcliffe, T. (2005). Physical activity levels in coeducational and single-gender high school physical education settings. *Journal of Teaching in Physical Education, 24,* 149-164.

National Association for Sport and Physical Education & American Heart Association. (2012). *2012 Shape of the Nation Report: Status of Physical Education in the USA.* Reston, VA: American Alliance for Health, Physical Education, Recreation and Dance.

O'Neill, J., Pate, R., & Liese, A. (2011). Descriptive epidemiology of dance participation in adolescents. *Research Quarterly for Exercise and Sport, 82* (3), 373-380.

Patnode, C., Lytle, L., Erikson, D., Sirard, J., Barr-Anderson, D., & Story, M. (2011). Physical activity and sedentary activity patterns among children and adolescents: A latent class analysis approach. *Journal of Physical Activity and Health, 8,* 457.

Portman, P. (2003). Are physical education classes encouraging students to be physically active?: Experiences of ninth graders in their last semester of required physical education. *The Physical Educator, 63* (3), 150-161.

Ruiz, L., Graupera, J., Moreno, J., & Rico, I. (2010). Social preferences for learning among adolescents. *Journal of Teaching in Physical Education, 29,* 3-20.

SHAPE America – Society of Health and Physical Educators. (2014). *National Standards & Grade-Level Outcomes for K-12 physical education.* Champaign, IL: Human Kinetics.

Stuart, J., Biddle, S., O'Donovan, T., & Nevill, M. (2005). Correlates of participation in physical activity for adolescent girls: A systematic review of literature. *Journal of Physical Activity and Health, 2,* 423-434.

Yli-Piipari, S., Leskinen, E., T., Jaakkola, & Liukkonen, J. (2012). Predictive role of physical education motivation: The developmental trajectories of physical activity during grades 7-9. *Research Quarterly for Exercise and Sport, 83* (4), 560-569.

Gender in High School Physical Education Curriculum

Bryan, C., Sims, S., Hester, D., & Dunaway, D. (2013). Fifteen years after the Surgeon General's Report: Challenges, changes, and future directions in physical education. *Quest, 65,* 139-150.

Cockburn, C. (2001). Year 9 girls and physical education: A survey of pupil perception. *The Bulletin of Physical Education, 37* (1), 5-24.

Couturier, L., Chepko, S., & Coughlin, M. (2007). Whose gym is it? Gendered perspectives on middle and secondary school physical education. *The Physical Educator, 64* (3), 152-157.

Derry, J.A. (2002). Single-sex and coeducation physical education: Perspectives of adolescent girls and female physical education teachers. *Melpomene Journal, 21* (3), 21-27.

Eime, R., Harvey, J., Sawyer, N., Craike, M., Symons, C., Polman, R., & Payne, W. (2013). Understanding contexts of adolescent female participation in sport and physical activity. *Research Quarterly for Exercise and Sport, 84,* 157-166.

Fagrell, B., Larsson, H., & Redelus, K. (2012). The game with the game: Girls' underperforming position in physical education. *Gender and Education, 24* (1), 101-118.

Gao, Z., Lee, A., & Harrison, L. (2012). Understanding students' motivation in sport and physical education: From expectancy-value model and self-efficacy theory perspectives. *Quest, 60,* 236-254.

Garn, A., Ware, D., & Solmon, M. (2011). Student engagement in high school physical education: Do social motivation orientations matter? *Journal of Teaching in Physical Education, 30,* 84-98.

Hannon, J., & Ratcliffe, T. (2005). Physical activity levels in coeducational and single-gender high school physical education settings. *Journal of Teaching in Physical Education, 24,* 149-164.

Hills, L. (2006). Playing the field(s): An exploration of change, conformity and conflict in girls' understandings of gendered physicality in physical education. *Gender and Education, 18* (5), 539-556.

O'Neill, J., Pate, R., & Liese, A. (2011). Descriptive epidemiology of dance participation in adolescents. *Research Quarterly for Exercise and Sport, 82* (3), 373-380.

Portman, P. (2003). Are physical education classes encouraging students to be physically active?: Experiences of ninth graders in their last semester of required physical education. *Physical Educator, 63* (3), 150-161.

Stuart, J., Biddle, S., O'Donovan, T., & Nevill, M. (2005). Correlates of participation in physical activity for adolescent girls: A systematic review of literature. *Journal of Physical Activity and Health, 2,* 423-434.

Wilkinson, C., & Bretzing, R. (2011). High school girls' perceptions of selected physical activities. *The Physical Educator, 68* (2), 58-65.

Skillfulness

Eime, R., Harvey, J., Sawyer, N., Craike, M., Symons, C., Polman, R., & Payne, W. (2013). Understanding contexts of adolescent female participation in sport and physical activity. *Research Quarterly for Exercise and Sport, 84,* 157-166.

Garn, A., Ware, D., & Solmon, M. (2011). Student engagement in high school physical education: Do social motivation orientations matter? *Journal of Teaching in Physical Education, 30,* 84-98.

Hands, B., Larkin, D., Parker, H., Straker, L., & Perry, M. (2009). The relationship among physical activity, motor competence and health-related fitness in 14-year-old adolescents. *Scandinavian Journal of Medicine & Science in Sports, 19,* 655-663.

Hardy, L., Barnett, L., Espinel, P., & Okely, A. (2013). Thirteen-year trends in child and adolescent fundamental movement skills: 1997-2010. *Medicine and Science in Sports and Exercise, 45* (10), 1965-1971.

Hardy, L., Reinten-Reynolds, T., Espinel, P., Zask, A., & Okely, A. (2012). Prevalence and correlates of low fundamental movement skill competency in children. *Pediatrics, 130* (2), e390-e398.

Luban, D., Morgan, P., Cliff, D., Barnett, L., & Okely, A. (2010). Fundamental movement skills in children and adolescents. *Sports Medicine, 40* (12), 1019-1035.

Ommundsen, Y. (2006). Pupils' self-regulation in physical education: The role of motivational climates and different achievement goals. *European Physical Education Review, 12* (3), 289-315.

Portman, P. (2003). Are physical education classes encouraging students to be physically active?: Experiences of ninth graders in their last semester of required physical education. The *Physical Educator, 63* (3), 150-161.

Velija, P., & Kumar, G. (2009). GCSE physical education and the embodiment of gender. *Sport, Education and Society, 14* (4), 383-399.

Wilkinson, C., & Bretzing, R. (2011). High school girls' perceptions of selected physical activities. *Physical Educator, 68* (2), 58-65.

Engagement (Relatedness, Cognitive Demand)

Chen, A., & Darst, P.W. (2001). Situational interest in physical education: A function of learning task design. *Research Quarterly for Exercise and Sport, 72* (2), 150-164.

Haerens, L., Kirk, D., Cardon, G., De Bourdeauhuij, I., & Vansteenkiste, M. (2010). Motivation profiles for secondary school physical education and its relationship to adoption of a physically active lifestyle among university students. *European Physical Education Review, 16* (2), 117-139.

Hamilton, K., & White, K. (2008). Extending the theory of planned behavior: The role of self and social influences in predicting adolescent regular moderate to vigorous physical activity. *Journal of Sport and Exercise Science, 30,* 56-74.

Ruiz, L., Graupera, J., Moreno, J., & Rico, I. (2010). Social preferences for learning among adolescents. *Journal of Teaching in Physical Education, 29,* 3-20.

Smith, M., & St. Pierre, P. (2009). Secondary students' perceptions of enjoyment in physical education: An American and English perspective. *The Physical Educator, 66* (4), 09-221.

Competence/Perceived Competence and Physical Activity

Patnode, C., Lytle, L., Erikson, D., Sirard, J., Barr-Anderson, D., & Story, M. (2011). Physical activity and sedentary activity patterns among children and adolescents: A latent class analysis approach. *Journal of Physical Activity and Health, 8,* 457-467.

Stuart, J., Biddle, S., O'Donovan, T., & Nevill, M. (2005). Correlates of participation in physical activity for adolescent girls: A systematic review of literature. *Journal of Physical Activity and Health, 2,* 423-434.

Yli-Piipari, S., Leskinen, E., Jaakkola, T., & Liukkonen, J. (2012). Predictive role of physical education motivation: The developmental trajectories of physical activity during grades 7-9. *Research Quarterly for Exercise and Sport, 83* (4), 560-569.

Chapter 4

Bryan, C., Sims, S., Hester, D., & Dunaway, D. (2013). Fifteen years after the Surgeon General's Report: Challenges, changes, and future directions in physical education. *Quest, 65,* 139-150.

Doolittle, S. (2014). Profiles of change: Lessons for improving high school physical education. *Journal of Physical Education, Recreation & Dance, 85* (3), 27-31.

Gallahue, D.L., Ozmun, J., & Goodway, J. (2012). *Understanding motor development: Infants, children, adolescents, adults.* New York: McGraw-Hill.

Hannon, J.C., & Ratcliffe, T. (2005). Physical activity levels in coeducational and single-gender high school physical education settings. *Journal of Teaching in Physical Education, 24,* 149-164.

Krause, T. (2014). Meeting the needs and interests of today's high school student. *Journal of Physical Education, Recreation & Dance, 85* (2), 10-13.

Ntoumanis, N., Pensgaard, A., Martin, C., & Pipe, K. (2004). An idiographic analysis of amotivation in compulsory school physical education. *Journal of Sport & Exercise Science, 26,* 197-214.

Ntoumanis, N. (2005). A prospective study of participation in optional school physical education using a self-determination theory framework. *Journal of Educational Psychology, 97* (3), 444-453.

Ryan, R.M., & Deci, E.L. (2000). Self-determination theory and the facilitation of intrinsic motivation, social development, and well-being. *American Psychologist, 55* (1), 68-78.

SHAPE America – Society of Health and Physical Educators. (2014). *National Standards & Grade-Level Outcomes for K-12 physical education.* Champaign, IL: Human Kinetics.

Vallerand, R.J., Pelletier, L.G., Blais, M.R., Briere, N.M., Senecal, C., & Vallieres, E.F. (1992). The academic motivation scale: A measure of intrinsic, extrinsic, and amotivation in education. *Educational and Psychological Measurement, 52* (4), 1003-1017.

Chapter 5

Louv, R. (2008). *Last child in the woods: Saving our children from nature-deficit disorder.* Chapel Hill, NC: Algonquin Books of Chapel Hill.

SHAPE America – Society of Health and Physical Educators. (2014). *National Standards & Grade-Level Outcomes for*

K-12 physical education. Champaign, IL: Human Kinetics.

The School of Fly Fishing. (1990). Learn how to fly fish: Student handbook: A guide to the fundamentals of fly fishing. Lincoln, NE: Author.

Chapter 6

SHAPE America – Society of Health and Physical Educators. (2014). *National Standards & Grade-Level Outcomes for K-12 physical education*. Champaign, IL: Human Kinetics.

Chapter 7

SHAPE America – Society of Health and Physical Educators. (2014). *National Standards & Grade-Level Outcomes for K-12 physical education*. Champaign, IL: Human Kinetics.

Siedentop, D., Hastie, P., & van der Mars, H. (2011). *Complete guide to sport education.* 2nd ed. Champaign, IL: Human Kinetics.

Chapter 8

SHAPE America – Society of Health and Physical Educators. (2014). *National Standards & Grade-Level Outcomes for K-12 physical education*. Champaign, IL: Human Kinetics.

Chapter 9

Couturier, L.E, Chepko, S., & Coughlin, M. (2007). Whose gym is it? Gendered perspectives on middle school and secondary school physical education. *The Physical Educator, 64* (3), 152-157.

Doan, R.J., MacDonald, L.C., Chepko, S. (2017). *Lesson planning for middle school physical education: Meeting the National Standards & Grade-Level Outcomes.* Reston, VA: SHAPE America; Champaign, IL: Human Kinetics.

SHAPE America – Society of Health and Physical Educators. (2014). *National Standards & Grade-Level Outcomes for K-12 physical education*. Champaign, IL: Human Kinetics.

Chapter 10

SHAPE America – Society of Health and Physical Educators. (2014). *National Standards & Grade-Level Outcomes for K-12 physical education*. Champaign, IL: Human Kinetics.

Chapter 11

Bompa, T., & Carrera, M. (2015). *Conditioning young athletes.* Champaign, IL: Human Kinetics

Faigenbaum, A., & Westcott, W. (2009). *Youth strength training programs for health, fitness, and sport.* Champaign, IL: Human Kinetics.

National Strength and Conditioning Association & Brown, L. (ed). (2017). *Strength training.* 2nd ed. Champaign, IL: Human Kinetics.

SHAPE America – Society of Health and Physical Educators. (2014). *National Standards & Grade-Level Outcomes for K-12 physical education*. Champaign, IL: Human Kinetics.

Glossary

Chen, A., Darst, P. W., & Pangrazi, R. P. (1999). What constitutes situational interest? Validating a construct in physical education. *Measurement in Physical Education and Exercise Science*, 3 (3), 157-180.

Ericsson, K. A. , Krampe, R., & Tesch-Roemer, C. (1993). The role of deliberate practice in the acquisition of expert performance. *Psychological Review*, 100: 363-406.

Haibach, P., Reid, G., & Collier, D. (2011). *Motor learning and development.* Champaign, IL: Human Kinetics.

Holt/Hale, S., & Hall, T. (2016). *Lesson planning for elementary physical education: Meeting the National Standards & Grade-Level Outcomes.* Reston, VA: SHAPE America; Champaign, IL: Human Kinetics.

Mitchell, S.A., Oslin, J.L, & Griffin, L.L. (2006). *Teaching sport concepts and skills: A tactical games approach.* 2nd ed. Champaign, IL: Human Kinetics.

SHAPE America – Society of Health and Physical Educators. (2014). *National Standards & Grade-Level Outcomes for K-12 physical education*. Champaign, IL: Human Kinetics.

Zhang, T., Solmon, M., Kosma, M., Carson, R.L., & Gu, X. (2011). Need support, need satisfaction, intrinsic motivation, and physical activity participation among middle school students. *Journal of Teaching in Physical Education*, 30, 51-68.

About the Editors

Lynn Couturier MacDonald, DPE, is a professor and chair of the physical education department at State University of New York at Cortland and is a former president of the National Association for Sport and Physical Education (NASPE), now called SHAPE America (Society of Health and Physical Educators). Dr. MacDonald earned her BS and DPE degrees in physical education from Springfield College and her MS in biomechanics from the University of Illinois at Champaign-Urbana. Dr. MacDonald chaired the NASPE's Curriculum Framework and K-12 Standards Revision Task Force, which spearheaded the 2013 revision of SHAPE America's National Standards for K-12 Physical Education and the development of SHAPE America's Grade-Level Outcomes for K-12 Physical Education. She also served as one of the three principal writers of SHAPE America's book National Standards & Grade-Level Outcomes for K-12 Physical Education, published by Human Kinetics. She has presented at the national level on the National Standards and Grade-Level Outcomes. She is a member of SHAPE America and the National Association for Kinesiology in Higher Education. Dr. MacDonald enjoys spending time with her family, being active outdoors (cycling, kayaking, gardening), and reading for pleasure.

Photo courtesy of SUNY.

Robert J. Doan, PhD, is an assistant professor of physical education in the University of Southern Mississippi's school of kinesiology. He previously taught physical education in elementary school. Dr. Doan serves as a board member for the Mississippi Association for Health, Physical Education, Recreation and Dance (MAHPERD), a SHAPE America state affiliate organization. He also serves as a teacher-education program reviewer for SHAPE America and as an article reviewer for two of SHAPE America's professional journals: Strategies and Journal of Physical Education, Recreation and Dance. Dr. Doan has conducted research on a variety of physical education topics and has presented at multiple conferences at the state, regional, and national levels. Dr. Doan earned his undergraduate degree from Grand Valley State University, attended Winthrop University for his master's degree, and completed his PhD in physical education with an emphasis in curriculum and assessment at the University of South Carolina.

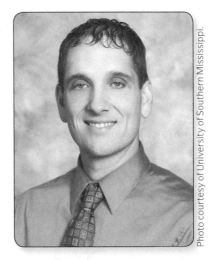

Photo courtesy of University of Southern Mississippi.

Photo courtesy of Winthrop University.

Stevie Chepko, EdD, is assistant dean for accreditation at the University of Nebraska at Omaha and is former senior vice president of accreditation for the Council for the Accreditation of Educator Preparation (CAEP). Dr. Chepko earned her EdD in curriculum and instruction and sport history from Temple University. She is a respected authority on performance-based standards, teaching for mastery, and assessment in physical education. Dr. Chepko served on the National Association for Sport and Physical Education's Curriculum Framework and K-12 Standards Revision Task Force, which spearheaded the 2013 revision of SHAPE America's National Standards for K-12 Physical Education and the development of SHAPE America's Grade-Level Outcomes for K-12 Physical Education. She also served as one of three principal writers of SHAPE America's book National Standards & Grade-Level Outcomes for K-12 Physical Education, published by Human Kinetics.

About the Contributors

Brandon Allen is an assistant teaching professor in sport management at the University of Southern Mississippi. He has taught activity classes and numerous undergraduate and graduate academic courses and activity courses in coaching education and sport management since 2006. Brandon formerly taught at the high school level and worked for the National Youth Sports Program.

Photo courtesy of University of Southern Mississippi

Joni M. Boyd is an assistant professor of exercise science at Winthrop University in Rock Hill, South Carolina, and a certified strength and conditioning specialist. Her research interests include health behaviors of elementary and college students and the impact of strength and conditioning programs on athletes. Joni teaches undergraduate- and graduate-level courses in health and exercise science and previously taught healthy habits as a school wellness teacher and coach.

Photo courtesy of Joni M. Boyd.

Rebecca Bryan is an assistant professor in the department of physical education at the State University of New York at Cortland, where she teaches undergraduate- and graduate-level courses in fitness education; curriculum, instruction, and assessment; adapted physical education; and physical education leadership. Rebecca formerly served as an adapted physical education consultant and taught physical education in California.

Photo courtesy of Rebecca Bryan.

Ericka Fangiullo is dean of students at Windsor High School in Windsor, Connecticut, where she previously taught physical education and health for 15 years. Along with serving as secretary of the Connecticut Association for Health, Physical Education, Recreation and Dance (CTAHPERD) for five years, she has presented at various local and district conferences. She proposed and wrote the curriculum for a semester-long yoga elective class, and she taught it for 10 years. Ericka has been coaching varsity swimming and diving for 18 years with numerous All-American and All-State athletes.

Photo courtesy of Ericka Fangiullo.

Photo courtesy of Isabelle Hart.

Aaron Hart is director of educational programs for US Games and is a lecturer at State University of New York at Cortland. In 2015, Hart launched Online Physical Education Network (OPEN) at OPENPhysEd.org as a public service of US Games. He also has cowritten several other curriculum projects, including the SPARK middle school and high school projects. Hart travels throughout the United States to provide professional development, conference presentations, and curriculum support to physical educators and the school communities in which they work.

Photo courtesy of HR Imaging Partners, Inc.

Lisa Jacob is a physical educator at Maine West High School in Des Plaines, Illinois, who specializes in dance education. She teaches all dance classes and directs the Maine West Variety Show, the Orchesis Dance Company, and Mr. Maine West. Jacob is the cochair of the Illinois High School Dance Festival, has presented on dance at the Illinois Association for Health, Physical Education, Recreation and Dance (IAHPERD) convention on numerous occasions, and she was the IAHPERD Dance Teacher of the Year for the northeastern region in 2014.

Photo courtesy of Adrienne Koesterer.

Adrienne Koesterer is an instructor in the physical education department at State University of New York at Cortland. She previously served as aquatics director at Humboldt State University in Arcata, California, and she has been an American Red Cross instructor since 1987.

Photo courtesy of Tracy Krause.

Tracy Krause has been a physical education teacher at Tahoma High School in Maple Valley, Washington, for more than 20 years. Tracy is a National Board–certified teacher who was named National Teacher of the Year by AAHPERD (now SHAPE America) in 2008 and PE Teacher of the Year by the NFL in 2012. Tracy thanks and acknowledges his original collaborators at Tahoma High School: language arts teacher Jamie Vollrath and science teacher Mike Hanson.

Photo courtesy of Patrice Lovdahl.

Patrice Lovdahl taught physical education for 30 years before retiring. She is a National Board–certified teacher and is presently an adjunct faculty member at the University of Southern Mississippi and William Carey University. Patrice was appointed to the Mississippi Governor's Commission on Physical Fitness and Sport in 1999 and reappointed in 2010 and was the first physical educator to be named to the Mississippi Hall of Master Teachers.

Melanie Perreault is an assistant professor of motor behavior at the State University of New York College at Brockport, where she also teaches tennis. Her research interests include examining motor learning and cognition in children to inform developmentally appropriate pedagogical practices and exploring student and teacher experiences using problembased learning in physical education classes.

Photo courtesy of Melanie Perreault.

Charlie Rizzuto is a health and physical education teacher at Oyster Bay High School in Long Island, New York. Charlie has presented at various conferences on topics relating to physical education, including TPSR, sport education, assessment, technology, growth mind-set, and the activity gap. He is currently working on a teacher resource website.

Photo courtesy of Charlie Rizzuto.

Anthony Smith is a visiting professor at the University of Southern Mississippi's school of kinesiology, where he teaches strength and conditioning programming, sport law, and pedagogy methods. Anthony began his career coaching club teams in volleyball and softball before joining the high school association to focus on basketball. Along with coaching, Anthony has trained several elite level athletes in soccer, basketball, and rugby through high school, college, and Olympic development programs.

Photo courtesy of University of Southern Mississippi.

Charla Tedder Krahnke taught physical education for 31 years. She is a past national teacher of the year named by AAHPERD (now SHAPE America) and a North Carolina high school teacher of the year. Charla is also a National Board–certified teacher who served as a member of the writing team for the Pipeline Teacher Models Curriculum (2011).

Photo courtesy of Charla T. Krahnke.

Mary Westkott is a professor in the department of health and physical education and associate head swimming and diving coach at the United States Coast Guard Academy in New London, Connecticut. She teaches classes in aquatics, wellness, and strength and conditioning. Mary is a USA Triathlon–certified coach and has been a race director for kids' triathlons. She has led swimming triathlon clinics through the Hartford Marathon Foundation.

Photo courtesy of Mary Westkott.

About SHAPE America

SHAPE America – Society of Health and Physical Educators is committed to ensuring that all children have the opportunity to lead healthy, physically active lives. As the nation's largest membership organization of health and physical education professionals, SHAPE America works with its 50 state affiliates and is a founding partner of national initiatives including the Presidential Youth Fitness Program, Active Schools, and the Jump Rope For Heart and Hoops For Heart programs.

Since its founding in 1885, the organization has defined excellence in physical education, most recently creating *National Standards & Grade-Level Outcomes for K-12 Physical Education* (2014), National Standards for Initial Physical Education Teacher Education (2016), National Standards for Health Education Teacher Education (2017) and *National Standards for Sport Coaches* (2006). Also, SHAPE America participated as a member of the Joint Committee on National Health Education Standards, which published *National Health Education Standards, Second Edition: Achieving Excellence* (2007). Our programs, products and services provide the leadership, professional development and advocacy that support health and physical educators at every level, from preschool through university graduate programs.

The SHAPE America website, www.shapeamerica.org, holds a treasure trove of free resources for health and physical educators, adapted physical education teachers, teacher trainers and coaches, including activity calendars, curriculum resources, tools and templates, assessments and more. Visit www.shapeamerica.org and search for Teacher's Toolbox.

Every spring, SHAPE America hosts its National Convention & Expo, the premier national professional-development event for health and physical educators.

Advocacy is an essential element in the fulfillment of our mission. By speaking out for the school health and physical education professions, SHAPE America strives to make an impact on the national policy landscape.

> **Our Vision:** A nation in which all children are prepared to lead healthy, physically active lives.

> **Our Mission:** To advance professional practice and promote research related to health and physical education, physical activity, dance and sport.

> **Our Commitment:** 50 Million Strong by 2029

Approximately 50 million students are enrolled currently in America's elementary and secondary schools (grades preK through 12). SHAPE America wants to ensure that by the time today's youngest students graduate from high school in 2029, all of America's young people are empowered to lead healthy and active lives through effective health and physical education programs. To learn more about 50 Million Strong by 2029, visit www.shapeamerica.org.

With one step, you'll join a national movement.

Membership will advance your career — and connect you to a national movement of educators who are preparing students to lead healthy, physically active lives.

Joining SHAPE America Is Your First Step Toward:

- **Improving your instructional practices.** Membership is your direct connection to the classroom resources, webinars, workshops, books, and all the professional development you need. **Members save up to 30%!**

- **Staying current on trends in education.** We will deliver the news to you through our weekly e-newsletter *Et Cetera,* our quarterly member newsletter *Momentum,* and peer-reviewed journals such as *Strategies: A Journal for Physical and Sport Educators,* the *American Journal of Health Education, Journal of Physical Education, Recreation & Dance,* and *Research Quarterly for Exercise and Sport.*

- **Earning recognition for you and your program.** Showcase your school's achievements and gain funding through grant and award opportunities.

- **Growing your professional network.** Whether it's a face-to-face event or online through the member-exclusive community—*Exchange*—you'll gain access to a diverse group of peers who can help you respond to daily challenges.

Join Today. shapeamerica.org/membership

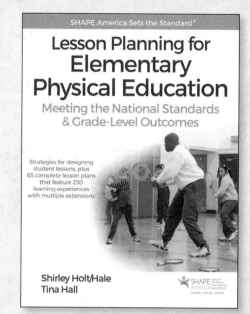
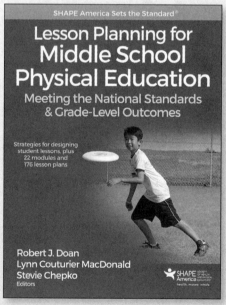

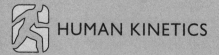